American Working Class History

American Working Class History

A Representative Bibliography

MAURICE F. NEUFELD
DANIEL J. LEAB
DOROTHY SWANSON

R. R. Bowker Company
New York and London, 1983

Published by R. R. Bowker Company
205 East Forty-second Street, New York, NY 10017

Printed and bound in the United States of America

Library of Congress Cataloging in Publication Data
Neufeld, Maurice F.
American working class history.

Includes index.
1. Labor and laboring classes—United States—History—Bibliography.
I. Leab, Daniel J. II. Swanson, Dorothy. III. Title.
Z7164.L1N54 1983 [HD8066] 016.331'0973 83-11845
ISBN 0-8352-1752-3

Contents

Introduction

This book is a thoroughly revised, greatly expanded reworking of Maurice F. Neufeld's *A Representative Bibliography of American Labor History*, published in 1964. Since then a veritable explosion in the field of working class history has taken place, especially in the past decade. It is our hope and belief that this edition accurately and usefully reflects that dynamic change.

Within each classification, items are arranged alphabetically by author whenever the author is indicated. Items without given authors are listed under their title in the case of films or when they appear in periodicals. In all other instances, they appear under the name of the organization, institution, or agency of origin, except that publications of the Congress and federal agencies generally appear under "U.S.," while publications of state and local agencies are found under the name of the state or political subdivision concerned. References to international unions are generally to those that operate in important sectors of the American economy or that represent the more significant types of American unionism. The cut-off date for inclusion of items is January 31, 1983.

The reader should note also that when bibliographies, guides, and reference and archival sources pertain to a specific industry, city, region, state, or leader, these items are listed under the classifications for those categories for the convenience of the user. For the same reason, when strikes pertain to a specific industry, they are listed under the classification for that industry. When specific industry strikes attained national importance, like the railroad strikes of 1877, they are listed under the pertinent "Period of Development."

As an added convenience, an overall index is provided at the end of this bibliography. The index covers all authors, agencies, organizations, and institutions, cited under each classification. A special appendix lists various sources for rental or purchase of the films listed under the various classifications.

This bibliography is not comprehensive and does not include titles that would merit attention in a bibliography aimed at full and complete coverage of American working class history. In recompense, the items selected represent a wide variety of *types* of useful materials: books ranging in nature from popular to technical; scholarly monographs; Ph.D. dissertations and M.A. theses; films; novels and plays; biographies and autobiographies; state and federal legislative investigations; government reports; union documents and management publications; articles from both learned journals and magazines of limited and mass circulation. Thus, by calling attention to examples of these diverse types and sources of information, this bibliography offers clues to additional possible sources of information and enlightenment. An annual bibliography covering periodicals and dissertations for the previous year is to be found in the Fall issue of *Labor History* (70 Washington Square South, New York, NY 10012).

Within its limitations, this bibliography also attempts to present different *points of view*. The items included range from those representing extreme left-wing attitudes to those that are clearly opposed to labor unions and to the entire process of collective bargaining as well as those without any sympathy for the working class.

A few notations of a housekeeping nature should be made at this point. When legislative committees are cited, the date in parentheses after the name of the committee indicates the year of appointment. An entry has sometimes been repeated when such an item covers more than one period or more than one union or industry. In the classification "Periods of Development," references dealing with a period earlier than the one under survey are sometimes listed with those devoted to a subsequent era so that all references to a given subject, which achieved importance during the later period under consideration, might be listed in one place. Periodical page references are handled in two ways: where a volume number is not given as with a magazine such as *The New Yorker*, we have included "pp" prior to the listing of the page reference; where the volume is given as with most learned journals, the page references are not preceded by "pp." Finally, it should be noted that some items are not readily available in most libraries, but have been listed because of their historical importance.

The cultivation of bibliographical files is a gentle, patient, exacting, thankless art. Every effort has been made to record all items with accuracy. Nonetheless, given the human condition, errors undoubtedly have survived our best efforts. The identification of such errors would be most welcome, and we would very much appreciate communications from anyone who finds them.

We would like to express our deep, heartfelt appreciation to Katharine Kyes Leab for her invaluable assistance with the creation of the data base from which this printed copy is drawn, and with the inputting of material. She played a vital role in the creation of this book. We would also like to thank Kathy Baker, Candy Verhulst, Bill King, and Joe Dupré of Inforonics, Inc., for their assistance in the development of camera-ready copy of this book. Thanks also must go to Jean Peters and Betty Sun of R. R. Bowker Company for their vision, concern, and support. Further, Maurice F. Neufeld would like to express his appreciation to Joyce N. Orzino for her exemplary efforts. Dorothy Swanson thanks Michael Brook for his work on the *Labor History* annual bibliographies. Daniel J. Leab wishes to express his thanks to Linda Gordon, Laura Schereschewsky, Stephen P. Skidgel, Kathleen Smith, and Carol Young, all of whom played a role in making this book possible, and without whom it could not have been completed.

July 11, 1983

MAURICE F. NEUFELD
ITHACA, NEW YORK

DANIEL J. LEAB
WASHINGTON, CONNECTICUT

DOROTHY SWANSON
NEW YORK, NEW YORK

Bibliographies, Guides, and Reference and Archival Sources

Note: When these items pertain to a specific industry, city, region, state, or leader, they are listed under the classifications for those categories for the convenience of the user.

1 AMERICAN FEDERATION OF LABOR. *American Federation of Labor History, Encyclopedia Reference Book.*, Vol 1. Wash.: AFL, 1919.

2 ———. *American Federation of Labor History, Encyclopedia Reference Book.*, Vol 2. Wash.: AFL, 1924.

3 ———. *American Federation of Labor History, Encyclopedia Reference Book.*, Vol 3 in 2 parts. Wash.: AFL-CIO, 1960.

4 "Annual Review of American Labor Developments." *Monthly Labor Review*, Jan or Feb, 1949-63, 1970-77. (Variously titled)

5 APTHEKER, HERBERT. "The W. E. B. Du Bois Papers." *Political Affairs*, Vol 44 (Mar 1966), 36-45.

6 BARNETT, GEORGE. *A Trial Bibliography of American Trade-Union Publications.* Balt.: Johns Hopkins Press, 1907.

7 BELL, DANIEL. *The Tamiment Library*. NY: New York U Libraries, 1969.

8 BERNER, RICHARD C. "Labor History: Sources and Perspectives." *Pacific Northwest Quarterly*, Vol 60 (1969), 31-33.

9 BLACK, J. WILLIAM. "References on the History of Labor and Some Contemporary Labor Problems." *Oberlin College Library Bulletin*, Vol I, No 2, 1893.

10 BLAZEK, RON. et al., comps. *The Black Experience: A Bibliography of Bibliographies....* Chicago: American Library Association, 1978.

11 BLOXOM, MARGUERITE D., comp. *Pickaxe and Pencil: References for the Study of the WPA*. Wash.: Library of Congress, 1982.

12 BLUM, ALBERT A. *An Annotated Bibliography of Industrial Relations and the Small Firm.* Ithaca: NY State School of Industrial and Labor Relations, Cornell U, 1960.

13 ———. "Local Union Archives in Michigan." *Labor History*, Vol 3 (1962), 335-40.

14 ———. "A Report on Research in Progress in American Labor History." *Labor History*, Vol 7 (1966), 78-92.

15 ———. "Research in Progress in American Labor History." *Labor History*, Vol 3 (1962), 218-25.

16 BOCCACCIO, MARY. "Labor Resources at the University of Maryland at College Park." *Labor History*, Vol 22 (1982), 498-501.

17 BRANDON, THOMAS, guest ed. "American Labor Films" *Film Library Quarterly*, Vol 12 (1979), entire issue.

18 BRICKETT, MARGARETT F. "Labor History Resources in the U.S. Department of Labor Library." *Labor History*, Vol 2 (1961), 236-40.

19 BROOK, MICHAEL. "Radical Literature in Swedish-America: A Narrative Survey." *Swedish Pioneer Historical Quarterly*, Vol 20 (1969), 111-32.

20 BROOKS, THOMAS R. *Labor and Migration: An Annotated Bibliography*. NY: Brooklyn College, Center for Migration Studies, 1970.

21 BROWNE, HENRY J. "Raiding Labor Records." *American Archivist*, Vol 17 (1954), 262-64.

22 BURKETT, WILBUR O., comp. *A Bibliography on Women and Minorities in the Workforce*. Ypsilanti, MI: Eastern Michigan U, 1980.

23 CHIN, FELIX. *Automation and Robots: A Selected Bibliography of Books*. Monticello, IL: Vance, 1982.

24 CONOVER, HELEN F., comp. *A Bibliography of Bibliographies of Trade Unions*. Wash.: Library of Congress, 1937. (Mimeo.)

25 CORNELL UNIVERSITY. LIBRARIES. Industrial and Labor Relations Library. *Library Catalog of the New York State School of Industrial and Labor Relations. No. 1.*, 12 vols. Bost.: G. K. Hall, 1967.

26 ———. ———. *Library Catalog of the New York State School of Industrial and Labor Relations. Cumulative Supplement.*, 9 vols. Bost.: G. K. Hall, 1976.

27 ———. ———. *Library Catalog of the New York State School of Industrial and Labor Relations. Supplement to the Cumulative Supplement.*, 5 vols. Bost.: G. K. Hall, 1977-1981.

28 DEVENS, R. M. "Labor Force Trends: a Bibliography." *Monthly Labor Review*, Vol 100 (Oct 1977), 12-15.

29 DI ROMA, EDWARD. "Notes on Resources for Research in Labor History in the Reference Department of the New York Public Library." *Labor History*, Vol 4 (1963), 93-99.

30 DINWIDDIE, ROBERT C., and LESLIE S. HOUGH. "The Southern Labor Archives." *Labor History*, Vol 22 (1982), 502-12.

31 "Directory of American Labor Films." *Film Library Quarterly*, Vol 12, No 2/3 (1979), 88-99.

32 DRESCHER, NUALA MCGANN. "Three Problems for the Labor Historian." *Pacific Northwest Quarterly*, Vol 60 (1969), 29-31.

33 DWYER, RICHARD. *Labor Education in the U.S.: An Annotated Bibliography*. Metuchen, NJ: Scarecrow Press, 1977.

34 EAST, DENNIS. "Labor History Resources in the Ohio Historical Society." *Labor History*, Vol 22 (1982), 513-15.

35 ECKERT, LEONE W., comp. *Guide to the Records [of the] Labor Management Documentation Center*. Ithaca: Library, NY State School of Industrial & Labor Relations, Cornell U, 1960.

36 FALER, PAUL. "Working Class Historiography." *Radical America*, Vol 3 (Mar-Apr 1969), 56-68.

37 FAUSS, RICHARD. *A Bibliography of Labor History in Newsfilm.*, 4 vols. Morgantown: Institute for Labor Studies, Division of Social and Economic Development, Center for Extension and Continuing Education, West Virginia U, 1980.

38 FILIPPELLI, RONALD L. "Labor Manuscripts in the Pennsylvania State University Library." *Labor History*, Vol 13 (1972), 79-88.

39 ———, and ALICE HOFFMAN. "Labor Sources at Penn State University." *Labor History*, Vol 22 (1982), 516-19.

40 FINK, GARY M., ed. *Labor Unions*. Westport, CT: Greenwood, 1977. (Vol 1 of Greenwood Encyclopedia of American Institutions Series)

41 FISHBEIN, LESLIE. "A Lost Legacy of Labor Films." *Film and History*, Vol 9 (1979), 33-39.

42 FISHBEIN, MEYER H. "Labor History Resources in the National Archives." *Labor History*, Vol 8 (1967), 330-51.

43 FOGARTY, ROBERT S., ed. *Dictionary of American Communal and Utopian History.* Westport, CT: Greenwood, 1980.

44 FONES-WOLF, KEN. "Sources for the Study of Labor History in the Urban Archives, Temple University." *Labor History*, Vol 22 (1982), 520-25.

45 FOX, JAMES, and MARY ANNE FOX. *Illegal Immigration: A Bibliography, 1968-1978.* Monticello, IL: Vance, 1978.

46 GAMBLE, ROBERT A., and GEORGE GREEN. "Labor Archives at the University of Texas at Arlington." *Labor History*, Vol 22 (1982), 526-27.

47 GATES, FRANCIS. "Labor Resources in the University of California (Berkeley) Libraries." *Labor History*, Vol I (1960), 196-205.

48 ———. *Reference Guides for Labor Research.* Berkeley: Labor Collection, Social Sciences Reference Service, General Library, U of California, 1957.

49 GEORGETOWN UNIVERSITY. International Labor Program *American Labor and World Affairs: A Bibliography.* Wash.: The Program, 1978.

50 GOLDSTEIN, ROBERT J. "The Anarchist Scare of 1908." *American Studies*, Vol 15 (Fall 1974), 55-78.

51 GOLDWATER, WALTER. *Radical Periodicals in America, 1890-1950: A Bibliography with Brief Notes.* 3rd Edition, with indexes. NY: University Place Bookshop, 1977.

52 GREEN, JAMES R. "Working Class History in the 1940s: a Bibliographical Essay." *Radical America*, Vol 9 (Jul-Aug 1975), 206-13.

53 GROSS, JAMES A. "Historians and the Literature of the Negro Worker." *Labor History*, Vol 10 (1969), 536-46.

54 HAM, GERALD. "Labor Manuscripts in the State Historical Society of Wisconsin." *Labor History*, Vol 7 (1966), 313-42.

55 ———. *Labor Manuscripts in the State Historical Society of Wisconsin.* Madison: Wisconsin State Historical Society, 1967.

56 HARRING, SIDNEY L. "Police Reports as Sources in Labor History." *Labor History*, Vol 18 (1977), 585-91.

57 HARVEY, O. L. "Inventory of Department of Labor Archives." *Labor History*, Vol 4 (1963), 196-98.

58 HEFFRON, PAUL T. "Manuscript Sources in the Library of Congress for a Study of Labor History." *Labor History*, Vol 10 (1969), 630-38.

59 HESLET, MARY R. *Trade Unions in the United States: References to Books on the Histories of Individual Trade Unions in the United States.* Wash.: Legislative Reference Service, Library of Congress, 1966.

60 HOERDER, DIRK. "Bibliographic and Archival Preservation of non-English-Language Labor and Radical Newspapers and Periodicals in North America, 1845 to 1976." *Immigration History Newsletter*, Vol 13 (1981), 11-12.

61 HOUKES, JOHN M., ed. *Industrial Relations Theses and Dissertations, 1949-1969: A Cumulative Bibliography.* Ann Arbor, MI: Xerox University Microfilms, 1973.

62 *Index to Labor Union Periodicals: A Subject Index to Materials from a Selected List of Newspapers and Journals Published by Major Labor Unions January-June 1960-67.* Ann Arbor: Bureau of Industrial Relations, U of Michigan, 1960-67.

63 INDUSTRIAL RELATIONS RESEARCH ASSOCIATION. "Publications Index, 1948-1960." *Proceedings of the Thirteenth Annual Meeting of the Industrial Relations Research Association*, Dec 28-29, 1960, pp 308-41. Madison: IRRA, 1961.

64 *Industrial Relations Theses and Dissertations.* (Abstracts sponsored by the Committee of University Industrial Relations Librarians, and printed by various publishers. Cumulation, 1949-69. Ann Arbor: University Microfilms, 1973.)

65 INTERNATIONAL ASSOCIATION OF LABOUR HISTORY INSTITUTIONS. *Directory / International Association of Labour History Institutions.* London: The Association, 1977.

66 INTERNATIONAL INSTITUTE FOR LABOUR STUDIES. *Directory of Institutes for Labour Studies*. Geneva: The Institute, 1978.

67 *An IWW Bibliography*. Chicago: Kerr, 1973.

68 JAMES, EDWARD T. et al, eds. *Papers of the Women's Trade Union League and its Principal Leaders: Guide to the Microfilm Edition*. Woodbridge, CT: Research Publications, 1981.

69 JOHNPOLL, BERNARD K. "Manuscript Sources in American Radicalism." *Labor History*, Vol 14 (1973), 92-97.

70 KENLLNER, H. T. "Library Service in the Garment District: Fashion Institute of Technology." *Wilson Library Bulletin*, Vol 55 (1981), 423-26.

71 KENNEDY, SUSAN E. *America's White Working-Class Women: A Historical Bibliography*. NY: Garland, 1981.

72 KIRKLEY, A. ROY, JR. *Labor Unions and the Black Experience: A Selected Bibliography*. New Brunswick, NJ: Institute of Management and Labor Relations, University Extension Division, Rutgers U, 1972.

73 LABOR HISTORY. "Annual Bibliography of Periodical Articles on American Labor History." *Labor History*, Annually from 1967.

74 LACKMAN, HAROLD, and GEORGE GREEN. "Origin and Progress of the Texas Labor Archives." *Labor History*, Vol 11 (1970), 341-44.

75 LAZAR, ROBERT E. "The International Ladies Garment Workers' Union Archives." *Labor History*, Vol 22 (1982), 528-33.

76 LERNER, GERDA. *Bibliography in the History of American Women*. Bronxville, NY: Sarah Lawrence College, 1978.

77 LEWINSON, PAUL. "The Archives of Labor." *American Archivist*, Vol 17 (1954), 19-24.

78 ———. "State Labor Agencies: Where Are Their Records?" *American Archivist*, Vol 19 (1956), 45-50.

79 ———, and MORRIS RIEGER. "Labor Union Records in the United States." *American Archivist*, Vol 25 (1962), 39-57.

80 LITOFF, JUDY BARRETT, and HAL LITOFF. "Working Women in Maine: A Note on Sources." *Labor History*, Vol 17 (1976), 88-95.

81 LOVETT, ROBERT W. *American Economic and Business History Information Sources: An Annotated Bibliography of Recent Works Pertaining to Economic, Business, Agricultural and Labor History and the History of Science and Technology for the United States and Canada*. Detroit: Gale Research, 1971.

82 ———. "Labor History Materials in the Harvard University Library." *Labor History*, Vol 4 (1963), 273-79.

83 LU, JOSEPH K. *U.S. Government Publications in the Social Sciences: An Annotated Guide*. Beverly Hills: Sage Publications, 1975.

84 MCBREARTY, JAMES C. *American Labor History and Comparative Labor Movements: A Selected Bibliography*. Tucson: U of Arizona Press, 1973.

85 MCCONNELL, STEPHEN R., and LESLIE A. MORGAN. *The Older Worker: A Selected Bibliography*. Los Angeles: Andrus Gerontology Center, U of Southern California, 1979.

86 MCCOY, RALPH E. *History of Labor Unionism in the United States: A Selected Bibliography*. Champaign, IL: Institute of Labor & Industrial Relations, 1962.

87 ———, and NED ROSEN, comps. *Doctoral Dissertations in Labor and Industrial Relations, 1933-1953*. Bibliographic Contributions No. 5. Champaign: Institute of Labor and Industrial Relations, U of Illinois, 1955.

88 MAIDA, PETER R., and JOHN L. MCCOY. *The Poor: A Selected Bibliography*. Wash.: G.P.O., 1969.

89 MARCLAY, ANNETTE. *Workers' Participation in Management: Selected Bibliography, 1950-1970*. Geneva: International Institute for Labour Studies, 1971.

90 MAROT, HELEN, comp. *A Handbook of Labor Literature*. Phila.: Free Library of Economics & Political Science, 1899.

91 MASON, PHILIP P. "The Archives of Labor and Urban Affairs, Walter P. Reuther Library, Wayne State University." *Labor History*, Vol 22 (1982), 534-45.

92 ———. "Labor Archives in the United States: Achievements and Prospects." *Labor History*, Vol 22 (1982), 487-97.

93 ———. "Preserving Labor's History." *AFL-CIO American Federationist*, Jan 1964, pp 22-24.

94 METZGER, BERTRAM L., and J. J. JEHRING. *An Extensive, Indexed Bibliography of American Publications on Profit Sharing Between 1940-1958....The Research Needs of Profit Sharing*. Evanston, IL: Profit Sharing Research Foundation, 1959.

95 MILLER, HAROLD L. "Labor Records at the State Historical Society of Wisconsin." *Labor History*, Vol 22 (1982), 546-52.

96 MUSGRAVE, GERALD L. *Social Security in the United States: A Classified Bibliography*. Monticello, IL: Vance, 1978.

97 NAAS, BERNARD G., and CARMELITA SAKR, comps. *American Labor Union Periodicals: A Guide to Their Location*. Ithaca: NY State School of Industrial and Labor Relations, Cornell U, 1956.

98 NAAS, BERNARD G., comp. *American Labor Unions' Constitutions and Proceedings: A Guide to the Microform Edition 1836-1978*. Sanford, NC: Microfilming Corporation of America, 1980.

99 NAJITA, JOYCE M., and HELENE S. TANIMOTO. *Guide to Statutory Provisions in Public Sector Collective Bargaining: Characteristics, Functions, and Powers of Administering Agencies*. Honolulu: Industrial Relations Center, U of Hawaii, 1981.

100 NATIONAL CENTER FOR PRODUCTIVITY AND QUALITY OF WORKING LIFE. *Directory of Labor-Management Committees*. Wash.: G.P.O., 1976.

101 O'DONNELL, L. A., comp. *American Unionism and the Catholic Church, with Special Emphasis on the Association of Catholic Trade Unionists: Bibliography*. San Francisco: Labor-Management School, U of San Francisco, 1959.

102 ONSI, PATRICIA WILSON. "Labor History Resources of the University of Illinois." *Labor History*, Vol 7 (1966), 209-15.

103 PETERS, EDWARD. "Recent Literature in American Labor History." *Proceedings of the Eighteenth Annual Winter Meeting of the Industrial Relations Research Association*, Dec 28-29, 1965, pp 333-46. Madison: IRRA, 1966.

104 PETTMAN, B. O. *Strikes: A Selected Bibliography*. Bradford: Institute of Scientific Business, 1976.

105 PFLUG, WARNER W., comp. *A Guide to the Archives of Labor History and Urban Affairs, Wayne State University*. Detroit: Wayne State U Press, 1974.

106 PORTER, DOROTHY B., comp. *The Negro in the United States: A Selected Bibliography*. Wash.: Library of Congress, 1970.

107 PRATT, NORMA F. "Archival Resources and Writing Immigrant American History: the Bund Archives of the Jewish Labor Movement." *Journal of Library History*, Vol 16 (1981), 166-76.

108 PRESTRIDGE, VIRGINIA, comp. *The Worker in American Fiction: An Annotated Bibliography*. Bibliographic Contributions No 4. Champaign: Institute of Labor and Industrial Relations, U of Illinois, 1954.

109 REEVES, DOROTHEA D. *Resources for the Study of Economic History: A Preliminary Guide to Pre-Twentieth Century Printed Material in Collections Located in Certain American and British Libraries*. Bost.: Baker Library, Harvard Graduate School of Business Administration, 1961.

110 REYNOLDS, LLOYD G., and CHARLES C. KILLINGSWORTH. *Trade Union Publications: The Official Journals, Convention Proceedings and Constitutions of International Unions and Federations, 1850-1941.*, 3 vols. Balt.: Johns Hopkins Press, 1944-45.

111 RIFKIN, BERNARD, and SUSAN RIFKIN. *American Labor Sourcebook*. NY: McGraw-Hill, 1979.

112 ROSE, FRED DUANE, comp. *American Labor in Journals of History: A Bibliography*. Bibliographic Contributions No 7. Champaign: Institute of Labor and Industrial Relations, U of Illinois, 1962.

113 SCANLAN, ELEANOR H. "The Labadie Collection." *Labor History*, Vol 6 (1965), 244-48.

114 SCHIFLETT, MARY, ed. *The Working Americans and the Humanities*. Houston: Center for Human Resources, U of Houston, 1977. (Selected reading list used in programs on the heritage and horizons of working Americans)

115 SHAUGHNESSY, D. F. "Labor in the Oral History Collection of Columbia University." *Labor History*, Vol 1 (1960), 177-95.

116 SILVER, SUSAN. "Women in the Workplace: A Variety of Viewpoints." *Monthly Labor Review*, Vol 97 (May 1974), 85-89.

117 SKOTNES, ANDOR, and JULIA WILLIAMS SKOTNES. *American Working-Class History in Historical Journals, 1961-1972: A Bibliography*. New Brunswick, NJ: Labor Education Center Center, Institute of Management and Labor Relations, University Extension Division, Rutgers U, 1974.

118 SOLTOW, MARTHA JANE. "Twenty-Year Cumulative Index to Labor History, Volumes 1-20, 1960-1979." *Labor History*, Vol 22 (1981), pp 57-135.

119 ———. "Women in Labor Unions in the U.S., 1825-1935: A Bibliography." *Review of Radical Political Economics*, Vol 4 (Jul 1972), 150-54.

120 ———. et al., comps. *Women in American Labor History, 1825-1935: An Annotated Bibliography*. East Lansing: Michigan State U, 1972.

121 ———, and MARY DIEBOLD. *American Labor History: A Guide to Sources in the Michigan State University Libraries*. East Lansing: Michigan State University School of Labor and Industrial Relations, 1980.

122 ———, and SUSAN GRAVELLE. *Worker Benefits: Industrial Welfare in America, 1900-1935—an Annotated Bibliography*. Metuchen, NJ: Scarecrow Press, 1983.

123 *State Labor Reports from the End of the Civil War to the Start of the Twentieth Century*. Westport, CT: Microfilm Division, Greenwood, 1970.

124 STATE UNIVERSITY OF IOWA. BUREAU OF LABOR AND MANAGEMENT. *A Guide to the Reference Collection*. Iowa City: The University, 1961.

125 STINEMEN, ESTHER, and CATHERINE LOEB. *Women's Studies: A Recommended Core Bibliography*. Littleton, CO: Libraries Unlimited, 1979.

126 STRASSBERG, RICHARD. "Labor History Resources in the Martin P. Catherwood Library of the New York State School of Labor and Industrial Relations at Cornell University." *Labor History*, Vol 22 (1982), 533-61.

127 STROUD, GENE S., and GILBERT E. DONAHUE, comps. *Labor History in the United States: A General Bibliography*. Bibliographic Contributions No 6. Urbana: Institute of Labor and Industrial Relations, U of Illinois, 1961.

128 SWANSON, DOROTHY. *Guide to the Manuscript Collection of the Tamiment Library*. NY: Garland, 1977.

129 ———. "Tamiment Institute/Ben Josephson Library and Robert F. Wagner Labor Archives." *Labor History*, Vol 22 (1982), 562-67.

130 TAMIMENT INSTITUTE LIBRARY. *Catalog of the Tamiment Institute Library of New York University*. Bost.: G. K. Hall, 1980.

131 TANIMOTO, HELENE S. *Topic Coded Titles on Public Employee Collective Bargaining, with Emphasis on State and Local Levels*. Honolulu: Industrial Relations Center, U of Hawaii, 1981.

132 TEEL, BARBARA, ed. *Undocumented Workers: Selected References*. Wash.: U.S. Department of Labor, 1977.

133 TICE, TERRENCE. *Employee Relations Bibliography: Public, Non-Profit and Professional Employment*. Wash.: G.P.O., 1978.

134 U.S. BUREAU OF LABOR STATISTICS. *BLS Publications, 1886-1971: Numerical Listings, Annotations, Subject Index*., Bulletin 1749. Wash.: G.P.O., 1972.

135 ———. *Implications of Automation and Other Technological Developments: A Selected Annotated Bibliography.*, Bulletin 1319-1. Wash.: G.P.O., 1964.

136 ———. *Subject Index of Bulletins Published by the Bureau of Labor Statistics, 1915-1959, with Annotated Listing of Bulletins, 1895-1959.*, Bulletin No 1281. Wash.: G.P.O., 1960.

137 U.S. CONGRESS. HOUSE. Committee on Education and Labor. *Applicability of Antitrust Legislation to Labor Unions: Selected Excerpts and Bibliography.* Wash.: G.P.O., 1961.

138 ———. SENATE. Committee on the Judiciary. *Selected Readings on U.S. Immigration Policy and Law.* Wash.: G.P.O., 1980.

139 U.S. LIBRARY OF CONGRESS. *The National Union Catalog of Manuscript Collections, 1959-* . Ann Arbor: J. W. Edwards, 1962; Hamden, CT: Shoestring Press, 1964; Wash.: Library of Congress, 1965- . (This book catalog of archival collections as of 1983 has reported on more than 39,000 collections located in over 1,000 institutions and has indexed more than 400,000 references)

140 U.S. NATIONAL ARCHIVES. *Black Studies.* Wash.: National Archives and Records Service, 1973.

141 ———. *Guide to the Records in the National Archives.* Wash.: G.P.O., 1948.

142 ———. *National Archives Accessions. A Supplement to the Guide.*, No 31- . Wash.: G.P.O., Jul 1947- . (Issued irregularly)

143 U.S. NATIONAL HISTORICAL PUBLICATIONS COMMISSION. *A Guide to Archives and Manuscripts in the United States.*, Philip M. Hamer, ed. New Haven: Yale U Press, 1961.

144 U.S. WOMEN'S BUREAU. *A Guide to Sources of Data on Women and Women Workers for the United States and for Regions, States, and Local Areas.* Wash.: The Bureau, 1972.

145 U.S. WORKS PROGRESS ADMINISTRATION. FEDERAL WRITERS' PROJECT, NEW YORK CITY. *A Trial Bibliography of Bibliographies Relating to Labor.* NY: The Administration, 1937. (Mimeo.)

146 VECOLI, RUDOLPH J. "Labor Related Collections in the Immigration History Research Center." *Labor History*, Vol 22 (1982), 568-74.

147 WASHINGTON, SYLVIA H., comp. *Bibliography: Labor Management Relations Act, 1947, as Amended by the Labor-Management Reporting and Disclosure Act, 1959. Supplement II, 1970.* Wash.: National Labor Relations Board, 1970.

148 WASON, JAMES R. "American Workers and American Studies," pp 104-30, *American Studies: Topics and Sources*, Robert Walker, ed. Westport, CT: Greenwood, 1976.

149 WEBER, EDWARD C. "The Labadie Collection in the University of Michigan Library." *Labor History*, Vol 22 (1982), 576-81.

150 WECHSLER, ROBERT. *New York Labor Heritage: A Selected Bibliography of New York City Labor History.* NY: Robert F. Wagner Labor Archives, Tamiment Institute Library, New York U, 1981.

151 *Who's Who in Labor.* NY: Arno, 1976. (Update of the earlier edition undertaken with the cooperation of the AFL-CIO)

152 WOODBRIDGE, MARK H., comp. *American Federation of Labor and Congress of Industrial Organizations Pamphlets, 1889-1955: A Bibliography and Subject Index to the Pamphlets Held in the AFL-CIO Library.* Westport, CT: Greenwood, 1977.

153 *Work Related Abstracts, 1950-* . Detroit: Information Service, 1950- . (A loose-leaf service which was known as Employment Related Abstracts to 1973, and includes c.30 labor periodicals, and bridges, in limited fashion, *Trade Union Publications* by Reynolds and Killingsworth and the *Index to Labor Union Periodicals* published at the U of Michigan)

154 WRIGHT, CARROLL D. *Index of All Reports Issued by Bureaus of Labor Statistics in the United States Prior to March 1902.* Wash.: G.P.O., 1902.

Theories of the American Labor Movement and Historiography

155 AITKEN, JOHN R. "Benjamin Franklin, Karl Marx, and the Labor Theory of Value." *Pennsylvania Magazine of History and Biography*, Vol 90 (1966), 378-84.

156 "American Labor Theory, Philosophy: Reappraisal of General Motivations and Aims of American Trade Union Movement—9 Articles." *Labor and Nation*, Winter 1951, pp 43-71.

157 ARONOWITZ, STANLEY. "The Labor Movement and the Left in the United States." *Socialist Revolution*, Vol 9 (Mar-Apr 1979), 9-16.

158 ———. "The Working Class: A Break with the Past." *Liberation*, Vol 17 (Aug 1972), 20-31.

159 ASKOL'DOVA, S. M. "Osiovnoe Napravlenie v Amerikanskoi Burzhauznoe Istoriografii Rabochego Dvizheniia." *Voprosy Istorii*, No 5 (1966), 41-53.

160 BARBASH, JACK. "American Unionism: from Protest to Going Concern." *Journal of Social Issues*, Vol 2 (1968), 45-59.

161 ———. "Labor Movement Theory and the Institutional Setting." *Monthly Labor Review*, Vol 104 (Sep 1981), 34-37.

162 ———. "The Legal Foundations of Capitalism and the Labor Problem." *Journal of Economic Issues*, Vol 10 (1976), 799-810.

163 BAUDER, RUSSELL. "Three Interpretations of the American Trade Union Movement." *Social Forces*, Vol 22 (1943), 214-24.

164 BENDIX, REINHARD. *Work and Authority in Industry: Ideologies of Management in the Course of Industrialization*. NY: Wiley, 1956.

165 BENNETT, LEAMON J. "When Employees Run the Company: an Interview with Leamon J. Bennett." *Harvard Business Review*, Vol 59 (Jan-Feb 1979), 75-90.

166 BILLINGTON, RAY ALLEN. *The American Frontier*., Publication No 8. Wash.: Service Center for Teachers of History, A Service of the American Historical Association, 1958.

167 BLUM, ALBERT A. "The Writing of Labor History." *Newsletter*, Michigan State University, School of Labor and Industrial Relations, Vol 16, No 12 (1972), 5-6.

168 BOOTH, D. E. "Collective Action, Marx's Class Theory, and the Union Movement." *JEI/ Journal of Economic Issues*, Vol 12 (1978), 163-85.

169 BRODY, DAVID. "Labor and the Great Depression: The Interpretative Prospects." *Labor History*, Vol 13 (1972), 231-44.

170 ———. "The Old Labor History and the New: In Search of an American Working Class." *Labor History*, Vol 20 (1979), 111-26.

171 ———. "Philip Taft: Labor Scholar." *Labor History*, Vol 19 (1978), 9-22.

172 ———. "Radical Labor History and Rank-and-File Militancy: *Rank and File: Personal Histories by Working Class Organizers* by Alice and Staughton Lynd." *Labor History*, Vol 16 (1975), 117-26.

173 ———. "Working Class History in the Great Depression." *Reviews in American History*, Vol 4 (1976), 262-67. (UAW 1936-39)

174 BUCKHOLZ, ROGENE A. "The Work Ethic Reconsidered." *Industrial and Labor Relations Review*, Vol 31 (1978), 450-59.

175 BURNHAM, JAMES. *The Managerial Revolution*. NY: John Day, 1941.

176 CHUDACOFF, HOWARD. "Integrating Working Class History." *Reviews in American History*, Vol 7 (1979), 535-41.

177 CLARK, JOHN M. et al. *The Impact of the Union: Eight Economic Theorists Evaluate the Labor Union Movement*. NY: Books for Libraries Press, 1969.

178 CLELAND, HUGH C. "The Effects of Radical Groups on the Labor Movement." *Pennsylvania History*, Vol 26 (1959), 119-32.

179 COCHRANE, JAMES L. *Industrialism and Industrial Man in Retrospect: A Critical Review of the Ford Foundation's Support for the Inter-University Study of Labor*. NY: Ford Foundation, 1979.

180 COMISSO, ELLEN. "Workers' Councils and Labor Unions: Some Objective Trade-Offs." *Politics and Society*, Vol 10 (1981), 251-79.

181 COMMONS, JOHN R. "The American Shoemakers, 1648-1895." chap. 14, *Labor and Administration*, NY: Macmillan, 1913.

182 DAVIS, MIKE. "Why the U.S. Working Class is Different." *New Left Review*, Vol 123 (Sep-Oct 1980), 3-44.

183 DAVIS, STEPHEN P. "The Concept of Poverty in the Encyclopaedia Britannica from 1810 to 1975." *Labor History*, Vol 21 (1980), 91-101.

184 DAWSON, ANDREW. "History and Ideology: Fifty Years of 'Job Consciousness'." *Literature and History*, Vol 8 (Autumn 1978), 223-41.

185 DEBRIZZI, JOHN A. *Ideology and the Rise of Labor Theory in America*. Ph D diss, SUNY-Buffalo, 1979.

186 DERBER, MILTON. *The American Idea of Industrial Democracy*. Urbana: U of Illinois Press, 1970.

187 ———. et al. *Plant Union-Management Relations: From Practice to Theory*. Urbana: Institute of Labor and Industrial Relations, U of Illinois, 1965.

188 DOLNICK, DAVID. "History and Theory of the Labor Movement." chap. 5, *Employment Relations Research: A Summary and Appraisal.*, NY: Harper, 1960.

189 DUNLOP, JOHN T. "The Development of Labor Organization: a Theoretical Frame-Work." pp 163-93, *Insights into Labor Issues*, Richard A. Lester & Joseph Shister, eds. NY: Macmillan, 1948.

190 DYE, HOWARD S. "A Bargaining Theory of Residual Income Distribution." *Industrial and Labor Relations Review*, Vol 21 (1967), 40-54.

191 EHRENREICH, JOHN, and BARBARA EHRENREICH. "Work and Consciousness." *Monthly Review*, Vol 28 (Jul-Aug 1976), 10-18.

192 FAHEY, DAVID M. "From Labor History to Working Class History." *Journal of Urban History*, Vol 6 (1979), 105-11.

193 FIELD, JOHN. "British Historians and the Concept of the Labor Aristocracy." *Radical History Review*, No 19 (1978-79), 61-85.

194 FILIPPELLI, RONALD L. "The Uses of History in the Education of Workers." *Labor Studies Journal*, Vol 5 (1980), 3-12.

195 FISHBEIN, LESLIE. "A Lost Legacy of Labor Films." *Film and History*, Vol 9 (1979), 33-40.

196 FONER, ERIC. "Redefining the Past: *Time On The Cross* by Robert Fogel and Stanley Engerman." *Labor History*, Vol 16 (1975), 127-38.

197 FOX, ALAN, and ALAN FLANDERS. "The Reform of Collective Bargaining: From Donovan to Durkeim." *British Journal of Industrial Relations*, Vol 7 (1969), 151-80.

198 GARSON, G. DAVID. "Radical Issues in the History of the American Working Class." *Politics and Society*, Vol 3 (Fall 1972), 25-32.

199 GEIS, ROBERT. *Liberty, Equality, Fraternity: The Ideology of the American Labor Movement from 1828 to 1848.* Ph D diss, U of Minnesota, 1971.

200 GIEBEL, GREGORY. *Alienation from Freedom: the Effect of the Loss of Union Power upon the Relationship between Technology and Work.* Ph D diss, Pennsylvania State U, 1981.

201 GINGER, RAY. "American Workers: Views From the Left." *Labor History*, Vol 14 (1973), 425-28.

202 GONCE, RICHARD ALLYN. *The Development of John R. Commons' System of Thought.* Ph D diss, U of Wisconsin, 1966.

203 GREEN, JAMES R. "Behavioralism and Class Analysis." *Labor History*, Vol 13 (1972), 89-106.

204 GREENBERG, ED S. "The Consequences of Worker Participation: a Clarification of the Theoretial Literature." *Social Science Quarterly*, Vol 56 (1975), 191-208.

205 GREENWOOD, DAVID C. *Contemporary Theories of Union-Management Relations.* Wash.: Public Affairs Press, 1956.

206 GROSSMAN, JONATHAN, and WILLIAM T. MOYE. "Labor History in the 1970s: A Question of Identity," chap. 8, *Industrial Relations Research in the 1970s: Review and Appraisal*, Thomas A. Hochan, et al., eds. Madison: IRRA, 1982.

207 GULICK, CHARLES A. *History and Theories of Working Class Movements: A Select Bibliography.* Berkeley: Institute of Industrial Relations, U of California, 1955. (Mimeo.)

208 ———, and MELVIN K. BERS. "Insight and Illusion in Perlman's Theory of the Labor Movement." *Industrial and Labor Relations Review*, Vol. ((1953), 510-31)

209 HAGEN, EVERETT E. "Some Implications of Personality Theory for the Theory of Industrial Relations." *Industrial and Labor Relations Review*, Vol 18 (1965), 339-51.

210 HARDMAN, J. B. S. "From Job-Consciousness to Power Accumulation." *Proceedings of the Third Annual Meeting of the Industrial Relations Research Association*, Dec 28-29, 1950, pp 146-57. Madison: IRRA, 1951.

211 HART, C. W. M. "Industrial Relations Research and Social Theory." *Canadian Journal of Economics and Political Science*, Feb 1949.

212 HARTER, LAFAYETTE G., JR. "John R. Commons: Social Reformer and Institutional Economist." *American Journal of Economics and Sociology*, Vol 24 (1965), 85-96.

213 HENDERSON, JEFF, and ROBIN COHEN. "Capital and the Work Ethic." *Monthly Review*, Vol 31 (Nov 1979), 11-26.

214 HENRETTA, JAMES A. "The Study of Social Mobility: Ideological Assumptions and Conceptual Bias." *Labor History*, Vol 18 (1977), 165-78.

215 HIGGINS, GEORGE G. *Voluntarism in Organized Labor in the United States, 1930-1940.* Wash.: Catholic U of America, 1944.

216 HOBSBAWM, E. J. "Labor History and Ideology." *Journal of Social History*, Vol 7 (1974), 371-81.

217 HOERDER, DIRK. "American Labor & Immigration History: Reports on the State of the Historiography Since 1945." *Labor History*, Vol 21 (1980), 261-76, 392-419.

218 HOERDER, DIRK, ed. *American Labor and Immigration History, 1877-1920: Recent European Research.* Urbana: U of Illinois Press, 1983.

219 HOLT, W. STULL. "Hegel, the Turner Hypothesis, and the Safety-Valve Theory." *Agricultural History*, Vol 22 (1948), 175-76.

220 HOWE, IRVING. "Sweet and Sour Notes: On Workers and Intellectuals." *Dissent*, Vol 19 (1972), 264-69.

221 HOXIE, ROBERT F. "A Sociopsychological Interpretation." pp 35-59, *Unions, Management and the Public*, E. Wight Bakke & Clark Kerr, eds. NY: Harcourt, Brace, 1948.

222 INDUSTRIAL RELATIONS RESEARCH ASSOCIATION. *Interpreting the Labor Movement.* Madison: IRRA, 1952.

223 JEFFREYS-JONES, RHODRI. "Theories of American Labour Violence." *Journal of American Studies*, Vol 13 (1979), 245-64.

224 JEVONS, W. STANLEY. *The State in Relation to Labour*. London: Macmillan, 1882.

225 JOSEPH, MYRON L. "The Concept of Bargaining in Industrial Relations." *Proceedings of the Eighteenth Annual Winter Meeting of the Industrial Relations Research Association*, Dec 28-29, 1965, pp 183-93. Madison: IRRA, 1966.

226 KAHN, HERMAN. "Some Problems in the Writing of Labor History." *Proceedings of the Eighteenth Annual Winter Meeting of the Industrial Relations Research Association*, Dec 28-29, 1965, pp 324-32. Madison: IRRA, 1966.

227 KEDDIE, WELLS. "Socialist Academics and the Labor Movement." *Monthly Review*, Vol 23 (Feb 1972), 44.

228 KERR, CLARK. et al. *Industrialism and Industrial Man*. Cambr.: Harvard U Press, 1960.

229 ———. "Postscript to *Industrialism and Industrial Man*." *International Labour Review*, Vol 103 (1971), 519-40.

230 ———, and ABRAHAM SIEGEL. "The Structuring of the Labor Force in Industrial Society: New Dimensions and New Questions." *Industrial and Labor Relations Review*, Vol 8 (1955), 151-68.

231 KESSLER-HARRIS, ALICE. "Women's Wage Work as Myth and History." *Labor History*, Vol 19 (1978), 287-307.

232 KONVITZ, MILTON R. "An Empirical Theory of the Labor Movement: W. Stanley Jevons." *Philosophical Review*, Vol 57 (1948), 59-76.

233 KRADITOR, AILEEN S. *The Radical Persuasion, 1890-1917: Aspects of the Intellectual History and the Historiography of Three American Radical Organizations*. Baton Rouge: Louisiana State U Press, 1981.

234 KRUEGER, THOMAS. "American Labor Historiography: Old and New, a Review Essay." *Journal of Social History*, Vol 4 (1971), 277-85.

235 LEAB, DANIEL J. "Confronting a Myth: Films About Work and Workers in America." *Film Library Quarterly*, Vol 12, No 2/3 (1979), 8-17.

236 ———. "Writing History With Film: Two Views of the 1937 Strike Against General Motors by the UAW." *Labor History*, Vol 21 (1980), 102-12.

237 LEBLANC, PAUL. "Socialism and Labor in the United States." *Monthly Review*, Vol 24 (Sep 1972), 30-40.

238 LESTER, RICHARD A. "Reflections on the 'Labor Monopoly' Issue." *Journal of Political Economy*, Vol 55 (1947), 513-36.

239 LEVINSON, DAVID. "Perlman's Theory and the Marginal Utility Theory." *Industrial and Labor Relations Review*, Vol 20 (1967), 665-66.

240 LEWIS, H. GREGG. "The Labor Monopoly Problem: A Positive Program." *Journal of Political Economy*, Vol 59 (1951), 277-87.

241 LINDBLOM, CHARLES E. *Unions and Capitalism*. New Haven: Yale U Press, 1949.

242 LIPSET, SEYMOUR MARTIN. "Trade Unions and Social Structure." *Industrial Relations*, Vol 1 (1962-63), 78-89, 89-110. (Parts 1 & 2)

243 MCNULTY, PAUL J. "Labor Problems and Labor Economics: the Roots of an Academic Discipline." *Labor History*, Vol ((1968), 239-61.

244 MARTIN, DONALD L. *An Ownership Theory of the Trade Union*. Berkeley: U of California Press, 1980.

245 MASQUERIER, LEWIS. *Sociology: Or, The Reconstruction of Society, Government, and Property*. NY: The Author, 1877.

246 MILLER, MARC. "Workers' Owned." *Southern Exposure 8(Winter, 1980), 12-21*

247 MOBERG, DAVID. "Work and American Culture: the Ideal of Self-Determination and the Prospects for Socialism." *Socialist Review*, Vol 10 (Mar-Jun 1980), 19-56.

248 MONDS, JEAN. "Workers' Control and the Historians: a New Economism." *New Left Review*, No 97 (May-Jun 1976), 81-104.

249 MONTGOMERY, DAVID. "Gutman's Nineteenth Century America." *Labor History*, Vol 19 (1978), 416-29.

250 ———. "The Past and Future of Workers' Control." *Radical America*, Vol 13 (Nov-Dec 1979), 7-23.

251 ———. "To Study The People: The American Working Class." *Labor History*, Vol 21 (1980), 485-512.

252 MOORE, W. E. *Industrialization and Labor*. Ithaca: Cornell U Press, 1951.

253 MULHERIN, JAMES. *The Sociology of Work and Organizations: Historical Context and Pattern of Development*. Ph D diss, U of California, 1980.

254 MURPHY, GEORGE G. S., and ARNOLD ZELLNER. "Sequential Growth, the Labor—Safety-Valve Doctrine and the Development of American Unionism." *Journal of Economic History*, Vol 19 (1959), 402-21.

255 NEUFELD, MAURICE F. "Portrait of the Labor Historian as Boy and Young Man: Excerpts from the Interviews of Philip Taft by Margaret Honig." *Labor History*, Vol 19 (1978), 39-71.

256 ———. "The Sense of History and the Annals of Labor." *Proceedings of the Fourteenth Annual Meeting of the Industrial Relations Research Association*, Dec 28-29, 1961, pp 214-25. Madison: IRRA, 1962.

257 NISSEN, BRUCE. "U.S. Workers and the U.S. Labor Movement." *Monthly Review*, Vol 33 (May 1981), 17-30.

258 O'CONNOR, JAMES. "Productive and Unproductive Labor." *Politics and Society*, Vol 5 (1975), 297-336.

259 OLLMAN, BERTELL. "Toward Class Consciousness Next Time: Marx and the Working Class." *Politics and Society*, Vol 3 (Fall 1972), 1-25.

260 OZANNE, ROBERT. "Trends in American Labor History." *Labor History*, Vol 21 (1980), 513-21.

261 PARKER, CARLETON H. *The Casual Laborer and Other Essays*. NY: Harcourt, Brace & Howe, 1920.

262 PECK, SIDNEY M. "The Sociology of Unionism: an Appraisal." *American Journal of Economics and Sociology*, Vol 25 (1966), 53-67.

263 PERLMAN, MARK. *Labor Union Theories in America: Background and Development*. Evanston, IL: Row, Peterson, 1958.

264 PERLMAN, SELIG. *A Theory of the Labor Movement*. NY: Macmillan, 1928.

265 PESSEN, EDWARD. "The 'Pessen Thesis': Brief Reflections by its Author." *New York History*, Vol 56 (1975), 456-60.

266 PHELPS, ORME W. "The Trade Unionism of Henry Simons." *Proceedings of the Seventh Annual Meeting of the Industrial Relations Research Association*, Dec 28-30, 1954, pp 280-85. Madison: IRRA, 1955.

267 "Philip Taft: Publications." *Labor History*, Vol 19 (1978), 130-36.

268 POLANYI, KARL. *The Great Transformation*. NY: Farrar & Rinehart, 1944.

269 POOLE, MICHAEL. *Theories of Trade Unionism: A Sociology of Industrial Relations*. Bost.: Routledge & Kegan Paul, 1981.

270 RADOSH, RONALD. "The Corporate Ideology of American Labor Leaders from Gompers to Hillman." *Studies on the Left*, Vol 6 (Nov-Dec 1966), 85-86.

271 RANDALL, JOHN H. *The Problem of Group Responsibility to Society: an Interpretation of the History of American Labor*. Ph D diss, Columbia U, 1922.

272 ROGIN, MICHAEL. "Voluntarism: The Political Functions of an Antipolitical Doctrine." *Industrial and Labor Relations Review*, Vol 15 (1962), 521-35.

273 ROPER, DONALD M. "Beyond the Jacksonian Era: a Comment on the Pessen Thesis." *New York History*, Vol 56 (1975), 227-33.

274 ROSS, ARTHUR M. "Labor Organizations and the Labor Movement in Advanced Industrial Society." *Virginia Law Review*, Vol 50 (1964), 1359-85.

275 SCOGGINS, WILL. "The Anti-Labor Bias in Schoolbooks." *AFL-CIO American Federationist*, Dec 1967, pp 10-14.

276 SHANNON, FRED A. "The Homestead Act and the Labor Surplus." *American Historical Review*, Vol 41 (1956), 637-51.

277 ———. "A Post Mortem on the Labor-Safety-Valve Theory." *Agricultural History*, Vol 19 (1945), 31-37.

278 SIEGEL, ABRAHAM. "The Extended Meaning and Diminished Relevance of 'Job Conscious' Unionism." *Proceedings of the Eighteenth Annual Winter Meeting of the Industrial Relations Research Association*, Dec 28-29, 1965, pp 166-82. Madison: IRRA, 1966.

279 SIEVERS, ALLEN MORRIS. *Has Market Capitalism Collapsed? A Critique of Karl Polanyi's New Economics*. NY: Columbia U Press, 1949.

280 SIMLER, NORMAN J. "The Safety-Valve Doctrine Re-evaluated." *Agricultural History*, Vol 32 (1958), 250-57.

281 SIMONS, HENRY C. "Some Reflections on Syndicalism." *The Journal of Political Economy*, Vol 52 (1944), 1-25.

282 SIVACHEV, N. V., and I. M. SAVEL'EVA. "American Labor in Recent Soviet Historiography." *Labor History*, Vol 18 (1977), 407-32.

283 SOFFER, BENSON. "A Theory of Trade Union Development: The Role of the 'Autonomous' Workman." *Labor History*, Vol 1 (1960), 141-63.

284 SOMERS, GERALD G., ed. *Essays in Industrial Relations Theory*. Ames: Iowa State U Press, 1969.

285 STEARNS, PETER. "The Effort at Continuity in Working-Class Culture." *Journal of Modern History*, Vol 52 (1980), 626-55.

286 STURMTHAL, ADOLF. "Comments on Selig Perlman's 'A Theory of the Labor Movement.'" *Industrial and Labor Relations Review*, Vol 4 (1951), 483-96.

287 TAFT, PHILIP. "Commons-Perlman Theory: A Summary." *Proceedings of the Fifth Annual Meeting of the Industrial Relations Research Association*, Dec 28-29, 1950, pp 140-45. Madison: IRRA, 1951.

288 ———. "Labor History and the Labor Movement Today." *Labor History*, Vol 7 (1966), 70-77.

289 ———. "Reflections on Selig Perlman as a Teacher and Writer." *Industrial and Labor Relations Review*, Vol 29 (1976), 249-57.

290 ———. "A Rereading of Selig Perlman's 'A Theory of the Labor Movement.'" *Industrial and Labor Relations Review*, Vol 4 (1950), 70-77.

291 TANNENBAUM, FRANK. *The Labor Movement: Its Conservative Functions and Social Consequences*. NY: Putnam, 1921.

292 ———. *A Philosophy of Labor*. NY: Knopf, 1951.

293 THOMPSON, MARK, and LARRY F. MOORE. "Managerial Attitudes toward Industrial Relations: a United States—Canadian Comparison." *Relations Industrielles-Industrial Relations*, Vol 30 (1975), 331-42.

294 TREMBLAY, LOUIS-MARIE. "La Theorie de Selig Perlman: une Etude Critique." *Relations Industrielles-Industrial Relations*, Vol 20 (1965), 295-339.

295 TUCKER, RUFUS S. "The Frontier as an Outlet for Surplus Labor." *Southern Economic Review*, Vol 7 (1940), 158-86.

296 TURNER, F. J. *The Frontier in American History*. NY: Holt, 1920.

297 TYLER, GUS. *A New Philosophy for Labor*. NY: Fund for the Republic, 1959.

298 ———. *The Political Imperative: The Corporate Character of Unions*. NY: Macmillan, 1968.

299 ULMAN, LLOYD. "Some Theories of the Labor Movement," chap. 18, *The Rise of the National Trade Union*, Cambr.: Harvard U Press, 1955.

300 VEBLEN, THORSTEIN. *The Engineers and the Price System*. NY: Viking, 1921.

301 WEBB, SIDNEY, and BEATRICE WEBB. *Industrial Democracy*. London: Longmans, Green, 1897.

302 WEINER, ROBERT. "Karl Marx's Vision of America: a Biographical and Bibliographical Sketch." *Review of Politics*, Vol 42 (1980), 465-503.

303 WELLENREUTHER, HERMANN. "Labor in the Era of the American Revolution: A Discussion of Recent Concepts and Theories." *Labor History*, Vol 22 (1981), 573-600.

304 ———. "Labor in the Era of the American Revolution: A Discussion of Recent Concepts and Theories." *Labor History*, Vol 22 (1981), 573-600.

305 WINGARD, JOEL D. *Toward a Workers' America: the Theory and Practice of the American Proletarian Novel, Based upon Four Selected Works*. Ph D diss, Louisiana State U, 1979.

306 WRIGHT, DAVID MCCORD, ed. *The Impact of the Labor Union*. NY: Harcourt, Brace, 1951.

307 ZIEGER, ROBERT H. "'Which Side Are You On?' Workers, Unions and Critics." *Labor History*, Vol 17 (1976), 279-90.

308 ———. "Workers and Scholars: Recent Trends in American Labor Historiography." *Labor History*, Vol 13 (Spring 1972), 245-66.

309 ZIMBALIST, ANDREW. "The Limits of Work Humanization." *Review of Radical Political Economics*, Vol 7 (Summer 1975), 50-59.

General Histories, Surveys, and Cross-Period Studies

310 AIKIN, WILLIAM E. *Technocracy and the American Dream: The Technocrat Movement, 1900-1941.* Berkeley: U of California Press, 1977.

311 ALEXANDER, KENNETH O. "The Evolving Status of American Unionism." *Relations Industrielles-Industrial Relations*, Vol 22 (1967), 344-56.

312 ALMAN, DAVID. *World Full of Strangers: the Labor Movement in Fiction and Non-Fiction.* NY: AMS Press, 1977.

313 ALTENBAUGH, RICHARD. *Forming the Structure of a New Society within the Shell of the Old: a Study of Three Labor Colleges and their Contributions to the American Labor Movement.* Ph D diss, U of Pittsburgh, 1980.

314 ANDERSON, JOHN C. et al. "Union Decertification in the U.S.: 1947-1977." *Industrial Relations*, Vol 19 (1980), 100-7.

315 ARMSTRONG, JAMES S. *The Labor Temple, 1910-1957: A Social Gospel in Action in the Presbyterian Church.* Ph D diss, U of Wisconsin, 1974.

316 ARONOWITZ, STANLEY. *False Promises: The Shaping of American Working Class Consciousness.* NY: McGraw-Hill, 1973.

317 ASHENFELTER, ORLEY, and JOHN H. PENCAVEL. "American Trade Union Growth: 1900-1960." *Quarterly Journal of Economics*, Vol 83 (1969), 434-48.

318 ATLESON, JAMES B. *Values and Assumptions in American Labor Law.* Amherst: U of Massachusetts Press, 1983.

319 AUERBACH, JEROLD S., ed. *American Labor: The Twentieth Century.* Indianapolis: Bobbs-Merrill, 1969.

320 BARKIN, SOLOMON. "The United States: A Time for Reassessment," chap. 10, *Worker Militancy and Its Consequences, 1965-1975: New Directions in Western Industrial Relations*, NY: Praeger, 1975.

321 ———, and ALBERT A. BLUM, eds.. "The Crisis in the American Trade-Union Movement." *Annals of the American Academy of Political and Social Science*, Phila: The Academy, Nov 1963, entire issue.

322 BARTON, BETTY L. *The Fellowship of Reconciliation: Pacifism, Labor and Social Welfare, 1915-60.* Ph D diss, Florida State U, 1974.

323 BEARD, MARY. *The American Labor Movement: A Short History.* NY: Macmillan, 1939.

324 BEIRNE, JOSEPH A. *Challenge to Labor: New Roles for American Trade Unions.* Englewood Cliffs, NJ: Prentice-Hall, 1969.

325 BERMAN, DANIEL M. *Death on the Job: Occupational Health and Safety in the United States.* NY: Monthly Review Press, 1978.

326 BERNSTEIN, IRVING. "The Growth of American Unions." *The American Economic Review*, Vol 44 (1954), 301-18.

327 ———. *Selected Works of Irving Bernstein.* Los Angeles: U of California, 1977.

328 ———. "Union Growth and Structural Cycles." *Proceedings of the Seventh Annual Meeting of the Industrial Relations Research Association*, Dec 28-30, 1954, pp 202-46. Madison: IRRA, 1955.

329 BERTHOFF, ROWLAND. *British Immigrants in Industrial America*. Cambr.: Harvard U Press, 1953.

330 BIMBA, ANTHONY. *The History of the American Working Class*. NY: International Publishers, 1933.

331 *Birth of a Union*. 1966. (Non-fiction film produced by National Educational Television)

332 BLACKMAN, JOHN L., JR. *Presidential Seizure in Labor Disputes*. Cambr.: Harvard U Press, 1967.

333 BLUM, ALBERT A. *The Development of American Labor*. NY: Macmillan, 1963. (Pamphlet)

334 ———. *Drafted or Deferred: Practices Past and Present*. Ann Arbor: Bureau of Industrial Relations, School of Business Administration, U of Michigan, 1967.

335 ———. "Labor and the Federal Government: 1850-1933." *Current History*, Vol 48 (1965), 328-33, 364.

336 ———. "Unions and Their Intellectuals." *Challenge*, Apr 1965, pp 23-25.

337 ———. "Why Unions Grow." *Labor History*, Vol 9 (1968), 39-72.

338 BODNER, JOHN. *Workers' World: Kinship, Community, and Protest in an Industrial Society, 1900-1940*. Balt.: Johns Hopkins Press, 1982.

339 BOK, DEREK C., and JOHN T. DUNLOP. *Labor and the American Community*. NY: Simon and Schuster, 1970.

340 BOLINO, AUGUST C. "The Duration of Unemployment: Some Tentative Historical Comparisons." *Quarterly Review of Economics and Business*, Vol. ((1966), 31-47)

341 ———. "Sequential Growth and the Development of American Unionism." *Journal of Economic History*, Vol 20 (1960), 314-17.

342 BOYER, RICHARD O., and HERBERT M. MORAIS. *Labor's Untold Story*. NY: United Electrical, Radio & Machine Workers of America, 1980.

343 BRANDES, STUART D. *American Welfare Capitalism*. Chicago: U of Chicago Press, 1976.

344 BRECHER, JEREMY. "Uncovering the Hidden History of the American Workplace." *Review of Radical Political Economics*, Vol 10 (1978), 1-23.

345 BROADWATER, MARGARET. *Labor and the First Amendment: Thornhill to Logan Valley Plaza*. Ph D diss, Rutgers U, 1977.

346 BRODY, DAVID. *Workers in Industrial America, Essays on the 20th Century Struggle*. NY: Oxford U Press, 1980.

347 BRODY, DAVID, ed. *The American Labor Movement*. NY: Harper & Row, 1971.

348 BRODY, DORIS COHEN. *American Labor Education Service, 1927-1962: an Organization in Workers' Education*. Ph D diss, Cornell U, 1973.

349 BROOKS, GEORGE W., and MARK THOMPSON. "Multiplant Units: the NLRB's Withdrawal of Free Choice." *Industrial and Labor Relations Review*, Vol 20 (1967), 363-80.

350 BROOKS, JOHN G. *Labor's Challenge to the Social Order: Democracy Its Own Critic and Educator*. NY: Macmillan, 1920.

351 BURRAGE, MICHAEL. "Democracy and the Mystery of the Crafts: Observations on Work Relationships in America and Britain." *Daedalus*, Vol 101 (Fall 1972), 141-62.

352 BURTT, EVERETT J. *Labor in the American Economy*. NY: St. Martin's Press, 1979.

353 CAHN, WILLIAM. *A Pictorial History of American Labor*. NY: Crown, 1972.

354 CANDELORO, DOMINIC. "The Single Tax Movement and Progressivism, 1880-1920." *American Journal of Economics and Sociology*, Vol 38 (1979), 113-27.

355 CANTOR, MILTON, ed. *American Workingclass Culture: Explorations in American Labor and Social History*. Westport, CT: Greenwood, 1979.

356 Carleton, Frank Tracy. *Organized Labor in American History.* NY: Appleton, 1920.

357 Chadwick-Jones, John K. et al. *Social Psychology of Absenteeism.* NY: Praeger, 1982.

358 Chamberlain, Lawrence H. *Loyalty and Legislative Action. A Survey of Activity by the New York State Legislature 1919-1949.* Ithaca: Cornell U Press, 1951.

359 Chandler, Margaret K. *Management Rights and Union Interests.* NY: McGraw-Hill, 1964.

360 Chang, Pei Yang. *Picketing.* Ph D diss, New York U, 1963.

361 Chapman, Frank. "New Challenge to Labor Rights." *Freedomways,* Vol 19 (1979), 137-42. (Anti-labor sentiments since the 1930s)

362 Chinloy, Peter. *Labor Productivity.* Cambr.: Abt Books, 1981.

363 Clark, Marjorie R., and S. Fanny Simon. *The Labor Movement in America.* NY: W. W. Norton, 1938.

364 Clawson, Dan. *Bureaucracy and the Labor Process: The Transformation of U.S. Industry, 1860-1920.* NY: Monthly Review Press, 1980.

365 Cobb, William H. "From Utopian Isolation to Radical Activism: Commonwealth College, 1925-1935." *Arkansas Historical Quarterly,* Vol 32 (1973), 132-47.

366 Coleman, John R. *Blue-Collar Journal: A College President's Sabbatical.* Phila.: Lippincott, 1974.

367 Committee for Economic Development. Research and Policy Committee *Union Powers and Union Functions: Toward a Better Balance.* NY: Committee for Economic Development, 1964.

368 Commons, John R. & Associates. *History of Labour in the United States.,* 2 vols. NY: Macmillan, 1918.

369 Conk, Margo A. "Occupational Classification int he United States Census: 1870-1970." *Journal of Interdisciplinary History,* Vol 9 (1978), 111-30.

370 ———. *The United States Census and Labor Force Change: A History of Occupational Statistics, 1870-1940.* Ann Arbor: U of Michigan Press, 1980.

371 *The Constitution and the Labor Union.* 1959. (Non-fiction film produced by National Educational Television)

372 Cooper, Patricia A. *From Handcraft to Mass Production: Men, Women, and Work Culture in American Cigar Factories, 1900-1919.* Ph D diss, U of Maryland, 1981.

373 Cornell, Fred. *History of the Rand School for Social Science.* Ph D diss, Columbia U, 1976.

374 Cory, Herbert Ellsworth. *The Intellectuals and the Wage Workers: A Study in Educational Psychoanalysis.* NY: Sunwise Turn, 1919.

375 Cotkin, George. *Working-Class Intellectuals and Evolutionary Thought in America, 1870-1915.* Ph D diss, Ohio State U, 1978.

376 Cumbler, John T. *Working-Class Community in Industrial America: Work, Leisure and Struggle in Two Industrial Cities, 1880-1930.* Westport, CT: Greenwood, 1979.

377 Czarnecki, Edgar R. *Factors Affecting the Growth of American Labor Unions.* Ph D diss, Georgetown U, 1967.

378 DeLorme, Charles D., Jr. *A Study of the Attitude of Organized Labor Toward Monetary Reform and Monetary Policy, 1866-1965.* Ph D diss, Louisiana State U, 1966.

379 Demeter, John. "Independent Film and Workingclass History: a Review of 'Northern Lights' and 'The Wobblies.'" *Radical America,* Vol 14 (Jan-Feb 1980), 17-26.

380 Derber, Milton. *The American Idea of Labor Democracy, 1865-1965.* Urbana: U of Illinois Press, 1970.

381 ———. "The Idea of Industrial Democracy in America; 1915-1935." *Labor History,* Vol 8 (1967), 3-29.

382 DOMMANGET, MAURICE. *Histoire du Premier Mai*. Paris: Editions de la tete de feuilles, 1972.

383 DOUTY, H. M. "Fifty Years of the MLR: An Appreciation." *Monthly Labor Review*, Vol 88 (1965), 771-77.

384 DUBOFSKY, MELVYN, ed. *American Labor Since the New Deal*. Chicago: Quadrangle, 1971.

385 DUDDEN, FAYE E. *From Help to Domestic: American Servants, 1800-1880*. Ph D diss, U of Rochester, 1981.

386 DULLES, FOSTER RHEA. *Labor in America*. NY: Thomas Y. Crowell, 1960.

387 DUNLOP, JOHN T. "Past and Future Tendencies in American Labor Organizations." *Daedalus*, Vol 107 (Winter 1978), 79-96.

388 DWYER, RICHARD. *An Examination of the Development of Labor Studies at Rutgers University, 1931-1974: a Study in Union-University Cooperation*. Ph D diss, Rutgers U, 1976.

389 ———. et al "Labor Studies: in Quest of Industrial Justice." *Labor Studies Journal*, Vol 2 (Fall 1977) 95-131.

390 EGLOFF, MARJORIE C. "From the Best of the Monthly Labor Review: Fifty Years of the MLR—A Special Section." *Monthly Labor Review*, Vol 88 (Jul 1965), 787-802.

391 EISNER, J. MICHAEL. *William Morris Leiserson: Economics in Action*. Ph D diss, U of Wisconsin, 1965.

392 ESTEY, MARTIN S. "Trends in Concentration of Union Membership, 1897-1962." *Quarterly Journal of Economics*, Vol 80 (1966), 343-60.

393 EVANS, ROBERT, JR. *Public Policy Toward Labor*. NY: Harper & Row, 1965.

394 FAULKNER, HAROLD U., and MARK STARR. *Labor in America*. NY: Oxford Book Co., 1957.

395 FELDSTEIN, STANLEY, and LAWRENCE COSTELLO, eds.. *The Ordeal of Assimilation: A Documentary History of the White Working Class*. Garden City, NY: Anchor, 1974.

396 FINK, GARY M. "The Rejection of Voluntarism." *Industrial and Labor Relations Review*, Vol 26 (1973), 805-19.

397 FINK, GARY M., ed. *AFL-CIO Executive Council Statements and Reports, 1956-1975*. Westport, CT: Greenwood Press, 1977.

398 FISHER, ROBERT. *The People's Institute of New York City, 1897-1934: Culture, Progressive Democracy and the People*. Ph D diss, New York U, 1974.

399 FONER, PHILIP S. *History of the Labor Movement in the United States.*, Vol 1: *From Colonial Times to the Founding of the American Federation of Labor*. NY: International, 1947.

400 ———, and REINHARD SCHULTZ. *Das Andere Amerika: Geschichte, Kunst, und Kultur der amerikanischen Arbeiterbewegung*. Berlin: Elefanten Press, 1983.

401 FONER, PHILIP S., comp. *American Labor Songs of the Nineteenth Century*. Urbana: U of Illinois Press, 1975.

402 FONER, PHILIP S., ed. *We, the Other People: Alternative Declarations of Independence by Labor Groups, Farmers, Woman's Rights Advocates, Socialists, and Blacks, 1829-1975*. Urbana: U of Illinois Press, 1976.

403 FRIED, ALBERT, ed. *Except to Walk Free: Documents and Notes in the History of American Labor*. Garden City, NY: Anchor, 1974.

404 FRISCH, MICHAEL, and DANIEL J. WALKOWITZ, eds. *Working Class America: Essays on Labor, Community, and American Society*. Urbana: U of Illinois Press, 1983.

405 GABRIEL, RONALD LEE. *A Critical Evaluation of the Role and Functions of the General Counsel of the NLRB in the Investigation and Prosecution of Unfair Labor Practice Charges, August 22, 1947 to June 25, 1971*. Ph D diss, American U 1974.

406 GARAFOLA, LYNN. "Hollywood and the Myth of the Working Class." *Radical America*, Vol 14 (Jan-Feb 1980), 7-16.

407 GARRATY, JOHN A. *Unemployment in History: Economic Thought and Public Policy*. NY: Harper & Row, 1977.

408 GILDEMEISTER, GLEN. *Prison Labor and Convict Competition with Free Workers in Industrializing America, 1849-1890.* Ph D diss, Northern Illinois U, 1977.

409 GOLDBERG, JOSEPH P. et al. *Federal Policies and Worker Status Since the Thirties.* Madison: IRRA, 1976.

410 GOLDEN, CARL, and SUSAN BONHOMME, eds.. *Organized Labor: Source Materials for the Study of Labor in America.* NY: United Federation of Teachers, 1976.

411 GORDON, DAVID M. et al. *Segmented Work, Divided Workers: The Historical Transformation of Labor in the United States.* Cambr., England: Cambridge U Press, 1982.

412 GOTTLIEB, SYLVIA B. "The Union Staff Intellectual in the Labor Movement." *Proceedings of the Sixteenth Annual Meeting of the Industrial Relations Research Association,* Dec 27-28, 1963, pp 259-68. Madison: IRRA, 1964.

413 GRAY, LOIS. "The American Way in Labor Education." *Industrial Relations,* Vol V (1966), 53-66.

414 GREEN, ARCHIE. "American Labor Lore: its Meanings and Uses." *Industrial Relations,* Vol 4 (1965), 51-68.

415 GREEN, JAMES R. *The World of the Worker.* NY: Hill & Wang, 1980.

416 GREEN, JAMES R., ed. *Workers' Struggles: A "Radical America" Reader.* Phila.: Temple U Press, 1983.

417 GREENFIELD, THOMAS. *Standing Before Kings: Work and the Work Ethic in American Drama, 1920-1970.* Ph D diss, U of Minnesota, 1980.

418 GREGORY, CHARLES OSCAR, and HAROLD A. KATZ. *Labor and the Law.,* 3d Edition. NY: Norton, 1978.

419 GROOM, PHYLLIS. "From Model-T to Medicare: Fifty Years of the MLR—A Special Section." *Monthly Labor Review,* Vol 88 (1965), 778-86.

420 GROSS, BEATRICE, and LEONARD GROSS, eds.. *The Children's Rights Movement: Overcoming the Oppression of Young People.* Garden City, NY: Anchor, 1977.

421 GROSS, JAMES A. *The Reshaping of the National Labor Relations Board: National Labor Policy in Transition, 1937-1947.* Albany, NY: SUNY Press, 1981.

422 GROSSMAN, JONATHAN. *The Department of Labor.* NY: Praeger, 1973.

423 ———. "The Labor Department's New England Ancestor." *Worklife,* Vol 1 (Jun 1976), 15-20.

424 ———. "The Origin of the United States Department of Labor." *Monthly Labor Review,* Vol 96 (Mar 1973), 3-7.

425 ———. "The People's Department." *Worklife,* Vol 1 (Aug 1976), 23-30.

426 ———. "Who Is the Father of Labor Day?" *Monthly Labor Review,* Vol 95 (Sep 1972), 3-6.

427 GUERIN, DANIEL. *100 Years of Labor in the USA.* London: Ink Links, 1979.

428 GUTMAN, HERBERT G. "Work, Culture, and Society in Industrializing America, 1815-1919." *American Historical Review,* Vol 77 (1973), 531-88.

429 ———. *Work, Culture, and Society in Industrializing America: Essays in American Working-Class and Social History.* NY: Vintage, 1977.

430 HABER, CAROLE. "Mandatory Retirement in Nineteenth Century America: the Conceptual Basis for a New Work Cycle." *Journal of Social History,* Vol 12 (1978), 77-96.

431 HABER, WILLIAM, ed. *Labor in a Changing America.* NY: Basic Books, 1966.

432 HAGGARD, THOMAS E. *Compulsory Unionism, the NLRB, and the Courts: a Legal Analysis of Union Security Agreements.* Phila.: U of Pennsylvania, 1977.

433 HAMERMESH, DANIEL S. *An Economic Theory of the Incidence and Growth of Trade Unionism.* Princeton: Industrial Relations Section, Princeton U, 1969.

434 HANSON, CHARLES G. et al. *The Closed Shop: A Comparative Study in Public Policy and Trade Union Security in Britain, the USA, and west Germany.* NY: St. Martin's Press, 1982.

435 Hareven, Tamara K., and Maris A. Vinovskis, eds. *Family and Population in Nineteenth-Century America.* Princeton: Princeton U Press, 1978.

436 Harrington, Michael. "Catholics in the Labor Movement: A Case History." *Labor History*, Vol 1 (1960), 231-63.

437 Hazelrigg, Lawrence E. "Occupational Mobility in 19th Century U.S. Cities: a Review of Some Evidence." *Social Forces*, Vol 53 (1974), 21-32.

438 Henle, Peter. "A Chronicle of Trade Union Positions on Government Ownership." *Monthly Labor Review*, Vol 88 (Jul 1965), 805-16.

439 Hiestand, Dale Leroy. *Economic Growth and the Opportunities of Minorities: an Analysis of Changes in the Employment of Negroes and Women.* Ph D diss, Columbia U, 1963.

440 Hildebrand, George H. *American Unionism: An Historical and Analytical Survey.* Reading, MA: Addison Wesley, 1979.

441 Hill, Stephen. *Competition and Control at Work: The New Industrial Sociology.* Cambr.: MIT Press, 1981.

442 Holland, Thomas. *The Labor Management Conferences.* Wash.: National Security Resources Board, 1950.

443 Horan, James D. *The Pinkertons: The Detective Dynasty That Made History.* NY: Crown, 1968.

444 ———, and Howard Swiggett. *The Pinkerton Story.* NY: Putnam, 1951.

445 Howe, Irving, ed. *The World of the Blue-Collar Worker.* NY: Quadrangle, 1972.

446 Howlett, Charles F. "Brookwood Labor College and Work Commitment to Social Reform." *Mid-America*, Vol 61 (1979), 47-66.

447 Hutchinson, John. *The Imperfect Union: A History of Corruption in American Trade Unions.* NY: Dutton, 1970.

448 *If You Don't Come In Sunday....* 1978. (Non-fiction film produced by the Manpower Education Institute)

449 Iman, Raymond S., and Thomas W. Koch. *Labor in American Society.* Chicago: Scott, Foresman, 1965.

450 "Important Events in American Labor History." *IBEW Journal*, Vol 71 (Mar 1972), 31-33.

451 *The Inheritance.* 1964. (Non-fiction film by Harold Mayer)

452 Jaher, Frederic Cople. "Industrialism and the American Aristocrat: a Social Study of John Hay and His Novel, *The Bread-Winners.*" *Illinois State Historical Society Journal*, Vol 45 (1972), 69-93.

453 James, John A. "Some Evidence on Relative Labor Scarcity in 19th Century American Manufacturing." *Explorations in Economic History*, Vol 18 (1981), 376-88.

454 Johnson, Haynes B., and Nick Kotz. *The Unions.* NY: Pocket Books, 1972.

455 Katz, Arthur. *A Study of Conflict and Cooperation in the Relationship between Organized Labor and Voluntary Social Welfare in America during the Years 1905-1955.* Ph D diss, New York U, 1968.

456 Katz, Michael. "Occupational Classification in History." *Journal of Interdisciplinary History*, Vol 3 (1972), 63-88.

457 Kaye, Stephen Arnold. *The Rhetoric of Song: Singing Persuasion in Social-Action Movements.* Ph D diss, U of Oregon, 1966.

458 Klein, Maury, and Harvey A. Kantor. *Prisoners of Progress: American Industrial Cities, 1850-1920.* NY: Macmillan, 1976. (See especially pp 285-329)

459 Koistinen, Paul A. C. *The Hammer and the Sword: Labor, the Military, and Industrial Mobilization, 1920-1945.* Ph D diss, U of California, 1964.

460 Kopald, Sylvia. *Rebellion in Labor Unions.* NY: Boni & Liveright, 1924.

461 Koretz, Robert F., ed. *Labor Organization.* NY: Chelsea House, 1970.

462 Kratz, Walter. *American Labor and the Intellectual.* NY: Vantage Press, 1956.

463 Krislov, Joseph. "Organizing, Union Growth, and the Cycle, 1949-1966." *Labor History*, Vol 11 (1970), 212-22.
464 ———. "Union Organizing of New Units, 1955-1966." *Industrial and Labor Relations Review*, Vol 21 (1967), 31-39.
465 "Labor's Centennial 1881-1981: 100 Years with the Union Label." *American Federationist*, Vol 88 (Apr 1981), 1-4.
466 Lane, Roger, and John J. Turner, eds.. *Riot, Rout, and Tumult: Readings in American Social and Political Violence.* Westport, CT: Greenwood, 1978.
467 Lanza, Aldo. "Teatro operaio e labor chatauquas' al Brookwood Labor College." *Movimento Operaio e Socialista*, New Series 3 (1980), 199-219.
468 Laslett, John H. M., comp. *The Workingman in American Life: Selected Readings.* Bost.: Houghton Mifflin, 1968.
469 Lasson, Kenneth. *The Workers: Portraits of Nine American Jobholders.* NY: Grossman, 1971.
470 Lauck, William J. *Political and Industrial Democracy, 1776-1926.* NY: Funk and Wagnalls, 1926.
471 Leab, Daniel J. "American History Through Film: Working Class History," pp 12-14, *American History Through Film*, Robert Toplin, ed. Bloomington, IN: Organization of American Historians, 1982.
472 ———. "The Use of Film in the Teaching of Labor History." *Organization of American Historians Newsletter*, Jul 1981, pp 19-23.
473 LeMasters, E. E. *Blue Collar Aristocrats: Life Styles at a Working Class Tavern.* Madison: U of Wisconsin Press, 1975.
474 Lens, Sidney. *The Labor Wars: from the Molly Maguires to the Sitdowns.* Garden City: Doubleday, 1973.
475 Levison, Andrew. *The Working Class Majority.* NY: Coward, McCann & Geoghegan, 1974.
476 Levitan, Sar A. *Blue-Collar Workers: A Symposium on Middle America.* NY: McGraw-Hill, 1971.
477 Lewis, Doris K. "Union-Sponsored Middle-Income Housing: 1927-65." *Monthly Labor Review*, Vol 88 (1965), 629-36.
478 Lindblom, Charles E. *Unions and Capitalism.* New Haven: Yale U Press, 1949.
479 Lorenz, Edward Charles. *Guidance and Work in the New York City Schools: a History of Vocational Guidance, 1898-1941.* Ph D diss, U of Chicago, 1978.
480 Lynd, Alice, and Staughton Lynd. *Rank and File: Personal Histories by Working-Class Organizers.* Princeton: Princeton U Press, 1981.
481 McBride, Paul W. "The Co-op Industrial Education Experiment, 1900-1917." *History of Education Journal*, Vol 14 (1974), 209-21.
482 Mackenzie, Gavin. *The Aristocracy of Labor: The Position of Skilled Craftsmen in the American Class Structure.* NY: Cambridge U Press, 1974.
483 McLaughlin, Doris B., and Christine F. Miller. *The Impact of Labor Unions on the Rate and Direction of Technological Innovation.* Ann Arbor: Institute of Labor and Industrial Relations, U of Michigan—Wayne State U, 1979.
484 McNulty, Paul J. *Economics and the Study of Labor.* Ph D diss, Cornell U, 1968.
485 Mader, Diane Castellano. *The Argumentation in the Trade Union Movement between 1902 and 1935.* Ph D diss, Northwestern U, 1966.
486 Magnuson, Norris Alden. *Salvation in the Slums: Evangelical Social Welfare Work, 1865-1920.* Ph D diss, U of Minnesota, 1968.
487 Matthews, H. "Labor and Humanities: Toward a Stronger Partnership." *Interface*, Vol 10 (1981), 6-7.
488 Mavrinac, Harry. *'Big' Labor and Education in Pennsylvania: a Study of the Educational Concerns of the AFL, the CIO, and the AFL-CIO, 1920-1970.* Ph D diss, U of Pittsburgh, 1978.

489 MELTZER, MILTON. *Bread—and Roses: The Struggle of American Labor, 1865-1915.* NY: Knopf, 1967.

490 MILLER, ROBERT S. *Business and Labor: the Social Gospel View.* Ph D diss, U of Kentucky, 1973.

491 MILLIS, HARRY A., and ROYAL E. MONTGOMERY. *Organized Labor.* NY: McGraw-Hill, 1945.

492 MILLS, ROBERT BRYANT. *The Generational Theory in Political Research: a Cohort Analysis of Public Opinion Toward Labor Unions 1937-1967.* Ph D diss, U of Iowa, 1972.

493 MONTGOMERY, DAVID. "New Tendencies in Union Struggles and Strategies in Europe and the United States, 1916-1922," pp 88-116, *Work, Community and Power: The Experience of Labor in Europe and America, 1900-1925*, James E. Cronin & Carmen Sirianni, eds. Phila: Temple U Press, 1983.

494 ———. "The 'New Unionism' and the Transformation of Workers' Consciousness in America, 1909-22." *Journal of Social History*, Vol 7 (1974), 509-29.

495 ———. "Workers Control of Machine Production in the 19th Century." *Labor History*, Vol 17 (1976), 485-509.

496 MORN, FRANK. *"The Eye That Never Sleeps": A History of the Pinkerton National Detective Agency.* Bloomington: Indiana U Press, 1982.

497 MORRIS, JAMES O. *Conflict Within the AFL: A Study of Craft Versus Industrial Unionism, 1901-1938.*, Cornell Studies in Industrial and Labor Relations, Vol 10. Ithaca: NY State School of Industrial and Labor Relations, Cornell U, 1958.

498 MORRIS, RICHARD B., ed. *The U.S. Department of Labor Bicentennial History of the American Worker.* Wash: G.P.O., 1976; new edition Princeton: Princeton U Press, 1983.

499 MOWDAY, RICHARD T. et al. *Employee-Organization Linkages: The Psychology of Commitment, Absenteeism, and Turnover.* NY: Academic Press, 1982.

500 MURPHY, GEORGE G. S., and ARNOLD ZELLNER. "Sequential Growth, the Labor—Safety-Valve Doctrine and the Development of American Unionism." *Journal of Economic History*, Vol 19 (1959), 402-21.

501 MUSSELMAN, BARBARA. "Working Class Unity and Ethnic Division: Trade Unionists and Cultural Pluralism 1893-1920." *Cincinnati Historical Society Bulletin*, Vol 34 (1976), 121-40.

502 NELSON, DANIEL. *Managers and Workers: Origins of the New Factory System in the United States, 1880-1920.* Madison: U of Wisconsin Press, 1975.

503 NEUFELD, MAURICE F. "The Historical Relationship of Liberals and Intellectuals to Organized Labor in the United States." *The Annals of the American Academy of Political and Social Science*, Nov 1963, pp 115-28.

504 NEWKIRK, WAYNE EUGENE. *The Implications of the Changing Status of Picketing on Labor Unions (1827-1963).* Ph D diss, Louisiana U, 1965.

505 NOVAK, ESTELLE GERSHGOREN. *Proletarian Poetry in the United States: Theory and Practice from 1926 to 1939.* Ph D diss, U of California, 1968.

506 O'CONNOR, JOHN JOSEPH. *The Supreme Court and Labor.* Ph D diss, Catholic U of America, 1932.

507 O'DONNELL, L. A. "Labor Discovers its Past." *Commonweal*, Vol 107 (Sep 1980), 490-95.

508 ORTH, SAMUEL P. *The Armies of Labor.* New Haven: Yale U Press, 1921.

509 OWEN, JOHN E. "The U.S. Labor Movement: its History and Current Problems." *Rivista Internazionale di Scienze Economiche e Commerciali*, Vol 23 (Jan 1976), 33-42.

510 PALMER, BRYAN D. "Class, Conception and Conflict: the Thrust for Efficiency; Managerial Views of Labor and the Working Class Rebellion, 1903-22." *Review of Radical Political Economics*, Vol 7 (Summer 1975), 31-49.

511 Patterson, James T. *America's Struggle Against Poverty*. Cambr.: Harvard U Press, 1981.

512 Pelling, Henry. *America and the British Left: From Bright to Bevan*. NY: New York U Press, 1957.

513 ———. *American Labor*. Chicago: U of Chicago Press, 1960.

514 Perkins, Frances, and J. Paul St. Sure. *Two Views of American Labor*. Los Angeles: Institute of Industrial Relations, U of California, 1965.

515 Perline, Martin M. *A Comparative Analysis of the Trade Union Press*. Ph D diss, Ohio State U, 1965.

516 ———. "The Trade Union Press: An Historical Analysis." *Labor History*, Vol 10 (1969), 107-14.

517 Perlman, Selig. *A History of Trade Unionism in the United States*. NY: Macmillan, 1922.

518 Pessen, Edward. "Labor from the Revolution to the Civil War." *Monthly Labor Review*, Vol 99 (Jun 1976), 17-24.

519 Pickering, John. *The Working Man's Political Economy*. Cincinnati: T. Varney, 1847.

520 Pierson, Frank C. *Unions in Postwar America: An Economic Assessment*. NY: Random House, 1967.

521 Piotrkowski, Chaya S. *Work and the Family System: A Naturalistic Study of Working-Class and Lower-Middle-Class Families*. NY: Free Press, 1979.

522 Pivan, Frances, and Richard A. Cloward. *Poor People's Movements: Why They Succeed, How They Fail*. NY: Pantheon, 1977.

523 Preis, Art. *Labor's Giant Step: Twenty Years of the CIO*. NY: Pathfinder Press, 1972.

524 Preston, William, Jr. *Aliens and Dissenters: Federal Suppression of Radicals, 1903-1933*. Cambr.: Harvard U Press, 1963.

525 Quart, Leonard, and Albert Auster. "The Working Class Goes to Hollywood," pp 163-75, *Cinema, Politics and Society in America*, Philip Davies & Brian Neve, eds. Manchester, England: Manchester U Press, 1981.

526 Radosh, Ronald. "The Corporate Ideology of American Labor Leaders from Gompers to Hillman." *Studies on the Left*, Vol 6 (Nov-Dec 1966), 66-68.

527 Ratner, Ronnie. "The Social Meaning of Industrialization in the United States: Determinants of the Scope of Coverage Under Wage and Hour Standards Legislation, 1900-1970." *Social Problems*, Vol 27 (1980), 448-66.

528 Rayback, Joseph G. *A History of American Labor*. NY: Macmillan, 1959.

529 Reuss, Richard A., ed. *Songs of American Labor, Industrialization, and the Work Experience*. Ann Arbor, MI: The Institute of Labor and Industrial Relations, U of Michigan, 1983.

530 Rimlinger, Gaston V. "Labor and the Government: a Comparative Historical Perspective." *Journal of Economic History*, Vol 37 (1977), 210-25.

531 ———. "The Legitimation of Protest: A Comparative Study in Labor History." *Comparative Studies in Society and History*, Vol 2 (1960), 329-43.

532 *The Rise of Labor*. 1958. (Documentary film directed by Arthur Barron)

533 Rodgers, Daniel T. "Tradition, Modernity, and the American Industrial Worker: Reflections and Critique." *Journal of Interdisciplinary History*, Vol 7 (1977), 655-81.

534 ———. *The Work Ethic in Industrial America, 1850-1920*. Chicago: U of Chicago Press, 1978.

535 Ross, Arthur M. "Labor Organizations and the Labor Movement in Advanced Industrial Society." *Virginia Law Review*, Vol 50 (1964), 1359-85.

536 Ross, Philip. *The Government as a Source of Union Power: The Role of Public Policy in Collective Bargaining*. Providence: Brown U Press, 1965.

537 ROTHSCHILD, EMMA. *Paradise Lost: The Decline of the Auto-Industrial Age.* NY: Vintage Books, 1973.

538 SAPOSS, DAVID J. *Case Studies in Labor Ideology: An Analysis of Labor, Political and Trade Union Activity as Influenced by Ideology; Philosophic, Structural and Procedural Adaptations Since World War I.* Honolulu: Industrial Relations Center, U of Hawaii, 1964.

539 SCHMIDT, EMERSON P. *Union Power and the Public Interest.* Los Angeles: Nash, 1973.

540 SCHRANK, ROBERT. *Ten Thousand Working Days.* Cambr.: MIT Press, 1978.

541 SCOVILLE, JAMES G. "The Development and Relevance of U.S. Occupational Data." *Industrial and Labor Relations Review*, Vol 19 (1965), 70-79.

542 SEASHORE, STANLEY E., and J. THAD BARNOWE. "Behind the Averages: A Closer Look at America's Lower-Middle-Income Workers." *Proceedings of the Twenty-Fourth Annual Winter Meeting of the Industrial Relations Research Association*, Dec 27-28, 1971, pp 358-65. Madison: IRRA, 1972.

543 SEATON, DOUGLAS P. *Catholic Church and the C.I.O.: the Case of the Association of Catholic Trade Unionists, 1937-1950.* Ph D diss, Rutgers U, 1976.

544 ———. *Catholics and Radicals: The Association of Catholic Trade Unionists and the American Labor Movement, from Depression to Cold War.* East Brunswick, NJ: Bucknell U Press, 1981.

545 SEIDMAN, HAROLD. *Labor Czars: A History of Labor Racketeering.* NY: Liveright, 1938.

546 SEIDMAN, JOEL. "Liberals and the Labor Movement: The Parting of the Ways?" *Proceedings of the Sixteenth Annual Meeting of the Industrial Relations Research Association*, Dec 27-28, 1963, pp 253-58. Madison: IRRA, 1964.

547 SEXTON, BRENDAN. "The Intellectuals and History." *Proceedings of the Sixteenth Annual Meeting of the Industrial Relations Research Association*, Dec 27-28, 1963, pp 245-52. Madison: IRRA, 1964.

548 SHEFLIN, TROY. et al. "Structural Stability in Models of American trade Union Growth." *Quarterly Journal of Economics*, Vol 96 (1981), 77-88.

549 SHERGOLD, PETER R. "Wage Differentials Based on Skill in the United States, 1889-1914: A Case Study." *Labor History*, Vol 18 (1977), 485-508.

550 ———. *Working Class Life: The "American Standard" in Comparative Perspective.* Pittsburgh: U of Pittsburgh Press, 1982.

551 SHISTER, JOSEPH. "The Direction of Unionism 1947-1967: Thrust or Drift?" *Industrial and Labor Relations Review*, Vol 20 (1967), 578-601.

552 "A Short History of American Labor" *American Federationist*, Vol 88 (Mar 1981), entire issue.

553 SHOSTAK, ARTHUR B., and WILLIAM GOMBERG, eds.. *Blue-Collar World: Studies of the American Worker.* Englewood Cliffs: Prentice Hall, 1964.

554 SHOVER, JOHN L. *The Attitude of American Intellectuals toward the Labor Movement, 1890-1900.* Ph D diss, Ohio State U, 1957.

555 SILVERMAN, BERTRAM, and MURRAY YANOWITCH, eds.. *The Worker in Post-Industrial Capitalism: Liberal and Radical Responses.* NY: Free Press, 1974.

556 SOLOMON, BENJAMIN. "Dimensions of Union Growth, 1900-1950." *Industrial and Labor Relations Review*, Vol 9 (1956), 544-61.

557 SOMERS, GERALD G., ed. *Labor, Management, and Social Policy: Essay in the John R. Commons Tradition.* Madison: U of Wisconsin Press, 1963.

558 "Songs and Stories of Labor." *Textile Labor*, Vol 30 (1972), 12-13. (Part of a series)

559 SORGE, FRIEDRICH. *Friedrich A. Sorge's Labor Movement in the United States: A History of the American Working Class from Colonial Times to 1890.* Westport, CT: Greenwood Press, 1977.

560 SPERRY, JAMES R. *Organized Labor and its Fight Against Military and Industrial Conscription, 1917-1945.* Ph D diss, U of Arizona, 1969.

561 Steinberg, Ronnie. *Wages and Hours: Labor and Reform in Twentieth-Century America.* New Brunswick, NJ: Rutgers U Press, 1982.

562 Stern, Sheldon M. "The Evolution of a Reactionary: Louis Arthur Coolidge, 1900-25." *Mid-America,* Vol 57 (1975), 89-105. (Successful campaign against child labor amendment in Massachusetts)

563 Stieber, Jack. "Forces Influencing the American Labor Movement: Past, Present and Future." *Relations Industrielles,* Vol 23 (1968), 591-604.

564 ———. et al, eds. *U.S. Industrial Relations 1950-1980: A Critical Assessment.* Madison: IRRA, 1981.

565 Strauss, George. "Labor and the Academicians." *Proceedings of the Sixteenth Annual Meeting of the Industrial Relations Research Association,* Dec 27-28, 1963, pp 234-44. Madison: IRRA, 1964.

566 Sultan, Paul E. *The Disenchanted Unionist.* NY: Harper & Row, 1963.

567 Summers, Clyde W., and Robert J. Rabin. *The Rights of Union Members: An American Civil Liberties Handbook.* NY: Avon, 1979.

568 Swados, Harvey. *A Radical at Large.* London: Hart-Davis, 1967.

569 Swanson, Catherine, and Philip Nusbaum, eds. "Occupational Folklore and the Folklore of Working." *Folklore Forum,* Vol 11 (1978), entire issue.

570 Taft, Philip. *The A. F. of L. From the Death of Gompers to the Merger.* NY: Harper, 1959.

571 ———. *Organized Labor in American History.* NY: Harper and Row, 1964.

572 ———, and Philip Ross. "American Labor Violence: Its Causes, Character, and Outcome," Vol I, pp 221-301, *Violence in America,* H. D. Graham & T. R. Gurr, eds. Wash.: G.P.O., 1969.

573 Taylor, Albion G. *Labor and the Supreme Court.* Ann Arbor, MI: Braun-Brumfield, 1961.

574 Thernstrom, Stephan. *Poverty and Progress: Social Mobility in a 19th-Century City.* Cambr.: Harvard U Press, 1964.

575 Thomson, Andrew William John. *The Reaction of the American Federation of Labor and the Trades Union Congress to Labor Law, 1900-1935.* Ph D diss, Cornell U, 1968.

576 Tomlins, Christopher. *The State and the Unions: Federal Labor Relations Policy and the Organized Labor Movement in America, 1935-1955.* Ph D diss, Johns Hopkins U, 1981.

577 Troy, Leo. *Distribution of Union Membership Among the States, 1939 and 1953.* NY: National Bureau of Economic Research, 1957.

578 ———. "The Growth of Union Membership in the South, 1939-1953." *Southern Economic Journal,* Vol 24 (1958), 407-20.

579 ———. "Trade Union Membership, 1897-1962." *Review of Economics and Statistics,* Vol 47 (1965), 93-113.

580 ———. *Trade Union Membership, 1897-1962.* NY: National Bureau of Economic Research, 1965.

581 Tyler, Gus. *Labor in the Metropolis.* Columbus, OH: C. E. Merril, 1972.

582 ———. *The Labor Revolution: Trade Unions in a New America.* NY: Viking, 1967.

583 Tyston, Luther Ewing. *The Function of Reconciliation in Industrial Mediation.* Ph D diss, Boston U, 1968.

584 U.S. Department of Labor. *200 Years of American Worklife.* Wash.: G.P.O., 1977.

585 ———. *Challenge and Change: A Brief History of the U.S. Department of Labor, 1913-1963.* Wash.: G.P.O., 1963.

586 ———. *Important Events in American Labor History, 1778-1978.* Wash.: G.P.O., 1979.

587 Ware, Norman J. *Labor in Modern Industrial Society.* Bost.: Heath, 1935.

588 WARNER, MALCOLM, and J. DAVID EDELSTEIN. "Factions in British Organization and American Trade Union Organizations: A Comparative Structural Approach." *Relations Industrielles*, Vol 28 (1973), 166-99.

589 WASON, JAMES R. "American Workers and American Studies." *American Studies*, AIN, Vol 13 (Winter 1974), 10-36.

590 WEBER, MICHAEL, and ANTHONY BOARDMAN. "Economic Growth and Occupational Mobility in 19th Century Urban America: a Reappraisal." *Journal of Social History*, Vol 11 (1977), 52-74.

591 WERSTEIN, IRVING. *The Great Struggle: Labor in America*. NY: Scribner, 1966.

592 WILENSKY, HAROLD L., and CHARLES N. LEBEAUX. *Industrial Society and Social Welfare: the Impact of Industrialization on the Supply and Organization of Social Welfare in the United States*. NY: Russell Sage, 1958.

593 WIRTZ, W. WILLARD. *Labor and the Public Interest*. NY: Harper & Row, 1964.

594 WISNIEWSKI, STANLEY C. *Factors in the Growth of Unionism: 1956-66*. Ph D diss, Catholic U of America, 1975.

595 WOLMAN, LEO. "Concentration of Union Membership." *Proceedings of the Fifth Annual Meeting of the Industrial Relations Research Association*, Dec 28-29, 1952, pp 214-19. Madison: IRRA, 1953.

596 ———. *Ebb and Flow in Trade Unionism*. NY: National Bureau of Economic Research, 1936.

597 ———. *The Growth of American Trade Unions, 1880-1923*. NY: National Bureau of Economic Research, 1924.

598 YELLOWITZ, IRWIN. *The Position of the Worker in American Society, 1865-1896*. Englewood Cliffs, NJ: Prentice-Hall, 1969.

599 ZIEGER, GAY P., and ROBERT H. ZIEGER. "Unions on the Silver Screen: A Review Essay on F.I.S.T., Blue Collar, and Norma Rae." *Labor History*, Vol 22 (1982), 67-78.

600 ZIMBALIST, SIDNEY E. *Historic Themes and Landmarks in Social Welfare Research*. NY: Harper & Row, 1977.

Periods of Development

American Labor before the Knights of Labor

601 Allis, Frederick S., Jr., ed. *Lemuel Shaw Papers.* Bost.: Massachusetts Historical Society, 1968.

602 Anderson, Samuel K. *A History of Labor in the Inland Empire during the Early Frontier Period.* Ph D diss, Washington State U, 1960.

603 Arky, Louis H. "The Mechanics' Union of Trade Associations and the Formation of the Philadelphia Workingmen's Movement." *Pennsylvania Magazine of History and Biography*, Vol 76 (1952), 142-76.

604 Bailey, Raymond C. "Racial Discrimination against Free Blacks in Antebellum Virginia: the Case of Harry Jackson." *West Virginia History*, Vol 39 (1978), 181-86.

605 Baker, Mary Roys. "Anglo-Massachusetts Trade Union Roots, 1130-1790." *Labor History*, Vol 14 (1973), 352-96.

606 Bisson, Wilfred J. *Some Conditions for Collective Violence: the Charlestown Convent Riot of 1834.* Ph D diss, Michigan State U, 1974.

607 Boston, Roy. "General Matthew Trumbull: Respectable Radical." *Illinois State Historical Society Journal*, Vol 46 (1973), 159-76.

608 Breen, T. H. "A Changing Labor Force and Race Relations in Virginia 1660-1710." *Journal of Social History*, Vol 7 (1973), 3-25.

609 Brook, Michael. "Lawrence Pitkethly, Dr. Smyles, and Canadian Revolutionaries in the United States, 1842." *Ontario History*, Vol 57 (1965), 79-84.

610 Burn, James Dawson. *Three Years among the Working-Classes in the United States during the War.* London: Smith, Elder, 1865.

611 Burns, Rex S. "The Yeoman Mechanic: 'Venturous Conservative'." *Rocky Mountain Social Science Journal*, Vol 14 (Oct 1967), 9-21.

612 Cale, Edgar B. *The Organization of Labor in Philadelphia, 1850-1870.* Phila.: the Author, 1940.

613 Chamberlain, Edwin Martin. *The Sovereigns of Industry.* Bost.: Lee & Shepard, 1875.

614 Champagne, Roger J. "Liberty Boys and Mechanics of New York City, 1764-1774." *Labor History*, Vol 8 (1967), 115-35.

615 Colton, Calvin. *The Rights of Labor.* NY: A. S. Barnes, 1847.

616 Commons, John R. "The American Shoemakers, 1648-1895," chap. 14, *Labor and Administration*, NY: Macmillan, 1913.

617 ———. & Associates. *A Documentary History of American Industrial Society.*, 11 vols in 10. Cleveland: A. H. Clark, 1910-11.

618 Conrad, James L. *Evolution of Industrial Capitalism in Rhode Island, 1790-1830: Almy, the Browns and the Slaters.* Ph D diss, U of Connecticut, 1973.

619 COPELAND, PETER F. *Working Dress in Colonial and Revolutionary America.* Westport, CT: Greenwood, 1977.

620 CUNLIFFE, MARCUS. *Chattel Slavery and Wage Slavery: the Anglo-American Context, 1830-1860.* Athens: U of Georgia Press, 1979.

621 CUNNINGHAM, REBECCA S. *Men on the Move: the Economic and Geographic Mobility of Farm Laborers in the Old Midwest, 1850-1870.* Ph D diss, Indiana U, 1977.

622 DEW, CHARLES B. "Disciplining Slave Ironworkers in the Antebellum South: Coercion, Conciliation, and Accommodation." *American Historical Review*, Vol 79 (1974), 398-410.

623 DUFFY, JULIA AGNES. *The Proper Objects of a Gratuitous Education: The Free-School Society of the City of New York, 1805 to 1826.* Ph D diss, Columbia U, 1968.

624 DYER, WALTER A. *Early American Craftsmen.* NY: Century, 1915.

625 EARLE, CARVILLE, and RONALD HOFFMAN. "The Foundation of the Modern Economy: Agriculture and the Costs of Labor in the U.S. and England, 1800-1860." *American Historical Review*, Vol 85 (1980), 1055-94.

626 EARLY, FRANCIS. "A Reappraisal of the New England Labour-Reform Movement of the 1840s: the Lowell Female Labor Reform Association and the New England Workingmen's Association." *Social History*, Vol 13 (1980), 33-54.

627 EKIRCH, A. ROGER. *"Poor Carolina": Politics and Society in Colonial North Carolina, 1729-1776.* Chapel Hill: U of North Carolina Press, 1981.

628 FELDBERG, MICHAEL. "The Crowd in Philadelphia History: A Comparative Perspective." *Labor History*, Vol 15 (1974), 323-36.

629 FELDBLUM, MARY. *The Formation of the First Factory Labor Force in the New England Cotton Textile Industry, 1800-1848.* Ph D diss, New School for Social Research, 1978.

630 FERGUSON, RUSSELL J. *The Rights and Privileges of Bond-Servants and Slaves in the English Colonies of America.* Ph D diss, Indiana U, 1928.

631 FICKETT, LAURA. "Wooddale: an Industrial Community." *Delaware History*, Vol 19 (1981), 229-42.

632 FITE, EMERSON D. *Social and Industrial Conditions in the North during the Civil War.* NY: Macmillan, 1910.

633 FONER, ERIC. *Politics and Ideology in the Age of the Civil War.* NY: Oxford U Press, 1980. (See especially pp 57-76 & 97-127)

634 FONER, PHILIP S. "Journal of an Early Labor Organizer." *Labor History*, Vol 10 (1969), 205-27. (S. C. Hewitt's New England Tour, 1844)

635 ———. "Marx's *Capital* in the United States." *Science & Society*, Vol 31 (1967), 461-66.

636 GALENSON, DAVID. "British Servants and the Colonial Indenture System in the Eighteenth Century." *Journal of Southern History*, Vol 44 (1978), 41-66.

637 ———. "Immigration and the Colonial Labor System." *Explorations in Economic History*, Vol 14 (1977), 360-77.

638 ———. "The Market Evaluation of Human Capital: the Case of Indentured Servitude." *Journal of Political Economy*, Vol 89 (1981), 446-67.

639 ———. "White Servitude and the Growth of Black Slavery in Colonial America." *Journal of Economic History*, Vol 41 (1981), 39-47.

640 ———. *White Servitude in Colonial America: An Economic Analysis.* NY: Cambridge U Press, 1982.

641 GEIS, ROBERT. *Liberty, Equality, Fraternity; the Ideology of the American Labor Movement from 1828 to 1848.* Ph D diss, U of Minnesota, 1971.

642 GETTLEMAN, MARVIN E., and NOEL P. CONLON, eds. "Responses to the Rhode Island Workingmen's Reform Agitation of 1833." *Rhode Island History*, Vol 28 (1969), 75-94.

643 GITELMAN, HOWARD M. "The Labor Force at Waltham Watch During the Civil War Era." *Journal of Economic History*, Vol 25 (1965), 214-43.

644 GREEN, BARBARA L. "Slave Labor at the Maramec Iron Works, 1828-1850." *Missouri Historical Review*, Vol 73 (1979), 150-64.

645 GRIFFEN, CLYDE. "Occupational Mobility in 19th Century America: Problems and Possibilities." *Journal of Social History*, Vol 5 (1972), 310-30.

646 GRIFFIN, J. DAVID. "Medical Assistance for the Sick Poor in Ante-Bellum Savannah." *Georgia Historical Quarterly*, Vol 53 (1969), 463-69.

647 GROB, GERALD N. "The Workers' War for Economic Opportunity." *Worklife*, Vol 1 (Apr 1976), 12-20.

648 GUTMAN, HERBERT G., ed. "English Labor Views the American Reconstruction: an Editorial in the Bee-Hive, September 26, 1874." *Labor History*, Vol 9 (1968), 110-12.

649 HALL, BOWMAN. "Joshua K. Ingalls, American Individualist." *American Journal of Economics and Society*, Vol 39 (1980), 383-96.

650 HALL, BRADLEY. *Work and Leisure in American Society*. Ph D diss, Carnegie-Mellon U, 1981. (Covers 1750-1850)

651 HARPER, C. W. "House Servants and Field Hands: Fragmentation in the Antebellum Slave Community." *North Carolina Historical Review*, Vol 55 (1978), 42-59.

652 HARRISON, JOHN F. C. "The Owenite Socialist Movement in Britain and the United States: a Comparative Study." *Labor History*, Vol 9 (1968), 323-37.

653 ———. "'The Steam Engine of the New Moral World' Owenism and Education, 1817-1829." *Journal of British Studies*, Vol 6 (1967), 76-98.

654 HEAVNER, ROBERT O. "Indentured Servitude: the Philadelphia Market, 1771-1773." *Journal of Economic History*, Vol 38 (1978), 701-13.

655 HENRETTA, JAMES A. "Families and Farms: *Mentalite* in Pre-Industrial America." *William and Mary Quarterly*, Vol 35 (1978), 3-32.

656 HERRICK, CHEESMAN ABIAH. *White Servitude in Pennsylvania: Indentures and Redemption Labor in Colony and Commonwealth*. Phila.: McVey, 1926.

657 HESFORD, WALTER. "Literary Contexts of *Life in the Iron-Mills*." *American Literature*, Vol 49 (1977), 70-85.

658 HIRSCH, SUSAN E. *The Industrialization of Crafts in Newark, 1800-1860*. Phila.: U of Pennsylvania Press, 1978.

659 HITZ, ELIZABETH. *A Technical and Business Revolution: American Woolens to 1832*. Ph D diss, New York U, 1979.

660 HUGHES, SARAH S. "Slaves for Hire: the Allocation of Black Labor in Elizabeth City County, Virginia, 1782 to 1810." *William and Mary Quarterly*, Vol 35 (1978), 260-86.

661 JENTZ, JOHN. *Artisans, Evangelicals, and the City: a Social History of Abolition and Labor Reform in Jacksonian New York*. Ph D diss, City U of NY, 1977.

662 JERNEGAN, MARCUS W. *Laboring and Dependent Classes in Colonial America, 1607-1783*. Chicago: U of Chicago Press, 1931.

663 JOHNSON, LELAND R. "Army Engineers on the Cumberland and Tennessee 1824-1854." *Tennessee Historical Quarterly*, Vol 31 (1972), 149-69.

664 JOHNSON, MICHAEL. "Runaway Slaves and the Slave Communities in South Carolina, 1777 to 1830." *William and Mary Quarterly*, Vol 38 (1981), 418-41.

665 KAGANOFF, NATHAN M. "Organized Jewish Welfare Activity in New York City (1848-1860)." *American Jewish Historical Quarterly*, Vol 56 (1966), 27-61.

666 KILIAN, MARTIN, and E. TATOM. "Marx, Hegel, and the Marxian of the Master Class: Eugene D. Genovese on Slavery." *Journal of Negro History*, Vol 66 (1981), 189-208.

667 KULIK, GARY. *The Beginnings of the Industrial Revolution in America: Pawtucket, Rhode Island, 1672-1829*. Ph D diss, Brown U, 1981.

668 LEMISCH, JESSE. "Listening to the 'Inarticulate': William Widger's Dream and the Loyalties of American Revolutionary Seamen in British Prisons." *Journal of Social History*, Vol 3 (1969), 1-29.

669 LESCOHIER, DON D. *The Knights of St. Crispen, 1867-1874.*, Bulletin 355. Madison: U of Wisconsin, 1910.

670 *A Letter, on the Present State of the Labouring Classes in America...By an Intelligent Emigrant at Philadelphia.* London: John Kay, 1827.

671 LEWIS, RONALD L. "Slave Families at Early Chesapeake Ironworks." *Virginia Magazine of History and Biography*, Vol 86 (1978), 169-79.

672 ———. "The Darkest Abode of Man,' Black Miners in the First Southern Coal Fields, 1780-1865." *Virginia Magazine of History and Biography*, Vol 87 (1979), 190-202.

673 ———. "The Use and Extent of Slave Labor in the Chesapeake Iron Industry: The Colonial Era." *Labor History*, Vol 17 (1976), 388-405.

674 ———. "The Use and Extent of Slave Labor in the Virginia Iron Industry: the Ante-Bellum Era." *West Virginia History*, Vol 38 (1977), 141-56.

675 MCCARTHY, JUSTIN. "The 'Mechanicks': Work Force of the Revolution." *Worklife*, Vol 1 (Jan 1976), 15-20.

676 MCKEE, SAMUEL, JR. *Labor in Colonial New York, 1664-1776.* NY: Columbia U Press, 1935.

677 MACKEY, HOWARD. "The Operation of the English Old Poor Law in Colonial Virginia." *Virginia Magazine of History and Biography*, Vol 72 (1965), 29-40.

678 ———. "Social Welfare in Colonial Virginia: The Importance of the English Old Poor Law." *Historical Magazine of the Protestant Episcopal Church*, Vol 36 (1967), 357-82.

679 MCMASTER, JOHN B. *The Acquisiton of Political, Social, and Industrial Rights of Man in America.* Cleveland: Imperial Press, 1903.

680 MCMURTRY, R. GERALD. "Lincoln Visited by a German Delegation of Workingmen in Cincinnati, Ohio, February 12, 1861." *Lincoln Lore*, No 1575 (May 1969), 1-3.

681 MARCUS, ROBERT D. "Wendell Phillips and American Institutions." *Journal of American History*, Vol 56 (1969), 41-58.

682 MESSNER, WILLIAM F. *Freedmen and the Ideology of Free Labor, Louisiana, 1862-1865.* Lafayette, LA: Center for Louisiana Studies, U of Southwestern Louisiana, 1978.

683 MEYER, STEPHEN. "*People vs. Fisher*: the Shoemakers' Strike of 1833." *New-York Historical Society Quarterly*, Vol 62 (1978), 6-21.

684 MILLER, RANDALL M. "The Fabric of Control: Slavery in Antebellum Southern Textile Mills." *Business History Review*, Vol 55 (1981), 471-90.

685 MOHL, RAYMOND A. "Poverty in Early America, a Reappraisal: the Case of Eighteenth-Century New York Citiy." *New York History*, Vol 50 (1969), 4-27.

686 MOHR, CLARENCE L. "Slavery in Oglethorpe County, Georgia, 1773-1865." *Phylon*, Vol 33 (1972), 4-21.

687 MONTGOMERY, DAVID. *Beyond Equality: Labor and the Radical Republicans, 1862-1872.* NY: Knopf, 1967.

688 ———. *Labor and the Radical Republicans: a Study of the Revival of the American Labor Movement, 1864-1868.* Ph D diss, U of Minnesota, 1962.

689 ———. "The Shuttle and the Cross: Weavers and Artisans in the Kensington Riots of 1844." *Journal of Social History*, Vol 5 (1972), 441-46.

690 ———. "The Working Classes of the Pre-Industrial American City, 1780-1830." *Labor History*, Vol 9 (1968), 3-22.

691 MORAIS, HERBERT M. "The Medical Profession and Workers' Health in Early Industrial America (1835-1860)." *Journal of Occupational Medicine*, Vol 7 (1965), 203-10.

692 MORRIS, RICHARD B. "A Bicentennial Look at the Early Days of American Labor." *Monthly Labor Review*, Vol 99 (May 1976), 21-28.

693 ———. *Government and Labor in Early America.* NY: Columbia U Press, 1946.

694 NASH, GARY B. "Up from the Bottom in Franklin's Philadelphia." *Past & Present*, Vol 77 (Nov 1977), 58-83.

695 NELLIS, ERIC G. *Communities of Workers: Free Labor in Provincial Massachusetts, 1690-1765.* Ph D diss, U of British Columbia, 1979.

696 ———. "Labor and Community in Massachusetts Bay: 1630-1660." *Labor History*, Vol 18 (1977), 525-44.

697 NELSON, OTTO M. "The Chicago Relief and Aid Society, 1850-1874." *Illinois State Historical Society Journal*, Vol 59 (1966), 48-66.

698 NEUFELD, MAURICE F. "The Persistence of Ideas in the American Labor Movement: the Heritage of the 1830s." *Industrial and Labor Relations Review*, Vol 35 (1982), 207-20.

699 ———. "Realms of Thought and Organized Labor in the Age of Jackson." *Labor History*, Vol 10 (1969), 5-43.

700 ———. "The Size of the Jacksonian Labor Movement: A Cautionary Account." *Labor History*, Vol 22 (1982), 599-607.

701 NICKLESS, PAMELA J. "A New Look at Productivity in the New England Cotton Textile Industry, 1830-1860." *Journal of Economic History*, Vol 39 (1979), 889-910.

702 OBERMANN, KARL. "The Communist League: a Forerunner of the American Labor Movement." *Science & Society*, Vol 30 (1966), 433-46.

703 O'DONNELL, CHARLES P. *Capitalism and Cities: a Critical Examination of the Rise of Industrial Capitalism and the Making of the First Modern Cities in America.* Ph D diss, U of California, 1979.

704 OLTON, CHARLES S. *Artisans for Independence: Philadelphia Mechanics and the American Revolution.* Syracuse: U of Syracuse Press, 1975.

705 ———. "Philadelphia Mechanics in the First Decade of the Revolution, 1765-1775." *Journal of American History*, Vol 49 (1972), 311-26.

706 PESSEN, EDWARD. "The Ideology of Stephen Simpson, Upperclass Champion of the Early Philadelphia Workingmen's Movement." *Pennsylvania History*, Vol 22 (1955), 328-40.

707 ———. *Jacksonian America: Society, Personality, and Politics.* Homewood, IL: Dorsey Press, 1969.

708 ———. *Most Uncommon Jacksonians: The Radical Leaders of the Early Labor Movement.* Albany: State U of New York Press, 1967.

709 ———. "Should Labor Have Supported Jackson?" *Labor History*, Vol 13 (1972), 427-37.

710 ———. "The Workingmen's Movement of the Jacksonian Era." *Mississippi Valley Historical Review*, Vol 43 (1956), 428-43.

711 PILLSBURY, WILLIAM M. "Earning a Living, 1788-1818: Job Danforth, Cabinetmaker." *Rhode Island History*, Vol 31 (1972), 81-93.

712 PUCKREIN, GARY. "Climate, Health and Black Labor in the English Americas." *Journal of American Studies*, Vol 13 (1979), 179-93.

713 RANDALL, EDWIN T. "Imprisonment for Debt in America: Fact and Fiction." *Mississippi Valley Historical Review*, Vol 39 (1952), 89-102.

714 RAYBACK, JOSEPH G. "The American Workingman and the Antislavery Crusade." *Journal of Economic History*, Vol 3 (1943), 152-63.

715 REZNECK, SAMUEL. "The Social History of an American Depression, 1837-1843." *American Historical Review*, Vol 40 (1935), 662-87.

716 ROCK, HOWARD B. "The American Revolution and the Mechanics of New York City: One Generation Later." *New York History*, Vol 57 (1976), 367-94.

717 ———. *Artisans of the New Republic: The Tradesmen of New York City in the Age of Jefferson.* NY: New York U Press, 1979.

718 ———. "A Delicate Balance: the Mechanics and the City in the Age of Jefferson." *New-York Historical Society Quarterly*, Vol 63 (1979), 93-114.

719 ———. *The Independent Mechanics: the Tradesmen of New York City in Labor and Politics during the Jeffersonian Era*. Ph D diss, New York U, 1974.

720 ———. "The Perils of Laissez-Faire: The Aftermath of the New York Bakers' Strike of 1801." *Labor History*, Vol 17 (1976), 372-87.

721 ROEDIGER, DAVID. "America's First General Strike: the St Louis 'Commune' of 1877." *Midwest Quarterly*, Vol 21 (1980), 196-206.

722 ———. *The Movement for a Shorter Working Day in the U.S. before 1866*. Ph D diss, Northwestern U, 1980.

723 ———. "Racism, Reconstruction and the Labor Press: the Rise and Fall of the St. Louis Daily Press, 1864-1866." *Science & Society*, Vol 42 (1978), 156-77.

724 ROSEMONT, HENRY P. "Benjamin Franklin and the Philadelphia Typographical Strikers of 1786." *Labor History*, Vol 22 (1981), 398-429.

725 ROSENBERG, NATHAN. "Anglo-American Wage Differences in the 1820's." *Journal of Economic History*, Vol 27 (1967), 221-29.

726 SALINGER, SHARON. "Colonial Labor in Transition: The Decline of Indentured Servitude in Late Eighteenth Century Philadelphia." *Labor History*, Vol 22 (1981), 165-91.

727 ———. *Labor and Indentured Servants in Colonial Pennsylvania*. Ph D diss, U of California, 1980.

728 SARTORIUS VON WALTERSHAUSEN, AUGUST JOHANN GEORG. *Die Arbeits-Verfassung der Englischen Kolonien in Nordamerika*. Strassburg: K. J. Truebner, 1894.

729 SCAFIDI, POLLY JOSE. "Doctor Pierre Didier and Early Industrial Medicine." *Delaware History*, Vol 15 (1972) 41-54. (DuPont Company in the 1st quarter of 19th century)

730 SCHLESINGER, ARTHUR M., JR. *The Age of Jackson*. Bost.: Little, Brown, 1945.

731 SCHMITT, DALE. "Labor in Early Connecticut." *Connecticut Review*, Vol 7 (Apr 1974), 16-24.

732 SHEPHERD, REBECCA. "Restless Americans: the Geographic Mobility of Farm Laborers in the Old Midwest, 1850-1870." *Ohio History*, Vol 89 (1980), 25-45.

733 SMITH, ABBOTT E. *Colonists in Bondage: White Servitude and Convict Labor in America, 1607-1776*. Chapel Hill: U of North Carolina Press, 1947.

734 SMITH, BILLY G. "The Material Lives of Laboring Philadelphians, 1750 to 1800." *William and Mary Quarterly*, Vol 38 (1981), 163-202.

735 SMITH, ROBERT A. *The Technologies and Working Conditions of Colonial Free Laborers*. Ph D diss, U of Illinois, 1950.

736 STEFFEN, CHARLES. *Between Revolutions: the Pre-Factory Urban Worker in Baltimore, 1780-1820*. Ph D diss, Northwestern U, 1978.

737 ———. "Changes in the Organization of Artisan Production in Baltimore, 1790 to 1820." *William and Mary Quarterly*, Vol 36 (1979), 101-17.

738 STEVENSON, GLORIA. "Cordwainers Put their Soles into Bargaining." *Worklife*, Vol 1 (Feb 1976), 22-24.

739 TAFT, PHILIP. "On the Origins of Business Unionism." *Industrial and Labor Relations Review*, Vol 17 (1963), 20-38.

740 TAMBURRO, FRANCIS. "A Tale of a Song! 'The Lowell Factory Girl'." *Southern Exposure*, Vol 2 (Spring-Summer 1974), 42-51.

741 TEMEN, PETER. "Labor Scarcity and the Problem of American Industrial Efficiency in the 1850's: a Reply." *Journal of Economic History*, Vol 28 (1968), 124-25.

742 TOWNER, LAWRENCE W. "The Indentures of Boston's Poor Apprentices: 1734-1805." *Colonial Society of Massachusetts. Publications,*, Vol 43: *Transactions,*, 1956-1963 (1966), 417-68.

743 TUCKER, BARBARA M. "The Family and Industrial Discipline in Ante-Bellum New England." *Labor History*, Vol 21 (1980), 55-74.

744 ———. "The Merchant, the Manufacturer, and the Factory Manager: the Case of Samuel Slater." *Business History Review*, Vol 55 (1981), 297-313.

745 ———. *Samuel Slater and Sons: the Emergence of an American Factory System, 1790-1860.* Ph D diss, U of California, 1974.

746 TURNER, MARJORIE B. *The Early American Labor Conspiracy Cases, Their Place in Labor Law: A Reinterpretation.* San Diego, CA: San Diego State College Press, 1967.

747 VAN BUREN, MARTIN. "Executive Order, March 31, 1840," Vol 3, p 602, *Messages and Papers of the Presidents*, James D. Richardson, ed. Wash.: G.P.O., 1900.

748 WARE, NORMAN J. *The Industrial Worker, 1840-1860.* Bost.: Houghton Mifflin, 1924.

749 WEISS, JANICE. "Educating Clerical Workers: the Nineteenth Century Private Commercial School." *Journal of Social History*, Vol 14 (1981), 407-24.

750 WOOD, GORDON S. "A Note on Mobs in the American Revolution," *William and Mary Quarterly*, 3d Series, Vol 23 (1966), 635-42.

751 WOOD, PETER H. "Whetting, Setting and Laying Timber: Black Builders in the Early South." *Southern Exposure*, Vol 8 (Spring 1980), 3-8.

752 WOOLEN, EVANS. "Labor Troubles between 1834 and 1837." *The Yale Review*, Vol 1 (1892), 87-100.

753 WRIGHT, GAVIN. "Cheap Labor and Southern Textiles before 1880." *Journal of Economic History*, Vol 39 (1979), 655-80.

The Era of Upheaval and the Growth of the Knights of Labor

754 *The Accused and the Accusers: The Famous Speeches of the Eight Chicago Anarchists in Court.* Chicago: Socialistic Publishing Co., 1886. (Haymarket Riot)

755 AVELING, EDWARD B., and ELEANOR MARX AVELING. *The Working-Class Movement in America.* NY: Scribner's, 1888.

756 BARRETT, TOM. *The Mollies Were Men.* NY: Vintage, 1969.

757 BEAN, RONALD. "A Note on the Knights of Labor in Liverpool, 1889-90." *Labor History*, Vol 13 (1972), 68-78.

758 BIMBA, ANTHONY. *The Molly Maguires.* NY: International Publishers, 1932.

759 BOUCHER, ARLINE, and JOHN TEHAN. *Prince of Democracy: James Cardinal Gibbons.* Garden City: Doubleday, 1962.

760 BROEHL, WAYNE G., JR. *The Molly Maguires.* Cambr.: Harvard U Press, 1964.

761 BROWNE, HENRY J. *The Catholic Church and the Knights of Labor.* Wash.: Catholic U of America Press, 1949.

762 BURBANK, DAVID T. *City of Little Bread: The St. Louis General Strike of 1877, the History of an American Strike.* St. Louis: David T. Burbank, 1957.

763 CASSITY, MICHAEL. "Modernization and Social Crisis: the Knights of Labor and a Midwest Community, 1885-1886." *Journal of American History*, Vol 66 (1979), 41-61.

764 CHRISTMAN, HENRY M., Ed. *The Mind and Spirit of John Peter Altgeld: Selected Writings and Addresse.* Urbana: U of Illinois Press, 1960.

765 COLEMAN, J. WALTER. *The Molly Maguire Riots: Industrial Conflict in the Pennsylvania Coal Region.* Richmond: Garrett, 1936.

766 DACUS, J. A. *Annals of the Great Strikes in the United States.* Chicago: L. T. Palmer, 1877.

767 DESTLER, CHESTER M. *American Radicalism, 1865-1901.* New London: Connecticut College, 1946.

768 DOHERTY, WILLIAM T., JR. "Berkeley's Non-revolution: Law and Order and the Great Railway Strike of 1877." *West Virginia History*, Vol 35 (1974), 271-89.

769 DOYLE, ARTHUR CONAN. *The Valley of Fear* (a novel). NY: A. L. Burt, 1920.

770 ELY, RICHARD T. *The Labor Movement in America.* NY: Crowell Publishing, 1886.

771 EWART, SHIRLEY. "Cornish Miners in Grass Valley: the Letters of John Coad, 1858-1860." *Pacific Historian,* Vol 25 (1981), 39-45.

772 FAHERTY, WILLIAM B. "The Clergyman and Labor Progress: Cornelius O'Leary and the Knights of Labor." *Labor History,* Vol 11 (1970), 175-89.

773 FAST, HOWARD. *The American* (a novel about John Peter Altgeld). NY: Duell, Sloan & Pearce, 1946.

774 FIESTER, KENNETH. "A Labor Movement Begins to Stir." *Worklife,* Vol 1 (Feb 1976), 13-21.

775 ———. "The Molly Maguires Were a Bloody Bunch." *Worklife,* Vol 1 (Apr 1976), 20-23.

776 FINE, SIDNEY, ed. "The Ely-Labadie Letters." *Michigan History,* Vol 36 (1952), 1-33.

777 FONER, PHILIP S. "The French Trade Union Delegation to the Philadelphia Centennial Exposition." *Science & Society,* Vol 40 (1976), 257-87.

778 ———. *The Great Labor Uprising of 1877.* NY: Monad, 1977.

779 ———. "A Labor Voice for Black Equality: the *Boston Daily Evening Voice,* 1864-1867." *Science & Society,* Vol 38 (1974), 304-25.

780 FREIFIELD, MARY. *The Emergence of the American Workingclasses: the Roots of Division, 1865-1885.* Ph D diss, New York U, 1980.

781 GARLOCK, JONATHAN. *Guide to the Local Assemblies of the Knights of Labor.* Westport, CT: Greenwood, 1982.

782 ———. *The Knights of Labor Data Bank: User's Manual and Index to Local Assemblies.* Ann Arbor: Inter-University Consortium for Political Research, 1973.

783 ———. *A Structural Analysis of the Knights of Labor: A Prolegomenon to the History of the Producing Classes.* Ph D diss, U of Rochester, 1975.

784 GARRATY, JOHN A., ed. *Labor and Capital in the Gilded Age.* Bost.: Little, Brown, 1968.

785 GELLER, RUTH. *The American Labor Novel, 1871-1884.* Ph D diss, SUNY-Buffalo, 1980.

786 GEMORAH, SOLOMON. *Lawrence Gronlund's Ideas and Influence, 1877-1899.* Ph D diss, New York U, 1965.

787 GILDEMEISTER, GLEN. "The Founding of the American Federation of Labor." *Labor History,* Vol 22 (1981), 262-68.

788 GINGER, RAY. *Altgeld's America.* NY: Funk & Wagnalls, 1958.

789 GLASSBERG, EUDICE. "Work, Wages, and the Cost of Living; Ethnic Differences and the Poverty Line, Philadelphia, 1880." *Pennsylvania History,* Vol 46 (1979), 17-58.

790 GOTTLIEB, AMY ZAHL. "The Influence of British Trade Unionists on the Regulation of the Mining Industry in Illinois, 1872." *Labor History,* Vol 19 (1978), 397-415.

791 GRANT, ROBERT (ANONYMOUSLY PUBLISHED). *Face to Face* (a novel). NY: Scribner, 1886.

792 GROB, GERALD N. "The Knights of Labor and the Trade Unions, 1878-1886." *Journal of Economic History,* Vol 18 (1958), 176-92.

793 ———. "Terence V. Powderly and the Knights of Labor." *Mid-America,* Vol 39, New Series, Vol 28, (1957), 39-55.

794 GROSSMAN, JONATHAN, and JUDSON MACLAURY. "The Creation of the Bureau of Labor Statistics." *Monthly Labor Review,* Vol 98 (Feb 1975), 25-31.

795 GUNTON, GEORGE. *Wealth and Progress: A Critical Examination of the Labor Problem.* NY: Appleton, 1887.

796 GUTMAN, HERBERT G. "The Failure of the Movement by the Unemployed for Public Works in 1873." *Political Science Quarterly,* Vol 80 (1965), 84-95.

797 ———. "The Knights of Labor and Patrician Anti-Semitism: 1891." *Labor History,* Vol 13 (1972), 63-67.

798 ———. "Protestantism and the American Labor Movement: the Christian Spirit in the Gilded Age." *American Historical Review*, Vol 52 (1966), 74-101.

799 HEYWOOD, EZRA H. *The Great Strike: Its Relation to Labor, Property and Government*. Princeton, MA: Cooperative Publishing, 1878.

800 HORNER, CLARE A. *Producers' Co-operatives in the United States, 1865-1890*. Ph D diss, U of Pittsburgh, 1979.

801 HOUGH, LESLIE S. *The Turbulent Spirit: Violence and Coaction among Cleveland Workers, 1877-1899*. Ph D diss, U of Virginia, 1979.

802 JAHER, FREDERIC COPLE. "*The New Nation*: an Introduction and Appraisal." *Labor History*, Vol 9 (1968), 376-79.

803 JAVERSAK, DAVID T. "One Place on This Great Green Planet where Andrew Carnegie Can't Get a Monument with his Money." *West Virginia History*, Vol 41 (1979), 7-19. (Ohio Valley Trades & Labor Assembly opposition to Carnegie Library in Wheeling, WV)

804 JEFFREYS-JONES, RHODRI. "Profit Over Class: A Study in American Industrial Espionage." *Journal of American Studies*, Vol. ((1972), 233-48)

805 KEARNS, DAVID. *The Social Mobility of New Orleans Laborers, 1870-1900*. Ph D diss, Tulane U, 1978.

806 KEMMERER, DONALD L., and EDWARD D. WICKERSHAM. "Reasons for the Growth of the Knights of Labor in 1885-1886." *Industrial and Labor Relations Review*, Vol 3 (1950), 213-20.

807 KENNEDY, DOUGLAS R. *The Knights of Labor in Canada*. London, Ontario: University of Western Ontario, 1956.

808 KIRKLAND, EDWARD C. *Industry Comes of Age: Business, Labor, and Public Policy, 1860-1897*. NY: Holt, Rinehart and Winston, 1961.

809 LABOR PUBLISHING COMPANY. *Labor: Its Rights and Wrongs, Statements and Comments by the Leading Men of our Nation on the Labor Question of To-day. With Platforms of the Various Labor Organizations, Knights of Labor, Federation of Trades, Agricultural Wheels of the South, Farmers' Alliance and Full Proceedings of the General Assembly of the Knights of Labor, at Cleveland, May 25 to June 3, 1886*. Wash.: The Company, 1886.

810 LANE, ANN J. "Recent Literature on the Molly Maguires." *Science & Society*, Vol 30 (1966), 309-19.

811 LEONARD, FRANK. "'Helping' the Unemployed in the Nineteenth Century: the Case of the American Tramp." *Social Service Review*, Vol 40 (1966), 429-34.

812 LEWIS, ARTHUR H. *Lament for the Molly Maguires*. NY: Harcourt, Brace & World, 1964.

813 LEWIS, FRANK D. "Explaining the Shift of Labor from Agriculture to Industry in the United States: 1869-1899." *Journal of Economic History*, Vol 39 (1979), 681-98.

814 LISSNER, WILL. "On the Centenary of *Progress and Poverty*." *American Journal of Economics and Sociology*, Vol 38 (1979), 1-16.

815 MCCABE, JAMES D. (E. W. MARTIN, PSEUD.). *History of the Great Riots*. Phila.: National Publishing, 1877.

816 MCCARTHY, CHARLES A. *The Great Molly Maguire Hoax, Based on Information Suppressed 90 Years. The Story of John J. Kehoe*. Wyoming, PA: Cro Woods, 1969.

817 MCLAURIN, MELTON A. *The Knights of Labor in the South*. Westport, CT: Greenwood, 1978.

818 MACLAURY, JUDSON. "The Selection of the First U.S. Commissioner of Labor." *Monthly Labor Review*, Vol 98 (Apr 1975), 16-19.

819 MCMATH, ROBERT C., JR. "Preface to Populism: the Origin and Economic Development of the 'Southern' Farmers' Alliance in Kansas." *Kansas Historical Quarterly*, Vol 42 (1976), 55-67.

820 MCNEILL, GEORGE E., ed. *The Labor Movement: The Problem of Today*. Bost.: A. M. Bridgman, 1887.

821 MARCUS, IRWIN M. *The Knights of Labor: Reform Aspects*. Ph D diss, Lehigh U, 1965.
822 MAROT, HELEN, comp. *A Handbook of Labor Literature*. Phila.: Free Library of Economics and Political Science, 1899.
823 MAYER, THOMAS. "Some Characteristics of Union Members in the 1880s and 1890s." *Labor History*, Vol 5 (1964), 57-66.
824 MONTGOMERY, DAVID. "American Labor, 1865-1902: the Early Industrial Era." *Monthly Labor Review*, Vol 99 (Jul 1976), 10-17.
825 MORRIS, JANE K. *Julie* (a novel). NY: McGraw-Hill, 1952.
826 OBERMANN, KARL. "Die Amerikareise Wilhelm Liebknechts im Jahre 1886." *Zeitschrift fuer Geschichtswissenschaft*, Vol 14 (1966), 611-17.
827 PELLING, HENRY M. "The Knights of Labor in Great Britain, 1880-1901." *Economic History Review*, Vol 9 (1956), 313-51.
828 PENNSYLVANIA GENERAL ASSEMBLY. Joint Committee Appointed to Investigate the Railroad Riots *Report of the Committee Appointed to Investigate the Railroad Riots in July 1877*. Harrisburg: Lane S Hart, 1879.
829 PERNICONE, CAROL GRONEMAN. *The 'Bloody Ould Sixth': A Society Analysis of a New York City Working-Class Communisty in the Mid-Nineteenth Century*. Ph D diss, U of Rochester, 1973.
830 PINKERTON, ALLAN. *The Molly Maguires and the Detectives*. NY: G. W. Carleton, 1878.
831 ———. *Strikers, Communists, Tramps and Detectives: Railroad Strike of 1877*. NY: Carleton, 1900.
832 POLLARD, JOHN A. "Whittier on Labor Unions." *New England Quarterly*, Vol 12 (1939), 99-102.
833 RHODES, JAMES FORD. "The Molly Maguires in the Anthracite Region of Pennsylvania." *American Historical Review*, Vol 15 (1910), 547-61.
834 SALVATORE, NICK. "Railroad Workers and the Great Strike of 1877: The View From a Small Midwest City." *Labor History*, Vol 21 (1980), 522-45.
835 SARTORIUS VON WALTERSHAUSEN, AUGUST JOHANN GEORG. *Die Nordamerikanischen Gewerkschaften unter dem Einfluss der Fortschreitenden Productionstechnik*. Berlin: H. Bahr, 1886.
836 SIGMUND, ELWIN W. "Railroad Strikers in Court: Unreported Contempt Cases in Illinois in 1877." *Journal of the Illinois State Historical Society,*, Vol 49 (1956), 190-209.
837 SINGER, AARON. *Labor-Management Relations at Steinway and Sons, 1853-1896*. Ph D diss, Columbia U, 1978.
838 SISCO, JOHN ISADORE. *Rhetoric in Failure: A Study of the Public Address of the Knights of Labor Movement*. Ph D diss, U of Minnesota, 1966.
839 SPEIZMAN, MILTON D. "The Radicals and the Poor." *Social Casework*, Vol 49 (1968), 102-10.
840 SUDERMAN, ELMER F. "The Social-Gospel Novelists' Criticisms of American Society." *Midcontinent American Studies Journal*, Vol 7 (1966), 45-60.
841 TRIPP, JOSEPH F. "Kansas Communities and the Birth of the Labor Problem, 1877-1883." *Kansas History*, Vol 4 (1981), 114-29.
842 TUCKER, MURRAY ALLEN. *The Effects of Three Unions on Wage and Employment Structures*. Ph D diss, U of Pittsburgh, 1964.
843 TUERK, RICHARD. "Jacob Riis and the Jews." *New-York Historical Society Quarterly*, Vol 63 (1979), 179-201.
844 ULLMO, SYLVIA. "The Great Strikes of 1877." *Revue Francaise d'Etudes Americaines*, Vol 1 (Oct 1976), 49-56.
845 U.S. CONGRESS. HOUSE. Select Committee on Depression in Labor and Business (1878). *The Causes of the General Depression in Labor and Business, etc*. Wash.: G.P.O., 1879.

846 ———. ———. Select Committee on Existing Labor Troubles. *Investigation of Labor Troubles in Missouri, Arkansas, Kansas, Texas, and Illinois.*, 1 vol, 2 parts. Wash.: G.P.O., 1887.

847 ———. Senate. Committee on Education and Labor (1883). *Report of the Committee of the Senate upon the Relations between Labor and Capital, and Testimony Taken by the Committee.*, 5 vols. Wash.: G.P.O., 1885.

848 Ware, Norman J. *The Labor Movement in the United States, 1860-1895.* NY: Appleton, 1929.

849 Warner, Beverly E. *Troubled Waters. A Problem of Today* (a novel). Phila.: Lippincott, 1885.

850 Watillon, Leon. *The Knights of Labor in Belgium.* Los Angeles: Institute of Industrial Relations, U of California, 1959.

851 Watts, Theodore. *The First Labor Day Parade, Tuesday, September 5, 1882: Media Mirrors to Labor's Icons.* Silver Spring, MD: Phoenix Rising, 1983.

852 Williams, Ben Ames. *Owen Glenn* (a novel about the Knights of Labor). Bost.: Houghton Mifflin, 1950.

853 Williamson, Jeffrey G. "Consumer Behavior in the Nineteenth Century: Carroll D. Wright's Massachusetts Workers in 1875." *Explorations in Entrepreneurial History*, 2d series, Vol 4 (1967), 98-135.

854 Wright, Carroll D. *The Industrial Evolution of the United States.* Meadville, PA: Flood & Vincent, 1895.

The Era of the Triumph of the American Federation of Labor to World War I

GENERAL

855 Adelman, William. *Touring Pullman.* Chicago: Illinois Labor Historical Society, 1972.

856 Akin, William E. "Arbitration and Labor Conflict: the Middle Class Panacea, 1886-1900." *The Historian*, Vol 29 (1967), 565-83.

857 Ames, Charles Francis, Jr. *Repression or Concession: Press and Party Leader Responses to the Threat of Social Upheaval, 1871-1903.* Ph D diss, Boston U, 1973.

858 Appel, John C. *The Relationship of American Labor to United States Imperialism, 1895-1905.* Ph D diss, U of Wisconsin, 1950.

859 Babcock, Robert H. "Sam Gompers and the Expansion of the A.F. of L., into Canada, 1882-1898." *Relations Industrielles-Industrial Relations*, Vol 27 (1972), 403-22.

860 Baker, B. Kimball. "The First Labor Day Parade." *Worklife*, Vol 1 (Sep 1976), 24-26.

861 Baker, Ray Stannard. *American Chronicle.* NY: Scribner, 1945.

862 Barbash, Jack. "John R. Commons and the Americanization of the Labor Problem." *Journal of Economic Issues*, Vol 1 (1967), 161-67.

863 Becker, Dorothy G. "Social Welfare Leaders as Spokesmen for the Poor." *Social Casework*, Vol 49 (1968), 82-89.

864 Bennett, S., and Carville Earle. "The Geography of Strikes in the U.S., 1881-1894." *Journal of Interdisciplinary History*, Vol 13 (Summer 1981), 63-84.

865 Brundage, David. "Denver's New Departure: Irish Nationalism and the Labor Movement in the Gilded Age." *Southwest Economy and Society*, Vol 5 (Winter 1981), 10-23, 24-25, 26-27. (See Comment by Sally Miller & response by Brundage following article)

866 BUBKA, TONY. "Jack London's Definition of a Scab." *American Book Collector*, Vol 17 (Nov 1966), 23-26.

867 BUCHIN, V. T., and A. M. DMITRIEV. "Otnoshenie Amerikanskikh Sotsialisticheskikh Organizatsii i AFT k Trestam (1895-1904), Leningrad. Universitet." *Vestnik. Seriia Istorii Iazyka i Literatury*, No 3 (1966), 128-32.

868 BUDER, STANLEY. *Pullman: An Experiment in Industrial Order and Community Planning, 1880-1930*. NY: Oxford U Press, 1967.

869 BURGOYNE, ARTHUR G. *The Homestead Strike of 1892*. Pitsburgh: U of Pittsburgh Press, 1979.

870 CAHN, WILLIAM. *Lawrence, 1912: The Bread and Roses Strike*. NY: Pilgrim 1980.

871 CARTER, PAUL J., JR. "Mark Twain and the American Labor Movement." *New England Quarterly*, Vol 30 (1957), 382-88.

872 CARWARDINE, WILLIAM H. *The Pullman Strike*. Chicago: Charles Kerr, 1894.

873 CASTROVINCI, J. L. "Prelude to Welfare Capitalism: the Role of Business in the Enactment of Workmen's Compensation Legislation in Illinois, 1905-1912." *Social Service Review*, Vol 50 (1976), 80-102.

874 "Centennial Minutes." *American Federationist.*, Vol 88 (Sep 1981), 14-15. (Illustrations)

875 CHAMBERS, CLARKE A., and ANDREA HINDING. "Charity Workers, the Settlements, and the Poor." *Social Casework*, Vol 49 (1968), 96-101. (A study of *Charities* and *The Commons* to their amalgamation in 1905)

876 CONELL, CAROL. *The Value of Union Sponsorship to Strikers*. Ph D diss, U of Michigan, 1981. (Deals with the years 1881-94)

877 DALRYMPLE, CANDICE. *Sexual Distinctions in the Law: Early Maximum Hour Decisions of the U.S. Supreme Court, 1905-17*. Ph D diss, U of Florida, 1980.

878 DARROW, CLARENCE. *The Story of My Life: An Autobiography*. NY: Scribner, 1932.

879 DAWSON, ANDREW. "The Paradox of Dynamic Technological Change and the Labor Aristocracy in the United States, 1880-1914." *Labor History*, Vol 20 (1979), 325-51.

880 DEMENTYEV, I.P. "Amerikanskaia Federatsiia Truda i Imperialisticheskaia Ekspansioo SShA na Rubezhe XX Veka." *Vestnik*, Series 9. Istoriia, No 2 (1969), 27-45.

881 DERBER, MILTON. "The Idea of Industrial Democracy in America, 1898-1915." *Labor History*, Vol 7 (1966), 259-86.

882 DEROLF, JOHN JOSEPH, III. *The Educational Philosophy of the American Federation of Labor and Its Influence upon the Social Studies Curriculum of the Secondary School*. Ph D diss, U of Nebraska, 1967.

883 DUBOFSKY, MELVYN. *Industrialism and the American Worker, 1865-1920*. NY: Crowell, 1975.

884 FONER, PHILIP S. *History of the Labor Movement in the United States.*, Vol 2: *From the Founding of the American Federation of Labor to the Emergence of American Imperialism*. NY: International, 1955.

885 ———. *History of the Labor Movement in the United States.*, Vol 3: *The Policies and Practices of the American Federation of Labor, 1900-1910*. NY: International, 1964.

886 ———. *History of the Labor Movement in the United States.*, Vol 5: *The AFL in the Progressive Era, 1910-1915*. NY: International, 1980.

887 ———. "Marti on the United States." *Monthly Review*, Vol 27 (Jan 1976), 52-59.

888 ———. "A Martyr to his Cause: The Scenario of the First Labor Film in the United States." *Labor History*, Vol 24 (1983), 103-11.

889 FONES-WOLF, ELIZABETH, and KENNETH FONES-WOLF. "Knights versus the Trade Unionists: The Case of the Washington, D.C. Carpenters, 1881-1896." *Labor History*, Vol 22 (1981), 192-212.

890 ———. "Voluntarism and Factional Disputes in the AFL—the Painters' Split in 1894-1900." *Industrial and Labor Relations Review*, Vol 35 (1981), 58-69.

891 GEORGE, HENRY. *The Condition of Labor: An Open Letter to Pope Leo XIII*. NY: United States Book Co., 1891.

892 Ghent, W. J. *Our Benevolent Feudalism.* NY: Macmillan, 1902.

893 Gilbert, James B. *Work Without Salvation: America's Intellectuals and Industrial Alienation, 1880-1910.* Balt.: Johns Hopkins U Press, 1977.

894 Gipe, George A. "Rebel in a Wing Collar." *American Heritage*, Vol 18 (Dec 1966), 25-29, 101. (Jacob S Coxey)

895 Gladden, Washington. *The Labor Question.* Bost.: Pilgrim Press, 1911.

896 Goldin, Claudia. "Household and Market Production of Families in a Late Nineteenth Century American City." *Explorations in Economic History*, Vol 16 (1979), 111-31.

897 Grayson, Carmen B. *W. Jett Lauck: Biography of a Reformer.* Ph D diss, U of Virginia 1975.

898 Graziosi, Andrea. "Common Laborers. Unskilled Workers: 1890-1915." *Labor History*, Vol 22 (1981), 512-44.

899 Greenberg, Irving. *Theodore Roosevelt and Labor, 1900-1918.* Ph D diss, Harvard U, 1960.

900 Griffiths, David B. "Far Western Populism: the Case of Utah, 1893-1900." *Utah Historical Quarterly*, Vol 37 (1969), 396-407.

901 ———. "Far-western Populist Thought: a Comparative Study of John R. Rogers and Davis H. Waite." *Pacific Northwest Quarterly*, Vol 60 (1969), 183-92.

902 Grossman, Jonathan. "The Coal Strike of 1902—Turning Point in U.S. Policy." *Monthly Labor Review*, Vol 98 ((ct 1975), 21-28.

903 ———, and Judson MacLaury. "The Creation of the Bureau of Labor Statistics." *Monthly Labor Review*, Vol 98 (Feb 1975), 25-31.

904 Hapgood, Hutchins. *The Spirit of Labor.* NY: Duffield, 1907.

905 Harris, Sheldon H. "Letters from West Virginia: Management's Version of the 1902 Coal Strike." *Labor History*, Vol 10 (1969), 228-40.

906 Helbing, Albert T. *The Departments of the American Federation of Labor.* Balt.: Johns Hopkins Press, 1931.

907 Henle, Peter. "A Chronicle of Trade Union Positions on Government Ownership." *Monthly Labor Review*, Vol 88 (1965), 804-16.

908 Herschbach, Dennis R. *Industrial Education Ideology, 1876-1917: a Social and Historical Analysis.* Ph D diss, U of Illinois, 1973.

909 Hogg, John B. *The Homestead Strike of 1892.* Ph D diss, U of Chicago, 1943.

910 Holmes, William F. "Whitecapping in Mississippi: Agrarian Violence in the Populist Era." *Mid-America*, Vol 55 (1973), 134-48.

911 Houghton, Virginia. "John W. Kern: Senate Majority Leader and Labor Legislation, 1913-17." *Mid-America*, Vol 57 (1975), 184-94.

912 Hoxie, Robert F. "The Trade Union Point of View." *Journal of Political Economy*, Vol 15 (1907), 345-63.

913 ———. "Trade Unionism in the United States." *Journal of Political Economy*, Vol 22 (1914), 201-17, 464-81.

914 ———. *Trade Unionism in the United States.* NY: Appleton, 1917.

915 James, Alfred P. "The First Convention of the American Federation of Labor, Pittsburgh, Pennsylvania, November 15th-18th, 1881: A Study in Contemporary Local Newspapers as a Source." *Western Pennsylvania Historical Magazine*, Vol 6 (1923), 201-33; Vol 7 (1924), 29-56, 106-20.

916 Jelley, Symmes M. *The Voice of Labor, Containing Special Contributions by Leading Workingmen Throughout the United States, with Opinions of Statesmen and Legislators upon the Great Issues of the Day: Plain Talk by Men of Intellect on Labor's Rights, Wrongs, Remedies, and Prospects.* Phila.: H. J. Smith, 1888.

917 Jones, Dallas L. *The Wilson Administration and Organized Labor 1912-1919.* Ph D diss, Cornell U, 1954.

918 Katzman, David M., and William M. Tuttle, Jr. (eds). *Plain Folk: The Life Stories of Undistinguished Americans.* Urbana: U of Illinois Press, 1982.

919 KELLEY, FLORENCE. *Some Ethical Gains through Legislation.* NY: Macmillan, 1905.

920 KIRKPATRICK, IVY E. *Struggle of Industrial Democracy: Croly, Lippmann, and Weyl, 1912-1917.* Ph D diss, Texas Christian U, 1974.

921 KREUTER, KENT, and GRETCHEN KREUTER. "The Lure of Law and Order: Cushman K. Davis and the Pullman Strike." *Mid-America*, Vol 50 (1969), 194-204.

922 LANG, LUCY ROBINS. *Tomorrow Is Beautiful.* NY: Macmillan, 1948.

923 LEGIEN, CARL RUDOLPH. *Aus Amerikas Arbeiterbewegung.* Berlin: Verlag der Generalkommission der Gewerkschaften Deutschlands, 1914.

924 LEIBY, JAMES. "State Welfare Institutions and the Poor." *Social Casework*, Vol 49 (1968), 90-95.

925 LEVASSEUR, EMILE. *The American Workman.* Balt.: John's Hopkins Press, 1900.

926 LIVINGSTON, JOHN CHARLES. *Clarence Darrow: Sentimental Rebel.* Ph D diss, U of Wisconsin, 1965.

927 LORWIN, LEWIS L. *The American Federation of Labor: History, Policies, and Prospects.* Wash.: Brookings Institution, 1933.

928 LUBOVE, ROY. "Economic Security and Social Conflicet in America: the Early Twentieth Century." *Journal of Social History*, Vol 1 (1967-68), 61-87, 325-50.

929 MCMURRY, DONALD L. *Coxey's Army: A Study of the Industrial Army Movement of 1894.* Bost.: Little, Brown, 1929.

930 MCQUAID, KIM. "An American Owenite: Edward A. Filene and the Parameters of Industrial Reform, 1890-1937." *American Journal of Economics and Sociology*, Vol 35 (1976), 77-94.

931 MAPES, LYNN G. *Iron Age: An Iron Manufacturer's Journal and the 'Labor Problem' in the Age of Enterprise.* Ph D diss, U of Rochester, 1973.

932 MAXWELL, WILLIAM JOSEPH. *Frances Kellor in the Progressive Era: a Case Study in the Professionalization of Reform.* Ph D diss, Columbia U, 1968.

933 MILKMAN, HOWARD. *Thomas Dewitt Talmage: an Evangelical 19th Century Voice on Technology, Urbanization, and Labor-Management Conflicts.* Ph D diss, New York U, 1980.

934 MONTGOMERY, DAVID. "For Labor, It was an Age of Frustration." *GBBA Horizons*, Vol 24 (Sep 1976), 8-10.

935 ———. "Labor and the Republic in Industrial America, 1860-1920." *Mouvement Social*, Vol 111 (1980), 201-15.

936 MORRIS, JOHN ROBERT. *Davis Hanson Waite: the Ideology of a Western Populist.* Ph D diss, U of Colorado, 1965.

937 MURPHY, PAUL L. "Labor-Management Relations: Consititutional Assumptions." *Current History*, Vol 48 (1965), 353-60, 366.

938 NELSON, DANIEL. "The Origins of Unemployment Insurance in Wisconsin." *Wisconsin Magazine of History*, Vol 51 (1968), 109-21.

939 RADER, BENJAMIN G. *The Professor as a Reformer: Richard T. Ely, 1854-1943.* Ph D diss, U of Maryland, 1964.

940 ———. "Richard T Ely: Lay Spokesman for the Social Gospel." *Journal of American History*, Vol 53 (1966), 61-74.

941 RAMIREZ, BRUNO. *Collective Bargaining and the Politics of Industrial Relations in the Progressive Era 1898-1916.* Ph D diss, U of Toronto, 1978.

942 ROBINSON, HARRY P. *Men Born Equal* (a novel). NY: Harper, 1895.

943 RODGERS, DANIEL T. *The Work Ethic in Industrial America, 1865-1917.* Ph D diss, Yale U, 1973.

944 ROLLINS, ALFRED B., JR. "Franklin Roosevelt's Introduction to Labor." *Labor History*, Vol 3 (1962), 3-18.

945 ROSENBERG, ARNOLD S. *John Adams Kingsbury and the Struggle for Social Justice in New York, 1906-1918.* Ph D diss, New York U, 1968.

946 ———. "The War on Poverty: John Kinsbury and the AICP, 1906-1918." *Connecticut Review*, Vol 2 (1968), 52-69. (Association for Improving the Condition of the Poor, New York City)

947 SCHEINBERG, STEPHEN J. "Progressivism in Industry: the Welfare Movement int he American Factory." *Historical Papers Presented at the Annual Meeting...Canadian Historical Association....*, (1968), 184-97.

948 SCHNEIDER, LINDA. "The Citizen Strike: Workers' Ideology in the Homestead Strike of 1892." *Labor History*, Vol 22 (1982), 47-66.

949 SCHRAMM, LEROY HENRY. *Organized Labor and the Muckrakers, 1900-1912*. Ph D diss, Cornell U, 1972.

950 SCHWANTES, CARLOS A. "Leftward Tilt on the Pacific Slope; Indigenous Unionism and the Struggle against AFL Hegemony in the State of Washington." *Pacific Northwestern Quarterly*, Vol 70 (1979), 24-34.

951 SHAPIRO, HERBERT. "Lincoln Steffens and the McNamara Case: a Progressive Response to Class Conflict." *American Journal of Economics and Sociology*, Vol 39 (1980), 397-412.

952 SHERGOLD, PETER R. "Wage Rates in Pittsburgh during the Depression of 1908." *Journal of American Studies*, Vol 9 (1975), 163-88.

953 ———. *Working-Class Life: The American Standard in Comparative Perspective, 1899-1913*. Pittsburgh: U of Pittsburgh Press, 1982.

954 SIVACHEV, N. V. "Iz Istoril Trudovogo Prava v SShA (1890-1918 gg.)." *Vestnik*, Series 9. Istoriia. No 3 (1968), 55-71.

955 SKEELS, JOYCE G. "The Early American Federation of Labor and Monetary Reform." *Labor History*, Vol 12 (1971), 530-50.

956 SMITH, JOHN S. "Organized Labor and Government in the Wilson Era; 1913-1921: Some Conclusions." *Labor History*, Vol 3 (1962), 265-86.

957 STEEPLES, DOUGLAS W. "The Panic of 1893: Contemporary Reflections and Reactions." *Mid-America*, Vol 47 (1965), 155-75.

958 STEFFENS, LINCOLN. *The Autobiography of Lincoln Steffens.*, 2 vols. NY: Harcourt, Brace, 1937.

959 STOWELL, MYRON R. *Fort Frick: Or the Siege of Homestead.* Pittsburgh: Pittsburgh Printing Co., 1893.

960 SUGIMOTO, HOWARD H. "Vancouver Riot and its International Significance." *Pacific Northwest Quarterly*, Vol 64 (1973), 163-74.

961 SZASZ, FERENC M., and RALPH BOGARDUS. "The Camera and the American Social Conscience: the Documentary Photography of Jacob A. Riis." *New York History*, Vol 40 (1974), 409-36. (Many photos of working conditions)

962 TAFT, PHILIP. *The A. F. of L. in the Time of Gompers*. NY: Harper, 1957.

963 ———. "Expansion of Unionization in the Early 20th Century." *Monthly Labor Review*, Vol 99 (Sep 1976), 32-35.

964 THOMPSON, ARTHUR W. "The Reception of Russian Revolutionary Leaders in America, 1904-1906." *American Quarterly*, Vol 18 (1966), 452-76.

965 TOBENKIN, ELIAS. *House of Conrad* (a novel). Phila.: Stokes, 1918.

966 U.S. COMMISSION ON INDUSTRIAL RELATIONS (1912). *Final Report and Testimony.*, 11 vols. Wash.: G.P.O., 1916.

967 U.S.INDUSTRIAL COMMISSION (1898). *Reports.*, 19 vols. Wash.: G.P.O, 1900-2. (See especially vols 7 & 14, *Report on the Relations and Conditions of Capital and Labor Employed in Manufactures and General Business,* 1901)

968 VOGEL, LISE. "Their Own Work: Two Documents from the Nineteenth Century Labor Movement." *Signs*, Vol 1 (1976), 787-802.

969 WADE, LOUISE C. "The Heritage from Chicago's Early Settlement Houses." *Journal of the Illinois State Historical Society*, Vol 60 (1967), 411-41.

970 WALLING, WILLIAM E. *American Labor and American Democracy*. NY: Harper, 1926.

971 WATKINS, B. J. *The Professors and the Unions: American Academic Social Theory and Labor Reform, 1883-1915*. Ph D diss, Yale U, 1977.

972 WEINSTEIN, JAMES. *The Corporate Ideal in the Liberal State, 1900-1918*. Bost.: Beacon, 1968.

973 WEISS, THOMAS. "The Industrial Distribution of the Urban and Rural Work-Forces: Estimates for the U.S., 1870-1910." *Journal of Economic History*, Vol 33 (1972), 919-37.

974 WESSER, ROBERT F. "Charles Evans Hughes and the Urban Sources of Urban Progressivism." *New York Historical Society Quarterly*, Vol 50 (1966), 365-400.

975 WHARTON, LESLIE. "Herbert N. Casson and the American Labor Church, 1893-1898." *Essex Institute Historical Collections*, Vol 117 (1981), 119-37.

976 WHITFORD, KATHRYN. "Miller of Boscobel: Hamlin Garland's Labor Play." *Midcontinent American Studies Journal*, Vol 8 (Fall, 1967), 33-42.

977 WIEBE, ROBERT H. "The Anthracite Strike of 1902: A Record of Confusion." *Mississippi Valley Historical Review*, Vol 48 (1961), 229-51.

978 WILHELM, CLARKE LAWSON. *William B. Wilson: the First Secretary of Labor*. Ph D diss, Johns Hopkins U, 1967.

979 WILSON, N. JAMES. *The Farmers' Search for Order: (1880-1910)*. Ph D diss, U of Oklahoma, 1974.

980 WISH, HARVEY. "The Pullman Strike: A Study in Violence." *Illinois State Historical Society Journal,* Vol 32 (1939), 289-312.

981 WOLFF, GERALD W. "Mark Hanna's Goal: American Harmony." *Ohio History*, Vol 79 (1970), 138-51.

982 WOLFF, LEON. *Lockout, the Story of the Homestead Strike of 1892: A Study of Violence, Unionism and the Carnegie Steel Empire*. NY: Harper & Row, 1965.

983 WOODMAN, HAROLD D. "Sequel to Slavery: the New History Views the Postbellum South." *Journal of Southern History*, Vol 43 (1977), 523-54.

984 YELLOWITZ, IRWIN. "The Origins of Unemployment Reform in the United States." *Labor History*, Vol 9 (1968), 338-60.

985 ———. "Skilled Workers and Mechanization: The Lasters in the 1890's." *Labor History*, Vol 18 (1977), 197-213.

986 ZISKA, PATRICK J. "The Violent Years of Labor's Youth." *Worklife*, Vol 1 (Jul 1976), 19-23.

CONDITIONS OF LABOR

987 ABRAMOVITZ, MIRIAM. *Business and Health Reform: Worker's Compensation and Health Insurance in the Progressive Era*. Ph D diss, Columbia U, 1981.

988 AMERICAN ACADEMY OF POLITICAL AND SOCIAL SCIENCE. *The Improvements of Labor Conditions in the United States*. Phila.: The Academy, 1906.

989 BAILEY, A. F. *The Progressives and Child Labour Reform*. Ph D diss, Manchester U, 1972.

990 BAILEY, HUGH C. "Edgar Gardner Murphy and the Child Labor Movement." *Alabama Review*, Vol 18 (1965), 47-59.

991 CLARK, DENNIS. "Babes in Bondage: Indentured Irish Children in Philadelphia in the 19th Century." *Pennsylvania Magazine of History and Biography*, Vol 101 (1977), 475-86.

992 FOSTER, JIM. "The Ten Day Tramps." *Labor History*, Vol 22 (1982), 608-23.

993 FRIEDMAN, LAWRENCE M., and MICHAEL M. SPECTOR. "Tenement House Legislation in Wisconsin: Reform and Reaction." *American Journal of Legal History*, Vol (1965), 41-63.

994 GOLDSTEIN, HAROLD. "Child Labor in America's History." *Children Today*, May-Jun 1976), 30-35.

995 JONES, ALTON DUMAR. "The Child Labor Reform Movement in Georgia." *Georgia Historical Quarterly*, Vol 49 (1965), 396-417.

996 KERR, THOMAS J., IV. *New York Factory investigating Commission and the Progressives.* Ph D diss, Syracuse U, 1965.

997 KOCH, CARL. *A Historical Review of Compulsory School Attendance Laws and Child Labor Laws.* Ph D diss, U of Wyoming, 1972.

998 LAUCK, WILLIAM J., and EDGAR SYDENSTRICKER. *Conditions of Labor in American Industries: A Summarization of the Results of Recent Investigations.* NY: Funk and Wagnalls, 1917.

999 LLOYD, GARY ARTHUR. *Social Work Concepts of the Causes and 'Treatment' of Poverty: 1893-1908.* Ph D diss, Tulane U, 1965.

1000 MCAHREN, ROBERT WILLARD. *Making the Nation Safe for Childhood: A History of the Movement for Federal Regulation of Child Labor, 1900-1038.* Ph D diss, U of Texas, 1967.

1001 MCCAULEY, ELFREIDA B. "The Manufacturers' and Village Library in Somersworth, New Hampshire." *Historical New Hampshire*, Vol 27 (1972), 89-107.

1002 NEW YORK STATE. Factory Investigating Commission (Robert Wagner, chairman) *Fourth Report Transmitted to Legislature, February 15, 1915.* Albany: J. B. Lyon Co., 1915. (Senate Document 43)

1003 ———. *Preliminary Report Transmitted to Legislature, March 1, 1912.* Albany: The Argus Co., 1912.

1004 ———. *Second Report Transmitted to Legislature, January 15, 1913.* Albany: J. B. Lyon Co., 1913. (Senate Document 36)

1005 ———. *Third Report Transmitted to Legislature, February 14, 1914.* Albany: J. B. Lyon Co., 1914. (Assembly Document 28)

1006 PRIDE, NANCY. "Incidents Preceding the Louisiana Child Labor Law of 1912." *Louisiana History*, Vol 19 (1978), 437-45.

1007 RODGERS, DANIEL T. "Socializing Middle-Class Children: Institutions, Fables, and Work Values in 19th Century America." *Journal of Social History*, Vol 13 (1980), 354-67.

1008 SHERGOLD, PETER R. *Standard of Life of Manual Workers in the First Decade of the 20th Century: A Comparative Study of Birmingham, U.K. and Pittsburgh, U.S.* Ph D diss, London School of Economics, 1972.

1009 SMITH, RUSSELL E. "The March of the Mill Children." *Social Science Review*, Vol 41 (1967), 298-303.

1010 SPEAKMAN, JOSEPH. *Unwillingly to School: Child Labor and its Reform in Pennsylvania and the Progressive Era.* Ph D diss, Temple U, 1976.

1011 STAMBLER, MOSES. "The Effect of Compulsory Education and Child Labor Laws on High School Attendance in New York City, 1898-1917." *History of Education QWuarterly*, Vol 8 (1968), 189-214.

1012 STEIN, LEON. *The Triangle Fire.* Phila.: J. B. Lippincott, 1962.

1013 SWANSON, MERWIN. "Professional Rural Social Work in America." *Agriculture History,*, Vol 46 (1972), 515-26.

1014 WALKER, ROGER W. "The A.F.L. and Child-Labor Legislation: An Exercise in Frustration." *Labor History*, Vol 11 (1970), 323-40.

EMPLOYERS ASSOCIATIONS AND OFFENSIVES, THE OPEN AND CLOSED SHOP CONTROVERSY, LABOR SPIES, LABOR INJUNCTIONS, AND LEGISLATION

1015 ASHER, ROBERT. "The 1911 Wisconsin Workmen's Compensation Law: a Study in Conservative Labor Reform." *Wisconsin Magazine of History*, Vol 57 (1973), 123-40.

1016 ———. "Business and Workers' Welfare in the Progressive Era: Workmen's Compensation Reform in Massachusetts, 1880-1911." *Business History*, Vol 43 (1969), 452-75.

1017 BERMAN, EDWARD. *Labor and the Sherman Act*. NY: Harper, 1930.

1018 BONNETT, C. E. *Employers' Associations in the United States*. NY: Macmillan, 1922.

1019 BURNS, WILLIAM J. *The Masked War*. NY: Doran, 1913.

1020 COMMONS, JOHN R. "Causes of the Union-Shop Policy." *Publications of the American Economic Association*, Vol 6, No 1, *Papers and Proceedings of the Seventeenth Annual Meeting, Part 1,* Feb 1905, 140-59.

1021 ELIOT, C. E. "Employers' Policies in the Industrial Strife." *Harper's*, Mar 1905.

1022 FRANKFURTER, FELIX, and NATHAN GREENE. *The Labor Injunction*. NY: Macmillan, 1930.

1023 FRIEDMAN, MORRIS. *The Pinkerton Labor Spy*. NY: Wilshire Book Co., 1907.

1024 GREEN, MARGUERITE. *The National Civic Federation and the American Labor Movement, 1900-1925*. Wash.: Catholic U of America Press, 1956.

1025 HACKER, BARTON C. "The United States Army as a National Police Force: the Federal Policing of Labor Disputes, 1877-1898." *Military Affairs*, Vol 33 (1969), 255-64.

1026 HEFLAND, BARRY F. "Labor and the Courts: The Common Law Doctrine of Criminal Conspiracy and its Application in the Buck's Stove Case." *Labor History*, Vol 18 (1977), 91-114.

1027 HOGG, JOHN B. "Public Reaction to Pinkertonism and the Labor Question." *Pennsylvania History*, Vol 11 (1944), 171-99.

1028 HUEBNER, GROVER G. *Blacklisting*. Madison: Wisconsin Free Library Commission, Legislative Reference Department, 1906.

1029 KUTLER, STANLEY I. "Labor, the Clayton Act, and the Supreme Court." *Labor History*, Vol 3 (1962), 19-38.

1030 LEA, ARDEN J. "Cotton Textiles and the Federal Child Labor Act of 1916." *Labor History*, Vol 16 (1975), 485-94.

1031 LUBOVE, ROY. "Workmen's Compensation and the Prerogatives of Voluntarism." *Labor History*, Vol 8 (1967), 254-79.

1032 MCLATCHY, PATRICK H. *The Development of the National Guard of Washington as an Instrument of Social Control, 1854-1916*. Ph D diss, U of Washington, 1973.

1033 MCLAUGHLIN, DORIS B. "The Second Battle of Battle Creek—The Open Shop Movement in the Early Twentieth Century." *Labor History*, Vol 14 (1973), 323-39.

1034 MARCOSSON, ISAAC F. "The Fight for the Open Shop." *World's Work*, Dec 1905.

1035 MASON, A. T. *Organized Labor and the Law, with Especial Reference to the Sherman and Clayton Acts*. Durham, NC: Duke U Press, 1925.

1036 MERRITT, WALTER G. *History of the League for Industrial Rights* (in this period known as the American Anti-Boycott Association). NY: League for Industrial Rights, 1925.

1037 MORN, FRANK. *The Eye that never Sleeps: a History of the Pinkerton National Detective Agency, 1850-1920*. Ph D diss, U of Chicago, 1976.

1038 SCHEINBERG, STEPHEN J. *The Development of Corporation Labor Policy, 1900-1940*. Ph D diss, U of Wisconsin, 1966.

1039 STEIGERWALT, ALBERT K. *The National Association of Manufacturers, 1895-1914: A Study in Business Leadership*. Ann Arbor: Graduate School of Business Administration, U of Michigan, 1964.

1040 STOCKTON, FRANK T. "The Closed Shop in American Unions." *Johns Hopkins University Studies in Historical and Political Science*, Series 29, 1911, 431-611.

1041 TAYLOR, ALBION G. *Labor Policies of the National Association of Manufacturers*. Urbana: U of Illinois, 1928.

1042 U.S. CONGRESS. HOUSE. Committee on the Judiciary. *Investigation of the Employment of Pinkerton Detectives in Connection with the Labor Troubles at Homestead, Pennsylvania.* Wash.: G.P.O., 1892.

1043 WARNE, COLSTON E., ed. *The Pullman Boycott of 1894: The Problem of Federal Intervention.* Bost.: Heath, 1955.

1044 WEINSTEIN, JAMES. "Big Business and the Origins of Workmen's Compensation." *Labor History*, Vol 8 (1967), 156-74.

1045 WETZEL, KURT. "Railroad Management's Response to Operating Employees Accidents, 1890-1913." *Labor History*, Vol 21 (1980), 351-68.

1046 WILLOUGHBY, WILLIAM FRANKLIN. "Employers' Associations for Dealing with Labor in the United States." *Quarterly Journal of Economics*, Vol 20 (1905), 110-50.

THE I.W.W.

1047 ANDERSON, BRYCE W. "The Bomb at the Governor's Gate." *American West*, Vol 2 (1965), 12-21, 75-76.

1048 ANDERSON, RONDO W. "Joe Hill—the Legend After Fifty Years." *Western Folklore*, Vol 25 (1966), 129-30.

1049 BERCUSON, DAVID JAY. "The One Big Union in Washington." *Pacific Northwest Quarterly*, Vol 69 (1978), 127-34.

1050 BETTEN, NEIL. "Riot, Revolution, Repression in the Iron Range Strike of 1916." *Minnesota History*, Vol 41 (1968), 82-94.

1051 BRAZIER, RICHARD. "The Mass I.W.W. Trial of 1918: A Retrospect." *Labor History*, Vol 7 (1966), 178-92.

1052 ———. "The Story of the I.W.W.'s 'Little Red Songbook.'" *Labor History*, Vol 9 (1968), 91-105.

1053 *Bread and Roses Too: Studies of the Wobblies.* Westport, CT: Greenwood, 1969.

1054 BRISSENDEN, PAUL F. *The I.W.W., A Study of American Syndicalism.* NY: Columbia U Press, 1920.

1055 ———. *The Launching of the Industrial Workers of the World.* Berkeley: U of California Press, 1913.

1056 BROOKS, JOHN G. *American Syndicalism: The I. W. W.* NY: Macmillan, 1913.

1057 BROWN, MYLAND RUDOLPH. *The I.W.W. and the Negro Worker.* Ph D diss, Ball State U, 1968.

1058 BROYLES, GLEN J. "The Spokane Free Speech Fight, 1909-1910: A Study in IWW Tactics." *Labor History*, Vol 19 (1978), 238-52.

1059 BUONFINO, GIANCARLO. "Il Muschio non cresce sui sassi che rotolano: Grafica e propaganda I.W.W." *Primo Maggio*, Vol 1 (Sep 1973), 67-88.

1060 CARTOSIO, BRUNO. "Note e documenti sugli Industrial Workers of the World." *Primo Maggio*, Vol 1 (Sep 1973), 43-56.

1061 CHAPLIN, RALPH. *Wobbly: The Rough-and-Tumble Story of an American Radical.* Chicago: U of Chicago Press, 1948.

1062 ———, and BEN HUR LAMPMAN. *The Centralia Case: Three Views on the Armistice Day Tragedy at Centralia, Washington, November 11, 1919: The Centralia Conspiracy. By Ralph Chaplin. Centralia: Tragedy and Trial. By Ben Hur Lampman. The Centralia Case: A Joint Report.* NY: Da Capo Press, 1971. (Originally published separately in 1920, 1924 & 1930)

1063 CHURCHILL, WINSTON. *The Dwelling Place of Light* (a novel). NY: Macmillan, 1917.

1064 CLARK, NORMAN H. "Everett, 1916, and after." *Pacific Northwest Quarterly*, Vol 57 (1966), 57-64.

1065 COBEN, STANLEY. *A. Mitchell Palmer: Politician.* NY: Columbia U Press, 1963.

1066 COLE, TERRY WAYNE. *Labor's Radical Alternative: the Rhetoric of the I.W.W.* Ph D diss, U of Oregon, 1974.

1067 CONLIN, JOSEPH R. *At the Point of Production: The Local History of the I.W.W.* Westport, CT: Greenwood Press, 1981.

1068 ———. *Bread and Roses Too: Studies of the Wobblies.* Westport, CT: Greenwood, 1969.

1069 ———. "The IWW and the Question of Violence." *Wisconsin Magazine of History*, Vol 51 (1968), 316-26.

1070 ———. "The I.W.W. and the Socialist Party." *Science & Society*, Vol 31 (1967), 22-36.

1071 ———. *The Wobblies: a Study of the Industrial Workers of the World before World War I.* Ph D diss, U of Wisconsin, 1966.

1072 CORTNER, RICHARD C. "The Wobblies and Fiske v. Kansas: Victory amid Disintegration." *Kansas History*, Vol 4 (1981), 30-38.

1073 DANIEL, CLETUS E. "In Defense of the Wheatland Wobblies: A Critical Analysis of the IWW in California." *Labor History*, Vol 19 (1978), 485-509.

1074 ———. "Wobblies on the Farm: the I.W.W. in the Yakima Valley." *Pacific Northwest Quarterly*, Vol 65 (1974), 166-75.

1075 DAVIS, MIKE. "Stop Watch and the Wooden Shoe: Scientific Management and the I.W.W." *Radical America*, Vol 9 (Jan-Feb 1975), 69-96.

1076 DE CAUX, LEN. *The Living Spirit of the Wobblies.* NY: International, 1978.

1077 DUBOFSKY, MELVYN. "Film as History: History as Drama—Some Comments on The Wobblies, a Play by Steward Bird and Peter Robilotta, and The Wobblies, a Film by Steward Bird and Deborah Shaffer." *Labor History*, Vol 22 (1981), 136-40.

1078 ———. "James H. Hawley and the Origins of the Haywood Case." *Pacific Northwest Quarterly*, Vol 53 (1967), 23-32.

1079 ———. *We Shall Be All: A History of the Industrial Workers of the World.* Chicago: Quadrangle, 1969.

1080 EBERT, JUSTUS. *The Trial of a New Society* (the Ettor, Giovannitti, and Caruso case). Cleveland: I.W.W. Publishing Bureau, 1913.

1081 EBNER, MICHAEL H. "The Passaic Strike of 1912 and the Two I.W.W.'s." *Labor History*, Vol 11 (1970), 452-66.

1082 ELDRIGE, P. W. "The Wheatland Hop Riot and the Ford and Suhr Case." *Industrial and Labor Relations Forum*, Vol 10 (May 1974), 165-95.

1083 FONER, PHILIP S. *The Case of Joe Hill.* NY: International, 1966.

1084 ———. *History of the Labor Movement in the United States.*, Vol 4: *The Industrial Workers of the World, 1905-1917.* NY: International, 1965.

1085 ———. "*United States of America vs. Wm. D. Haywood, et al.*: The I.W.W. Indictment." *Labor History*, Vol 11 (1970), 500-30.

1086 ———. "The IWW and the Black Worker." *Journal of Negro History*, Vol 55 (1970), 45-64.

1087 FONER, PHILIP S., ed. *Fellow Workers and Friends: I.W.W. Free Speech Fights as Told by Participants.* Westport, CT: Greenwood, 1981.

1088 ———. *The Letters of Joe Hill.* NY: Oak, 1965.

1089 GAMBS, JOHN. *The Decline of the I.W.W.* NY: Columbia U Press, 1932.

1090 GENINI, RONALD. "Industrial Workers in the World and their Fresno Free Speech Fight, 1910-1911." *California Historical Quarterly*, Vol 53 (1974), 100-28.

1091 GEORGE, HARRISON. *The I.W.W. Trial.* Chicago: IWW, 1918.

1092 GOMEZ, JOSEPH A. "History, Documentation and Audience Manipulation: A View of the Wobblies." *Labor History*, Vol 22 (1981), 141-45.

1093 GRONQUIST, ROY. *The Ideology of the IWW as Represented in the Discursive Acts of William D. Haywood.* Ph D diss, Washington State U, 1976.

1094 GUNNS, ALBERT F. "Ray Becker, The Last Centralia Prisoner." *Pacific Northwest Quarterly*, Vol 59 (1968), 88-99.

1095 GUTFELD, ARNON. "The Murder of Frank Little: Radical Labor Agitation in Butte, Montana, 1917." *Labor History*, Vol 10 (1969), 177-92.

1096 HOKANSON, NELS. "Swedes and the I.W.W." *Swedish Pioneer Historical Quarterly*, Vol 23 (1972), 25-36.

1097 HOUSTON, ROBERT. *Bisbee '17* (a novel). NY: Pantheon, 1979.

1098 HOXIE, ROBERT F. "The Truth about the I.W.W." *Journal of Political Economy*, Vol 21 (1913), 785-97.

1099 KOPPES, CLAYTON R. "The Industrial Workers of the World and County-Jail Reform in Kansas, 1915-20." *Kansas Historical Quarterly*, Vol 41 (1975), 63-86.

1100 ———. "The Kansas Trial of the IWW, 1917-1919." *Labor History*, Vol 16 (1975), 338-58.

1101 KORNBLUH, JOYCE L., ed. *Rebel Voices, an I. W. W. Anthology*. Ann Arbor: U of Michigan Press, 1964.

1102 LEWARNE, CHARLES P. "The Aberdeen, Washington, Free Speech Fight of 1911-12." *Pacific Northwest Quarterly*, Vol 66 (1975), 1-12.

1103 ———. "The Bolsheviks Land in Seattle: the Shilka Incident of 1917." *Arizona and the West*, Vol 20 (1978), 107-22.

1104 ———. "On the Wobbly Train to Fresno." *Labor History*, Vol 14 (1973), 264-89.

1105 LINDQUIST, JOHN H. "The Jerome Deportation of 1917." *Arizona and the West*, Vol 11 (1969), 233-46.

1106 ———, and JAMES FRASER. "A Sociological Interpretation of the Bisbee Deportation." *Pacific Historical Review*, Vol 38 (1968), 401-22.

1107 LOVIN, HUGH T. "Idaho and the 'Reds,' 1919-1926." *Pacific Northwest Quarterly*, Vol 69 (1978), 107-15.

1108 ———. "Moses Alexander and the Idaho Lumber Strike of 1917." *Pacific Northwest Quarterly*, Vol 66 (1975), 115-22.

1109 MCCLELLAND, JOHN M., JR. "Terror on Tower Avenue." *Pacific Northwest Quarterly*, Vol 57 (1966), 65-72. (Centralia, 1919)

1110 MILLER, CHARLES. "Our Great Neglected Wobbly." *Michigan Quarterly Review*, Vol 6 (1967), 57-61. (About novelist known as B. Traven, Traven Torsvan, or Hal Croves)

1111 NOCHLIN, LINDA. "The Paterson Strike Pageant of 1913." *Art in America*, Vol 62 (May-Jun 1974), 64-68.

1112 NOMURA, TATSURO. "McKees Rocks Strike and the I.W.W. Activities in the Pittsburgh District Steel Industry." *Journal of the Faculty of Foreign Studies, Aichi Prefectural University*, No 12 (Mar 1979), 23-66. (In Japanese)

1113 ———. *Partisan Politics in and around the I.W.W.: The Earliest Phase*. (Journal of the Faculty of Foreign Studies/Aichi Prefectural University), No 10(Mar 1977), 86-139

1114 PATTERSON, K. "Lion and the Fox; B. Haywood Trial of 1906." *American History Illustrated*, Vol 13 (Apr 1978), 12-21.

1115 PETERSON, H. C., and GILBERT C. FITE. *Opponents of War, 1917-1918*. Madison: U of Wisconsin Press, 1957.

1116 "R. D. Ginther, Working Man, Artist and Historian of Skid Row." *California Historical Quarterly*, Vol 54 (1975), 263-71.

1117 REED, MERL E. "The IWW and Individual Freedom in Western Louisiana, 1913." *Louisiana History*, Vol 10 (1969), 61-69.

1118 ———. "Lumberjacks and Longshoremen: The I.W.W. in Louisiana." *Labor History*, Vol 13 (1972), 41-59.

1119 RENSHAW, PATRICK. "The IWW and the Red Scare, 1917-24." *Journal of Contemporary History*, Vol 3 (Oct 1968), 63-72.

1120 ———. *The Wobblies: The Story of Syndicalism in the United States*. Garden City: Doubleday, 1967.

1121 REUSS, RICHARD A. "The Ballad of 'Joe Hill' Revisited." *Western Folklore*, Vol 26 (1967), 187-88.

1122 ROBINSON, LELAND WALTER. *Social Movement Organizations in Decline: a Case Study of the I.W.W.* Ph D diss, Northwestern U, 1973.

1123 ROCHA, GUY LOUIS. "The IWW and the Boulder Canyon Project: the Final Death Throes of American Syndicalism." *Nevada Historical Society Quarterly*, Vol 21 (Spring 1978), 3-24.

1124 ———. "Radical Labor Struggles in the Tonopah-Goldfield Mining District, 1901-1922." *Nevada Historical Society Quarterly*, Vol 20 (1977), 3-45.

1125 RODNITZSKY, JEROME L. "The Evolution of the American Protest Song." *Journal of Popular Culture*, Vol 3 (1969), 35-45.

1126 SERAILE, WILLIAM. "Ben Fletcher, I.W.W. Organizer." *Pennsylvania History*, Vol 46 (1979), 213-32.

1127 SMITH, WALKER C. *The Everett Massacre: A History of the Class Struggle in the Lumber Industry*. Chicago: IWW, 1917.

1128 TAFT, PHILIP. "The Bisbee Deportation." *Labor History*, Vol 13 (1972), 3-40.

1129 ———. "The Federal Trials of the I.W.W." *Labor History*, Vol 3 (1962), 57-91.

1130 ———. "The I.W.W. in the Grain Belt." *Labor History*, Vol 1 (1960), 53-67.

1131 ———. "Mayor Short and the I.W.W. Agricultural Workers." *Labor History*, Vol 7 (1966), 173-77.

1132 TOBIN, EUGENE M. "Direct Action and Conscience: The 1913 Paterson Strike as Example of hte Relationship Between Labor Radicals and Liberals." *Labor History*, Vol 20 (1979), 73-88.

1133 TRAVEN, B. *The Cotton-Pickers* (a novel). NY: Hill & Wang, 1966. (First published as *Der Wobbly*, Berlin, 1926)

1134 TYLER, ROBERT L. "The I.W.W. and the West." *American Quarterly*, Vol 12 (1960), 175-87.

1135 ———. *Rebels of the Woods and Fields: A Study of the I.W.W. in the Pacific Northwest*. Ph D diss, U of Oregon, 1953.

1136 ———. *Rebels of the Woods: The I.W.W. in the Pacific Northwest*. Eugene: U of Oregon Books, 1967.

1137 WAGAMAN, DAVID. "The Industrial Workers of the World in Nebraska." *Nebraska History*, Vol 56 (1975), 295-337.

1138 WERSTEIN, IRVING. *Pie in the Sky, an American Struggle: The Wobblies and Their Time*. NY: Delacorte, 1969.

1139 WETZEL, KURT. "The Defeat of Bill Dunne: an Episode in the Montana Red Scare." *pacific Northwest Quarterly*, Vol 64 (1973), 12-20.

1140 WHITE, EARL BRUCE. "Might is Right: Unionism and Goldfield, Nevada, 1904 to 1908." *Journal of the West*, Vol 16 (Jul 1977), 75-84.

1141 ———. *The Wichita Indictments and Trial of the I.W.W., 1917-1919 and the Aftermath*. Ph D diss, U of Colorado, 1981.

1142 WILLIAMS, WILLIAM J. "Bloody Sunday Revisited." *Pacific Northwest Quarterly*, Vol 71 (1980), 50-62.

1143 *The Wobblies*. 1979. (Documentary film by Stewart Bird & Deborah Shaffer)

1144 WORTMAN, ROY. *The I.W.W. in Ohio, 1905-1950*. Ph D diss, Ohio State U, 1971.

1145 ———. "The Resurgence of the I.W.W. in Cleveland." *Northwest Ohio Quarterly*, Vol 47 (1974-75), 20-29.

1146 ZEIGER, ROBERT H. "Robin Hood in the Silk City: the I.W.W. and the Paterson Silk Strike of 1913" *New Jersey Historical Society. Proceedings*, Vol 84 (1966), 182-95.

SCIENTIFIC MANAGEMENT

1147 AITKEN, HUGH G. J. *Taylorism at Watertown Arsenal: Scientific Management in Action, 1908-1915*. Cambr.: Harvard U Press, 1960.

1148 BLACKFORD, MANSEL. "Scientific Management and Welfare Work in Early 20th Century American Business: the Buckeye Steel Casting Co." *Ohio History*, Vol 90 (1981), 238-58.

1149 BRANDEIS, LOUIS D. "Organized Labor and Efficiency." *Survey*, Apr 22, 1911, 148-51.

1150 BURNHAM, JAMES. *The Managerial Revolution*. NY: John Day, 1941.

1151 HABER, SAMUEL. *Efficiency and Uplift: Scientific Management in the Progressive Era, 1890-1920*. Chicago: U of Chicago Press, 1964.

1152 HOXIE, ROBERT F. *Scientific Management and Labor*. NY: Appleton, 1915.

1153 KAKAR, SUDHIR. *Frederick Taylor: A Study in Personality and Innovation*. Cambr.: MIT Press, 1970.

1154 KRAINES, OSCAR. "Brandeis and Scientific Management." *Publication of the American Jewish Historical Society*, Vol 51 (1951), 41-60.

1155 MCKELVEY, JEAN T. *AFL Attitudes Toward Production, 1900-1932*. Ithaca: NY State School of Industrial and Labor Relations, Cornell U, 1952.

1156 MERRILL, HARWOOD F., ed. *Classics in Management: Selections from the Historic Literature of Management*. NY: American Management Association, 1960.

1157 NADWORNY, MILTON J. *Scientific Management and the Unions, 1900-1932*. Cambr.: Harvard U Press, 1955.

1158 NELSON, DANIEL. *Frederick W. Taylor and the Rise of Scientific Management*. Madison: U of Wisconsin Press, 1980.

1159 ———, and STUART CAMPBELL. "Trylorism versus Welfare Work in American Industry: H. L. Gantt and the Bancrofts." *Business History Review*, Vol 46 (1972), 1-16.

1160 PATRY, BILL. "Taylorism Comes to the Social Services." *Monthly Review*, Vol 30 (Oct 1978), 30-37.

1161 TAYLOR, FREDERICK WINSLOW. *Scientific Management: Comprising Shop Management, The Principles of Scientific Management, Testimony Before the Special House Committee*. NY: Harper, 1947.

1162 VEBLEN, THORSTEIN. *The Engineers and the Price System*. NY: Viking, 1921.

World War I and the Golden Aftermath

1163 BENNETT, DIANNE, and WILLIAM GRAEBNER. "Safety First: Slogan and Symbol of the Industrial Safety Movement." *Illinois State Historical Society Journal*, Vol 68 (1975), 243-56.

1164 BERNSTEIN, IRVING. *The Lean Years: A History of the American Worker, 1920-1933*. Bost.: Houghton Mifflin, 1960.

1165 BEST, GARY DEAN. "President Wilson's Second Industrial Conference, 1919-1920." *Labor History*, Vol 16 (1975), 505-20.

1166 BRADLEY, HAROLD CHARLES. *Frank P. Walsh and Postwar America*. Ph D diss, St. Louis U, 1966.

1167 BRODY, DAVID. *Labor in Crisis: The Steel Strike of 1919*. Phila.: Lippincott, 1965.

1168 CHURCHILL, THOMAS. *Centralia Dead March*. Willimantic, CT: Curbstone, 1980.

1169 COHEN, WILLIAM. "Riots, Racism, and Hysteria: the Response of Federal Investigative Officials to the Race Riots of 1919." *Massachusetts Review*, Vol 13 (1972), 373-400.

1170 CONNOR, VALERIE J. *The National War Labor Board: 1918-1919*. Ph D diss, U of Virginia, 1974.

1171 ———. "'The Mothers of the Race' in World War I: The National War Labor Board and Women in Industry." *Labor History*, Vol 21 (1980), 31-54.

1172 COOK, PHILIP L. "Red Scare in Denver." *Colorado Magazine*, Vol 43 (1966), 309-26.

1173 CUFF, ROBERT D. "The Politics of Labor Administration During World War I." *Labor History*, Vol 21 (1980), 546-69.

1174 ———. *The War Industries Board: Business-Government Relations during World War I.* Balt.: Johns Hopkins Press, 1973.

1175 DENISOFF, R. SERGE. "Songs of Persuasion: a Sociological Analysis of Urban Propaganda Songs." *Journal of American Folklore*, Vol 79 (1966), 581-89.

1176 DESMARAIS, RALPH H. "Military Intelligence Reports on Arkansas Riots: 1919-1920." *Arkansas Historical Quarterly*, Vol 33 (1974), 175-91.

1177 "Documents of the Race Riot at East St. Louis." *Illinois State Historical Society Journal*, Vol 45 (1972), 327-36. (Introduction and notes by Robert Asher)

1178 DUBOFSKY, MELVYN. "Abortive Reform: The Wilson Administration and Organized Labor, 1913-1920" pp 173-96, *Work, Community and Power: The Experience of Labor in Europe and America, 1900-1925*, James E. Cronin & Carmen Sirianni, eds. Phila: Temple U Press, 1983.

1179 DUBREUIL, HYACINTHE. *Robots or Men?: A French Workman's Experience in American Industry*. NY: Harper, 1930.

1180 DUNN, ROBERT W. *The Americanization of Labor: The Employers' Offensive Against the Trade Unions*. NY: International Publishers, 1927.

1181 ———. *Company Unions, Employers' "Industrial Democracy."* NY: Vanguard, 1927.

1182 ———. "The Industrial Welfare Offensive," chap. 19, *American Labor Dynamics*, J. B. S. Hardman, ed. NY: Harcourt, Brace, 1928.

1183 FONER, PHILIP S. *The Bolshevik Revolution: Its Impact on American Radicals, Liberals, and Labor. A Documentary Study*. NY: International, 1967.

1184 FOSTER, WILLIAM Z. *The Great Steel Strike and Its Lessons*. NY: Huebsch, 1920.

1185 FRANKLIN, VINCENT P. "The Philadelphia Race Riot of 1918." *Pennsylvania Magazine of History and Biography*, Vol 99 (1975), 336-50.

1186 FRIEDHEIM, ROBERT L. "Prologue to a General Strike: The Seattle Shipyard Strike of 1919." *Labor History*, Vol 6 (1965), 121-42.

1187 ———. *The Seattle General Strike*. Seattle: U of Washington, 1964.

1188 GAGLIARDO, DOMENICO. *The Kansas Industrial Court*. Lawrence: U of Kansas Press, 1941.

1189 GENGARELLY, W. ANTHONY. "Secretary of Labor William B. Wilson and the Red Scare, 1919-1920." *Pennsylvania History*, Vol 46 (1980), 311-30.

1190 GENTRY, CURT. *Frame-Up: The Incredible Case of Tom Mooney and Warren Billings*. NY: Norton, 1967.

1191 GIBBS, CHRISTOPHER. "The Lead Belt Riots and World War I." *Missouri Historical Review*, Vol 71 (1977), 396-418.

1192 GOMPERS, SAMUEL. *American Labor and the War*. NY: Doran, 1919.

1193 GREEN, JAMES R. "Comments on the Montgomery Paper." *Journal of Social History*, Vol 7 (1974), 530-35.

1194 GREENWALD, MAURINE W. "Women Workers and World War I: the American Railroad Industry, a Case Study." *Journal of Social History*, Vol 9 (1975), 154-77.

1195 GRIN, CAROLYN. "The Unemployment Conference of 1921: an Experiment in National Cooperative Planning." *Mid-America*, Vol 55 (1973), 83-107.

1196 GRUBBS, FRANK L., JR. "Council and Alliance Labor Propaganda: 1917-1919." *Labor History*, Vol 7 (1966), 156-72.

1197 ———. *The Struggle for Labor Loyalty: Gompers, the A.F.L., and the Pacifists, 1917-1920*. Durham: Duke U Press, 1968.

1198 HENDRICKSON, KENNETH E., JR. "The Pro-War Socialists, the Social Democratic League, and the Ill-Fated Drive for Industrial Democracy in America, 1917-1920." *Labor History*, Vol 11 (1970), 304-22.

1199 HERBST, JOSEPHINE. *The Executioner Waits* (a novel). NY: Harcourt, Brace, 1934.

1200 HOFFMAN, DENNIS. *An Exploratory Analysis of the Response of Urban Police to Labor Radicalism*. Ph D diss, Portland State U, 1980.

1201 HOPKINS, ERNEST J. *What Happened in the Mooney Case.* NY: Brewer, Warren & Putnam, 1932.
1202 HOSTETTER, GORDON L., and THOMAS Q. BEESLEY. *It's a Racket!* Chicago: Les Quin Books, 1929.
1203 HOWARD, SIDNEY. *The Labor Spy.* NY: Republic Publishing, 1924.
1204 HURVITZ, HAGGAI. "Ideology and Industrial Conflict: President Wilson's First Industrial Conference of October, 1919." *Labor History*, Vol 18 (1977), 509-24.
1205 INGALLS, ROBERT P. "Murder of Joseph Shoemaker." *Southern Exposure*, Vol 8 (Summer 1980), 64-68.
1206 INTERCHURCH WORLD MOVEMENT OF NORTH AMERICA. *Public Opinion and the Steel Strike.* NY: Harcourt, Brace, 1921.
1207 JAFFE, JULIAN. *Crusade against Radicalism: New York during the Red Scare, 1914-1924.* Port Washington, NY: Kennikat, 1972.
1208 ———. "Red Scare and the New York Schools: 1917-1920." *Montclair Journal of Social Sciences and the Humanities*, Vol 1 (1972), 53-65.
1209 JENSON, CAROL ELIZABETH. *Agrarian Pioneer in Civil Liberties: The Nonpartisan League in Minnesota during World War I.* Ph D diss, U of Minnesota, 1968.
1210 JOHNSON, OAKLEY C. "1919, Crucial Year on the Left: A Study of the Proletarian Party." *Political Affairs*, Vol 53 (Dec 1974), 34-38.
1211 JOUGHIN, LOUIS. "Problemes historiques poses par un proces Celebre: L'Affaire Sacco-Vanzetti." *Revue d'Histoire Economique et Sociale*, Vol 47 (1969), 92-107.
1212 KARLSRUD, ROBERT A. *The Hoover Labor Department: a Study in Bureaucratic Divisiveness.* Ph D diss, U of California, 1972.
1213 KRIVY, LEONARD PHILIP. "American Organized Labor and the First World War, 1917-1918: a History of Labor Problems and the Development of a Government War Labor Program." *Ph D diss, New York U, 1965*
1214 KUTLER, STANLEY I. *The Judicial Philosophy of Chief Justice Taft and Organized Labor, 1921-1930.* Ph D diss, Ohio State U, 1960.
1215 LAIDLER, HARRY W. *Social-Economic Movements.* NY: Thomas Y. Crowell, 1945. (See pp 589-96)
1216 LANFEAR, VINCENT W. *Business Fluctuations and the American Labor Movement, 1915-1922.* NY: Columbia U, 1924.
1217 LARSON, BRUCE L. "Kansas and the Nonpartisan League: The Response to the Affair at Great Bend, 1921." *Kansas Historical Quarterly*, Vol 34 (1968), 51-71.
1218 LAUCK, WILLIAM J., and CLAUDE S. WATTS. *The Industrial Code.* NY: Funk and Wagnalls, 1922.
1219 LYONS, RICHARD L. "The Boston Police Strike of 1919." *New England Quarterly*, Vol 20 (1947), 147-68.
1220 MERRITT, WALTER G. *Destination Unknown: Fifty Years of Labor Relations.* NY: Prentice-Hall, 1951.
1221 ———. *History of the League for Industrial Rights.* NY: League for Industrial Rights, 1925.
1222 MILLER, ROBERT MOATS. *American Protestantism and Social Issues, 1919-1939,*, Part 3. Chapel Hill: U of North Carolina Press, 1958.
1223 MILLIS, HARRY A., and ROYAL E. MONTGOMERY. "Employee Representation Plans and Independent Unions," chap. 15, *Organized Labor*, NY: McGraw-Hill, 1945.
1224 MURRAY, ROBERT K. "Communism and the Great Steel Strike of 1919." *Mississippi Valley Historical Review*, Vol 38 (1951), 445-66.
1225 ———. "The Outer World and the Inner Light: A Case Study." *Pennsylvania History*, Vol 36 (1969), 265-89. (A. Mitchell Palmer)
1226 ———. *Red Scare: A Study in National Hysteria, 1919-1920.* Minneapolis: U of Minnesota Press, 1955.
1227 NASH, GERALD D. "Franklin D. Roosevelt and Labor: The World War I Origins of Early New Deal Policy." *Labor History*, Vol 1 (1960), 39-52.

1228 National Industrial Conference, 1919. *Proceedings of the First Industrial Conference (Called by the President) October 6 to 23, 1919.* Wash.: G.P.O., 1920.

1229 National Industrial Conference, 1919-1920. *Report of the Industrial Conference Called by the President, March 6, 1920* (convened Dec 1, 1919 & reconvened Jan 12, 1920). NY: M. B. Brown & Co., 1920.

1230 National Industrial Conference Board. *Collective Bargaining through Employee Representation.* NY: The Board, 1933.

1231 ———. *Experience with Works Councils in the United States.*, Research Report 50. NY: Century, 1922.

1232 Olds, Marshall. *Analysis of the Interchurch World Movement Report on the Steel Strike.* NY: G. P. Putnam, 1922.

1233 Panunzio, Constantine M. *The Deportation Cases of 1919-1920.* NY: Da Capo Press, 1970.

1234 Perlman, Selig, and Philip Taft. *History of Labor in the United States, 1896-1932.* NY: Macmillan, 1935. (See pp 403-620)

1235 Robinson, James W. "The Expulsion of Brookwood Labor College from the Workers' Education Bureau." *Labour History*, [Canberra] No 15 (1968), 64-69.

1236 Russell, Francis. *A City in Terror: 1919, the Boston Police Strike.* NY: Viking, 1975.

1237 ———. *Tragedy in Dedham: The Story of the Sacco-Vanzetti Case.* NY: McGraw-Hill, 1962.

1238 Savage, Marion Dutton. *Industrial Unionism in America.* NY: Ronald Press, 1922.

1239 Seattle Union Record Publishing Co., Inc. *The Seattle General Strike: An Account of What Happened in Seattle and Especially in the Seattle Labor Movement during the General Strike, February 6 to 11, 1919.* Seattle: The Company, 1919.

1240 Selekman, Sylvia K. *Rebellion in Labor Unions.* NY: Boni and Liveright, 1924.

1241 Shapiro, Stanley. "The Great War and Reform: Liberals and Labor, 1917-19." *Labor History*, Vol 12 (1971), 323-44.

1242 Shepherd, Allen LaVerne. *Federal Railway Labor Policy, 1913-1926.* Ph D diss, U of Nebraska, 1971.

1243 Slichter, Sumner H. *Union Policies and Industrial Management.* Wash.: Brookings Institution, 1941. (See chaps. 15 & 16)

1244 Stricker, Frank. "Affluence for Whom?—Another Look at Prosperity and the Working Classes in the 1920s." *Labor History*, Vol 24 (1983), 5-33.

1245 ———. "The Wages of Inflation: Worker's Earnings in the World War I Era." *Mid-America*, Vol 63 (1981), 93-105.

1246 Swan, L. Alex. "When Whites Riot—the East St. Louis Massacre." *International Socialist Review*, Vol 34 (Oct 1973), 12-24.

1247 Taylor, Albion G. *Labor Policies of the National Association of Manufacturers.* Urbana: U of Illinois, 1928.

1248 Tippett, Thomas. *When Southern Labor Stirs.* NY: J. Cape & H. Smith, 1931.

1249 Tomlins, Christopher. "AFL Unions in the 1920s: Their Performance in Historical Perspective." *Journal of American History*, Vol 65 (1979), 1021-42.

1250 Tripp, Joseph F. "Toward an Efficient and Moral Society: Washington State Minimum Wage Law, 1913-1925." *Pacific Northwest Quarterly*, Vol 67 (1976), 97-112.

1251 Tuttle, William M., Jr. "Violence in a 'Heathen' Land: the Longview Race Riot of 1919." *Phylon*, Vol 33 (1972), 324-33.

1252 U.S. Children's Bureau. *Suffer the Little Children: Two Children's Bureau Bulletins.* NY: Arno, 1977.

1253 U.S. Department of Labor. Bureau of Labor Statistics *Characteristics of Company Unions.*, Bulletin 634. Wash.: G.P.O., 1938.

1254 Van der Slice, Austin. *International Labor, Diplomacy and Peace, 1914-1919* (labor movements of France, Great Britain, and the U.S. during the period of the war and the peace). Phila.: U of Pennsylvania Press, 1941.

1255 Wakstein, Allen M. "The National Association of Manufacturers and Labor Relations in the 1920s." *Labor History*, Vol 10 (1969), 163-76.

1256 ———. *The Open Shop Movement, 1919-1933.* Ph D diss, U of Illinois, 1961.

1257 ———. "The Origins of the Open Shop Movement, 1919-1920." *Journal of American History*, Vol 51 (1964), 460-75.

1258 Wander, Paul. "The Challenge of Company-Made Unionism," chap. 20, *American Labor Dynamics*, J. B. S. Hardman, ed. NY: Harcourt, Brace, 1928.

1259 Warne, Colston E., ed. *The Steel Strike of 1919.* Bost.: Heath, 1963.

1260 Warne, Frank J. *The Workers at War.* NY: Century, 1920.

1261 Watkins, Gordon S. *Labor Problems and Labor Administration in the United States during the World War.* Urbana: U of Illinois Press, 1920.

1262 Wise, Leah. "The Elaine Massacre." *Southern Exposure*, Vol 1 (1973), 9-10.

1263 Zibel, Howard J. "The Role of Calvin Coolidge in the Boston Police Strike of 1919." *Industrial and Labor Relations Forum*, Vol 6 (1969), 299-318.

1264 Zieger, Robert H. "Herbert Hoover, the Wage-earner, and the 'New Economic System,' 1919-1929." *Business History Review*, Vol 51 (1977), 161-89.

1265 Zimand, Savel. *The Open Shop Drive.* NY: Bureau of Industrial Research, 1921.

The Great Depression, the New Deal, and the Rise of the CIO

1266 Ajay, Abe. "Working for the W.P.A." *Art in America*, Vol 60 (Sep-Oct 1972), 70-75.

1267 Argersinger, Jo Ann E. "Assisting the 'Loafers': Transient Relief in Baltimore, 1933-1937." *Labor History*, Vol 22 (1982), 226-45.

1268 Auerbach, Jerold S. "The Influence of the New Deal." *Current History*, Vol 47 (1965), 334-39, 365.

1269 ———. *The La Follette Committee: Labor and Civil Liberties in the New Deal.* Ph D diss, Columbia U, 1965.

1270 ———. *Labor and Liberty: The LaFollette Committee and the New Deal.* Indianapolis: Bobbs-Merrill, 1966.

1271 Baker, B. Kimball. "The Great Depression." *Worklife*, Vol 1 (Sep 1976), 11-18.

1272 Baskin, Alex. *Education and the Great Depression: an Inquiry into the Social Ideas and Activities of Radical American Educators during the Economic Crisis of the 1930s.* Ph D diss, Wayne State U, 1966.

1273 ———. "The Ford Hunger March—1932." *Labor History*, Vol 13 (1972), 331-60.

1274 Battista, Carmine. *The San Francisco Longshoremen's and General Strike, in 1934: An Episode in the Emergence of a New Labor Movement in the 1930s.* MA thesis, New York U, 1965.

1275 Beecher, John. "In Egypt Land." *Southern Exposure*, Vol 1 (1973), 33-37. (Poem recording the Reeltown gunbattle during S.T.F.U. organizing)

1276 Beezer, Bruce G. "Arthurdale: An Experiment in Community Education." *West Virginia History*, Vol 36 (1974), 17-37.

1277 Bellush, Bernard. *The Failure of the N.R.A.* NY: Norton, 1976.

1278 Bernard, Dan. "The NLRB, the Courts, and Employer Free Speech." *Industrial and Labor Relations Forum*, Vol 2 (1965), 1-21.

1279 Bernstein, Irving. *The New Deal Collective Bargaining Policy.* Berkeley: U of California Press, 1950.

1280 ———. *The New Deal Collective Bargaining Policy: A Legislative History.* Ph D diss, Harvard U, 1948.

1281 ———. *The Turbulent Years: A History of the American Worker 1933-1941.* Bost.: Houghton Mifflin, 1970.
1282 BETTEN, NEIL. *Catholicism and the Industrial Worker during the Great Depression.* Ph D diss,U of Minnesota, 1969.
1283 ———. "The Great Depression and the Activities of the Catholic Worker Movement." *Labor History,* Vol 12 (1971), 243-358.
1284 ———. "Urban Catholicism and Industrial Reform, 1937-1940." *Thought,* Vol 44 (1969), 434-50.
1285 BLANTZ, THOMAS EDWARD. *Francis J. Haas: Priest in Public Service.* Ph D diss, Columbia U, 1968.
1286 BLUMBERG, BARBARA. *The New Deal and the Unemployed: The View from New York City.* Lewisburg, PA: Bucknell U Press, 1979.
1287 ———. *The WPA in New York City: A Case Study of the New Deal in Action.* Ph D diss, Columbia U, 1974.
1288 BONNIFIELD, PAUL. *The Dust Bowl: Men, Dirt, and Depression.* Albuquerque: U of New Mexico Press, 1979.
1289 BOWMAN, ROBERT A. *The National Committee for the Extension of Labor Education 1942-1950: a Study of the Committee's Attempt to Establish a Labor Extension Service.* Ph D diss, Rutgers U, 1979.
1290 BRAEMAN, JOHN. "The New Deal and the 'Broker State': A Review of the Recent Scholarly Literature." *Business History Review,* Vol 45 (1972), 409-29.
1291 BRANTON, THOMAS. "Survival List—Films of the Great Depression." *Film Library Quarterly,* Vol 12, No 2/3 (1979), 33-40.
1292 BREMER, WILLIAM W. "Along the 'American Way': The New Deal's Work Relief Programs for the Unemployed." *Journal of American History,* Vol 62 (1975), 636-52.
1293 BROOKS, GEORGE W., and MARK THOMPSON. "Multiplant Units: the NLRB's Withdrawal of Free Choice." *Industrial and Labor Relations Review,* Vol 20 (1967), 363-80.
1294 BROOKS, ROBERT R. R. *Unions of Their Own Choosing: An Account of the National Labor Relations Board and Its Work.* New Haven: Yale U Press, 1939.
1295 ———. *When Labor Organizes.* New Haven: Yale U Press, 1937.
1296 BURRAN, JAMES A. "The W.P.A. in Nashville, 1935-43." *Tennessee Historical Quarterly,* Vol 34 (1975), 298-306.
1297 CALKINS, CLINCH. *Spy Overhead.* NY: Harcourt, Brace, 1937.
1298 CHAMBERS, JOHN W. "The Big Switch: Justice Roberts and the Minimum-Wage Cases." *Labor History,* Vol 10 (1969), 44-73.
1299 CHANDLER, LESTER V. *America's Greatest Depression, 1929-1941.* NY: Harper & Row, 1970.
1300 COBB, WILLIAM H., and DONALD H. GRUBBS. "Arkansas' Commonwealth College and the Southern Tenant Farmers' Union." *Arkansas Historical Quarterly,* Vol 25 (1966), 293-311.
1301 COODE, THOMAS, and DENNIS FABBIN. "The New Deal's Arthurdale Project in West Virginia." *West Virginia History,* Vol 36 (1975), 291-308.
1302 COOKE, MORRIS L., and PHILIP MURRAY. *Organized Labor and Production: Next Steps in Industrial Democracy.* NY: Harper, 1940.
1303 CORTNER, RICHARD C. *The Jones and Laughlin Case.* NY: Random House, 1970.
1304 CURLEE, JOAN E. *Some Aspects of the New Deal Rationale: The Pre-1936 Writings of Six of Roosevelt's Advisers.* Ph D diss, Vanderbilt U, 1957.
1305 DANIEL, CLETUS E. *The ACLU and the Wagner Act: An Inquiry into the Depression-Era Crisis of American Liberalism.* Ithaca: NY State School of Industrial and Labor Relations, Cornell, U, 1980.
1306 DANIELS, ROGER. *The Bonus March: An Episode of the Great Depression.* Westport, CT: Greenwood, 1971.

1307 DARBY, MICHAEL R. "Three-and-a-half Million U.S. Employees Have Been Mislaid: or, an Explanation of Unemployment, 1934-1941." *Journal of Political Economy*, Vol 84 (1976), 1-16.

1308 DAUGHERTY, CARROLL R. *Labor under the N.R.A.* Bost.: Houghton Mifflin, 1934.

1309 DEARING, C. L. et al. *The ABC of the NRA.* Wash.: Brookings Institution, 1934.

1310 DENISOFF, R. SERGE, and RICHARD A. REUSS. "The Protest Songs and Skits of American Trotskyists." *Journal of Popular Culture*, Vol 6 (1972), 407-24.

1311 DENNING, DENNIS F. *The Theme of Poverty as Reflected in Plays by Six Depression Playwrights.* Ph D diss, U of Kansas, 1966.

1312 *The Depression Years as Reported by The New York Times.* NY: Arno Press, 1977.

1313 DERBER, MILTON, and EDWIN YOUNG, eds. *Labor and the New Deal.* Madison: U of Wisconsin Press, 1957.

1314 DINWOODIE, D. H. "Deportation: the Immigration Service and the Chicano Labor Movement in the 1930s." *New Mexico Historical Review*, Vol 52 (1977), 193-206.

1315 DUBAY, ROBERT W. "The Civilian Conservation Corps: A Study of Opposition, 1933-1935." *Southern Quarterly*, Vol 6 (1968), 341-58.

1316 DUBOFSKY, MELVYN. "Not so 'Turbulent Years': Another Look at the American 1930's." *Amerkiastudien/American Studies*, Vol 24 (1979), 5-20.

1317 DUNNE, WILLIAM F. *The Great San Francisco General Strike.* NY: Workers Library Publishers, 1934.

1318 DURAM, JAMES C. "The Labor Union Journals and the Constitutional Issues of the New Deal." *Labor History*, Vol 15 (1974), 216-38.

1319 DWYER, RICHARD. "Evolution of the Affiliated Schools in Workers' Education from Coordination to Educational Service." *Labor Studies Journal*, Vol 2 (Spring 1977), 37-49.

1320 ELLIS, EDWARD ROBB. *A Nation in Torment: The Great American Depression, 1929-1939.* NY: Coward-McCann, 1970.

1321 ERICKSON, HERMAN. "WPA Strike and Trials of 1939." *Minnesota History*, Vol 42 (1971), 202-14.

1322 FARBER, MILTON L., JR. *Changing Attitudes of the American Federation of Labor toward Business and Government, 1929-1933.* Ph D diss, Ohio State U, 1959.

1323 FELT, JEREMY P. "The Child Labor Provisions of the Fair Labor Standards Act." *Labor History*, Vol 11 (1970), 467-81.

1324 FICKLE, JAMES E. "The Southern Pine Association and the N.R.A.: a Case Study of the Blue Eagle in the South." *Southwestern Historical Quarterly*, Vol 79 (1976), 253-78.

1325 FINE, SIDNEY. "Frank Murphy, the Thornill Decision, and Picketing as Free Speech." *Labor History*, Vol 6 (1965), 99-120.

1326 FISCHER, ADAM JACOB. *Formula for Utopia: the American Proletarian Novel, 1930-1939.* Ph D diss, U of Massachusetts, 1974.

1327 FOX, BONNIE R. "Unemployment Relief in Philadelphia, 1930-1932: a Study of the Depression's Impact on Voluntarism." *Pennsylvania Magazine of History and Biography*, Vol 93 (1969), 86-108.

1328 FUCHS, DAVID. *An Analysis of Unemployment Situations Proposed in Selected American Journals of Opinion during the Great Depression.* Ph D diss, New York U, 1968.

1329 GALBRAITH, JOHN K. *The Great Crash, 1929.* NY: Avon, 1980.

1330 GALENSON, WALTER. *The CIO Challenge to the AFL: A History of the American Labor Movement, 1935-1941.* Cambr.: Harvard U Press, 1960.

1331 ———. *Rival Unionism in the United States.* NY: American Council on Public Affairs, 1940.

1332 GALL, GILBERT J. "Heber Blankenhorn, the LaFollette Committee, and the Irony of Industrial Repression." *Labor History*, Vol 22 (1982), 246-53.

1333 GANGER, DAVID W. *Impact of Mechanization and the New Deal's Acreage Reduction Programs on Cotton Farmers during the 1930s.* Ph D diss, U of California, 1973.

1334 GARRATY, JOHN A. "The New Deal, National Socialism and the Great Depression." *American Historical Review,* Vol 78 (1973), 907-44.

1335 ———. "Unemployment During The Great Depression." *Labor History,* Vol 17 (1976), 133-59.

1336 GINGER, ANN FAGAN. "Organizing Lawyers to, inter alia, Pack the Supreme Court." *Guild Practitioner,* Vol 38 (1981) 83-98. (Formation of the National Lawyers Guild)

1337 GOLDSTON, ROBERT C. *The Great Depression: The United States in the Thirties.* Indianapolis: Bobbs-Merrill, 1968.

1338 GOTTLIEB, PETER. "The Complicated Equation: Worker Rebellion and Unionization." *Appalachean Journal,* Vol 6 (1979), 321-25.

1339 GOWER, CALVIN W. "'Camp William James': A New Deal Blunder?" *New England Quarterly,* Vol 38 (1965), 475-93.

1340 ———. "The C.C.C. Indian Division: Aid for Depressed Americans, 1933-1942." *Minnesota History,* Vol 43 (1972), 3-136.

1341 GRAHAM, OTIS L. *An Encore for Reform: The Old Progressives and the New Deal.* NY: Oxford U Press, 1967.

1342 GREEN, JAMES R. "Working Class Militancy in the Depression." *Radical America,* Vol 6 (Nov-Dec 1972), 1-35.

1343 GREENE, NATHAN. "Civil Liberties and the NLRB." *Guild Practitioner,* Vol 38 (1981) 101-9.

1344 GROSS, JAMES A. *The Making of the National Labor Relations Board: A Study in Economics, Politics, and the Law.* Albany: State U of NY Press, 1974.

1345 HALVERSON, GUY, and WILLIAM E. AMES. "The Butte *Bulletin*: Beginnings of a Labor Daily." *Journalism Quarterly,* Vol 46 (1969), 260-66.

1346 HANSON, JAMES AUSTIN. *The Civilian Conservation Corps in the Northern Rocky Mountains.* Ph D diss, U of Wyoming, 1973.

1347 HARRIS, HERBERT. *American Labor.* New Haven: Yale U Press, 1939.

1348 ———. *Labor's Civil War.* NY: Knopf, 1940.

1349 HARRISON, HELEN A. "American Art and the New Deal." *Journal of American Studies,* Vol 6 (1972), 289-96.

1350 HASKETT, WILLIAM. *Ideological Radicals: The American Federation of Labor and Federal Labor Policy in the Strikes of 1934.* Ph D diss, U of California, 1957.

1351 HAYNES, JOHN EARL. "The 'Rank and File' Movement in Private Social Work." *Labor History,* Vol 16 (1975), 78-98.

1352 HEINEMANN, RONALD. "Blue Eagle or Black Buzzard? The NRA in Virginia." *Virginia Magazine of History and Biography,* Vol 89 (1981), 90-100.

1353 HENDRICKSON, KENNETH E., JR. "The Civilian Conservation Corps in Pennsylvania: a Case Study of a New Deal Relief Agency in Operation." *Pennsylvania Magazine of History and Biography,* Vol 100 (1976), 66-96.

1354 HICKS, FLOYD W., and C. ROGER LAMBERT. "Food for the Hungry: Federal Food Programs in Arkansas, 1933-1942." *Arkansas Historical Quarterly,* Vol 37 (1978), 23-43.

1355 HIGGINS, GEORGE G. *Voluntarism in Organized Labor in the United States, 1930-1940.* Wash.: Catholic U of America Press, 1944.

1356 HOLLAND, REID. "Civilian Conservation Corps in the City: Tulsa and Oklahoma City in the 1930s." *Chronicles of Oklahoma,* Vol 53 (1975), 367-75.

1357 HOOK, SIDNEY. "*Modern Quarterly,* a Chapter in American Radical History: V. F. Calverton and his Periodicals." *Labor History,* Vol 10 (1969), 241-49.

1358 HUBERMAN, LEO. *The Labor Spy Racket.* NY: Modern Age Books, 1937.

1359 *Hunger: The National Hunger March to Washington.* 1932. (Workers Film and Photo League Production)

1360 HUNTER, JOHN O. "Marc Blitzstein's 'The Cradle Will Rock' as a Document of America, 1937." *American Quarterly*, Vol 18 (1966), 227-33.

1361 HURD, CHARLES. *When the New Deal Was Young and Gay*. NY: Hawthorn, 1965.

1362 HURD, RICK. "New Deal Labor Policy and the Containment of Radical Union Activity." *Review of Radical Political Economics*, Vol 8 (Fall 1976), 32-43.

1363 ISSERMAN, ABRAHAM J. "CIO v Hague: the Battle of Jersey City." *Guild Practitioner*, Vol 36 (1979), 14-32.

1364 JEANSONNE, GLEN. "Challenge to the New Deal: Huey P. Long and the Redistribution of National Wealth." *Louisiana History*, Vol 21 (1980), 331-39.

1365 JOHNSON, JAMES P. "The Apple Sellers of the Great Depression." *American History Illustrated*, Vol 14 (Jan 1980), 22-24.

1366 JOHNSON, JOSEPHINE W. *Jordanstown* (a novel). NY: Simon and Schuster, 1937.

1367 JOHNSON, WILLIAM R. "Rural Rehabilitation in the New Deal: the Ropesville Project." *Southwestern Historical Quarterly*, Vol 79 (1976), 279-95.

1368 KEMPTON, MURRAY. *Part of Our Time: Some Ruins and Monuments of the Thirties*. NY: Simon and Schuster, 1955.

1369 KIMBERLY, CHARLE M. *The Depression and New Deal in Maryland*. Ph D diss, American U, 1974.

1370 KOCH, RAYMOND LOUIS. *The Development of Public Relief Programs in Minnesota, 1929-1941*. Ph D diss, U of Minnesota, 1967.

1371 LA GUMINA, SALVATORE J. *Vito Marcantonio, Labor and the New Deal, (1935-1940)*. Ph D diss, St. John's U, 1966.

1372 LACY, LESLIE ALEXANDER. *The Soil Soldiers: The Civilian Conservation Corps in the Great Depression*. Radnor, PA: Chilton, 1976.

1373 LALLY, KATHLEEN A. *A History of the Federal Dance Theatre of the WPA, 1935-1939*. Ph D diss, Texas Woman's U, 1979.

1374 LAMBERT, C. ROGER. "Want and Plenty: the Federal Surplus Relief Corporation and the A.A.A." *Agricultural History*, Vol 46 (1972), 390-400.

1375 LANGE, DOROTHEA, and PAUL S. TAYLOR. *An American Exodus: A Record of Human Erosion in the Thirties*. New Haven: Yale U Press, 1969.

1376 LANSKY, LEWIS. *Isador Lubin: the Ideas and Career of a New Deal Labor Economist*. Ph D diss, Case Western Reserve U, 1977.

1377 LARROWE, CHARLES P. "The Great Maritime Strike of '34." *Labor History*, Vol 11 (1970), 403-51; Vol 12 (1971), 3-37.

1378 LASHBROOK, LAURENCE. *Work Relief in Maine: the Administration and Programs of the W.P.A.* Ph D diss, U of Maine 1978.

1379 LEAB, DANIEL J. "Barter and Self-help Groups, 1932-33." *Midcontinent American Studies Journal*, Vol 7 (1966), 15-24.

1380 ———. "'United We Eat': the Creation and Organization of the Unemployed Councils in 1930." *Labor History*, Vol 8 (1967), 300-15.

1381 LEVINE, RHONDA. *Class Struggle and the Capitalist State: the National Industrial Recovery Act and the New Deal*. Ph D diss, SUNY-Binghamton, 1980.

1382 LEVINSON, EDWARD. *Labor on the March*. NY: Harper, 1938.

1383 LISIO, DONALD J. "A Blunder Becomes Catastrophe: Hoover, the Legion and the Bonus Army." *Wisconsin Magazine of History*, Vol 51 (1967), 37-50.

1384 ———. *The President and Protest: Hoover, Conspiracy, and the Bonus Riot*. Columbia: U of Missouri Press, 1974.

1385 LONGIN, THOMAS C. "Coal, Congress and the Courts: the Bituminous Coal Industry and the New Deal." *West Virginia Magazine*, Vol 35 (1974), 101-30.

1386 MCELVAINE, ROBERT S. *Thunder without Lightning: Working Class Discontent in the U.S., 1929-1937*. Ph D diss, SUNY/Binghamton, 1974.

1387 MCFARLAND, CHARLES K. "Coalition of Convenience: Lewis and Roosevelt, 1933-1950." *Labor History*, Vol 13 (1972), 400-14.

1388 ———. *Coalition of Convenience: The Roosevelt-Lewis Courtship, 1933 to 1941.* Ph D diss, West Virginia U, 1965.

1389 ———. *Roosevelt, Lewis, and the New Deal, 1933-1940.* Fort Worth: Texas Christian U Press, 1970.

1390 McLeod, Norman. *The Bitter Roots* (a novel). NY: Smith & Durrell, 1941.

1391 Malamont, B. C. "British Labour and Roosevelt's New Deal: the Response of the Left and the Unions." *Journal of British Studies*, Vol 17 (Sep 1978), 136-67.

1392 Mal'kov, V. L. "Rabochaia politika F. Ruzvel'ta (1933-1940 gg.)." *Voprosy Istorii*, Vol 40 (1965), 88-101.

1393 Marcello, Ronald Ely. *The North Carolina Works Progress Administration and the Politics of Relief.* Ph D diss, Duke U, 1969.

1394 Marquart, Frank. "From a Labor Journal: Unions and Radicals in the Depression Era." *Dissent*, Vol 21 (1974), 421-30.

1395 Martin, Charles H. "Southern Labor Relations in Transition: Gadsden, Alabama, 1930-1943." *Journal of Southern History*, Vol 47 (1981), 545-68.

1396 Mathews, Jane De Hart. "Arts and the People: The New Deal Quest for a Cultural Democracy." *Journal of American History*, Vol 42 (1975), 316-39.

1397 ———. *Art Relief, and Politics: the Federal Theatre, 1935-39.* Ph D diss, Duke U, 1966.

1398 May, Irvin M. "Cotton and Cattle: the F.S.R.C. and Emergency Work Relief." *Agricultural History*, Vol 46 (1972), 938-57.

1399 Meltzer, Milton. *Brother, Can You Spare a Dime: The Great Depression, 1929-1933.* NY: Knopf, 1969.

1400 Miller, Donald L. *The New American Radicalism: Alfred M. Bingham and Non-Marxian Insurgency in the New Deal Era.* Port Washington, NY: Kennikat, 1979.

1401 Miller, John E. "Progressivism and the New Deal: the Wisconsin Workers Bill of 1935." *Wisconsin Magazine of History*, Vol 62 (1978), 25-40.

1402 Miller, M. Lawrence. *Original Federal Theatre Protest Plays—1936-1939: New Deal Contributions to the American Drama of Social Concern.* Ph D diss, U of California, 1968.

1403 Miller, Richard Lurie. "The Enigma of Section 8(5) of the Wagner Act." *Industrial and Labor Relations Review*, Vol 18 (1965), 166-85.

1404 Millett, John David. *The Works Progress Administration in New York City.* Chicago: Public Administration Service, 1938.

1405 Millis, Harry A., and E. C. Brown. *From the Wagner Act to Taft-Hartley: A Study of National Labor Policy and Labor Relations.* Chicago: U of Chicago Press, 1950.

1406 ———, and Royal E. Montgomery. "Employee Representation Plans and Independent Unions," chap. 15, *Organized Labor*, NY: McGraw-Hill, 1945.

1407 Milton, David. *The Politics of Economism: Organized Labor Fights its Way into the American System under the New Deal.* Ph D diss, U of California, 1981.

1408 Mitchell, Broadus. *Depression Decade: From New Era through New Deal, 1929-1941.* NY: Rinehart, 1947.

1409 *Modern Times.* 1936. (Charlie Chaplin feature film)

1410 Monroe, Gerald M. "The '30s: Art, Ideology and the W.P.A." *Art in America*, Vol 63 (Nov-Dec 1975), 64-67.

1411 Morgan, Thomas S., Jr. "A 'Folly, Manifest to Everyone': the Movement to Enact Unemployment Insurance Legislation in North Carolina, 1935-36." *North Carolina Historical Review*, Vol 52 (1975), 283-302.

1412 Morton, Herbert Charles. *Public Contracts and Private Wages: Experience under the Walsh-Healey Act.* Ph D diss, U of Minnesota, 1964.

1413 Mottram, Eric. "Living Mythically: the Thirties." *Journal of American Studies*, Vol 6 (1972), 267-87.

1414 Mullins, William H. "Self-help in Seattle, 1931-1932: Herbert Hoover's Concept of Cooperative Individualism and the Unemployed Citizen's League." *Pacific Northwest Quarterly*, Vol 72 (1981), 11-19.

1415 Muste, Abraham J. *The A. F. of L. in 1931.* NY: National Executive Commission of the Conference for Progressive Labor Action, 1932.

1416 Naison, Mark. "Great Depression: the Threads of a Lost Tradition." *Journal of Ethnic Studies*, Vol I (Fall 1973), 31-52. (S.T.F.U. affiliation with C.I.O./U.C.A.P.A.W.A.)

1417 *National Hunger March.* 1931. (Workers Film and Photo League Production)

1418 *Native Land.* 1942. (Frontier Films production)

1419 Nelson, Daniel. "The Beginnings of the Sit-down Era: The Reminiscences of Rex Murray." *Labor History*, Vol 15 (1974), 89-97.

1420 ———. "Origins of the Sit-Down Era: Worker Militancy and Innovation in the Rubber Industry, 1934-38." *Labor History*, Vol 22 (1982), 198-225.

1421 Nelson, Lawrence J. "Oscar Johnston, the New Deal and the Cotton Subsidy Payments Controversy, 1936-37." *Journal of Southern History*, Vol 40 (1974), 399-416.

1422 Noble, Richard A. "Paterson's Response to the Great Depression." *New Jersey History*, Vol 90 (1978), 87-98.

1423 Nye, Ronald L. "The Challenge to Philanthropy: Unemployment Relief in Santa Barbara, 1930-1932." *California History*, Vol 56 (1978), 310-27.

1424 Ober, Michael J. "The CCC Experience in Glacier National Park." *Montana: Magazine of Western History*, Vol 26 (Summer 1976), 30-39.

1425 O'Brien, David. "American Catholics and Organized Labor in the 1930's." *Catholic Historical Review*, Vol 56 (1966), 323-49.

1426 O'Conner, John. "'King Cotton': the Federal Theatre Project." *Southern Exposure*, Vol 6 (Spring 1978) 74-81.

1427 O'Neill, Robert. "The Federal Writers' Project Files for Indiana." *Indiana Magazine of History*, Vol 77 (1980), 85-96.

1428 Ortquist, Richard T. "Unemployment and Relief; Michigan's Response to the Depression during the Hoover Years." *Michigan History*, Vol 45 (1973), 209-36.

1429 Parker, Robert V. "The Bonus March of 1932: a Unique Experience in North Carolina Political and Social Life." *North Carolina Historical Review*, Vol 51 (1974), 64-89.

1430 Parman, Donald Lee. *The Indian Civilian Conservation Corps.* Ph D diss, U of Oklahoma, 1967.

1431 Patterson, James T., ed. "Life on Relief in Rhode Island, 1934: a Contemporary View from the Field." *Rhode Island History*, Vol 39 (1980), 79-93. (Photographs)

1432 Paulsen, George E. *The Legislative History of the Fair Labor Standards Act.* Ph D diss, Ohio State U, 1959.

1433 Peeler, David. *America's Depression Culture: Social Art and Literature of the 1930s.* Ph D diss, U of Wisconsin, 1981.

1434 Penington, Ralph Alden. *The National Labor Relations Board: Three Decades of Operation.* Ph D diss, Purdue U, 1968.

1435 Perkins, Frances. *The Roosevelt I Knew.* NY: Viking Press, 1946.

1436 Petty, Anne W. *Dramatic Activities and Workers' Education at Highlander Folk School, 1932-1942.* Ph D diss, Bowling Green State U, 1979.

1437 President's Research Committee on Social Trends. *Recent Social Trends in the United States.* NY: Whittlesey House, McGraw-Hill, 1934.

1438 Reeves, William Dale. *The Politics of Public Works 1933-1935.* Ph D diss, Tulane U, 1968.

1439 ———. "P.W.A. and Competitive Administration in the New Deal." *Journal of American History*, Vol 40 (1973), 357-72.

1440 RISON, DAVID. *Arkansas during the Great Depression.* Ph D diss, U of California, 1974.

1441 ROGERS, MICHAEL D. *Collective Bargaining in the Tennessee Valley Authority: the Trades and Labor Experience.* Ph D diss, U of Tennessee, 1973.

1442 ROSENZWEIG, ROY. "Organizing the Unemployed: the Early Years of the Great Depression, 1929-1933." *Radical America*, Vol 10 (Jul-Aug 1976), 37-60.

1443 ———. "Radicals and the Jobless: The Musteites and the Unemployed Leagues, 1932-1936." *Labor History*, Vol 16 (1975), 52-77.

1444 ———. "'Socialism in our Time': The Socialist Party and the Unemployed, 1929-1936." *Labor History*, Vol 20 (1979), 485-509.

1445 ———. "Working Class Struggles in the Great Depression: The Film Record." *Film Library Quarterly*, Vol 13, No 1 (1980), 5-14.

1446 SALMOND, JOHN A. *The Civilian Conservation Corps, 1933-1942: A New Deal Case Study*. Durham, NC: Duke U Press, 1967.

1447 ———. *'Roosevelt's Tree Army': a History of the Civilian Conservation Corps, 1933-1942.* Ph D diss, Duke U, 1967.

1448 SCHLESINGER, ARTHUR M., JR. *The Age of Roosevelt.*, Vol 1: *The Crisis of the Old Order;* Vol 2: *The Coming of the New Deal*; Vol 3: *The Politics of Upheaval.* Bost.: Houghton Mifflin, 1957-60.

1449 SCHUYLER, MICHAEL W. "Federal Drought Relief Activities in Kansas, 1934." *Kansas Historical Quarterly*, Vol 42 (1976), 403-24.

1450 SCHWARTZ, BONNIE. *The Civil Works Administration, 1933-1934: The Business of Emergency Employment in the New Deal.* Ph D diss, Columbia U, 1980.

1451 ———. "New Deal Work Relief and Organized Labor: the CWA and the AFL Building Trades." *Labor History*, Vol 17 (1976), 38-57.

1452 SERETAN, L. GLEN. "The 'New' Workingclass and Social Banditry in Depression America." *Mid-America*, Vol 63 (1981), 107-17.

1453 SHAPIRO, EDWARD S. "Decentralist Intellectuals and the New Deal." *Journal of American History*, Vol 58 (1972), 938-57.

1454 SHAPIRO, WILLIAM. *Public Educational Interests and Positions of the C.I.O. during the Era of the New Deal: an Historical Overview.* Ph D diss, Columbia U Teachers College, 1980.

1455 SIMMONS, JEROLD. "Dawson County Responds to the New Deal, 1933-1940." *Nebraska History*, Vol 62 (1981), 47-72.

1456 SIPE, DANIEL A. *A Moment of the State: the Enactment of the National Labor Relations Act, 1935.* Ph D diss, U of Pennsylvania, 1981.

1457 SMILEY, SAM. "Friends of the Party: The American Writers' Congresses." *Southwest Review*, Vol 54 (1969), 290-300.

1458 STERNSHER, BERNARD. "Depression and New Deal in Ohio: Lorena A. Hickok's Reports to Harry Hopkins, 1934-36." *Ohio History*, Vol 86 (1977), 258-77.

1459 ———. "Victims of the Great Depression: Self Blame/Non Self Blame, Radicalism and Pre-1929 Experiences." *Social Science History*, Vol 1 (1977), 169-81.

1460 STOLBERG, BENJAMIN. *The Story of the CIO.* NY: Viking Press, 1938.

1461 SUGAR, MAURICE. *The Ford Hunger March.* Berkeley, CA: Meiklejohn Civil Liberties Institute, 1980.

1462 SULLIVAN, EDWARD D. *This Labor Union Racket.* NY: Hillman-Curl, 1936.

1463 TANASOCA, DONALD. "CCC: Six Months in Garden Valley; edited by Elmo Richardson." *Idaho Yesterdays*, Vol 11 (Summer, 1967), 17-24.

1464 TEAD, ORDWAY, and H. C. METCALF. *Labor Relations under the Recovery Act.* NY: McGraw-Hill, 1933.

1465 TOMLINS, CHRISTOPHER. "AFL Unions in the 1930s: Their Presence in Historical Perspective." *Journal of American History*, Vol 65 (1979), 1021-42.

1466 TSELOS, GEORGE. "Self-help and Sauerkraut: the Organized Unemployed, Inc., of Minneapolis." *Minnesota History*, Vol 45 (1977), 307-20.

1467 TERKEL, STUDS. *Hard Times: An Oral History of the Depression.* NY: Pantheon, 1970.

1468 U.S. CONGRESS. SENATE. Committee on Education and Labor (Robert M. LaFollette, Jr., chairman). *Violations of Free Speech and the Rights of Labor.*, Parts 1-75. Wash.: G.P.O., 1937049.

1469 U.S. DEPARTMENT OF LABOR. Bureau of Labor Statistics *Characteristics of Company Unions.*, Bulletin 634. Wash.: G.P.O., 1938.

1470 U.S. NATIONAL LABOR RELATIONS BOARD. *Legislative History of the National Labor Relations Act, 1935.*, 2 vols. Wash.: G.P.O., 1949.

1471 VACHA, J. E. "The Case of the Runaway Opera: the Federal Theatre and Marc Blitzstein's *The Cradle Will Rock.*" *New York History*, Vol 62 (1981), 133-52.

1472 VAN DEWATER, PETER E. "The Workers' Education Service." *Michigan History*, Vol 60 (1976), 99-113.

1473 VERBA, SIDNEY, and KAY LEHMAN SCHLOZMAN. "Unemployment, Class Consciousness, and Radical Politics: What Didn't Happen in the 1930s." *Journal of Politics*, Vol 34 (1977), 291-323.

1474 VERDICCHIO, JOSEPH. *New Deal Work Relief and New York City, 1933-1938.* Ph D diss, New York U, 1980.

1475 VITTOZ, STANLEY. *The American Industrial Economy and the Political Origins of Federal Labor Policy Between the World Wars.* Ph D diss, York U, 1980.

1476 VITZ, ROBERT C. "Struggle and Response: American Artists and the Great Depression." *New York History*, Vol 57 (1976), 81-98.

1477 VIVIAN, JAMES F., and JEAN H. VIVIAN. "The Bonus March of 1932: the Role of General George Van Horn Moseley." *Wisconsin Magazine of History*, Vol 51 (1967), 26-36.

1478 VORSE, MARY H. *Labor's New Millions.* NY: Modern Age Books, 1938.

1479 WALLIS, JOHN J. *Work Relief and Unemployment in the 1930s.* Ph D diss, U of Washington, 1981.

1480 WALSH, J. R. *C.I.O.—Industrial Unionism in Action.* NY: Norton, 1937.

1481 WARE, JAMES. "The Sooner NRA: New Deal Recovery in Oklahoma." *Chronicles of Oklahoma*, Vol 54 (1977), 339-51.

1482 WEISS, STUART. "Thomas Amlie and the New Deal." *Mid-America*, Vol 59 (1977), 19-38.

1483 WHATLEY, LARRY. "The Works Progress Administration in Mississippi." *Journal of Mississippi History*, Vol 30 (1968), 35-50.

1484 WOLVIN, ANDREW DAVIS. *The 1933 Blue Eagle Campaign: a Study in Persuasion and Coercion.* Ph D diss, Purdue U, 1968.

1485 WOODRUFF, NAN. "The Failure of Relief during the Arkansas Drought of 1930-1931." *Arkansas Historical Quarterly*, Vol 39 (1980), 301-13.

1486 *Workers Newsreel, Unemployment Special.* 1931. (Workers Film and Photo League Production)

1487 WUTKE, EUGENE ROGER. *Technocracy: It Failed to Save the Nation.* Ph D diss, U of Missouri 1964.

1488 WYATT, BRYANT N. "Experimentation as Technique: the Protest Novels of John Steinbeck." *Discourse*, Vol 12 (1969), 143-53.

1489 WYCHE, BILLY H. "Southern Newspapers View Organized Labor in the New Deal Years." *South Atlantic Quarterly*, Vol 74 (1975), 178-96.

1490 YASKO, KAREL. "Treasures from the Depression." *Historic Preservation*, Vol 24 (Jul-Sep 1972), 26-31.

1491 YORK, HILDRETH. "The New Deal Arts Projects in New Jersey." *New Jersey History*, Vol 98 (1980), 133-74.

Labor in World War II

1492 ANDERSON, KAREN. *Wartime Women: Sex Roles, Family Relations, and the Status of Women During World War II.* Westport, CT: Greenwood, 1981.

1493 BLACKMAN, JOHN L., JR. "Navy Policy Toward the Labor Relations of Its War Contractors." *Military Affairs*, Vol 18 (1954), 176-87; Vol 19 (1955), 21-31.

1494 BLUM, ALBERT A. "Roosevelt, the M-Day Plans and the Military-Industrial Complex." *Military Affairs*, Vol 36 (1972), 44-46.

1495 ———. "Sailor or Worker: A Manpower Dilemma during the Second World War." *Labor History*, Vol 6 (1965), 232-43.

1496 ———. "Soldier or Worker: A Reevaluation of the Selective Service System." *Midwest Quarterly*, Vol 13 (1972), 147-67.

1497 ———. "Working to Win World War II." *Worklife*, Vol 1 (Oct 1976), 12-18.

1498 CUFF, ROBERT D. "Harry Garfield, the Fuel Administration and the Search for a Cooperative Order During World War I." *American Quarterly*, Vol 30 (1978), 39-53.

1499 DERBER, MILTON. "Labor-Management in World War II." *Current History*, Vol 48 (1965), 340-45.

1500 DI BACCO, THOMAS V. "'Draft the Strikers (1946) and Seize the Mills (1952)': the Business Reaction." *Duquesne Review*, Vol 13 (1968), 63-75.

1501 DUFFY, DORIS. *The Role of Government in Labor-Management Production Committees.* Wash.: Catholic U of America Press, 1947.

1502 FIRST, EDYTHE W. *Industry and Labor Advisory Committee in the National Defense Advisory Commission and the Office of Production Management May 1940 to January 1942.* Wash.: U.S. Civilian Production Administration, 1946.

1503 FLYNN, GEORGE Q. *The Mess in Washington: Manpower Mobilization in World War II.* Westport, CT: Greenwood, 1979.

1504 FREEMAN, JOSHUA B. "Delivering the Goods: Industrial Unionism During World War II." *Labor History*, Vol 19 (1978), 570-93.

1505 GLABERMAN, MARTIN. *Wartime Strikes: The Struggle Against the No-Strike Pledge in the UAW during World War II.* Detroit: Bewick, 1980.

1506 GREEN, JAMES R. "Fighting on Two Fronts: Working Class Militancy in the 1940s." *Radical America*, Vol 9 (Jul-Aug 1975), 7-48.

1507 HOWELL, JOHN HARRIS. *The Right To Manage: Industrial Relations Policies of American Business in the 1940s.* Madison: U of Wisconsin Press, 1982.

1508 JENNINGS, ED. "Wildcat! The Wartime Strike wave in Auto." *Radical America*, Vol 9 (Jul-Aug 1975), 77-105.

1509 KEEZER, DEXTER. "Observations on the Operations of the National War Labor Board." *American Economic Review*, Jun 1946.

1510 KOISTINEN, PAUL A. C. "Mobilizing the World War II Economy: Labor and the Industrial-Military Alliance." *Pacific Historical Review*, Vol 42 (1973), 443-78.

1511 LICHTENSTEIN, NELSON. "Ambiguous Legacy: The Union Security Problem During World War II." *Labor History*, Vol 18 (1977), 214-38.

1512 ———. "Defending the No-Strike Pledge: C.I.O. Politics during World War II." *Radical America*, Vol 9 (Jul-Aug 1975), 49-75.

1513 ———. *Industrial Unionism under the No-strike Pledge: A Study of the C.I.O. during the Second World War.* Ph D diss, U of California, 1974.

1514 ———. *Labor's War at Home: The CIO in World War II.* NY: Cambridge U Press, 1982.

1515 MCNEAL, PATRICIA. "Catholic Conscientious Objection during World War II." *Catholic Historical Review*, Vol 61 (1975), 222-42. (Catholic Workers Movement)

1516 MILLER, GLENN W. *American Labor and the Government.* NY: Prentice-Hall, 1948.

1517 NATIONAL WAR LABOR BOARD. *The Termination Report: Industrial Disputes and Wage Stabilization in Wartime, January 12, 1942-December 31, 1945.*, 3 vols. Wash.: G.P.O., 1948-49.

1518 PESSEN, EDWARD. "A Young Industrial Worker in Early World War II in New York City." *Labor History*, Vol 22 (1981), 269-81.

1519 PLUTH, EDWARD. "Prisoner of War Employment in Minnesota during World War II." *Minnesota History*, Vol 44 (1975), 290-303.

1520 PURCELL, RICHARD J. *Labor Policies of the National Defense Advisory Commission and the Office of Production Management, May 1940 to April, 1942*. Wash.: U.S. Civilian Production Administration, 1946.

1521 RICHARDS, ALLAN RENE. *War Labor Boards in the Field*. Chapel Hill: U of North Carolina Press, 1953.

1522 ROCKOFF, HUGH. "The Response of the Giant Corporations to Wage and Price Controls in World War II." *Journal of Economic History*, Vol 41 (1981), 123-28.

1523 SCHWEITZER, MARY. "World War II and Female Labor Force Participation Rates." *Journal of Economic History*, Vol 40 (1980), 89-95.

1524 SEIDMAN, JOEL. *American Labor from Defense to Reconversion*. Chicago: U of Chicago Press, 1953.

1525 STEIN, BRUNO. "Labor's Role in Government Agencies During World War II." *Journal of Economic History*, Vol 17 (1957), 389-408.

1526 U.S. DEPARTMENT OF LABOR. *The National Wage Stabilization Board, January 1, 1946-February 24, 1947*. Wash: G.P.O., 1950.

1527 ———. Bureau of Labor Statistics *Historical Studies of Wartime Problems.*, Nos 1-78. Wash.: BLS, 1941-45.

1528 ———. *Problems and Policies of Dispute Settlement and Wage Stabilization during World War II.*, Bulletin 1009. Wash.: G.P.O., 1950.

1529 ———. *Report of the Work of the National Defense Mediation Board, March 19, 1941-January 12, 1942.*, Bulletin 714. Wash.: G.P.O., 1942.

1530 ———. *Report on the Work of the National Defense Mediation Board, March 19, 1941-January 12, 1942.*, Bulletin 714. Wash.: G.P.O., 1942.

1531 ———. Division of Labor Standards *The President's National Labor-Management Conference November 5-30, 1945: Summary and Committee Reports.*, Bulletin 77. Wash.: G.P.O., 1946.

1532 WARNE, COLSTON E. et al, eds. *War Labor Policies*. NY: Philosophical Library, 1945.

1533 WITNEY, FRED. *Wartime Experiences of the National Labor Relations Board, 1941-1945*. Urbana: U of Illinois Press, 1949.

Post World War II through the 1950s

1534 "The AFL-CIO Merger." *Industrial and Labor Relations Review*, Vol 9 (Apr 1956), entire issue.

1535 ASH, PHILIP. "The Periodical Press and the Taft-Hartley Act." *Public Opinion Quarterly*, Vol 12 (1948), 266-71.

1536 BARBASH, JACK. *The Taft-Hartley Law in Action*. NY: League for Industrial Democracy, 1954.

1537 BARTELL, H. ROBERT, JR. "National Union Assets, 1959-61." *Industrial and Labor Relations Review*, Vol 9 (1965), 80-91.

1538 BEGGS, VANCE M. "Assumption of Union Contracts by Successors: Court Decisions and Arbitration Awards." *Arbitration Journal*, Vol 20 (1965), 20-33.

1539 BEIER, EMERSON H. "Financing Supplemental Unemployment Benefit Plans." *Monthly Labor Review*, Vol 92 (1969), 31-35.

1540 ———. "Terminations of Pension Plans: 11 Years' Experience." *Monthly Labor Review*, Vol 90 (June, 1967), 26-30.

1541 BELL, DANIEL. "Labor in the Post-Industrial Society." *Dissent*, Vol 19 (Winter 1972), 163-89.

1542 ———. "The Next American Labor Movement." *Fortune*, Apr 1953, 120ff.

1543 BERNSTEIN, BARTON J. "The Truman Administration and its Reconversion Wage Policy." *Labor History*, Vol 6 (1965), 214-31.

1544 ———. "The Truman Administration and the Steel Strike of 1946." *Journal of American History*, Vol 52 (1966), 791-803.

1545 BERNSTEIN, IRVING. "The Growth of American Unions, 1945-1960." *Labor History*, Vol 2 (1961), 131-57.

1546 BLOOMBERG, WARNER, JR. et al. *The State of the Unions*. Wash.: National Publishing, 1960.

1547 BONETTE, SAMUEL J. *A Critical Analysis of Union Trusteeships under Title III of Labor-Management Reporting and Disclosure Act of 1959*. Ph D diss, American U, 1973.

1548 BROOKS, GEORGE W. "Reflections on the Changing Character of American Labor Unions." *Proceedings of the Ninth Annual Meeting of the Industrial Relations Research Association*, Dec 28-29, 1956, pp 33-43. Madison: IRRA, 1957.

1549 ———. *The Sources of Vitality in the American Labor Movement*., Bulletin No 41. Ithaca: NY State School of Industrial and Labor Relations, Cornell U, 1960.

1550 BROWN, EMILY C. *National Labor Policy: Taft-Hartley after Three Years and the Next Steps*. Wash.: Public Affairs Institute, 1950.

1551 BUKOWSKI, CHARLES. *Post Office* (a novel). Santa Barbara, CA: Black Sparrow Press, 1974.

1552 CAMMER, HAROLD I. "The Labor Law Committee of the National Lawyers Guild." *Guild Practitioner*, Vol 33 (1976), 52-60.

1553 CAPOZZOLA, JOHN M. *The New York City Regional Office of the National Labor Relations Board: A Study of Field-Headquarters Relationships*. Ph D diss, Pennsylvania State U, 1964.

1554 CHAMBERLAIN, NEIL W. "The Role of Unions in Society," chap. 24, *Sourcebook on Labor*, NY: McGraw-Hill, 1958.

1555 ———. *The Union Challenge to Management Control*. NY: Harper, 1948.

1556 CHAMBERLIN, EDWARD H. et al. *Labor Unions and Public Policy*. Wash.: American Enterprise Association, 1958.

1557 COCHRAN, BERT, ed. *American Labor in Midpassage*. NY: Monthly Review Press, 1959.

1558 COHEN, DORIS. "American Labor Education Service International Education Project: 1951-1961." *Labor Studies Journal*, Vol 4 (1979), 131-47.

1559 COX, ARCHIBALD. *Law and the National Labor Policy*. Los Angeles: U of California, 1960.

1560 CRAYPO, CHARLES. "The National Union Convention as an Internal Appeal Tribunal." *Industrial and Labor Relations Review*., Vol 22 (1969), 487-511.

1561 DALE, ERNEST. *Greater Productivity Through Labor-Management Cooperation*. NY: American Management Association, 1949.

1562 DESCHWEINITZ, DOROTHEA. *Labor and Management in a Common Enterprise*. Cambr.: Harvard U Press, 1949.

1563 DUBIN, ROBERT. "Industrial Conflicts: The Power of Prediction." *Industrial and Labor Relations Review*, Vol 18 (1965), 352-63.

1564 ———. "Union-Management Co-operation and Productivity." *Industrial and Labor Relations Review*, Vol 2 (1949), 20-25.

1565 EMSPAK, FRANK. *The Break Up of the Congress of Industrial Organizations, 1945-1950*. Ph D diss, U of Wisconsin 1972.

1566 FARR, GRANT N. *The Origins of Recent Labor Policy*. Boulder: U of Colorado Press, 1959.

1567 FERGUSON, C. E., and WILLIAM J. STOBER. "Estimate of Union Membership from Reports Filed under the Labor-Management Reporting and Disclosure Act." *Southern Economic Journal*, Vol 33 (1966), 166-86.

1568 FOSTER, JAMES C. "1954: A CIO Victory?" *Labor History*, Vol 12 (1971), 392-408.

1569 GALENSON, WALTER. "Why the American Labor Movement is Not Socialist." *The American Review*, Vol 1 (1961), 1-19.

1570 ———, and SEYMOUR MARTIN LIPSET. *Labor and Trade Unionism: An Interdisciplinary Reader*. NY: John Wiley, 1960.

1571 GARBER, PHILIP E. "Taft-Hartley: Section 304. A Legislative History." *Industrial and Labor Relations Forum*, Vol 7 (1970), 59-102.

1572 GILPATRICK, ELEANOR GOTTESFOCHT. *Unemployment and Aggregate Demand: A Study of Postwar Employment and Unemployment in the United States, 1948-1962*. Ph D diss, Cornell U, 1964.

1573 GOLDBERG, ARTHUR J. *AFL-CIO: Labor United*. NY: McGraw-Hill, 1956.

1574 GOLDBERG, JOSEPH P. "Labor-Management Since World War II." *Current History*, Vol 48 (1965), 356-52, 365-66.

1575 "Government and Labor in the United States." *Current History*, Vol 37 (1959), 129-80.

1576 GUJARATI, DAMODAR. "Labor's Share in Manufacturing Industries, 1949-1964." *Industrial and Labor Relations Review*, Vol 23 (1969), 65-77.

1577 HARRINGTON, MICHAEL, and PAUL JACOBS, eds. *Labor in a Free Society*. Berkeley: U of California Press, 1959.

1578 HILLS, RODERICK M. "A Close Look at Three Administration Policies." *Industrial Relations*, Vol 3 (1964), 5-20.

1579 HUTCHINSON, JOHN. "Corruption in American Trade Unions." *The Political Quarterly*, Vol 28 (Jul-Sep 1957).

1580 INTERNATIONAL LABOUR OFFICE. *The Trade Union Situation in the United States: Report of a Mission from the International Labour Office*. Geneva: ILO, 1960.

1581 JACOBS, PAUL. *Old Before Its Time: Collective Bargaining at 28*. Santa Barbara, CA: Center for the Study of Democratic Institutions, 1963.

1582 JOHNSON, MALCOLM. *Crime on the Labor Front*. NY: McGraw-Hill, 1950.

1583 KASSALOW, EVERETT M. "Occupational Frontiers of Trade Unionism in the United States." *Proceedings of the Thirteenth Annual Meeting of the Industrial Relations Research Association*, Dec 28-29, 1960, pp 183-208. Madison: IRRA, 1961.

1584 KAUN, DAVID E. "Wage Adjustments in the Appalachian States." *Southern Economic Journal*, Vol 32 (1965), 127-36.

1585 KEMPTON, MURRAY. "Labor: The Alliance on the Plateau." *The Reporter*, Jun 30, 1955, pp 26-30.

1586 KENNEDY, ROBERT F. *The Enemy Within*. NY: Harper, 1960.

1587 KERR, CLARK. *Unions and Union Leaders of Their Own Choosing*. NY: The Fund for the Republic, 1957.

1588 KESEY, KEN. *Sometimes a Great Notion* (a novel). New York: Viking, 1963.

1589 KORNHAUSER, RUTH. "Some Social Determinants and Consequences of Union Membership." *Labor History*, Vol 2 (1961), 30-61.

1590 KRISLOV, JOSEPH. "New Organizing by Unions During the 1950's." *Monthly Labor Review*, Vol 83 (1960), 922-24.

1591 ———. "Union Organizing of New Units, 1955-1966." *Industrial and Labor Relations Review*, Vol 21 (1967), 31-39.

1592 ———, and VIRGIL L. CHRISTIAN, JR. "Union Organizing and the Business Cycle, 1949-1966." *Southern Economic Journal*, Vol 36 (1969), 185-88.

1593 "Labor Relations and the Public." *Annals of the American Academy of Political and Social Science*, (1946), entire issue.

1594 "Labor Violence and Corruption." *Business Week*, Aug 31, 1957.

1595 LAMMIE, WAYNE D. *Unemployment in the Truman Administration: Political, Economic and Social Aspects*. Ph D diss, Ohio State U, 1973.

1596 LANDIS, BROOK I. *The Role of Personal Values in Arbitration: a Case Study of Saul Wallen*. Ph D diss, Cornell U, 1974.

1597 LEE, R. ALTON. *Truman and Taft-Hartley: A Question of Mandate*. Lexington: U of Kentucky Press, 1966.

1598 LENS, SIDNEY. *The Crisis of American Labor*. NY: Sagamore Press, 1959.

1599 ———. "Labor Unity is No Panacea." *The Antioch Review*, Summer 1955, pp 180-94.

1600 ———. "Will Merged Labor Set New Goals?" *Harvard Business Review*, Vol 34 (1956), 57-63.

1601 LESIEUR, FREDERICK G., ed. *Scanlon Plan: A Frontier in Labor-Management Cooperation*. NY: Wiley, 1958.

1602 LESTER, RICHARD A. "Labor Policy in a Changing World." *Industrial Relations*, Vol 2 (1962), 39-52.

1603 LIPSITZ, GEORGE. *Class and Culture in Cold War America*. South Hadley, MA: J. F. Bergin, 1982.

1604 ———. "Rank and File Fantasy in Films of the Forties." *Jump Cut*, Dec 1976, pp 12-13.

1605 MCADAMS, ALAN K. *Power Politics in Labor Legislation* (Landrum-Griffin Act, 1959). NY: Columbia U Press, 1964.

1606 MCCLURE, ARTHUR F. *The Truman Administration and the Problems of Post-War Labor, 1945-1948*. Rutherford, NJ: Fairleigh Dickinson U Press, 1969.

1607 MACDONALD, ROBERT M. "Collective Bargaining in the Postwar Period." *Industrial and Labor Relations Review*, Vol 20 (1967), 553-77.

1608 MAGOUN, F. ALEXANDER. *Cooperation and Conflict in Industry*. NY: Harper, 1960.

1609 MARCUS, MAEVA. *Truman and the Steel Seizure Case: The Limits of Presidential Power*. NY: Columbia U Press, 1977.

1610 MARSHALL, F. RAY. "Some Factors Influencing the Growth of Unions in the South." *Proceedings of the Thirteenth Annual Meeting of the Industrial Relations Research ASsociation*, Dec 18-19, 1960, pp 166-82. Madison: IRRA, 1961.

1611 MEANY, GEORGE. "What Labor Means by 'More.'" *Fortune*, Mar 1955, pp 1-12.

1612 METZ, HAROLD, and MEYER JACOBSTEIN. *A National Labor Policy*. Wash.: Brookings Institution, 1947.

1613 MILLER, RICHARD ULRIC. "Arbitration of New Contract Wage Disputes: Some Recent Trends." *Industrial and Labor Relations Review*, Vol 20 (1967), 250-64.

1614 NATIONAL ASSOCIATION OF MANUFACTURERS. *Some Facts about the AFL-CIO Merger*. NY: The Association, 1956.

1615 NICHOLS, OSGOOD. *Partners in Production—A Basis for Labor-Management Understanding*. NY: Twentieth Century Fund, 1949.

1616 OSHINSKY, DAVID M. *Senator Joseph McCarthy and the American Labor Movement*. Columbia: U of Missouri Press, 1976.

1617 PATTEN, THOMAS H., JR. "An Evaluation of the Marginal Man Concept in Industrial Sociology." *Social Science*, Vol 40 (1965), 11-21.

1618 PETERS, RONALD J. *Factors Affecting Labor Extension Legislation, 1945-1950*. Ph D diss, Michigan State U, 1977.

1619 PETERSON, FRANK ROSS. "Protest Songs for Peace and Freedom: People's Songs and the 1948 Progressives." *Rocky Mountain Social Science Journal*, Vol 9 (Jan 1972), 1-10.

1620 PETRO, SYLVESTER. *Labor Policy of the Free Society*. NY: Ronald Press, 1957.

1621 POMPER, GERALD. "Labor and Congress: The Repeal of Taft-Hartley." *Labor History*, Vol 2 (1961), 323-43.

1622 ———. "Labor Legislation: The Revision of Taft-Hartley in 1953-1954." *Labor History*, Vol 6 (1965), 143-58.

1623 POUND, ROSCOE. *Labor Unions and the Concept of Public Service.* Wash.: American Enterprise Association, 1959.

1624 RASKIN, A. H. "The Outlook for Labor under Eisenhower." *Commentary*, Apr 1953, pp 365-73.

1625 REZLER, JULIUS. *Union Growth Reconsidered: A Critical Analysis of Recent Growth Theories.* NY: Kossuth Foundation, 1961.

1626 ROBERTS, BENJAMIN C. *Trade Unions in a Free Society: Studies in the Organisation of Labour in Britain and the U.S.A.* L: Hutchinson, 1962.

1627 ———. *Unions in America: A British View.* Princeton: Industrial Relations Section, Princeton U, 1959.

1628 ROE, WELLINGTON. *Juggernaut: American Labor in Action.* Phila.: Lippincott, 1948.

1629 ROUKIS, GEORGE S. *American Labor and the Conservative Republicans, 1946-48: a Study in Economic and Political Conflict.* Ph D diss, New York U, 1973.

1630 RYBACKI, K. C. *A Case Study of Organizational Apologia: the American Federation of Labor, 1945-1956.* Ph D diss, U of Iowa, 1980.

1631 SAMOFF, BERNARD L. "The Impact of Taft-Hartley Job Discrimination Victories." *Industrial Relations*, Vol 4 (1965), 77-94.

1632 SCHAEFER, ARTHUR MCCLUNY. *Presidential Intervention in Labor Disputes During the Truman Administration: A History and Analysis of Experience.* Ph D diss, U of Pennsylvania, 1967.

1633 SEIDMAN, JOEL. *Democracy in the Labor Movement.*, Bulletin 39. Ithaca: NY State School of Industrial and Labor Relations, Cornell U, Feb 1958.

1634 SGONTZ, LARRY GENE. *The Experience with the Provisions of the Labor-Management Reporting and Disclosure Act Regulating the Internal Affairs of Labor Unions.* Ph D diss, U of Illinois, 1964.

1635 SHAW, CHARLES E. "Management-Labor Committees." *Industrial and Labor Relations Review*, Vol 3 (1950), 229-41.

1636 SHEFFERMAN, NATHAN. *The Man in the Middle.* Garden City: Doubleday, Sep 1961.

1637 SHISTER, JOSEPH. "The Logic of Union Growth." *The Journal of Political Economy*, Vol 51 (1953), 413-33.

1638 ———. et al., eds. *Public Policy and Collective Bargaining.* NY: Harper & Row, 1962.

1639 SIMONS, JOHN H. "The Union Approach to Health and Welfare." *Industrial Relations*, Vol 4 (1965), 61-76.

1640 SLICHTER, SUMNER H. "The Position of Trade Unions in the American Economy." pp 17-44, *Labor in a Free Society*, Michael Harrington & Paul Jacobs, eds. Berkeley: U of California Press, 1959.

1641 SMITH, RUSSELL A. "Government Intervention in the Substantive Areas of Collective Bargaining." *Proceedings of the Fifteenth Annual Meeting of the Industrial Relations Research Association*, Dec 27-28, 1962, pp 237-47. Madison: IRRA, 1963.

1642 SOMERS, GERALD G., ed. *Labor, Management, and Social Policy: Essays in the John R. Commons Tradition.* Madison: U of Wisconsin Press, 1963.

1643 STEIN, BRUNO. *Labor Participation in Stabilization Agencies: the Korean War Period as a Case Study.* Ph D diss, New York U, 1959.

1644 STEVENSON, THOMAS MARTIN, JR. *The Origins and Objectives of the Labor-Management Reporting and Disclosure Act of 1959.* Ph D diss, U of Illinois, 1964.

1645 STIEBER, JACK. "Labor's Walkout from the Korean War Wage Stabilization Board." *Labor History*, Vol 21 (1980), 239-60.

1646 STIEBER, JACK, ed. *U.S. Industrial Relations: The Next Twenty Years.* East Lansing: Michigan State U Press, 1958.

1647 TAFT, PHILIP. *Corruption and Racketeering in the Labor Movement.*, Bulletin 38. Ithaca: NY State School of Industrial and Labor Relations, Cornell U, Feb 1958.

1648 ———. "Reflections on the Present State of the Labor Movement." *Proceedings of the Fourteenth Annual Meeting of the Industrial Relations Research Association*, Dec 28-29, 1961, pp 3-14. Madison: IRRA, 1962.

1649 ———. "The Responses of the Bakers, Longshoremen and Teamsters to Public Exposure." *The Quarterly Journal of Economics,* Vol 74 (1960), 393-412.

1650 "The Taft-Hartley Act after Ten Years: a Symposium." *Industrial and Labor Relations Review,* Vol 11 (1958), 327-412.

1651 TAYLOR, BENJAMIN. *An Evaluation of the National Labor Relations Board in the Administration of the Taft-Hartley Act in Indiana.* Ph D diss, Indiana U, 1966.

1652 TEMPLETON, RONALD K. *The Campaign of the American Federation of Labor and the Congress of Industrial Organizations to Prevent the Passage of the Labor-Management Relations Act of 1947.* Ph D diss, Ball State U, 1967.

1653 TURNER, EMERY CARL. *The Impact of the Labor-Management Reporting and Disclosure Act on Labor Union Financial Administration.* Ph D diss, Washington U, 1966.

1654 TWENTIETH CENTURY FUND. Labor Committee *Partners in Production: A Basis for Labor-Management Understanding.* NY: The Fund, 1949.

1655 U.S. NATIONAL LABOR RELATIONS BOARD. *Legislative History of the Labor Management Relations Act, 1947.,* 2 vols. Wash.: G.P.O., 1948.

1656 ———. *Legislative History of the Labor-Management Reporting and Disclosure Act of 1959.,* 2 vols. Wash.: G.P.O., 1959.

1657 WARNE, COLSTON E., ed. *Labor in Postwar America.* Brooklyn, NY: Remsen Press, 1949.

1658 WEIR, STAN. "American Labor on the Defensive: a 1950s Odyssey." *Radical America,* Vol 9 (Jul-Aug 1975), 163-85.

1659 "What the AFL-CIO Merger Means." *U.S. News and World Report,* Dec 16, 1955, pp 23-30.

1660 *The Whistle at Eaton Falls.* 1951. (Feature film produced by Louis de Rochmont)

1661 WOLMAN, LEO. "Labor Unions and Labor Policy." *Yale Review,* Vol 36 (1947), 86-95.

The 1960s to the Present

1662 ADLER, JOHN S. "Section 6 of the Norris-LaGuardia Act: the Chameleons Are Coming." *Labor Law Journal,* Vol 24 (1973), 131-41.

1663 AFL-CIO. Department of Research *Union Membership and Employment, 1959-1979.* Wash.: The Department, 1980.

1664 ALLISON, ELISABETH K. "Financial Analysis of the Local Union." *Industrial Relations,* Vol 14 (1975), 145-55.

1665 *Anatomy of a Lie.* 1962. (A film produced by the International Association of Machinists as a counter to *And Woman Must Weep*)

1666 *And Woman Must Weep.* 1960. (A film produced by the National Right to Work Committee)

1667 ANDERSON, JAMES E. "Poverty, Unemployment, and Economic Development: the Search for a National Antipoverty Policy." *Journal of Politics,* Vol 29 (1967), 70-93.

1668 ANDERSON, JOHN C. "Local Union Participation, a Re-Examination." *Industrial Relations,* Vol 18 (1979), 18-31.

1669 APPELBAUM, LEON, and HARRY BLAINE. "The 'Iron Law' Revisited: Oligarchy in Trade Union Locals." *Labor Law Journal,* Vol 26 (1975), 597-600.

1670 ARNDT, ROBERT. "Coping with Job Stress: the Role of the Union Safety and Health Committee." *Labor Studies Journal,* Vol 6 (1981), 53-61.

1671 *Assembly Line.* 1960. (Documentary film produced by the U of Pennsylvania)

1672 AUSTER, ALBERT. et al. "Hollywood and the Working Class: a Discussion." *Socialist Review,* Vol 9 (Jul-Aug 1979), 109-21.

1673 BABSON, STEVE. "The Multinational Corporation and Labor." *Review of Radical Political Economics,* Vol 5 (Spring 1973), 19-36.

1674 BAKER, JOSEPH B. *An Analysis of Organizational Union Representation Elections Conducted Under the National Labor Relations Act.* Ph D diss, SUNY/Albany, 1971.

1675 BARBASH, JACK. "The Tensions of Work: Can We Reduce Costs of Industrialism?" *Dissent*, Vol 19 (1972), 240-48.

1676 BARKIN, SOLOMON. *The Decline of the Labor Movement and What Can Be Done About It.* Santa Barbara, CA: Center for the Study of Democratic Institutions, 1961.

1677 ———. "New Labor Relations Policies and Remedies Suggested by Different Industrial Settings." *Proceedings of the Fifteenth Annual Meeting of the Industrial Relations Research Association*, Dec 27-28, 1962, pp 220-36. Madison: IRRA, 1963.

1678 BELLACE, JANICE R., and ALAN D. BERKOWITZ. *The Landrum-Griffin Act: Twenty Years of Federal Protection of Union Members' Rights.* Phila.: U of Pennsylvania, 1979.

1679 BENSON, H. W. "Apathy and Other Axioms: Expelling the Union Dissenter from History." *Dissent*, Vol 19 (1972), 211-24.

1680 ———. "Divided Soul of Labor Leadership." *Dissent*, Vol 27 (1980), 352-55.

1681 BLINDER, ALAN S. *Who Joins Unions?* Princeton: Industrial Relations Section, Princeton U, 1972.

1682 *Blue Collar Capitalism.* 1977. (Non-fiction film produced by Joelle Shefts)

1683 *The Blue Collar Trap.* 1972. (Non-fiction film produced by NBC-TV)

1684 BOK, DEREK C., and JOHN T. DUNLOP. "How Trade Union Policy Is Made." *Monthly Labor Review*, Vol 93 (Feb 1970), 17-20.

1685 ———. *Labor and the American Community.* NY: Simon and Schuster, 1970.

1686 BORNSTEIN, TIM. "Unions, Critics and Collective Bargaining." *Labor Law Journal*, Vol 27 (1976), 614-22.

1687 BOTT, WILLIAM L., and EDGAR WEINBERG. "Labor-Management Cooperation Today." *Harvard Business Review*, Vol 56 (Jan-Feb 1978), 96-104.

1688 BOULD, SALLY. "Unemployment as a Factor in Early Retirement Decisions." *American Journal of Economics and Sociology*, Vol 39 (1980), 123-36.

1689 BRAND, H. "On the Economic Condition of American Workers." *Dissent*, Vol 28 (1981), 331-38.

1690 BRETT, J. M. "Why Employees Want Unions." *Organizational Dynamics*, Vol 8 (Spring 1980), 47-59.

1691 BRONFENBRENNER, MARTIN. "Some Reactionary Suggestions on the Labor Front." *South Atlantic Quarterly*, Vol 74 (1975), 237-43.

1692 BURDETSKY, BENJAMIN. *An Analysis of Sections 201 and 205 of the Labor-Management Reporting and Disclosure Act of 1959 and Their Impact on Labor Union Financial Management Policies and Practices.* Ph D diss, American U, 1968.

1693 BUREAU OF NATIONAL AFFAIRS. *Labor Relations in an Economic Recession: Job Losses and Concession Bargaining.* Wash.: BNA Books, 1982.

1694 BURKITT, BRIAN, and DAVID BOWERS. *Trade Unions and the Economy.* NY: Holmes & Meier, 1979.

1695 BURROWS, RONNIE. *Accounting and Reporting Practice at National Labor Unions.* Ph D diss, Pennsylvania State U, 1980.

1696 CAMMER, HAROLD I. "The Burger Court and Labor." *Guild Practitioner*, Vol 4 (1976), 113-29.

1697 CAPLAN, MARVIN. "What the Washington Labor Lobbyists Do." *Dissent*, Vol 22 (1975), 193-95.

1698 CARNEGIE-MELLON UNIVERSITY. Department of Engineering and Public Policy *The Impacts of Robotics on the Workforce and Workplace.* Pittsburgh: The Department, 1981.

1699 CENTER TO PROTECT WORKERS RIGHTS. *From Brass Knuckles to Briefcases: The Changing Art of Union-Busting in America.* Wash.: The Center, 1979.

1700 CHAISON, GARY. "Federation Expulsions and Union Mergers in the United States." *Relations Industrielles-Industrial Relations*, Vol 28 (1973), 343-60.

1701 ———. "Union Growth and Union Mergers." *Industrial Relations*, Vol 20 (1981), 98-107.

1702 CHAMBER OF COMMERCE OF THE U.S. *The Case for Voluntary Unionism.* Wash.: The Chamber, 1964.

1703 CHARTIER, ROGER. "Collective Bargaining and the Public Interest." *Labor Law Journal*, Aug 1963, pp 733-38.

1704 CHEESEMAN, ROBERT H. *A Survey of the Pre-Retirement Education Policies and Programs among National Labor Unions of the United States.* Ph D diss, U of Southern Mississippi, 1978.

1705 CHERNOW, RON. "Grey Flannel Goons: the Latest in Union Busting." *Working Papers for a New Society*, Vol 8 (Jan-Feb 1981), 19-25.

1706 CHITAYAT, GIDEON. *Trade Union Mergers and Labor Conglomerates.* NY: Praeger, 1979.

1707 CLOSE, WILLIAM EDWARD. *An Historical Study of the American Federation of Labor—Congress of Industrial Organization's Involvement in Higher Education with an Emphasis on the Period 1960-1969.* Ph D diss, Catholic U of America, 1972.

1708 CLOVER, VERNON T. "Compensation in Union and Nonunion Plants, 1960-1965." *Industrial and Labor Relations Review*, Vol 31 (1968), 226-33.

1709 COGHILL, MARY ANN. *Efforts to Repeal 14(b): A Review of Legislative Action by the 89th Congress on the Controversial Taft-Hartley Section.* Ithaca: NY State School of Industrial and Labor Relations, Cornell U, 1966. (Right-to-work state legislation)

1710 COHANY, HARRY P. "Trends and Changes in Union Membership." *Monthly Labor Review*, Vol 89 (1966), 510-13.

1711 COLFAX, J. DAVID. "Labor Responds to Compulsory Arbitration: Organizational Correlates of Protest and Acquiescence." *Industrial and Labor Relations Review*, Vol 20 (1966), 76-87, 450-52.

1712 COMMITTEE FOR ECONOMIC DEVELOPMENT. Research and Policy Committee *Union Powers and Union Functions: Toward a Better Balance.* NY: The Committee, 1964.

1713 COMPA, LANCE. "Back to Basics for the Labor Movement." *Working Papers for a New Society*, Vol 8 (Sep-Oct 1981), 13-16.

1714 CROWN, PAUL, and MARTIN JAY LEVITT. "How to Start/Stop a Union." *Guild Practitioner*, Vol 35 (1978), 33-53.

1715 DALTON, MELVILLE. "The Prospects of Formal Union-Management Cooperation." *Proceedings of the Seventeenth Annual Meeting of the Industrial Relations Research Association*, Dec 89-89, 1964, pp 252-60. Madison: IRRA, 1965.

1716 DAVIS, LOUIS E., and ALBERT B. CHERNS, eds.. *The Quality of Working Life.*, 2 vols. NY: The Free Press, 1975.

1717 DAVIS, MIKE. "The AFL-CIO's Second century." *New Left Review*, Nov-Dec 1982, pp 43-54.

1718 DAVIS, WILLIAM, and LILY MARY DAVIS. "Pattern of Wage and Benefit Changes in Manufacturing." *Monthly Labor Review*, Vol 91 (1968), 40-48.

1719 DENKER, JOEL. *Unions and Credentials: an Examination of Labor Studies in the University.* Ph D diss, Harvard U, 1979.

1720 *Depressed Area, U.S.A.* 1964. (Documentary film by Willard Van Dyke for the CBS-TV show 20th Century)

1721 DERBER, CHARLES. "Unemployment and the Entitled Worker: Job Entitlement and Radical Political Attitudes among the Youthful Unemployed." *Social Problems*, Vol 26 (1978), 26-37.

1722 DERBER, MILTON. "Crosscurrents in Workers Participation." *Industrial Relations*, Vol 9 (1970), 123-36.

1723 ———. "Labor Participation in Management: Some Impressions of Experience in the Metal Working Industries of Britain, Israel and the United States." *Proceedings of the Seventeenth Annual Meeting of the Industrial Relations Research Association*, Dec 28-29, 1964, pp 261-69. Madison: IRRA, 1965.

1724 ———. et al. "Types and Variants in Local Union-Management Relationships." *Human Organization*, Vol 21 (1962-63), pp 264-70.

1725 ———. "Union Participation in Plant Decision-Making." *Industrial and Labor Relations Review*, Vol 15 (1961), 83-101.

1726 DINGES, R. "Ruzicka vs. General Motors: an Unlikely Hero of the Trade Trade Union Movement—the Individual Employee in a Section 301 Case who has been a Victim of Union Negligence." *Wayne Law Review*, Vol 24 (1978), 1773-86.

1727 DUBOFF, RICHARD B. "Full Employment: the History of a Receding Target." *Politics and Society*, Vol 7 (1977), 1-25.

1728 DUNBAR, TONY, and BOB HALL. "Union Busters: Who, Where, When, How and Why?" *Southern Exposure*, Vol 8 (Summer 1980), 27-48.

1729 DUNCAN, GREG, and FRANK P. STAFFORD. "Do Union Members Receive Compensating Wage Differentials?" *American Economic Review*, Vol 70 (1980), 355-71.

1730 DUNLOP, JOHN T. "The American Industrial Relations System in 1975." *U.S. Industrial Relations: The Next Twenty Years*, Jack Stieber, Ed., pp, 27-54, 205-6. East Lansing: Michigan State U Press, 1958.

1731 ———. "The Future of the American Labor Movement," *The Third Century: America as a Post-Industrial Society*, Seymour Martin Lipset, ed. Stanford: Hoover Institution Press, 1979.

1732 ———. "Guideposts, Wages, and Collective Bargaining." *Monthly Labor Review*, Vol 89 (1966), 630-33.

1733 DWORKIN, JAMES B., and M. EXTEJT. "Union-Shop Deauthorization Poll: a New Look after Twenty Years." *Monthly Labor Review*, Vol 102 (Nov 1979), 36-40.

1734 DWYER, RICHARD. "Workers' Education, Labor Education, Labor Studies: an Historical Delineation." *Review of Educational Research*, Vol 47 (Winter 1977), 179-207.

1735 DYER, LEE. et al. "Union Satisfaction and Participation." *Industrial Relations*, Vol 16 (1977), 145-51.

1736 EDELSTEIN, J. DAVID, and MALCOLM WARNER. "Research Areas in National Union Democracy." *Industrial Relations*, Vol 16 (1977), 186-98.

1737 EIGER, NORMAN. "Labor Education in a Hostile Environment." *Labor Studies Journal*, Vol 4 (1979), 25-38.

1738 ELLIOT, RALPH D. "Do Right to Work Laws have an Impact on Union Organizing Activities?" *Journal of Social and Political Studies*, Vol 4 (1979), 81-93.

1739 EVANS, ROBERT, JR. *Public Policy Toward Labor*. NY: Harper & Row, 1965.

1740 FARBER, HENRY, and DANIEL SAKS. "Why Workers Want Unions: the Role of Relative Wages and Job Characteristics." *Journal of Political Economy*, Vol 88 (1980), 349-69.

1741 FEDERAL BAR COUNCIL. Committee on Labor Law "Recommendations of the Committee on Labor Law of the Federal Bar Council: Sweetheart Contracts." *Industrial and Labor Relations Review*, Vol 23 (1969), 105-8.

1742 FELTON, NADINE. et al. "A New Generation of Workers." *Liberation*, Vol 17 (Aug 1972), 32-48.

1743 FERNANDEZ, JOHN P. *Racism and Sexism in Corporate Life: Changing Values in American Business*. Lexington, MA: Lexington Books, 1981.

1744 FORKOSCH, MORRIS D. "Workers' Councils and Worker Participation in Management in Theory and in Actuality." *Washburn Law Journal*, Vol 10 (1971), 339-55.

1745 FRASER, CHRISTOPHER R. *The Impact of Collective Bargaining on Job Satisfaction*. Ph D diss, U of Wisconsin, 1977.

1746 Freeman, John, and Jack Brittain. "Union Merger Process and Industrial Environment." *Industrial Relations*, Vol 16 (1977), 173-85.

1747 Freeman, Richard, and James Medoff. "New Estimates of Private Sector Unionism in the United States." *Industrial and Labor Relations Review*, Vol 32 (1979), 143-74.

1748 ———. "The Two Faces of Unionism." *Public Interest*, Vol 57 (1979), 69-93.

1749 Furlong, James. *Labor in the Boardroom: The Peaceful Revolution*. Princeton: Dow Jones Books, 1977.

1750 Galin, Amira, and Joseph Krislov. "Mediation Techniques in Four Countries: Some Common Trends and Differences." *Labor Studies Journal*, Vol 4 (1979), 119-30.

1751 Gamm, Sara. "The Election Base of National Union Executive Boards." *Industrial and Labor Relations Review*, Vol 32 (1979), 295-311.

1752 Garbarino, Joseph W., and Bill Aussieker. "Creeping Unionism Revisited." *Proceedings of the Twenty-Sixth Annual Winter Meeting of the Industrial Relations Research Association*, Dec 28-29, 1973, pp 259-66. Madison: IRRA, 1974.

1753 Gillespie, David. *Tenant Unions and Collective Bargaining*. Ph D diss, U of Wisconsin, 1978.

1754 Gillett, Alexander. "Current Developments in Labor-Management Relations: Notes." *Industrial and Labor Relations Forum*, Vol 5 (1969), 328-32.

1755 Gilman, Tamara. *Union Administration: Strategy, Structure and Organizing Behavior*. Ph D diss, Harvard U, 1981.

1756 Ginger, Ann Fagan. "The Nixon-Burger Court and What to Do About It." *Guild Practitioner*, Vol 33 (1976), 143-51.

1757 Glick, William. et al. "Union Satisfaction and Participation." *Industrial Relations*, Vol 16 (1977), 145-51.

1758 Gold, Charlotte. *Employer-Employee Committees and Worker Participation*. Ithaca: NY State School of Industrial and Labor Relations, Cornell U, 1976.

1759 Goldberg, Stephen. "Current Decisions of the NLRB and of the Courts." *Proceedings of the Twenty-First Annual Winter Meeting of the Industrial Relations Research Association*, Dec 29-30, 1968, pp 195-205. Madison: IRRA, 1969.

1760 Goode, Billy M. *The Motivational Orientations of Trade Unionists for Attending College*. Ph D diss, Rutgers U, 1981.

1761 Gordon, R. A. "Unemployment Patterns with 'Full Employment'." *Industrial Relations*, Vol 8 (1968), 46-72.

1762 Gordon, Suzanne. "Half-time Blues." *Working Papers for a New Society*, Vol 8 (May-Jun 1981), 36-41.

1763 Gray, Lois. "Trends in Selection and Training of International Union Staff: Implications for University and College Labor Education." *Labor Studies Journal*, Vol 5 (1980), 13-24.

1764 ———. "Unions Implementing Managerial Techniques." *Monthly Labor Review*, Vol 104 (Jun 1981), 3-13.

1765 Grodin, Joseph R. "The Kennedy Labor Board." *Industrial Relations*, Vol 3 (1964), 33-45.

1766 Gunn, Christopher. "The Fruits of Rath: a New Model of Self-Management." *Working Papers for a New Society*, Vol 8 (Mar-Apr 1981), 17-21.

1767 Haas, Ain. *Workers' Control in Working Class Consciousness*. Ph D diss, U of Wisconsin, 1978.

1768 Hall, Burton. *Autocracy and Insurgency in Organized Labor*. NY: Transaction Books, 1972.

1769 Hanagan, Michael, and C. Stephenson. "The Skilled Worker and Working-Class Protest." *Social Science History*, Vol 4 (1980), 5-14.

1770 Harrington, Michael. "Old Working Class, New Working Class." *Dissent*, Vol 19 (1972), 146-62.

1771 HARVEY, BRUCE S., and RUDOLPH L. KAGERER. "Marginal Workers and their Decisions to Work or Quit." *American Journal of Economics and Sociology*, Vol 35 (1976), 137-47.

1772 HAUSER, D. "Union-Busting Hustle: Work of Modern Management Methods." *New Republic*, Aug 25, 1979, pp 16-18.

1773 HAYMAN, MICHELE. *Labor Unions and Civil Rights Compliance*. Ph D diss, U of Michigan, 1978.

1774 HERLING, JOHN. "Change and Conflict in the AFL-CIO." *Dissent*, Vol 21 (1974), 479-85.

1775 HIRSCHORN, L. "The Post-Industrial Labor Process." *New Political Science*, Vol 2 (Fall 1981), 11-32.

1776 HOESCHEN, DANIEL. *Workplace Democratization: a Case Study of the Implementation of Worker Participation in Decision Making*. Ph D diss, American U, 1981.

1777 HOLLAND, SUSAN S. "Long-Term Unemployment in the 1960s." *Monthly Labor Review*, Vol 88 (1965), 1069-76.

1778 HOWE, IRVING, ed. *The World of the Blue Collar Worker*. NY: Quadrangle, 1972.

1779 HOWELLS, JOHN, and S. CATHRO. "Union Growth and Concentration Revisited." *Journal of Industrial Relations*, Vol 23 (Mar 1981), 23-32.

1780 HUNNIUS, GERRY. et al., eds. *Workers' Control: A Reader on Labor and Social Change*. NY: Random House, 1973.

1781 HUTCHINSON, JOHN. "The Anatomy of Corruption in Trade Unions." *Industrial Relations*, Vol 7 (1969), 133-50.

1782 "The Impact on Labor of Changing Corporate Structure and Technology." *Labor Studies Journal*, Vol 3 (1979), entire issue.

1783 INGLE, SUD. *Quality Circles Master Guide: Increasing Productivity with People Power*. Englewood Cliffs, NY: Prentice-Hall, 1982.

1784 JACKSON, GORDON E. *When Labor Trouble Strikes: An Action Handbook*. Englewood Cliffs, NJ: Prentice-Hall, 1981.

1785 JACOBS, L. A., and G. W. SPRING. "Fair Coverage in Internal Union Periodicals." *Industrial Relations Law Journal*, Vol 4 (1981), 204-57.

1786 JACOBS, ROGER B. "*Dewey v. Reynolds Metal Company:* Arbitration and Judicial Review under the 1964 Civil Rights Act." *Labor Law Journal*, Vol 24 (1973), 100-18.

1787 JOHNSON, RALPH ARTHUR. "World Without Workers: Prime Time's Presentation of Labor." *Labor Studies Journal*, Vol 5 (1980), 199-206.

1788 JONES, DEREK C., and JAN SVEJNAR, eds.. *Participatory and Self-Managed Firms: Evaluating Economic Performance*. Lexington, MA: Lexington Books, 1982.

1789 KAHN, LAWRENCE M. "Unionism and Relative Wages: Direct and Indirect Effects." *Industrial and Labor Relations Review*, Vol 32 (1979), 520-32.

1790 KANTER, R. M. "Work in a New America." *Daedalus*, Vol 107 (Winter 1978), 44-77.

1791 KATZ, ARNOLD, and JOSEPH HIGHT, eds. "The Economics of Unemployment Insurance: a Symposium." *Industrial and Labor Relations Review*, Vol 30 (1977), 431-526.

1792 KENNEDY, DONALD. et al., eds. *Labor and Technology: Union Response to Changing Environment*. University Park: Pennsylvania State U, 1982.

1793 KILGOUR, JOHN G. *Preventive Labor Relations*. NY: AMACCM, 1981.

1794 KING, CHARLES D., and MARK VAN DE VALL. "Dimensions of Workers' Participation in Managerial Decision-Making." *Proceedings of the Twenty-Second Annual Winter Meeting of the Industrial Relations Research Association*, Dec 29-30, 1969, pp 164-77. Madison: IRRA, 1970.

1795 KIRSLOV, J. "Decertification Elections Increase but Remain No Major Burden to Unions." *Monthly Labor Review*, Vol 102 (Nov 1979), 30-32.

1796 KISTLER, ALAN. "Trends in Union Growth." *Labor Law Journal*, Aug 1977, pp 539-45.

1797 KOCHAN, T. A. "How American Workers View Labor Unions." *Monthly Labor Review*, Vol 102 (Apr 1979), 23-31.

1798 LAWRENCE, ANNE. "Union Democracy: a Conference Report." *Socialist Revolution*, No 55 (Jan-Feb 1981), 105-11.

1799 LEAHY, WILLIAM H. "Grievances over Union Business on Company Time and Premises." *Arbitration Journal*, Vol 30 (1975), 191-98.

1800 LENS, SIDNEY. "'Big Labor,' Big Trouble." *New Politics*, Vol 11 (Spring 1974), 28-37.

1801 LESIEUR, FREDERICK G., and ELBRIDGE S. PUCKETT. "The Scanlon Plan: Past, Present and Future." *Proceedings of the Twenty-First Annual Winter Meeting of the Industrial Relations Research Association*, Dec 29-30, 1968, pp 71-80, 90-95. Madison: IRRA, 1969.

1802 LEVITAN, SAR A., ed. *Blue Collar Workers: A Symposium on Middle America*. NY: McGraw-Hill, 1971.

1803 LIPSET, SEYMOUR MARTIN, and WILLIAM SCHNEIDER. *The Confidence Gap: Business, Labor, and Government in the Public Mind*. NY: Free Press, 1983.

1804 LOVELL, FRANK. "Wage Controls and the Unions: What the Record Shows." *International Socialist Review*, Vol 30 (Apr 1972), 24-31.

1805 LUNDEN, LEON E. "AFL-CIO Focus: Economy, Farmworkers, and Women's Rights." *Monthly Labor Review*, Vol 98 (Dec 1975), 42-46.

1806 LUXENBERG, S. "Labor Studies Blossom in Community Colleges; Cooperation with Unions." *Change*, Vol 11 (Jul 1979), 58-59.

1807 LYND, STAUGHTON. "Workers' Control in a Time of Diminished Workers' Rights." *Radical America*, Vol 10 (Sep-Oct 1976), 5-19.

1808 MCBREARTY, JAMES C. *Public Policy Implications of NLRB and Court Interpretations of Employer Unfair Labor Practices, 1961-1966*. Ph D diss, U of Illinois, 1968.

1809 MCDERMOTT, JOHN. *The Crisis in the Working Class and Some Arguments for a New Labor Movement*. Bost.: South End Press, 1980.

1810 MCKENZIE, RICHARD B., ed. *Plant Closings: Public or Private Choices?* Wash.: Cato Institute, 1982.

1811 MERKER, STEVEN. *Alienation and Life Styles of Blue-Collar Workers*. Ph D diss, U of Louisville, 1981.

1812 MEYERS, GEORGE. "Taking Stock in Labor in 1976." *Political Affairs*, Vol 55 (Jan 1976), 4-13.

1813 MILLER, EDWARD B. *An Administrative Appraisal of the NLRB*. Phila: U of Pennsylvania, 1980.

1814 MILLER, RICHARD ULRIC. "Arbitration of New Contract Wage Disputes: Some Recent Trends." *Industrial and Labor Relations Review*, Vol 20 (1967), 250-64.

1815 ———. "The Enigma of Section 8 (5) of the Wagner Act." *Industrial and Labor Relations Review*, Vol 18 (1965), 166-85.

1816 MILLS, D. Q. "Flawed Victory in Labor Law Reform." *Harvard Business Review*, Vol 57 (May-Jun 1979), 92-102.

1817 MIRENGOFF, WILLIAM. et al. *CETA, Accomplishments, Problems, Solutions: A Report*. Kalamazoo, MI: W. E. Upjohn Institute for Employment Research, 1982.

1818 MISHEL, LARRY. "Corporate Structure and Bargaining Power: the Coordinated Bargaining Experience." *Labor Studies Journal*, Vol 3 (1979), 308-32.

1819 MKRTCHIAN, ANATOLII. *US Labour Unions Today: Basic Problems and Trends*. Moscow: Progress, 1978.

1820 MOBERG, DAVID. "What's Left for Labor?" *Working Papers for a New Society*, Vol 8 (May-Jun 1981), 21-23.

1821 MOORE, WILLIAM J., and ROBERT J. NEWMAN. "Determinants of Differences in Union Membership Among the States." *Proceedings of the Twenty-Sixth Annual Winter Meeting of the Industrial Relations Research Association*, Dec 28-29, 1973, pp 188-96. Madison: IRRA, 1974.

1822 ———, and DOUGLAS K. PEARCE. "Union Growth: A Test of the Ashenfelter-Pencavel Model." *Industrial Relations*, Vol 15 (1976), 244-47.

1823 MORRISON, WALBERT. *Community College-Labor Union Cooperation: Programs in Labor Studies*. Ph D diss, Columbia U Teachers College, 1980.

1824 MURPHY, MICHAEL E. "Workers on the Board: Borrowing a European Idea." *Labor Law Journal*, Vol 27 (1976), 751-62.

1825 NATIONAL COMMISSION FOR MANPOWER POLICY. *Labor's Views on Employment Policy: Conference Report*. Wash.: The Commission, 1978.

1826 NELSON, WALLACE B. "Union Representation During Investigatory Interviews." *Arbitration Journal*, Vol 31 (1976), 181-90.

1827 NESBITT, FREDERICK. *The Impact of a Labor Endorsement on the Voting Behavior of Rank-and-File Members: a Case Study of the 1974 General Election in Pennsylvania*. Ph D diss, West Virginia U, 1976.

1828 NEUFELD, MAURICE F. "Lifetime Jobs and Wage Security: Vintage Wine in New Containers." *Monthly Labor Review*, Vol 100 (Sep 1977), 27-28.

1829 NORTHRUP, HERBERT R., and RICHARD L. ROWAN. *Employee Relations and Regulation in the '80s*. Phila.: U of Pennsylvania, 1982.

1830 ———, and HARVEY A. YOUNG. "The Causes of Industrial Peace Revisited." *Industrial and Labor Relations Review*, Vol 22 (1968), 31-47.

1831 O'CLEIREACAIN, CAROL. "Getting Serious about Pension Funds." *Working Papers for a New Society*, Vol 8 (Jul-Aug 1981), 17-21.

1832 OLSEN, DAVID. "Labor's Stake in a Democratic Workplace." *Working Papers for a New Society*, Vol 8 (Mar-Apr 1981), 12-17.

1833 *On the Line*. 1976. (Documentary film produced by Barbara Margolis)

1834 OPPENHEIMER, MARTIN. "What Is the New Working Class?" *New Politics*, Vol 10 (Fall 1972), 29-43.

1835 O'ROURKE, WILLIAM, ed. *On the Job: Fiction about Work by Contemporary American Writers*. NY: Vintage, 1977.

1836 PARSLEY, C. J. "Labor Union Effects on Wage Gains: a Survey of Recent Literature." *Journal of Economic Liberature*, Vol 18 (Mar 1980), 1-31.

1837 PECK, SIDNEY M. "Trends in American Labor." *New Politics*, Vol 11 (Spring 1974), 9-27.

1838 PENCAVEL, JOHN H. "The Demand for Union Services: An Exercise." *Industrial and Labor Relations Review*, Vol 24 (1971), 180-90.

1839 PETERKA, GERALD. *Some General Determinants of the Future Trends and a Forecast of Labor Union Membership in the U.S. for the 1980's*. Ph D diss, U.S. International U, 1980.

1840 PIERSON, FRANK C. "Agenda for Wage-Price Policy." *Proceedings of the Fifteenth Annual Meeting of the Industrial Relations Research Association*, Dec 27-28, 1962, pp 283-93. Madison: IRRA, 1963.

1841 PODGURSKY, MICHAEL. *Trade Unions and Income Inequality*. Ph D diss, U of Wisconsin, 1981.

1842 PONAK, ALLEN, and C. R. P. FRASER. "Union Activists' Support for Joint Programs." *Industrial Relations*, Vol 18 (1979), 197-209.

1843 PROSTEN, R. "Rise in NLRB Election Delays: Measuring Business' New Resistance." *Monthly Labor Review*, Vol 102 (Feb 1979), 38-40.

1844 PYRON, TIMOTHY WINSTON. *Labor Union Membership: an Empirical Evaluation of Some of the Proposed Explanation of Membership Growth*. Ph D diss, Louisiana State U, 1971.

1845 QUINN, CORNELIUS. et al. *Maintaining Nonunion Status*. Bost.: CBI Publishing, 1982.

1846 *Rank and File*. 1970. (Documentary film produced by National Educational Television)

1847 RICHE, MARTHA F. "Union Election Challenges Under the LMRDA." *Monthly Labor Review*, Vol 88 (1965), 1-7.

1848 RICHTER, IRVING. "American Labor." *Center Magazine*, Vol 12 (1979), 34-43.

1849 RIFKIN, JEREMY. *Own Your Own Job: Economic Democracy for Working Americans.* NY: Bantam, 1977.

1850 ROACH, JOHN M. *Worker Participation: New Voices in Management.* NY: The Conference Board, 1973.

1851 ROOMKIN, MYRON, and H. A. JURIS. "Changing Character of Unionism in Traditionally Organized Sectors." *Monthly Labor Review*, Vol 102 (Feb 1979), 36-38.

1852 ROSEN, SUMNER M. "Union-Management Cooperation: Is There an Agenda for Tomorrow?" *Proceedings of the Twenty-First Annual Winter Meeting of the Industrial Relations Research Association*, Dec 29-30, 1968, pp 81-95. Madison: IRRA, 1969.

1853 ROSS, ARTHUR M. "Where We Are and Why." *Monthly Labor Review*, Vol 89 (1966), 624-29.

1854 ROSS, PHILIP. *The Government as a Source of Union Power: The Role of Public Policy in Collective Bargaining.* Providence: Brown U Press, 1965.

1855 ROTHERBERG, ISADORE H., and STEVEN B. SILVERMAN. *Labor Unions; How to: Avert Them, Beat Them, Out-Negotiate Them, Live with Them, Unload Them.* Elkins Park, PA: Management Relations, 1973.

1856 RUH, ROBERT A. et al. "Management Attitudes and the Scanlon Plan." *Industrial Relations*, Vol 12 (1973), 282-88.

1857 SAYLES, JOHN. *Union Dues* (a novel). Bost.: Little, Brown, 1977.

1858 SCHACHHUBER, DIETER. "The Missing Link in Labor Education." *Labor Studies Journal*, Vol 4 (1979), 148-56. (See comment by Dale Brickner, pp 157-58)

1859 SCHEFFER, MARTIN WARNE. *The Poor: Separate Class of Working Class, a Comparative Study.* Ph D diss, U of Utah, 1972.

1860 SCHLOZMAN, KAY LEHMAN, and SIDNEY VERBA. *Injury to Insult: Unemployment, Class, and Political Response.* Cambr.: Harvard U Press, 1979.

1861 SCHRANK, ROBERT. "Work in America: What Do Workers Really Want?" *Industrial Relations*, Vol 13 (1974), 124-29.

1862 SCHRANK, ROBERT, ed. *American Workers Abroad: A Report to the Ford Foundation.* Cambr.: MIT Press, 1979.

1863 SCHREGLE, JOHANNES. "Forms of Participation in Management." *Industrial Relations*, Vol 9 (1970), 117-22.

1864 SCOVILLE, JAMES G. "Research Note: Influences on Unionization in the U.S. in 1966." *Industrial Relations*, Vol 10 (1971), 354-61.

1865 SEIDMAN, JOEL. "The Sources for Future Growth and Decline in American Trade Unions." *Proceedings of the Seventeenth Annual Meeting of the Industrial Relations Research Association*, Dec 28-29, 1964, pp 98-108. Madison: IRRA, 1965.

1866 SEXTON, BRENDAN. "Progressive Stirrings in the American Unions." *Dissent*, Vol 24 (1977), 347-51.

1867 SEXTON, PATRICIA CAYO. "Organizing a Labor College" *Dissent*, Vol 20 (1973), 349-52.

1868 ———. and BRENDAN SEXTON. *Blue Collars and Hard Hats: The Working Class and the Future of American Politics.* NY: Random House, 1971.

1869 SHAIKEN, HARLEY. "Numerical Control of Work: Workers and Automation in the Computer Age." *Radical America*, Vol 13 (Nov-Dec 1979), 25-38.

1870 SHAPIRO, DAVID. "Relative Wage Effects of Unions in the Public and Private Sectors." *Industrial and Labor Relations Review*, Vol 31 (1978), 193-203.

1871 SHEPPARD, HAROLD L., and NEAL HERRICK. *Where Have All the Robots Gone? Workers Dissatisfaction in the 1970's.* NY: Free Press, 1972.

1872 SHISTER, JOSEPH. "The Outlook for Union Growth." *Annals of the American Academy of Political and Social Science*, Vol 350 (1963), 55-62.

1873 SIEGEL, IRVING H., and EDGAR WEINBERG. *Labor-Management Cooperation: The American Experience.* Kalamazoo, MI: W. E. Upjohn Institute for Employment Research, 1982.

1874 SINGER, DANIEL DERRICK, III. *Labor Force Participation in Poverty Areas.* Ph D Diss, U of Colorado, 1971.

1875 SINGH, SETHI, and STUART J. DIMMOCK, eds.. *Industrial Relations and Health Services.* NY: St. Martin's, 1982.

1876 SOMERS, GERALD G., ed. *Collective Bargaining: Contemporary American Experience.* Madison: Industrial Relations Research Association, 1980.

1877 SOUTAR, DOUGLAS H. "Co-Determination, Industrial Democracy, and the Role of Management." *Proceedings of the Twenty-Sixth Annual Winter Meeting of the Industrial Relations Research Association*, Dec 28-29, 1973, pp 1-7. Madison: IRRA, 1974.

1878 STAINES, GRAHAM, and ROBERT QUINN. "American Workers Evaluate the Quality of their Jobs." *Monthly Labor Review*, Vol 102 (Jan 1979), 3-12.

1879 STEPHEN, FRANK H., ed. *The Performance of Labor-Managed Firms.* NY: St. Martin's, 1982.

1880 STERN, JAMES. "The Kennedy Policy: A Favorable View." *Industrial Relations*, Vol 3 (1964), 21-32.

1881 STERN, ROBERT N. *The Community Context of Industrial Conflict.* Ph D diss, Vanderbilt U, 1974.

1882 ———. et al. *Employee Ownership in Plant Shutdowns: Prospects for Employment Stability.* Kalamazoo, MI: W. E. Upjohn Institute for Employment Research, 1979.

1883 STIEBER, JACK. "The President's Committee on Labor-Management Policy." *Industrial Relations*, Vol 5 (1966), 1-19.

1884 STODDER, JIM. "Old and New Working Class." *Radical America*, Vol 3 (Sep-Oct 1973), 99-118. (With a response by Albert Szymanski)

1885 STRAUSS, GEORGE. "Union Government in the U.S." *Industrial Relations*, Vol 16 (1977), 215-42.

1886 ———. et al. "Implications for Industrial Relations," chap. 8, *Organizational Behavior: Research and Issues*, Madison: IRRA, 1974.

1887 ———, and ELIEZER ROSENSTEIN. "Workers Participation: A Critical View." *Industrial Relations*, Vol 9 (1970), 197-214.

1888 STURMTHAL, ADOLF. "Industrial Democracy in the Affluent Society." *Proceedings of the Seventeenth Annual Meeting of the Industrial Relations Research Association*, Dec 28-29, 1964, pp 270-79. Madison: IRRA, 1965.

1889 ———. "Workers' Participation in Management: A Review of United States Experience." *International Institute for Labour Studies Bulletin*, June 1968, pp 1-38.

1890 SWANSON, C. R. "Participation in Unions: an Analysis of the Literature and a Research Agenda." *Journal of Collective Negotiating*, Vol 10 (1981), 1-18.

1891 TAYLOR, R. "How Democratic are the Trade Unions?" *Political Quarterly*, Vol 47 (Jan 1976), 29-38.

1892 TCHOBANIAN, R. "Trade Unions and the Humanization of Work." *International Labour Review*, Vol 3 (1975), 199-217.

1893 TERKEL, STUDS. "A Steelworker Speaks: Interview with Mike Fitzgerald." *Dissent*, Vol 19 (1972), 9-20.

1894 ———. *Working.* NY: Pantheon, 1972.

1895 TRECKEL, KARL F. *The Rise and Fall of the Alliance for Labor Action (1968-1972).* Kent, OH: Kent State U, 1976.

1896 TROY, LEO. "American Unions and their Wealth." *Industrial Relations*, Vol 14 (1975), 134-44.

1897 ———. "Trade Union Growth in a Changing Economy." *Monthly Labor Review*, Vol 92 (Sep 1969), 3-7.

1898 TUBBESING, CARL DOUGLAS. *Attitude Consensus and Conflict in an Interest Group: the Case of Two St. Louis Labor Unions.* Ph D diss, Washington U, 1971.

1899 TYLER, GUS. "White Worker/Blue Mood." *Dissent*, Vol 19 (1972), 190-96.

1900 ULMAN, LLOYD. "The Labor Policy of the Kennedy Administration." *Proceedings of the Fifteenth Annual Meeting of the Industrial Relations Research Association*, Dec 27-28, 1962, pp 248-62. Madison: IRRA, 1963.

1901 U.S. CONGRESS. SENATE. Committee on Human Resources. *Labor Reform Act of 1977.* Wash.: G.P.O., 1977.

1902 ———. ———. Committee on Labor and Human Resources. *Workers and the Evolving Economy of the Eighties.* Wash.: G.P.O., 1981.

1903 ———. ———. Committee on Labor and Public Welfare. Subcommittee on Labor. *Equal Treatment of Craft and Industrial Workers.* Wash.: G.P.O., 1975.

1904 ———. ———. *Legislative History of the Federal Coal Mine Health and Safety Act of 1969.* Wash.: G.P.O., 1975.

1905 U.S. DEPARTMENT OF HEALTH EDUCATION AND WELFARE. *The Measure of Poverty: A Report to Congress as Mandated by the Education Amendments of 1974.* Wash.: The Department, 1976.

1906 USERY, W. J., and D. HENNE. "The American Labor Movement in the 1980's." *Employee Relations Law Journal*, Vol 7 (Autumn 1981), 251-59.

1907 VELIE, LESTER. *Labor U. S. A. Today.* NY: Harper & Row, 1964.

1908 WAGGENER, RON. "Right-to-Work—The Missouri Decision." *American Federationist*, Vol 86 (Jan 1979), 18-21.

1909 WALKER, J. MALCOLM, and JOHN LAWLER. "Dual Unions and Political Processes in Organizations." *Industrial Relations*, Vol 18 (1979), 32-43.

1910 WALTON, RICHARD E. "Work Innovations in the U.S." *Harvard Business Review*, Vol 59 (Jul-Aug 1979), 88-98.

1911 WARREN-BOULTON, FREDERICK. "Vertical Control by Labor Unions." *American Economics Review*, Vol 67 (1977), 309-21.

1912 WEBER, ARNOLD R. "The Craft-Industrial Issue Revisited: A Study of Union Government." *Industrial and Labor Relations Review*, Vol 16 (1963), 381-404.

1913 WECKSLER, A. N., and EDGAR WEINBERG, eds.. *Recent Initiatives in Labor-Management Cooperation.* Wash.: National Center for Productivity and Quality of Working Life, 1976.

1914 WEINBERG, EDGAR. "Labor-Management Cooperation: a Report on Recent Initiatives." *Monthly Labor Review*, vol 99 (Apr 1976), 13-22.

1915 WEINSTEIN, HARRIET G. *A Comparison of Three Alternative Work Schedules: Flexible Work Hours, Compact Work Week, and Staggered Work Hours.* Phila.: U of Pennsylvania, 1975.

1916 WELLINGTON, HARRY. "Union Fines and Workers' Rights." *Yale Law Journal*, Vol 85 (1976), 1022-1059.

1917 WESTCOTT, DIANE. "The Youngest Workers: 14 and 15 Year Olds." *Monthly Labor Review*, Vol 104 (Feb 1981), 65-69.

1918 WHITE, BERNARD J. *Union Response to Job Dissatisfaction and Work Innovations.* Ph D diss, U of Michigan, 1975.

1919 *Why Work.* 1976. (Documentary film produced by WNET-TV in New York)

1920 WIDICK, B. J. *Labor Today: The Triumphs and Failures of Unionism in the United States.* Bost.: Houghton Mifflin, 1964.

1921 ———. "New Trends in the Unions." *Dissent*, Vol 20 (1973), 281-83.

1922 WILKEN, FOLKERT. *The Liberation of Work: The Elimination of Strikes and Strife in Industry Through Associative Organization of Enterprise.* NY: Roy, 1969.

1923 WILSON, CHARLES. "The Struggle for the Shorter Work Week Today." *Political Affairs*, Vol 55 (May 1976), 4-10.

1924 WINDMULLER, JOHN. "Concentration Trends in Union Structure: an International Comparison." *Industrial and Labor Relations Review*, Vol 35 (1981), 43-57.

1925 Winpisinger, William W. *A Trade Union View of U.S. Manpower Policy*. Wash.: British-North American Committee, 1980.

1926 Wirtz, W. Willard. *Labor and the Public Interest*. NY: Harper & Row, 1964.

1927 Witte, John F. *Democracy, Authority, and Alienation in Work: Workers' Participation in an American Corporation*. Chicago: U of Chicago Press, 1980.

1928 *Work*. 1970. (Documentary film directed by Fred Wardenburg)

1929 "Worker and Unions Participation in Decision-Making: Introduction." *Proceedings of the Twenty-Second Annual Winter Meeting of the Industrial Relations Research Association*, Dec 29-30, 1969, pp 162-63. Madison: IRRA, 1970.

1930 Wren, Daniel Alan. *Governmental Intervention in Labor-Management Disputes: 1961-1963*. Ph D diss, U of Illinois, 1964.

1931 Wycke, Bill. "The Work Shortage: Class Struggle and Capital Reproduction." *Review of Radical Political Economics*, Vol 7 (Summer 1975), 11-13.

1932 Young, Harvey A. *The Causes of Industrial Peace—Twenty Years Later*. Ph D diss, U of Pennsylvania, 1968.

1933 Zwerdling, Daniel. "Saving Jobs by Buying the Plant. Employee Ownership: How Well is it Working?" *Working Papers for a New Society*, Vol 7 (May-Jun 1979), 15-27.

1934 ———. *Workplace Democracy: A Guide to Workplace Ownership, Participation and Self-Management Experiments in the United States and Europe*. NY: Harper & Row, 1980.

Labor and Political Action, (including Ideological Unionism and History of Radical Parties)

1935 AARON, DANIEL. "*Good Morning* and 'Art' Young: an Introduction and Appraisal." *Labor History*, Vol 20 (1969), 100-4.

1936 ALEXANDER, ROBERT J. "Schisms and Unification in the American Old Left, 1923-1940." *Labor History*, Vol 14 (1973), 536-61.

1937 ANDREUCCI, FRANCO. "Socialismo e Marxismo per pochi cents: Charles H. Kerr editore." *Movimento Operaio e Socialista*, New Series 3 (1980), 269-76.

1938 ARNOLD, DELBERT D. *The CIO's Role in American Politics, 1936-1948*. Ph D diss, U of Maryland, 1953.

1939 BAISDEN, RICHARD N. *Labor Unions in Los Angeles Politics*. Ph D diss, U of Chicago, 1958-59.

1940 BARBASH, JACK. "The Structure of Union Political Action—A Trial Analytic Framework." *Labor Law Journal*, Aug 1965, pp 491-99.

1941 BARITZ, LOREN, ed. *The American Left: Radical Political Thought in the Twentieth Century*. NY: Basic, 1971.

1942 BARNES, JACK, and STEVE CLARK, eds.. *The Changing Face of U.S. Politics: Building a Party of Socialist Workers: Reports and Resolutions of the Socialist Workers Party*. NY: Pathfinder, 1981.

1943 BASSETT, MICHAEL EDWARD RAINTON. *The Socialist Party of America, 1912-1919: Years of Decline*. Ph D diss, Duke U, 1964.

1944 BASSETT, THEODORE. et al., eds. *Highlights of a Fighting History: 60 Years of the Communist Party, USA*. NY: International, 1979.

1945 BEAN, WALTON. *Boss Ruef's San Francisco: The Story of the Union Labor Party, Big Business, and the Graft Prosecution*. Berkeley: U of California Press, 1952.

1946 BEAUD, MICHEL. "The Winter of Socialism." *Cross Currents*, Vol 30 (1980), 252-61.

1947 BEDFORD, HENRY F. *Socialism and the Workers in Massachusetts, 1889-1912*. Amherst: U of Massachusetts Press, 1966.

1948 BELL, DANIEL. "The Background and Development of Marxian Socialism in the United States," chap., *Socialism and American Life*, Vol 1, Donald Drew Egbert & Stow Persons, eds. Princeton: Princeton U Press, 1952.

1949 ———. "*The Modern Review*: an Introduction and Appraisal." *Labor History*, Vol 9 (1968), 380-83.

1950 BERG, GORDON. "The Workingmen's Party—A First in Labor Politics." *Worklife*, Vol 1 (1976), 23-26.

1951 BERNSTEIN, IRVING, ed. "Samuel Gompers and Free Silver, 1896." *Mississippi Valley Historical Review*, Vol 69 (1942), 394-400.

1952 BERNSTEIN, SAMUEL. *The First International in America*. NY: Kelley, 1962.

1953 BICHA, KAREL DENIS. "Liberalism Frustrated: the League for Independent Political Action, 1928-1933." *Mid-America*, Vol 47 (1966), 19-28.

1954 BIEMILLER, ANDREW J. "Labor Issues in the 1960 Political Campaign: A Labor View." *Proceedings of the Thirteenth Annual Meeting of the Industrial Relations Research Association*, Dec 18-19, 1960, pp 218-29. Madison: IRRA, 1961.

1955 BLUM, ALBERT A. "The Political Alternatives of Labor." *Labor Law Journal*, Sep 1959, pp 623-31.

1956 BORNET, VAUGHN D. *Labor and Politics in 1928.* Ph D diss, Stanford U, 1951.

1957 BRAVERMAN, HARRY. "Labor and Politics." *Monthly Review*, Jul-Aug 1958, pp 134-45.

1958 BROWN, W. R. "State Regulation of Union Political Action." *Labor Law Journal*, Nov 1955, pp 769-76.

1959 BUHLE, PAUL. *Marxism in the United States, 1900-1950.* Ph D diss, U of Wisconsin, 1976.

1960 BURBANK, GARIN. "Disruption and Decline of Oklahoma Socialist Party." *Journal of American Studies*, Vol 7 (1973), 133-52.

1961 BURKI, MARY ANN MASON. "The California Progressives: Labor's Point of View." *Labor History*, Vol 17 (1976), 24-37.

1962 BYRDSALL, FITZWILLIAM. *The History of the Loco-foco, or Equal Rights Party: Its Movements, Conventions, and Proceedings, with Short Characteristic Sketches of its Prominent Men.* NY: Clement & Packard, 1842.

1963 CADDY, DOUGLAS. *The Hundred Million Dollar Payoff: How Big Labor Buys Its Democrats*. New Rochelle, NY: Arlington House, 1974.

1964 CALKINS, FAY. *The CIO and the Democratic Party*. Chicago: U of Chicago Press, 1952.

1965 CANNON, JAMES P. *Socialism on Trial: The Official Court Record of James P. Cannon's Testimony in the Famous Minneapolis "Sedition" Trial.* NY: Merit, 1969.

1966 CANTOR, MILTON. *The Divided Left: American Radicalism, 1900-1975.* NY: Hill & Wang, 1978.

1967 CARRIGAN, D. OWEN. "A Forgotten Yankee Marxist." *New England Quarterly*, Vol 52 (1969), 23-43.

1968 CARROLL, MOLLIE RAY. *Labor and Politics: The Attitude of the American Federation of Labor Toward Legislation and Politics*. Bost.: Houghton Mifflin, 1923.

1969 CARTER, ROBERT FREDERICK. *Pressure from the Left: The American Labor Party, 1936-1954*. Ph D diss, Syracuse U, 1965.

1970 CATCHPOLE, TERRY. *How to Cope with COPE: The Political Operations of Organized Labor*. New Rochelle, NY: Arlington House, 1968.

1971 CHAMBERLAIN, NEIL W. "Political Activity," chap. 6, *Sourcebook on Labor*, NY: McGraw-Hill, 1958.

1972 CHERN, KENNETH S. "The Politics of Patriotism: War, Ethnicity, and the New York Mayoral Campaign, 1917." *New York Historical Quarterly*, Vol 63 (1979), 291-313.

1973 CHILDS, HARWOOD LAWRENCE. *Labor and Capital in National Politics*. Columbus: Ohio State U Press, 1930.

1974 CHRISTOPULOS, DIANA. *American Radicals and the Mexican Revolution, 1900-1925*. Ph D diss, SUNY-Binghamton, 1980.

1975 CLELAND, HUGH C. *The Political History of a Local Union: Local 601 of the CIO Electrical Workers Union*. Ph D diss, Western Reserve U, 1957.

1976 COBURN, DAVID R. "Governor Alfred E. Smith and the Red Scare, 1919-1920." *Political Science Quarterly*, Vol 88 (1973), 423-44.

1977 COCHRAN, BERT. *Labor and Communism: The Coflict that Shaped American Unions*. Princeton: Princeton U Press, 1977.

1978 COLES, ROBERT. *A Spectacle Unto the World: The Catholic Worker Movement*. NY: Viking Press, 1973.

1979 COMMONS, JOHN R. "Labor Organization and Labor Politics, 1827-37." *Quarterly Journal of Economics*, Vol 21 (1907), 323-29.

1980 *COPE: Good Work for Democracy*. 1971. (Non-fiction film produced by the AFL-CIO Committee on Political Education)

1981 CRAVENS, HAMILTON. "The Emergence of the Farmer-Labor Party in Washington Politics, 1919-20." *Pacific Northwest Quarterly*, Vol 57 (1966), 148-57.

1982 CUMBERLAND, WILLIAM H. "The Red Flag Comes to Iowa." *Annals of Iowa*, 3rd Series, Vol 39 (1968), 441-54.

1983 CURRIE, HAROLD W. "A Socialist Edits the *Detroit Times*." *Michigan History*, Vol 52 (1968), 1-11. (Allan L. Benson)

1984 CURTIS, BRUCE. "Sinclair and Sumner: the Private Background of a Public Confrontation." *Mid-America*, Vol 60 (1978), 185-90.

1985 DARLING, ARTHUR B. "The Workingmen's Party in Massachusetts, 1833-1834." *American Historical Review*, Vol 29 (1923), 81-86.

1986 DAVID, HENRY. "One Hundred Years of Labor in Politics," chap. 5, *The House of Labor*, J. B. S. Hardman & Maurice F. Neufeld, eds. NY: Prentice-Hall, 1951.

1987 DAVIN, ERIC LEIF, and STAUGHTON LYND. "Picket LIne and Ballot Box: The Forgotten Legacy of the Local Labor Party Movement, 1932-1936." *Radical History Review*, Vol 22 (1979-80), 43-60.

1988 DAVIS, MIKE. "The Barren Marriage of American Labour and the Democratic Party." *New Left Review*, Vol 124 (Nov-Dec 1980, 43-84.

1989 DELEON, DAVID. *The American as Anarchist: Reflections on Indigenous Radicalism*. Balt.: Johns Hopkins U Press, 1978.

1990 DICK, WILLIAM M. *Labor and Socialism in America: The Gompers Era*. Port Washington, NY: Kennikat Press, 1972.

1991 DORFMAN, JOSEPH. "The Jackson Wage-Earner Thesis." *American Historical Review*, Vol 54 (1949), 296-306. (See also communication of Arthur M. Schlesinger, Jr. Apr 1949, 785-86)

1992 DRAPER, THEODORE. "Communists and Miners, 1928-1933." *Dissent*, Vol 19 (1972), 371-92.

1993 DRESCHER, NAULA MCGANN. "Organized Labor and the Eighteenth Amendment." *Labor History*, Vol 8 (1967), 28-99.

1994 DRESSNER, RICHARD B. *Christian Socialism: a Response to Industrial America in the Progressive Era*. Ph D diss, Cornell U, 1972.

1995 DUBOFSKY, MELVYN. "The Origins of Western Working Class Radicalism, 1890-1905." *Labor History*, Vol 7 (1966), 131-54.

1996 ———. "Success and Failure of Socialism in New York City, 1900-1918: a Case Study." *Labor History*, Vol 9 (1968), 361-75.

1997 DYCHE, JOHN A. *Bolshevism in American Labor Unions: A Plea for Constructive Unionism*. NY: Boni and Liveright, 1926.

1998 DYSON, B. PATRICIA, and LOWELL K. DYSON. "An Honest Light." *Labor History*, Vol 22 (1982), 422-23. (Review of the film *Northern Lights*)

1999 DYSON, LOWELL K. *Red Harvest: the Communist Party and American Farmers*. Lincoln: U of Nebraska Press, 1982.

2000 ———. "Red Peasant International in America." *Journal of American History*, Vol 58 (1972), 958-73.

2001 ELDRIDGE, SEBA. "Labor and Independent Politics," chap. 22, *American Labor Dynamics*, J. B. S. Hardman, ed. NY: Harcourt, Brace, 1928.

2002 ELLISON, ROBERT A. "The Attitudes of Government Employee Unions Toward the Hatch Act and Its Impact Upon Them Since 1939." *Industrial and Labor Relations Forum*, Vol 7 (1970), 1-58.

2003 EPSTEIN, ALBERT, and NATHANIEL GOLDFINGER. "Communist Tactics in American Unions." *Labor and Nation*, Vol 6 (1950), 36-43.

2004 EVANS, GEORGE HENRY. "History of the Origin and Progress of the Working Man's Party in New York." *Radical*, Granville, NJ, Jan 1842 to Apr 1843. (Radical was a continuation of the Working Man's Advocate)

2005 EVERETT, EDWARD. *A Lecture on the Working Men's Party*. Bost.: Gray and Bowen, 1830.

2006 FINE, NATHAN. *Labor and Farmer Parties in the United States, 1828-1928*. NY: Rand School of Social Science, 1928.

2007 FINK, GARY M. *Labor's Search for Political Order: The Political Behavior of the Missouri Labor Movement, 1890-1940*. Columbia: U of Missouri Press, 1973.

2008 FINK, LEON. "'Irrespective of Party, Color of Social Standing': The Knights of Labor and Opposition Politics in Richmond, Virginia." *Labor History*, Vol 19 (1978), 325-49.

2009 ———. *Workingman's Democracy: The Knights of Labor in Local Politics, 1886-1896*. Ph D diss, U of Rochester, 1977.

2010 FINN, J. F. "American Federation of Labor Leaders and the Question of Politics in the early 1890s." *Journal of American Studies*, Vol 7 (1973), 243-65.

2011 FOLK, RICHARD A. "Socialist Party of Ohio—War and Free Speech." *Oral History*, Vol 58 (1969), 104-15.

2012 FORM, WILLIAM H. "Job vs. Political Unionism: A Cross-National Comparison." *Industrial Relations*, Vol 12 (1973), 224-38.

2013 FOSTER, JAMES C. *The Union Politic: The CIO Political Action Committee*. Columbia: U of Missouri Press, 1975.

2014 FREEMAN, JOSHUA B. "Catholics, Communists, and Republicans: Irish Workers and the Organization of the Transport Workers Union," pp 256-83, *Working Class America: Essays on Labor, Community, and American Society*, Michael Frisch & Daniel J. Walkowitz, eds. Urbana: U of Illinois Press, 1983.

2015 FRENCH, JOHN D. "'Reaping the Whirlwind': the Origins of the Allegheny County Greenback Labor Party in 1877." *Western Pennsylvania Historical Magazine*, Vol 64 (1981), 97-119.

2016 FRIEDBERG, GERALD. "Sources for the Study of Socialism in America, 1901-19." *Labor History*, Vol 6 (1965), 159-65.

2017 GAER, JOSEPH. *The First Round: The Story of the CIO Political Action Committee*. NY: Duell, Sloan and Pearce, 1944.

2018 GAFFIELD, CHAD. "Big Business, the Working-Class, and Socialism in Schenectady, 1911-1916." *Labor History*, Vol 19 (1978), 350-72.

2019 GALENSON, WALTER. "Communists and Trade Union Democracy." *Industrial Relations*, Vol 13 (1974), 228-37.

2020 GAMBATESE, JOSEPH M. *Business and the Unions in Politics: A Post-Election Appraisal*. NY: Personnel Division, American Management Association, 1961.

2021 GARLID, GEORGE W. "The Antiwar Dilemma of the Farmer-Labor Party." *Minnesota History*, Vol 40 (1967), 354-74.

2022 GIESKE, MILLARD L. *Minnesota Farmer-Laborism: The Third-Party Alternative*. Minneapolis: U of Minnesota Press, 1979.

2023 GOLDBERG, BARRY H. *Beyond Free Labor: Labor, Socialism, and the Idea of Wage Slavery, 1890-1920*. Ph D diss, Columbia U, 1979.

2024 GOODMAN, CARY. *Choosing Sides: Labor, Capital and the Rise of Organized Play*. Ph D diss, Union Graduate School, 1978.

2025 GOODMAN, JAY S. "A Note on Legislative Research: Labor Representation in Rhode Island." *American Political Science Review*, Vol 59 (1967), 468-73.

2026 GORDON, MAX. "The Communists and the Drive to Organized Steel, 1936." *Labor History*, Vol 22 (1982), 254-65.

2027 GOTSCH, CHARLES E. *The Albany Workingmen's Party and the Rise of Popular Politics*. Ph D diss, SUNY-Albany, 1977.

2028 GREEN, JAMES R. *Socialism and the Southwestern Class Struggle, 1898-1918: A Study of Radical Movements in Oklahoma, Texas, Louisiana and Arkansas.* Ph D diss, Yale U, 1972.

2029 GREENSTONE, J. DAVID. *Labor in American Politics.* Chicago: U of Chicago Press, 1977.

2030 GROAT, CHARLES VINCENT. *Political Greenbackism in New York State, 1876-1885.* Ph D diss, Syracuse U, 1963.

2031 GROB, GERALD N. "The Knights of Labor, Politics, and Populism." *Mid-America*, Vol 40, New Series Vol 29, (1958), 3-21.

2032 ———. "Reform Unionism: The National Labor Union." *Journal of Economic History*, Vol 14 (1954), 126-42.

2033 ———. *Workers and Utopia: A Study of Ideological Conflict in the American Labor Movement 1865-1900.* Evanston: U of Illinois Press, 1961.

2034 GUROWSKY, DAVID. *Factional Dispute within the ILGWU, 1919-1928.* Ph D diss, SUNY-Binghamton, 1978.

2035 HARRIS, LEM. "Communists in Farm Struggles." *Political Affairs*, Vol 58 (Aug-Sep 1979), 66-69.

2036 HARVEY, ROWLAND H. *A Comparison of the Approach toward Socialism of British and American Labor since 1900.* Ph D diss, Stanford U, 1924.

2037 HAYNES, JOHN. "Communists and Anti-Communists int he Northern Minnesota CIO, 1936-1949." *Upper Midwest History*, Vol 1 (1981), 55-73.

2038 ———. *Liberals, Communists, and the Popular Front in Minnesota: the Struggle to Control the Political Direction of the Labor Movement and Organized Liberalism, 1936-1950.* Ph D diss, U of Minnesota, 1978.

2039 HENDRICKSON, GORDON O. "The Red Special in Colorado." *Colorado Magazine*, Vol 51 (1974), 216-27.

2040 HENDRICKSON, KENNETH E., JR. "George R. Lunn and the Socialist Era in Schenectady, New York, 1909-1916." *New York History*, Vol 47 (1966), 22-40.

2041 HERMAN, ALAN. "Dust, Depression and Demagogues: Political Radicals of the Great Plains, 1930-36." *Journal of the West*, Vol 16 (Jan 1977), 57-62.

2042 HESSELTINE, WILLIAM BEST. *The Rise and Fall of Third Parties.* Wash.: Public Affairs Press, 1948.

2043 HILLQUIT, MORRIS. *History of Socialism in the United States.* NY: Funk and Wagnalls, 1910.

2044 HOFMANN, BENJAMIN GUY. *The Political Thought of James Burnham.* Ph D diss, U of Michigan, 1969.

2045 HOLLOWAY, HARRY. "Interest Groups in the Postpartisan Era: the Political Machine of the AFL-CIO." *Political Science Quarterly*, Vol 94 (1979), 117-33.

2046 HOLT, JAMES. "The Trade Unions and Socialism in the United States." *Journal of American Studies*, Vol 7 (1973), 321-27.

2047 HOROWITZ, RUTH L. *Political Ideologies of Organized Labor: the New Deal Era.* New Brunswick, NJ: Transaction Books, 1978.

2048 ———. *Political Ideologies of the AFL and CIO During the New Deal.* Ph D diss, Washington U, St. Louis, 1972.

2049 HUGINS, WALTER E. *Jacksonian Democracy and the Working Class, a Study of the New York Workingmen's Movement, 1829-1837.* Stanford: Stanford U Press, 1960.

2050 HUNTER, ROBERT. *Labor in Politics.* Chicago: Socialist Party, 1915.

2051 HURT, R. DOUBLAS. "John R. Rogers: the Union Labor Party, Georgism, and Agrarian Reform." *Journal of the West*, Vol 16 (Jan 1977), 10-15.

2052 HYFLER, ROBERT. *American Socialist Thought: from Debs to Harrington.* Ph D diss, U of Massachusetts, 1980.

2053 ISSERMAN, MAURICE. "Inheritance Lost: Socialism in Rochester, 1917-1919." *Rochester History*, Vol 39 (Oct 1977), 1-24.

2054 ———. *Peat Bog Soldiers: the American Communist Party during World War II, 1939-1945.* Ph D diss, U of Rochester, 1979.

2055 JACKSON, SIDNEY L. "Labor, Education, and Politics in the 1830's." *Pennsylvania Magazine of History and Biography*, Vol 66 (1942), 279-93.

2056 JAFFE, PHILIP J. "The Rise and Fall of Earl Browder." *Survey*, Vol 18 (Spring 1972), 14-65.

2057 JAMES, EDWARD T. *American Labor and Political Action, 1865-1896: The Knights of Labor and Its Predecessors.* Ph D diss., Harvard U, 1954.

2058 ———. "Ben Butler Runs for President: Labor, Greenbackers, and Anti-Monopolists in the Election of 1884." *Essex Institute Historical Collection*, Vol 113 (1977), 65-88.

2059 JOHNPOLL, BERNARD K., and MARK R. YERBURGH. *The League for Industrial Democracy: A Documentary History.* Westport, CT: Greenwood, 1980.

2060 JOHNSON, EDWARD CLAYTON. *An Analysis of the Origins and Programs of the Alliance for Labor Action.* Ph D diss, Georgia State U, 1973.

2061 JUDD, RICHARD W. *Socialist Cities: Explorations into the Grass Roots of American Socialism.* PhD diss, U of Caoifornia, 1980.

2062 KAMPELMAN, MAX M. *The Communist Party vs. the C.I.O.: A Study in Power Politics.* NY: F. A. Praeger, 1957.

2063 KARSON, MARC. *American Labor Unions and Politics, 1900-1918.* Carbondale: Southern Illinois U Press, 1958.

2064 KEERAN, ROGER. *The Communist Party and the Auto Workers Unions.* Bloomington: Indiana U Press, 1980.

2065 KERSEY, E. R. *Labor Organizations and Political Development: An Historical Comparative Analysis.* Ph D diss, U of Minnesota, 1972.

2066 KISER, G. GREGORY. "The Socialist Party in Arkansas, 1900-1912." *Arkansas Historical Quarterly*, Vol 40 (1981), 119-53.

2067 KORNHAUSER, ARTHUR W. et al. *When Labor Votes: A Study of Auto Workers.* NY: University Books, 1956.

2068 KRADITOR, AILEEN S. *The Radical Persuasion, 1890-1917: Aspects of the Intellectual History and the Historiography of Three American Radical Organizations.* Baton Rouge: Louisiana State U Press, 1981.

2069 KREUTER, KENT, and GRETCHEN KREUTER. "The Vernacular History of A. M. Simons." *Journal of American Studies*, Vol 2 (1968), 65-91.

2070 LACYK, WALTER M. *Illinois Labor Unions in the Election of 1924.* MA thesis, U of Illinois, 1955.

2071 LADER, LAWRENCE. *Power on the Left: American Radical Movements since 1946.* NY: Norton, 1979.

2072 LAIDLER, HARRY W. *Social-Economic Movements.* NY: Thomas Y. Crowell, 1945. (See chap. 37, pp 577-89)

2073 LASLETT, JOHN H. M. *Labor and the Left: A Study of Socialist and Radical Influences in the American Labor Movement.* NY: Basic Books, 1970.

2074 ———. "Socialism and the American Labor Movement: Some New Reflections." *Labor History*, Vol (1967), 136-55.

2075 ———, and SEYMOUR MARTIN LIPSET, eds.. *Failure of a Dream? Essays in the History of American Socialism.* Garden City, NY: Anchor, 1974.

2076 LEINENWEBER, CHARLES. "The American Socialist Party and 'New' Immigrants." *Science & Society*, Vol 32 (1968), 1-25.

2077 ———. "Socialists in the Streets: the New York City Socialist Party in Working Class Neighborhoods, 1908-18." *Science & Society*, Vol 41 (1977), 152-71.

2078 LEISERSON, AVERY. "Organized Labor as a Pressure Group." *The Annals of the American Academy of Political and Social Science*, Vol 274, Mar 1951, pp 108-17.

2079 LENS, SIDNEY. *Left, Right and Center: Conflicting Forces in American Labor.* Hinsdale, IL: Regnery, 1949.

2080 ———. *Radicalism in America.* NY: Crowell, 1969.

2081 LEVENSTEIN, HARVEY A. *Communism, Anti-Communism, and the CIO.* Westport, CT: Greenwood, 1981.

2082 ———. "Leninists Undone by Leninism: Communism and Unionism in the United States and Mexico, 1935-1939." *Labor History*, Vol 22 (1981), 237-69.

2083 LEVINE, GENE N. *Workers Vote: The Political Behavior of Men in the Printing Trade.* Totowa, NJ: Bedminster Press, 1963.

2084 LICHTENSTEIN, NELSON. "The Communist Experience in American Trade Unions." *Industrial Relations*, Vol 19 (1980), 119-39. (Replies by Robert Zieger & Roger Keeran)

2085 LOMBARDI, JOHN. *Labor's Voice in the Cabinet: A History of the Department of Labor from Its Origin to 1921.* NY: Columbia U Press, 1942.

2086 LOVIN, HUGH T. "The Automobile Workers Unions and the Fight for Labor Parties in the 1930s." *Indiana Magazine of History*, Vol 77 (1981), 123-49.

2087 ———. "Persistence of Third Party Dreams of the American Labor Movement, 1930-1938." *Mid-America*, Vol 58 (1976), 141-57.

2088 ———. "Red Scare in Idaho, 1916-1918." *Idaho Yesterdays*, Vol 17 (Fall 1973), 2-13.

2089 LOVING, HUGH L. "The 'Farmer-Labor' Movement in Idaho, 1933-1938." *Journal of the West*, Vol 28 (1979), 21-29.

2090 LYND, STAUGHTON. "A Chapter from History: the United Labor Party, 1946-1952." *Liberation*, Vol 18 (Dec 1973), 38-45.

2091 ———. "The United Front in America: a Note." *Radical America*, Vol 8 (Jul-Aug 1974), 29-37.

2092 LYND, STAUGHTON, ed. *American Labor Radicalism: Testimonies and Interpretations.* NY: Wiley, 1973.

2093 LYONS, PAUL H. *The Communist as Organizer: the Philadelphia Experience, 1936-1956.* Ph D diss, Bryn Mawr College, 1981.

2094 MCCLURE, STEWART E. *Making Tracks: Lobbying for Rail Labor.* Glenn Dale, MD: Merkle Press, 1979.

2095 MCCORMACK, ANDREW. *The Origins and Extent of Western Labor Radicalism, 1896-1919.* Ph D diss, U of Western Ontario, 1973.

2096 MACKAY, KENNETH C. *The Progressive Movement of 1924.* NY: Octagon Books, 1966.

2097 MASTERS, MARICK F., and JOHN THOMAS DELANEY. "The AFL-CIO's Political Record, 1974-1980." *Proceedings of the Thirty-Fourth Annual Meeting of the Industrial Relations Research Association*, Dec 28-30, 1981, pp 351-59. Madison: IRRA, 1982.

2098 MAY, TIMOTHY C. *Trade Unions and Pressure Group Politics.* Lexington, MA: Lexington Books, 1975.

2099 MILTON, DAVID. *The Politics of U.S. Labor: From the Great Depression to the New Deal.* NY: Monthly Review Press, 1982.

2100 MITAU, G. THEODORE. "The Democratic-Farmer-Labor Party Schism of 1948." *Minnesota History*, Vol 34 (1955), 187-94.

2101 MITTELMAN, EDWARD B. "Chicago Labor in Politics 1877-1896." *Journal of Political Economy*, Vol 28 (1920), 68-79.

2102 MONROY, DOUGLAS. "Anarquismo y Comunismo: Mexican Radicalism and the Communist Party in Los Angeles during the 1930s." *Labor History*, Vol 24 (1983), 34-59.

2103 MORLAN, ROBERT L. "The Nonpartisan League and the Minnesota Campsign of 1918." *Minnesota History*, Vol 34 (1955), 221-32.

2104 MORRIS, GEORGE. "Left Expulsions from the CIO—Thirty Years After." *Political Affairs*, Vol 58 (Oct 1979), 23-30.

2105 ———. "Sixty Years of Communist Trade Union Work." *Political Affairs*, Vol 58 (Aug-Sep 1979), 5-12.

2106 NADWORNY, MILTON J. "New Jersey Workingmen and the Jacksonians." *New Jersey Historical Society Proceedings: A Magazine of New Jersey History*, Vol 67 (1949), 185-98.

2107 NAFTALIN, ARTHUR. "The Tradition of Protest and the Roots of the Farmer-Labor Party." *Minnesota History*, Vol 35 (1956), 53-63.

2108 NASH, MICHAEL. *Conflict and Accomodation: Coal Miners, Steel Workers, and Socialism 1890-1920.* Westport, CT: Greenwood, 1982.

2109 ———. *Conflict and Accomodation: Some Aspects of the Political Behavior of America's Coal Miners and Steel Workers, 1890-1920.* Ph D diss, SUNY/Binghamton, 1975.

2110 NELSON, NELS E. "Union Dues and Political Spending." *Labor Law Journal*, Vol 28 (1977), 109-19.

2111 NORD, DAVID PAUL. "The *Appeal to Reason* and American Socialism, 1901-1920." *Kansas History*, Vol 1 (1978), 75-89.

2112 *Northern Lights.* 1978. (A "dramatized account" of the Non-Partisan League directed by John Hanson & Rob Nilson)

2113 O'BRIEN, F. S. "The 'Communist-Dominated' Unions in the United States Since 1950." *Labor History*, Vol 9 (1968), 184-209.

2114 ODEGARD, PETER H., and E. ALLEN HELMS. *American Politics: A Study in Political Dynamics.* NY: Harper, 1938.

2115 OLSSEN, ERIK. "The Making of a Political Machine: The Railroad Unions Enter Politics." *Labor History*, Vol 19 (1978), 373-96.

2116 O'NEILL, WILLIAM L. "Labor Radicalism and the 'Masses,'" *Labor History*, Vol 7 (1966), 197-208.

2117 OWEN, HOMER LEROY. *The Role of the CIO-PAC in the 1944 Elections.* MS thesis, NY State School of Industrial and Labor Relations, Cornell U, 1952.

2118 PACHECO, BLANCA S. *Puerto Rican Workers and the Socialist Party, 1932-1940.* Ph D diss SUNY/Albany, 1973.

2119 PAHL, THOMAS L. "G-string Conspiracy, Political Reprisal or Armed Revolt?; the Minneapolis Trotskyite Trial." *Labor History*, Vol 8 (1967), 30-51.

2120 PIEHL, MEL. *The Catholic Worker and the Origin of Catholic Radicalism in America.* Ph D diss, Stanford U, 1980.

2121 ———. *The Catholic Worker Movement and the Origin of Catholic Radicalism in America.* Phila.: Temple U Press, 1982.

2122 PRAGO, ALBERT. *The Organization of the Unemployed and the Role of the Radicals, 1929-1935.* Ph D diss, Union Graduate School, 1977.

2123 *Prairie Fire.* 1976. (Non-fiction film by John Hanson & Rob Nilsson about the Non-Partisan League)

2124 PRICKETT, JAMES R. "Anti-Communism and Labor History." *Industrial Relations*, Vol 15 (1976), 349-54.

2125 ———. "Anti-Communism and Labor History." *Industrial Relations*, Vol 13 (1974), 219-27.

2126 ———. "Communist Conspiracy or Wage Dispute?: The 1941 Strike at North American Aviation." *Pacific Historical Review*, Vol 50 (1981), 215-33.

2127 ———. "Some Aspects of the Communist Controversy in the CIO." *Science & Society*, Vol 33 (1969), 299-321.

2128 PUBLIC OPINION INDEX FOR INDUSTRY. *Labor Union Power.* Princeton: The Index, May 1957.

2129 REESE, WILLIAM. "'Partisans of the Proletariat': the Socialist Workingclass and the Milwaukee Schools, 1890-1920." *History of Education Quarterly*, Vol 21 (1981), 3-50.

2130 REHMUS, CHARLES M., and DORIS B. MCLAUGHLIN. *Labor and American Politics: A Book of Readings.* Ann Arbor: U of Michigan Press, 1967.

2131 RENSHAW, PATRICK. "Rose of the World: the Pastor-Stokes Marriage and the American Left, 1905-1925." *New York History*, Vol 62 (1981), 415-38.

2132 RICE, STUART ARTHUR. *Farmers and Workers in American Politics.* NY: Columbia U, 1924.

2133 RIKER, WILLIAM H. *The CIO in Politics 1936-1946.* Ph D diss, Harvard U, 1948.

2134 ROGIN, LAWRENCE. *Central Labor Bodies and Independent Political Action in New York City, 1918-1922.* MA thesis, Columbia U, 1931.

2135 ROGIN, MICHAEL. "Voluntarism: The Political Functions of an Antipolitical Doctrine." *Industrial and Labor Relations Review*, Vol 14 (1962), 521-35.

2136 ROSEN, ELLEN. *Peasant Socialism in America?: the Socialist Party in Oklahoma before World War I.* Ph D diss, City U of NY, 1976.

2137 ———. "Socialism in Oklahoma: a Theoretical Overview." *Politics and Society*, Vol 8 (1978), 109-29.

2138 ROSEN, HARVEY. *The Quest for a New Social Order: Harry W. Laidler and the League for Industrial Democracy.* Ph D diss, New York U, 1976.

2139 ROSEN, SIDNEY. "A Study of DRIVE: The Political Organization of the International Brotherhood of Teamsters." *Industrial and Labor Relations Forum*, Vol 6 (1969), 259-98.

2140 ROSSI, WAGNER. *A Work Pedagogy: a Study of the Relationship between Productive Work and Education in the Socialist Tradition.* Ph D diss, Bowling Green State U, 1981.

2141 RUDE, LESLIE G. "The Rhetoric of Farmer-Labor Agitators." *Central States Speech Journal*, Vol 20 (1969), 280-85.

2142 RUMINSKI, HENRY J. *A Content Analysis of Political Coverage in Selected Labor Union Publications during 8 Presidential Campaigns.* Ph D diss, U of Illinois, 1972.

2143 RYAN, JAMES G. *Earl Browder and American Communism at High Tide: 1934-1945.* Ph D diss, Notre Dame U, 1981.

2144 SAENGER, MARTHA LEE. *Labor Political Action at Mid-Twentieth Century: A Case Study of the CIO-PAC Campaign of 1944 and the Textile Workers Union of America.* Ph D diss, Ohio State U, 1959.

2145 SAPOSS, DAVID J. *Case Studies in Labor Ideology: An Analysis of Labor, Political and Trade Union Activity as Influenced by Ideology; Philosophic, Structural and Procedural Adaptations Since World War I.* Honolulu: Industrial Relations Center, U of Hawaii, 1964.

2146 ———. *Communism in American Politics.* Wash.: Public Affairs Press, 1960.

2147 ———. *Communism in American Unions.* NY: McGraw-Hill, 1959.

2148 ———. *Left-Wing Unionism.* NY: International Publishers, 1926.

2149 SAVETSKY, SEYMOUR. *The New York Working Men's Party.* MA thesis, Columbia U, 1948.

2150 SCHAPPES, MORRIS U. "The Political Origins of the United Hebrew Trades, 1888." *Journal of Ethnic Studies*, Vol 5 (Spring 1977), 13-44.

2151 SCHARNAU, RALPH. "Thomas J. Morgan and the United Labor Party of Chicago." *Illinois State Historical Society Journal*, Vol 46 (1973), 41-61.

2152 SCHEINBERG, STEPHEN J. "Theodore Roosevelt and the A. F. of L.'s Entry into Politics, 1906-1908." *Labor History*, Vol 3 (1962), 131-48.

2153 SCHNEIDER, D. M. *The Workers' (Communist) Party and American Trade Unions.* Balt.: Johns Hopkins Press, 1928.

2154 SCHWANTES, CARLOS A. *Left-wing Unionism in the Pacific Northwest: a Comparative History of Organized Labor and Socialist Politics in Washington and British Columbia, 1885-1917.* Ph D diss, U of Michigan, 1976.

2155 SEATON, DOUGLAS P. *Catholics and Radicals: The Association of Catholic Trade Unionists and the American Labor Movement, from Depression to Cold War.* Lewisburg: Bucknell U Press, 1981.

2156 SHAFFER, RALPH E. "Formation of the California Communist Labor Party." *Pacific Historical Review*, Vol 36 (1967), 59-78.

2157 SHANNON, THOMAS. *Variation and Change in the Political Strategies of Major American Labor Unions: 1946-1966*. Ph D diss, U of Michigan, 1976.

2158 SHAPIRO, STANLEY. *Hand and Brain: the Farmer-Labor Party of 1920*. Ph D diss, U of Michigan, 1968.

2159 SHATTUCK, HENRY L. "The Loyalty Review Board of the U.S. Civil Service Commission, 1947-1953." *Proceedings of the Massachusetts Historical Society*, Vol 77 (1966), 63-80.

2160 SHIELDS, ART. "What the Communist Party Means to Me." *Political Affairs*, Vol 42 (Sep 1973), 10-24.

2161 SHOVER, JOHN L. "The Progressives and the Working Class Vote in California." *Labor History*, Vol 10 (1969), 584-601.

2162 SKEELS, JOYCE G. "The Early American Federation of Labor and Monetary Reform." *Labor History*, Vol 12 (1971), 530-50.

2163 SOMKIN, FRED. "How Vanzetti Said Goodby." *Journal of American History*, Vol 68 (1981), 298-312.

2164 SPENCER, THOMAS T. "'Labor is with Roosevelt': The Pennsylvania Labor Non-Partisan League and the Election of 1936." *Pennsylvania History*, Vol 46 (1979), 3-16.

2165 STABILE, DONALD R. *The Provisional Arbiters: a Study of the Contradictory Location of Engineering Reformers, American Socialists and Thorstein Veblen*. Ph D diss, U of Massachusetts, 1980.

2166 STAVE, BRUCE MARTIN. "The 'La Follette Revolution' and the Pittsburgh Vote, 1932." *Mid-America*, Vol 49 (1967), 244-51.

2167 STEDMAN, J. C., and R. A. LEONARD. *The Workingmen's Party of California*. San Francisco: Bacon and Co., 1878.

2168 STEDMAN, MURRAY S., and SUSAN W. STEDMAN. *Discontent at the Polls: A Study of Farmer and Labor Parties, 1827-1948*. NY: Columbia University Press, 1950.

2169 STEIN, JUDITH. "The Impact of the New Deal on New York Politics." *New-York Historical Society Quarterly*, Vol 56 (1972), 29-53.

2170 STEIN, LEON, and PHILIP TAFT, eds.. *Labor Politics: Collected Pamphlets*. NY: Arno, 1971.

2171 STEVENS, HARRY R. "Did Industrial Labor Influence Jacksonian Land Policy?" *Indiana Magazine of History*, Vol 43 (1947), 159-67.

2172 STUART, JACK MEYER. *William English Walling: a Study in Politics and Ideas*. Ph D diss, Columbia U, 1968.

2173 STUHLER, BARBARA. "The One Man Who Voted 'Nay': the Story of John T. Barnard's Quarrel with American Foreign Policy, 1937-1939." *Minnesota History*, Vol 43 (1972), 83-92.

2174 STURMTHAL, ADOLF. "Some Thoughts on Labor and Political Action." *Relations Industrielles-Industrial Relations*, Vol 17 (1962), 244-58.

2175 SVIRIDOFF, MITCHELL. "Political Participation by Unions: The 1960 Situation." *Labor Law Journal*, Jul 1960, pp 639-45.

2176 SYLVERS, MALCOLM. "Sicilian Socialists in Houston, Texas, 1896-98." *Labor History*, Vol 11 (1970), 77-81.

2177 SYMES, LILLIAN, and TRAVERS CLEMENT. *Rebel America*. NY: Harper, 1934.

2178 TAFT, PHILIP. *Labor Politics American Style: The California State Federation of Labor*. Cambr.: Harvard U Press, 1968.

2179 TAYLOR, JOHN BERWICK. *The Politics of the Labor Injunction*. Ph D diss, Princeton U, 1972.

2180 THURNER, ARTHUR W. "The Mayor, the Governor and the People's Council." *Illinois State Historical Society Journal*, Vol 46 (1973), 125-43.

2181 TILLERY, WINSTON L. "National Politics Dominates AFL-CIO Convention." *Monthly Labor Review*, Vol 96 (Dec 1973), 59-60.

2182 TYLER, GUS. *The Political Imperative: The Corporate Character of Unions.* NY: Macmillan, 1968.

2183 U.S. CONGRESS. HOUSE. Committee on Un-American Activities. *Hearings regarding Communist Activities in the Territory of Hawaii.*, 4 vols. Wash.: G.P.O., 1951.

2184 ———. SENATE. Committee on Labor and Public Welfare. Subcommittee on Labor and Labor-Management Relations. *Communist Domination of Certain Unions.*, Document 89. Wash.: G.P.O., 1951.

2185 URMANN, MICHAEL F. *Rank and File Communists and the CIO.* Ph D diss, U of Utah, 1981.

2186 VADNEY, THOMAS E. "The Politics of Repression, a Case Study of the Red Scare in New York." *New York History*, Vol 49 (1968), 56-75.

2187 VALE, VIVIAN. "American Labour's Political Freedom: a British View." *Political Studies*, Vol 13 (1965), 281-99.

2188 ———. *Labour in American Politics.* NY: Barnes and Noble, 1971.

2189 WAKSMUNDSKI, JOHN. "Governor McKinley and the Workingman." *The Historian*, Vol 38 (1976), 629-47.

2190 ———. *McKinley Politics and the Changing Attitudes Towards American Labor, 1870-1900.* Ph D diss, Ohio State U, 1972.

2191 WALD, ALAN. "From Antinomianism to Revolutionary Marxism: John Wheelwright and the New England Rebel Tradition." *Marxist Perspectives*, Vol 3 (1980), 44-68.

2192 WALWIK, THEODORE JOSEPH. *Speaking of American Socialists in Opposition to World War I.* Ph D diss, Ohio U, 1967.

2193 WANCZYCKI, JAN K. "Union Dues and Political Contributions—Great britain, United States, Canada—A Comparison." *Relations Industrielles-Industrial Relations*, Vol 21 (1966), 143-205.

2194 WEINSTEIN, JAMES. "Labor and Socialism in America." *Labor History*, Vol 14 (1973), 429-34.

2195 ———. "Radicalism in the Midst of Normalcy." *Journal of American History*, Vol 52 (1966), 773-90. (National Farmer-Labor Politics, 1919-24)

2196 WEST, JAMES. "The Communist Party and the Organization of the Unorganized." *Political Affairs*, Vol 56 (Sep 1977), 18-37.

2197 WESTERGARD, THORPE. *Revolutionary Syndicalist Internationalism, 1913-1923: the Origins of the International Workingmen's Association.* Ph D diss, U of British Columbia, 1980.

2198 WHEELER, ROBERT HULINGS LAPPE. *American Communists: Their Ideology and Their Interpretation of American Life 1917-1939.* Ph D diss, Yale U, 1953.

2199 WHITFIELD, STEPHEN J. *Scott Nearing and the Ambiguity of American Radicalism.* Ph D diss, Brandeis U, 1972.

2200 WHITMAN, ALDEN. *Labor Parties, 1827-1834.* NY: International Publishers, 1943.

2201 WILLIAMSON, JOHN. "Some Strands from the Past: The Y.W.L. Meets Gompers." *Political Affairs*, Vol 44 (1965), 36-45.

2202 WILSON, GRAHAM K. *Unions in American National Politics.* NY: St. Martin's Press, 1979.

2203 WILSON, JOHN SCOTT. *Norman Thomas, Critic of the New America.* Ph D diss, U of North Carolina, 1966.

2204 WOLFE, ALAN. "The Withering Away of the American Labor Party." *Journal of the Rutgers University Library*, Vol 31 (1968), 46-47.

2205 WOLFE, ARTHUR C. "Trends in Labor Union Voting Behavior, 1948-1968." *Industrial Relations*, Vol 9 (1969), 1-10.

2206 "The Workingmen's Party of California, 1877-1882." *California Historical Quarterly*, Vol 55 (1976), 58-71.

2207 YORBURG, BETTY G. *People in Protest: Three Generations of American Socialists.* Ph D diss, New School for Social Research, 1968.

2208 ZAHLER, HELENE S. *Eastern Workingmen and National Land Policy, 1829-1862.* NY: Columbia U Press, 1941.

2209 ZIEGER, ROBERT H. *Republicans and Labor 1919-1929.* Lexington: U of Kentucky Press, 1969.

2210 ———. *The Republicans and Labor: Politics and Policies, 1919-1929.* Ph D diss, U of Maryland, 1965.

2211 ———. "Senator George Wharton Pepper and Labor Issues in the 1920s." *Labor History*, Vol 9 (1968), 163-83.

American Labor and International Affairs

2212 ABELLA, I. M. "The CIO, the Communist Party and the Formation of the Canadian Congress of Labour, 1936-1941." *Historical Papers*, Canadian Historical Association, (1969), 112-28.

2213 ADAMS, R. J. "Canada-United States Labor Link under Stress." *Industrial Relations*, Vol 15 (1976), 295-312.

2214 AFL-CIO. RESEARCH DEPARTMENT. *AFL-CIO Looks at Foreign Trade: A Policy for the Sixties*. Wash.: The Department, 1961.

2215 "AFL-CIO Merger Seen Strengthening the ICFTU." *Industrial Bulletin*, Feb 1956, pp 12-13.

2216 ALEXANDER, ROBERT J. "International Labor Groups in the Americas." *Labor Law Journal*, Vol 13 (1962), 507-15.

2217 ———. "Labor and Inter-American Relations." *The Annals of the American Academy of Political and Social Science*, Vol 334, Mar 1961, pp 41-53.

2218 AMERICAN FEDERATION OF LABOR. *Labor and the War: American Federation of Labor and the Labor Movements of Europe and Latin America*. Wash.: A. F. of L., 1918.

2219 ———. Free Trade Union Committee *American Labor Looks at the World.*, Vols 1-9. NY: Free Trade Union Committee, 1947-55.

2220 AMERICAN INSTITUTE FOR FREE LABOR DEVELOPMENT. *A Union to Union Program for the Americas*. Wash.: The Institute, 1979.

2221 *American Laborer Devoted to the Cause of Protection to Home Industry*. NY: Greeley & Moblrath, 1843.

2222 ARNOW, PHILIP. "Foreign Trade and Collective Bargaining." *Monthly Labor Review*, Vol 83 (1960), 693-99.

2223 BARKIN, SOLOMON. "European Industrial Relations: a Resource for the Reconstruction of the American System." *Relations Industrielles-Industrial Relations*, Vol 35 (1980), 439-46.

2224 ———. "Labor's Position on Tariff Reduction." *Industrial Relations*, Vol 1 (1962), 49-63.

2225 BEIGBEDER, YVES. "The U.S. Withdrawal from the I.L.O." *Relations Industrielles-Industrial Relations*, Vol 34 (1979), 223-40.

2226 BERGER, HENRY. "American Labor Overseas." *The Nation*, Jan 16, 1967.

2227 ———. *Union Diplomacy: American Labor's Foreign Policy in Latin America, 1932-1955*. Ph D diss, U of Wisconsin, 1966.

2228 ———. "Unions and Empire: Organized Labor and American Corporations Abroad." *Peace and Change*, Vol 3 (Spring 1976), 34-48.

2229 BERKOWITZ, MONROE. "Labor's International Relations." *Proceedings of the Conference on Labor, New York University*, NY, 1961, pp 239-59.

2230 BRUCKNER, MOLLY ACREMAN. *The Role of Labor in the Conduct of United States Foreign Affairs.* Ph D diss, U of Chicago, 1950.

2231 CARWELL, JOSEPH. *The International Role of American Labor.* Ph D diss, Columbia U, 1956.

2232 CHAIKIN, SOL C. *A Labor Viewpoint: Another Opinion.* NY: Library Research Associates, 1980.

2233 COPP, ROBERT. "The Labor Affairs Function in a Multinational Firm." *Labor Law Journal,* Vol 24 (Aug 1973), 453-58.

2234 CORNELL UNIVERSITY. NY STATE SCHOOL OF INDUSTRIAL AND LABOR RELATIONS. *American Labor's Role in Less Developed Countries: AS Report on a Conference Held at Cornell University, October 12-17, 1958.* Ithaca: The School, 1959.

2235 COX, ROBERT W. "Labor and the Multinationals." *Foreign Affairs,* Vol 54 (1976), 344-65.

2236 ———. "Labor and Transnational Relations." *International Organization,* Vol 25 (1971), 554-84.

2237 CREGAN, JAMES F. "Public Law 78: a Tangle of Domestic and International Relations." *Journal of Inter-American Studies,* Vol 7 (1965), 541-56. (The bracero question)

2238 DALE, L. "La Participation du Mouvement Syndical Americain a l'establissement de l'Organisation internationale du travail." *Relations Industrielles-Industrial Relations,* Quebec, Vol 17 (1962), 34-42.

2239 DAVIES, MARGARET M. *The Role of the American Trade Union Representatives in the Aid-to-Greece Program.* Ph D diss, U of Washington, 1960.

2240 DELANEY, GEORGE P. "American Federation of Labor's International Activities." *Proceedings of the Fourth Annual Meeting of the Industrial Relations Research Association,* Dec 28-29, 1951, pp 86-95. Madison: IRRA, 1952.

2241 DERBER, MILTON. "Collective Bargaining, Mutuality, and Workers Participation in Management: an International Analysis." *Relations Industrielles-Industrial Relations,* Vol 35 (1980), 187-201.

2242 DUBINSKY, DAVID. "Rift and Realignment in World Labor." *Foreign Affairs,* Vol 27 (1949), 232-45.

2243 EDELMAN, MURRAY. "Labor's Influence in Foreign Policy." *Labor Law Journal,* May 1954, pp 323-29.

2244 FINE, MARTIN. "Syndicalisme et Reformisme: Samuel Gompers et le Mouvement Ouvrier Francais (1918-1919)." *Mouvement Social,* No 53 (1969), 3-33.

2245 FINGER, ELEANOR. "Labor and European Recovery," chap. 12, *The House of Labor,* J. B. S. Hardman & Maurice F. Neufeld, eds. NY: Prentice-Hall, 1951.

2246 FONER, PHILIP S. *American Labor and the Indochina War: The Growth of Union Opposition.* NY: International, 1971.

2247 GERSHMAN, CARL. *The Foreign Policy of American Labor.* Wash.: Center for Strategic and International Studies, Georgetown U, 1975.

2248 GIBSON, DONALD E. *Multinationals and Socialism in the United States.* Ph D diss, U of Delaware, 1979.

2249 GODSON, ROY. "The AFL Foreign Policy Making Process from the End of World War II to the Merger." *Labor History,* Vol 16 (1975), 325-37.

2250 ———. *American Labor and European Politics: The AFL as a Transnational Force.* NY: Crane, Russak, 1976.

2251 ———. "American Labor's Continuing Involvement in World Affairs." *Orbis,* Vol 19 (1975), 93-116.

2252 ———. *Non-Governmental Organizations in International Politics: the A. F. of L., the International Labor Movement, and French Politics, 1945-1952.* Ph D diss, Columbia U, 1976.

2253 GOMBERG, WILLIAM. "Labor's Participation in the European Productivity Program: A Study of Frustration." *Political Science Quarterly,* Vol 74 (1959), 240-55.

2254 GOMPERS, SAMUEL. *Seventy Years of Life and Labor*. NY: Dutton, 1925. (See Vol 2, chaps. 17 & 37-46)

2255 GORDON, GERALD RUSSELL. *The AFL, the CIO, and the Quest for a Peaceful World Order, 1914-1946*. Ph D diss, U of Maine, 1967.

2256 "Government and Labor Abroad." *Current History*, Vol 37 (Aug 1959), 65-100.

2257 HARDY, MARGARET. *The Influence of Organized Labor on the Foreign Policy of the United Staes*. Liege, Belgium: H. Vaillant-Carmanne, 1936.

2258 HEAPS, DAVID. "Union Participation in Foreign Aid Programs." *Industrial and Labor Relations Review*, Vol 9 (1955), 100-8.

2259 HENDLEY, WILLIAM J. "American Labor and World Affairs." *The Annals of the American Academy of Political and Social Science*, Vol 274, Mar 1951, pp 131-38.

2260 HERLING, JOHN. "U.S. Labor vs. Khrushchev." *The New Leader*, Oct 5, 1959, pp 7-10.

2261 HERO, ALFRED O. *The Reuther-Meany Foreign Policy Dispute*. NY: Oceana Publication, 1970.

2262 ———. *The UAW and World Affairs*. Bost: World Peace Foundation, 1965.

2263 HILDEBRAND, GEORGE H. "Organized Labor and Foreign Trade." *Proceedings of the Twenty-Fourth Annual Winter Meeting of the Industrial Relations Research Association*, Dec 27-28, 1971, pp 2-13. Madison: IRRA, 1972.

2264 ———. "Unions, Devaluation, and Foreign Trade." *Monthly Labor Review*, Vol 95 (Apr 1972), 15-18.

2265 JACOBSON, H. R. "Labor, the U.N. and the Cold War." *International Organization*, Vol 11 (1957), 55-67.

2266 KAISER, PHILIP. "American Labor in International Affairs." *Proceedings of the Fourth Annual Meeting of the Industrial Relations Research Association*, Dec 28-29, 1951, pp 100-9. Madison: IRRA, 1952.

2267 KOSHIRO, KAZUTOSHI. "Labor and the Multinationals: A View from Japan." *Japan Labor Bulletin*, Vol 14 (1975), 5-8.

2268 KUJAWA, DUANE, ed. *American Labor and the Multinational Corporation*. NY: Praeger, 1973.

2269 "Labor's Role Abroad." *Fortune*, Jan 1957, pp 186-88.

2270 LARSON, SIMEON. *Labor and Foreign Policy: Gompers, the AFL, and the First World War, 1914-1918*. Cranbury, NJ: Fairleigh Dickinson U Press, 1975.

2271 LASSER, DAVID. "Labor and World Affairs." *Foreign Policy Reports*, Nov 15, 1949.

2272 LAWRENCE, JAMES R. "The American Federation of Labor and the Philippine Independence Question, 1920-1935." *Labor History*, Vol 7 (1966), 62-69.

2273 LENBURG, LEROY JONES. *The CIO and American Foreign Policy, 1934-1955*. Ph D diss, Pennsylvania State U, 1973.

2274 LEUCK, MIRIAM SIMONS. *The American Socialist and Labor Mission to Europe 1918; Background, Activities and Significance: An Experiment in Democratic Diplomacy*. Ph D diss, Northwestern U, 1941.

2275 LEVENSTEIN, HARVEY A. "The AFL and Mexican Immigration in the 1920s: An Experiment in Labor Diplomacy." *Hispanic American Historical Review*, Vol 48 (1968), 206-19.

2276 ———. *Labor Organizations in the United States and Mexico: A History of Their Relations*. Westport, CT: Greenwood, 1971.

2277 ———. *The United States Labor Movement and Mexico, 1910-1951*. Ph D diss, U of Wisconsin, 1966.

2278 LITVAK, I. A., and C. J. MAULE. "The Union Response to International Corporations." *Industrial Relations*, Vol 11 (1972), 62-71.

2279 LODGE, GEORGE C. *Spearheads of Democracy: Labor in the Developing Countries*. NY: Harper and Row, 1962.

2280 LORWIN, LEWIS L. *The International Labor Movement*. NY: Harper, 1953.

2281 ———. *Labor and Internationalism*. NY: Macmillan, 1929.

2282 LORWIN, VAL R. "Labor's International Relations," chap. 11, *The House of Labor*, J. B. S. Hardman & Maurice F. Neufeld, eds. NY: Prentice-Hall, 1951.

2283 LOVESTONE, JAY. "American Labor and the World Crisis." *Proceedings of the Ninth Annual Meeting of the Industrial Relations Research Association*, Dec 28-29, 1956, pp 50-66. Madison: IRRA, 1957.

2284 LYNCH, MARIE ELIZABETH, SISTER. *Labor and Tariff Issues in the Majority Party Platforms, 1900-1932.* Wash.: Catholic U of America Press, 1953.

2285 MCCARTHY, JAMES E. "Contrasting Experiences with Trade Adjustment Assistance." *Monthly Labor Review*, Vol 98 (Jun 1975), 25-30.

2286 MCKEE, DELBER L. *The American Federation of Labor and American Foreign Policy*. Ph D diss, Stanford U, 1953.

2287 ———. "Samuel Gompers, the A. F. of L., and Imperialism, 1895-1900." *The Historian*, Vol 21 (1959), 197-99.

2288 MADDOX, WILLIAM P. "Labor's Stake in American Foreign Policy." *Political Science Quarterly*, Vol 50 (1935), 405-18.

2289 MANGOLD, GEORGE B. *The Labor Argument in the American Protective Tariff Discussion.* Madison: U of Wisconsin, 1908.

2290 MECHLING, T. B. "Can Labor Cope with Multi-Nationals?" *Business and Society Review*, Vol 17 (1980), 4-9. (Interview with W. Winpisinger)

2291 MITCHELL, DANIEL J. B. *Essays on Labor and International Trade*. Los Angeles: Institute of Industrial Relations, U of California, 1970.

2292 ———. "Labor and the Tariff Question." *Industrial Relations*, Vol 9 (1970), 268-76.

2293 MOLLENHOFF, CLARK R. "What United States Labor and Management Can Contribute Abroad." *Labor Law Journal*, Jul 1962, pp 520-24.

2294 MOREHOUSE, WARD, ed. *American Labor in a Changing World.* NY: Praeger, 1978.

2295 MORRIS, GEORGE. *The CIA and American Labor: The Subversion of the AFL-CIO's Foreign Policy*. NY: International, 1967.

2296 MORSE, DAVID A. "Labor and American Foreign Policy." *Industrial and Labor Relations Review*, Vol 1 (1947), 18-28.

2297 MURPHY, ROBERT D. "Labor's Concern with Foreign Affairs." *Department of State Bulletin*, Vol 32 (Jan 1955), 84-91.

2298 NEWBOUND, GERALD D., and PETER BUCKLEY. "Collective Bargaining in the Conglomerate Multinational Firm: Litton's Shutdown of Imperial Typewriter." *Labor Studies Journal*, Vol 4 (1979), 109-18.

2299 OSTROWER, GARY B. "The American Decision to Join the International Labor Organization." *Labor History*, Vol 16 (1975), 495-504.

2300 POLISHOOK, S. S. "American Federation of Labor, Zionism, the First World War." *American Jewish Historical Quarterly*, Vol 65 (1976), 228-44.

2301 POLLIN, ROBERT. "The Multinational Mineral Industry in Crisis." *Monthly Review*, Vol 31 (Apr 1980), 245-37.

2302 RADOSH, RONALD. *American Labor and United States Foreign Policy*. NY: Random House, 1969.

2303 REPAS, ROBERT. "Laborites Look at World Issues." *Labor and Nation*, Fall, 1951, pp 44-46.

2304 RICHE MARTHA F. "The American Institute for Free Labor Development: A Catalyst for Latin American Labor Through Union Lender Training and Social Projects Sponsorship." *Monthly Labor Review*, Vol 83 (Sep 1965), 1049-55.

2305 ROMUALDI, SERAFINO. *Presidents and Peons: Recollections of a Labor Ambassador in Latin America*. NY: Funk and Wagnalls, 1967.

2306 ROSS, MICHAEL. "American Labor's World Responsibilities." *Foreign Affairs*, Vol 30 (1951), 112-22.

2307 ———. "American Unions and West European Recovery." *Proceedings of the Fourth Annual Meeting of hte Industrial Relations Research Association*, Dec 28-29, 1951, pp 94-99. Madison: IRRA, 1952.

2308 ROTONDARO, RUBEN O. J. *The American Federation of Labor Policies Toward Latin America in the Time of Gompers.* MS thesis, Cornell U, 1963.

2309 SCOTT, JACK. *Yankee Unions, Go Home: How the AFL Helped the U.S. Build an Empire in Latin America.* Vancouver: New Star, 1978.

2310 SEIDMAN, BERT. "ILO Accomplishments—Organized Labor's View." *Monthly Labor Review*, Vol 98 (May 1975), 37-39.

2311 SHELTON, WILLIAM C. "The Changing Attitude of U.S. Labor Unions Toward World Trade." *Monthly Labor Review*, Vol 93 (May 1970), 51-54.

2312 SILVER, A. HITCHCOCK. *U.S. Labor and Europe.* Los Angeles: MacGuffin Press, 1945.

2313 SMITSENDONK, ANTON G. O. *Trade and Labor: Two American Policies.* NY: Vantage, 1971.

2314 SNOW, SINCLAIR. *The Pan-American Federation of Labor.* Durham, NC: Duke U Press, 1965.

2315 ———. *Samuel Gompers and the Pan-American Federation of Lasbor.* Ph D diss, U of Virginia, 1960.

2316 STURMTHAL, ADOLF. "The Labor Movement Abroad," chap. 6, *A Decade of Industrial Relations Research 1945-1956*, Neil Chamberlain et al, eds. NY: Harper, 1958.

2317 TAFT, PHILIP. *Defending Freedom: American Labor and Foreign Affairs.* Los Angeles: Nash, 1973.

2318 ———. "Is Labor Really the Villain in the Foreign Trade Story?" *Columbia Journal of World Business*, Vol 1 (1966), 97-101.

2319 TIPTON, JOHN B. *Participation of the United States in the International Labor Organization.* MS thesis, U of Illinois, 1959.

2320 TORRENCE, DONALD. *American Imperialism and Latin American Labor, 1959-1970: a Study of the Role of the Organizacion Regional Inter-Americana de Trabajadores in the Latin American Policy of the U.S.* Ph D diss, Northern Illinois U, 1976.

2321 TOTH, CHARLES W. "The Pan American Federation of Labor: Its Political Nature." *Western Political Quarterly*, Vol 18 (1965), 615-20.

2322 ———. "Samuel Gompers, Communism, and the Pan American Federation of Labor." *The Americas*, Vol 23 (1967), 273-78.

2323 ULMAN, LLOYD. "Multinational Unionism: Incentives, Barriers, and Alternatives." *Industrial Relations*, Vol 14 (1975), 1-31.

2324 U.S. CONGRESS. HOUSE. Committee on Ways and Means. Subcommittee on Trade. *Trade Adjustment Assistance for Workers, Firms, and Communities.* Wash.: G.P.O., 1981.

2325 VAN DER SLICE, AUSTIN. *International Labor, Diplomacy and Peace, 1914-1919.* Phila.: U of Pennsylvania, 1941.

2326 WEILER, PETER. "The U.S., International Labor, and the Cold War: the Breakup of the World Federation of Trade Unions." *Diplomatic History*, Vol 5 (1981), 1-22.

2327 WHITTAKER, WILLIAM GEORGE. "The Santiago Iglesias Case, 1901-1902: Origins of American Trade Union Involvement in Puerto Rico." *The Americas*, Vol 24 (1968), 378-93.

2328 WILLIAMS, CHARLES BRIAN. *Canadian-American Trade Union Relations—A Study of the Development of Binational Unionism.* Ph D diss, Cornell U, 1964.

2329 ———. "Development of Relations between Canadian and American National Trade Union Centers—1886-1925." *Relations Industrielles-Industrial Relations*, Vol 20 (1965), 340-71.

2330 WINDMULLER, JOHN P. *American Labor and the International Labor Movement 1940 to 1953.* Ithaca: The Institute of International Industrial and Labor Relations, Cornell U, 1954.

2331 ———. "Foreign Affairs and the AFL-CIO." *Industrial and Labor Relations Review*, Vol 9 (1956), 419-32.

2332 ———. "The Foreign Policy Conflict in American Labor." *Political Science Quarterly*, Vol 82 (1967), 205-34.

2333 ———. "ICFTU After Ten Years: Problems and Prospects." *Industrial and Labor Relations Review*, Vol 14 (1961), 257-72.

2334 ———. "Labor: A Partner in American Foreign Policy?" *Annals of the American Academy of Political and Social Science*, Vol 350 (1963), 104-14.

Leadership

General

2335 Bakke, E. Wight. "Union Leadership and the Public Interest." *Proceedings of the Twenty-First Annual Winter Meeting of the Industrial Relations Research Association*, Dec 29-30, 1968, pp 173-82, 192-94. Madison: IRRA, 1969.

2336 Barbash, Jack. "Perspectives on the Problems of Union Leadership: Introduction." *Proceedings of the Twenty-First Annual Winter Meeting of the Industrial Relations Research Association*, Dec 29-30, 1968, pp 167-72. Madison: IRRA, 1969.

2337 ———. "Prospects for Future Union Growth—The Union Leadership Factor." *Proceedings of the Fifteenth Annual Meeting of the Industrial Relations Research Association*, Dec 27-28, 1962, pp 208-18. Madison: IRRA, 1963.

2338 Barbash, Jack, ed. *Unions and Union Leadership: Their Human Meaning*. NY: Harper, 1959.

2339 Benson, H. W. "Labor Leaders, Intellectuals, and Freedom in the Unions." *Dissent*, 20 (1973), 206-19.

2340 Conway, Jack T. "Challenges to Union Leadership in an Era of Change." *Proceedings of the Twenty-First Annual Winter Meeting of the Industrial Relations Research Association*, Dec 29-30, 1968, pp 183-91. Madison: IRRA, 1969.

2341 Cook, Roy A. P. *Leaders of Labor*. Phila.: Lippincott, 1966.

2342 England, George W. et al. "Union Leaders and Managers: A Comparison of Value Systems." *Industrial Relations*, Vol 19 (1971), 211-26.

2343 Fink, Gary M., ed. *Biographical Dictionary of American Labor Leaders*. Westport, CT: Greenwood, 1974.

2344 Friedman, Abraham. *The Leaders of National and International Labor Unions*. Ph D diss, U of Chicago, 1969.

2345 Gaer, Joseph. *Our Lives: American Labor Stories*. NY: Boni & Gaer, 1948.

2346 Ginzberg, Eli. *The Labor Leader: An Exploratory Study*. NY: Macmillan, 1948.

2347 Gouldner, Alvin W., ed. *Studies in Leadership: Leadership and Democratic Action*. NY: Harper, 1950.

2348 Herberg, Will. "Bureaucracy and Democracy in Labor Unions." *Antioch Review*, Fall, 1943.

2349 Imberman, A. A. "Labor Leaders and Society." *Harvard Business Review*, Vol 28 (1950), 52-60.

2350 Kelly, Richard. *Nine Lives for Labor*. NY: Praeger, 1956.

2351 Kirshbaum, Louis. *America's Labor Dictators*. NY: Industrial Forum, 1940.

2352 Licht, Walter, and Hal Seth Barron. "Labor's Men: A Collective Biography of Union Officialdom During the New Deal Years." *Labor History*, Vol 19 (1978), 532-45.

2353 MacDonald, Lois. et al. *Leadership Dynamics and the Trade-Union Leader*. NY: New York U Press, 1959.

2354 McNeill, George E. *The Labor Movement: The Problem of Today*. Bost.: A. M. Bridgman, 1887. (See Appendix, pp 617-27, biographies of labor leaders, 1880-1890)

2355 Madison, Charles A. *American Labor Leaders: Personalities and Forces in the Labor Movement*. NY: Harper, 1950.

2356 Miles, Raymond E., and J. B. Ritchie. "Leadership Attitudes Among Union Officials." *Industrial Relations*, Vol 8 (1968), 108-17.

2357 Miller, Robert W. et al. *The Practice of Local Union Leadership: A Study of Five Local Unions*. Columbus: Ohio State U Press, 1965.

2358 Mills, C. Wright. *The New Men of Power: America's Labor Leaders*. NY: Harcourt, Brace, 1948.

2359 Minton, Bruce (Richard Bransten, pseud.), and John Stuart. *Men Who Lead Labor*. NY: Modern Age Books, 1937.

2360 National Planning Association. *Why I Am a Member of the Labor Movement, by 15 Labor Leaders*., Special Report No 20. Wash.: The Association, 1949. (Solomon Barkin, James B. Carey,l Nelson H. Cruikshank, Katherine P. Ellickson, Frank P. Fenton, Sander Genis, Clinton Golden, Marion H. Hedges, Carl Holderman, Eric Peterson, Samuel E. Roper, Ted F. Silvey,l William S. Townsend, Edward H. Weyler, Arnold S. Zander)

2361 Peck, Sidney M. *The Rank and File Leader*. New Haven: College & University Press, 1963.

2362 Petro, Sylvester. *Power Unlimited: The Corruption of Union Leadership: A Report on the McClellan Committee Hearings*. NY: Ronald Press, 1959.

2363 Phelps, Orme W. "Community Recognition of Union Leaders." *Industrial and Labor Relations Review*, Vol 7 (1954), 419-33.

2364 Radosh, Ronald. *The Development of the Corporate Ideology of American Labor Leaders, 1914-1933*. Ph D diss, U of Wisconsin, 1967.

2365 Rischin, Moses. "From Gompers to Hillman: Labor Goes Middle Class." *Antioch Review*, Summer 1953, pp 191-201.

2366 Seidman, Harold. *Labor Czars: A History of Labor Racketeering*. NY: Liveright, 1938.

2367 ———. et al. "Leadership in a Local Union." *American Journal of Sociology*., Vol 56 (1950), 229-37.

2368 Selekman, Ben M. "Wanted: Mature Labor Leaders." *Harvard Business Review*, Vol 24 (1946), 405-26.

2369 Sorokin, Pitirim A. "Leaders of Labor and Radical Movements in the United States and Foreign Countries." *American Journal of Sociology*, Vol 33 (1927), 382-411.

2370 Stanley, Louis. "A Cross-Section of American Labor Leadership," Appendix 3, *American Labor Dynamics*, J. B. S. Hardman, ed. NY: Harcourt, Brace, 1928.

2371 "Ten Who Deliver." *Fortune*, Nov 1946, pp 146-51.

2372 U.S. Bureau of Labor Statistics. *Case Studies in Union Leadership Training, 1951-1952*., Bulletin 1114. Wash.: G.P.O., 1952.

2373 Van Tine, Warren R. *The Making of the Labor Bureaucrat: Union Leadership in the United States, 1870-1920*. Amherst: U of Massachusetts Press, 1973.

2374 Walton, Richard E. "Leadership Strategies for Achieving Membership Consensus During Negotiations." *Proceedings of the Eighteenth Annual Winter Meeting of the Industrial Relations Research Association*, Dec 28-29, 1965, pp 99-110. Madison: IRRA, 1966.

2375 *Who's Who in Labor: The Authorized Biographies of the Men and Women Who Lead Labor in the United States and Canada and of Those Who Deal with Labor*. NY: Dryden, 1946.

2376 Won, George. "Local Union Leadership Orientation and Union Democracy." *Canadian Review of Sociology and Anthropology*, Vol 1 (1964), 103-14.

Individual Leaders (Male)

2377 ABEL, I. W. Herling, John. "Labor's New Voice." *The New Leader*, Jun 21, 1965, pp 13-18.

2378 AMERINGER, OSCAR. Meredith, H. L. "Oscar Ameringer and the Concept of Agrarian Socialism." *Chronicles of Oklahoma*, Vol 45 (1967), 77-83.

2379 ANTONINI, LUIGI. "Luigi Antonini: A Half Century Recalled." *Industrial Bulletin*, Vol 43 (Apr 1964), 2-5.

2380 ———. "Luigi Antonini Is Dead at 85: Leader in Union and Politics." *The New York Times*, Dec 30, 1968, p 31.

2381 ———. Crawford, John S. *Luigi Antonini: His Influence on Italian-American Relations*. NY: International Ladies' Garment Workers' Union, Local 89, 1950.

2382 BALDANZI, GEORGE. "George Baldanzi of Textile Union. President Since 1958 Dies—Began as Miner at 16." *The New York Times*, Apr 18, 1972, p 46.

2383 BECK, DAVE. "President Pardons Dave Beck." *The New York Times*, May 24, 1975, p 14.

2384 ———. "Teamsters' Dave Beck." *Fortune*, Dec 1948, 191-98.

2385 ———. Hass, Eric. *Dave Beck, Labor Merchant*. NY: NY Labor News Co., 1955.

2386 ———. McCallum, John D. *Dave Beck*. Mercer Island, WA: Writing Works, 1978.

2387 ———. Miller, Joe. "Dave Beck Comes Out of the West." *The Reporter*, Dec 8, 1953, pp 20-23.

2388 BEIRNE, JOSEPH A. Naughton, James M. "A Forward-Looking Union Leader: Joseph Anthony Beirne." *The New York Times*, Jul 15, 1971, p 21.

2389 ———. Weisman, Steven K. "Joseph A. Beirne of Phone Union Dies." *The New York Times*, Sep 3, 1974, p 34.

2390 BELLANCA, AUGUST. "August Bellanca Is Dead at 89: Helped Found Clothing Union." *The New York Times*, Nov 14, 1969, p 47.

2391 BIEMILLER, ANDREW J. "Andrew J. Biemiller Dies at 75; Was AFL-CIO's Top Lobbyist." *The New York Times*, Apr 4, 1982, p 36.

2392 BILLINGS, WARREN K. "Warren K. Billings, '16 Blast Figure Freed with Mooney in 1939, Is Dead." *The New York Times*, Sep 5, 1972, p 34.

2393 BISNO, ABRAHAM. *Abraham Bisno, Union Pioneer: An Autobiographical Account of Bisno's Early Life and the Beginnings of Unionism in the Women's Garment Industry*. Madison: U of Wisconsin Press, 1967.

2394 BLUESTONE, IRVING. "Director of Union's G.M. Section: Irving Bluestone." *The New York Times*, Sep 17, 1970, p 80.

2395 BOLAND, JOHN P. "Msgr. Boland, 80, The Labor Priest. First Head of State Labor Relations Board Is Dead." *The New York Times*, Jul 2, 1968, p 41.

2396 BOMMARITO, PETER. "Leader of Rubber Strike: Peter Bommarito." *The New York Times*, Apr 22, 1976, p 26.

2397 BOWERS, MICHAEL. "Mickey Bowers, Led I.L.A. Local: Ex-Convict and Enforcer on Waterfront a Crash Victim." *The New York Times*, Jun 29, 1966, p 41.

2398 BOYLE, WILLIAM A. "Mine Union Victor: William Anthony Boyle." *The New York Times*, Dec 11, 1969, p 28.

2399 BRADLEY, WILLIAM V. "William Bradley, Dock Union Head—President of Longshoremen 10 Years Dies in Crash." *The New York Times*, Apr 25, 1973, p 40.

2400 BRENNAN, PETER JOSEPH. "A Patriotic Union Man at Head of Labor Department: Peter Joseph Brennan." *The New York Times*, Nov 30, 1972, p 37.

2401 BRIDGES, HARRY. Larrowe, Charles P. *Harry Bridges: The Rise and Fall of Radical Labor in the United States*. NY: L. Hill, 1972.

2402 ———. Ledbetter, Les. "Harry Bridges Ends his Last Convention: Two Candidates Are Nominated to Succeed the Longshore Leader After 40 Years at Helm." *The New York Times*, Apr 24, 1977, p 23.

2403 ———. Schwartz, Harvey. "Harry Bridges and the Scholars Looking at History's Verdict." *California History*, Vol 59 (1980), 66-79.

2404 BROPHY, JOHN. *A Miner's Life: An Autobiography*. Madison: U of Wisconsin Press, 1964.

2405 ———. Mullay, M. Camilla, Sister. *John Brophy, Militant Labor Leader and Reformer: The CIO Years*. Ph D diss, Catholic U of America, 1966.

2406 BROUN, HEYWOOD. Moreau, John A. "The Often Enraged Heywood." *Journalism Quarterly*, Vol 44 (1967), 497-507.

2407 ———. O'Connor, Richard. *Heywood Broun: A Biography*. NY: Putnam, 1975.

2408 BROWN, ELMER. "Elmer Brown of the I.T.U. Dies; President of Union for 10 Years." *The New York Times*, Feb 28, 1968, p 43.

2409 BUCHANAN, JOSEPH R. *The Story of a Labor Agitator*. NY: Outlook, 1903.

2410 ———. Marlatt, Gene. *Joseph R. Buchanan: Spokesman for Labor during the Populist and Progressive Eras*. Ph D diss, U of California, 1976.

2411 BUCKMASTER, L. S. "L. S. Buckmaster, Union Chief, Dies: Leader of Rubber Workers from 1945 to 1960." *The New York Times*, Jan 4, 1967, p 39.

2412 BURKE, JOHN P. "John P. Burke, 82, Led Pulp Laborers." *The New York Times*, Apr 26, 1966, p 41.

2413 BURNS, MATTHEW J. "Matthew J. Burns, Headed Paper Union." *The New York Times*, Jun 20, 1967, p 35.

2414 CASSESE, JOHN J. "John J. Cassese, 64, Converted City's P.B.A. 'Into a Labor Union'." *The New York Times*, Jun 11, 1977, p 22.

2415 CHAIKIN, SOL CHICK. Stetson, Damon. "New I.L.G.W.U. Head: Sol Chick Chaikin." *The New York Times*, May 30, 1975, p 52.

2416 CHATMAN, ABRAHAM. "He's Called 'Mr. Labor'." *Times Union*, (Rochester, NY), Jun 19, 1982, pp 4-5.

2417 CHAVEZ, CESAR. Day, Mark. *Forty Acres: Cesar Chavez and the Farm Workers*. NY: Praeger, 1971.

2418 ———. Fodell, Beverly. *Cesar Chavez and the United Farm Workers: A Selective Bibliography*. Detroit: Wayne State U Press, 1974.

2419 ———. Levy, Jacques E. *Cesar Chavez: Autobiography of La Causa*. NY: Norton, 1975.

2420 ———. Matthiessen, Peter. *Sal Si Puedes: Cesar Chavez and the New American Revolution*. NY: Random House, 1970.

2421 ———. Pitrone, Jean M. *Chavez, Man of the Migrants*. Staten Island, NY: Alba House, 1971.

2422 ———. Yinger, Winthrop. *Cesar Chavez: The Rhetoric of Nonviolence*. Hicksville, NY: Exposition, 1975.

2423 CLAESSENS, AUGUST. *Didn't We Have Fun!* NY: Rand School Press, 1953.

2424 COLLENS, T. WHARTON. Reinders, Robert C. "T. Wharton Collens and the Christian Labor Union." *Labor History*, Vol 8 (1967), 53-70.

2425 CONNOLLY, EUGENE P. "Eugene P. Connolly Dead at 70; Labor Figure Sat on City Council." *The New York Times*, Dec 2, 1971, p 50.

2426 CORRIDAN, JOHN M. Raymond, Allen. *Waterfront Priest*. NY: Holt, 1955.

2427 CROSSWAITH, FRANK. Marcus, Irwin M. "Frank Crosswaith: Black Socialist, Labor Leader, and Reformer." *Negro History Bulletin*, Vol 37 (1974), 287-88.

2428 ———. Walter, John C. "Frank R. Crosswaith and the Negro Labor Committee in Harlem, 1925-1939." *Afro-Americans in New York Life and History*, Vol 3 (Jul 1979), 35-49.

2429 CURRAN, JOSEPH. Bamberger, Werner. "Curran Retires as N.M.U. Head: Aide Is Named Acting President." *The New York Times*, Mar 6, 1973, p 70.

2430 ———. Barbanel, Josh. "Joseph Curran, 75, Founder of National Maritime Union." *The New York Times*, Aug 15, 1981, p 47.

2431 Daniel, Franz. Dodson, Ann Fair. "Death of Franz Daniel Is Widely Mourned." *Springfield (MO) Leader-Press*, Aug 20, 1976, p 15.

2432 Davis, Hal. Flint, Peter B. "Hal Davis, 63, Head of Musicians Union. Was Also an Arts Council Member and an A.F.L.-C.I.O. Official." *The New York Times*, Jan 13, 1978, p 82.

2433 Davis, James J. *The Iron Puddler: My Life in the Rolling Mills and What Came of It*. NY: Grosset & Dunlap, 1922.

2434 ———. Dudley, John Bruce. *James J. Davis: Secretary of Labor Under Three Presidents 1921-1930*. Ph D diss, Ball State U, 1972.

2435 Davis, Leon Julius. McFadden, Robert D. "Complex Chief of Hospital Union." *The New York Times*, Nov 10, 1973, p 32.

2436 De Andrade, Anthony J. "Anthony J. De Andrade Dead: President of Pressmen's Union." *The New York Times*, Jan 22, 1970, p 37.

2437 De Caux, Len. *Labor Radical: From the Wobblies to CIO, a Personal History*. Bost.: Beacon, 1970.

2438 Debs, Eugene V. "Eugene Victor Debs Birthday Issue." *Tamiment Institute Library Bulletin*, Dec 1960.

2439 ———. *Writings and Speeches of Eugene V. Debs*. NY: Hermitage, 1948.

2440 ———. Brommel, Bernard J. "Debs' Cooperative Commonwealth Plan for Workers." *Labor History*, Vol 12 (1971), 560-69.

2441 ———. ———. *Eugene V. Debs: Spokesman for Labor and Socialism*. Ph D diss, Indiana U, 1964.

2442 ———. ———. *Eugene V. Debs: Spokesman for Labor and Socialism*. Chicago: Charles H. Kerr, 1978.

2443 ———. ———. "Eugene V. Debs: the Agitator as Speaker." *Central States Speech Journal*, Vol 20 (1969), 202-14.

2444 ———. Corbin, David. "Betrayal in the West Virginia Coal Fields: Eugene Debs and the Socialist Party of America 1912-1914." *Journal of American History*, Vol 64 (1978), 987-1009.

2445 ———. Cumbler, John T., and Bernard J. Brommel. "Debs and the Social Democracy: An Exchange." *Labor History*, Vol 13 (1972), 615-21.

2446 ———. Currie, Harold W. *Eugene V. Debs*. Bost.: Twayne, 1976.

2447 ———. Fouts, Kenneth Burr. *Eugene V. Debs: Champion of Free Speech*. Ph D diss, Southern Illinois U, 1968.

2448 ———. Ginger, Ray. *The Bending Cross: A Biography of Eugene Victor Debs*. New Brunswick, NJ: Rutgers U Press, 1949.

2449 ———. Kaufman, Murray. *The Image of Eugene V. Debs in the American Popular Mind: 1894-1926*. Ph D diss, Carnegie-Mellon U, 1981.

2450 ———. Morgan, H. Wayne. *Eugene V. Debs, Socialist for President*. Syracuse, NY: Syracuse U Press, 1962.

2451 ———. Nissenson, Aaron. *Song of Man: A Novel Based Upon the Life of Eugene V. Debs*. New Haven: Whittier, 1964.

2452 ———. Noble, Iris. *Labor's Advocate, Eugene V. Debs*. NY: Messner, 1966.

2453 ———. Oestreicher, Richard. "A Note of the Origins of Eugene V. Debs' 'Bending cross' Speech." *Indiana Magazine of Hisotry*, Vol 77 (1980), 55-56.

2454 ———. Radosh, Ronald. *Debs*. Englewood Cliffs, NJ: Prentice-Hall, 1971.

2455 ———. Salvatore, Nick. *Eugene V. Debs: Citizen and Socialist*. Urbana: U of Illinois Press, 1982.

2456 ———. ———. *A Generation in Transition: Eugene V. Debs and the Emergence of Modern Corporate America*. Ph D diss, U of California, 1978.

2457 ———. Selvin, David F. *Eugene Debs: Rebel, Labor Leader, Prophet. A Biography*. NY: Lothrop, Lee & Shepard, 1966.

2458 ———. Shannon, David A. "Eugene V. Debs: Conservative Labor Editor." *Indiana Magazine of History*, Vol 47 (1951), 357-64.

2459 ———. White, Anne Terry. *Eugene Debs: American Socialist.* NY: Lawrence Hill, 1974.

2460 DELANEY, GEORGE P. "Former OLA Director George Delaney Dies." *Front Lines,* Feb 24, 1972, p 3.

2461 DELEON, DANIEL. Buhle, Paul. "Daniel De Leon: Enigmatic Giant of the Left." *Reviews in American History,* Vol 8 (1980), 264-71.

2462 ———. DeLeon, Solon. "Daniel DeLeon Bibliography." *Tamiment Institute Library Bulletin,* Sep-Oct 1959.

2463 ———. Johnpoll, Bernard K. "A Note on Daniel DeLeon." *Labor History,* Vol 17 (1976), 606-12.

2464 ———. McKee, Don K. "Daniel De Leon: A Reappraisal." *Labor History,* Vol 1 (1960), 264-97.

2465 ———. Seretan, L. Glen. "Daniel De Leon as American." *Wisconsin Magazine of History,* Vol 61 (19978), 210-23.

2466 ———. ———. *Deniel DeLeon: The Odyssey of an American Marxist.* Cambr.: Harvard U Press, 1979.

2467 ———. Stevenson, James. "Daniel De Leon and European Socialism, 1890-1914." *Science & Society,* Vol 44 (1980), 199-223.

2468 ———. ———. *Daniel De Leon: the Relationship of Socialist Labor Party to European Marxism, 1890-1914.* Ph D diss, U of Wisconsin, 1978.

2469 ———. ———. "Letters to Daniel De Leon: The Intra-party Constituency for his Policy of Strict Party Discipline, 1896-1904." *Labor History,* Vol 18 (1977), 382-96.

2470 ———. Young, James D. "Daniel DeLeon and Anglo-American Socialism." *Labor History,* Vol 17 (1976), 239-50.

2471 DELURY, JOHN. Kleiman, Dena. "John DeLury, Union Chief, Dies: Sanitationmen's Leader 40 Years." *The New York Times,* Feb 13, 1980, p D17.

2472 DENNIS, CHARLES L. Smith, Robert M. "President of the Railway Clerks: Charles Leslie Dennis." *The New York Times,* Dec 11, 1970, p 36.

2473 DIETZ, PETER E. Fox, Mary Harrita. *Peter E. Dietz, Labor Priest.* Notre Dame, IN: Notre Dame Press, 1953.

2474 DINSKY, LAZAR. "Lazar Dinsky, 85, Poet and Fur Workers Organizer." *The New York Times,* Aug 22, 1976, p 40.

2475 DUBINSKY, DAVID. Dewey, John. *David Dubinsky: A Pictorial Biography.* NY: Inter-allied, 1951.

2476 ———. Hardman, J. B. S. "David Dubinsky, Labor Leader and Man." *Labor History,* Vol 9 (1968), Special Supplement, 69-81.

2477 ———. Jacobs, Paul. "David Dubinsky: Why his Throne Is Wobbling." *Harper's,* Dec 1962, pp 74-84.

2478 ———. Lubell, Samuel. "Dictator in Sheep's Clothing." *Saturday Evening Post,* Nov 19, 1949, pp 19-21, 66-72.

2479 ———. Oko, Dorothy Kuhn. "David Dubinsky and the I.L.G.W.U., A Selected Bibliography." *Labor History,* Vol 9 (1968), Special Supplement, 116-26.

2480 ———. Raskin, A. H. *David Dubinsky: A Life with Labor.* NY: Simon & Schuster, 1977.

2481 ———. ———. "Dubinsky: Herald of Change." *Labor History,* Vol 9 (1968), Special Supplement, 14-25.

2482 ———. Rich, J. C. "David Dubinsky: The Young Years." *Labor History,* Vol 9 (1968), Special Supplement, 5-13.

2483 ———. Taft, Philip. "David Dubinsky and the Labor Movement." *Labor History,* Vol 9 (1968), Special Supplement, 26-42.

2484 EDELMAN, JOHN W. "John W. Edelman, a Trade Unionist: Ex-Head of Senior Citizens Unit, Consumer Aide, Dies." *The New York Times,* Dec 28, 1971, p 33.

2485 ERVIN, CHARLES W. *Homegrown Liberal: the Autobiography of Charles Ervin.* NY: Dodd, 1954.

2486 EVANS, GEORGE H. Jeffrey, Newman. *The Social Origins of George Henry Evans, Workingman's Advocate*. MA thesis, Wayne State U, 1960.

2487 FAY, JOSEPH. "Joseph Fay Dead: Ex-Labor Leader." *The New York Times*, Aug 11, 1972, p 28.

2488 FEINBERG, ISRAEL. "Israel Feinberg (1887-1952)." *L.I.D. News Bulletin*, Vol 16 (Oct 1952), 3.

2489 FELDMAN, HARRY. "Harry Feldman, Led Deliverers. Second Head of Union Dies—Aide of Flushing News." *The New York Times*, Dec 10, 1971, p 46.

2490 FILBEY, FRANCIS. "Francis Filbey, President of Postal Workers Union, Dies in Washington at 69." *The New York Times*, May 19, 1977, p 38.

2491 FINLEY, MURRAY HOWARD. "Merged Union's Head: Murray Howard Finley." *The New York Times*, Jun 4, 1976, p A11.

2492 FITZMAURICE, DAVID J. "David J. Fitzmaurice Is Dead: Leader of Electrical Workers." *The New York Times*, Nov 14, 1982, p 48.

2493 ———. Raskin, A. H. "The Labor Scene: Unflappable Jogger a Key Man in G.E. Talks." *The New York Times*, May 21, 1976, p D5.

2494 FITZPATRICK, JOHN. Keiser, John H. *John Fitzpatrick and Progressive Unionism 1915-1925*. Ph D diss, Northwestern U, 1965.

2495 FITZSIMMONS, FRANK EDWARD. "Hoffa's Loyal Heir: Frank Edward Fitzsimmons." *The New York Times*, Jun 5, 1971, p 30.

2496 FLETCHER, BENJAMIN. Marcus, Irwin M. "Benjamin Fletcher: Black Labor Leader." *Negro History Bulletin*, Vol 35 (1972), 138-40.

2497 FLORE, EDWARD. Rubin, Jay, and M. J. OBERMEIER. *Growth of a Union: The Life and Times of Edward Flore*. NY: Historical Union Association, 1943.

2498 FOSCO, PETER. "Peter Fosco, 82, President of Laborers Union, Is Dead." *The New York Times*, Oct 28, 1975, p 34.

2499 FOSTER, FRANK KEYES. *The Evolution of a Trade Unionist*. Bost.: Allied Printing Trades Council, 1901.

2500 FOSTER, WILLIAM Z. *Misleaders of Labor*. Chicago: Trade Union Educational League, 1927.

2501 ———. *More Pages from a Worker's Life*. NY: American Institute for Marxist Studies, 1979.

2502 ———. *Pages from a Worker's Life*. NY: International, 1939.

2503 ———. Douglass, Paul F. *Six Upon the World*. Bost.: Little, Brown, 1954.

2504 ———. Lee, Mark Wilcox. *An Analysis of Selected Speeches of William Z. Foster During the Reconstruction Period of the Communist Party, U.S.A., 1945-1950*. Ph D diss, U of Washington, 1966.

2505 ———. Zipser, Arthur. *Workingclass Giant: the Life of William Z. Foster*. NY: International, 1981.

2506 FRASER, DOUGLAS A. "Beyond Collective Bargaining: Interview with Douglas Fraser." *Challenge*, Vol 22 (Mar-Apr 1979), 33-39.

2507 ———. "Mr. Fraser Takes Over." *The New York Times*, May 22, 1977, p E5.

2508 ———. Stevens, William K. "A Down-to-Earth Union Chief: Douglas Andrew Fraser." *The New York Times*, May 20, 1977, p 10.

2509 FRUMKIN, JACOB. "Jacob Frumkin, ORT Aide, was 91." *The New York Times*, Sep 29, 1971, p 34.

2510 FURUSETH, ANDREW. *Andrew Furuseth, A Bibliographical List*. Wash.: Library of Congress, 1942.

2511 ———. Axtell, Silas B., comp. *A Symposium on Andrew Furuseth*. New Bedford, MA: Darwin, 1948.

2512 ———. Johnson, Alvin S. "Andrew Furuseth." *New Republic*, Nov 11, 1916.

2513 ———. Rygg, A. N. "Andrew Furuseth." *American-Scandinavian Review*, Vol 26 (1938), 123-33.

2514 ———. Weintraub, Hyman G. *Andrew Furuseth: Emancipator of the Seamen.* Berkeley: U of California Press, 1959.

2515 GERMER, ADOLPH. "Adolph Germer, Union Aide, Dies." *The New York Times*, May 28, 1966, p 27.

2516 ———. Cary, Lorin Lee. "Adolph Germer and the 1890's Depression." *Illinois State Historical Society Journal*, Vol 68 (1975), 337-43.

2517 ———. ———. *Adolph Germer: From Labor Agitator to Labor Professional.* Ph D diss, U of Wisconsin, 1968.

2518 GOMPERS, SAMUEL. *The Liquid Fire.* 1966. (Documentary film about Gompers produced by the George Meany Foundation)

2519 ———. *Seventy Years of Life and Labor.*, 2 vols. NY: Dutton, 1925.

2520 ———. Babcock, Robert H. *Gompers in Canada: A Study in American Continentalism Before the First World War.* Toronto: U of Toronto Press, 1975.

2521 ———. Chasan, Will. *Samuel Gompers: Leader of American Labor.* NY: Praeger, 1971.

2522 ———. Cotkin, George B. "The Spencerian and Comtian Nexus in Gompers' Labor Philosophy: The Impact of Non-Marxian Evolutionary Thought." *Labor History*, Vol 20 (1979), 510-23.

2523 ———. Dick, William M. "Samuel Gompers and American Consensus." *Historical Papers*, Canadian Historical Association, 1969, 192-40.

2524 ———. Greenbaum, Fred. "The Social Ideas of Samuel Gompers." *Labor History*, Vol 7 (1966), 35-61.

2525 ———. Griffen, Clyde. "Christian Socialism Instructed by Gompers." *Labor History*, Vol 12 (1971), 195-213.

2526 ———. Harvey, Rowland H. *Samuel Gompers, Champion of the Toiling Masses.* Stanford: Stanford U, 1935.

2527 ———. Hughes, Rupert. *The Giant Wakes: A Novel about Samuel Gompers.* Los Angeles: Borden, 1950.

2528 ———. Kaufman, Stuart B. *Samuel Gompers and the Origins of the American Federation of Labor, 1848-1896.* Westport, CT: Greenwood, 1973.

2529 ———. Levenstein, Harvey A. "Samuel Gompers and the Mexican Labor Movement." *Wisconsin Magazine of History*, Vol 51 (1968), 155-63.

2530 ———. Livesay, Harold C. *Samuel Gompers and Organized Labor in America.* Bost.: Little, Brown, 1978.

2531 ———. Mandel, Bernard. *Samuel Gompers, a Biography.* Yellow Springs, OH: Antioch Press, 1963.

2532 ———. Mann, Arthur. "Gompers and the Irony of Racism." *Antioch Review*, Summer 1953, pp 203-14.

2533 ———. Reed, Louis S. *Labor Philosophy of Samuel Gompers.* NY: Columbia U Press, 1930.

2534 ———. Selvin, David F. *Sam Gompers: Labor's Pioneer.* NY: Abelard-Schuman, 1964.

2535 ———. Stearn, Gerald E. *Gompers.* Englewood Cliffs, NJ: Prentice-Hall, 1971.

2536 ———. Thorne, Florence C. *Samuel Gompers, American Statesman.* NY: Philosophical Library, 1957.

2537 ———. Toth, Charles W. "Samuel Gompers, World Peace, and the Pan-American Federation of Labor." *Caribbean Studies*, Vol 7 (Oct 1967), 59-64.

2538 ———. Weisberger, Bernard A. *Samuel Gompers.* Morristown, NJ: Silver Burdett, 1967.

2539 ———. Whittaker, William George. "Samuel Gompers, Anti-Imperialist." *Pacific Historical Review*, Vol 38 (1969), 429-45.

2540 ———. ———. "Samuel Gompers, Labor, and the Mexican-American Crisis of 1916: The Carrizal Incident." *Labor History*, Vol 17 (1976), 551-67.

2541 Gorman, Patrick E. Hanna, Hilton E., and Joseph Belsky. *Picket and the Pen: The Pat Gorman Story*. Yonkers, NY: American Institute of Social Science, 1960.

2542 ———. Raskin, A. H. "Old-Timer Moves Up at Butchers' Union." *The New York Times*, May 21, 1976, p D5.

2543 Gosser, Richard T. "Richard T. Gosser, Ex-Official of U.A.W. From Toledo, Dead." *The New York Times*, Dec 2, 1969, p 51.

2544 Gotbaum, Victor H. "Municipal Unionist." *The New York Times*, May 24, 1967, p 31.

2545 ———. Dembart, Lee. "Fiery Yet Quiet Chief: Victor Harry Gotbaum." *The New York Times*, Jul 12, 1975, p 9.

2546 Gray, Richard J. "Richard Gray, 79, Union Chief, Dies." *The New York Times*, May 3, 1966, p 47.

2547 Green, William. Danish, Max D. *William Green*. NY: Inter-Allied Publications, 1952.

2548 ———. Held, Adolph. *A Tribute to William Green*. NY: Jewish Labor Committee, 1952.

2549 Guinan, Matthew. "Firm T.W.U. Leader: Matthew Guinan." *The New York Times*, Dec 27, 1971, p 34.

2550 ———. "A Quiet, but Tough Union Leader: Matthew Guinan." *The New York Times*, Dec 30, 1969, p 31.

2551 Gunton, George. Blicksilver, Jack. "George Gunton: Pioneer Spokesman for a Labor-Big Business Entente." *Business History Review*, Vol 31 (1957), 1-22.

2552 Haggerty, Cornelius J. "C. J. Haggerty, 77, Labor Chief, Dies." *The New York Times*, Oct 13, 1971, p 48.

2553 Hardman, J. B. S. "J. B. S. Hardman, 85, Unionist, Is Dead. Ex-Editor of Advance Urged Labor to Widen Role." *The New York Times*, Jan 31, 1968.

2554 Harris, James Alexander. Maeroff, Gene I. "New Head of N.E.A.: James Alexander Harris." *The New York Times*, Jul 4, 1974, p 10.

2555 Harrison, George. "George Harrison, Union Head, Dies." *The New York Times*, Dec 3, 1968, p 47.

2556 Harrison, George M. Denton, Nixson. *History of the Brotherhood of Railway & Steamship Clerks, Freight Handlers, Express and Station Employees, with Emphasis on the Years in which George M. Harrison was President*. Cincinnati: George M. Harrison Biographical Committee, 1965.

2557 Hartman, Richard. Kennedy, Shawn G. "P.B.A.'s New Negotiator: Richard Hartman." *The New York Times*, Mar 11, 1978, p 35.

2558 Haywood, Allan S. "Allan S. Haywood of CIO Dies at 64." *The New York Times*, Feb 23, 1953, p 25.

2559 Haywood, William D. *Bill Haywood's Book*. NY: International, 1929.

2560 ———. Carlson, Peter. *Roughneck: The Life and Times of Big Bill Haywood*. NY: Norton, 1983.

2561 ———. Conlin, Joseph R. *Big Bill Haywood and the Radical Union Movement*. Syracuse: Syracuse U Press, 1969.

2562 ———. ———. "The Haywood Case: an Enduring Riddle." *Pacific Northwest Quarterly*, Vol 59 (1968), 23-32.

2563 ———. Grover, David H. *Debaters and Dynamiters: The Story of the Haywood Trial*. Corvallis: Oregon State U Press, 1964.

2564 ———. Koolsch, Charles F. *The Haywood Case*. Boise: Idaho Mining Assoc., 1946.

2565 ———. Palmer, Bryan D. "Big Bill Haywood's Defection to Russia and the IWW: Two Letters." *Labor History*, Vol 17 (1976), 271-78.

2566 ———. Preston, William. "Shall This Be All? U.S. Historians versus William D. Haywood, et al." *Labor History*, Vol 12 (1971), 435-53.

2567 Held, Adolph. "Adolph Held Dies: Labor Activist, 84." *The New York Times*, May 15, 1969, p 43.

2568 HELLER, PHILIP. "Phillip Heller, 65, Dies: Former Labor Official Was in Foreign Service." *The New York Times*, Dec 7, 1976, p 44.

2569 HILL, HERBERT. Hunter, Charlayne. "Month of Victories Marks Herbert Hill's 25th Year as N.A.A.C.P. Labor Director." *The New York Times*, Dec 17, 1974, p 21.

2570 HILL, JOE. *Joe Hill*. 1971. (Feature film produced & directed by Bo Widerberg.)

2571 ———. Ebner, Michael H. "'I Never Died': The Case of Joe Hill v. the Historians." *Labor History*, Vol 12 (1971), 139-43.

2572 ———. Foner, Philip S. *The Case of Joe Hill*. NY: International, 1966.

2573 ———. Foner, Philip S., ed. *The Letters of Joe Hill*. NY: Oak, 1965.

2574 ———. Smith, Gibbs M. *Joe Hill*. Salt Lake City: U of Utah Press, 1969.

2575 ———. Stavis, Barrie. *The Man Who Never Died: A Play about Joe Hill, with Notes on Joe Hill and his Times*. NY: Haven Press, 1954.

2576 ———. Stegner, Wallace. *The Preacher and the Slave* (a novel about Joe Hill). Bost.: Houghton Mifflin, 1950.

2577 HILLMAN, SIDNEY. Gould, Jean. *Sidney Hillman: Great American*. Bost.: Houghton, Mifflin, 1952.

2578 ———. Hardman, J. B. S., and LEN GIOVANNITTI. *Sidney Hillman: Labor Statesman*. NY: Amalgamated Clothing Workers of America, 1948.

2579 ———. Josephson, Matthew. *Sidney Hillman, Statesman of American Labor*. Garden City, NY: Doubleday, 1952.

2580 ———. Soule, George. *Sidney Hillman, Labor Statesman*. NY: Macmillan, 1939.

2581 HILLQUIT, MORRIS. Fox, Richard W. "The Paradox of 'Progressive Socialism': The Case of Morris Hillquit, 1901-1914." *American Quarterly*, Vol 26 (1974), 127-40.

2582 ———. Pratt, Norma F. *Morris Hillquit: A Political History of an American Jewish Socialist*. Westport, CT: Greenwood, 1979.

2583 ———. Yellowitz, Irwin. "Morris Hillquit: American Socialism and Jewish Concerns." *American Jewish History*, Vol 68 (1978), 163-88.

2584 HOCHMAN, JULIUS. "Julius Hochman of I.L.G.W.U. Dies." *The New York Times*, Mar 21, 1970, p 29.

2585 ———. Lyons, Eugene. "A Remarkable Union—And Union Leader." *Reader's Digest*, Vol 48 (Apr 1946), 52-55.

2586 HOFFA, JAMES R. "Ex-Investigator Says Hoffa Had Aid of Ehrlichman and Chotiner." *The New York Times*, Jan 18, 1973, p 22.

2587 ———. "Hoffa Ruled 'Presumed' Dead." *The New York Times*, Dec 10, 1982, p D17.

2588 ———. ———. *The Name Is Hoffa*. St. Louis: International Brotherhood of Teamsters, Joint Council No 13, 1956.

2589 ———. *The Trials of Jimmy Hoffa, an Autobiography*. Chicago: Regnery, 1970.

2590 ———. Brill, Steven. *The Teamsters*. NY: Simon & Schuster, 1978.

2591 ———. Clay, James. *Hoffa! Ten Angels Swearing: An Authorized Biography*. Beaverdam, VA: Beaverdam Books, 1965.

2592 ———. Darnton, John. "Hard-Driving Ex-Teamster Chief: James Riddle Hoffa." *The New York Times*, Dec 24, 1971, p 12.

2593 ———. Hannibal, Edward, and Robert Boris. *Blood Feud* (a novel). NY: Ballantine, 1980.

2594 ———. Martin, John B. *Jimmy Hoffa's Hot*. Greenwich, CT: Fawcett, 1959.

2595 ———. Moldea, Dan E. *The Hoffa Wars: Teamsters, Rebels, Politicians and the Mob*. NY: Paddington, 1978.

2596 ———. Mollenhoff, Clark R. *Tentacles of Power, the Story of Jimmy Hoffa*. Cleveland: World, 1965.

2597 ———. Salpukas, Agis. "A Friend of Prisoners: James Riddle Hoffa." *The New York Times*, Sep 8, 1972, p 4.

2598 ———. Sheridan, Walter. *The Fall and Rise of Jimmy Hoffa*. NY: Saturday Review Press, 1973.

2599 HOLLANDER, LOUIS. Ledbetter, Les. "Louis Hollander, Long a Leader of Amalgamated Clothing Union." *The New York Times*, Jan 5, 1980, p 26.
2600 HOUSEWRIGHT, JAMES T. "James T. Housewright Dead at 55: Led Retail Clerks International." *The New York Times*, Sep 21, 1977, p 36.
2601 HUTCHESON, MAURICE. "Maurice Hutcheson, 85, Is Dead: Led Carpenters Union 2 Decades." *The New York Times*, Jan 11, 1983, p B14.
2602 HUTCHESON, WILLIAM L. "Big Bill Retires." *Time*, Dec 31, 1951, pp 11-12.
2603 ———. Raddock, Maxwell. *Portrait of an American Labor Leader: William L. Hutcheson*. NY: American Institute of Social Science 1955.
2604 HUTCHINSON, ALBERT E. "Albert E. Hutchinson Dies; Headed Asbestos Workers." *The New York Times*, Jun 21, 1972, p 40.
2605 IGLESIAS, SANTIAGO. Senior, Clarence. *Santiago Iglesias, Labor Crusader*. Hato Rey, Puerto Rico: Inter American U Press, 1973.
2606 JENNINGS, PAUL. "Norman Thomas Award Presented to Union Chief." *The New York Times*, Feb 1, 1970.
2607 KENIN, HERMAN D. "Herman D. Kenin, Musicians' Chief. Union President Since 1958 Dies—Won TV Pacts." *The New York Times*, Jul 22, 1970, p 37.
2608 KENNEDY, WILLIAM P. "William P. Kennedy Dies at 76: Led Trainmen's Union 13 Years." *The New York Times*, May 15, 1968, p 41.
2609 KIRKLAND, LANE. "A.F.L.-C.I.O. Official Gets Eugene V. Debs Award." *The New York Times*, Mar 25, 1976, p 32.
2610 ———. Raskin, A. H. "A Reporter at Large: After Meany." *The New Yorker*, Aug 25, 1980, 36-51.
2611 KROLL, JACK. "Jack Kroll, Led C.I.O. in Politics." *The New York Times*, May 28, 1971, p 32.
2612 LAWSON, JOHN R. Beshoar, Barron B. *Out of the Depths: The Story of John R. Lawson, a Labor Leader*. Denver: Colorado Labor Historical Committee of the Denver Trades and Labor Assembly, 1942.
2613 LEIGHTY, GEORGE E. "George E. Leighty, Rail Union Head." *The New York Times*, Jul 19, 1973, p 36.
2614 LEWIS, JOHN L. *John L. Lewis and the International Union, United Mine Workers of America: The Story from 1917 to 1952*. Wash.: The Union, 1952.
2615 ———. "John L. Lewis, Labor's Thunderer, Led Mine Union and Helped Found the CIO." *The New York Times*, Jun 13, 1969, p 34.
2616 ———. Alinsky, Saul. *John L. Lewis*. NY: Putnam, 1949.
2617 ———. Bernstein, Irving. "John L. Lewis and the Voting Behavior of the CIO." *Public Opinion Quarterly*, Jun 1941.
2618 ———. Carnes, Cecil. *John L. Lewis: Leader of Labor*. NY: Speller, 1936.
2619 ———. Danish, Max D. "Lewis Takes Another Walk. What Next?" *New Leader*, Dec 20, 1947, pp 1, 15.
2620 ———. Dubofsky, Melvyn, and Warren R. Van Tine. *John L. Lewis*. NY: Quadrangle, 1977.
2621 ———. Fast, Howard. *Power* (a novel about John L. Lewis.). Garden City, NY: Doubleday, 1962.
2622 ———. Fine, Sidney. "John L. Lewis Discusses the General Motors Sit-Down Strike: A Document." *Labor History*, Vol 15 (1974), 563-70.
2623 ———. Hardman, J. B. S. "John L. Lewis, Labor Leader and Man: An Interpretation." *Labor History*, Vol 2 (1961), 3-29.
2624 ———. Hass, Eric. *John L. Lewis Exposed*. NY: NY Labor News Co., 1938.
2625 ———. Hutchinson, John. "John L. Lewis: To the Presidency of the UMWA." *Labor History*, Vol 19 (1978), 185-203.
2626 ———. McCarthy, Justin. "John L. Lewis Organized the Unorganized." *Worklife*, Vol 1 (Sep 1976), 19-22.

2627 ———. Raskin, A. H. "Secrets of John L. Lewis' Great Power." *The New York Times Magazine*, Oct 5, 1952, pp 15, 59.

2628 ———. Ross, Hugh. "John L. Lewis and the Election of 1940." *Labor History*, Vol 17 (1976), 160-90.

2629 ———. Selvin, David F. *The Thundering Voice of John L. Lewis*. NY: Lothrop, Lee & Shepard, 1969.

2630 ———. Sulzberger, C. L. *Sit Down with John L. Lewis*. NY: Random House, 1938.

2631 ———. Wechsler, James A. *Labor Baron: A Portrait of John L. Lewis*. NY: Morrow, 1944.

2632 LONDON, MEYER. Frieburger, William J. *The Lone Socialist Vote: a Political Study of Meyer London*. Ph D diss, U of Cincinnati, 1980.

2633 ———. Rogoff, Hillel. *An East Side Epic: The Life and Work of Meyer London*. NY: Vanguard, 1930.

2634 LUCY, WILLIAM. Perlmutter, Emanuel. "Back in Key Union Job: William Lucy." *The New York Times*, Jun 1, 1972, p 26.

2635 LUTHER, SETH. Gersuny, Carl. "Seth Luther—The Road from Chepachet." *Rhode Island History*, Vol 33 (1974), 47-55.

2636 ———. Hartz, Louis. "Seth Luther: The Story of a Working-Class Revel." *New England Quarterly*, Vol 13 (1940), 401-18.

2637 MCBRIDE, LLOYD. Dembart, Lee. "New Head of Steel Union: Lloyd McBride." *The New York Times*, Feb 11, 1977, p 15.

2638 MCCARTHY, JUSTIN G. "Justin McCarthy, Editor for U.M.W." *The New York Times*, Apr 6, 1978, p 34.

2639 MCDONALD, DAVID J. *Union Man*. NY: Dutton, 1969.

2640 ———. Daniels, Lee A. "David J. McDonald, Retired Head of Steelworkers Union, Dies at 76." *The New York Times*, Aug 10, 1979, p A12.

2641 ———. Dembart, Lee. "David McDonald, Retired Since 1965, Misses Steel Union." *The New York Times*, Sep 9, 1975, p 25.

2642 ———. Kelly, George E., and Edwin Beachler. *Man of Steel: The Story of David J. McDonald*. NY: North American Book Co., 1954.

2643 MCGUIRE, P. J. Lyon, David Nicholas. *The World of P. J. McGuire: A Story of the American Labor Movement, 1870-1890*. Ph D diss, U of Minnesota, 1972.

2644 MACMAHON, DOUGLAS. Asbury, Edith Evans. "Man Who Takes Up Quill Baton Was Once his Foe." *The New York Times*, Jan 5, 1966, p 14.

2645 MARTIN, HOMER. "Homer Martin, 66, of U.A.W. is Dead." *The New York Times*, Jan 24, 1968, p 39.

2646 MATLES, JAMES J. Whitman, Alden. "James J. Matles, a Top Official of Electrical Workers, 66, Dies." *The New York Times*, Sep 14, 1975, p 38.

2647 MEANY, GEORGE. "A Collection of 29 Paintings by George Meany, President of the A.F.L.-C.I.O., Is on Exhibition...." *The New York Times*, May 20, 1972, p 19.

2648 ———. Dubofsky, Melvyn. "George Meany, the Perfect Bureaucrat." *New Politics*, Vol 10 (Winter 1973), 30-36.

2649 ———. Flint, Jerry. "George Meany Is Dead at 85; Pioneer in Labor Merged the A.F.L. and the C.I.O." *The New York Times*, Jan 12, 1980, p 25.

2650 ———. Goulden, Joseph C. *Meany*. NY: Atheneum, 1972.

2651 ———. Hausknecht, Murray. "The Finished World of George Meany." *Dissent*, Vol 20 (1973), 177-82.

2652 ———. Raskin, A. H. "At 81, George Meany Is Still Mr. Labor." *The New York Times*, Oct 5, 1975, p E3.

2653 ———. ———. "George Meany: A Life Remembered." *The New York Times*, Jan 13, 1980, p E5.

2654 ———. Robinson, Archie. *George Meany and his Times: A Biography*. NY: Simon & Schuster, 1981.

2655 MILLER, ARNOLD RAY. Dembart, Lee. "Two Adversaries from Coal Mining Country: Arnold Ray Miller and Guy Farmer." *The New York Times*, Nov 15, 1974, p 24.

2656 MILLER, MARVIN. Berkow, Ira. "Sports of The Times: The Master Bargainer." *The New York Times*, Jan 1, 1983, p 15.

2657 MITCHELL, HARRY L. *Mean Things Happening in This Land: The Life and Times of H. L. Mitchell, Cofounder of the Southern Tenant Farmers' Union*. Montclair, NJ: Allanheld, Osmun, 1979.

2658 MITCHELL, JOHN. Glueck, Elsie. *John Mitchell, Miner: Labor's Bargain with the Gilded Age*. NY: John Day, 1929.

2659 ———. Gowaskie, Joseph Michael. *John Mitchell: A Study in Leadership*. Ph D diss, Catholic U of America, 1968.

2660 ———. Morris, James O. "The Acquisitive Spirit of John Mitchell UMW President (1899-1908)." *Labor History*, Vol 20 (1979), 5-43.

2661 MOONEY, FRED. *Struggle in the Coal Fields: The Autobiography of Fred Mooney*. Morgantown: West Virginia U Library, 1967.

2662 ———. *Struggle in the Coal Fields: The Autobiography of Fred Mooney*. Morgantown: West Virginia U Library, 1967.

2663 MOONEY, TOM. *The Mooney-Billings Report: Suppressed by the Wickersham Commission*. NY: Gotham House, 1932.

2664 ———. *The Strange Case of Tom Mooney*. 1933. (Documentary film by Independent Productions)

2665 ———. Frost, Richard H. *The Mooney Case*. Stanford, CA: Stanford U Press, 1968.

2666 MORTIMER, WYNDHAM. *Organize! My Life as a Union Man*. Bost.: Beacon, 1971.

2667 ———. "Wyndham Mortimer Dies at 82: Ex-Auto Industry Labor Leader." *The New York Times*, Aug 28, 1966, p 92.

2668 MURPHY, FRANK. Fine, Sidney. *Frank Murphy: The Detroit Years*. Ann Arbor: U of Michigan Press, 1975.

2669 ———. ———. *Frank Murphy: The New Deal Years*. Chicago: U of Chicago Press, 1979.

2670 ———. Lunt, Richard D. *The High Ministry of Government: The Political Career of Frank Murphy*. Detroit: Wayne State U Press, 1965.

2671 MURPHY, VINCENT J. "Vincent Murphy, Labor Leader, 83. Headed Jersey A.F.L.-C.I.O. and Was Mayor of Newark." *The New York Times*, Jun 10, 1976, p 38.

2672 MURRAY, PHILIP. Chamberlain, John. "Philip Murray." *Life*, Feb 1946, pp 78-80, 82, 84, 86, 89-90.

2673 ———. Tate, Juanita Diffay. *Philip Murray as a Labor Leader*. Ph D diss, New York U, 1962.

2674 MUSTE, ABRAHAM J. "My Experience in the Labor and Radical Struggles of the 1930s," pp 123-50, *As We Saw the Thirties: Essays on Social and Political Movements of a Decade*, Rita Simon, ed. Urbana: U of Illinois Press, 1967, pp 123-50.

2675 ———. *The Reminiscences of A. J. Muste*. Glen Rock, NJ: Microfilming Corp of America, 1972. (Recorded in the early 1950s)

2676 MYERS, ISAAC. Artison, Richard E. *Isaac Myers of Baltimore, Maryland (1835 to 1891)*. Ithaca: Africana Studies and Research Center, Cornell U, 1974.

2677 NAGLER, ISIDORE. Haskel, Harry. *A Leader of the Garment Workers: The Biography of Isidore Nagler*. NY: ILGWU, Local 10, 1950.

2678 NELSON, LOUIS. "Louis Nelson, 75, I.L.G.W.U. Officer." *The New York Times*, Oct 15, 1969, p 41.

2679 OSMAN, ARTHUR. "Arthur Osman Is Dead at 62: Started First Drygoods Union." *The New York Times*, Nov 7, 1969, p 45.

2680 Owen, Robert. Cole, Margaret. *Robert Owen of New Lanark, 1771-1858.* NY: Oxford U Press, 1953.

2681 ———. Lightfoot, Alfred. *The Educational Philosophy and Practices of Robert Owen: Educational Iconoclast of the 19th Century.* Ph D diss, Marquette U, 1968.

2682 Owens, John. "John Owens, President, District 6 (Ohio) United Mine Workers, AFL." *Fortune,* Nov 1946, p 148.

2683 Pachler, William J. "William J. Pachler, Utility Union Head." *The New York Times,* May 29, 1970, p 29.

2684 Parsons, Albert R. Calmer, Alan. *Labor Agitator: The Story of Albert R. Parsons.* NY: International, 1937.

2685 Perlis, Leo. "A Look at Leo Perlis." *Industrial Bulletin,* Vol 43 (May 1964), 8-10.

2686 Phillips, Paul. "Paul Phillips, Led Papermakers Union." *The New York Times,* Feb 13, 1975, p 36.

2687 Pine, Max. Fliegal, Hyman J. *The Life and Time of Max Pine; A History of the Jewish Labor Movement in the U.S.A. during the Last Part of the 19th Century and the First Part of the 20th Century.* NY: no publisher indicated, 1959.

2688 Policastro, Thomas F. "Thomas F. Policastro, 57; New England Labor Chief." *The New York Times,* Aug 12, 1977, p B2.

2689 Pollock, William. "William Pollock, Unionist, Is Dead. Retired in 1972 as the Leader of the Textile Workers." *The New York Times,* Mar 5, 1982, p B8.

2690 Potofsky, Jacob S. "Potofsky Praised as Labor Chief; People Called his 'Real Concern'." *The New York Times,* Aug 10, 1979, p A13.

2691 ———. Pace, Eric. "Jacob Potofsky, Longtime Leader of Clothing Workers, Is Dead at 84." *The New York Times,* Aug 6, 1979, p A1.

2692 Powderly, Terence V. *The Path I Trod.* NY: Columbia U Press, 1940.

2693 ———. *Thirty Years of Labor.* Columbus, OH: Excelsior, 1889.

2694 ———. Bloch, Herman D. "Terence V. Powderly and Disguised Discrimination." *American Journal of Economics and Sociology,* Vol 33 (1974), 145-60.

2695 ———. Falzone, Vincent J. *Terence V. Powderly: Mayor and Labor Leader, 1849-1893.* Ph D diss, U off Maryland, 1970.

2696 ———. ———. *Terence V. Powderly, Middle Class Reformer.* Wash: U Press of America, 1978.

2697 ———. ———. "Terence V. Powderly: Politician and Progressive Mayor of Scranton, 1878-1884." *Pennsylvania History,* Vol 41 (1974), 289-310.

2698 ———. Grob, Gerald N. "Terence V. Powderly and the Knights of Labor." *Mid-America,* New Series, Vol 28 (1957), 39-55.

2699 ———. Walker, Samuel. "Terence V. Powderly, Machinist: 1866-1877." *Labor History,* Vol 19 (1978), 165-84.

2700 ———. Walsh, J. C. "Powderly of the Knights of Labor." *Journal of the American Irish Historical Society.,* Vol 32 (1941), 85-91.

2701 Quill, Michael J. "Quill Dies of Heart Attack: T.W.U. President Was 60." *The New York Times,* Jan 29, 1966, p 1.

2702 ———. Whittemore, L. H. *The Man Who Ran the Subways: The Story of Mike Quill.* NY: Holt, Rinehart & Winston, 1968.

2703 Quintiliano, Luigi. "Luigi Quintiliano Is Dead; I.L.G.W.U. Unit Head Was 77." *The New York Times,* Feb 14, 1970, p 27.

2704 Randolph, A. Philip. "Randolph, 80 Years Old Today, Reflects on his Fights for Labor." *The New York Times,* Apr 15, 1969, p 49.

2705 ———. Anderson, Jervis. *A. Philip Randolph: A Biographical Portrait.* NY: Harcourt Brace Jovanovich, 1973.

2706 ———. Brooks, Thomas R., and A. H. Raskin. "A. Philip Randolph, 1889-1979." *New Leader,* Jun 4, 1979, 6-9

2707 ———. Davis, Daniel S. *Mr. Black Labor: The Story of A. Philip Randolph, Father of the Civil Rights Movement.* NY: Dutton, 1972.

2708 ———. Delaney, Paul. "A. Philip Randolph, Rights Leader, Dies: President Leads Tributes." *The New York Times*, May 18, 1979, p B4.

2709 ———. Harris, William H. "A. Philip Randolph as a Charismatic Leader, 1925-1941." *Journal of Negro History*, Vol 64 (1979), 301-15.

2710 ———. Marable, Manning. "A. Philip Randolph and the Foundations of Black American Socialism." *Radical America*, Vol 14 (Mar-Apr 1980), 7-29.

2711 ———. Terrill, Tom E. "A. Philip Randolph." *Reviews in American History*, Vol 7 (1979), 107-11.

2712 RAPIER, JAMES. Schweninger, Loren. "James Rapier and the Negro Labor Movement, 1869-1872." *Alabama Review*, Vol 28 (1975), 185-201.

2713 RAPOPORT, JOE. Kann, Kenneth. *Joe Rapoport, the Life of a Jewish Radical*. Phila.: Temple U Press, 1981.

2714 REUTHER, VICTOR. Raskin, A. H. "Last of the Reuthers." *The New York Times*, Jun 21, 1971, p 29.

2715 REUTHER, WALTER. "Reuther Aiming for A.F.L.-C.I.O. Presidency, Most Union Officials Believe." *The New York Times*, May 22, 1966, p 83.

2716 ———. "Reuther, Wife, 4 Others Die in Crash of Small Jet." *The New York Times*, May 11, 1970, p 1.

2717 ———. "Walter Philip Reuther, 1907-1970." *Solidarity*, Vol 13 (Jun 1970), memorial issue.

2718 ———. Christman, Henry M., ed. *Walter P. Reuther, Selected Papers*. NY: Macmillan, 1961.

2719 ———. Cook, Fred J. *Walter Reuther: Building the House of Labor*. Chicago: Encyclopaedia Britannica Press, 1963.

2720 ———. Cormier, Frank, and William J. Eaton. *Reuther*. Englewood Cliffs, NJ: Prentice-Hall, 1970.

2721 ———. Dayton, Eldorous L. *Walter Reuther: The Autocrat at the Bargaining Table* NY: Devin-Adair, 1958.

2722 ———. Gould, Jean, and Lorena Hickok. *Walter Reuther: Labor's Rugged Individualist*. NY: Dodd, Mead, 1972.

2723 ———. Howe, Irving, and B. J. Widick. *The UAW and Walter Reuther*. NY: Random House, 1949.

2724 ———. Neikind, Claire. "Beck and Reuther." *The Reporter*, Jul 5, 1949.

2725 ———. Slack, Walter Harmon. *Walter Reuther: A Study of Ideas*. Ph D diss, U of Iowa, 1965.

2726 ———. Tyler, Robert L. *Walter Reuther*. Grand Rapids, MI: W. B. Eerdmans, 1973.

2727 ———. Wechsler, James A. "Labor's Bright Young Man." *Harper's*, Mar 1948, p 264.

2728 ———. Yahrmatter, Arthur Joseph. *The Speaking of Walter P. Reuther on Labor and Social Reform Issues*. Ph D diss, Southern Illinois U, 1968.

2729 RIEVE, EMIL. Saxon, Wolf. "Emil Rieve Dead: Key Labor Leader." *The New York Times*, Jan 26, 1975, p 49.

2730 RIFFE, JOHN. Grogan, William. *John Riffe of the Steelworkers: American Labor Statesman*. NY: Coward-McCann, 1959.

2731 ROGERS, RAYMOND F., JR. Jensen, Michael C. "Union Strategist on Wall Street." *The New York Times*, Mar 26, 1978, p F5.

2732 ROMUALDI, SERAFINO. "Serafino Romualdi, 66, Is Dead; A.F.L.-C.I.O. Aide to Latins." *The New York Times*, Nov 13, 1967, p 47.

2733 RONEY, FRANK. *Frank Roney, Irish Rebel and California Labor Leader*. Berkeley: U of California, 1931.

2734 ROSE, ALEX. Raskin, A. H. "Alex Rose of Liberal Party, a Power in Politics, Is Dead." *The New York Times*, Dec 29, 1976, p 1.

2735 ROSENBLUM, FRANK. "Frank Rosenblum, 85, Leader in Amalgamated Union, Dead." *The New York Times*, Feb 10, 1973, p 30.

2736 ROSENSTOCK, ARTHUR. "Arthur Rosenstock, 72, Dies; ExHead of Newspaper Guild." *The New York Times*, Apr 11, 1975, p 34.

2737 RUEF, ABRAHAM. Thomas, Lately. *A Debonaire Scoundrel: An Episode in the Moral History of San Francisco.* NY: Holt, Rinehart & Winston, 1962.

2738 RYOR, JOHN EDWARD. Maeroff, Gene I. "Teachers' New Leader: John Edward Ryor." *The New York Times*, Jul 9, 1975, p 38.

2739 SCHERER, EMANUEL. "Emanuel Scherer, at 75, Long Active as a Leader of Jewish Labor Bund." *The New York Times*, May 5, 1977, p 42.

2740 SCHLOSSBERG, JOSEPH. "Joseph Schlossberg Dies at 95; Co-Founder of Clothing Union." *The New York Times*, Jan 16, 1971, p 32.

2741 SCHOLLE, AUGUST. "August Scholle, Labor Leader, 67." *The New York Times*, Feb 17, 1972, p 38.

2742 SHANKER, ALBERT. Cunnings, Judith. "Shanker, a Skilled Negotiator, Faces a Straightforward Rival." *The New York Times*, Sep 14, 1975, p 38.

2743 ———. Maeroff, Gene I. "Teacher Union Chief: Albert Shanker." *The New York Times*, Aug 22, 1974, p 40.

2744 ———. Stevens, William K. "Shanker's Foes Call his Rule Autocratic." *The New York Times*, Feb 24, 1971, pp 43, 82.

2745 SHANNON, DANIEL JAMES. Dembart, Lee. "'Open' Teamster Aide: Daniel James Shannon." *The New York Times*, Jul 10, 1976, p 8.

2746 ———. Stetson, Damon. "The 2 Leaders Who Cast Union's New Militancy." *The New York Times*, Jun 4, 1974, p 22.

2747 SHELLEY, JOHN F. "John F. Shelley, Labor Leader, Legislator, Coast Mayor, Dies." *The New York Times*, Sep 2, 1974, p 18.

2748 SINEY, JOHN. Killeen, Charles Edward. *John Siney: The Pioneer in American Industrial Unionism and Industrial Government*. Ph D diss, U of Wisconsin, 1942.

2749 ———. Pinkowski, Edward. *John Siney, the Miners' Martyr*. Phila.: Sunshine Press, 1963.

2750 STANLEY, MILES. "Miles Stanley, 49, Labor Leader, Dies." *The New York Times*, May 5, 1974, p 77.

2751 STEINBOCK, MAX. "Max Steinbock, of Retail Union. Labor Editor, Organizer and Executive Dies on L.I." *The New York Times*, Jun 19, 1975, p 36.

2752 STEWARD, IRA. Commons, John R. "Ira Steward and the Hours of Labor," chap. 3 of Vol 9, *A Documentary History of American Industrial Society*, Cleveland, A. H. Clark, 1910-11.

2753 ———. Douglas, Dorothy W. "Ira Steward on Consumption and Unemployment." *Journal of Political Economy*, Vol 40 (1932), 532-43.

2754 STONE, M. HEDLEY. "M. Hedley Stone, 73, Is Dead: Ex-Officer of Seamen's Union." *The New York Times*, Oct 8, 1970, p 48.

2755 STRASSER, ADOLPH. Cooper, Patricia A. "Whatever Happened to Adolph Strasser?" *Labor History*, Vol 20 (1979), 414-19.

2756 ———. Gitelman, Howard M. "Adolph Strasser and the Origins of Pure and Simple Unionism." *Labor History*, Vol 6 (1965), 71-83.

2757 STULBERG, LOUIS. Stetson, Damon. "Louis Stulberg, Former President of Garment Union, Is Dead at 76." *The New York Times*, Dec 15, 1977, p D23.

2758 ———. ———. "Stulberg Retiring as I.L.G.W.U. Chief." *The New York Times*, May 29, 1975, p 63.

2759 SUFFRIDGE, JAMES. Healy, Paul F. "He Runs a White-Collar Union." *Saturday Evening Post*, Mar 16, 1957, pp 49, 125-26.

2760 SULLENS, FRED. Skates, John Ray. "Fred Sullens and the Growth of Organized Labor." *Southern Quarterly*, Vol 10 (1972), 341-76.

2761 SULLIVAN, DAVID. "David Sullivan, 71, Dead; Ex-Head of Service Union." *The New York Times*, Jan 26, 1976, p 21.

2762 SWAYDUCK, EDWARD. "Swayduck Resigns Post as Head of Lithographers." *The New York Times*, Aug 28, 1975, p 34.

2763 SWINTON, JOHN. Reuter, Frank T. "John Swinton's Paper." *Labor HIstory*, Vol 1 (1960), 298-307.

2764 ———. Ross, Marc. *John Swinton, Journalist and Reformer: the Active Years, 1857-1887.* Ph D diss, New York U, 1969.

2765 SYLVIS, WILLIAM. Grossman, Jonathan. *William Sylvis, Pioneer of American Labor.* NY: Columbia U Press, 1945.

2766 ———. Sylvis, James C. *The Life, Speeches, Labors and essays of William H. Sylvis, Late President of the Iron-moulders' International Union; and also of the National Labor Union.* Phila.: Claxton, Remsen & Haffelfinger, 1872.

2767 ———. Todes, Charlotte. *William H. Sylvis and the National Labor Union.* NY; International, 1942.

2768 TAIBI, CALOGERO. "Calogero Taibi, 40, Aide of Seafarers Union, Dead." *The New York Times*, Jan 6, 1968, p 29.

2769 TALARICO, SAMUEL J. "Profile of a Labor Leader: President 'Sam' Talarico." *Industrial Bulletin*, Vol 47 (Feb 1968), 12-16.

2770 ———. "What Makes a Labor Leader? Three Unionists Surveyed: Talarico, Young, Butler." *Industrial Bulletin*, Vol 42 (Apr 1963), 17-22.

2771 TITLER, GEORGE. Morrow, Elsie. "Portrait of a Union Boss." *Saturday Evening Post*, Feb 28, 1948, pp 25, 110-14.

2772 TRACY, DANIEL W. Wanek, Meriemmi G. *Daniel William Tracy, 1886-1954: A Contribution to the History of Leadership in the American Labor Movement.* Ph D diss, Georgetown U, 1959.

2773 TRAVIS, ROBERT. "Robert Travis Dies at 73: Led G.M. Strike in 1936." *The New York Times*, Nov 27, 1979, p B17.

2774 TREVELLICK, RICHARD. Hicks, Obadiah. *The Life of Richard Trevellick, the Labor Orator, or the Harbinger of the Eight-Hour System.* Joliet, IL: J. F. Williams, 1896.

2775 ———. Yearley, Clifton K., Jr. "Richard Trevellick: Labor Agitator." *Michigan History*, Vol 39 (1955), 425-44.

2776 VAN ARSDALE, HARRY, JR. "Unionist in the Middle." *The New York Times*, Nov 15, 1968, p 34.

2777 VAN RIPER, ELLIS. Dugan, George. "Quiet Union President: Ellis Van Riper." *The New York Times*, Apr 1, 1974, p 24.

2778 WALINSKY, OSSIP J. "Ossip J. Walinsky, Union Head and Jewish Leader, Dies at 86." *The New York Times*, Mar 6, 1973, p 40.

2779 WALL, SHANNON JEROME. "Ex-Sailor Takes Helm." *The New York Times*, Jun 11, 1973, p 41.

2780 WALSH, FRANK. Bradley, Harold Charles. *Frank P. Walsh and Post-War America.* Ph D diss, St. Louis U, 1966.

2781 ———. Meehan, Maria Eucharia, Sister. *Frank Walsh and the American Labor Movement.* Ph D diss, New York U, 1962.

2782 WARD, MARTIN. "Martin Ward, Head of Plumbers' Union, Dies." *The New York Times*, Oct 11, 1982, p D12.

2783 WATCHORN, ROBERT. West, Herbert F., ed. *The Autobiography of Robert Watchorn.* Oklahoma City: Watchorn Charities, Ltd, 1959.

2784 WEINBERG, NAT. "An Abrasive Bargainer." *The New York Times*, Jul 11, 1967, p 37.

2785 WEINTRAUB, MILTON. "Milton Weintraub, Stage Labor Leader." *The New York Times*, Nov 18, 1968, p 47.

2786 WEISBORD, ALBERT. "Albert Weisbord, 76, A Radical Who Led Passaic Strike in '26." *The New York Times*, Apr 28, 1977, p 38.

2787 Wenzl, Theodore Charles. "State Strike Leader: Theodore Charles Wenzl." *The New York Times*, Apr 3, 1972, p 43.

2788 Wertheimer, Val. "Val Wertheimer, 53, High Official in Union of clothing Workers." *The New York Times*, Nov 21, 1978, p 12.

2789 Widman, Michael F., Jr. Kleiman, Dena. "Michael F. Widman, Jr. Dies at 77: Helped to Unionize Ford Motor Co." *The New York Times*, Aug 17, 1977, p 62.

2790 Williams, Claude C. Johnson, Thomas A. "Claude C. Williams; Organized Blacks." *The New York Times*, Jul 7, 1979, p 24.

2791 Williams, John E. Clark, Donald Otis. *John Elias Williams (1853-1919)—Labor Peacemaker*. MA thesis, U of Illinois, 1957.

2792 ———. Potofsky, J. S., ed. *John E. Williams, First Chairman of the Board of Arbitration under the Hart, Schaffner and Marx Labor Agreement, 1912-1919, in Tribute*. Chicago: The Amalgamated Clothing Workers of America, Chicago Joint Board, n.d.

2793 Wilson, John M. *The Dark and the Damp: An Autobiography*. NY: Dutton, 1951.

2794 Wilson, William B. Babson, Roger. *W. B. Wilson and the Department of Labor*. NY: Brentano's, 1919.

2795 ———. Pritchard, Paul W. "William B. Wilson, Master Workman." *Pennsylvania History*, Vol 12 (1945), 81-108.

2796 ———. ———. *William B. Wilson: The Evolution of a Central Pennsylvania Mine Union Leader*. Ph D diss, U of Pennsylvania, 1942.

2797 Wittes, David. "David Wittes, 67, of Teacher Union: Federation Treasurer Dies—An Expert on Pensions." *The New York Times*, Jan 4, 1972, p 34.

2798 Wolchok, Samuel. Kihss, Peter. "Samuel Wolchok, Ex-Unionist, 82, Dies." *The New York Times*, Jan 18, 1979, p D15.

2799 Woodcock, Leonard. "Choice for Auto Union President: Leonard Freel Woodcock." *The New York Times*, May 22, 1970, p 12.

2800 ———. "Woodcock Approved for China Post." *The New York Times*, Jun 30, 1977, p 31.

2801 ———. Mohr, Charles. "Woodcock Among Those Considered for Post in Peking." *The New York Times*, Apr 6, 1977, p A8.

2802 Wright, Carroll D. Leiby, James. *Carroll wright and Labor Reform: The Origin of Labor Statistics*. Cambr.: Harvard U Press, 1960.

2803 ———. MacLaury, Judson. "The Selection of the First U.S. Commissioner of Labor." *Monthly Labor Review*, Vol 98 (1975), 16-19.

2804 Wurf, Jerry. "Jerry Wurf, 62, Union Chief, Dies; Was head of municipal Workers." *The New York Times*, Dec 12, 1981, p 32.

2805 ———. "Public Employees' Voice: Jerome Wurf." *The New York Times*, Sep 3, 1968, p 37.

2806 Young, Thomas G. "What Makes a Labor Leader? Three Unionists Surveyed: Talarico, Young, Butler." *Industrial Bulletin*, Vol 42 (Apr 1963), 17-22.

2807 Zander, Arnold S. "Arnold S. Zander, Labor Chief, Dies: Ex-Head of State, County, Municipal Employees was 74." *The New York Times*, Jul 21, 1975, p 24.

2808 Zaritsky, Max. Lewis, Marx. *Max Zaritsky at Fifty. The Story of an Aggressive Labor Leadership*. NY: Atlanta Printing Co., 1935.

2809 Zausner, Philip. *Unvarnished: The Autobiography of a Union Leader*. NY: Brotherhood Publishers, 1941.

Women (including Women Leaders)

2810 Abbott, Edith. "Harriet Martineau and the Employment of Women in 1836." *Journal of Political Economy*, Vol 14 (1906), 614-26.

2811 ———. "History of Industrial Employment of Women in the U.S.: An Introductory Study." *Journal of Politicsl Economics*, Vol 14 (1906), 461-501.

2812 Abicht, Minoka. *Women's Leadership Roles in Two Selected Labor Unions in the U.S. and Belgium: a Comparative, Descriptive Study*. Ph D diss, U of Cincinnati, 1976.

2813 Adam, Ruth. *A Woman's Place, 1910-1975*. NY: Norton, 1977.

2814 Adams, Arvil V. *Toward Fair Employment and the EEOC: A Study of Compliance Procedures Under Title VII of the Civil Rights Act of 1964; Final Report*. Wash.: G.P.O., 1973.

2815 Agassi, Judith Buber. "Women Who Work in Factories." *Dissent*, Vol 19 (1972), 233-39.

2816 Aiken, John R. "New Netherlands Arbitration in the 17th Century." *Arbitration Journal*, Vol 29 (1974), 145-57. (Earliest example of a woman serving as a labor arbitrator)

2817 Aldrich, Mark. "State Reports on Women and Child Wage Earners, 1870-1908." *Labor History*, Vol 21 (1980), 86-90.

2818 ———, and Randy Albelda. "Determinants of Working Women's Wages during the Progressive Era." *Explorations in Economic History*, Vol 17 (1980), 323-41.

2819 *American Association for Labor Legislation Papers, 1905-1943*. Glen Rock, NJ: Microfilming Corporation of America, 1974. (Originals in Martin P. Catherwood Library, Cornell U)

2820 Anderson, James R. *The New Deal Career of Frances Perkins, Secretary of Labor, 1933-1939*. Ph D diss, Western Reserve U, 1968.

2821 Anderson, Karen. *Wartime Women: Sex Roles, Family Relations, and the Status of Women During World War II*. Westport, CT: Greenwood, 1981.

2822 Anderson, Mary. *Woman at Work: The Autobiography of Mary Anderson as Told to Mary N. Winslow*. Minneapolis: U of Minnesota Press, 1951.

2823 Anderson, Ruth D. *The Character and Communication of a Modern-Day Prophet: a Rhetorical Analysis of Dorothy Day and the Catholic Worker Movement*. Ph D diss, U of Oregon, 1980.

2824 Andrews, John B., and W. D. P. Bliss. "History of Women in Trade Unions." *Report on Condition of Woman and Child Wage-Earners in the United States*, Vol 10 (1911), U.S. Bureau of Labor. Wash.: G.P.O., 1910-13. (U.S. Senate Document 645, 61st Congress, 2d Session, 19 volumes)

2825 Andrisani, Paul J. "Job Satisfaction among Working Women." *Signs*, Vol 3 (1978), 588-621.

2826 Antos, Joseph R. et al. "Sex Differences in Union Membership." *Industrial and Labor Relations Review*, Vol 33 (1980), 162-69.

2827 ATKINSON, LINDA. *Mother Jones, the Most Dangerous Woman in America.* NY: Crown, 1978.

2828 BARNHART, JACQUELINE. *Working Women: Prostitution in San Francisco from the Gold Rush to 1900.* Ph D diss, U of California, 1977.

2829 BARTOL, KATHRYN M., and ROBERT A. BARTOL. "Women in Managerial and Professional Positions: The United States and the Soviet Union." *Industrial and Labor Relations Review,* Vol 28 (1975), 524-34.

2830 BASIL, DOUGLAS C. *Women in Management.* NY: Dunellen, 1972.

2831 BAXANDALL, ROSALYN. et al. *America's Working Women: a Documentary History, 1600 to the Present.* NY: Vintage Books, 1976.

2832 BEECHER, MAUREEN. "Women's Work on the Mormon Frontier." *Utah Historical Quarterly,* Vol 49 (1981), 276-90.

2833 BENNION, SHERILYN. "Enterprising Ladies: Utah's Nineteenth Century Women Editors." *Utah Historical Quarterly,* Vol 49 (1981), 291-304.

2834 BENSON, EDWARD, and SHARON STROM. "Crystal Lee, Norma Rae, and All Their Sisters: Working Women on Film." *Film Library Quarterly,* Vol 12, No 2/3 (1979), 18-25.

2835 BENSON, SUSAN P. "Business Heads and Sympathizing Hearts: the Women of the Providence (Rhode Island) Employment Society." *Journal of Social History,* Vol 12 (1978), 302-12.

2836 ———. "'The Clerking Sisterhood,' Rationalization and the Work Culture of Saleswomen in American Department Stores, 1890-1960." *Radical America,* Vol 12 (Mar-Apr 1978), 41-55.

2837 BERG, GORDON. "Champion of Labor Law in a Tricorn Hat." *Worklife,* Vol 1 (Oct 1976), 23-27. (Frances Perkins)

2838 BERGQUIST, VIRGINIA A. "Women's Participation in Labor Organizations." *Monthly Labor Review,* Vol 97 (Oct 1974), 3-9.

2839 BIRD, CAROLINE. *The Two-Paycheck Marriage: How Women at Work Are Changing Life in America.* NY: Rawson, Wade, 1979.

2840 BLACKWELDER, JULIA KIRK. "Women in the Work Force: Atlanta, New Orleans, and San Antonio, 1930 to 1940." *Journal of Urban History,* Vol 4 (1978), 331-58.

2841 BLEWETT, MARY H. "Women in American History: A History Through Film." *Film and History,* Vol 4 (Dec 1974), 1-11.

2842 BLITZ, RUDOLPH C. "Women in the Professions, 1870-1970." *Monthly Labor Review,* Vol 97 (May 1974), 34-39.

2843 BLOOR, ELLA R. *We Are Many: An Autobiography.* NY: International, 1940.

2844 BLUMBERG, DOROTHY ROSE. *Florence Kelley: The Making of a Social Pioneer.* NY: Augustus M. Kelley, 1966.

2845 BOLIN, WINIFRED. "The Economics of Middle-Income Family Life: Working Women during the Great Depression." *Journal of American History,* Vol 65 (1978), 60-73.

2846 ———. *Past Ideas and Present Pleasures: Women, Work and the Family, 1920-40.* Ph D diss, U of Minnesota, 1977.

2847 BOONE, GLADYS. *The Women's Trade Union Leagues in Great Britain and the United States of America.* NY: Columbia U Press, 1942.

2848 BOULDING, ELISE. *Women in the Twentieth Century World.* Beverly Hills, CA: Sage, 1977.

2849 BRAND, BARBARA. *The Influence of Higher Education on Sex Typing in Three Professions, 1870-1920: Librarianship, Social Work, and Public Health.* Ph D diss, U of Washington, 1978.

2850 BROWNLEE, W. ELLIOT, and MARY M. BROWNLEE. *Women in the American Economy: A Documentary History, 1675-1929.* New Haven: Yale U Press, 1976.

2851 Bryant, Keith L., Jr. "Kate Barnard, Organized Labor, and Social Justice in Oklahoma during the Progressive Era." *Journal of Southern History*, Vol 35 (1969), 145-64.

2852 Buhle, Mari Jo. *Feminism and Socialism in the U.S., 1820-1920.* Ph D diss, U of Wisconsin, 1974.

2853 ———. *Women and American Socialism, 1870-1920.* Urgana: U of Illinois Press, 1981.

2854 Burns, John E., and Catherine G. Burns. "An Analysis of the Equal Pay Act." *Labor Law Journal*, Vol 24 (1973), 92-99.

2855 Burstein, Paul. "Equal Employment Opportunity Legislation and the Income of Women and Non-Whites." *American Sociological Review*, Vol 44 (1979), 67-391.

2856 Campbell, D'Ann. "Women's Life in Utopia: the Shaker Experiment in Sexual Equality Reappraised, 1810 to 1860." *New England Quarterly*, Vol 51 (1978), 23-28.

2857 Cantor, Milton, and Bruce Laurie, eds. *Class, Sex, and the Woman Worker.* Westport, CT: Greenwood, 1977.

2858 Caroli, Betty Boyd. "Italian Women in America: Sources for Study." *Italian Americana*, Vol 2 (1976), 242-54.

2859 Carrigan, D. Owen. "Martha Moore Avery: Crusader for Social Justice." *Catholic Historical Review*, Vol 54 (1968), 17-38.

2860 Center for Women Policy Studies. *Harrassment and Discrimination of Women in Employment: Working Paper Prepared for the Conference on Harassment in the Workplace, July 7-9, 1981.* Wash.: The Center, 1981.

2861 Chernow, Ron. "All in a Day's Work: Housekeepers, Mostly Black Women, are the Last Frontier of Labor Organizing." *Mother Jones*, Vol 1 (Aug 1976), 11-16.

2862 Clark, Sue Ainslie, and Edith Wyatt. *Making Both Ends Meet: The Income and Ouutlay of New York Working Girls.* NY: Macmillan, 1911.

2863 Clive, Alan. "Women Workers in World War II: Michigan as a Test Case." *Labor History*, Vol 20 (1979), 44-72.

2864 Coalition of Labor Union Women. *Statement of Purpose, Structure, and Guidelines Adopted by the Coalition of Labor Union Women, Founding Conference, March 23-24, 1974, Chicago, Illinois.* Detroit: The Coalition, 1974.

2865 Cohen, R. C. *Fannia Cohen and the International Ladies Garment Workers Union* Ph D diss, U of Southern California, 1976.

2866 Connor, Valerie J. "'The Mothers of the Race' in World War I: The National War Labor Board and Women in Industry." *Labor History*, Vol 21 (1980), 31-54.

2867 Cook, Alice H. "Equal Pay: Where Is It?" *Industrial Relations*, Vol 14 (1975), 158-77.

2868 Cooney, Rosemary S. "Changing Labor Force Participation of Mexican American Wives: a Comparison with Anglos and Blacks." *Social Science Quarterly*, Vol 56 (1975), 252-61.

2869 Corcoran, Catherine T., Sister. *Vida Dutton Scudder: the Progressive Years.* Ph D diss, Georgetown U, 1973.

2870 Costin, Lela B. "Grace Abbott of Nebraska." *Nebraska History*, Vol 56 (165-91.

2871 Cowl, Margaret. "Women's Struggles for Equality." *Political Affairs*, Vol 53 (May 1974), 40-44.

2872 *Crystal Lee Jordan.* 1974. (Non-fiction film produced by KERA-TV (Dallas) in association with MS Magazine)

2873 Cummings, Ariel Ivers. *The Factory Girl...* (a novel). Lowell, MA: J. E. Short & Co., 1847.

2874 Daly, John Marie, Sister. *Mary Anderson, Pioneer Labor Leader.* Ph D diss, Georgetown U, 1968.

2875 Dancis, Bruce. "Socialism and Women in the United States, 1900-1917." *Socialist Revolution*, Vol 6 (Jan-Mar 1976), 81-144.

2876 DANIELS, DORIS G. *Lillian D. Wald: the Progressive Woman and Feminism*. Ph D diss, City U of NY, 1977.

2877 DAVIES, MARGARET W. "Woman's Place is at the Typewriter: the Feminization of the Clerical Labor Force." *Radical America*, Vol 8 (Jul-Aug 1974), 1-28.

2878 ———. *Woman's Place is at the Typewriter: the Feminization of Clerical Workers and Changes in Clerical Work in the United States, 1870-1930*. Ph D diss, Brandeis U, 1979.

2879 DAVIS, HOWARD. "Employment Gains of Women by Industry, 1968-1978." *Monthly Labor Review*, Vol 103 (July 1980), 3-9.

2880 DAY, DOROTHY. *The Long Loneliness*. NY: Harper, 1952.

2881 DEITCH, CYNTHIA. *Sex Inequality and the Labor Market: Earnings Differences between Men and Women Workers, 1959 and 1976*. Ph D diss, U of Massachusetts, 1981.

2882 DELGADO, JEANNE HUNNICUTT, ed. "Nellie Kedzie Jones' Advice to Farm Women: Letters from Wisconsin, 1912-1916." *Wisconsin Magazine of History*, Vol 57 (1973), 3-27.

2883 DEWEY, LUCRETIA M. "Women in Labor Unions." *Monthly Labor Review*, Vol 94 (1971), 42-48.

2884 DICKASON, GLADYS. "Women in Labor Unions." *Annals of the American Academy of Political and Social Science*, Vol 251 (1947), 70-78.

2885 DICKINSON, JOAN YOUNGER. *The Role of the Immigrant Women in the U.S. Labor Force, 1890-1910*. Ph D diss, U of Pennsylvania, 1974.

2886 DIXLER, ELSA JANE. *The Woman Question: Women and the American Communist Party 1929-41*. Ph D diss, Yale U, 1974.

2887 DREIER, MARY. *Margaret Dreier Robins: Her Life, Letters and Work*. NY: Island Press Cooperative, 1950.

2888 DRINNON, RICHARD. *Rebel in Paradise: A Biography of Emma Goldman*. Chicago: U of Chicago Press, 1961.

2889 DUBLIN, THOMAS. "The Hodgdon Family Letters: a View of Women in the Early Textile Mills, 1830-1840." *Historical New Hampshire*, Vol 33 (1978), 283-95.

2890 ———. *Women at Work: The Transformation of Work and Community in Lowell, Massachusetts, 1826-1860*. NY: Columbia U Press, 1979.

2891 ———. *Women at Work: The Transformmation of Work and Community in Lowell, Mass., 1826-1860*. Ph D diss, Columbia U, 1975.

2892 DUBLIN, THOMAS, ed. *Farm to Factory: Women's Letters, 1830-1860*. NY: Columbia U Press, 1981.

2893 DUNNIGAN, KATE. et al "Working Women: Images of Women at Work in Rhode Island, 1880-1925." *Rhode Island History*, Vol 38 (1979), 3-21.

2894 DUPONT, JULIE A. *Women: Their Social and Economic Status. Selected References, December 1970*. Wash.: U.S. Department of Labor Library, 1970.

2895 DYE, NANCY SCHROM. *The Womens Trade Union League of New York, 1903-1920*. Ph D diss, U of Wisconsin, 1974.

2896 ECKERT, LEONE W. *A Preliminary Bibliography of American Labor Leader Biographies*. Ithaca: Library, NY State School of Industrial and Labor Relations, Cornell U, 1961.

2897 EDWARDS, HARRY T. "Sex Discrimination under Title VII: Some Unresolved Issues." *Labor Law Journal*, Vol 24 (1973), 411-23.

2898 ENDELMAN, GARY. *Solidarity Forever: Rose Schneiderman and the Women's Trade Union League*. Ph D diss, U of Delaware, 1978.

2899 ESTES, BARBARA. *Margaret Dreier Robins: Social Reformer and Labor Organizer*. Ph D diss, Ball State U, 1978.

2900 EWEN, ELIZABETH. *Immigrant Women in the Land of Dollars, 1890-1920*. Ph D diss, SUNY-Stonybrook, 1980.

2901 FEE, TERRY. "Domestic Labor: an Analysis of Housework and its Relation to the Production Process." *Review of Radical Political Economics*, Vol 8 (Spring 1976), 1-8.

2902 FERMAN, LOUIS A. et al, comp. *Negroes and Jobs: A Book of Readings*. Ann Arbor: U of Michigan Press, 1968.

2903 FERNANDES, MARIA T. *Women and the Wage Labor System: A Theoretical Approach*. Ph D diss, Brandeis U, 1982.

2904 FERREE, M. M. "Working Class Feminism: a Consideration of the Consequences of Employment." *Sociology Quarterly*, Vol 21 (1980), 173-84.

2905 FETHERLING, DALE. *Motner Jones, the Miners' Angel: A Portrait*. Carbondale: Southern Illinois U Press, 1974.

2906 FIELD, JANA. "The Coalition of Labor Union Women." *Political Affairs*, Vol 54 (Mar 1975), 3-12.

2907 FLORER, JOHN H. *NOW: The Formative Years. National Effort to Acquire Federal Action on Equal Employment Rights for Women in the 1960s*. Ph D diss, Syracuse U, 1972.

2908 FLYNN, ELIZABETH G. *The Rebel Girl: An Autobiography. My First Life (1906-1926)*. NY: International, 1973.

2909 FONER, PHILIP S. "Caroline Hollingsworth Pemberton: Philadelphia Socialist Champion of Black Equality." *Pennsylvania History*, Vol 43 (1976), 227-51.

2910 ———. "A Pioneer Proposal for a Women's Library." *Journal of Library History*, Vol 13 (1978), 157-59.

2911 ———. *Women and the American Labor Movement: From Colonial Times to the Eve of World War I*. NY: Free Press, 1979.

2912 FONER, PHILIP S., ed. *The Factory Girls: A Collection of Writings....* Urbana: U of Illinois Press, 1977.

2913 *Four Years in the Underbrush: Adventures of a Working Woman in New York*. NY: Scribner, 1921.

2914 FRAZER, WINIFRED L. "Two Revolutionaries: Gertrude Stein and Emma Goldman." *Science/Technology and the Humanities*, Vol 1 (Winter 1978), 70-78.

2915 FREDERICKSON, MARY. *A Place to Speak our Minds: The Southern School for Women Workers*. Ph D diss, U of North Carolina, 1981.

2916 FUCHS, VICTOR R. "Recent Trends and Long-Run Prospects for Female Earnings." *American Economic Review*, Vol 64 (1974), 236-42.

2917 FURIO, COLOMBA. *Immigrant Women and Industry; a Case Study. The Italian Immigrant Women and the Garment Industry, 1880-1950*. Ph D diss, New York U, 1980.

2918 GABIN, NANCY. "Women Workers and the UAW in the Post-World War II Period: 1945-1954." *Labor History*, Vol 21 (1980), 5-30.

2919 GARCIA, MARIO T. "Chicana in American History: the Mexican Women of El Paso, 1880-1920—a Case Study." *Pacific Historical Review*, Vol 49 (1980), 315-70.

2920 GARFINKLE, STUART H. "Occupations of Women and Black Workers, 1962-74." *Monthly Labor Review*, Vol 98 (Nov 1975), 25-35.

2921 GARRISON, DEE. "The Tender Technicians: The Feminization of Public Librarianship, 1876-1905." *Journal of Social History*, Vol 6 (Winter 1972), 131-59.

2922 GAUMER, GARY L. "Sex Discrimination and Job Tenure." *Industrial Relations*, Vol 14 (1975), 121-29.

2923 GINGER, RAY, and VICTORIA GINGER. "Feminist and Family History: Some Pitfalls." *Labor History*, Vol 12 (1971), 614-18.

2924 GIRALDO, Z. I. *Public Policy and the Family: Wives and Mothers in the Labor Force*. Lexington, MA: Lexington Books, 1980.

2925 GLAZER-MALBIN, NONA. "Housework (a review essay)." *Signs*, Vol 1 (Spring 1976), 905-22.

2926 GOLDEN, RENNY. "Sisters Reclaim Labor History—Theologizing as Workers." *Cross Currents*, Vol 31 (1981), 52-61.

2927 GOLDIN, CLAUDIA. "The Work and Wages of Single Women, 1870-1920." *Journal of Economic History*, Vol 40 (1980), 81-88.

2928 GOLDMAN, EMMA. *Living My Life*. NY: Knopf, 1931.

2929 GOLDMARK, JOSEPHINE. *Impatient Crusader: Florence Kelley's Life Story*. Urbana: U of Illinois Press, 1953.

2930 GRAEBNER, WILLIAM. "'Uncle Sam Just Loves the Ladies': Sex Discrimination in the Federal Government, 1917." *Labor History*, Vol 21 (1980), 75-85.

2931 GREENFIELD, SUSAN. *Attitudes toward Work and Success of Women Employed in Male vs. Famale Dominated Jobs*. Ph D diss, U of Southern California, 1978.

2932 GREENWALD, MAURINE W. *Women, War, and Work: the Impact of World War I on Women Workers in the United States*. Ph D diss, Brown U, 1978.

2933 ———. *Women, War, and Work: The Impact of World War I on Women Workers in the United States*. Westport, CT: Greenwood Press, 1980.

2934 GREGORY, CHESTER WOODROW. *The Problem of Labor during World War II: The Employment of Women in Defense Production*. Ph D diss, Ohio State U, 1969.

2935 GROSS, JOEL. *Maura's Dream* (a novel). NY: Seaview Books, 1981.

2936 GRUENFELD, ELAINE F. *Promotion: Practices, Policies, and Affirmative Action*. Ithaca: NY State School of Industrial and Labor Relations, Cornell U, 1975.

2937 HAMMERMAN, HERBERT, and MARVIN ROGOFF. "Unions and Title VII of the Civil Rights Act of 1964." *Monthly Labor Review*, Vol 99 (Apr 1976), 34-37.

2938 HARTMANN, HEIDI I. "Women's Work in the U.S." *Current History*, Vol 70 (1976), 215-19, 229.

2939 HATCH, CAROL. "Socialist-Feminism and the Workplace." *Socialist Review*, Vol 9 (Sep-Oct 1979), 119-30.

2940 HAYDEN, DOLORES. "Two Utopian Feminists and their Campaigns for Kitchenless Houses." *Signs*, Vol 4 (1978), 274-90.

2941 HEDGES, JANICE NEIPERT. "Women Workers and Manpower Demands in the 1970's." *Monthly Labor Review*, Vol 93 (Jun 1970), 19-29.

2942 HELSON, RAVENNA. "The Changing Image of the Career Woman." *Journal of Social Issues*, Vol 28 (1972), 33-46.

2943 HENRY, ALICE. *The Trade Union Woman*. NY: Appleton, 1915.

2944 ———. *Women and the Labor Movement*. NY: Doran, 1923.

2945 HERRON, BELVA M. *Labor Organization Among Women*. Urbana: U of Illinois Press, 1905.

2946 HEWES, AMY, and HENRIETTE R. WALTER. *Women as Munition-Makers: A Study of Conditions in Bridgeport, Connecticut*. NY: Russell Sage Foundation, 1917.

2947 HILL, VICKI L. *Strategy and Breadth: the Socialist-Feminist in American Fiction*. Ph D diss, SUNY-Buffalo, 1980.

2948 HOGLER, RAYMOND. "Labor History as Drama: 'The Trial of Mother Jones'." *Labor Studies Journal*, Vol 5 (1980), 146-49.

2949 HOLCOMB, JOSEPHINE. *Women in the Labor Force in the U.S., 1940-50*. Ph D diss, U of South Carolina, 1977.

2950 HORNE, G. M. *Mary Anderson and the Development of Protective Legislation for Women in the United States, 1890-1938*. Ph D diss, London School of Economics, 1972.

2951 HOURWICH, ANDRIA T., and GLADYS PALMER, eds. *I Am a Woman Worker: A Scrapbook of Autobiographies*. NY: Affiliated Schools for Workers, 1936.

2952 HOWE, LOUISE K. *Pink Collar Workers: Inside the World of Women's Work*. NY: Putnam, 1977.

2953 HUMMER, PATRICIA M. *The Decade of Elusive Promise: Professional Women in the United States, 1920-1930*. Ann Arbor, MI: UMI Research Press, 1978.

2954 Hutchinson, Emilie J. *Women's Wages*. NY: Columbia U Press, 1919.
2955 Illinois Bureau of Labor Statistics. "Working Women in Chicago." *Seventh Biennial Report, 1892*, Part 1. Springfield, IL: The Bureau, 1893.
2956 International Labour Office. *Bibliography on Women Workers (1861-1963)*. Geneva: ILO, 1974.
2957 Janiewski, Dolores. "Making Common Cause; the Needlewomen of New York, 1831-1869." *Signs*, Vol 1 (1976), 777-86.
2958 Jensen, Joan. "Cloth, Butter and Boarders: Women's Household Production for the Market." *Review of Radical Political Economics*, Vol 12 (Summer 1980), 14-24.
2959 Jessup, Mary F. *Women in the Railroad Industry during and after World War I.*, Historical Studies of Wartime Problems No 70. Wash.: U.S. Bureau of Labor Statistics (Division of Historical Studies of Wartime Problems, 1941-1945), 1944. (Mimeo.)
2960 Johnson, George, and Frank P. Stafford. "The Earnings and Promotion of Women Faculty." *American Economic Review*, vol 64 (1974), 888-903.
2961 Johnson, Oakley C. "Marxism and Women's Rights." *Political Affairs*, Vol 44 (1965), 40-51.
2962 Johnston, Laurie. "Lillian Roberts, Gotbaum Aide 'Keeps Management on Toes.'" *The New York Times*, Jun 19, 1978, p B1.
2963 Jones, Mary. *Autobiography of Mother Jones*. Chicago: Kerr, 1925.
2964 Jones, Nancy Baker. "A Forgotten Feminist: the Early Writings of Ida Husted Harper, 1878-1894." *Indiana Magazine of History*, Vol 73 (1977), 79-101. (Wrote monthly column "The Woman's Department" in the *Locomotive Firemen's Magazine*)
2965 Kahne, Hilda, and Andrew Kohen. "Economic Perspectives on the Roles of Women in the American Economy." *Journal of Economic Literature*, Vol 13 (1975), 1249-92.
2966 Katzman, David M. *Seven Days a Week: Women and Domestic Service in Industrializing America*. NY: Oxford U Press, 1978.
2967 Kenneally, James J. *Women and American Trade Unions*. St. Albans, VT: Eden Press, 1978.
2968 Kennedy, Susan E. *If All We Did Was to Weep at Home: A History of White Working Class Women in America*. Bloomington: Indiana U Press, 1979.
2969 ———. "Poverty, Respectability, and Ability to Work." *International Journal of Women's Studies*, Vol 2 (1979), 401-18.
2970 Kessler-Harris, Alice. "Organizing the Unorganizable: Three Jewish Women and Their Union." *Labor History*, Vol 17 (1976), 5-23.
2971 ———. *Out to Work: A History of Wage-Earning Women in the United States*. NY: Oxford U Press, 1982.
2972 ———. *Women Have Always Worked: A Historical Overview*. Old Westbury: Feminist Press, 1981.
2973 ———. "Women's Wage Work as Myth and History." *Labor History*, Vol 19 (1978), 287-307.
2974 Kessner, Thomas, and Betty Boyd Caroli. "New Immigrant Women at Work: Italians and Jews in New York City, 1880-1905." *Journal of Ethnic Studies*, Vol 5 (Winter 1978), 19-32.
2975 King, Allan G. "Industrial Structure, the Flexibility of Working Hours, and Women's Labor Force Participation." *Review of Economics and Statistics*, Vol 60 (1978), 399-407.
2976 Kizer, Benjamin H. "Elizabeth Gurley Flynn." *Pacific Northwest Quarterly*, Vol 57 (1966), 110-12.
2977 Klaczynska, Barbara. "Why Women Work: A Comparison of Various Groups —Philadelphia, 1910-1930." *Labor History*, Vol 17 (1976), 73-87.
2978 ———. *Working Women in Philadelphia, 1900-1930*. Ph D diss, Temple U, 1976.

2979 KLEINBERG, SUSAN J. *Technocracy's Stepdaughters: the Impact of Industrialization upon Working Class Women, Pittsburgh, 1865-1890.* Ph D diss, U of Pittsburgh, 1973.

2980 ———. "Technology and Women's Work: The Lives of Working Class Women in Pittsburgh, 1870-1900." *Labor History*, Vol 17 (1976), 58-72.

2981 KLEMESRUD, JUDY. "Director of Hospital Walkout: Lillian Roberts." *The New York Times*, Aug 5, 1976, p 52.

2982 KOLKO, GABRIEL. "Working Wives: their Effects on the Structure of the Working Class." *Science & Society*, Vol 42 (1978), 257-77.

2983 KOONTZ, ELIZABETH DUNCAN. "The Women's Bureau Looks to the Future." *Monthly Labor Review*, Vol 93 (Jun 1970), 3-9.

2984 KOZIARA, KAREN, and D. A. PIERSON. "The Lack of Female Union Leaders: a Look at Some Reasons." *Monthly Labor Review*, Vol 104 (May, 1981), 30-32.

2985 KUGLER, ISRAEL. "The Trade Union Career of Susan B. Anthony." *Labor History*, Vol 2 (1961), 90-100.

2986 KYRK, HAZEL. "Who Works and Why." *Annals of the American Academy of Political and Social Science*, Vol 251 (1947), 44-52.

2987 "The Labor of Women: Work and Family." *Signs*, Vol 4 (1979), entire issue.

2988 LAWSON, DON. *Frances Perkins: First Lady of the Cabinet*. NY: Abelard-Schuman, 1966.

2989 LEDGERWOOD, DONNA. *An Analysis of the Satisfaction/Dissatisfaction of U.S. Female Unionists with their Local Trade Union Organization: a View of the Coalition of Labor Union Women.* Ph D diss, U of Oklahoma, 1980.

2990 LEHRER, SUSAN. *Origins of Protective Labor Legislation for Women, 1900-1925.* Ph D diss, SUNY-Binghamton, 1980.

2991 LEIBOWITZ, ARLEEN. "Education and Home Production." *American Economic Review*, Vol 64 (1974), 243-50.

2992 LEMOV, PENELOPE. "Tailoresses Gave Wage the Needle." *Worklife*, Vol 1 (Feb 1976), 25-26.

2993 LERNER, GERDA. "The Lady and the Mill Girl: Changes in the Status of Women in the Age of Jackson." *Midcontinent American Studies Journal*, Vol 10 (Spring, 1969), 5-15.

2994 LEVIN, SUSAN B. *Their Own Sphere: Women's Work, the Knights of Labor and the Transformation of the Carpet Trade, 1870-1890.* Ph D diss, City U of NY, 1980.

2995 LICHTMAN, SHEILA T. *Women at Work, 1941-1945: Wartime Employment in the San Francisco Bay Area.* Ph D diss, U of California, 1981.

2996 LINDEN, FABIAN. *Women: A Demographic, Social and Economic Presentation.* NY: Conference Board, 1973.

2997 LITOFF, JUDY BARRETT. "Forgotten Women: American Wives at the Turn of the Century." *Historian*, Vol 40 (1978), 235-51.

2998 ———, and HAL LITOFF. "Working Women in Maine: A Note on Sources." *Labor History*, Vol 17 (1976), 88-95.

2999 LLOYD, CYNTHIA B. "The Role of Women in Modern Economic Life: A Working Bibliography." *Review of Radical Political Economics*, Vol 4 (Jul 1972), 129-31.

3000 ———. et al. *Women in the Labor Market.* NY: Columbia U Press, 1979.

3001 LOESER, HERTA. *Women, Work, and Volunteering.* Bost.: Beacon, 1974.

3002 LOFTIN, BERNADETTE K. "A Woman Liberated: Lillian C. West." *Florida Historical Quarterly*, Vol 52 (Apr 1974), 396-410. (editor of *Panama City Pilot,* 1917-37)

3003 LONG, JAMES, and ETHEL JONES. "Labor Force Entry and Exit by Married Women." *Review of Economics and Statistics*, Vol 62 (1980), 1-6.

3004 LOPATE, CAROL. "Women and Pay for Housework." *Liberation*, Vol 18 (May-Jun 1974), 8-11. (See responses in Sep-Oct issue)

3005 LOPEZ DE LA CRUZ, JESSIE. "My Life as Told to Ellen Cantarow." *Radical America*, Vol 12 (Nov-Dec 1978), 26-40.

3006 LOWRY, TOM. "Little David Blues." *Southern Exposure*, Vol 1 (Winter 1973), 137-43. (Interview with Fran Ansley, Brenda Bell & Florence Reece)

3007 LUBLIN, JOANN S. "Discrimination Against Women in Newsrooms: Fact or Fantasy?" *Journalism Quarterly*, Vol 49 (1972), 357-60.

3008 LUSSIER, VIRGINIA LEE. "Academic Collective Bargaining: Panaceas or Palliative for Women and Minorities?" *Labor Law Journal*, Vol 27 (1976), 565-72.

3009 LYLE, JEROLYN R. "An Empirical Study of the Occupational Standing of Women in Multinational Corporations." *Labor Law Journal*, Vol 24 (Aug 1973), 458-68.

3010 MCCOURT, KATHLEEN. *Working-Class Women and Grass-Roots Politics*. Bloomington: Indiana U Press, 1977.

3011 MCGAW, JUDITH A. "'A Good Place to Work,' Industrial Workers and Occupational Choice: the Case of Berkshire Women." *Journal of Interdisciplinary History*, Vol 10 (1979), 227-48.

3012 MACLAURY, JUDSON. "A Senator's Reaction to Report on Working Women and Children." *Monthly Labor Review*, Vol 98 (Oct 1975), 36-38.

3013 MADDALENA, LUCILLE A. *The Goals of the Bryn Mawr Summer School for Women Workers as Established during its First Five Years*. Ph D diss, Rutgers U, 1979.

3014 MALOS, ELLEN. "Housework and the Politics of Women's Liberation." *Socialist Review*, Vol 8 (1978), 41-71.

3015 MANCKE, RICHARD B. "Lower Pay for Women: A Case of Economic Discrimination?" *Industrial Relations*, Vol 10 (1971), 316-26.

3016 MANNING, CAROLINE. *The Immigrant Woman and her Job*. Wash.: G.P.O., 1930.

3017 MARSH, MARGARET. "The Anarchist Feminist Response to the 'Woman Question' in late Nineteenth Century America." *American Quarterly*, Vol 30 (1978), 533-47.

3018 MARTIN, GEORGE. *Madam Secretary: Frances Perkins*. Bost.: Houghton Mifflin, 1976.

3019 MASON, LUCY R. *To Win These Rights: A Personal Story of the CIO in the South*. NY: Harper, 1952.

3020 MATTHAEI, JULIE. *An Economic History of Women in America*. NY: Schocken Books, 1982.

3021 MATTHEWS, LILLIAN RUTH. *Women in Trade Unions in San Francisco*. Berkeley: U of California Press, 1913.

3022 MAY, ELAINE TYLER. "Expanding the Past: Recent Scholarship on Women in Politics and Work." *Reviews in American History*, Vol 10 (1982), 216-33.

3023 MEYER, ANNIE N., ed. *Woman's Work in America*. NY: Holt, 1891.

3024 MILDEN, JAMES W. "Women, Public Libraries, and Library Unions: the Formative Years." *Journal of Library History*, Vol 12 (1977), 150-58.

3025 MILKMAN, RUTH. "Organizing the Sexual Division of Labor: Historical Perspectives on 'Women's Work' and the American Labor Movement." *Socialist Review*, Vol 10 (Jan-Feb 1980), 95-150.

3026 ———. "Women's Work and Economic Crisis: Some Lessons of the Great Depression." *Review of Radical Political Economics*, Vol 8 (Spring 1976), 73-97.

3027 MILLER, FRANK, and MARY ANN COGHILL. "Sex and the Personnel Manager." *Industrial and Labor Relations Review*, Vol 18 (1964), 32-44.

3028 ———, and MARY ZITWER. "Women Workers Win One in New York." *Labor Law Journal*, Vol 28 (1977), 703-6.

3029 MILLER, MARC. "Working Women and World War II." *New England Quarterly*, Vol 53 (1980), 42-61.

3030 MILLER, SALLY M. "From Sweatshop Worker to Labor Leader: Theresa Malkiel, a Case Study." *American Jewish History*, Vol 68 (1978), 189-205.

3031 ———. "Other Socialists; Native-Born and Immigrant Women in the Socialist Party of America, 1901-1917." *Labor History*, Vol 24 (1983), 84-102.

3032 MILLER, WILLIAM D. *A Harsh and Dreadful Love: Dorothy Day and the Catholic Worker Movement*. NY: Liveright, 1973.

3033 MOHR, LILLIAN H. *Frances Perkins: That Woman in FDR's Cabinet.* Croton-on-Hudson, NY: North River Press, 1979.

3034 MORAN, ROBERT D. "Reducing Discrimination: Role of the Equal Pay Act." *Monthly Labor Review*, Vol 93 (Jun 1970), 30-34.

3035 MOTT, FRANK L. et al. *Women, Work, and Family: Dimensions of Change in American Society.* Lexington, MA: Lexington Books, 1978.

3036 MUNTS, RAYMOND, and DAVID C. RICE. "Women Workers: Protection or Equality?" *Industrial and Labor Relations Review*, Vol 24 (1970), 3-13.

3037 MURPHY, MIRIAM B. "The Working Women of Salt Lake City: a Review of the *Utah Gazetteer*, 1892-1893." *Utah Historical Quarterly*, Vol 46 (1978), 121-35.

3038 NASH, GARY B. "The Failure of Female Factory Labor in Colonial Boston." *Labor History*, Vol 20 (1979), 165-88.

3039 NESTOR, AGNES. *Woman's Labor Leader: An Autobiography.* Rockford, IL: Bellevue Books, 1954.

3040 *Nine to Five.* 1976. (Documentary film produced by WNET-TV in New York)

3041 NORDSTROM, BYRON. "Evelina Mansson and the Memoir of an Urban Labor Migrant." *Swedish Pioneer Historical Quarterly*, Vol 31 (1980), 182-95.

3042 NORTHRUP, HERBERT R., and JOHN A. LARSON. *The Impact of the AT&T-EEO Consent Decree.* Phila.: U of Pennsylvania, 1979.

3043 OAKLEY, ANN. *Woman's Work: The Houswife, Past and Present.* NY: Pantheon, 1975.

3044 ODENCRANTZ, LOUISE C. *Italian Women in Industry: A Study of Conditions in New York City.* NY: Russell Sage Foundation, 1919.

3045 ONDERCIN, DAVID G. *The Compleat Woman: the Equal Rights Amendment and Perception of Womanhood, 1920-1972.* Ph D diss, U of Minnesota, 1973.

3046 OPPENHEIMER, VALERIE KINCADE. *The Female Labor Force in the United States.* Westport, CT: Greenwood, 1970.

3047 ———. *The Female Labor Force in the United States: Factors Governing its Growth and Changing Composition.* Ph D diss, U of California, 1966.

3048 PALMER, PHYLLIS MARYNICK. *Frances Wright D'Arusmont: Case Study of a Reformer.* Ph D diss, Ohio State U, 1973.

3049 PAM, DOROTHY. *Exploitation, Independence and Solidarity: the Changing Role of American Working Women as Refelcted in the Working-Girl Melodrama, 1870-1910.* Ph D diss, New York U, 1980.

3050 PEARLSON, JEANNE S. *Equal Pay for Women; Its Development in the United States.* Ph D diss, Harvard U, 1953.

3051 PESOTTA, ROSE. *Bread Upon the Waters.* NY: Dodd, Mead, 1945.

3052 PETERSON, JOHN M. "Employment Effects of State Minimum Wages for Women: Three Historical Cases Re-examined." *Industrial and Labor Relations Review*, Vol 12 (1959), 406-22.

3053 PETRIK, PAULA. "Capitalists with Rooms: Prostitution in Helena, Montana, 1865-1900." *Montana Magazine of Western History*, Vol 31 (Apr 1981), 24-41.

3054 PICHLER, JOSEPH A., and H. GORDON FITCH. "And Women Must Weep: the NLRB as Film Critic." *Industrial and Labor Relations Review*, Vol 28 (1975), 395-410.

3055 PIDGEON, MARY E. *Employed Women under NRA Codes.*, Women's Bureau Bulletin 130. Wash.: G.P.O., 1935.

3056 ———. *Women in the Economy of the United States of America.* Wash.: G.P.O., 1937.

3057 PORTER, LORLE ANN. "Amelia Bloomer: An Early Iowa Feminist's Sojourn on the Way West." *Annals of Iowa*, Vol 41 (1973), 1242-57. (Her employment of women led to printers' strike 1854)

3058 POSNER, LESLIE. *Male-Female Worker Relations in a Traditionally Male Industrial Setting: the Case of the First Women Workers in a 'Co-Town' Steel Mill.* Ph D diss, U of Pittsburgh, 1980.

3059 PRATT, WILLIAM C. "Women and American Socialism, the Reading Experience." *Pennsylvania Magazine of History and Biography*, Vol 99 (1975), 72-91.

3060 PRZYBYLA, BARBARA. *The Experience of Taking Responsibility in Leadership Roles Among Selected Labor Union Women.* Ph D diss, U of Michigan, 1980.

3061 PUCKETT, PATTY LOU. *Yankee Reformer in a Man's World: Frances Perkins as Secretary of Labor.* Ph D diss, Michigan STate U, 1979.

3062 QUICK, PADDY. "Women's Work." *Review of Radical Political Economics,* Vol 4 (Jul 1972), 2-19.

3063 RAPER, ARTHUR M. "The Southern Negro and the NRA." *Georgia Historical Quarterly,* Vol 64 (1980), 128-45.

3064 RAPHAEL, EDNA E. "Working Women and the Membership in Labor Unions." *Monthly Labor Review,* Vol 97 (May 1974), 27-33.

3065 RAPONE, ANITA J. *Clerical Labor Force Formation: The Office Woman in Albany, 1870-1930.* Ph D diss, New York U, 1981.

3066 RATNER, RONNIE. "The Paradox of Protection: Maximum Hours Legislation in the U.S." *International Labour Review,* Vol 119 (1980), 185-87.

3067 "Report of the President's Commission on the Status of Women." *Monthly Labor Review,* Vol 86 (Oct 1963), 1166-69.

3068 REVERBY, SUSAN. "An Epilogue...or Prologue to C.L.U.W.?" *Radical America,* Vol 9 (Nov-Dec 1975), 111-14.

3069 RITTER, ELLEN M. "Elizabeth Morgan: Pioneer Female Labor Agitator." *Central States Speech Journal,* Vol 22 (1972), 242-51.

3070 ROBINSON, HARRIET H. et al. *Women of Lowell.* NY: Arno Press, 1974.

3071 ROSENBERG, BERNARD, and SAUL WEINMAN. "Young Women Who Work: An Interview with Myra Wolfgang." *Dissent,* Vol 19 (1972), 29-36.

3072 *Rosie the Riveter.* 1980. (Documentary produced & directed by Connie Field)

3073 ROTELLA, ELYCE. "Women's Labor Force Participation and the Decline of the Family Economy in the U.S." *Explorations in Economic History,* Vol 17 (1980), 95-117.

3074 ———. *Women's Labor Force Participation and the Growth of Clerical Employment in the United States, 1870-1930.* Ph D diss, U of Pennsylvania 1978.

3075 ROYDHOUSE, M. *The Universal Sisterhood of Women: Women and Labor Reform in North Carolina, 1900-1932.* Ph D diss, Duke U, 1980.

3076 RUBIN, MARILYN. "Debunking the Myth: Working Women in Suburbia." *New York Affairs,* Vol 5 (1979), 78-83.

3077 RURY, JOHN L. *Women, Cities and Schools: Education and the Development of an Urban Female Labor Force, 1890-1930.* Ph D diss, U of Wisconsin, 1982.

3078 SAFA, HELEN. "Runaway Shops and Female Employment: the Search for Cheap Labor." *Signs,* Vol 7 (1981), 418-33.

3079 SANDLER, B. "Women: the Last Minority." *Journal of College Placement,* Vol 32 (1972), 49-50.

3080 SCHARF, LOIS. *The Employment of Married Women during the Depression, 1929-1941.* Ph D diss, Case Western Reserve U, 1977.

3081 ———. *To Work and To Wed: Female Employment, Feminism, and the Great Depression.* Westport, CT: Greenwood, 1980.

3082 SCHNEIDERMAN, ROSE, and LUCY GOLDTHWAITE. *All for One.* NY: Paul Eriksson, 1967.

3083 SCHOFIELD, ANN. *The Rise of the Pig-Headed Girl: an Analysis of the American Labor Press for their Attitudes towards Women, 1877-1920.* Ph D diss, SUNY-Binghamton, 1980.

3084 SCORESBY, WILLIAM. *American Factories and Their Female Operatives, with an Appeal on Behalf of the British Factory Population and Suggestion for the Improvement of Their Condition.* Bost.: Ticknor, 1945.

3085 SCOTT, ANN FIROR. "Jane Addams and the City." *Virginia Quarterly Review,* Vol 43 (1967), 53-62.

3086 SEALANDER, JUDITH. *The Women's Bureau, 1920-1950: Federal Reaction to Female Wage Earning*. Ph D diss, Duke U, 1978.

3087 SECOMBE, WALLY. "The Housewife and her Labour under Capitalism." *New Left Review*, No 83 (Jan-Feb 1974), 3-24.

3088 SELLER, MAXINE S. "Beyond the Stereotype: a New Look at the Immigrant Woman 1880-1924." *Journal of Ethnic Studies*, Vol 3 (Spring 1975), 59-70.

3089 SEMEL, ROCHELLE, ed. *Union Women View Their Past*. Ithaca: NY State School of Industrial and Labor Relations, Cornell U, 1976.

3090 SEVERN, WILLIAM. *Frances Perkins: A Member of the Cabinet*. NY: Hawthorn, 1976.

3091 SEXTON, PATRICIA CAYO. "Workers (Female) Arise!" *Dissent*, Vol 21 (1974), 380-95. (On the founding of Coalition of Labor Union Women)

3092 SHARP, KATHLEEN A. *Rose Pastor Stokes: Radical Champion of the American Working Class, 1879-1933*. Ph D diss, Duke U, 1979.

3093 SHIELDS, E. L. *Negro Women in Industry*., Womens Bureau Bulletin No 20. Wash.: G.P.O., 1922.

3094 SHULER, ALEXANDERINA. "Clara Beyer: AID Advisor Made U.S. Labor History." *Front Lines*, Aug 29, 1974, p 8.

3095 SHULMAN, ALIX. *To the Barricades: The Anarchist Life of Emma Goldman*. NY: Crowell, 1971.

3096 SIDEL, RUTH. *Urban Survival, the World of Working Class Women*. Bost.: Beacon Press, 1978.

3097 SILLITO, JOHN. "Women and the Socialist Party in Utah, 1900-1920." *Utah Historical Quarterly*, Vol 49 (1981), 220-38.

3098 SILVER, SUSAN. "Women in the Work Place: a Variety of Viewpoiints." *Monthly Labor Review*, Vol 97 (May 1974), 85-89.

3099 SIPSER, MARGARET ANN. "Maternity Leave: Judicial and Arbitral Interpretation 1970-1972." *Labor Law Journal*, Vol 24 (1973), 173-90.

3100 SLAIGHT, WILMA RUTH. *Alice Hamilton: First Lady of Industrial Medicine*. Ph D diss, Case Western Reserve U, 1974.

3101 SMITH, CAROL J. *Women, Work and Use of Government Benefits: a Case Study of Hispanic Women Workers in New York's Garment Industry*. Ph D diss, Adelphi U, 1980.

3102 SMITH, HILDA WORTHINGTON. *Opening Vistas in Workers' Education: An Autobiography of Hilda Worthington Smith*. Wash.: publisher not indicated, 1978.

3103 SMUTS, ROBERT W. *Women and Work in America*. NY: Columbia U Press, 1959.

3104 "Socialist Women and Labor Struggles, 1934-45—a Report by Participants." *International Socialist Review*, Vol 36 (1975), 20-25, 36-38.

3105 SOKOLOFF, NATALIE J. *Women in the Labor Market: a Critique of Theoretical Perspectives in Sociology, Marxism, and Feminism*. Ph D diss, City U of NY, 1979.

3106 SPECTOR, ROBERT M. "Woman against the Law: Myra Bradwell's Struggle for Admission to the Illinois Bar." *Illinois State Historical Society Journal*, Vol 68 (1975), 228-42.

3107 SPOFFORD, HARRIET E. *The Servant Girl Question*. Bost.: Houghton, Mifflin, 1881.

3108 SREBNICK, AMY. *True Womanhood and Hard Times; Women and Early New York Industrialization, 1840-1860*. Ph D diss, SUNY-Stonybrook, 1979.

3109 STANSELL, CHRISTINE. "The Origins of the Sweatshop: Women and Early Industrialization in New York City," pp 78-103, *Working Class America: Essays on Labor, Community, and American Society*, Michael Frisch & Daniel J. Walkowitz, eds. Urbana: U of Illinois Press, 1983.

3110 ———. *Women of the Laboring Poor in New York City, 1820-1860*. Ph D diss, Yale U, 1980.

3111 STAPEN, CANDYCE. *The Novel Form and Woodhull and Claflin's Weekly, 1870-1876: a Little Magazine Edited by Women and Published for Suffragists, Socialists, Free Lovers and other Radicals*. Ph D diss, U of Maryland, 1980.

3112 STEVENSON, GLORIA. "That's No Lady, That's Mother Jones." *Worklife*, Vol 1 (Jul 1976), 24-28.

3113 STOVER, ED. "Inflation and the Female Labor Force." *Monthly Labor Review*, Vol 26 (Jan 1975), 50-58.

3114 STRASSER, SUSAN. *Never Done: the Ideology and Technology of Household Work, 1850-1930.* Ph D diss, SUNY-Stonybrook, 1978.

3115 STRICKER, FRANK. "Cookbooks and Law Books: the Hidden History of Career Women in Twentieth Century America." *Journal of Social History*, Vol 10 (1976), 1-19.

3116 STROM, SHARON. "Old Barriers and New Opportunities: Working Women in Rhode Island, 1900-1940." *Rhode Island History*, Vol 39 (1980), 43-55.

3117 SUMNER, HELEN L. "History of Women in Industry in the United States." *Report on Condition of Woman and Child Wage-Earners in the United States*, Vol IX (1910), U. S. Bureau of Labor. Wash.: G.P.O., 1910-13. (U.S. Senate Document 645, 61st Congress, 2nd Session, 19 volumes)

3118 SUTHERLAND, SHARON L. "The Unambitious Female: Women's Low Professional Aspirations." *Signs*, Vol 3 (1978), 774-94.

3119 TARR-WHELAN, L. "Women Workers and Organized Labor." *Social Policy*, Vol ((May 1978), 13-17.

3120 TAX, MEREDITH. "The United Front of Women." *Monthly Review*, Vol 32 (Oct 1980), 30-48.

3121 TAYLOR, JUDITH. *The Struggle for Work and Love: Working Women in American Novels, 1890-1925.* Ph D diss, U of California, 1978.

3122 TENTLER, LESLIE WOODCOCK. *Wage-Earning Women: Industrial Work and Family Life in the United States, 1900-1930.* NY: Oxford U Press, 1979.

3123 ———. *Women and Work: Industrial Employment and Sex Roles, 1900-1929.* Ph D diss, U of Michigan, 1976.

3124 TILLY, LOUISE, and JOAN W. SCOTT. *Women, Work, and Family*. NY: Holt, Rinehart & Winston, 1978.

3125 TRAVIS, ANTHONY R. "Sophonisba Beckinridge, Militant Feminist." *Mid-America*, Vol 58 (1976), 111-35.

3126 TREY, J. E. "Women in the War Economy, World War II." *Review of Radical Political Economics*, Vol 4 (Jul 1972), 40-57.

3127 TROGER, ANNE MARIE. "Coalition of Labor Union Women: Strategic Hope, Tactical Despair." *Radical America*, Vol 9 (Nov-Dec 1975), 85-110.

3128 TURBIN, CAROLE. *Woman's Work and Woman's Rights: A Comparative study of the woman's Trade Union Movement and the Woman Suffrage Movement in the Mid-Nineteenth Century*. Ph D diss, New School for Social Research, 1979.

3129 TURNER, MARJORIE B. *Women and Work*. Los Angeles: Institute of Industrial Relations, U of California, 1964.

3130 *The Twentieth Century Trade Union Woman: Vehicle for Social Change, an Oral History Collection—Part I.* Sanford, NC: Microfilming Corp. of America, 1979. (Microfiche)

3131 TWIN, STEPHANIE L. *Jack and Jill: Aspects of Women's Sports History in America, 1870-1940.* Ph D diss, Rutgers U, 1979.

3132 TYLER, GUS. "Sexism and the Unions." *New Leader*, Dec 17, 1979, pp 24-27.

3133 "U.M.W.A. Women: from Mother Jones to Brookside." *United Mine Workers Journal*, Vol 87 (Mar 1976), 10-27.

3134 UNDERWOOD, LORRAINE A. *Women in Federal Employment Programs*. Wash.: Urban Institute, 1979.

3135 *Union Maids*. 1976. (Non-fiction film directed by Julia Reichert, et al.)

3136 U.S. BUREAU OF LABOR. *Report on Condition of Woman and Child Wage-Earners in the United States.*, 19 vols. Wash.: G.P.O., 1910-13. (U.S. Senate Document 645, 61st Congress, 2nd Session)

3137 U.S. DEPARTMENT OF LABOR. Manpower Administration *Dual Careers: A Longitudinal Study of Labor Market Experience of Women.* Wash.: G.P.O., 1970.

3138 U.S. EQUAL EMPLOYMENT OPPORTUNITY COMMISSION. *Hearings...on Utilization of Minority and Women Workers in the Public Utilities Industry. Hearings Held in Washington, D.C., November 15-17, 1971.* Wash.: G.P.O., 1972.

3139 U.S. WOMEN'S BUREAU. *A Guide to Sources of Data on Women and Women Workers for the United States and for Regions, States, and Local Areas.* Wash.: The Bureau, 1972.

3140 ———. *Towards Better Working Conditions for Women: Methods and Policies of the National Women's Trade Union League.* Wash.: G.P.O., 1953.

3141 URY, CLAUDE M. "Women in Trade Unions: an Historical Overview." *Social Studies,* Vol 72 (1981), 280-83.

3142 VAN KLEECK, MARY. *Women in the Bookbinding Trade.* NY: Survey Associates, 1913.

3143 VAN VORST, MARIE. *The Woman Who Toils.* NY: Doubleday, Page, 1903.

3144 VOGEL, LISE. *Beyond Domestic Labor: Women's Oppression and the Reproduction of Labor Power.* Ph D diss, Brandeis U, 1981.

3145 ———. "'Humorous Incidents and Sound Common Sense': More on the New England Mill Women." *Labor History,* Vol 19 (1978), 280-86.

3146 WALDMAN, ELIZABETH. "Changes in the Labor Force Activity of Women." *Monthly Labor Review,* vol 93 (Jun 1970), 10-18.

3147 WALKOWITZ, DANIEL J. "Workingclass Women in the Gilded Age: Factory, Community and Family Life Among Cohoes, New York, Cotton Workers." *Journal of Social History,* Vol 5 (1972), 464-90.

3148 WALSHOK, MARY LINDENSTEIN. *Blue-Collar Women: Pioneers on the Male Frontier.* Garden City, NY: Anchor, 1981.

3149 WANDERSEE, WINIFRED D. *Women's Work and Family Values, 1920-1940.* Cambr.: Harvard U Press, 1981.

3150 WAYSKI, MARGARET. "Women and Mining in the Old West." *Journal of the West,* Vol 20 (1981), 38-47.

3151 WEIGLEY, EMMA SEIFRIT. "It Might have been Euthenics: the Lake Placid Conferences and the Home Economics Movement." *American Quarterly,* Vol 26 (1974), 79-96.

3152 WEINER, LOIS. "Women Trade Unionists Organize." *New Politics,* Vol 9 (Winter 1974), 31-35.

3153 WEINER, LYNN. *From the Working Girl to the Working Mother: the Debate over Women, Work, and Morality in the U.S., 1820-1980.* Ph D diss, Boston U, 1981.

3154 ———. "Our 'Sister's Keepers': the Minneapolis Christian Association and Housing for Working Women." *Minnestoa History,* Vol 46 (19790, 189-200.

3155 WEISSKOFF, FRANCINE BLAU. "Women's 'Place' in the Labor Market." *American Economic Review,* Vol 42 (1972), 161-66.

3156 WERTHEIMER, BARBARA M. *Labor Education for Women Workers.* Phila.: Temple U Press, 1981.

3157 ———. *We Were There: The Story of Working Women in America.* NY: Pantheon, 1977.

3158 ———, and ANNE H. NELSON. *Trade Union Women: A Study of Their Participation in New York City Locals.* NY: Praeger, 1975.

3159 WEST, ELLIOTT. "Scarlet West: the Oldest Profession in the Trans-Mississippi West." *Montana: The Magazine of Western History,* Vol 31 (Apr 1981), 16-27.

3160 WILLACY, HAZEL M., and HARVEY J. HILASKI. "Working Women in Urban Poverty Neighborhoods." *Monthly Labor Review,* Vol 93 (Jun 1970), 35-38.

3161 WILLETT, MABEL H. *The Employment of Women in the Clothing Trade, New York.* NY: Columbia U Press, 1902.

3162 WITHORN, ANN. "The Death of the Coalition of Labor Union Women." *Radical America,* Vol 10 (Mar-Apr 1976), 47-51.

3163 WOLFE, ALLIS ROSENBERG. "Letters of a Lowell Mill Girl and Friends." *Labor History*, Vol 17 (1976), 96-102.

3164 WOLFSON, THERESA. *The Woman Worker and the Trade Unions.* NY: International Publishers, 1926.

3165 ———, and ALICE J. G. PERKINS. *Frances Wright: Free Enquirer; the Study of a Temperament.* NY: Harper, 1939.

3166 "Women in the Labor Force." *Industrial and Labor Relations Forum.*, Vol 7 (Oct 1971), entire issue.

3167 "Women in the Workplace: A Special Section." *Monthly Labor Review*, Vol 97 (May 1974), 3-58, 85-89.

3168 "Women Workers—Employment Trends, 1900 to 1950." *Monthly Labor Review*, Vol 72 (1951), 52.

3169 WOMEN'S TRADE UNION LEAGUE OF MASSACHUSETTS. *The History of Trade Unionism among Women in Boston.* Bost.: The League, 1915.

3170 "Working Women and the War: Four Narratives." *Radical America*, Vol 9 (Jul-Aug 1975), 133-61.

3171 ZELMAN, PATRICIA. *Development of Equal Employment Opportunity for Women as a National Policy, 1960-1967.* Ph D diss, Ohio State U, 1981.

3172 ———. *Women, Work, and National Policy: The Kennedy-Johnson Years.* Ann Arbor: U of Michigan Press, 1982.

Immigration, Ethnicity, and Minority Groups

3173 ABRAMSON, EDWARD A. *The Immigrant Experience in American Literature*. Durham, UK: British Association for American Studies, 1982. (Pamphlet)

3174 ADAMS, ARVIL V. *Toward Fair Employment and the EEOC: A Study of Compliance Procedures Under Title VII of the Civil Rights Act of 1964: Final Report*. Wash.: G.P.O., 1973.

3175 ———. et al. "Plantwide Seniority, Black Employment, and Employer Affirmative Action." *Industrial and Labor Relations Review*, Vol 26 (1972), 686-90.

3176 ALLEN, FAYETTA A. "Blacks in Appalachia." *Black Scholar*, Vol 5 (Jun 1974), 42-52.

3177 ANDERSON, BERNARD E. *Negro Employment in Public Utilities: A Study of Racial Policies in the Electric Power, Gas, and Telephone Industries*. Phila.: U of Pennsylvania Press, 1970.

3178 ARMENTROUT-MA, L. EVE. "Chinese in California's Fishing Industry, 1850-1941." *California History*, Vol 60 (1981), 142-57.

3179 ASHENFELTER, ORLEY. "Racial Discrimination and Trade Unionism." *Journal of Political Economy*, Vol 80 (1972), 435-64.

3180 ———, and LAMOND I. GODWIN. "Some Evidence on the Effect of Unionism on the Average Wage of Black Workers Relative to White Workers, 1900-1967." *Proceedings of the Twenty-Fourth Annual Winter Meeting of the Industrial Relations Research Association,*, Dec 27-28, 1971, pp 217-24. Madison: IRRA, 1972.

3181 ASHER, R. "Jewish Unions and the American Federation of Labor Power Structure, 1903-1935." *American Jewish Historical Quarterly*, Vol 65 (1976), 215-27.

3182 ASHER, ROBERT. "Union Nativism and the Immigrant Response." *Labor History*, Vol 22 (1982), 325-48.

3183 ATTAWAY, WILLIAM. *Blood on the Forge* (a novel). NY: Doubleday, Doran, 1941.

3184 BACA-RAMIREZ, REYNALD, and DEXTER BRYAN. "The Undocumented Mexican Worker: a Social Problem?" *Journal of Ethnic Studies*, Vol 8 (Spring 1980), 55-70.

3185 BAILEY, KENNETH. "A Judicious Mixture: Negroes and Immigrants in the West Virginia Mines, 1880-1917." *West Virginia History*, Vol 34 (1973), 168-86.

3186 BAILY, SAMUEL L. "The Adjustment of Italian Immigrants in Buenos Aires and New York, 1870-1914." *American Historical Review*, Vol 88 (1983), 281-305.

3187 BALDWIN, STEPHEN E. "The Effect of Fixed-Wage Rises on Discriminated-Against Minorities." *Industrial and Labor Relations Review*, Vol 21 (1968), 581-82.

3188 BARKEY, FRED. "Socialist Influence in the West Virginia State Federation of Labor: the John Nugent Case." *West Virginia History*, Vol 38 (1977), 275-90.

3189 BARNUM, DAROLD T. *The Negro in the Bituminous Coal Mining Industry*. Phila.: U of Pennsylvania Press, 1970.

3190 BARTON, JOSEF J. *Peasants and Strangers: Italians, Rumanians, and Slovaks in an American City*. Cambr.: Harvard U Press, 1975.

3191 BATCHELDER, ALAN B. *The Negro in the Rubber Tire Industry*. Phila.: U of Pennsylvania Press, 1969.

3192 BAUMAN, JOHN F. "Black Slums/Black Projects: the New Deal and Negro Housing in Philadelphia." *Pennsylvania History*, Vol 41 (1974), 311-38.

3193 BELL, DANIEL. "Reflections on the Negro and Labor." *The New Leader*, Jan 21, 1963, pp 18-20.

3194 ———, and SEYMOUR MARTIN LIPSET, eds. "Trade Unions and Minority Groups." *The Journal of Social Issues*, Vol 9, 1953. (Special issue)

3195 BENNETT, LERONE, JR. *Confrontation: Black and White.* Chicago: Johnson Publishing Co., 1970.

3196 BERGMANN, BARBARA R., and WILLIAM R. KRAUSE. "Evaluating and Forecasting Progress in Racial Integration of Employment." *Industrial and Labor Relations Review*, Vol 25 (1972), 399-409.

3197 BJORKLUND, ROBERT L. et al. "Project Step-Up: A Systems Approach to Upgrading Laid-Off Disadvantaged Workers." *Proceedings of the Twenty-Third Annual Winter Meeting of the Industrial Relations Research Association*, Dec 28-29, 1970, pp 286-95, 318-19. Madison: IRRA, 1971.

3198 "Blacks and Organized Labor." *Black Enterprise*, Vol 2 (Jul 1972), 16-18.

3199 BLACKWELL, JAMES E., and MARIE HAUG. "Relations between Black Bosses and Black Workers." *Black Scholar*, Vol 4 (Feb 1973), 36-43.

3200 BLOCH, HERMAN D. *The Circle of Discrimination: An Economic and Social Study of the Black Man in New York*. NY: New York U Press, 1969.

3201 ———. "Craft Unions and the Negro in Historical Perspective." *Journal of Negro History*, Vol 43 (1958), 10-33.

3202 ———. "Discrimination against the Negro in Employment in New York, 1920-1963." *American Journal of Economics and Sociology*, Vol 24 (1965), 361-82.

3203 ———. "Labor and the Negro, 1866-1910." *Journal of Negro History*, Vol 50 (1965), 163-84.

3204 ———. "The National Labor Union and Black Workers." *Journal of Ethnic Studies*, Vol 1 (1973), 13-21.

3205 BLOOM, GORDON F., and F. MARION FLETCHER. *The Negro in the Supermarket Industry*. Phila.: U of Pennsylvania Press, 1972.

3206 *Blue Collar*. 1978. (Feature film co-written & directed by Paul Schraeder)

3207 BLUM, BILL. "Undocumented Workers: America's Clandestine Proletariat." *Socialist Revolution*, No 55 (Jan-Feb 1981), 139-58.

3208 BLUME, NORMAN. "Union Worker Attitudes toward Open Housing; the Case of the U.A.W. in the Toledo Metropolitan Area." *Phylon*, Vol 34 (1973), 63-72.

3209 BLUMROSEN, ALFRED W. "Craft Unions and Blacks: The View from Newark—The Need for Result-Oriented Research." *Proceedings of the Twenty-Fourth Annual Winter Meeting of the Industrial Relations Research Association,*, Dec 27-28, 1971, pp 210-16. Madison: IRRA, 1971.

3210 ———. "The Individual Right to Eliminate Employment Discrimination by Litigation." *Proceedings of the Nineteenth Annual Winter Meeting of the Industrial Relations Research Association*, Dec 28-29, 1967, pp 88-98. Madison: IRRA, 1967.

3211 ———. "A Survey of Remedies for Discrimination in the Union and on the Job." *Proceedings of the Twenty-First Annual Winter Meeting of the Industrial Relations Research Association*, Dec 29-30, 1968, pp 283-91, 303-305. Madison: IRRA, 1969.

3212 BODNAR, JOHN. *Immigration and Industrialization: Ethnicity in an American Mill Town, 1870-1940*. Pittsburgh: U of Pittsburgh Press, 1977.

3213 ———. "Immigration and Modernization: the Case of Slavic Peasants in Industrial America." *Journal of Social History*, Vol 10 (1976), 44-71.

3214 ———. "Immigration, Kinship, and the Rise of Working-Class Realism in Industrial America." *Journal of Social History*, Vol 14 (1980), 45-65.

3215 ———. "The Impact of the 'New Immigration on the Black Worker: Steelton, Pennsylvania, 1880-1920." *Labor History*, Vol 17 (1976), 214-29.

3216 ———. "The Procurement of Immigrant Labor: Selected Documents." *Pennsylvania History*, Vol 41 (1974), 189-206.

3217 ———. "Socialization and Adoptation: Immigrant Families in Scranton, 1880-1890." *Pennsylvania History*, Vol 43 (1976), 147-62.

3218 ———. et al. *Lives of Their Own: Blacks, Italians, and Poles in Pittsburgh, 1900-1960.* Pittsburgh, U of Pittsburgh Press, 1982.

3219 BRACEY, JOHN H., JR. et al, eds. *Black Workers and Organized Labor*. Belmont, CA: Wadsworth Publishing Co., 1971.

3220 BRAGAW, DONALD H. "Status of Negroes in a Southern Port City in the Progressive Era; Pensacola, 1896-1920." *Florida Historical Quarterly*, Vol 41 (1973), 281-302.

3221 BREEN, T. H., and STEPHEN INNES. "Seventeenth Century Virginia's Forgotten Yeomen: The Free Blacks." *Virginia Cavalcade*, Vol 32 (Summer 1982), 10-19.

3222 BRIER, STEPHEN. "Labor Politics and Race: A Black Worker's Life." *Labor History*, Vol 22 (1982), 416-21.

3223 BRODERICK, FRANCIS L., and AUGUST MEIER, eds. *Negro Protest Thought in the Twentieth Century*. Indianapolis: Bobbs-Merrill, 1966.

3224 BROOKS, TOM. "Negro Militants, Jewish Liberals, and the Unions." *Commentary*, Sep 1961, pp 209-16.

3225 BULLOCK, PAUL. "Employment Problems of the Mexican-American." *Industrial Relations*, Vol 3 (1964), 37-50.

3226 BUREAU OF NATIONAL AFFAIRS. *The Equal Employment Opportunity Act of 1972: Editorial Analysis, Discussion of Court Decisions Under 1964 Act, Text of Amended Act, Congressional Reports, Legislative History*. Wash.: The Bureau, 1973.

3227 BUSTAMANTE, J., and J. CROCKCRAFT. "One More Time: the Undocumented." *Radical America*, Vol 15 (Nov-Dec 1981), 7-15.

3228 CAHAN, ABRAHAM. *The Education of Abraham Cahan.* Phila.: Jewish Publication Society of America, 1969.

3229 ———. *The Rise of David Levinsky* (a novel). NY: Harper, 1917.

3230 CAMARILLO, ALBERT. *Chicanos in a Changing Society: From Mexican Pueblos to American Barrios in Santa Barbara and Southern California, 1848-1930.* Cambr.: Harvard U Press, 1979.

3231 CAMPBELL, JOEL T., and LEON BELCHER. "Changes in Non-White Employment, 1960-1966." *Phylon*, Vol 28 (1967), 325-37.

3232 CANTOR, MILTON, ed. *Black Labor in America.* Westport, CT: Negro Universities Press, 1969.

3233 CARDOSO, LAURENCE A. "Labor Emigration to the Southwest, 1916 to 1920: Mexican Attitudes and Policy." *Southwestern Historical Quarterly*, Vol 79 (1976), 400-16.

3234 CARTAGENA, E. PEREZ. *Education Labor Organizations in Puerto Rico since 1974: an Analysis of the Perspectives of Mainland and Puerto Rican Educational Labor Leaders.* Ph D diss, U of Connecticut, 1981.

3235 CARTER, DAN THOMAS. *The Scottsboro Case, 1931-1950.* Ph D diss, U of North Carolina, 1967.

3236 CASSELL, FRANK H. "Black Merchant Seamen of Newport, 1803-1865: A Case Study in Foreign Commerce." *Journal of Negro History*, Vol 8 (1972), 156-68.

3237 ———. "Chicago 1960-1970: One Small Step Forward." *Industrial Relations*, Vol 9 (1970), 277-93.

3238 ———. et al. "Discrimination Within Internal Labor Markets." *Industrial Relations*, Vol 14 (1975), 337-44.

3239 CAYTON, HORACE R., and GEORGE S. MITCHELL. *Black Workers and the New Unions.* Chapel Hill: U of North Carolina Press, 1939.

3240 Chen, Ta. *Chinese Migrations, with Special Reference to Labor Conditions.*, Bureau of Labor Statistics Bulletin 340. Wash.: G.P.O., 1923.

3241 *Children of Labor*. 1977. (Documentary film produced by Richard Broadman, et al.)

3242 Chiu, Ping. *Chinese Labor in California, 1850-1880: An Economic Study*. Madison: State Historical Society of Wisconsin, 1967.

3243 ———. *Chinese Labor in California, 1850-1880: An Economic Study*. Ph D diss, U of Wisconsin, 1960.

3244 Christian, Virgil L., Jr., and F. Ray Marshall. "Black Economic Progress in the South: The Role of Education." *Proceedings of the Twenty-Seventh Annual Winter Meeting of the Industrial Relations Research Association*, Dec 28-29, 1974, pp 287-93. Madison: IRRA, 1975.

3245 ———, and Adamantios Pepelasis. "Negro Agricultural Employment and Surplus Labor in the Economy of the South." *Proceedings of the Twenty-Third Annual Winter Meeting of the Industrial Relations Research Association*, Dec 28-29, 1970, pp 55-64, 67-68. Madison: IRRA, 1971.

3246 Coelho, Anthony. *A Row of Nationalities: Life in a Working Class Community, the Irish, English and French Canadians of Fall River, Mass., 1850-1890*. Ph D diss, Brown U, 1981.

3247 Cohen, A. P. "Notes on a Chinese Workingclass Bookshelf." *American Oriental Society Journal*, Vol 96 (1976), 419-30.

3248 Conk, Margo A. "Immigrant Workers in the City, 1870-1930: Agents of Growth or Threats to Democracy." *Social Science Quarterly*, Vol 62 (1981), 704-20.

3249 Cook, Fannie. *Mrs. Palmer's Honey* (a novel). NY: Doubleday, 1946.

3250 Corbett, P. Scott, and Nancy P. Corbett. "The Chinese in Oregon 1870-1880." *Oregon Historical Quarterly*, Vol 78 (1977), 73-85.

3251 Cramer, M. R. "Race and Southern White Workers' Support for Unions." *Phylon*, Vol 39 (1978), 311-21.

3252 Critchlow, Donald T. "Communist Unions and Racism: A Comparative Study of the Responses of the United Electrical Radio and Machine Workers and the National Maritime Union to the Black Question During World War II." *Labor History*, Vol 17 (1976), 230-44.

3253 Crowell, Elizabeth. *An Analysis of Discrimination Against the Negro in the Building Trades' Unions*. Ph D diss, Indiana U, 1971.

3254 Curry, Leonard P. *The Free Black in Urban America, 1800-1850*. Chicago: U of Chicago Press, 1981.

3255 Dann, Martin. "Black Populism: A Study of the Colored Farmers' Alliance through 1891." *Journal of Ethnic Studies*, Vol 2 (Fall 1974), 58-71.

3256 ———. *'Little Citizens': Working Class and Immigrant Childhood in New York City, 1890-1915*. Ph D diss, City U of NY, 1978.

3257 Das, Rajani K. *Hindustani Workers on the Pacific Coast*. Berlin: Walter de Gruyten, 1923.

3258 Davies, Shane, and Gary Fowler. "The Disadvantaged Urban Migrant in Indianapolis." *Economic Geography*, Vol 48 (1972), 153-67.

3259 ———, and David L. Hoff. "Impact of Ghettoization on Black Employment." *Economic Geography*, Vol 48 (1972), 421-27.

3260 Davis, Angela. "Reflections on the Black Women's Role in the Community of Slaves." *Massachusetts Review*, Vol 13 (1972), 81-100. (With Response by Johnetta Cole)

3261 Davis, J. Treadwell. "Nashoba: Frances Wright's Experiment in Self-Emancipation." *Southern Quarterly*, Vol 11 (1972), 63-90.

3262 Davis, W. G. "Black Worker in America." *Crisis*, Vol 83 (Fall 1976), 56-62.

3263 Denby, Charles. *Indignant Heart: A Black Worker's Journal*. Bost.: South End Press, 1978.

3264 DICKINSON, JOAN YOUNGER. "Aspects of Italian Immigration to Philadelphia." *Pennsylvania Magazine of History and Biography*, Vol 90 (1966), 445-64.

3265 DIGGINS, JOHN P. "The Italo-American Anti-Fascist Opposition." *Journal of American History*, Vol 54 (1967), 579-98.

3266 DINNERSTEIN, LEONARD, and DAVID M. REIMERS. *Ethnic Americans: A History of Immigration and Assimilation.*

3267 DOERINGER, PETER B. "Promotion Systems and Equal Employment Opportunity." *Proceedings of the Nineteenth Annual Winter Meeting of the Industrial Relations Research Association*, Dec 28-29, 1966, pp 278-89. Madison: IRRA, 1967.

3268 ———, and MICHAEL J. PIORE. "Equal Employment Opportunity in Boston." *Industrial Relations*, Vol 9 (1970), 324-39.

3269 DROTNING, JOHN E., and DAVID B. LIPSKY. "How Union Leaders View Job Training Programs." *Monthly Labor Review*, Vol 94 (Apr 1971), 65-66.

3270 DUBINSKY, IRWIN. *Reform in Trade Union Discrimination in the Construction Industry: Operation Dig and its Legacy*. NY: Praeger, 1973.

3271 DUBOFSKY, MELVYN. "Organized Labor and the Immigrant in New York City, 1900-1918." *Labor History*, Vol 2 (1961), 182-201.

3272 DUFOUR, WILLIAM D. *The Early Black Labor Movement: The Case of the Brotherhood of Sleeping Car POrters.* MS thesis, West Virginia U, 1972.

3273 ECKERT, EDWARD K. "Contract Labor in Florida During Reconstruction." *Florida Historical Quarterly*, Vol 47 (1968), 34-40.

3274 EHRLICH, RICHARD L. "Immigrant Strikebreaking Activity: A Sampling of Opinion Expressed in the *National Labor Tribune*, 1878-1885." *Labor History*, Vol 15 (1974), 528-42.

3275 EHRLICH, RICHARD L., ed. *Immigrants in Industrial America, 1850-1920.* Charlottesville: U Press of Virginia, 1977.

3276 ELGIE, ROBERT. "Industrialization and Racial Inequality within the American South, 1950-1970." *Social Science Quarterly*, Vol 61 (1980), 458-72.

3277 ELKINS, W. F. "'Unrest among the Negroes,' a British Document of 1919." *Science & Society*, Vol 32 (1968), 6-79.

3278 "Employment of Negroes by Government Contractors." *Monthly Labor Review*, Vol 87 (1964), 789-93.

3279 EPSTEIN, MELECH. *Jewish Labor in the U.S.A., 1914-1952.*, 2 vols. NY: Trade Union Sponsoring Committee, 1953.

3280 ———. *Jewish Labor in the U.S.A.: An Industrial, Political and Cultural History of the Jewish Labor Movement.* NY: Ktav Publishing House, 1969.

3281 ERENBURG, MARK. "Obreros Unidos in Wisconsin." *Monthly Labor Review*, Vol 91 (June 1968), 17-23.

3282 ERICKSON, CHARLOTTE. *American Industry and the European Immigrant, 1860-1885.* Cambr.: Harvard U Press, 1957.

3283 EZEANI, E. C. "Economic Conditions and Freed Black Slaves in the U.S., 1870-1920." *Review of Black Political Economy*, Vol × (1977), 104-18.

3284 FELDBERG, MICHAEL JAY. *The Philadelphia Riots of 1844: A Study of Ethnic Conflict.* Westport, CT: Greenwood, 1975.

3285 FENTON, EDWIN. *Immigrants and Unions, a Case Study: Italians and American Labor, 1870-1920.* NY: Arno Press, 1975.

3286 ———. "Italians in the Labor Movement." *Pennsylvania History*, Vol 26 (1959), 133-48.

3287 FERGUSON, RUSSELL J. *The Rights and Privileges of Bond-Servants and Slaves in the English Colonies of America.* Ph D diss, Indiana U, 1928.

3288 FERMAN, LOUIS A., comp. *Negroes and Jobs: A Book of Readings.* Ann Arbor: U of Michigan Press, 1968.

3289 FERRARIS, LUIGI VITTORIO. "L'Assassinio di Umberto I e gli Anarchici di Paterson." *Rassegna Storica del Risorgimento*, Vol 50 (1968), 47-64.

3290 *Finally Got the News.* 1970. (Non-fiction film by Black Star Productions)

3291 FINNEY, JOHN DUSTIN, JR. *A Study of Negro Labor During and After World War I.* Ph D diss, Georgetown U, 1967.

3292 FITZGERALD, RICHARD A. "The San Francisco *Illustrated Wasp* and Chinese Labor in the 1870s." *Southwest Economy and Society*, Vol 5 (Winter 1981), 3-9.

3293 FLETCHER, F. MARION. *The Negro in the Drug Manufacturing Industry*. Phila: U of Pennsylvania Press, 1970.

3294 ———. *The Negro in the Drugstore Industry*. Phila.: U of Pennsylvania Press, 1971.

3295 FLETCHER, LINDA P. *The Negro in the Insurance Industry*. Phila.: U of Pennsylvania Press, 1970.

3296 FLYNN, CHARLES. *White Land, Black Labor: Property, Ideology and the Political Economy of late Nineteenth Century Georgia.* Ph D diss, Duke U, 1981.

3297 FOGEL, ROBERT WILLIAM, and STANLEY ENGERMAN. *Time on the Cross: the Economics of American Negro Slavery*. Bost.; Little, Brown, 1974.

3298 FOGEL, WALTER. "Blacks in Meatpacking: Another View of The Jungle." *Industrial Relations*, Vol 10 (1971), 338-53.

3299 ———. "Illegal Alien Workers in the U.S." *Industrial Relations*, Vol 16 (1977), 243-63.

3300 ———. *Mexican Illegal Alien Workers in the United States*. Los Angeles: U of California, 1978.

3301 ———. *The Negro in the Meat Industry*. Phila.: U of Pennsylvania Press, 1970.

3302 FONER, PHILIP S. "Blacks and the Labor Movement in Pennsylvania: the Beginnings." *Pennsylvania Heritage*, Vol 4 (1977), 34-38.

3303 ———. *Organized Labor and the Black Worker, 1619-1973*. NY: Praeger, 1974.

3304 ———. "Peter H. Clark: Pioneer Black Socialist." *Journal of Ethnic Studies*, Vol 5 (Fall 1977), 17-35.

3305 ———, and RONALD L. LEWIS, eds.. *The Black Worker: A Documentary History from Colonial Times to the Present*. Phila.: Temple U Press, 1978- .

3306 FONER, PHILIP S., ed. "The Knights of Labor." *Journal of Negro History*, Vol 53 (1968), 70-77.

3307 FRANKLIN, CHARLES L. *The Negro Labor Unionist of New York: Problems and Conditions.* NY: Columbia U Press, 1936.

3308 FREDERICKSON, MARY. "Four Decades of Change: Black Workers in Southern Textiles, 1941-1981." *Radical America*, Vol 16 (Nov-Dec 1982), 27-44.

3309 FRIEND, BRUCE I. *The Literature of the Negro worker, 1877-1968: A Critical Analysis.* MS thesis, Cornell U, 1970.

3310 GAMBOA, ERASMO. "Mexican Migration into Washington State: a History, 1940-1950." *Pacific Northwest Quarterly*, Vol 72 (1981), 121-31.

3311 GARCIA, JUAN RAMON. *Operation Wetback: The Mass Deportation of Mexican Undocumented Workers in 1954*. Westport, CT: Greenwood, 1980.

3312 GARCIA, MARIO T. "Americanization and the Mexican Immigrant, 1880-1930." *Journal of Ethnic Studies*, Vol 6 (Summer 1978), 19-34.

3313 ———. "On Mexican Immigration, the U.S. and Chicano History." *Journal of Ethnic Studies*, Vol 7 (Spring 1979), 80-88.

3314 GATEWOOD, LUCIAN B. "The Black Artisan in the U.S., 1890-1930." *Review of Black Political Economy*, Vol 5 (Fall 1974), 19-44.

3315 GAZDA, HENRY. "Frances Perkins' Interest in a New Deal for Blacks." *Monthly Labor Review*, Vol 103 (Apr 1980), 31-35.

3316 GENOVESE, EUGENE. *From Rebellion to Revolution: Afro American Slave Revolts in the Making of the Modern World.* Baton Rouge: Louisiana State U Press, 1979.

3317 ———. *The Political Economy of Slavery: Studies in the Economy and Society of the Slave South.* NY: Pantheon, 1965.

3318 Geschwender, James A. "League of Revolutionary Black Workers: Problems Confronting Black Marxist-Leninist Organizations." *Journal of Ethnic Studies*, Vol 2 (Fall 1974), 1-23.

3319 ———. "Marxist-Leninist Organization: Prognosis among Black Workers." *Journal of Black Studies*, Vol 8 (1978), 279-98.

3320 Ginger, Ray. "Were Negroes Strikebreakers?" *Negro History Bulletin*, Vol 15 (1952), 73-74.

3321 Giordano, Paul A. *The Italians of Louisiana: their Cultural Background and their Many Contributions in the Fields of Literature, the Arts, Education, Politics, Business and Labor*. Ph D diss, Indiana U, 1979.

3322 Glanz, Rudolph. "Some Remarks on Jewish Labor and American Public Opinion in the pre-World War I Era." *YIVO Annual of Jewish Social Science*, Vol 16 (1976), 178-201.

3323 Glaser, David. "Migration in Idaho's History." *Idaho Yesterdays*, Vol 11 (1967), 22-31.

3324 Gordon, Milton M. "Recent Trends in the Study of Minority and Race Relations." *Annals of the American Academy of Political and Social Science*, Vol 350 (1963), 148-56.

3325 Gould, William B. "Black Workers in White Unions." *Black Enterprise*, Vol 8 (Oct 1977), 67-69.

3326 ———. *Black Workers in White Unions: Job Discrimination in the United States*. Ithaca: Cornell U Press, 1977.

3327 ———. "Racial Discrimination, the Courts, and Construction." *Industrial Relations*, Vol 11 (1972), 380-93.

3328 Graham, Joseph. "Chicano Workers: Their Status and Struggles." *Political Affairs*, Vol 41 (Jan 1972), 26-35.

3329 Gray, Lois. *Case Study No. 7: The Labor Unions and Puerto Ricans in New York City*. Paris: Organisation for Economic Co-Operation and Development, 1963.

3330 Greeley, Andrew M. "New Ethnicity and Blue Collars: Cultural Pluralism in the Working Class." *Dissent*, Vol 19 (1972), 270-77.

3331 Green, James R. "Tenant Farmer Discontent and Socialist Protest in Texas, 1901-17." *Southwestern Historical Quarterly*, Vol 81 (1977), 133-54.

3332 Greene, Lorenzo J., ed. "Negro Sharecroppers." *Negro History Bulletin*, Vol 31 (Feb 1968), 17-19.

3333 Greene, Victor R. "The Poles and Anthracite Unions in Pennsylvania." *Polish American Studies*, Vol 22 (1965), 10-16.

3334 Greer, Edward. "Racism and United States Steel, 1906-1974." *Radical America*, Vol 10 (Sep-Oct 1976), 45-66.

3335 Greer, Scott A. *Last Man In: Racial Access to Union Power*. Glencoe, IL: Free Press, 1959.

3336 Grob, Gerald N. "Organized Labor and the Negro Worker, 1865-1900." *Labor History*, Vol 1 (1960), 164-76.

3337 Gross, James A. "Historians and the Literature of the Negro Worker." *Labor History*, Vol 10 (1969), 536-46.

3338 Gross, Joel. *Maura's Dream* (a novel). NY: Seaview Books, 1981.

3339 Grossman, Jonathan. "Black Studies in the Department of Labor, 1897-1907." *Monthly Labor Review*, Vol 97 (Jun 1974), 17-27.

3340 Gutman, Herbert G. "Black Coal Miners and the Greenback-Labor Party in Redeemer, Alabama: 1878-1879. The Letters of Warren D. Kelley, Willia Johnson Thomas, 'Dawson,' and Others." *Labor History*, Vol 10 (1969), 506-35.

3341 ———. *The Black Family in Slavery and Freedom, 1750-1925*. NY: Pantheon, 1974.

3342 ———. "Documents on Negro Seamen during the Reconstruction Period." *Labor History*, Vol 7 (1966), 307-11.

3343 ———. "Five Letters of Immigrant Workers from Scotland to the United States, 1867-1869: William Latta, Daniel M'Lachlan, and Allan Pinkerton." *Labor History*, Vol 9 (1968), 384-408.

3344 ———. "Reconstruction in Ohio: Negroes in the Hocking Valley Coal Mines in 1873 and 1874." *Labor History*, Vol 3 (1962), 243-64.

3345 ———. *Slavery and the Numbers Game: A Critique of Time on the Cross*. NY: Pantheon, 1978.

3346 HAMMERMAN, HERBERT. "Minority Workers in Construction Referral Unions." *Monthly Labor Review*, Vol 95 (May 1972), 17-26.

3347 ———, and MARVIN ROGOFF. "Unions and Title VII of the Civil Rights Act of 1964." *Monthly Labor Review*, Vol 99 (Apr 1976), 34-37.

3348 HANDLIN, OSCAR. *The Newcomers: Negroes and Puerto Ricans in a Changing Metropolis*. Cambr.: Harvard U Press, 1959.

3349 HANSEN, KAREN T. *American Indians and Work in Seattle: Associations, Ethnicity and Class*. Ph D diss, U of Washington, 1979.

3350 HAREVEN, TAMARA K. "Un-American America and the 'Jewish Daily Forward'" *YIVO Annual of Jewish Social Science*, Vol 4 (1969), 234-50.

3351 HARLAN, LOUIS R. *The Negro in American History*. Wash.: Service Center for Teachers of History, American Historical Association, 1965.

3352 HARNEY, ROBERT F. "The Padrone and the Immigrant." *Canadian Review of American Studies*, Vol 5 (1974), 101-18.

3353 HARRIS, WILLIAM H. "Federal Intervention in Union Discrimination: FEPC and West Coast Shipyards During World War II." *Labor History*, Vol 22 (1981), 325-47.

3354 ———. *The Harder We Run: Black Workers Since the Civil War*. NY: Oxford U Press, 1982.

3355 ———. "Work and the Family in Black Atlanta, 1880." *Journal of Social History*, Vol 9 (1976), 319-30.

3356 HARRISON, BENNETT. "Human Capital, Black Poverty and 'Radical' Economics." *Industrial Relations*, Vol 10 (1971), 277-86.

3357 HAWLEY, ELLIS W. "The Politics of the Mexican Labor Issue, 1950-1965." *Agricultural History*, Vol 40 (1966), 157-76.

3358 HAYES, LAURENCE J. W. *The Negro Federal Government Worker*. Wash.: Howard University, 1941.

3359 HAYES, MARION. "A Century of Change: Negroes in the U.S. Economy, 1860-1960." *Monthly Labor Review*, Vol 85 (1962), 1359-65.

3360 HAYNES, GEORGE E. *The Negro at Work in New York City*. NY: Columbia U Press, 1912.

3361 HAYWOOD, HARRY. *Black Bolshevik: Autobiography of an Afro-American Communist*. Chicago: Liberator, 1978.

3362 HEALD, MORRELL. *Business Attitudes toward European Immigration, 1861-1914*. Ph D diss, Yale U, 1951.

3363 HEARNS, JACKIE P. "New Approaches to Meet Post-Hiring Difficulties of Disadvantaged Workers." *Proceedings of the Twenty-First Annual Winter Meeting of the Industrial Relations Research Association*, Dec 29-30, 1968, pp 207-16. Madison, IRRA, 1969.

3364 HELLWIG, DAVID. "Black Attitudes Towards Immigrant Labor in the South, 1865-1910." *Filson Club Historical Quarterly*, Vol 54 (1980), 151-68.

3365 HENDERSON, THOMAS MCLEAN. *Tammany Hall and the New Immigrants*. Ph D diss, U of Virginia, 1973.

3366 HENRY, KEITH S. "Caribbean Migrants in New York: the Passage from Political Quiescence to Radicalism." *Afro-Americans in New York Life and History*, Vol 2 (Jul 1978), 29-41.

3367 HERBST, ALMA. *The Negro in the Slaughtering and Meat Packing Industry in Chicago.* Ph D diss, U of Chicago, 1930.

3368 HERRING, GEORGE S. *A Study of an Inter-Institutional Effort for Preparing Minority Trade Union Leaders: a Programmatic Alternative for Higher Education* Ph D diss, U of California, 1978.

3369 HERTZ, JACOB S., comp. *The Jewish Labor Bund: A Pictorial History, 1897-1957.* NY: Farlag Unser Tsait, 1958.

3370 *Hester Street.* 1975. (Feature film by Joan Micklin Silver)

3371 HIESTAND, DALE L. "Equal Employment in New York City." *Industrial Relations,* Vol ((1970), 294-307.

3372 HIGGINBOTHAM, A. LEON, JR. "Civil Action 71-2698—The Commonwealth of Pennsylvania and Raymond Williams, et al. vs. Local Union 542, International Union of Operating Engineers, et al." *Journal of Negro History,* Vol 60 (1975), 360-98.

3373 HILL, C. RUSSELL. "Migrant-Nonmigrant Earnings Differentials in a Local Labor Market." *Industrial and Labor Relations Review,* Vol 28 (1975), 411-23.

3374 HILL, HERBERT. "Affirmative Action and the Quest for Job Equality." *Review of Black Political Economy,* Vol 6 (Spring 1976), 263-78.

3375 ———. *Black Labor and the American Legal System.* Wash.: Bureau of National Affairs, 1977.

3376 ———. "Black Labor, the N.L.R.B., and the Developing Law of Equal Employment Opportunity." *Labor Law Journal,* Vol 26 (1975), 207-23.

3377 ———. "In the Age of Gompers and After—Racial Practices of Organized Labor" *New Politics,* Vol 4 (1965), 26-46.

3378 ———. *NAACP Labor Manual.* NY: NAACP, 1968.

3379 ———. "Organized Labor and the Negro Wage Earner: Ritual and Reality." *New Politics,* Vol 1 (1962), 8-19.

3380 ———. "Racial Inequality in Employment: The Patterns of Discrimination." *Annals of the American Academy of Political and Social Science,* Vol 357 (1965), 30-47.

3381 HILL, RICHARD CHILD. "Unionization and Racial Income Inequality in the Metropolis." *American Sociological Review,* Vol 39 (1974), 507-22.

3382 HIMES, CHESTER B. *Lonely Crusade* (a novel). NY: Knopf, 1947.

3383 HINCKLEY, TED C. "Prospectors, Profits & Prejudice." *American West,* Vol 2 (1965), 58-65. (Chinese miners in late 19th-century Alaska)

3384 HOERDER, DIRK, ed. *American Labor and Immigration History, 1877-1920s: Recent European Research.* Urbana: U of Illinois Press, 1983.

3385 HOFFMAN, ABRAHAM. "A Note on the Field Research Interviews of Paul S. Taylor for the Mexican Labor in the U.S. Monographs." *Pacific Historian,* Vol 20 (1976), 123-31.

3386 ———. "An Unusual Monument: Paul S. Taylor's *Mexican Labor in the U.S.* Monograph Series." *Pacific Historical Review,* Vol 45 (1976), 255-70.

3387 HOGG, THOMAS C. "Black Man in White Town." *Pacific Northwest Quarterly,* Vol 63 (1972), 14-21.

3388 HOLLEMAN, JERRY R. "The Job Ahead for the President's Committee on Equal Employment Opportunity." *Labor Law Journal,* Jul 1961, pp 618-21. (Proceedings, Spring Meeting, Industrial Relations Research Association, May 4-5, 1961)

3389 HOLM, TOM. "Fighting a White Man's War: the Extent and Legacy of American Indian Participation in World War II." *Journal of Ethnic Studies,* Vol 9 (Summer 1981), 69-82.

3390 HOLMES, MICHAEL S. "The Blue Eagle as 'Jim Crow Bird': The NRA and Georgia's Black Workers." *Journal of Negro History,* Vol 17 (1972), 276-83.

3391 ———. "The New Deal and Georgia's Black Youth." *Journal of Southern History,* Vol 38 (1972), 443-60.

3392 Holmes, William F. "Demise of the Colored Farmers' Alliance." *Journal of Southern History*, Vol 41 (1975), 187-200.

3393 ———. "The Leflore County Massacre and the Demise of the Colored Farmers' Alliance." *Phylon*, Vol 34 (1973), 267-74.

3394 Hope, John, II. "Trade Unions and Minority Problems—'The Self-Survey of the Packinghouse Union: A Technique for Effecting Change.'" *The Journal of Social Issues*, Vol 9 (1953).

3395 Horton, Aimee. "The Highlander Folk School: Pioneer of Integration in the South." *Teachers College Record*, Vol 68 (1966), 242-50.

3396 Hourwich, Isaac A. *Immigration and Labor: The Economic Aspects of European Immigration to the United States*. NY: Putnam, 1912.

3397 Howard, John C. *The Negro in the Lumber Industry*. Phila.: U of Pennsylvania Press, 1970.

3398 Howe, Irving. *World of Our Fathers*. NY: Harcourt Brace Jovanovich, 1976.

3399 Hummasti, Paul. *Finnish Radicals in Astoria, Oregon, 1904-1940: a Study in Immigrant Socialism*. Ph D diss, U of Oregon, 1976.

3400 Hunter, Gary J. *"Don't buy from where you can't work": Black Urban Boycott Movements during the Depression, 1929-1941*. Ph D diss, U of Michigan, 1977.

3401 Hutchinson, Edward P. *Legislative History of American Immigration Policy, 1798-1965*. Phila: U of Pennsylvania Press, 1981.

3402 Hyman, Bennett. *Racial Dualism in the Chicago Labor Market* Ph D diss, Northwestern U, 1968.

3403 Ichioka, Yuji. "Japanese Immigrant Labor Contractors and the Northern Pacific and the Great Northern Railroad Companies, 1898-1907." *Labor History*, Vol 21 (1980), 325-50.

3404 Ignatin, George, and Brian S. Rungeling. "The Economics of Discrimination: Theory and Practice." *Proceedings of the Twenty-Fourth Annual Winter Meeting of the Industrial Relations Research Association*, Dec 27-28, 1971, pp 70-78. Madison, IRRA, 1972.

3405 Ignatin, Noel. "Black Workers, White Workers." *Radical America*, Vol 8 (Jul-Aug 1974), 41-60.

3406 Ingle, Edward. *The Negro in the District of Columbia*. Balt.: Johns Hopkins Press, 1893.

3407 Jacobson, Julius, ed. *The Negro and the American Labor Movement*. Garden City: Doubleday, 1968.

3408 Janis, Ralph. "The Watsonville Anti-Filipino Riot of 1930: A Case Study of the Great Depression and Ethnic Conflict in California." *Southern California Quarterly*, Vol 61 (1979), 291-302.

3409 Jeffress, Philip W. *The Negro in the Urban Transit Industry*. Phila: U of Pennsylvania Press, 1970.

3410 Johnsen, Leigh D. "Equal Rights and the 'Heathen Chinee': Black Activism in San Francisco, 1865-1875." *Western Historical Quarterly*, Vol 11 (1980), 57-68.

3411 Johnson, Charles. "The Army, the Negro and the Civilian Conservation Corps: 1933-1942." *Military Affairs*, Vol 36 (1972), 82-88.

3412 Johnston, Esther. "A Square Mile of New York." *New York Public Library. Bulletin*, Vol 70 (1966), 524-36. (The Lower East Side, 1916-21)

3413 Jones, James E. *Disestablishment of Labor Unions for Engaging in Racial Discrimination—A New Use for an Old Remedy*. Madison: Institute for Research on Poverty, U of Wisconsin, 1972.

3414 Jones, Lamar B., and Loren C. Scott. "Minimum Wages and Black Employment in the Louisiana Sugarcane Industry." *Proceedings of the Twenty-Fourth Annual Winter Meeting of the Industrial Relations Research Association, Dec 27-28, 1971, pp 89-99.*, Madison: IRRA, 1972.

3415 KAHN, TOM. *The Economics of Equality.* NY: League for Industrial Democracy, 1964.

3416 KAIN, JOHN F., comp. *Race and Poverty: The Economics of Discrimination.* Englewood Cliffs, NJ: Prentice-Hall, 1969.

3417 KALMAR, KAREN. "Southern Black Elites and the New Deal: a Case Study of Savannah, Georgia." *Georgia Historical Quarterly*, Vol 66 (1981), 341-55.

3418 KARLIN, JULES ALEXANDER. "The Anti-Chinese Outbreak in Tacoma, 1885." *Pacific Historical Review*, Vol 23 (1954), 271-83.

3419 ———. "The Anti-Chinese Outbreaks in Seattle, 1885-1886." *Pacific Northwest Quarterly,* Vol 39 (1948), 103-30.

3420 KEISER, JOHN H. "Black Strikebreakers and Racism in Illinois, 1865-1900." *Illinois State Historical Society Journal*, Vol 45 (1972), 313-26.

3421 KELLY, MYRA. *Little Citizens: The Humours of School Life.* NY: McClure, 1904.

3422 ———. *Wards of Liberty.* NY: McClure, 1907.

3423 KELSEY, CARL. *The Negro Farmer.* Chicago: Jennings & Pye, 1903.

3424 KERR, LOUISE. *Chicano Experience in Chicago: 1920-70.* Ph D diss, U of Illinois, 1977.

3425 KESSLER, SIDNEY H. "The Organization of Negroes in the Knights of Labor." *Journal of Negro History*, Vol 37 (1952), 248-76.

3426 KESSLER-HARRIS, ALICE. *the Lower Class as a Factor in Reform: New York, the Jews, and the 1890s.* Ph D diss, Rutgers U, 1968.

3427 KESSNER, THOMAS. *The Golden Door: Immigrant Mobility in New York City, 1880-1915.* Ph D diss, Columbia U, 1975.

3428 ———. *The Golden Door: Italian and Jewish Immigrant Mobility in New York City, 1880-1915.* NY: Oxford U Press, 1977.

3429 ———. "Jobs, Ghettoes and the Urban Economy, 1880-1935." *American Jewish History*, Vol 71 (1981), 218-38.

3430 ———, and BETTY BOYD CAROLI. *Today's Immigrants: Their Stories.* NY: Oxford U Press, 1982.

3431 KIDDER, ALICE H. "Federal Compliance Efforts in the Carolina Textile Industry: A Summary Report." *Proceedings of the Twenty-Fifth Anniversary Meeting of the Industrial Relations Research Association*, Dec 28-29, 1972, pp 353-61.

3432 ———. "Paths from Poverty to Employment: Job Search Among Negroes." *Labor Law Journal*, Vol 19 (1968), pp 482-88.

3433 KIFER, ALLEN. "Changing Patterns of Negro Employment." *Industrial Relations*, Vol 3 (May 1964), 23-35.

3434 KIM, KWANG CHUNG. et al. "Job Information Deprivation in the U.S.: a Case Study of Korean Immigrants." *Ethnicity*, Vol 8 (1981), 219-32.

3435 KING, ALLAN G., and CHARLES B. KNAPP. "An Interracial Analysis of the Determinants of On-the-Job Training." *Proceedings of the Twenty-Seventh Annual Winter Meeting of the Industrial Relations Research Association*, Dec 28-29, 1974, pp 279-86.

3436 KING, CARL B., and HOWARD W. RISHER, JR.. *The Negro in the Petroleum Industry.* Phila.: U of Pennsylvania Press, 1969.

3437 KIRSTEIN, PETER NEIL. *Anglo over Bracero: a History of the Mexican Worker in the U.S. from Roosevelt to Nixon.* Ph D diss, St Louis U, 1973.

3438 KORMAN, GERD. "Americanization at the Factory Gate." *Industrial and Labor Relations Review*, Vol 18 (1965), 396-419.

3439 KORNHAUSER, WILLIAM. "The Negro Union Official: A Study of Sponsorship and Control." *American Journal of Sociology*, Vol 57 (1952), 443-52.

3440 KORNWEIBEL, THEODORE, JR. "An Economic Profile of Black Life in the Twenties." *Journal of Black Studies*, Vol 6 (1976), 307-20.

3441 KOVACH, K. A. "Blacks in the U.S. Labor Movement." *Michigan State University Business Topics*, Vol 25 (Autumn 1977), 11-16.

3442 KOZIARA, EDWARD C., and KAREN KOZIARA. *The Negro in the Hotel Industry*. Phila.: U of Pennsylvania Press, 1968.

3443 KRAUS, GEORGE. "Chinese Laborers and the Construction of the Central Pacific." *Utah Historical Quarterly*, Vol 37 (1969), 41-57.

3444 KRISLOV, SAMUEL. *The Negro in Federal Employment: The Quest for Equal Opportunity*. Minneapolis: U of Minnesota Press, 1967.

3445 KRUMAN, MARK W. "Quotas for Blacks: The Public Works Administration and The Black Construction Worker." *Labor History*, Vol 16 (1975), 37-51.

3446 KWONG, PETER. *The Politics of the Labor Movement in New York City's Chinatown, 1930-1950.* Ph D diss, Columbia U, 1980.

3447 LA GUMINA, SALVATORE J. *The Immigrants Speak: Italian Americans Tell Their Story*. NY: Center for Migration Studies, 1979.

3448 LADENSON, ALEX. "The Background of the Hawaiian-Japanese Labor Convention of 1886." *Pacific Historical Review*, Vol 9 (1940), 389-400.

3449 LAMM, ROGER. "Black Union Leaders at the Local Level." *Industrial Relations*, Vol 14 (1975), 220-32.

3450 LANDOLT, ROBERT G. *The Mexican-American Workers of San Antonio, Texas*. NY: Arno Press, 1976.

3451 LANE, A. T. "American Labour and European Immigrants in the late 19th Century." *Journal of American Studies*, Vol 11 (1977), 241-60.

3452 LANG, JANE, and HARRY N. SCHEIBER. "The Wilson Administration and the Wartime Mobilization of Black Americans." *Labor History*, Vol 10 (1969), 433-58.

3453 LANGLEY, HAROLD D. "The Negro in the Navy and Merchant Service—1789 [misprint for 1798]-1860." *Journal of Negro History*, Vol 52 (1967), 273-86.

3454 LARSON, RALPH V. *A Study of American Influences in the Finnish Trade Union Movement from 1890-1920.* Ph D diss, Indiana U, 1972.

3455 LAURENTZ, ROBERT. *Racial/Ethnic Conflict in the New York City Garment Industry, 1933-1980.* Ph D diss, SUNY-Binghamton, 1980.

3456 LAURIE, BRUCE. et al. "Immigrants and Industry: the Philadelphia Experience, 1850-1880." *Journal of Social History*, Vol 9 (1975), 219-48.

3457 LAWRENCE, ELWOOD P. *Immigrant in American Fiction.* Ph D diss, Western Reserve U, 1943.

3458 LEAB, DANIEL J. "*Rocky*: The Blue Collar Ethnic in Bi-Centennial America," pp 257-72, *American History/American Film: Interpreting the Hollywood Image*, Martin Jackson & John O'Connor, eds. NY: Ungar, 1979.

3459 LEIGH, DUANE. "Unions and Nonwage Racial Discrimination." *Industrial and Labor Relations Review*, Vol 32 (1979), 439-50.

3460 ———, and V. LANE RAWLING. "Racial Differentials in Male Unemployment Rates: Evidence from Low-Income Urban Areas." *Review of Economics and Statistics*, Vol 56 (1974), 150-57.

3461 LEINENWEBER, CHARLES. *Immigration and the Decline of Internationalism in the American Working Class Movement, 1864-1919.* Ph D diss, U of California, 1968.

3462 LEISERSON, WILLIAM M. *Adjusting Immigrant and Industry*. NY: Harper, 1924.

3463 LEONE, RICHARD D. *The Negro in the Trucking Industry*. Phila.: U of Pennsylvania Press, 1970.

3464 LEVINE, MARVIN J. *The Untapped Human Resource: The Urban Negro and Employment Equality*. Morristown, NJ: General Learning Press, 1972.

3465 LEVITAN, SAR A. et al. *Economic Opportunity in the Ghetto: The Partnership of Government and Business.* Baltimore: Johns Hopkins Press, 1970.

3466 LEVSTIK, FRANK R. "The Toledo Riot of 1862: A Study of Midwest Negrophobia." *Northwest Ohio Quarterly*, Vol 44 (1972), 100-6.

3467 LEWIS, RONALD L. *Coal, Iron, and Slaves: Industrial Slavery in Maryland and Virginia, 1715-1865*. Westport, CT: Greenwood, 1979.

3468 LIEBERSON, STANLEY. *A Piece of the Pie: Black and White Immigrants since 1880.* Berkeley: U of California Press, 1980.

3469 LIGGETT, MALCOLM H. "The Efficacy of State Fair Employment Practices Commissions." *Industrial and Labor Relations Review*, Vol 22 (1969), 559-67.

3470 ———. *Employment Patterns for Negro Males: The Decade of the Fifties.* Ph D diss, Cornell U, 1966.

3471 ———. "Unions and Title VII: Remedies for Insiders and Outsiders." *Proceedings of the Twenty-Fourth Annual Winter Meeting of the Industrial Relations Research Association*, Dec 27-28, 1971, pp 225-31. Madison: IRRA, 1972.

3472 LINDMARK, STURE. "The Swedish-Americans and the Depression Years, 1929-1932." *Swedish Pioneer Historical Quarterly*, Vol 19 (1968), 3-31.

3473 LIPSKY, DAVID B. "Employer Role in Hard-Core Trainee Success." *Industrial Relations*, Vol 12 (1973), 125-36.

3474 ———, and JOSEPH B. ROSE. "Craft Entry for Minorities: The Case of Project JUSTICE." *Industrial Relations*, Vol 10 (1971), 327-37.

3475 LOFTON, WILLISTON H. "Northern Labor and the Negro During the Civil War." *Journal of Negro History*, Vol 34 (1949), 251-73.

3476 LONG, DURWARD. "'*La Resistencia*': Tampa's Immigrant Labor Union." *Labor History*, Vol 6 (1965), 193-213.

3477 ———. "An Immigrant Co-operative Medical Program in the South, 1887-1963." *Journal of Southern History*, Vol 31 (1965), 416-34.

3478 LUNDEN, LEON E. "Antidiscrimination Provisions in Major Contracts, 1961." *Monthly Labor Review*, Vol 85 (1962), 643-51.

3479 MCELROY, KATHLEEN M. *Labor Relocation Assistance: the Alabama Experience. A Case-Study of the Tuskegee Institute Labor Mobility Demonstration Project, 1965-66.* Ph D diss, Case Western Reserve U, 1974.

3480 MCKEE, DELBER L. "'The Chinese must go!' Commissioner General Powderly and Chinese Immigration, 1897-1902." *Pennsylvania History*, Vol 44 (1977), 37-51.

3481 MCKERSIE, ROBERT B. "The Civil Rights Movement and Employment." *Industrial Relations*, Vol 3 (May 1964), 1-21.

3482 MCLAURIN, MELTON A. "The Racial Policies of the Knights of Labor and the Organization of Southern Black Workers." *Labor History*, Vol 17 (1976), 568-85.

3483 MCMATH, ROBERT C., JR. "Southern White Farmers and the Organization of Black Farm Workers: A North Carolina Document." *Labor History*, Vol 18 (1977), 115-19.

3484 MAN, ALBON P., JR. "Labor Competition and the New York Draft Riots." *Journal of Negro History*, Vol 36 (1951), 375-405.

3485 MANDEL, BERNARD. "Anti-Slavery and the Southern Worker." *Negro History Bulletin*, Vol 17 (1954), 99-105.

3486 ———. *The Northern Working Class and the Abolition of Slavery.* Ph D diss, Western Reserve U, 1952.

3487 ———. "Samuel Gompers and the Negro Workers, 1886-1914." *Journal of Negro History*, Vol 40 (1955), 34-60.

3488 ———. "Slavery and the Southern Workers." *Negro History Bulletin*, Vol 17 (1953), 57-62.

3489 MARCUS, IRWIN M. "The Southern Negro and the Knights of Labor." *Negro History Bulletin*, Vol 30 (1967), 5-7.

3490 MARGOLIS, RICHARD J. "Last Chance for Desegregation: Will Black and White Worker Live Together?" *Dissent*, Vol 19 (1972), 249-56.

3491 MARKOWITZ, STEVEN. "Paths from Poverty to Employment: Training and Job Creation—A Case Study." *Labor Law Journal*, Aug 1968, pp 488-96.

3492 MARKS, SAMUEL B. "Employer Techniques for Upgrading Low-Skill Workers." *Proceedings of the Twenty-First Annual Winter Meeting of the Industrial Relations Research Association*, Dec 29-30, 1968, pp 217-27. Madison: IRRA, 1969.

3493 MARSHALL F. RAY. "Black Workers and the Unions." *Dissent*, Vol 19 (1972), 295-302.

3494 ———. "Ethnic and Economic Minorities: Unions' Future or Unrecruitable?" *Annals of the American Academy of Political and Social Science*, Vol 350 (1963), 63-73.

3495 ———. *The Negro and Organized Labor.* NY: Wiley, 1965.

3496 ———. *The Negro Worker.* NY: Random House, 1967.

3497 ———. "Some Factors Influencing Union Racial Practices." *Proceedings of the Fourteenth Annual Meeting of the Industrial Relations Research Association*, Dec 28-29, 1961, pp 104-19. Madison: IRRA, 1962.

3498 ———. "Union Racial Problems in the South." *Industrial Relations*, Vol 1 (1962), 117-28.

3499 ———. "Unions and the Negro Community." *Industrial and Labor Relations Review*, Vol 17 (1964), 179-202, 619-26.

3500 ———, and ARVIL V. ADAMS. "Negro Employment in Memphis." *Industrial Relations*, Vol 9 (1970), 308-23.

3501 ———, and VERNON M. BRIGGS, JR.. *The Negro and Apprenticeship*. Balt.: Johns Hopkins Press, 1967.

3502 ———. "Remedies for Discrimination in Apprenticeship Programs." *Industrial Relations*, Vol 6 (1967), 303-20.

3503 ———, and JAMES HEFNER. "Black Employment in Atlanta." *Proceedings of the Twenty-Third Annual Winter Meeting of the Industrial Relations Research Association*, Dec 28-29, 1970, pp 45-54, 65-68. Madison: IRRA, 1971.

3504 MARTIN, CHARLES H. "Communists and Blacks: the International Labor Defense and the Angelo Herdon Case." *Journal of Negro History*, Vol 64 (1979), 131-41.

3505 MATERA, VINCENT L. "Steel Industry Equal Employment Consent Decress." *Proceedings of the Twenty-Seventh Annual Winter Meeting of the Industrial Relations Research Association*, Dec 28-29, 1974, pp 217-24. Madison: IRRA, 1975.

3506 MATISON, SUMNER ELIOT. "The Labor Movement and the Negro During Reconstruction." *Journal of Negro History*, Vol 33 (1948), 426-68.

3507 MATTHEWS, GLENNA. "An Immigrant Community in Indian Territory" *Labor History*, Vol 22 (1982), 374-94.

3508 MAURIZI, ALEX. "Minority Membership in Apprenticeship Programs in the Construction Trades." *Industrial and Labor Relations Review*, Vol 25 (1972), 200-6; Vol 26 (1972), 696-705; Vol 27 (1973), 93-102.

3509 MAY, J. THOMAS. "The Freedmen's Bureau at the Local Level: a Study of a Louisiana Agent." *Louisiana History*, Vol 9 (1968), 5-19.

3510 MAYER, MAGRIT. "American Labor and Immigration History, 1877-1972: Recent Research; Bericht ueber die gleichnamige Tagung in Bermen, 13-17 Nov 1978." *Amerikastudien/American Studies*, Vol 24 (1979), 163-64.

3511 MEADOR, BRUCE S. *"Wetback" Labor in the Lower Rio Grande Valley*. San Francisco: R & E Research Associates, 1973.

3512 MEIER, AUGUST, and ELLIOTT RUDWICK. "Communist Unions and the Black Community: the Case of the Transport Workers Union, 1934-1944." *Labor History*, Vol 22 (1982), 165-97.

3513 ———. "The Rise of Segregation in the Federal Bureaucracy, 1900-1930." *Phylon*, Vol 28 (1967), 178-84.

3514 MENDELSOHN, EZRA. "The Russian Roots of the American Jewish Labor Movement." *YIVO Annual of Jewish Social Science*, Vol 16 (1976), 150-77.

3515 MEREDITH, H. L. "Agrarian Socialism and the Negro in Oklahoma, 1900-1918." *Labor History*, Vol 11 (1970), 277-84.

3516 MERGEN, BERNARD. "Another Great Prize: the Jewish Labor Movement in the Context of the American Labor Movement." *YIVO Annual of Jewish Social Science*, Vol 16 (1976), 394-423.

3517 Meyer, Stephen. "Adapting the Immigrant to the Line: Americanization in the Ford Factory, 1914-1921." *Journal of Social History*, Vol 14 (1981), 67-82.

3518 Miles, Raymond E. "Introduction to Discrimination in Employment: A Complementary Collection." *Industrial Relations*, Vol 10 (1971), 272-76.

3519 Miller, Floyd J. "Black Protest and White Leadership: A Note on the Colored Farmers' Alliance." *Phylon*, Vol 33 (1972), 169-74.

3520 Miller, Randall M., and Thomas D. Marzik. *Immigrants and Religion in Urban America*. Phila.: Temple U Press, 1977.

3521 Miller, Sally M. *The Radical Immigrant*. NY: Twayne, 1974.

3522 Mitchell, Brian. *Immigrants in Utopia: the Early Irish Community of Lowell, Mass., 1821-1861*. Ph D diss, U of Rochester, 1981.

3523 Modell, John. "Class or Ethnic Solidarity: the Japanese American Company Union." *Pacific Historical Review*, Vol 38 (1969), 193-206.

3524 Mogull, Robert G. "Discrimination in the Labor Market." *Journal of Black Studies*, Vol 3 (1972), 237-49.

3525 ———. "The Pattern of Labor Discrimination." *Negro History Bulletin*, Vol 35 (1972), 54-59.

3526 Mohl, Raymond A., and Neil Betten. "Paternalism and Pluralism: Immigrants and Social Welfare in Gary Indiana, 1906-1940." *American Studies*, Vol 15 (Spring 1974), 5-30.

3527 Mondello, Salvatore. "The Magazine *Charities* and the Italian Immigrants, 1903-14." *Journalism Quarterly*, Vol 44 (1967), 91-98.

3528 Monroy, Douglas. "Anarquismo y Comunismo: Mexican Radicalism and the Communist Party in Los Angeles during the 1930s." *Labor History*, Vol 24 (1983), 34-59.

3529 ———. "An Essay on Understanding the Work Experience of Mexicans in Southern California, 1900-1939." *Aztlan*, Vol 12 (Spring 1981), 59-74.

3530 Moore, Howard. "Black Labor: Slavery to Fair Hiring." *Black Scholar*, Vol 4 (Feb 1973), 22-31.

3531 Moore, R. Laurence. "Flawed Fraternity—American Socialist Response to the Negro, 1901-1912." *The Historian*, Vol 32 (1969), 1-18.

3532 Morgan, Philip D. "Work and Culture: The Task System and the World of Low Country Blacks, 1700-1880." *William and Mary Quarterly*, Vol 39 (1982), 563-99.

3533 Muraskin, William. "The Harlem Boycott of 1934: Black Nationalism and the Rise of Labor-Union Consciousness." *Labor History*, Vol 13 (1972), 361-73.

3534 Murphy, James T. et al. "Black Employment in New Orleans." *Proceedings of the Twenty-Fourth Annual Winter Meeting of the Industrial Relations Research Association*, Dec 27-28, 1971, pp 79-88. Madison: IRRA, 1972.

3535 Murray, Hugh T., Jr. "The NAACP versus the Communist Party: the Scottsboro Rape Cases, 1931-1932." *Phylon*, Vol 28 (1967), 276-87.

3536 Myers, John B. "The Alabama Freedman and the Economic Adjustments During Presidential Reconstruction, 1865-1867." *Alabama Review*, Vol 26 (1973), 252-67.

3537 Myers, Robin. *Black Craftsmen Through History*. NY: Institute of the Joint Apprenticeship Program, Workers Defense League, A. Philip Randolph Educational Fund, 1970.

3538 Myrdal, Gunnar. et al. *An American Dilemma: The Negro Problem and Modern Democracy*. NY: Harper, 1962.

3539 National Urban League. *Negro Membership in American Labor Unions*. NY: Alexasnder Press, 1930.

3540 ———. *Negro Membership in American Labor Unions*. NY: Negro Universities Press, 1969.

3541 Nelli, Humbert S. "The Italian Padrone System in the United States." *Labor History*, Vol 5 (1964), 153-67.

3542 ———. "The Padrone System: An Exchange of Letters." *Labor History*, Vol 17 (1976), 406-12.
3543 NEW YORK UNIVERSITY CONFERENCE ON LABOR. "Management, Unions and Minority Groups." *Proceedings...*, Wash.: Bureau of National Affairs, 1964.
3544 NIEMI, ALBERT W., JR. "Wage Discrimination Against Negroes and Puerto Ricans in the New York SMSA." *Social Science Quarterly*, Vol 55 (1974), 112-20.
3545 NORGREN, PAUL H. "Governmental Fair Employment Agencies: An Appraisal of Federal and State and Municipal Efforts to End Job Discrimination." *Proceedings of the Fourteenth Annual Meeting of the Industrial Relations Research Association*, Dec 28-29, 1961, pp 120-38. Madison: IRRA, 1962.
3546 ———. et al. *Employing the Negro in American Industry*. NY: Industrial Relations Counselors, 1959.
3547 NORTHRUP, HERBERT R. *The Negro in the Aerospace Industry*. Phila.: U of Pennsylvania Press, 1968.
3548 ———. *The Negro in the Automobile Industry*. Phila.: U of Pennsylvania Press, 1968.
3549 ———. *The Negro in the Paper Industry*. Phila.: U of Pennsylvania Press, 1969.
3550 ———. *The Negro in the Tobacco Industry*. Phila.: U of Pennsylvania Press, 1970.
3551 ———. *Organized Labor and the Negro*. NY: Harper, 1944.
3552 ———. et al. *Negro Employment in Basic Industry: A Study of Racial Policies in Six Industries*. Phila.: U of Pennsylvania Press, 1970.
3553 ———. *The Negro in the Air Transport Industry*. Phila.: U of Pennsylvania Press, 1970.
3554 ———, and GORDON R. STORHOLM. *Restrictive Labor Practices in the Supermarket Industry*. Phila.: U of Pennsylvania Press, 1967.
3555 *Nothing but a Man*. 1964. (Feature film directed & co-produced by Michael Roemer)
3556 OFARI, EARL. "Black Activists and 19th Century Radicalism." *Black Scholar*, Vol 5 (Feb 1974), 19-25.
3557 "An 'Old Warrier' Offers New Perspective for Young Activists." *Black Enterprise*, Vol 2 (Jul 1972), 19-21.
3558 OLIN, SPENCER C., JR. "European Immigrant and Oriental Alien: Acceptance and Rejection by the California Legislature of 1913." *Pacific Historical Review*, Vol 35 (1966), 303-15.
3559 OLSON, JAMES S. *The Ethnic Dimension in American History*. NY: St. Martin's, 1980
3560 ———. "Organized Black Leadership and Industrial Unionism: The Racial Response, 1936-1945." *Labor History*, Vol 10 (1969), 475-86.
3561 ONG, PAUL M. "Chinese Labor in Early San Francisco: Racial Segmentation and Industrial Expansion." *Amerasia Journal*, Vol 3 (1981), 69-92.
3562 ———. "The Ethnic Trade: the Chinese Laundries in Early California." *Journal of Ethnic Studies*, Vol 8 (Winter 1981), 95-113.
3563 ORNSTEIN, MICHAEL DAVID. *Entry into the American Labor Force*. Ph D diss, Johns Hopkins U, 1971.
3564 OZANNE, ROBERT. *The Negro in the Farm Equipment and Construction Machinery Industries*. Phila.: U of Pennsylvania Press, 1972.
3565 *Packingtown, U.S.A.* 1968. (Docu-drama produced by William Adelman)
3566 PAGANO, JULES. "Union-Management Adaptation to Needs of Disadvantaged New Employees." *Proceedings of the Twenty-First Annual Winter Meeting of the Industrial Relations Research Association*, Dec 29-30, 1968, pp 228-35.
3567 PAINTER, NELL I. *The Narrative of Hosea Hudson, His Life as a Negro Communist in the South*. Cambr.: Harvard U Press, 1979.
3568 PALMER, PAUL C. "Servant into Slave: the Evolution of the Legal Status of the Negro Laborer in Colonial Virginia." *South Atlantic Quarterly*, Vol 55 (1966), 355-70.
3569 PAPANIKOLAS, HELEN ZEESE. "Life and Labor Among the Immigrants of Bingham Canyon." *Utah Historical Quarterly*, Vol 33 (1965), 289-314.

3570 PAROT, JOSEPH. "Ethnic versus Black Metropolis: The Origins of Polish-Black Housing Tensions in Chicago." *Polish American Studies*, Vol 29 (1972), 5-33.

3571 PERDUE, CHARLES L. et al, eds. *Weevils in the Wheat: Interviews with Virginia Ex-Slaves*. Charlottesville: U of Virginia Press, 1976.

3572 PEROTTI, ANTONIO. "L'Evoluzione della Politica Sindacale verso l'Immigrazione Operaia negli Stati Uniti (1850-1945) (Saggio d'Interpretazione)." *Studi Emigrazione*, Vol 6 (1969), 129-88.

3573 PERRY, JOSEPH MCGARITY. *The Impact of Immigration on Three American Industries, 1865-1914*. Ph D diss, Northwestern U, 1966.

3574 PFEFFER, J., and J. ROSS. "Unionization and Income Inequality." *Industrial Relations*, Vol 20 (1981), 271-85.

3575 PICHLER, JOSEPH A. "The Job Corps Transition." *Industrial and Labor Relations Review*, Vol 25 (1972), 336-53.

3576 PIOTT, STEVEN. "The Lesson of the Immigrant: Views of Immigrants in Muckraking Magazines, 1900-1909." *American Studies*, Vol 19 (1978), 21-33.

3577 PLASTRIK, STANLEY. "Coalition of Black Trade Unionists." *Dissent*, Vol 20 (1973), 12-13.

3578 POLLARD, WILLIAM E. "The Need for Expanded EEOC Conciliation Efforts Under Title VII." *Proceedings of the Twenty-Seventh Annual Winter Meeting of the Industrial Relations Research Association*, Dec 28-29, 1974, pp 235-41. Madison: IRRA, 1975.

3579 PORTER, KENNETH. "Negro Labor in the Western Cattle Industry 1866-1900." *Labor History*, Vol 10 (1969), 346-74.

3580 PORTER, KENNETH W. "Negro Labor in the Western Cattle Industry, 1866-1900." *Labor History*, Vol 10 (1969), 346-74.

3581 POSADAS, BARBARA M. "The Hierarchy of Color and Psychological Adjustment in an Industrial Environment: Filipinos, The Pullman Company and the Brotherhood of Sleeping Car Porters." *Labor History*, Vol 22 (1982), 349-73.

3582 POSTON, DUDLEY L., JR. et al. "Earnings Differences between Anglo and Mexican American Male Workers in 1960 and 1970: Changes in the 'Cost' of being Mexican American." *Social Science Quarterly*, Vol 57 (1976), 618-31.

3583 POWELL, WILLIAM E. "European Settlement in the Cherokee-Crawford Coal Field of Southeastern Kansas." *Kansas Historical Quarterly*, Vol 41 (1975), 150-65.

3584 POWERS, THOMPSON, ed. *Now Hear This! Equal Employment Opportunity: Compliance and Affirmative Action. Questions and Answers from Four Industry-Government Meetings on the Administration and Enforcement Activities of the Equal Employment Opportunity Commission and the Office of Federal Contract Compliance*. NY: National Association of Manufacturers, 1969.

3585 "Progress of U.S. Negroes during the 1960's." *Monthly Labor Review*, Vol 93 (Apr 1970), 64-65.

3586 PURCELL, THEODORE V., and GERALD F. CAVANAGH. *Blacks in the Industrial World: Issues for the Manager*. NY: Pree Press, 1972.

3587 ———, and DANIEL P. MULVEY. *The Negro in the Electrical Manufacturing Industry*. Phila.: U of Pennsylvania Press, 1971.

3588 PYCIOR, JULIE. *La Raza Organizes: Mexican American Life in San Antonio, 1915-1930, as Reflected in Mutualista Activities*. Ph D diss, Notre Dame U, 1979.

3589 QUAY, WILLIAM HOWARD. *The Negro in the Chemical Industry*. Phila.: U of Pennsylvania Press, 1969.

3590 RABKIN, PEGGY A. "Affirmative Action and Reverse Discrimination: the Implications of Herbert Hill's *Black Labor and the American Legal System* and William B. Gould's *Black Workers in White Unions*." *Afro-Americans in New York Life and History*, Vol 3 (1979), 69-78.

3591 RAPPAPORT, JOSEPH. *Jewish Immigrants and World War I: A Study of American Yiddish Press Reactions*. Ph D diss, Columbia U, 1951.

3592 RASKIN, A. H. "Management Experiences in Dealing with the Disadvantaged: A Public View of the Contribution of the Private Sector." *Labor Law Journal*, Vol 22 (Aug 1968), 469-71.

3593 RECORD, WILSON. *The Negro and the Communist Party*. Chapel Hill: U of North Carolina Press, 1951.

3594 ———. *Race and Radicalism: The NAACP and the Communist Party in Conflict*. Ithaca: Cornell U Press, 1964.

3595 REED, MERL E. "The F.E.P.C., the Black Worker, and the Southern Shipyards." *South Atlantic Quarterly*, Vol 74 (1975), 446-67.

3596 REINDERS, ROBERT C. "The Free Negro in the New Orleans Economy, 1850-1860." *Louisiana History*, Vol 6 (1965), 273-85.

3597 REISLER, MARK. "Always the Laborer, Never the Citizen: Anglo Perceptions of the Mexican Immigrant during the 1920s." *Pacific Historical Review*, Vol 45 (1976), 231-54.

3598 ———. *By the Sweat of Their Brow: Mexican Immigrant Labor in the United States*. Westport, CT: Greenwood, 1976.

3599 ———. "Mexican Immigrant in the Chicago Area during the 1920's." *Illinois State Historical Society Journal*, Vol 46 (1973), 144-58.

3600 ———. "Mexican Unionization in California Agriculture, 1927-1936." *Labor History*, Vol 14 (1973), 562-79.

3601 ———. *Passing through our Egypt: Mexican Labor in the U.S., 1900-1940*. Ph D diss, Cornell U, 1973.

3602 REUTLINGER, A. S. "Reflections on the Anglo-American Jewish Experience; Immigrants, Workers and Entrepreneurs in New York and London." *American Jewish Historical Quarterly*, Vol 66 (1977), 473-84.

3603 RISCHIN, MOSES. *The Promised City: New York's Jews, 1870-1914*. Cambr.: Harvard U Press, 1962.

3604 RISHER, HOWARD W., JR. *The Negro in the Railroad Industry*. Phila.: U of Pennsylvania Press, 1970.

3605 RISTORUCCI, CARMEN. "The Puerto Rican Worker." *Political Affairs*, Vol 41 (1972), 39-44.

3606 RITTENOURE, ROBERT LYNN. "Negro Employment in the Federal Government." *Proceedings of the Twenty-Third Annual Winter Meeting of the Industrial Relations Research Association*, Dec 28-29, 1970, pp 34-44, 65-68.

3607 ———. *Negro Employment in the Federal Service in the South*. Ph D diss, U of Texas, 1970.

3608 ROBBINS, LYNN A. "Navajo Labor and the Establishment of a Voluntary Workers Association." *Journal of Ethnic Studies*, Vol 6 (Fall 1978), 97-112.

3609 ROBERTS, MARKLEY. "Some Factors Affecting Employment and Earnings of Disadvantaged Youths." *Industrial and Labor Relations Review*, Vol 25 (1972), 376-82.

3610 ROGERS, WILLIAM WARREN. "Negro Knights of Labor in Arkansas: A Case Study of the 'Miscellaneous' Strike." *Labor History*, Vol 10 (1969), 498-505.

3611 ROGOFF, ABRAHAM M. *Formative Years of the Jewish Labor Movement in the United States (1890-1900)*. Ph D diss, Columbia U, 1945.

3612 ROSALES, FRANCISCO. *Mexican Immigration to the Urban Midwest during the 1920s*. Ph D diss, Indiana U, 1978.

3613 ———, and D. SIMON. "Mexican Immigrant Experience in the Urban Midwest: East Chicago, Indiana, 1919-1945." *Indiana Magazine of History*, Vol 77 (1981), 333-57.

3614 ROSENBLUM, GERALD. *Immigrant Workers: Their Impact on American Radicalism*. NY: Basic, 1973.

3615 ———. *Modernization, Immigration, and the American Labor Movement*. Ph D diss, Princeton U, 1968.

3616 ROSS, ARTHUR M., and HERBERT HILL, eds.. *Employment, Race, and Poverty*. NY: Harcourt, Brace & World, 1967.

3617 ROVERE, RICHARD H. "Letter from Washington." *New Yorker*, Sep 11, 1965, pp 116-30.

3618 ROWAN, EUGENE F. "Management Experiences in Dealing with the Disadvantaged: What We Are Doing on the Retail Front." *Labor Law Journal*, Vol 22 (1968), 467-69.

3619 ROWAN, RICHARD L. *The Negro and Employment Opportunity: Problems and Practices*. Ann Arbor: Graduate School of Business Administration, U of Michigan, 1965.

3620 ———. *Negro Employment in Southern Industry: A Study of Racial Policies in Five Industries*. Phila.: U of Pennsylvania Press, 1970.

3621 ———. "Negro Employment in the Basic Steel Industry." *Industrial and Labor Relations Review*, Vol 23 (1969), 29-39.

3622 ———. *The Negro in the Steel Industry*. Phila.: U of Pennsylvania Press, 1968.

3623 ———. *The Negro in the Textile Industry*. Phila.: U of Pennsylvania Press, 1970.

3624 ———, and ROBERT J. BRUDNO. "Fair Employment in Building: Imposed and Hometown Plans." *Industrial Relations*, Vol 11 (1972), 394-406.

3625 ROWLAND, DONALD. "The United States and the Contract Labor Question in Hawaii, 1862-1900." *Pacific Historical Review*, Vol 2 (1933), 249-69.

3626 RUBIN, LESTER. *The Negro in the Shipbuilding Industry*. Phila.: U of Pennsylvania Press, 1970.

3627 RUDOLPH, FREDERICK. "Chinamen in Yankeedom: Anti-Unionism in Massachusetts in 1870." *American Historical Review*, Vol 53 (1947), 1-29.

3628 RUSTIN, BAYARD. "The Blacks and the Unions." *Harper's*, May 1971, pp 36-45.

3629 RYON, RODERICK. "An Ambiguous Legacy: Baltimore Blacks and the C.I.O., 1936-1941." *Journal of Negro History*, Vol 65 (1980), 18-33.

3630 SALMOND, JOHN A. "The Civilan Conservation Corps and the Negro." *Journal of American History*, Vol 52 (1965), 75-88.

3631 SAMORA, JULIAN. *Los Mojados: The Wetback Story*. Notre Dame: Notre Dame Press, 1971.

3632 SANDERS, RONALD. *The Downtown Jews*. NY: Harper & Row, 1969.

3633 SANDMEYER, ELMER C. "California Anti-Chinese Legislation and the Federal Courts: A Study in Federal Relations." *Pacific Historical Review*, Vol 5 (1936), 189-211.

3634 SASSEN-KOOB, SASKIA. "Immigrant and Minority Workers in the Organization of the Labor Process." *Journal of Ethnic Studies*, Vol 8 (Spring 1980), 1-34.

3635 SAXTON, ALEXANDER. *Bright Web in the Darkness* (a novel). NY: St. Martin's Press, 1958.

3636 ———. *The Indispensable Enemy: Labor and the anti-Chinese Movement in California*. Berkeley: U of California Pres,s 1971.

3637 SCARPACI, JEAN ANN. "Immigrants in the New South: Italians in Louisiana's Sugar Parishes, 1880-1910." *Labor History*, Vol 16 (1975), 165-83.

3638 SCHMIDT, FRED H. "Job Caste in the Southwest." *Industrial Relations*, Vol 9 (1969), 100-10.

3639 ———. "Los Angeles: Show, Little Substance." *Industrial Relations*, Vol ((1970), 340-55.

3640 ———. *Spanish Surnamed American Employment in the Southwest*. Wash.: Equal Employment Opportunity Commission, 1970.

3641 SCOTT, FRANKLIN D. "Literature in Periodicals of Protest of Swedish-America." *Swedish Pioneer Historical Quarterly*, Vol 16 (1965), 193-215.

3642 SCRUGGS, OTEY M. *A History of Mexican Agricultural Labor in the United States, 1942-1954*. Ph D diss, Harvard U, 1958.

3643 SHAPIRO, JUDAH J. *The Friendly Society: A History of the Workmen's Circle*. NY: Media Judaica, 1970.

3644 SHEPPARD, HAROLD L., and HERBERT E. STRINER. *Civil Rights, Employment, and the Social Status of American Negroes*. Kalamazoo: W. E. Upjohn Institute for Employment Research, 1966.

3645 SHERIDAN, FRANK J. *Italian, Slavic, and Hungarian Unskilled Immigrant Laborers in the U.S.* Wash.: G.P.O., 1907.

3646 SHOFNER, JERRELL. "Florida and the Black Migration." *Florida History Quarterly*, Vol 57 (1979), 267-88.

3647 ———. "The Labor League of Jacksonville: A Negro Union and White Strikebreakers." *Florida Historical Quarterly*, Vol 50 (1972), 278-82. (lumber mill workers, 1873)

3648 ———. "The Legacy of Racial Slavery: Free Enterprise and Freed Labor in Florida in the 1940s." *Journal of Southern History*, Vol 47 (Aug 1981), 411-26.

3649 ———. "Militant Negro Laborers in Reconstruction Florida." *Journal of Southern History*, Vol 39 (1973), 397-413.

3650 ———. "The Pensacola Workingman's Association." *Labor History*, Vol 13 (1972), 555-59.

3651 SIMBA, MALIK. *The Black Laborer, the Black Legal Experience, and the United States Supreme Court, with Emphasis on the Neo-Concept of Equal Employment*. Ph D diss, U of Minnesota, 1978.

3652 SIMON, HAL. "The Struggle for Jobs and for Negro Rights in the Trade Unions." *Political Affairs*, Vol 29 (Feb 1950), 33-48.

3653 SIVACHEV, N. V. "Negritianskii Vopros v Rabochem Dvizhenii SShA (1919-1939 gg.)." *Voprosy Istorii*, No 8 (1966), 47-61.

3654 SLAIMAN, DONALD. "Equal Employment and Unions." *The AFL-CIO American Federationist*, Dec 1967, pp 14-17.

3655 SMALLWOOD, JAMES. "Perpetuation of Caste: Black Agriculture Workers in Reconstruction Texas." *Mid-America*, Vol 61 (1979), 5-24.

3656 SMITH, ELSIE J. "Regional Origin and Migration: Impact on Black Workers." *Journal of Black Studies*, Vol 8 (1978), 309-20.

3657 SOBIN, DENNIS P. *The Working Poor: Minority Workers in Low-wage, Low-skill Jobs*. Port Washington, NY: Kennikat, 1973.

3658 SORRELL, RICHARD S. "Life, Work and Acculturation Patterns of Eastern European Immigrants in Lackawanna, New York: 1900-1922." *Polish Review*, Vol 14 (Autumn, 1969), 65-91.

3659 SOVERN, MICHAEL I. *Legal Restraints on Racial Discrimination in Employment*. NY: Twentieth Century Fund, 1966.

3660 ———. "Race Discrimination and the National Labor Relations Act: The Brave New World of Miranda." *Proceedings of the Conference on Labor*, New York U, 1963, pp 3-18.

3661 SOWELL, THOMAS. *Ethnic America*. NY: Basic Books, 1981.

3662 SPERO, STERLING D., and ABRAM L. HARRIS. *The Black Worker: The Negro and the Labor Movement*. NY: Columbia U Press, 1931.

3663 SPIVEY, DONALD. *Schooling for the New Slavery: Black Industrial Education, 1868-1915*. Westport, CT: Greenwood Press, 1978.

3664 SPRIGGS, WILLIAM. "The Virginia Colored Farmers' Alliance: a Case Study of Race and Class Identity." *Journal of Negro History*, Vol 64 (1979), 191-204.

3665 STANBACK, HOWARD. *Racism, Black Labor and the Giant Corporation*. Ph D diss, U of Massachusetts, 1981.

3666 STANFIELD, J. EDWIN. *In Memphis: More than a Garbage Strike, with Supplements Issued April 3, 1968 and April 28, 1968*. Atlanta: Southern Regional Council, 1968.

3667 STAR, JACK. "A National Disgrace: What Unions Do to Blacks." *Look*, Nov 12, 1968, pp 26-34.

3668 STAROBIN, ROBERT. "Disciplining Industrial Slaves in the Old South." *Journal of Negro History*, Vol 53 (1968), 111-28.

3669 ———. *Industrial Slavery in the Old South.* NY: Oxford U Press, 1970.
3670 STEALEY, JOHN EDMUND, III. "The Responsibilities and Liabilities of the Bailee of Slave Labor in Virginia." *American Journal of Legal History*, Vol 12 (1968), 336-53.
3671 STEWART, FRED MUSTARD. *Ellis Island* (a novel). NY: Morrow, 1983.
3672 STIPANOVICH, JOSEPH. *"In Unity is Strength": Immigrant Workers and Immigrant Intellectuals in Progressive America: a History of the South Slav Social Democratic Movement, 1900-1918.* Ph D diss, U of Minnesota, 1978.
3673 SYLVERS, MALCOLM. "Sicilian Socialists in Houston, Texas, 1896-98." *Labor History*, Vol 11 (1970), 77-81.
3674 SZAJKOWSKI, ZOSA. "The Yohudi and the Immigrant: a Reappraisal." *American Jewish Historical Quarterly*, Vol 43 (1973), 13-27. (Jewish labor leader's attitudes toward immigrants)
3675 SZYMANSKI, AL. "Trends in Economic Discrimination Against Blacks in the U.S. Working Class." *Review of Radical Political Economics*, Vol 7 (Fall 1975), 1-21.
3676 TCHERIKOWER, ELIAS, ed. *History of the Jewish Labor Movement in the United States* (in Yiddish), 2 vols. NY: Yiddish Scientific Institute, 1943, 1945. (Translated into English and revised by Aaron Antonovsky under the title *The Early Jewish Labor Movement in the United States,* NY: Yivo Institute for Jewish Research, 1961)
3677 TERWILLIGER, MARLENE. *Jews and Italians and the Socialist Party in New York City, 1901-1917: a Study of Class Ethnicity and Class Consciousness.* Ph D diss, Union Graduate School, 1978.
3678 THIEBLOT, ARMAND J., JR. *The Negro in the Banking Industry.* Phila.: U of Pennsylvania Press, 1970.
3679 ———, and LINDA P. FLETCHER. *Negro Employment in Finance: A Study of Racial Policies in Banking and Insurance.* Phila.: U of Pennsylvania Press, 1970.
3680 THOMAS, RICHARD. "The Detroit Urban League, 1916-1924." *Michigan History*, Vol 60 (1976), 315-38.
3681 ———. *From Peasant to Proletarian: the Formation and Organization of the Black Industrial Working Class in Detroit, 1915-1945.* Ph D diss, U of Michigan, 1976.
3682 THOMPSON, MINDY. *The National Negro Labor Council: A History.* NY: AIMS, 1978.
3683 TODD, ARTHUR C. *The Cornish Miner in America: The Contribution to the Mining History of the United States by Emigrant Cornish Miners: The Men Called Cousin Jacks.* Glendale, CA: Clark, 1967.
3684 TORRES, LORENZO. "Short History of Chicano Workers." *Political Affairs*, Nov 1973, pp 88-99; Oct 1975, pp 14-27.
3685 TROTTER, JOE W. *The Making of an Industrial Proletariat: Black Milwaukee, 1915-1945.* Ph D diss, U of Minnesota, 1981.
3686 TRUNK, ISAIAH. "The Cultural Dimension of the American Jewish Labor Movement." *YIVO Annual of Jewish Social Science*, Vol 16 (1976), 342-93.
3687 TUTTLE, WILLIAM M., JR. "Labor Conflict and Racial Violence: the Black Worker in Chicago, 1894-1919." *Labor History*, Vol 10 (1969), 408-32.
3688 "Union Program for Eliminating Discrimination." *Monthly Labor Review*, Vol 86 (1963), 58-59.
3689 U.S. BUREAU OF LABOR STATISTICS. *Work Attitudes of Disadvantaged Black Men: A Methodological Inquiry.* Wash.: G.P.O., 1972.
3690 U.S. CONGRESS. SENATE. Committee on Labor and Public Welfare. Subcommittee on Labor. *Legislative History of the Equal Employment Opportunity Act of 1972 (H.R. 1746, P.L. 92-261), Amending Title VII of the Civil Rights Act of 1964.* Wash.: G.P.O., 1972.
3691 U.S. DEPARTMENT OF LABOR. DIVISION OF NEGRO ECONOMICS. *Negro Migration in 1916-17: Reports by R. H. Leavell and Others.* NY: Negro Universities Press, 1969.
3692 U.S. EQUAL EMPLOYMENT OPPORTUNITY COMMISSION. *Hearings...on Utilization of Minority and Women Workers in the Public Utilities Industry. Hearings Held in Washington, D.C., November 15-17, 1971.* Wash.: GPO, 1972.

3693 Van Arsdol, Maurice D., Jr. *Non-Apprehended and Apprehended Undocumented Residents in the Los Angeles Labor Market: An Exploratory Study*. Springfield, VA: National Technical Information Service, U.S. Department of Commerce, 1980.

3694 Van Zanten, John W. "Communist Theory and the American Negro Question." *Review of Politics*, Vol 29 (1967), 435-56.

3695 Vinyard, Jo Ellen. "Inland Urban Immigrants: the Detroit Irish, 1850." *Michigan History*, Vol 47 (1973), 121-39.

3696 Vroman, Wayne. "Changes in the Labor Market Position of Black Men Since 1964." *Proceedings of the Twenty-Seventh Annual Winter Meeting of the Industrial Relations Research Association*, Dec 28-29, 1974, pp 294-301. Madison: IRRA, 1975.

3697 Wade, Richard. *Slavery in the Cities: The South 1820-1860*. NY: Oxford U Press, 1964.

3698 Wadley, Janet K., and Everett S. Lee. "The Disappearance of the Black Farmer." *Phylon*, Vol 35 (1974), 276-83.

3699 Wagstaff, Thomas. "Call Your Old Master—'Master': Southern Political Leaders and Negro Labor During Presidential Reconstruction." *Labor History*, Vol 10 (1969), 323-45.

3700 Walker, Joseph E. "A Comparison of Negro and White Labor in a Charcoal Iron Community." *Labor History*, Vol 10 (1969), 487-97.

3701 ———. "Negro Labor in the Charcoal Industry of Southeastern Pennsylvania." *Pennsylvania Magazine of History and Biography*., Vol 93 (1969), 466-86.

3702 Walker, Lee. "Racism and Speed Up in an Auto Plant." *Political Affairs*, Vol 42 (Nov 1973), 41-44.

3703 Warne, Frank J. *The Immigrant Invasion*. NY: Dodd, Mead, 1913.

3704 Warren, Samuel E. "A Partial Background for the Study of the Development of Negro Labor: An Adventure in Teaching Certain Aspects of American Labor History." *Journal of Negro History*, Vol 25 (1940), 45-59.

3705 Washington-Bolder, Jacqueline. *American Socialism: Its Origin, Nature, and Impact on the Black Working Class and the Socio-Economic Development of the U.S.* Ph D diss, Howard U, 1977.

3706 Watkins, Beverly. "Efforts to Encourage Immigration to Arkansas, 1865-1874." *Arkansas History Quarterly*, Vol 38 (1979), 32-62.

3707 Weaver, Robert C. *Negro Labor: A National Problem*. NY: Harcourt, Brace, 1946.

3708 Weiss, Bernard J., ed. *American Education and the European Immigrant, 1840-1940*. Urbana: U of Illinois Press, 1982.

3709 Wheeler, John H. "The Impact of Race Relations on Industrial Relations in the South." *Labor Law Journal*, Vol 15 (1964), 474-81.

3710 White, David Laurence. *Factors Influencing Non-White Participation in Apprenticeship Programs in Selected Building Trades in New Jersey*. Ph D diss, Rutgers U, 1973.

3711 Wilcox, B. P. "Anti-Chinese Riots in Washington." *Washington Historical Quarterly*, Vol 20 (1929), 204-12.

3712 Wilentz, Robert Sean. "Industrializing America and the Irish: Towards the New Departure." *Labor History*, Vol 20 (1979), 579-95.

3713 Winn, Charles Carr. *Mexican-Americans in the Texas Labor Movement*. Ph D diss, Texas Christian U, 1972.

3714 Wolkinson, Benjamin W. "The Effectiveness of EEOC Policy in the Construction Industry." *Proceedings of the Twenty-Fifth Anniversary Meeting of the Industrial Relations Research Association*, Dec 28-29, 1972, pp 362-69. Madison: IRRA, 1973.

3715 ———. "Labor and the Jewish Tradition—a Reappraisal." *Jewish Social Studies*, Vol 40 (1978), 231-38.

3716 ———. *Promise or Illusion: Examination of the Efficacy of the EEOC's Conciliation Process in Remedying Racially Discriminatory Union Practices Under the Civil Rights Act of 1964.* Ph D diss, Cornell U, 1972.

3717 Wolters, Raymond. *Negroes and the Great Depression: The Problem of Economic Recovery.* Westport, CT: Greenwood, 1970.

3718 ———. *Negroes and the New Deal Economic Recovery Program.* Ph D diss, U of California, 1968.

3719 ———. "Section 7a and the Black Worker." *Labor History*, Vol 10 (1969), 459-74.

3720 Wong, Charles C. "The Continuity of Chinese Grocers in Southern California." *Journal of Ethnic Studies*, Vol 8 (Summer 1980), 63-82.

3721 ———. *Ethnicity, Work and Community: the Case of Chinese in Los Angeles.* Ph D diss, U of California 1979.

3722 Worthman, Paul B. "A Black Worker and the Bricklayers and Masons' Union, 1903." *Journal of Negro History*, Vol 54 (1969), 398-404.

3723 ———. "Black Workers and Labor Unions in Birmingham, Alabama, 1897-1904." *Labor History*, Vol 10 (1969), 375-407.

3724 Wortman, Roy. "Denver's Anti-Chinese Riot, 1880." *Colorado Magazine,* Vol 42 (1965), 275-91.

3725 Wye, Christopher. "New Deal and the Negro Community: Toward a Broader Conceptualization." *Journal of American History*, Vol 49 (1972), 621-39.

3726 Wynne, Robert E. "American Labor Leaders and the Vancouver Anti-Oriental Riots." *Pacific Northwest QWuarterly*, Vol 57 (1966), 172-79.

3727 Yans-McLaughlin, Virginia. "A Flexible Trade: South Italian Immigrants Confront a New Work Experience." *Journal of Social History*, Vol 7 (1974), 429-45. (See also Comments by Alice Kessler-Harris & Louise A. Tilly on pp 446-51 & 452-59)

3728 Yearley, Clifton K., Jr. *Britons in American Labor: A History of the Influence of the United Kingdom Immigrants on American Labor, 1820-1914.* Balt.: Johns Hopkins Press, 1957.

3729 Yellowitz, Irwin. "American Jewish Labor: Historiographical Problems and Prospects." *American Jewish Historical Quarterly*, Vol 66 (1976), 203-14.

3730 ———. "Black Militancy and Organized Labor: An Historical Parallel." *Midwest Quarterly*, Vol 13 (1972), 169-83.

3731 ———. "Jewish Immigrants and the American Labor Movement, 1900-1920." *American Jewish History*, Vol 71 (1981), 188-217.

3732 Yetman, Norman, ed. *Life Under the "Peculiar Institution": Selections from the Slave Narrative Collection.* NY: Holt, Rinehart & Winston, 1970.

3733 Yoneda, Karl G. "A Brief History of the U.S. Asian Labor." *Political Affairs*, Vol 55 (Sep 1976), 28-42.

3734 "Zum 65 Yorikes Yubillee fun Arbeter Ring." *Bund Archives Bulletin*, Vol 7 (Apr 1966), 2-4.

Communitarian Movements, Anarchism, and Cooperatives

3735 ABRAHAMS, EDWARD H. "Ignatius Donnelly and the Apocalyptic Style." *Minnesota History*, Vol 46 (1978), 102-11.

3736 ABRAMS, ANN. "The Ferrer Center: New York's Unique Meeting of Anarchism and the Arts." *New York History*, Vol 59 (1978), 307-25.

3737 ADAMIC, LOUIS. *Grandsons* (a novel concerning the Haymarket Riot and the subsequent generation). NY: Harper, 1935.

3738 ANGLE, PAUL. "An Illinois Paradise: the Icarians at Nauvoo." *Chicago History*, Vol 7 (1965), 199-209.

3739 ARMSTRONG, GARY W. "Utopians in Clayton County, Iowa." *Annals of Iowa*, Vol 41 (1972), 923-38.

3740 ARNDT, KARL J. "Bismarck's Socialist Law of 1878 and the Harmonists." *Western Pennsylvania Historical Magazine*, Vol 59 (1976), 55-69.

3741 ———. "George Rapp's Harmonists and the Beginnings of Norwegian Migration to America." *Western Pennsylvania Historical Magazine*, Vol 60 (1977), 241-63.

3742 ———. "*The Pittsburgh Leader's* Analysis of the 1890 Crisis in the Harmony Society and its International Repercussions." *Western Pennsylvania Historical Magazine*, Vol 55 (1972), 319-46.

3743 ———. "The Strange and Wonderful New World of George Rapp and his Harmony Society." *Western Pennsylvania Historical Magazine*, Vol 57 (1974), 141-66.

3744 ARRINGTON, LEONARD J. "Cooperative Community in the North: Brigham City, Utah." *Utah Historical Quarterly*, Vol 33 (1965), 198-217.

3745 AVRICH, PAUL. "Kropotkin in America." *International Review of Social History*, Vol 25 (1980), 1-34.

3746 BERTZ, EDUARD. "'Not for the Moment Only': Eduard Bertz to Mary Percival, February 18, 1886." *Tennesee Historical Quarterly*, Vol 24 (1965), 54-62. (A German Socialist and the Rugby Colony, TN; edited by Ben Harris McClary)

3747 BLICK, BORIS, and H. ROGER GRANT. "Life in New Icaria, Iowa: a 19th-Century Utopian Community." *Annals of Iowa*, Vol 42 (1974), 198-204.

3748 BURT, DONALD CHARLES. *Utopia and the Agrarian Tradition in America, 1865-1900.* Ph D diss, U of New Mexico, 1973.

3749 BUTLER, ANN C. *Josiah Warren: Peaceful Revolutionist*. Ph D diss, Ball State U, 1979.

3750 CARMONY, DONALD, and JOSEPHINE ELLIOTT. "New Harmony, Indiana: Robert Owen's Seed Bed for Utopia." *Indiana Magazine of History*, Vol 77 (1980), 161-261.

3751 CARY, FRANCINE. "*The World a Department Store*: Bradford Peck and the Utopian Endeavor." *American Quarterly*, Vol 29 (1977), 370-84.

3752 ———. *Shaping the Future in the Gilded Age: a Study of Utopian Thought, 1888-1900.* Ph D diss, U of Wisconsin, 1976.

3753 CASWELL, JERRY V. "'A New Civilization Radically Higher Than The Old': Adin Ballou's Search for Social Perfecting." *Journal of the Universalist Historical Society*, Vol 7 (1967-68), 70-96.

3754 CUMMINS, ROGER WILLIAM. *The Second Eden: Charles Lane and American Transcendentalism*. Ph D diss, U of Minnesota, 1967.

3755 DAVID, HENRY. *The History of the Haymarket Affair*. NY: Farrar & Rinehart, 1936.

3756 DAVIDSON, RONDEL V. "Victor Considerant and the Failure of La Reunion." *Southwestern Historical Quarterly*, Vol 86 (1973), 277-96.

3757 DEAKIN, JAMES. *The Lobbyists*. Wash.: Public Affairs Press, 1967.

3758 DEPILLIS, MARIO STEPHEN. *The Development of Mormon Communitarianism 1826-1846*. Ph D diss, Yale U, 1960.

3759 DOUGLAS, PAUL H. *The Material Culture of the Communities of the Harmony Society*. Ph D diss, George Washington U, 1973.

3760 DUBIN, BARBARA HINDA. *A Critical Revolution of the Social and Educational Theories of Josiah Warren and his Individualist School of Anarchism*. Ph D diss, U of Illinois, 1973.

3761 EGERTON, JOHN. "Visions of Utopia." *Southern Exposure*, Vol 7 (Spring 1979), 38-47. (Rugby, TN)

3762 FEUER, LEWIS S. "The Influence of the American Communist Colonies on Engels and Marx." *Western Political Quarterly*, Vol 19 (1966), 456-74.

3763 FINE, HOWARD D. "The Koreshan Unity: the Chicago Years of a Utopian Community." *Illinois State Historical Society Journal*, Vol 68 (1975), 213-27.

3764 FISH, JOHN O. "The Christian Commonwealth Colony: A Georgia Experiment, 1896-1900." *Georgia Historical QWuarterly*, Vol 47 (1973), 213-26.

3765 FOGARTY, ROBERT S. "American Communes, 1865-1914" *Journal of American Studies*, Vol 9 (1975), 145-62.

3766 ———. *Dictionary of American Communal and Utopian History*. Westport, CT: Greenwood, 1980.

3767 ———. "Oneida: A Utopian Search for Religious Security." *Labor History*, Vol 14 (1973), 202-27.

3768 ———. *The Oneida Community, 1848-1880: a Study in Conservative Christian Utopianism*. Ph D diss, U of Denver, 1968.

3769 ———, and H. ROGER GRANT. "Free Love in Ohio: Jacob Beilhart and the Spirit Fruit Colony." *Ohio History*, Vol 89 (1980), 206-21.

3770 FONER, PHILIP S., comp. *The Autobiographies of the Haymarket Martyrs*. NY: Humanities Press, 1969.

3771 FRIESEN, GERHARD K. "An Additional Source on the Harmony Society of Economy, Pennsylvania." *Western Pennsylvania Historical Magazine*, Vol 61 (1978), 301-14.

3772 GILMAN, MUSETTA. "Bookwalter, Agricultural Commune in Nebraska." *Nebraska History*, Vol 54 (1973), 91-105.

3773 GRANT, H. ROGER. "Blueprint for Co-operative Communities." *Journal of the West*, Vol 13 (Jul 1974), 74-82. (The Labor Exchange and the Colorado Co-operative Company)

3774 ———. "Henry Olerich and the Utopian Ideal." *Nebraska History*, Vol 56 (1975), 249-58.

3775 ———. "Henry Olerich and Utopia: the Iowa Years, 1870-1902." *Annals of Iowa*, Vol 43 (1977), 349-61.

3776 ———. "One Who Dares to Plan: Charles W. Caryl and the New Era Union." *Colorado Magazine*, Vol 51 (1974), 13-27.

3777 ———. "Portrait of a Workers' Utopia: the Labor Exchange and the Freedom, Kansas, Colony." *Kansas Historical Quarterly*, Vol 42 (1977), 56-66.

3778 GUARNERI, CARL JOSEPH. *Utopian Socialism and American Ideas: the Origins and Doctrine of American Fourierism, 1832-1848*. Ph D diss, Johns Hopkins U, 1979.

3779 HARRIS, FRANK. *The Bomb* (a novel about the Haymarket Riot). NY: Mitchell Kennerley, 1909.

3780 HARRISON, JOHN F. C. "The Owenite Socialist Movement in Britain and the United States." *Labor History*, Vol 9 (1968), 323-37.

3781 HUXLEY, ALDOUS, and PAUL KAGAN. "A Double Look at Utopia; Llano del Rio. I. Ozymandias, the Utopia that Failed by Huxley. II. Portrait of a California Utopia by Kagan." *California Historical Quarterly*, Vol 41 (1972), 117-54.

3782 ICKSTADT, HEINZ. "Fiction Shows Fact the Future: Amerikanische Utopien des spaeten 19. Jahrhunderts." *American Studies/Amerika Studien*, Vol 22 (1977), 295-308.

3783 JOHNSON, MICHAEL. "Albert R. Parsons: an American Architect of Syndicalism." *Midwest Quarterly*, Vol 9 (1968), 376-79.

3784 JOHNSTON, DALE ALLEN. *An American Anarchist: An Analysis of the Individualist Anarchism of Benjamin R. Tucker* Ph D diss, U of New Mexico, 1973.

3785 KEITH, JOHN M, JR. "The Early Manufacturing and Selling of the Shakers at South Union, Kentucky." *Kentucky Historical Society Register*, Vol 70 (1972), 187-99.

3786 KELLOGG, MINER K. "Miner K. Kellogg: Recollections of New Harmony; edited by Lorna Lutes Sylvester; Contributed by C. W. Hackensmith." *Indiana Magazine of History*, Vol 54 (1968), 137-46.

3787 KERN, LOUIS. *Love, Labor, and Self-Control: Sex Roles and Sexuality in Three Nineteenth Century American Utopian Communities*. Ph D diss, Rutgers U, 1978.

3788 KIRCHMANN, GEORGE. "Unsettled Utopias: the North American Phalanx and the Raritan Bay Union." *New Jersey History*, Vol 117 (1929), 25-36.

3789 KIRK, CLARA, and RUDOLF KIRK. "William Dean Howells, George William Curtis and the 'Haymarket Affair.'" *American Literature*, Vol 40 (1968), 487-98.

3790 KLEHR, HARVEY. "Marxist Theory in Search of America." *Journal of Politics*, Vol 35 (1973), 311-31.

3791 KOGAN, BERNARD R., ed. *The Chicago Haymarket Riot: Anarchy on Trial*. Bost.: Heath, 1959.

3792 LEWARNE, CHARLES P. "The Anarchist Colony at Home, Washington, 1901-1902." *Arizona and the West*, Vol 14 (1972), 155-68.

3793 ———. "Equality Colony: The Plan to Socialize Washington." *Pacific Northwest Quarterly*, Vol 59 (1968), 137-46.

3794 LOCKWOOD, MAREN. "The Experimental Utopia in America." *Daedalus*, Vol 97 (1965), 401-18.

3795 LOWRY, CHARLES B. "'The City on a Hill' and Kibbutzim: 17th Century Utopias versus Ideal Types." *American Jewish Historical Quarterly*, Vol 64 (1974), 25-41.

3796 MCCORMICK, JOHN S. "An Anarchist Defends the Mormons: the Case of Dyer D. Lum." *Utah Historical Quarterly*, Vol 44 (1976), 156-69.

3797 MCHUGH, CHRISTINE. *Edward Bellamy and the Populists: the Agrarian Response to Utopia, 188-1898*. Ph D diss, U of Illinois, 1977.

3798 MCQUAID, KIM. "Industry and the Co-Operative Commonwealth: William P. Hapgood and the Columbia Conserve Company, 1917-1943." *Labor History*, Vol 17 (1976), 510-29.

3799 MANCINI, MATTHEW J. *The Covert Themes of American Anarchism, 1881-1908: Time, Space, and Consciousness as Anarchist Myth*. Ph D diss, Emory U, 1974.

3800 MAY, DEAN L. "Mormon Co-operatives in Paris, Idaho, 1869-1896." *Idaho Yesterdays*, Vol 19 (Summer 1975), 21-30.

3801 MERCER, DUANE D. "The Colorado Co-operative Company, 1894-1904." *Colorado Magazine*, Vol 44 (1967), 293-306.

3802 MILLER, ERNEST. "Utopian Communities in Warren County, Pennsylvanias." *Western Pennsylvania Historical Magazine*, Vol 49 (1966), 301-17.

3803 MILLER, KENNETH E. "Danish Socialism and the Kansas Prairie." *Kansas Historical Quarterly*, Vol 38 (1972), 157-68. (Attempt of Louis Albert Francois Pio, leader of the Danish Socialist Party, to establish a colony in Kansas 1877)

3804 MONTGOMERY, HORACE. "Georgia's Koinonia: a Heritage of Communitarian Ideas and Ordeals." *Americana-Austriaca*, Vol 3 (1974), 151-80.

3805 MORRIS, JAMES K. "Outpost of the Cooperative Commonwealth: the History of the Llano del Rio Colony in Gila, New Mexico, 1932-1935." *New Mexico Historical Quarterly*, Vol 56 (1981), 177-95.

3806 MURRAH, BILL. "Llana Cooperative Colony, Louisiana." *Southern Exposure*, Vol 1 (Winter 1973), 88-104.

3807 MYERS, ELEANOR. "Oneida Community. Land Records Wouldn't Help Here!" *National Genealogical Society Quarterly*, Vol 54 (1966), 193-210. (State census returns, 1855, 1865, 1875)

3808 NELSON, RONALD E. "The Bishop Hill Colony and Its Pioneer Economy." *Swedish Pioneer Historical Quarterly*, Vol 18 (1966), 32-48.

3809 NORTON, JOHN E. "'And Utopia Became Bishop Hill'." *Historic Preservation*, Vol 24 ((ct-Dec 1972), 4-7.

3810 OLSEN, DEBORAH M., and CLARK M. WEIL. "Musical Heritage of the Aurora Colony." *Oregon Historical Quarterly*, Vol 79 (1978), 233-67.

3811 *Our Daily Bread*. 1934. (Feature film produced & directed by King Vidor)

3812 OWEN, CAROLINE DALE SNEDEKER. *Seth Way: A Romance of the New Harmony Community*. Bost.: Houghton Mifflin, 1917.

3813 PITZER, DONALD E. "The Harmonist Heritage of Three Towns." *Historic Preservation*, Vol 29 (Oct-Dec 1977), 5-10.

3814 ———, and JOSEPHINE ELLIOTT. "New Harmony's First Utopians, 1814-1824." *Indiana Magazine of History*, Vol 75 (1979), special issue.

3815 REICHERT, WILLIAM O. "Toward a New Understanding of Anarchism." *Western Political Quarterly*, Vol 20 (1967), 856-65.

3816 RUDIN, A. JAMES. "Bad Axe, Michigan: an Experiment in Jewish Agriculture Settlement." *Michigan History*, Vol 46 (1972), 119-30.

3817 SARGENT, LYMAN TOWER. "The Icarians in Iowa." *Annals of Iowa*, Vol 41 (1972), 957-68.

3818 SCHWANTES, CARLOS A. "Free Love and Free Speech on the Pacific Northwest Frontier." *Oregon Historical Quarterly*, Vol 82 (1981), 271-93.

3819 SEARS, HAL D. "Alcander Longley, Missouri Communist: a History of Reunion Community and a Study of the Constitutions of Reunion and Friendship." *Bulletin of the Missouri Historical Society*, Vol 25 (1969), 123-37.

3820 SHIROM, ARIE. "The Industrial Relations Systems of Industrial Cooperatives in the United States, 1880-1935." *Labor History*, Vol 13 (1972), 533-51.

3821 SMITH, MARTHA BROWNING. "The Story of Icaria." *Annals of Iowa*, 3rd series, Vol 38 (1965), 36-64.

3822 SOKOLOW, JAYME A. "Culture and Utopia: the Raritan Bay Union." *New Jersey History*, Vol 94 (1976), 89-100.

3823 STAGG, BRIAN L. "America's Rugby." *Historic Preservation*, Vol 19 (1967), 76-79.

3824 STEVENSON, BILLIE. *The Ideology of American Anarchism, 1880-1910*. Ph D diss, U of Iowa, 1972.

3825 SWEETLAND, JAMES. "Federal Sources for the Study of Collective Communities." *Government Publications Review*, No 7A (1980), 129-38.

3826 TAGER, FLORENCE M. *A Radical Approach to Education: Anarchist Schooling—the Modern School of New York and Stelton*. Ph D diss, Ohio State U, 1979.

3827 VALLANCE, MARGARET. "Rudolf Rocker—A Biographical Sketch." *Journal of Contemporary History*, Vol 8 (Jul 1973), 75-95.

3828 WALKER, ROBERT HOWARD. *Charles Lane and the Fruitlands Utopia*. Ph D diss, U of Texas, 1967.

3829 Weisbrod, Carol. *The Boundaries of Utopia.* NY: Pantheon, 1980.

3830 Werstein, Irving. *Strangled Voices: The Story of the Haymarket Affair.* NY: Macmillan, 1970.

3831 Whisenhunt, Donald W. "Old Moneyless: His Search for Utopia." *Southwest Review*, Vol 54 (1969), 413-24. (H. C. McCowen)

3832 Wilson, John B. "Emerson and the 'Communities.'" *Emerson Society Quarterly*, Vol 53 (1966), 56-62.

3833 Wilson, R. Jackson. "Experience and Utopia: The Making of Edward Bellamy's *Looking Backward.*" *Journal of American Studies*, Vol 11 (1977), 45-60.

3834 Wilson, William E. *The Angel and the Serpent: The Story of New Harmony.* Bloomington: Indiana U Press, 1964.

3835 Wolski, Kalikst. "A Visit to the North American Phalanx." *Proceedings of the New Jersey Historical Society*, Vol 83 (1965), 149-60. (Translated by Marion Moore Coleman)

3836 Wright, Langdon. "In Search of Peace and Harmony: New York Communities in the 17th Century." *New York History*, Vol 60 (1980), 5-21.

Strikes and Strike Legislation

Note: When strikes pertain to a specific industry, they are listed under the classification for that industry for the convenience of the reader. When specific-industry strikes attained national importance, like the railroad strikes of 1877 or the Pullman strike of 1894, they are listed under the pertinent Period of Development.

3837 AARON, BENJAMIN. "Emergency Disputes in the Private Sector—National Emergency Disputes: Some Current Proposals." *Labor Law Journal*, Vol 22 (Aug 1971), pp 461-74.

3838 ———. "Emergency Disputes: Recent British and American Experience." *Proceedings of the Twenty-Fifth Anniversary Meeting of the Industrial Relations Research Association*, Dec 28-29, 1972, pp 1-14. Madison: IRRA, 1973.

3839 ———. "Labor Injunctions in the State Courts: Part I: A Survey; Part II: A Critique." *Virginia Law Review*, Vol 50 (1964), 951-1033, 1147-64.

3840 ———. "Public-Interest Disputes and Their Settlement: Observations on the United States Experience." *Labor Law Journal*, Aug 1963, pp 746-52.

3841 ———. "Strikes in Breach of Collective Agreements: Some Unanswered Questions." *Columbia Law Review*, Vol 63 (1963), 1027-52.

3842 ADAMIC, LOUIS. *Dynamite*. NY: Viking Press, 1931.

3843 ADAMS, GRAHAM, JR. *The Age of Industrial Violence, 1910-15: The Activities and Findings of the United States Commission on Industrial Relations*. NY: Columbia U Press, 1966.

3844 ATLESON, JAMES B. "Work Group Behavior and Wildcat Strike: the Causes and Functions of Industrial Civil Disobedience." *Industrial Relations Law Digest*, Vol 17 (Summer 1974), 45-65.

3845 BAKER, RAY STANNARD. *The New Industrial Unrest*. NY: Doubleday, Page, 1920.

3846 BARKAS, EILEEN. "Non-Stoppage Strike Agreement." *Industrial and Labor Relations Forum*, Vol 5 (1969), 333-55.

3847 BERMAN, EDWARD. *Labor Disputes and the President of the United States*. NY: Columbia U, 1924.

3848 BERNSTEIN, IRVING. et al, eds. *Emergency Disputes and National Policy*. NY: Harper, 1955.

3849 BING, A. *War-Time Strikes and Their Adjustment*. NY: Dutton, 1921.

3850 BLACKMAN, JOHN L., JR. *Presidential Seizure in Labor Disputes*. Cambr.: Harvard U Press, 1967.

3851 BLAKE, FAY M. *The Strike in the American Novel*. Metuchen, NJ: Scarecrow Press, 1972.

3852 Blanchard, John, and Dorothy Terrill. *Strikes in the Pacific Northwest, 1927-1940: A Statistical Analysis*. Portland, OR: Northwest Regional Council, 1942.

3853 Bloch, Joseph W., and Julian Malnak. "The Dimensions of Major Work Stoppages." *Monthly Labor Review*, Vol 84 (1961), 335-43.

3854 Braun, Kurt. *Labor Disputes and Their Settlement*. Balt.: Johns Hopkins Press, 1955.

3855 Brecher, Jeremy. *Strike!* San Francisco: Straight Arrow Books, 1972.

3856 Byrnes, Robert E. "Emergency Stoppages in the Private Sector—A Discussion." *Labor Law Journal*, Vol 22 (Aug 1971), 475-77.

3857 Cabe, J. Carl. *Governmental Intervention in Labor Disputes from 1945 to 1952*. Ph D diss, U of Illinois, 1952.

3858 Carney, James T. "The Forgotten Man on the Welfare Roll: a Study of Public Subsidies for Strikers." *Industrial Relations Law Digest*, Vol 17 (Summer 1974), 23-36.

3859 Cass, Millard. "The Relationship of Size of Firm and Strike Activity." *Monthly Labor Review*, Vol 80 (1957), 1330-34.

3860 Chamberlain, Neil W. *The Impact of Strikes*. NY: Harper, 1954.

3861 ———. *Social Responsibility and Strikes*. NY: Harper, 1953.

3862 ———. "Strikes in Contemporary Context." *Industrial and Labor Relations Review*, Vol 20 (1967), 602-16.

3863 Corbin, David. "The *Socialist and Labor Star:* Strike and Suppression in West Virginia, 1912-1913." *West Virginia History*, Vol 34 (1973), 168-86.

3864 Crook, Wilfrid H. *The General Strike: A Study of Labor's Tragic Weapon in Theory and Practice*. Chapel Hill: U of North Carolina Press, 1931.

3865 Crowther, Samuel. *Why Men Strike*. NY: Doubleday, 1920.

3866 Cullen, Donald E. *National Emergency Strikes*. Ithaca: NY State School of Industrial and Labor Relations, Cornell U, 1968.

3867 ———. "The Taft-Hartley Act in National Emergency Disputes." *Industrial and Labor Relations Review*, Vol 7 (1953), 15-30.

3868 Currier, Thomas Franklin. "Whittier and the Amesbury-Salisbury Strike." *New England Quarterly*, Vol 8 (1935), 105-12.

3869 Eaton, B. Curtis. "The Worker and the Profitability of the Strike." *Industrial and Labor Relations Review*, Vol 26 (1972), 670-79.

3870 Edwards, Paul K. *Strikes in the United States, 1881-1974*. (NY: St. Martin's Press, 1981)

3871 Eisele, C. Frederick. "Organization of Size, Technology, and Frequency of Strikes." *Industrial and Labor Relations Review*, Vol 27 (1974), 560-71.

3872 Fisher, Waldo E. "The Strike as a Socio-Economic Institution." *Proceedings of the Third Annual Meeting of the Industrial Relations Research Association*, Dec 28-29, 1950, pp 297-316. Madison: IRRA, 1951.

3873 Fitch, John. *The Causes of Industrial Unrest*. NY: Harper, 1924.

3874 Fleming, R. W. "Emergency Strikes and National Policy." *Labor Law Journal*, Vol 11 (Apr 1960), 267-76, 336.

3875 Gennard, John. *Financing Strikers*. NY: Wiley, 1977.

3876 Gephart, Ronald M. "Poltiticians, Soldiers and Strikes: The Reorganizations of the Nebraska Militia and the Omaha Strike of 1882." *Nebraska History*, Vol 44 (1965), 89-120.

3877 Gouldner, Alvin W. *Wildcat Strike*. Yellow Spring, OH: Antioch Press, 1954.

3878 Griffin, John I. *Strikes: A Study in Quantitative Economics*. NY: Columbia U Press, 1939.

3879 Grossman, Jonathan. "The Coal Strike of 1902—Turning Point in U.S. Policy." *Monthly Labor Review*, Vol 98 (Oct 1975), 21-28.

3880 HALL, FREDERICK S. *Sympathetic Strikes and Sympathetic Lockouts*. NY: Columbia U Press, 1898.
3881 HAMMETT, HUGH B. "Labor and Race: The Georgia Railroad Strike of 1909." *Labor History*, Vol 16 (1975), 470-84.
3882 HARTMANN, GEORGE W., and THEODORE NEWCOMB, eds. *Industrial Conflict: A Psychological Interpretation*. NY: The Gordon Co., 1939.
3883 HILLER, ERNEST T. *The Strike: A Study in Collective Action*. Chicago: U of Chicago Press, 1928.
3884 HIRSCH, JOHN S., JR. "Strike Insurance and Collective Bargaining." *Industrial and Labor Relations Review*, Vol 22 (1969), 399-415.
3885 HOMANS, GEORGE, and JEROME F. SCOTT. "Reflections on the Wildcat Strikes." *American Sociological Review*, Vol 12 (1947), 278-87.
3886 HUNTER, ROBERT. *Violence and the Labor Movement*. NY: Macmillan, 1914.
3887 HUTT, WILLIAM H. *The Strike-Threat System: The Economic Consequences of Collective Bargaining*. New Rochelle, NY: Arlington House, 1973.
3888 JANES, GEORGE M. *Control of Strikes in American Trade Unions*. Balt.: Johns Hopkins U, 1916.
3889 KANAREK, HAROLD K. "Disaster for Hard Coal: The Anthracite Strike of 1925-1926." *Labor History*, Vol 15 (1974), 44-62.
3890 KLINE, SHELDON M. "Strike Benefits of National Unions." *Monthly Labor Review*, Vol 98 (Mar 1975), 17-23.
3891 KORNHAUSER, ARTHUR W. et al. *Industrial Conflict*. NY: McGraw-Hill, 1954.
3892 LAIDLER, HARRY W. *Boycotts and Labor Struggle: Economic and Legal Aspects*. NY: J. Lane, 1914.
3893 LAZAR, JOSEPH. et al. "The Tripartite Commission in Public Interest Labor Disputes in Minnesota, 1940-1960." *Labor Law Journal*, Vol 14 (May 1963), 419-33.
3894 LEVINSON, EDWARD. *I Break Strikes! The Technique of Pearl L. Bergoff*. NY: McBride & Co., 1935.
3895 LEWIS, GEORGE D. *Syndicalism and the General Strike*. Bost.: Small, Maynard, 1912.
3896 LISTON, ROBERT A. *The Limits of Defiance: Strikes, Rights, and government*. NY: F. Watts, 1971.
3897 MCCALMONT, DAVID B. "The Semi-Strike." *Industrial and Labor Relations Review*, Vol 15 (1962), 191-208.
3898 MCCARTHY, EUGENE. et al. *The Strike: For and Against*. NY: Hart, 1971.
3899 MCLEAN, D. A. *The Morality of the Strike*. NY: P. J. Kennedy, 1921.
3900 MANTOVANI, RICHARD E. *A Quantitative Analysis of the Impact of Federal Regulative Activities on Labor Disputes*. Ph D diss, Johns Hopkins U, 1979.
3901 MONTGOMERY, DAVID. "Strikes in 19th Century America." *Social Sciences History*, Vol 4 (1980), 81-104.
3902 MORRIS, RICHARD B. "Andrew Jackson, Strikebreaker." *American Historical Review*, Vol 55 (1949), 54-68.
3903 NATIONAL COUNCIL OF THE CHURCHES OF CHRIST (COMMITTEE ON THE CHURCH AND ECONOMIC LIFE). *The Right to Strike and the General WElfare*. NY: The Council Press, 1967.
3904 NORTHRUP, HERBERT R. *Compulsory Arbitration and Government Intervention in Labor Disputes: An Analysis of Experience*. Wash.: Labor Policy Association, 1966.
3905 OLDS, MARSHALL. *The High Cost of Strikes*. NY: Putnam, 1921.
3906 PATCH, BUAL W. "Industry-Wide Bargaining and Industry-Wide Strikes." *Editorial Research Reports*, Vol 1 (1953), 261-77.
3907 PAYNE, BARBARA. *The Division of Labor Power and Collective Action: a Study of Industrial Strike Activity*. Ph D diss, Stanford U, 1977.
3908 PECK, GUSTAVE. *Collective Bargaining and the Strike Limitation Issue, 1933-46*. Wash.: Library of Congress, 1946.

3909 PETERSON, FLORENCE. *Strikes in the United States, 1880-1936*. Wash.: G.P.O., 1938.

3910 RAINS, HARRY H. "Should Strikers Receive Unemployment Insurance Benefits?" *Labor Law Journal*, Vol 30 (Nov 1979), 700-8.

3911 RECCOW, LOUIS. *The Orange County Citrus Strike of 1935-1936: The 'Forgotten People' in Revolt*. Ph D diss, U of Southern California, 1971.

3912 REDER, MELVIN, and GEORGE NEUMANN. "Conflict and Contract: the Case of Strikes." *Journal of Political Economy*, Vol 88 (1980), 876-86.

3913 RIMLINGER, GASTON V. "The Legitimation of Protest: A Comparative Study in Labor History." *Comparative Studies in Society and History*, Vol 2 (1960), 329-43.

3914 ROOMKIN, MYRON. "Union Structure, Internal Control, and Strike Activity." *Industrial and Labor Relations Review*, Vol 29 (1976), 198-217.

3915 ROSS, ARTHUR M. "The Prospects for Industrial Conflict." *Industrial Relations*, Vol 1 (1961), 57-64.

3916 SCHNEIDER, LINDA. *American Nationality and Workers' Consciousness in Industrial Conflict: 1870-1920. Three Case Studies*. Ph D diss, Columbia U, 1975. (Strikes in coal & iron industries, 1873, Homestead strike, 1892, & steel strike, 1919)

3917 SENTURIA, J. J. *Strikes*. Chicago: U of Chicago Press, 1935.

3918 SHAIR, DAVID I. "The Sit-Down as a Union Weapon." *Fairleigh Dickinson University Business Review*, Vol 7 (1967), 12-22.

3919 SHELTON, BRENDA K. "The Buffalo Grain Shovellers' Strike of 1899." *Labor History*, Vol 9 (1968), 210-38.

3920 SHULTZ, GEORGE P. "The Massachusetts Choice-of-Procedures to Emeregency Disputes." *Industrial and Labor Relations Review*, Vol 10 (1957), 359-74.

3921 SIEMILLER, P. L. "Special Government Dispute Settlement Panels." *Labor Law Journal*, Vol 15 (Jul 1964), 419-23.

3922 SIGAL, BENJAMIN C. "National Emergency Strikes and the Public Interest." *North Carolina Law Review*, Vol 27 (1949), 213-19.

3923 SKEELS, JACK W. "Measures of U.S. Strike Activity." *Industrial and Labor Relations Review*, Vol 24 (1971), 515-25.

3924 SMITH, OSCAR S. "Are Public Service Strikes Necessary?" *Public Personnel Review*, Vol 21 (1960), 169-73.

3925 ———. "The Effect of the Public Interest on the Right to Strike and to Bargain Collectively." *North Carolina Law Review*, Vol 27 (1949), 204-12.

3926 SMYTHE, CYRUS F. "Public Policy and Emergency Disputes." *Labor Law Journal*, Vol 14 (Oct 1963), 827-33.

3927 SNARR, D. NEIL. "Strikers and Nonstrikers: A Social Comparison." *Industrial Relations*, Vol 14 (1975), 371-74.

3928 SNYDER, DAVID. "Early North American Strikes: a Reinterpretation." *Industrial and Labor Relations Review*, Vol 30 (1977), 325-41.

3929 SOCIETY FOR THE PSYCHOLOGICAL STUDY OF SOCIAL ISSUES. *Industrial Conflict: A Psychological Interpretation* (a study of Detroit). NY: Cordon, 1939.

3930 SOSNICK, STEPHEN H. "Non-Stoppage Strikes: A New Approach." *Industrial and Labor Relations Review*, Vol 18 (1964), 73-80.

3931 STERN, JAMES. "Declining Utility of the Strike." *Industrial and Labor Relations Review*, Vol 18 (1964), 60-72.

3932 STERN, ROBERT N. "Intermetropolitan Patterns of Strike Frequency." *Industrial and Labor Relations Review*, Vol 29 (1976), 218-35.

3933 STEUBEN, JOHN. *Strike Strategy*. NY: Gaer, 1950.

3934 STIEBER, JACK. "Unauthorized Strikes under the American and British Industrial Relations Systems." *British Journal of Industrial Relations*, Vol 6 (1968), 232-38.

3935 STROH, PAUL. *Catholic Clergy and American Labor Disputes*. Ph D diss, Catholic U, 1949.

3936 STYLES, PAUL L. "Special Government Dispute Settlement Procedure." *Labor Law Journal*, Vol 15 (Jul 1964), 413-16.

3937 SWINTON, JOHN. *Striking for Life: Labor's Side of the Labor Question*. Phila.: Keller, 1894.

3938 SYLVESTER, JOAN. *Strikes and Monopoly Capitalism*. Ph D diss, U of Maryland, 1981.

3939 TAFT, PHILIP. "Violence in American Labor Disputes." *Annals of the American Academy of Political and Social Science*, Vol 344 (1966), 127-40.

3940 THIEBLOT, ARMAND J., JR, and RONALD M. COWAN. *Welfare and Strikes: the Use of Public Funds to Support Strikers*. Phila.: U of Pennsylvania, 1972.

3941 THOMPSON, DUANE E., and RICHARD P. BORGLUM. "A Case Study of Employee Attitudes and Labor Unrest." *Industrial and Labor Relations Review*, Vol 27 (1973), 74-83.

3942 TODES, CHARLOTTE. *Dynamite*. NY: Viking, 1931.

3943 U.S. BUREAU OF LABOR STATISTICS. *Analysis of Work Stoppages*. Wash.: G.P.O., 1936- . (Annual bulletin)

3944 ———. *National Emergency Disputes under the Labor Management Relations (Taft-Hartley) Act, 1947-61*. Wash.: G.P.O., 1962.

3945 U.S. FEDERAL MEDIATION AND CONCILIATION SERVICE. *Synopsis: Presidential Boards of Inquiry Created Under National Emergency Provisions of Labor Management Relations Act, 1947, September 1960*. Wash.: The Service, 1961.

3946 U.S. LIBRARY OF CONGRESS. Legislative Reference Service *Collective Bargaining and the Strike Limitation Issue 1933-1946.*, Public Affairs Bulletin 39. Wash.: The Library, 1946.

3947 ———. *Federal Legislation to End Strikes: A Documentary History*. Wash.: G.P.O., 1967.

3948 U.S. NATIONAL WAR LABOR BOARD. *The Termination Report of the National War Labor Board; Industrial Disputes and Wage Stabilization in Wartime*. Wash.: G.P.O., 1948.

3949 WALKER, MICHAEL. "Sitdown Strikes Grabbed Attention." *Worklife*, Vol 1 (Sep 1976), 22-24.

3950 WARNER, W. L., and J. O. LOW. *The Social System of the Modern Factory: The Strike, a Social Analysis*. New Haven: Yale U Press, 1947.

3951 WARREN, EDGAR L. "Thirty-Six Years of 'National Emergency' Strikes." *Industrial and Labor Relations Review*, Vol 5 (19510, 3-19.

3952 WEINTRAUB, ANDREW R. "Prosperity versus Strikes: an Empirical Approach." *Industrial and Labor Relations Review*, Vol 19 (1966), 231-38.

3953 WILCOX, BERTRAM F., and ELIZABETH S. LANDIS. "Government Seizures in Labor Disputes." *Cornell Law Quarterly*, Vol 34 (1948), 155-81.

3954 WILSON, WALTER, and ALBERT DEUTSCH. *Call Out the Militia! A Survey of the Use of Troops in Strikes*. NY: American Civil Liberties Union, 1938.

3955 WITTE, EDWIN E. *The Government in Labor Disputes*. NY: McGraw-Hill, 1932.

3956 WRIGHT, CARROLL D. *The Battles of Labor*. Phila.: Jacobs, 1906.

3957 ———. "Strikes and Lockouts Occurring Prior to 1881." chap. 4, *Third Annual Report of the Commissioner of Labor 1887: Strikes and Lockouts.*, Wash.: G.P.O., 1888.

3958 YABROFF, BERNARD, and DANIEL P. WILLIS, JR. "Federal Seizures in Labor-Management Disputes, 1917-52." *Monthly Labor Review*, Vol 76 (1953), 611-16.

3959 YELLEN, SAMUEL. *American Labor Struggles*. NY: Harcourt, Brace, 1936.

3960 ZIBEL, HOWARD J. "The Role of Calvin Coolidge in the Boston Police Strike of 1919." *Industrial and Labor Relations Forum*, Vol 6 (1969), 299-318.

City, Regional, and State Labor Movements and Conditions

City

GENERAL

3961 SEIDMAN, JOEL. "Community Influences on Industrial Relations Patterns." *Industrial Relations*, Vol 4 (1965), 1-7.

ALBANY

3962 GREENBERG, BRIAN. *Work and Community: the Social Structure of a 19th-Century American City, Albany, New York, 1850-1884.* Ph D diss, Princeton U, 1980.

3963 RAPONE, ANITA J. *Clerical Labor Force Formation: The Office Woman in Albany, 1870-1930.* Ph D diss, New York U, 1981.

BALTIMORE

3964 ARGERSINGER, JO ANN E. "Assisting the 'Loafers': Transient Relief in Baltimore, 1933-1937." *Labor History*, Vol 22 (1982), 226-45.

3965 GLOCKER, THEODORE W. *Trade Unionism in Baltimore Before the War of 1812.* Balt.: Johns Hopkins U, 1907.

BENNINGTON, VT

3966 SPARGO, JOHN. *The Potters and Potteries of Bennington.* Bost.: Houghton, Mifflin, 1926.

BOSTON

3967 DODD, JILL SIEGEL. "The Working Classes and the Temperance Movement in Ante-Bellum Boston." *Labor History*, Vol 19 (1978), 510-31.

3968 LAZEROW, JAMA. "'The Workingman's Hour': The 1886 Labor Uprising in Boston." *Labor History*, Vol 21 (1980), 200-20.

3969 *Mission Hill and the Miracle of Boston.* 1978. (Documentary film by Richard Boardman, et al.)

3970 ROBOFF, SARI. *Boston's Labor Movement: An Oral History of Work and Union Organizing.* Bost.: Boston 200 Corporation, 1977.

3971 SCHREIBER, HENRY M. *The Working People of Boston in the Middle of the Nineteenth Century.* Ph D diss, Boston U, 1950.

3972 THERNSTROM, STEPHAN. *The Other Bostonians: Poverty and Progress in the American Metropolis, 1880-1970.* Cambr.: Harvard U Press, 1973.

3973 WHITEHILL, WALTER M. "Boston Artists and Craftsmen at the Opening of the Twentieth Century." *New England Quarterly*, Vol 50 (1977), 387-408.

3974 ZIBEL, HOWARD J. "The Role of Calvin Coolidge in the Boston Police Strike of 1919." *Industrial and Labor Relations Forum*, Vol 6 (1969), 299-318.

BUFFALO

3975 MCDONNELL, JAMES R. *The Rise of the CIO in Buffalo, New York, 1936-1942.* Ph D diss, U of Wisconsin, 1970.

BUTTE

3976 U.S. COMMISSION ON INDUSTRIAL RELATIONS (1912). "Mining Conditions and Industrial Relations at Butte, Montana," Vol 4, pp 3681-4095, *Final Report*, Wash.: G.P.O., 1916.

CHICAGO

3977 BEHEN, DAVID M. *The Chicago Labor Movement, 1874-1896: Its Philosophical Bases.* Ph D diss, U of Chicago, 1954.

3978 HALPER, ALBERT. *The Chute* (a novel). NY: Viking, 1937.

3979 HOGAN, DAVID. "Education and the Making of the Chicago Working Class, 1880-1930." *History of Education Quarterly*, Vol 18 (1978), 227-70.

3980 MORRIS, JANE K. *Julie* (a novel about a labor organizer and leader during the late 19th century). NY: McGraw-Hill, 1952.

3981 MOTLEY, WILLARD. *We Fished All Night* (a novel). NY: Appleton-Century-Crofts, 1951.

3982 NEWELL, BARBARA W. *Chicago and the Labor Movement: Metropolitan Unionism in the 1930's.* Urbana: U of Illinois Press, 1961.

3983 O'BRIEN, HOWARD V. *New Men for Old* (a novel). NY: M. Kennerley, 1914.

3984 PIERCE, BESSIE L. *A History of Chicago.*, Vol III, *The Rise of a Modern City: 1871-1893.* NY: Knopf, 1957.

3985 STEAD, WILLIAM THOMAS. *Chicago Today: Or, The Labour War in America.* London: Review of Reviews Office, 1894.

3986 U.S. COMMISSION ON INDUSTRIAL RELATIONS (1912). "Industrial Conditions in Chicago," Vol 4, pp 3173-457, *Final Report*, Wash.: G.P.O, 1916.

CINCINNATI

3987 DUGGAN, EDWARD. "Machines, Markets, and Labor: the Carriage and Wagon Industry in late 19th Century Cincinnati." *Business History Review*, Vol 51 (1977), 308-25.

3988 HARDING, LEONARD. "The Cincinnati Riots of 1862." *Bulletin of the Cincinnati Historical Society*, Vol 25 (1967), 229-39.

3989 MORRIS, JAMES M. "No Haymarket for Cincinnati." *Ohio History*, Vol 83 (1974), 17-32. (Strike for 8-hour day in Cincinnati)

3990 ———. *The Road to Trade Unionism: Organized Labor in Cincinnati to 1893.* Ph D diss, U of Cincinnati, 1969.

3991 MUSSELMAN, BARBARA. *The Quest for Collective Improvement: Cincinnati Workers, 1893 to 1920.* Ph D diss, U of Cincinnati, 1976.

3992 ROSS, STEVEN J. *Workers on the Edge: Work, Leisure, and Politics in Industrializing Cincinnati, 1830-1890.* Ph D diss, Princeton U, 1980.

CLEVELAND

3993 HOUGH, LESLIE S. *The Turbulent Spirit: Violence and Co-Action Among Cleveland Workers, 1877-1890.* Ph D diss, U of Virginia, 1977.

3994 WEINBERG, DANIEL E. "Ethnic Identity in Industrial Cleveland: the Hungarians, 1900-20." *Ohio History*, Vol 86 (1977), 171-86.

COHOES, NY

3995 WALKOWITZ, DANIEL J. *Worker City, Company Town: Iron and Cotton Worker Protest in Troy and Cohoes, New York, 1855-1884.* Urbana: U of Illinois Press, 1978.

DECATUR, IL

3996 DERBER, MILTON. "A Small Community's Impact on Labor Relations." *Industrial Relations*, Vol 4 (1965), 27-41.

DENVER

3997 MERGEN, BERNARD M. "Denver and the War on Unemployment." *Colorado Magazine*, Vol 47 (1970), 326-37.

DETROIT

3998 ALPERN, RON. et al. *Union Town: A Labor History Guide to Detroit.* Detroit: Workers Education Local 189, Labor History Task Force, 1979.

3999 BICKNELL, CATHERINE. "Detroit's Capuchin Soup Kitchen." *Labor History*, Vol 24 (1983), 112-24.

4000 *Detroit Workers News Special: The Ford Massacre.* 1932. (Workers Film and Photo League Production)

4001 LEGGETT, JOHN C. *Class, Race, and Labor: Working Class Consciousness in Detroit.* NY: Oxford U Press, 1968.

4002 OESTREICHER, RICHARD. "Socialism and the Knights of Labor in Detroit, 1877-1886." *Labor History*, Vol 22 (1981), 5-30.

4003 ———. *Solidarity and Fragmentation: Working People and Class Consciousness in Detroit, 1877-1895.* Ph D diss, Michigan State U, 1979.

4004 SULLIVAN, MARTIN EDWARD. *'On the dole': the Relief Issue in Detroit, 1929-1939.* Ph D diss, Notre Dame U, 1974.

4005 WIDICK, B. J. "Black Cities, Black Unions? Detroit Experiences a Painful Tension." *Dissent*, Vol 19 (1972), 138-45.

DURHAM

4006 JANIEWSKI, DOLORES. *From Field to Factory: Race, Class, Sex, and the Woman Worker in Durham, 1880-1940.* Ph D diss, Duke U, 1979.

FALL RIVER, MA

4007 SILVIA, PHILIP T. *The Spindle City: Labor and Politics, and Religion in Fall River, Massachusetts, 1870-1905.* Ph D diss, Fordham U, 1973.

FLINT, MI

4008 CHAFE, WILLIAM H. "Flint and the Great Depression." *Michigan History*, Vol 53 (1969), 225-39.

KANSAS CITY

4009 U.S. CONGRESS. HOUSE. Committee on Education and Labor. *Strikes and Racketeering in the Kansas City Area.* Wash.: G.P.O., 1953.

LANSING, MI

4010 BLUM, ALBERT A., and IRA SPAR. "The Lansing Labor Holiday." *Michigan History*, Vol 49 (1965), 1-11.

LAWRENCE, MA

4011 COLE, DONALD B. *Immigrant City: Lawrence, Massachusetts, 1845-1921*. Chapel Hill: U of North Carolina Press, 1963.

LOS ANGELES

4012 BERNSTEIN, IRVING. "Labor Relations in Los Angeles." *Industrial Relations*, Vol 4 (1965), 8-26.

4013 LEWIN, DAVID. "Local Government Relations in Transition: The Case of Los Angeles." *Labor History*, Vol 17 (1976), 191-213.

4014 PERRY, LOUIS B., and RICHARD S. PERRY. *A History of the Los Angeles Labor Movement*. Berkeley: U of California Press, 1963.

4015 ROMO, RICARDO. *Mexican Workers in the City: Los Angeles, 1915-1930*. Ph D diss, U of California, 1976.

4016 SCHIESL, MARTIN J. "Progressive Reform in Los Angeles under Mayor Alexander, 1909-13." *California Historical Quarterly*, Vol 54 (1975), 37-56.

4017 STIMSON, GRACE HEILMAN. *Rise of the Labor Movement in Los Angeles*. Berkeley: U of California Press, 1955.

4018 TIPTON, GENE B. *The Labor Movement in the Los Angeles Area During the Nineteen-Forties*. Ph D diss, U of California, 1953.

4019 U.S. COMMISSION ON INDUSTRIAL RELATIONS (1912). "The Open and Closed Shop Controversy in Los Angeles," Vol 6, pp 5485-999, *Final Report*, Wash.: G.P.O., 1916.

4020 VAN ARSDOL, MAURICE D., JR. *Non-Apprehended and Apprehended Undocumented Residents in the Los Angeles Labor Market: An Exploratory Study*. Springfield, VA: National Technical Information Service, U.S. Department of Commerce, 1980.

LOWELL

4021 BLEWETT, MARY H., ed. *Surviving Hard Times: the Working People of Lowell*. Lowell, MA: Lowell Museum, 1982.

LYNN, MA

4022 DAWLEY, ALAN. *Class and Community: The Industrial Revolution in Lynn*. Cambr.: Harvard U Press, 1976.

4023 FALER, PAUL. *Mechanics and Manufacturers in the Early Industrial Revolution, Lynn, Massachusetts, 1780-1860*. Albany, NY: SUNY Press, 1981.

MANCHESTER, NH

4024 HAREVEN, TAMARA K. *Family Time and Industrial Time: The Relationship Between the Family and Work in a New England Industrial Community*. NY: Cambridge U Press, 1982.

MEMPHIS

4025 BORN, KATE. "Organized Labor in Memphis, Tennessee, 1826-1901." *Papers of the West Tennessee Historical Society*, Vol 21 (1967), 60-79.

4026 GREEN, E., JR. *Labor in the South: a Case Study of Memphis—the 1968 Sanitation Strike and Its Effects on an Urban Community*. Ph D diss, New York U, 1980.

4027 STANFIELD, J. EDWIN. *In Memphis: More than a Garbage Strike, with Supplements Issued April 3, 1968 and April 28, 1968*. Atlanta: Southern Regional Council, 1968.

MILWAUKEE

4028 Gavett, Thomas W. *Development of the Labor Movement in Milwaukee.* Madison: U of Wisconsin Press, 1965.

4029 Korman, Gerd. *Industrialization, Immigrants, and Americanizers: The View from Milwaukee, 1866-1921.* Madison: The State Historical Society of Wisconsin, 1967.

4030 Mayer, Jonathan. *The Journey-to-work, Ethnicity, and Occupation in Milwaukee, 1860-1900.* Ph D diss, U of Michigan, 1978.

MINNEAPOLIS-ST. PAUL

4031 D'Urso, Joe. "Mass Strike in Minneapolis, 1934: Interviews with Strikers." *Red Buffalo*, double issue 2 & 3 (1972), 55-90.

4032 Romer, Sam. "Twin Cities: National Patterns and Sibling Rivalry." *Industrial Relations*, Vol 4 (1965), 42-50.

4033 Walker, Charles R. *American City: A Rank-and-File History.* NY: Farrar and Rinehart, 1937.

MUSCATINE

4034 Federal Council of the Churches of Christ in America. Commission on the Church and Social Service *Report on the Industrial Situation at Muscatine, Iowa, by a Special Committee* (Button Workers Strike, 1911). NY: The Council, 1912.

NEW BRUNSWICK, NJ

4035 Leggett, John C., and Jerry Gioglio. "Break Out the Double Digit: Mass Unemployment in the City of New Brunswick." *Review of Radical Political Economics*, Vol 10 (Spring,, 1978), 32-46.

NEW ORLEANS

4036 Shugg, Roger Wallace. "The New Orleans General Strike of 1892." *Louisiana Historical Quarterly*, Vol 21 (1938), 547-60.

NEW YORK CITY

4037 Cook, Alice H. "Public Employee Bargaining in New York City." *Industrial Relations*, Vol 9 (1970), 249-67.

4038 ———, and Lois Gray. "Labor Relations in New York City." *Industrial Relations*, Vol 5 (1966), 86-104.

4039 Costello, Lawrence. *The New York City Labor Movement, 1861-1873.* Ph D diss, Columbia U, 1967.

4040 Degler, Carl N. *Labor in the Economy and Politics of New York City, 1850-1860.* Ph D diss, Columbia U, 1952.

4041 Dubofsky, Melvyn. *New York City Labor in the Progressive Era, 1910-1918: A Study of Organized Labor in an Era of Reform.* Ph D diss, U of Rochester, 1960.

4042 ———. *When Workers Organize: New York City in the Progressive Era.* Amherst: U of Massachusetts Press, 1968.

4043 Goldschmidt, Eli. "Labor and Populism: New York City, 1891-1896." *Labor History*, Vol 13 (1972), 520-32.

4044 Gordon, Michael A. "The Labor Boycott in New York City, 1880-1886." *Labor History*, Vol 16 (1975), 184-229.

4045 Gutman, Herbert G. "The Tompkins Square 'Riot' in New York City on January 13, 1874: A Re-examination of its Causes and its Aftermath." *Labor History*, Vol 6 (1965), 44-70.

4046 Hayes, Alfred. *Shadow of Heaven* (a novel). NY: Howell, Soskin, 1947.

4047 Hayes, Dorsha. *Who Walk with the Earth* (a novel). NY: Harper, 1945.

4048 HORTON, RAYMOND D. *The Municipal Labor Relations System in New York City: 1954-1970.* Ph D diss, Columbia U, 1971.

4049 HYMAN, PAULA E. "Immigrant Women and Consumer Protest: the New York City Kosher Meat Boycott of 1902." *American Jewish History*, Vol 70 (1980), 91-105.

4050 INGALLS, ROBERT P. *Herbert H. Lehman and New York's Little New Deal.* Ph D diss, Columbia U, 1973.

4051 LAWSON, RONALD, and STEPHEN BOITAR. "Sex Roles in Social Movements: a Case Study of the Tenant Movement in New York City." *Signs*, Vol 6 (1980), 230-47.

4052 LYND, STAUGHTON. "The Mechanics in New York Politics, 1774-1788." *Labor History*, Vol 5 (1964), 225-46.

4053 MOHL, RAYMOND A. "Poverty, Politics and the Mechanics of New York City, 1803." *Labor History*, Vol 12 (1971), 38-51.

4054 PERRIER, HUBERT. "The Socialists and the Working Class in New York, 1890-1896." *Labor History*, Vol 22 (1981), 485-511.

4055 PERRY, ELIZABETH ISRAELS. "Industrial Reform in New York City: Belle Moskowitz and the Protocol of Peace, 1913-1916." *Labor History*, Vol 22 (1982), 5-31.

4056 PESSEN, EDWARD. "Who has Power in the Democratic Capitalistic Community? Reflections on Antebellum New York City." *New York History*, Vol 58 (1977), 129-55.

4057 ———. "A Young Industrial Worker in Early World War II in New York City." *Labor History*, Vol 22 (1981), 269-81.

4058 ROCK, HOWARD B. *Artisans of the New Republic: The Tradesmen of New York City in the Age of Jefferson.* NY: New York U Press, 1979.

4059 STANSELL, CHRISTINE. "The Origins of the Sweatshop: Women and Early Industrialization in New York City," pp 78-103, *Working Class America: Essays on Labor, Community, and American Society*, Michael Frisch & Daniel J. Walkowitz, eds. Urbana: U of Illinois Press, 1983.

4060 WECHSLER, ROBERT. *New York Labor Heritage: A Selected Bibliography of New York City Labor History.* NY: Robert F. Wagner Labor Archives, Tamiment Institute Library, New York U, 1981.

NEWARK, NJ

4061 BLOOMBERG, SUSAN E. H. *Industrialization and Skilled Workers: Newark 1826 to 1860.* Ph D diss, U of Michigan, 1974.

4062 BROOKS, THOMAS R. "Breakdown in Newark." *Dissent*, Vol 19 (1972), 128-37.

4063 GUTMAN, HERBERT G. "Industrial Invasion of the Village Green." *Trans-action*, May-Jun 1966, pp 39-42.

4064 HIRSCH, SUSAN E. *Roots of the American Working Class: The Industrialization of Crafts in Newark, 1800-1860.* Phila.: U of Pennsylvania Press, 1978.

PADUCAH

4065 TRIPP, L. REED. et al. *Labor-Management Relations in the Pasducah Area of Western Kentucky*., Bureau of Business Research Bulletin No 28. Lexington: U of Kentucky, 1954.

PEKIN, IL

4066 BRUNE, LESTER H. "'Union Holiday—Closed til Further Notice': The 1936 General Strike at Pekin, Illinois." *Journal of the Illinois State Historical Society*, Vol 75 (1982), 48-67.

PATERSON

4067 U.S. COMMISSION ON INDUSTRIAL RELATIONS (1912). "Industrial Conditions and Relations in Paterson, N. J," Vol 3, pp 2411-2645, *Final Report*, Wash.: G.P.O., 1916.

PENSACOLA, FL

4068 FLYNT, WAYNE. "Pensacola Labor Problems and Political Radicalism, 1908." *Florida Historical Quarterly*, Vol 43 (1965), 315-32.

PHILADELPHIA

4069 ADAMS, DONALD R., JR. *Wage Rates in Philadelphia, 1790-1830.* Ph D diss, U of Pennsylvania, 1967.

4070 ———. "Wage Rates in the Early National Period: Philadelphia 1785-1830." *Journal of Economic History*, Vol 28 (1968), 404-26.

4071 BERNSTEIN, LEONARD. "The Working People of Philadelphia from Colonial Times to the General Strike of 1835." *Pennsylvania Magazine of History and Biography*, Vol 74 (1950), 322-39.

4072 BROWN, SCOTT C. *Migrants and Workers in Philadelphia, 1850 to 1880.* Ph D diss, U of Pennsylvania, 1981.

4073 CALE, EDGAR B. *The Organization of Labor in Philadelphia, 1850-1870.* Ph D diss, U of Pennsylvania, 1940.

4074 ERICKSEN, EUGENE, and WILLIAM YANCEY. "Work and Residence in Industrial Philadlephia." *Journal of Urban History*, Vol 5 (1979), 147-82.

4075 FELDBERG, MICHAEL JAY. *The Philadelphia Riots of 1844: A Study of Ethnic Conflict.* Westport, CT: Greenwood, 1975.

4076 HERSHBERG, THEODORE, ed. *Philadelphia: Work, Space, Family and Group Experience in the Nineteenth Century: Essays toward an Interdisciplinary History of the City.* NY: Oxford U Press, 1981.

4077 LANE, ROGER. *Violent Death in the City: Suicide, Accident and Murder in Nineteenth-Century Philadelphia.* Cambr.: Harvard U Press, 1979.

4078 LAURIE, BRUCE. *Working People of Philadelphia, 1800-1850.* Phila.: Temple U Press, 1980.

4079 OLTON, CHARLES S. *Artisans for Independence: Philadelphia Mechanics and the American Revolution.* Syracuse, NY: Syracuse U Press, 1975.

4080 SULLIVAN, WILLIAM A. "Philadelphia Labor During the Jackson Era." *Pennsylvania History*, Vol 15 (1948), 305-20.

4081 SUTHERLAND, JOHN F. *A City of Homes: Philadelphia Slums and Reformers, 1880-1918.* Ph D diss, Temple U, 1973.

4082 U.S. COMMISSION ON INDUSTRIAL RELATIONS (1912). "General Industrial Relations and Conditions in Philadelphia," Vol 3, pp 2647-730, *Final Report*, Wash.: G.P.O., 1916.

PITTSBURGH

4083 COUVARES, FRANCIS. *Work, Leisure, and Reform in Pittsburgh: the Transformation of an Urban Culture, 1860-1920.* Ph D diss, U of Michigan, 1980.

4084 JOSEPH, MYRON L. *The Operation and Effects of the Taft-Hartley Law in the Pittsburgh District.* Ph D diss, U of Wisconsin, 1953.

4085 KLEINBERG, SUSAN J. "Technology and Women's Work: The Lives of Working Class Women in Pittsburgh, 1870-1900." *Labor History*, Vol 17 (1976), 58-72.

4086 RUSSELL SAGE FOUNDATION. *The Pittsburgh Survey.*, 6 vols. NY: Charities Publication Committee, 1909-1914.

PORTLAND

4087 Pilcher, William W. *The Portland Longshoremen: A Dispersed Urban Community.* NY: Holt, Rinehart & Winston, 1972.

4088 U.S. Commission on Industrial Relations (1912). "General Industrial Conditions and Relations in Portland, Oregon," Vol 5, pp 4573-770, *Final Report*, Wash.: G.P.O., 1916.

POUGHKEEPSIE

4089 Griffen, Clyde, and Sally Griffen. *Natives and Newcomers: The Ordering of Opportunity in Mid-Nineteenth-Century Poughkeepsie.* Cambr.: Harvard U Press, 1978.

PULLMAN

4090 Buder, Stanley. *Pullman: An Experiment in Industrial Order and Community Planning, 1880-1930.* NY: Oxford U Press, 1967.

ROCHESTER

4091 McKelvey, Blake. *Rochester: An Emerging Metropolis, 1925-1961.* Rochester: Christopher Press, 1961. (Chap. on labor)

4092 ———. *Rochester, the Flower City, 1855-1890.* Cambr.: Harvard U Press, 1949. (Chaps. on labor)

4093 ———. *Rochester: The Quest for Quality, 1890-1925.* Cambr.: Harvard U Press, 1956. (Chaps. on labor)

4094 ———. *Rochester, the Water-Power City, 1812-1854.* Cambr.: Harvard U Press, 1945. (Chaps. on labor)

4095 ———. "Rochester's Near Northeast." *Rochester History*, Vol 29 (1967), 1-23.

ST. LOUIS

4096 Fink, Gary M. "The Paradoxical Experiences of St. Louis Labor during the Depression of 1837." *Bulletin of the Missouri Historical Society*, Vol 26 (1969), 53-63.

4097 Forsythe, Edwin James. *The St. Louis Central Trades and Labor Union, 1887-1945.* Ph D diss, U of Missouri, 1956.

4098 Nolen, Russell M. "The Labor Movement in St. Louis from 1860 to 1890." *Missouri Historical Review*, Vol 34 (1940), 157-81.

4099 ———. "The Labor Movement in St. Louis Prior to the Civil War." *Missouri Historical Review*, Vol 34 (1939), 18-37.

SAN FRANCISCO

4100 Averbach, Alvin. "San Francisco's South of Market District, 1850-1950: the Emergence of a Skid Row." *California Historical Quarterly*, Vol 42 (1973), 197-223.

4101 Chiles, Frederic. "General Strike: San Francisco, 1934—An Historical Compilation Film Storyboard." *Labor History*, Vol 22 (1981), 430-65.

4102 Clements, Jayce. *The San Francisco Maritime and General Strikes of 1934 and the Dynamics of the Repression.* Ph D diss, U of California, 1976.

4103 Cronin, Bernard C. *Father Yorke and the Labor Movement in San Francisco, 1900-1910.* Wash.: Catholic U of America Press, 1943.

4104 Dancis, Bruce. "Social Mobility and Class Consciousness: San Francisco's International Workmen's Association in the 1880's." *Journal of Social History*, Vol 11 (1977), 75-98.

4105 Decker, Peter R. *Fortunes and Failures: White-Collar Mobility in Nineteenth Century San Francisco.* Cambr.: Harvard U Press, 1978.

4106 DUNNE, WILLIAM F. *The Great San Francisco General Strike.* NY: Workers Library, 1934.

4107 "Four Dacades Later-'Bloody Thursday' Still Lives." *Dispatcher,* Jul 5, 1974, pp 4-5.

4108 GIANNINI, RALPH. *San Francisco: Labor's City, 1900-1910.* Ph D diss, U of Florida, 1976.

4109 HICHBORN, FRANKLIN. *The System as Uncovered by the San Francisco Graft Prosecution.* San Francisco: Barry, 1915.

4110 ISSEL, WILLIAM. "Class and Ethnic Conflict in San Francisco Political History: The Reform Charter of 1898." *Labor History,* Vol 18 (1977), 341-59.

4111 KAHN, LAWRENCE M. "Union and Internal Labor Markets: The Case of the San Francisco Longshoremen." *Labor History,* Vol 21 (1980), 369-91.

4112 KNIGHT, ROBERT E. L. *Industrial Relations in the San Francisco Bay Area, 1900-1918.* Berkeley: U of California Press, 1960.

4113 LAWRENCE, JOHN A. *Behind the Palaces: the Working Class and the Labor Movement in San Francisco, 1877-1901.* Ph D diss, U of California, 1980.

4114 LEVI, STEVEN C. "The Battle for the Eight Hour Day in San Francisco." *California History,* Vol 57 (1978), 343-53.

4115 ———. "San Francisco's Law and Order Committee, 1916." *Journal of the West,* Vol 12 (1973), 53-70.

4116 RYAN, FREDERICK L. *Industrial Relations in the San Francisco Building Trades.* Norman: U of Oklahoma Press, 1936.

4117 SAXTON, ALEXANDER. "San Francisco Labor and the Populist and Progressive Insurgencies." *Pacific Historical Review,* Vol 34 (1965), 421-38.

4118 SHUMSKY, NEIL. "San Francisco's Workingmen Respond to the Modern City." *California Historical Quarterly,* Vol 55 (1976), 46-57.

4119 TYGIEL, JULES. *Workingmen in San Francisco, 1880-1901.* Ph D diss, U of California, 1977.

4120 U.S. COMMISSION ON INDUSTRIAL RELATIONS (1912). "General Industriall Relations and Conditions in San Francisco," Vol 6, pp 5421-472, *Final Report,* Wash.: G.P.O., 1916.

4121 VARCADOS, PETER RICHARD. *Labor and Politics in San Francisco, 1880-1892.* Ph D diss, U of California, 1968.

SEATTLE

4122 FRIEDHAM, ROBERT L. *The Seattle General Strike.* Seattle: U of Washington Press, 1964.

4123 SEATTLE UNION RECORD PUBLISHING CO., INC. *The Seattle General Strike: An Account of What Happened in Seattle and Especially in the Seattle Labor Movement during the General Strike, February 6 to 11, 1919.* Seattle: The Company 1919.

4124 U.S. COMMISSION ON INDUSTRIAL RELATIONS (1912). "Industrial Relations and Remedies, Seattle, Washington," Vol 5, pp 4097-571, *Final Report,* Wash.: G.P.O., 1916.

SPRINGFIELD, MA

4125 HARDWICK, A. F., ed. *History of the Central Labor Union of Springfield, Massachusetts, with Some of the Pioneers: Brief Sketches of Affiliated Unions, 1887-1912.* Springfield: The Union, 1912.

STOCKTON, CA

4126 U.S. COMMISSION ON INDUSTRIAL RELATIONS (1912). "Open and Closed Shop Controversies in Stockton, California," Vol 5, pp 4771-909, *Final Report,* Wash.: G.P.O., 1916.

TOLEDO, OH

4127 CARY, LORIN LEE. "The Bureau of Investigation and Radicalism in Toledo, Ohio: 1918-1920." *Labor History*, Vol 21 (1980), 340-440.

4128 CLAPP, TOM. "Toledo Industrial Peace Board, 1935-1943." *Northwest Ohio Quarterly*, Vol 50 (1968), 50-67, 97-110, Vol 51 (1969), 24-51, 70-86.

4129 LYONS, SCHLEY R. "The Labor Press and Its Audience: the Case of the Toledo *Union Journal*." *Journalism Quarterly*, Vol 46 (1969), 558-64.

4130 MEAD, JOHN F. *An Economic Analysis of the Toledo Labor-Management-Citizens Committee after Twenty Years of Operation*. Ph D diss, U of Kentucky, 1968.

4131 ZIEREN, GREGORY R. *The Propertied Worker: Working Class Formation in Toledo, Ohio, 1870-1900*. Ph D diss, U of Delaware, 1981.

TROY, NY

4132 WALKOWITZ, DANIEL J. *Worker City, Company Town: Iron and Cotton Worker Protest in Troy and Cohoes, New York, 1855-1884*. Urbana: U of Illinois Press, 1978.

WALTHAM, MA

4133 GITELMAN, HOWARD M. *Workingmen of Waltham: Mobility in American Urban Industrial Development, 1850-1890*. Balt.: Johns Hopkins U Press, 1974.

Regional

MIDWEST

4134 KAPSTEIN, ISRAEL J. *Something of a Hero* (a novel). NY: Knopf, 1941.

4135 WALKER, KENNETH R. "The Era of Industrialization: Capital and Labor in the Midwest in 1901." *Northwest Ohio Quarterly*, Vol 37 (1965), 49-60.

4136 WILKINS, ROBERT P. "The Nonpartisan League and Upper Midwest Isolationism." *Agricultural History*, Vol 39 (1965), 102-9.

NEW ENGLAND

4137 BUELL, CHARLES CHAUNCEY. *The Workers of Worcester: Social Mobility and Ethnicity in a New England City, 1850-1880*. Ph D diss, New York U, 1974.

4138 FIELD, BEN. *Piper Tompkins* (a novel). NY: Doubleday, 1946.

4139 FREEMAN, MARY E. WILKINS. *The Portion of Labor* (a novel). NY: Harper, 1901.

4140 PAUL ELLIOT H. *The Stars and Stripes Forever* (a novel set in a New England town about workers who organize and strike under the impetus of the Wagner Act). NY: Random House, 1939.

4141 ROBINSON, HARRIET H. *Early Factory Labor in New England*. Bost.: Wright & Potter, 1889.

4142 TURNER, GEORGE K. *The Taskmasters* (a novel). NY: McClure, Phillips, 1902.

4143 ZUGSMITH, LEANE. *Summer Soldier* (a novel). NY: Random House, 1938.

NORTHWEST

4144 KERR, CLARK. "Collective Bargaining on the Pacific Coast." *Monthly Labor Review*, Vol 64 (1947), 650-74.

4145 STONE, HARRY W. "Beginnings of Labor Movement in the Pacific Northwest." *Oregon Historical Quarterly*, Vol 47 (1946), 155-64.

4146 THORSETH, MATTHEA. *Color of Ripening* (a novel). Seattle: Superior Publishers, 1949.

4147 WHITE, WILLIAM T. *A History of Railroad Workers in the Pacific Northwest, 1883-1934.* Ph D diss, U of Washington, 1981.

SOUTH

4148 BERGLUND, ABRAHAM. et al. *Labor in the Industrial South: A Survey of Wages and Living Conditions in Three Major Industries of the New Industrial South.*, Institute for Research in the Social Sciences, Monograph No 9. Charlottesville: U of Virginia, 1930.

4149 CARPENTER, CHARLES G. *Southern Labor and the Southern Urban Continuum, 1919-1929.* Ph D diss, Tulane U, 1973.

4150 COOK, SYLVIA J. *The Southern Poor White in Fiction.* Chapel Hill: U of North carolina Press, 1976.

4151 DE VYVER, FRANK T. "The Present Status of Labor Unions in the South, 1948." *The Southern Economic Journal*, Vol 16 (1949), 15-24.

4152 ELLER, RONALD D. *Miners, Millhands, and Mountaineers: Industrialization of the Appalachian South, 1880-1930.* Knoxville: U of Tennessee Press, 1982.

4153 FINK, GARY M., and MERL E. REED. *Essays in Southern Labor History.* Westport, CT: Greenwood, 1977.

4154 FLYNT, WAYNE. *Dixie's Forgotten People: The South's Poor Whites.* Bloomington: U of Indiana Press, 1979.

4155 "Labor Drives South." *Fortune*, Nov 1946, 52-59.

4156 LAWRENCE, KEN. "The Roots of Class Struggle in the South." *Radical America*, Vol 9 (Mar-Apr 1975), 15-35.

4157 MCCOY, A. D. *Thoughts on Labor in the South: Past, Present and Future.* New Orleans: Blelock, 1865.

4158 MCMATH, ROBERT C. *The Farmers' Alliance in the South: the Career of an Agrarian Institution.* Ph D diss, U of North Carolina, 1972.

4159 MALIZIA, EMIL. "Organizing to Overcome Uneven Development: the Case of the U.S. South." *Review of Radical Political Economics*, Vol 10 (Fall 1978), 87-94.

4160 MARKS, GEORGE P., III. "The New Orleans Screwmen's Benevolent Association 1850-1861." *Labor History*, Vol 14 (1973), 259-63.

4161 MARSHALL, F. RAY. *Labor in the South.* Cambr.: Harvard U Press, 1967.

4162 MEIKLEJOHN, KENNETH, and PETER NEHEMKIS. *Southern Labor in Revolt.* NY: Intercollegiate Student Council of the League for Industrial Democracy, 1930.

4163 NEWMAN, DALE. "Work and Community Life in a Southern Town." *Labor History*, Vol 19 (1978), 204-25.

4164 NOVAK, DANIEL A. *Peonage: Negro Contract Labor, Sharecropping Tenantry and the Law in the South, 1865-1970.* Ph D diss, Brandeis U, 1975.

4165 *People of the Cumberland.* 1938. (Frontier Films production)

4166 "Southern Campaign, 1946." *Labor and Nation*, Apr-May 1946, pp 32-46.

4167 "A Special Issue on Labor in the South." *Monthly Labor Review*, Vol 91 (Mar 1968).

4168 STAROBIN, ROBERT. *Industrial Slavery in the Old South.* NY: Oxford U Press, 1970.

4169 ———. *Industrial Slavery in the Old South, 1790-1861: a Study in Political Economy.* Ph D diss, U of Missouri, 1968.

4170 STEELE, H. ELLSWORTH, and HOMER FISHER, JR.. "A Study of the Effects of Unionism in Southern Plants." *Monthly Labor Review*, Vol 87 (1964), 258-70.

4171 THRASHER, SUE, and LEAH WISE. "The Southern Tenant Farmers' Union." *Southern Exposure*, Vol 1 (Winter 1973), 5-8, 11-32. (6 first-person accounts by active participants in the union: George Stith, Clay East, Naomi Williams, J. R. Butler & H. L. Mitchell)

4172 TIPPETT, THOMAS. *When Southern Labor Stirs.* NY: J. Cape and H. Smith, 1931.

SOUTHWEST

4173 CULLISON, WILLIAM EUGENE. *An Examination of Union Membership in Arkansas, Louisiana, and Oklahoma.* Ph D diss, U of Oklahoma, 1967.

4174 FOSTER, JAMES C. *American Labor in the Southwest: The First One Hundred Years.* Tucson: U of Arizona Press, 1982.

4175 GREEN, GEORGE. "The Union Movement in the Southwest." *Dissent*, Vol 27 (1980), 485-92.

4176 LOPEZ, DAVID E. "Cowboy Strikes and Unions." *Labor History*, Vol 18 (1977), 325-40.

State

ALABAMA

4177 BROWN, JAMES SEAY, JR. *Up Before Daylight: Life Histories from the Alabama Writers' Project.* Tuscaloosa: U of Alabama Press, 1982.

4178 FLYNT, WAYNE. "Spindle, Mine, and Mule: the Poor White Experience in Post-Civil War Alabama." *Alabama Review*, Vol 34 (1981), 243-86.

4179 FONER, PHILIP S. "An Additional Short Note on the Alabama State Federation of Labor." *Labor History*, Vol 18 (1977), 120-21.

4180 KUNDAHL, GEORGE GUSTAUS, JR. *Organized Labor in Alabama State Politics.* Ph D diss, U of Alabama, 1967.

4181 MARTIN, CHARLES H. "Southern Labor Relations in Transition: Gadsden, Alabama, 1930-1943." *Journal of Southern History*, Vol 47 (1981), 545-68.

4182 NELSON, DANIEL. "A CIO Organizer in Alabama, 1941." *Labor History*, Vol 18 (1977), 570-84.

4183 SCHARNAU, RALPH. "Elizabeth Morgan, Crusader for Labor Reform." *Labor History*, Vol 14 (1973), 340-51.

4184 TAFT, PHILIP. "A Short Note on the Alabama State Federation of Labor." *Labor History*, Vol 16 (1975), 410-11.

4185 ———, and GARY M. FINK. *Organizing Dixie: Alabama Workers in the Industrial Era.* Westport, CT: Greenwood, 1981.

4186 WARD, ROBERT DAVID, and WILLIAM WARREN ROGERS. *Labor Revolt in Alabama: The Great Strike of 1894.* Tuscaloosa: U of Alabama Press, 1965.

ALASKA

4187 MASSON, JACK, and DONALD L. GUIMARY. "Asian Labor Contractors in the Alaskan Canned Salmon Industry: 1800-1937." *Labor History*, Vol 22 (1981), 377-97.

4188 U.S. BUREAU OF LABOR STATISTICS. *The Status of Labor in Puerto Rico, Alaska, Hawaii.*, Bulletin No 1191. Wash.: G.P.O., 1956.

ARIZONA

4189 BYRKIT, JAMES W. *Forging the Copper Collar: Arizona's Labor Management War, 1901-1921.* Tucson, U of Arizona Press, 1982.

ARKANSAS

4190 HOLMES, WILLIAM F. "The Arkansas Cotton Pickers Strike of 1891 and the Demise of the Colored Farmers' Alliance." *Arkansas Historical Quarterly*, Vol 32 (1973), 107-19.

4191 SIMON, CHARLIE M. *The Share-Cropper* (a novel). NY: Dutton, 1937.

CALIFORNIA

4192 CROSS, IRA BROWN. *History of the Labor Movement in California*. Berkeley: U of California Press, 1935.

4193 EVES, LUCILE. *A History of California Labor Legislastion: With an Introductory Sketch of the San Francisco Labor Movement*. Berkeley, U of California, 1910.

4194 GALARZA, ERNESTO. *Farm Workers and Agri-Business in California, 1947-1960*. Notre Dame, IN: Notre Dame U Press, 1977.

4195 GRUBBS, DONALD H. "Prelude to Chavez: The National Farm Labor Union in California." *Labor History*, Vol 16 (1975), 453-69.

4196 JANIS, RALPH. "The Watsonville Anti-Filipino Riot of 1930: A Case Study of the Great Depression and Ethnic Conflict in California." *Southern California Quarterly*, Vol 61 (1979), 291-302.

4197 KAUER, RALPH. "The Workingmen's Party of California." *Pacific Historical Review*, Vol 13 (1944), 278-91.

4198 MCENTIRE, DAVIS. *The Labor Force in California: A Study of Characteristics and Trends in Labor Force, Employment, and Occupations in California, 1900-1950*. Berkeley: U of California Press, 1952.

4199 SELVIN, DAVID F. *Sky Full of Storm: A Brief History of California Labor*. San Francisco: California Historical Society, 1975.

4200 SHOVER, JOHN L. "The Progressives and the Working Class Vote in California." *Labor History*, Vol 10 (1969), 584-601.

4201 SLOBODEK, MITCHELL. *A Selective Bibliography of California Labor History*. Los Angeles: Institute of Industrial Relations, U of California, 1964.

4202 STEIN, WALTER J. *California and the Dust Bowl Migration*. Westport, CT: Greenwood, 1973.

4203 VISELTEAR, ARTHUR J. "Compulsory Health Insurance in California, 1915-18." *Journal of the History of Medicine and Allied Sciences*, Vol 24 (1969), 151-82.

4204 WHITE, DAVID MAGON. *The West Coast Waterfront and Sympathy Strikes of 1934*. Ph D diss, U of California, 1966.

4205 WHITTEN, WOODROW C. "Criminal Syndicalism and the Law in California: 1919-1927." *Transactions of the American Philosophical Society*, New Series Vol 59 (1969), 1-73.

4206 ———. *Criminal Syndicalism and the Law in California: 1919-1927*. Ph D diss, U of California, 1946.

4207 WOLLENBERG, CHARLES. "Race and Class in Rural California: The El Monte Berry Strike of 1933." *California Historical Quarterly*, Vol 51 (1972), 155-64.

COLORADO

4208 BARDWELL, GEORGE E., and HARRY SELIGSON. *Organized Labor and Political Action in Colorado, 1900-1960*. Denver: College of Business Administration, U of Denver, 1969.

4209 KNIGHT, HAROLD V. *Working in Colorado: A Brief History of the Colorado Labor Movement*. Boulder: Center for Labor Education and Research, U of Colorado, 1971.

4210 LONSDALE, DAVID L. "The Fight for an Eight-Hour Day." *Colorado Magazine*, Vol 43 (1966), 339-53.

4211 MCGOVERN, GEORGE S. *The Colorado Coal Strike, 1913-1914*. Ph D diss, Northwestern U, 1952.

4212 SUGGS, GEORGE G., JR. *Colorado Conservatives versus Organized Labor: A Study of the James Hamilton Peabody Administration, 1903-19*. Ph D diss, U of Colorado, 1964.

4213 ———. *Colorado's War on Militant Unionism: James H. Peabody and the Western Federation of Miners*. Detroit: Wayne State U Press, 1972.

4214 Tank, Robert M. "Mobility and Occupational Structure on the Late Nineteenth Century Urban Frontier: the Case of Denver, Colorado." *Pacific Historical Review*, Vol 47 (1978), 189-216.

4215 U.S. Bureau of Labor. *A Report on Labor Disturbances in the State of Colorado, from 1880 to 1904, Inclusive, with Correspondence Relating Thereto*. Wash.: G.P.O., 1905. (Printed as Senaste Document No 122, 58th Congress, 3rd Session)

4216 Willis, Edmund P. *Colorado Industrial Disturbances, 1903-1904*. MA thesis, U of Wisconsin, 1955.

CONNECTICUT

4217 Brecher, Jeremy. et al, eds. *Brass Valley: The Story of Working People's Lives and Struggles in an American Industrial Region*. Phila.: Temple U Press, 1982.

4218 Burr, Nelson R. *The Early Labor Movement in Connecticut, 1790-1860*. West Hartford, CT: Burr, 1972.

4219 Heath, Frederick M. "Labor and the Progressive Movement in Connecticut." *Labor History*, Vol 12 (1971), 52-67.

4220 Nelson, Nels Edward. *Unemployment and Labor Force Participation Rates in Connecticut Towns*. Ph D diss, U of Connecticut, 1972.

4221 Preston, John H. *The Liberals* (a novel). NY: Day, 1938.

4222 Steiner, B. C. *History of Slavery in Connecticut*. Balt.: Johns Hopkins Press, 1893.

DELAWARE

4223 Gibson, George H. "Labor Piracy on the Brandywine." *Labor History*, Vol 8 (1967), 175-82.

DISTRICT OF COLUMBIA

4224 Fones-Wolf, Elizabeth, and Kenneth Fones-Wolf. "Knights versus the Trade Unionists: The Case of the Washington, D.C. Carpenters, 1881-1896." *Labor History*, Vol 22 (1981), 192-212.

FLORIDA

4225 Flynt, Wayne. "Florida Labor and Political 'Radicalism,' 1919-1920." *Labor History*, Vol 9 (1968), 73-90.

4226 Long, Durward. "'La Resistencia': Tampa's Immigrant Labor Union." *Labor History*, Vol 6 (1965), 193-213.

4227 ———. "Labor Relations in the Tampa Cigar Industry, 1885-1911." *Labor History*, Vol 12 (1971), 551-59.

4228 Mormino, Gary. "'We Worked Hard and Took Care of Our Own': Oral History and Italians in Tampa." *Labor History*, Vol 22 (1982), 395-415.

4229 Pozzetta, George E. "A Padrone Looks at Florida: Labor Recruiting and the Florida East Coast Railroad." *Florida Historical Quarterly*, Vol 53 (1975), 74-84.

4230 Shofner, Jerrell. "The Legacy of Racial Slavery: Free Enterprise and Forced Labor in Florida in the 1940s." *Journal of Southern History*, Vol 47 (1981), 411-26.

GEORGIA

4231 Brooks, Robert P. *History of Agricultural Labor in Georgia, 1865-1910*. Ph D diss, U of Wisconsin, 1912.

4232 Cimbala, Paul A. "The 'Talisman Power': Davis Tillson, the Freedmen's Bureau, and Free Labor in Reconstruction Georgia, 1865-1866." *Civil War History*, Vol 28 (1982), 153-71.

4233 Martin, Charles H. "White Supremacy and Black Workers: Georgia's 'Black Shirts' Combat the Great Depression." *Labor History*, Vol 18 (1977), 366-81.

4234 WHIE, LEE ANN. *Southern Ladies and Mill Hands: the Domestic Economy and Class Politics: Augusta, Georgia, 1870-1890.* Ph D diss, U of California, 1982.

HAWAII

4235 JOHANNESSEN, EDWARD. *The Hawaiian Labor Movement: A Brief History.* Bost.: Bruce Humphries, 1956.

4236 LADENSON, ALEX. "The Background of the Hawaiian-Japanese Labor Convention of 1886." *Pacific Historical Review*, Vol 9 (1940), 389-400.

4237 PENDLETON, EDWIN C. *Labor in Hawaii: A Bibliography.* Honolulu: Industrial Relations Center, College of Business Administration, U of Hawaii, 1971.

4238 PERLMAN, MARK. "Organized Labor in Hawaii." *Labor Law Journal*, Vol 3 (1952), 263-75.

4239 ———, and JOHN B. FERGUSON. *Trade Unionism and the Competitive Menace in Hawaii.* Honolulu: Industrial Relations Center, U of Hawaii, 1952.

4240 REINECKE, JOHN E., comp. *Labor Unions of Hawaii: A Chronological Checklist.* Honolulu: Industrial Relations Center, U of Hawaii, 1966.

4241 ROBERTS, HAROLD S., ed. *Labor-Management Relations in Hawaii.*, 3 parts. Honolulu: U of Hawaii, 1955-56.

4242 ROWLAND, DONALD. "The United States and the Contract Labor Question in Hawaii." *Pacific Historical Review*, Vol 2 (1933), 249-69.

4243 TAKAKI, RONALD. "'An Entering Wedge': The Origins of the Sugar Plantation and a Multi-ethnic Working Class in Hawaii." *Labor History*, Vol 22 (1982), 32-46.

4244 U.S. BUREAU OF LABOR STATISTICS. *The Status of Labor in Puerto Rico, Alaska, Hawaii.*, Bulletin No 1191. Wash.: G.P.O., 1956.

4245 U.S. CONGRESS. SENATE. Committee on Labor and Public Welfare. *Hawaiian Labor Situation.* Wash.: G.P.O., 1949.

IDAHO

4246 GABOURY, WILLIAM JOSEPH. "From Statehouse to Bull Pen: Idaho Populism and the Coeur d'Alene Troubles of the 1890's." *Pacific Northwest Quarterly*, Vol 58 (1967), 14-22.

4247 HARRIMAN, JOB. *The Class Struggle in Idaho.* NY: Labor Publishing Association, 1904.

4248 SMITH, ROBERT WAYNE. *The Idaho Antecedents of the Western Federation of Miners, 1890 to 1893.* Ph D diss, U of California, 1938.

4249 WELLS, MERLE W. "Fred T. Dubois and the Nonpartisan League in the Idaho Election of 1918." *Pacific Northwest Quarterly*, Vol 56 (1965), 17-29.

ILLINOIS

4250 DESTLER, CHESTER M. "Consummation of a Labor-Populist Alliance in Illinois, 1894." *Mississippi Valley Historical Review*, Vol 27 (1942), 589-602.

4251 MAURER, DAVID J. "Unemployment in Illinois During the Great Depression," pp 120-32, *Essays in Honor of Glen Huron Seymour*, Donald F. Tingley, ed. Carbondale, IL: Southern Illinois U Press, 1968.

4252 OREAR, LESLIE F., ed. *On the Job: A Bicentennial Photographic Exhibition.* Chicago: Illinois Labor History Society, 1976.

4253 STALEY, EUGENE. *History of the Illinois State Federation of Labor.* Chicago: U of Chicago Press, 1930.

INDIANA

4254 AYER, HUGH M. *Hoosier Labor in the Second World War.* Ph D diss, Indiana U, 1957.

4255 BROOK, ANTHONY. "Gary, Indiana: Steeltown Extraordinary." *Journal of American Studies*, Vol 9 (1975), 35-53.

4256 VAN VALER, RALPH WALDEN. "The Indiana State Federation of Labor." *Indiana Magazine of History*, Vol 11 (1915), 40-58.

IOWA

4257 DOWNEY, EZEKIAL H. *History of Labor Legislation in Iowa.* Iowa City: The State Historical Society of Iowa, 1910.

4258 JOHNSON, KEACH. "Iowa's Industrial Roots, 1890-1910." *Annals of Iowa*, Vol 44 (1978), 163-90, 247-77.

4259 MERGEN, BERNARD. "A Quantitative Study of Wage Workers in Iowa, 1894." *Annals of Iowa*, Vol 41 (1972), 371-82.

4260 STUCKEY, LORIN. *The Iowa State Federation of Labor.* Iowa City: U of Iowa, 1916.

KANSAS

4261 GAGLIARDO, DOMENICO. "The Gompers-Allen Debate on the Kansas Industrial Court." *Kansas Historical Quarterly*, Vol 3 (1934), 385-95.

4262 WALKER, EDITH, and DOROTHY LEIBENGOOD. "Labor Organizations in Kansas in the Early Eighties." *Kansas Historical Quarterly*, Vol 4 (1935), 283-90.

KENTUCKY

4263 CURRIS, CONSTANTINE WILLIAM. "State Public Welfare Developments in Kentucky." *Register of the Kentucky Historical Society*, Vol 44 (1966), 299-336.

4264 ELLIS, WILLIAM. "Labor-Management Relations in the Progressive Era: a Profit-Sharing Experiment in Louisville." *Kentucky Historical Society Register*, Vol 78 (Spring 1980), 140-56.

4265 EWEN, LYNDA ANN. *Which Side Are You On? The Brookside Mine Strike in Harlan County, Kentucky.* Chicago: Vanguard, 1979.

4266 WHISENHUNT, DONALD W. "The Great Depression in Kentucky: the Early Years." *Register of the Kentucky Historical Society*, Vol 67 (1969), 55-62.

LOUISIANA

4267 BECNEL, THOMAS. *Labor, Church, and the Sugar Establishment: Louisiana, 1887-1976.* Baton Rouge: Louisiana State U Press, 1980.

4268 CRETE, LILIANE. *Daily Life in Louisiana: 1815-1830.* Baton Rouge: Louisiana State U Press, 1981.

4269 MESSNER, WILLIAM F. *Freedmen and the Ideology of Free Labor, Louisiana, 1862-1865.* Lafayette, LA: Center for Louisiana Studies, U of Southwestern Louisiana, 1978.

4270 WEBB, BERNICE LARSON. "Company Town—Louisiana Style." *Louisiana History*, Vol 9 (1968), 325-39.

MAINE

4271 SCONTRAS, CHARLES ANDREW. *Two Decades of Organized Labor and Labor Politics in Maine, 1880-1900.* Ph D diss, U of Maine, 1968.

MARYLAND

4272 HARVEY, KATHERINE A. "The Knights of Labor in the Maryland Coal Fields, 1878-1882." *Labor History*, Vol 10 (1969), 555-83.

4273 HOFFMAN, WILLIAM. *The Dark Mountains* (a novel). Garden City, NY: Doubleday, 1963.

4274 McCormac, Eugene I. *White Servitude in Maryland.* Ph D diss, Yale U, 1901.

4275 Muller, Edward K., and Paul Groves. "The Changing Location of the Clothing Industry: a Link to the Social Geography of Baltimore in the 19th Century." *Maryland Historical Magazine*, Vol 71 (1976), 403-20.

MASSACHUSETTS

4276 Bedford, Henry F. *Socialism and the Workers in Massachusetts, 1889-1912.* Amherst: U of Massachusetts Press, 1966.

4277 Heintz, Albert M., and John R. Whitney. *History of the Massachusetts State Federation of Labor, 1887-1935.* Worcester: The Federation, 1935.

4278 Kingsbury, Susan M., ed. *Labor Laws and Their Enforcement with Special Reference to Massachusetts.* NY: Longmans, Green, 1911.

4279 Siracusa, Carl. *A Mechanical People: Perceptions of the Industrial Order in Massachusetts, 1815-1880.* Middletown, CT: Wesleyan U Press, 1979.

4280 Towner, Lawrence W. *A Good Master Well Served: A Social History of Servitude in Massachusetts, 1620-1750.* Ph D diss, Northwestern U, 1955.

MICHIGAN

4281 Blum, Albert A., and Dan Georgakas. *Michigan Labor and the Civil War.* Lansing: Michigan Civil War Centennial Observance Commission, 1964.

4282 Brophy, Jacqueline. "The Merger of the AFL and the CIO in Michigan." *Michigan History*, Vol 50 (1966), 139-57.

4283 Clive, Alan. "Women Workers in World War II: Michigan as a Test Case." *Labor History*, Vol 20 (1979), 44-72.

4284 Glazer, Sidney. *Labor and the Agrarian Movements in Michigan, 1876-1896.* Ph D diss, U of Michigan, 1932.

4285 ———. "The Michigan Labor Movement." *Michigan History Magazine*, Vol 29 (1945), 73-82.

4286 McLaughlin, Doris B. *Michigan Labor: A Brief History from 1818 to the Present.* Ann Arbor: Institute of Labor and Industrial Relations, U of Michigan—Wayne State U, 1970.

MINNESOTA

4287 Asher, Robert. "Origins of Workmen's Compensation in Minnesota." *Minnesota History,* Vol 44 (1974), 142-53.

4288 Engberg, George B. "The Knights of Labor in Minnesota." *Minnesota History*, Vol 22 (1941), 367-90.

4289 ———. "The Rise of Organized Labor in Minnesota." *Minnesota History*, Vol 21 (1940), 372-94.

4290 Engdahl, Walfrid. "Magnus Johnson—Colorful Farmer-Labor Senator from Minnesota." *Swedish Pioneer Historical Quarterly*, Vol 16 (1965), 122-36.

4291 Lawson, George W. *Organized Labor in Minnesota.* St. Paul: Minnesota State Federation of Labor, 1955.

4292 Sofchalk, Donald G. "Organized Labor and the Iron Ore Miners of Northern Minnesota, 1907-1936." *Labor History*, Vol 12 (1971), 214-42.

4293 Weiner, Lynn. "'Who Are Wanted In Minnesota': Workers as Described in Antebellum 'Booster Literature.'" *Labor History*, Vol 18 (1977), 403-6.

MISSISSIPPI

4294 Barton, Bill. "Mississippi: Battlefront for Labor." *The AFL-CIO American Federationist*, Oct 1965, pp 19-21.

4295 Currie, George Franklin. *The Impact of Minimum Wage Legislation on the Economy of Mississippi.* Ph D diss, U of Illinois, 1964.

4296 Mosley, Donald Crumpton. *A History of Labor Unions in Mississippi.* Ph D diss, U of Alabama, 1965.

MISSOURI

4297 Fink, Gary M. *The Evolution of Social and Political Attitudes in the Missouri Labor Movement, 1900-1940.* Ph D diss, U of Missouri, 1968.

4298 ———. *Labor's Search for Political Order: The Political Behavior of the Missouri Labor Movement, 1890-1940.* Columbia: U of Missouri Press, 1973.

4299 ———. "The Unwanted Conflict: Missouri Labor and the CIO." *Missouri Historical Review*, Vol 54 (1970), 432-47.

4300 Meriwether, Lee. "A Century of Labor in Missouri." *The Missouri Historical Review*, Vol 15 (1920), 163-75.

MONTANA

4301 Clinch, Thomas Anthony. "Coxey's Army in Montana." *Montana: The Magazine of Western History*, Vol 15 (1965), 2-11.

4302 ———. *Populism and Bimetallism in Montana.* Ph D diss, U of Oregon 1964.

NEBRASKA

4303 Lawson, Michael. "Omaha, a City in Ferment: Summer of 1919." *Nebraska History*, Vol 58 (1977), 385-417.

4304 Wagaman, David. "The Evolution of Some Legal-Economic Aspects of Collective Bargaining by Public Employees in Nebraska Since 1919." *Nebraska History*, Vol 58 (1977), 475-89.

NEVADA

4305 Zanjani, Sally Springmeyer. *The Unspiked: Memoir of a Nevada Rebel.* Reno: U of Nevada Press, 1981.

NEW HAMPSHIRE

4306 Hanlan, J. P. *The Working Population of Manchester, New Hampshire, 1840-86.* Ph D diss, Clark U, 1980.

4307 McKinney, Gordon. "The Politics of Protest: the Labor Reform and Greenback Parties in New Hampshire." *Historical New Hampshire*, Vol 36 (1981), 149-70.

4308 Williams, David. "'Sowing the Wind': the Deportation Raids of 1920 in New Hampshire." *Historical New Hampshire*, Vol 34 (1979), 1-31.

NEW JERSEY

4309 Troy, Leo. *Organized Labor in New Jersey.* Princeton: Van Nostrand, 1965.

4310 Weinberg, William Martin. *An Administrative History of the New Jersey State Board of Mediation.* Ph D diss, U of Pennsylvania, 1964.

NEW YORK

4311 Felt, Jeremy P. *Hostages of Fortune: Child Labor Reform in New York State.* Syracuse: Syracuse U Press, 1965.

4312 Groat, George C. *Trade Unions and the Law in New York.* NY: Columbia U Press, 1905.

4313 Hurwitz, Howard L. *Theodore Roosevelt and Labor in New York State, 1880-1900.* NY: Columbia U Press, 1943.

4314 Ingalls, Robert P. "New York and the Minimum-Wage Movement, 1933-1937." *Labor History*, Vol 15 (1974), 179-98.

4315 KERR, THOMAS J., IV. *New York Factory Investigating Commission and the Progressives.* D S Sc thesis, Syracuse U, 1965.

4316 MCKEE, SAMUEL, JR. *Lasbor in Colonial New York, 1664-1776.* NY: Columbia U Press, 1935.

4317 NEW YORK STATE. FACTORY INVESTIGATING COMMISSION. (Robert Wagner, Chairman). *Fourth Report Transmitted to Legislature, February 15, 1915.*, Senate Document 43. Albany: J. B. Lyon Co., 1915.

4318 ———. ———. *Preliminary Report Transmitted to Legislature, March 1, 1912.* Albany: The Argus Co., 1912.

4319 ———. ———. *Second Report Transmitted to Legislature, January 15, 1913.*, Senate Document 36. Albany: J. B. Lyon Co., 1913.

4320 ———. ———. *Third Report Transmitted to Legislature, February 14, 1914.*, Assembly Document 28. Albany: J. B. Lyon Co., 1915.

4321 NORDSTROM, CARL. "The New York Slave Code." *Afro-Americans in New York Life and History*, Vol 4 (1980), 7-26.

4322 PESSEN, EDWARD. "A Variety of Panaceas: the 'Social Problem' and Proposed Solutions to it in Mid-Nineteenth Century New York State." *New York History*, Vol 59 (1978), 198-222.

4323 RINGENBACH, PAUL T. *Tramps and Reformers, 1873-1916: The Discovery of Unemployment in New York.* Westport, CT: Greenwood, 1973.

4324 WALKOWITZ, DANIEL J. *Worker City, Company Town: Iron and Cotton-Worker Protest in Troy and Cohoes, New York, 1855-84.* Urbana: U of Illinois Press, 1978.

4325 WESSER, ROBERT F. "Conflict and Compromise: The Workmen's Compensation Movement in New York, 1890's-1913." *Labor History*, Vol 12 (1971), 345-72.

4326 WINDMULLER, JOHN P. *Union Organization and Collective Bargaining in Manufacturing and Public Utility Industries in Chemung County, New York.* MS thesis, NY State School of Industrial and Labor Relations, Cornell U, 1949.

4327 YELLOWITZ, IRWIN. *Labor and the Progressive Movement in New York State, 1897-1916.* Ithaca: Cornell U Press, 1965.

NORTH CAROLINA

4328 EKIRCH, A. ROGER. *"Poor Carolina": Politics and Society in Colonial North Carolina, 1729-1776.* Chapel Hill: U of North Carolina Press, 1981.

4329 JOLLEY, HARLEY E. "The Labor Movement in North Carolina, 1880-1922." *North Carolina Historical Review*, Vol 30 (1953), 354-75.

OHIO

4330 BAUGHMAN, JAMES L. *The 1937 Little Steel Strike in Three Ohio Communities.* MA thesis, Columbia U, 1975.

4331 BORYCZKA, RAYMOND, and LORIN LEE CARY. *No Strength Without Union: an Illustrated History of Ohio Workers, 1803-1980.* Columbus: Ohio Historical Society, 1983.

4332 BRITO, PATRICIA. "Protective Legislation in Ohio; the Inter-War Years." *Ohio History*, Vol 88 (1979), 173-97.

4333 CLOPPER, EDWARD S. "The Ohio Mechanics Institute—Its 125th Anniversary." *Bulletin of the Historical asnd Philosophical Society of Ohio*, Vol 11 (1953), 79-191.

4334 HATCHER, HARLAN H. *Central Standard Time* (a novel). NY: Farrar & Rinehart, 1937.

4335 JAVERSAK, DAVID T. *The Ohio Valley Trades and Labor Assembly: the Formative Years, 1882-1915.* Ph D diss, West Virginia U, 1978.

4336 MEADE, ROGER A., and MARJORIE J. MYERS, comps. *Guide to Primary Sources in Ohio Labor History.* Columbus: Ohio Labor History Project, Ohio Historical Society, 1980.

4337 PECKMAN, CHARLES A. "The Ohio National Guard and its Police Duties, 1894." *Ohio History*, Vol 83 (1974), 51-67.

4338 ROSE, PATRICIA T. *Design and Expediency: the Ohio State Federation of Labor as a Legislative Lobby, 1883-1935*. Ph D diss, Ohio State U 1975.

4339 ———. *The Ohio State Federation of Labor as a Legislative Lobby, 1883-1935*. Ph D diss, Ohio State U, 1975.

OKLAHOMA

4340 BRYANT, KEITH L. "Labor in Politics: The Oklahoma State Federation of Labor During the Age of Reform." *Labor History*, Vol 11 (1970), 259-76.

4341 PICKENS, DONALD K. "Oklahoma Populism and Historical Interpretation." *Chronicles of Oklahoma*, Vol 43 (1965), 275-83.

4342 U.S. WORK PROJECTS ADMINISTRATION. FEDERAL WRITERS' PROJECT. Oklahoma Writers' Program. *Labor History of Oklahoma*. Oklahoma City: A. M. Van Horn, 1940.

4343 WARRICK, SHERRY. "Radical Labor in Oklahoma: the Working Class Union." *Chronicles of Oklahoma*, Vol 52 (1974), 180-95.

OREGON

4344 LOVIN, HUGH T. "Toward a Farmer-Labor Party in Oregon, 1933-1938." *Oregon Historical Quarterly*, Vol 76 (1975) 135-51.

4345 TOBIE, HARVEY ELMER. "Oregon Labor Disputes, 1919-23." *Oregon Historical Quarterly*, Vol 47 (1947), 7-24, 195-213, 309-21.

PENNSYLVANIA

4346 COLEMAN, JAMES W. *Labor Disturbances in Pennsylvania, 1850-1880*. Wash.: Catholic U of America, 1936.

4347 GEISER, KARL F. *Indented Servants in the Colony and Commonwealth of Pennsylvania*. Ph D diss, Yale U, 1900.

4348 ———. *Redemptioners and Indentured Servants in the Colony and Commonwealth of Pennsylvania*. New Haven: Yale U Press, 1901.

4349 HERRICK, CHEESMAN ABIAH. *White Servitude in Pennsylvania: Indentured and Redemption Labor in Colony and Commonwealth*. Phila.: McVey, 1926.

4350 KURITZ, HYMAN. *The Pennsylvania State Government and Labor Controls from 1865 to 1922*. Ph D diss, Columbia U, 1953.

4351 RICKER, RALPH R. *The Greenback-Labor Movement in Pennsylvania, 1865-1880*. Ph D diss, Pennsylvania State U, 1955.

4352 SULLIVAN, WILLIAM A. *The Industrial Worker in Pennsylvania 1800-1840*. Harrisburg: Historical and Museum Commission, 1955.

4353 WALLACE, ANTHONY F. C. *Rockdale: The Growth of an American Village in the Early Industrial Revolution*. NY: Knopf, 1978.

RHODE ISLAND

4354 RHODE ISLAND LABOR HISTORY FORUM. "Labor and Community Militance in Rhode Island." *Radical History Review*, Vol 17 (Spring 1978), entire issue on labor history.

SOUTH CAROLINA

4355 SNOWDEN, YATES. *Notes on Labor Organizations in South Carolina, 1742-1861.*, Bulletin 38, Part 4. Columbia: U of South Carolina, 1914.

SOUTH DAKOTA

4356 U.S. Commission on Industrial Relations (1912). "Industrial Conditions and Relations in the Gold-Mining Operations Lead and Black Hills, S. D.," Vol 4, pp 3537-697, *Final Report*, Wash.: G.P.O., 1916.

TENNESSEE

4357 Ayers, Edward. "Northern Business and the Shape of Southern Progress: the Case of Tennessee's Model City." *Tennessee Historical Quarterly*, Vol 39 (1980), 208-22.

4358 Givens, Charles G. *The Devil Takes a Hill Town* (a novel). Indianapolis: Bobbs-Merrill, 1939.

TEXAS

4359 Allen, Ruth A. *Chapters in the History of Organized Labor in Texas.* Austin: U of Texas, 1941.

4360 Brewer, Thomas B. "State Anti-Labor Legislation: Texas—A Case Study." *Labor History*, Vol 11 (1970), 58-76.

4361 McCain, Johnny. "Texas and the Mexican Labor Question, 1942-1947." *Southwestern Historical Quarterly*, Vol 85 (1981), 45-64.

4362 Meyers, Frederic. "The Growth of Collective Bargaining in Texas—A Newly Industrialized Area." *Proceedings of the Seventh Annual Meeting of the Industrial Relations Research Association*, Dec 28-30, 1954, pp 286-97. Madison: IRRA, 1955.

4363 Reed, Jimmy F. *The Effect of a Central Labor Council on Selected Public Employee Groups in a Texas County*. Ph D diss, Texas A&M U, 1974.

4364 Reese, James V. "The Early History of Labor Organizations In Texas, 1838-1876." *Southwestern Historical Quarterly*, Vol 72 (1968), 1-20.

4365 ———. *The Worker in Texas, 1821-1876.* Ph D diss, U of Texas, 1964.

4366 Sylvers, Malcolm. "Sicilian Socialists in Houston, Texas, 1896-98." *Labor History*, Vol 11 (1970), 77-81.

4367 *Talkin' Union: A Film About Working Women.* 1980. (Documentary film produced by People's History in Texas, Inc.)

UTAH

4368 Allen, James B. "The Company Town: a Passing Phase of Utah's Industrial Development." *Utah Historical Quarterly*, Vol 34 (1966), 138-60.

4369 Davies, Joseph Kenneth. *Deseret's Sons of Toil: A History of the Worker Movement of Territorial Utah.* Salt Lake City: Olympus, 1977.

4370 ———. "The Secularization of the Utah Labor Movement." *Utah Historical Quarterly*, Vol 45 (1977), 108-34.

4371 ———. "Utah Labor before Statehood." *Utah Historical Quarterly*, Vol 34 (1966), 202-17.

4372 Pawar, Sheelwant B. "The Structure and Nature of Labor Unions in Utah, an Historical Perspective, 1890-1920." *Utah Historical Quarterly*, Vol 35 (1967), 236-55.

4373 Pierce, Virgil Caleb. "Utah's First Convict Labor Camp." *Utah Historical Quarterly*, Vol 42 (1974), 245-57.

4374 Randa, Ernest W., and Reed C. Richardson. *Union Membership in Utah: A County and Industry Study*. Salt Lake City: Institute of Industrial Relations, U of Utah, 1960.

4375 Rees, W. D. *The Professional Education Association Movement and Utah: an Interpretive History*. Ph D diss, U of Utah, 1977.

4376 Stipanovich, Joseph. "South Slav Settlements in Utah, 1890-1935." *Utah Historical Quarterly*, Vol 43 (1975), 144-71.

VERMONT

4377 NELSON, MARGARET T. "Vermont Female Schoolteachers in the Nineteenth Century." *Vermont History*, Vol 51 (1981), 5-30.

VIRGINIA

4378 BALLAGH, JAMES C. *White Servitude in the Colony of Virginia: A Study of the System of Indentured Labor in the American Colonies*. Ph D diss, Johns Hopkins U, 1895.

4379 COPE, ROBERT S. *Slavery and Servitude in the Colony of Virginia in the Seventeenth Century*. Ph D diss, Ohio State U, 1950.

4380 PERDUE, CHARLES L. et al, eds. *Weevils in the Wheat: Interviews with Virginia Ex-Slaves*. Charlottesville: U of Virginia Press, 1976.

WASHINGTON

4381 DEMBO, JONATHAN. *An Historical Bibliography of Washington State Labor and Laboring Classes*. Seattle: no publisher indicated, 1978.

4382 ———. *A History of the Washington State Labor Movement, 1885-1935*. Ph D diss, U of Washington, 1979.

4383 SCHWANTES, CARLOS A. *Radical Heritage: Labor, Socialism and Reform in Washington and British Columbia, 1885-1917*. Seattle: U of Washington Press, 1979.

4384 ———. "Washington State's Pioneer Labor-Reform Press: a Bibliographical Essay and Annotated Checklist." *Pacific Northwest Quarterly*, Vol 71 (1980), 112-26.

4385 TRIPP, JOSEPH F. *Progressive Labor Laws in Washington State (1900-1925)*. Ph D diss, U of Washington, 1973.

WEST VIRGINIA

4386 ANSON, CHARLES P. *A History of the Labor Movement in West Virginia*. Ph D diss, U of North Carolina, 1940.

4387 CORBIN, DAVID. *Life, Work, and Rebellion in the Coal Fields; The Southern West Virginia Miners, 1880-1922*. Urbana: U of Illinois Press, 1981.

4388 HARRIS, EVELYN L. K., and FRANK J. KREBS. *From Humble Beginnings: West Virginia State Federation of Labor, 1903-1957*. Charleston: West Virginia Labor History Publishing Fund, 1960.

4389 LEE, HOWARD B. *Bloodletting in Appalachia: the Story of West Virginia's Four Major Mine Wars....* Morgantown: West Virginia U Press, 1969.

4390 LUNT, RICHARD D. *Law and Order vs the Miners, West Virgina, 1907-1933*. Hamden, CT: Archon, 1979.

4391 POSEY, THOMAS EDWARD. *The Labor Movement in West Virginia, 1900-1948*. Ph D diss, U of Wisconsin, 1948.

WISCONSIN

4392 ALTMEYER, ARTHUR J. *The Industrial Commission of Wisconsin: A Case Study in Labor Law Administration*. Madison: U of Wisconsin, 1932.

4393 ASHER, ROBERT. "The 1911 Wisconsin Workmen's Compensation Law: a Study in Conservative Labor Reform." *Wisconsin Magazine of History*, Vol 59 (1973), 123-40.

4394 LENIHAN, PATRICK MINER. *The Economic Effects of the Wisconsin Minimum Wage Orders*. Ph D diss, U of Wisconsin, 1968.

4395 MARSDEN, K. GARALD. "Patriotic Societies and American Labor: The American Protective Association in Wisconsin." *Wisconsin Magazine of History*, Vol 41 (1958), 287-94.

4396 OSHINSKY, DAVID M. "Wisconsin Labor and the Campaign of 1951." *Wisconsin Magazine of History*, Vol 56 (1973), 109-18.

4397 WITTE, EDWIN E. "Labor in Wisconsin History." *Wisconsin Magazine of History*, Vol 35 (1951), 83-86, 137-42.

Individual Occupations, Trades, and Industries

Agriculture

4398 ADAMS, LEONARD P. et al. *Viable Farmer-Worker Relationships.*, Bulletin 1019. Ithaca: Cornell Agricultural Experiment Station, NY State College of Agriculture, and NY State School of Industrial and Labor Relations, 1967.

4399 ALLEN, T. C. "Management Experiences in Dealing with the Disadvantaged: Achievements of an Industry-Operated Job Corps Center." *Labor Law Journal*, Vol 19 (Aug 1968), 463-66.

4400 *America's Disinherited.* 1936. (Documentary film produced by the Sharecropper Film Committee for the Southern Tenant Farmers Union)

4401 AMUNDSON, RICHARD J. "Henry S. Sanford and Labor Problems in the Florida Orange Industry." *Florida Historical Quarterly*, Vol 43 (1965), 229-43.

4402 ANDERSON, NELS. *Men on the Move.* Chicago: U of Chicago Press, 1940.

4403 APPLEN, ALLEN. "Labor Casualization in Great Plains Wheat Production: 1865-1902." *Journal of the West*, Vol 16 (Jan 1977), 5-9.

4404 ———. *Migratory Harvest Labor in the Midwestern Wheat Belt, 1870-1940.* Ph D diss, Kansas State U, 1974.

4405 AUERBACH, JEROLD S. *Southern Tenant Farmers: Socialist Critics of the New Deal.* (Labor History), Vol 7(1966), 3-18

4406 BECKER, WILLIAM. "Conflict as a Source of Solidarity: Some Notes on the California Farm Labor Scene." *The Journal of Social Issues*, Vol 9 (1953). (Special issue, Trade Unions and Minority Problems, ed by Daniel Bell & Seymour Martin Lipset)

4407 BECNEL, THOMAS. *With Benefit of Clergy: Catholic Church Support for the National Agriculture Workers Union in Louisiana, 1894-1958.* Ph D diss, Louisiana State U, 1973.

4408 BENSON, JACKSON, and ANNE LOFTIS. "John Steinbeck and Farm Labor Unionization: the Background of *In Dubious Battle*" *American Literature*, Vol 52 (1980), 194-223.

4409 BROOKS, ROBERT P. *History of Agricultural Labor in Georgia, 1865-1910.* Ph D diss, U of Wisconsin, 1912.

4410 CANTOR, LOUIS. "A Prologue to the Protest Movement: the Missouri Sharecropper Roadside Demonstration of 1939." *Journal of American History*, Vol 55 (1969), 804-22.

4411 CHANDLER, DAVID. *¡Huelga!* NY: Simon and Schuster, 1970.

4412 CHAVEZ, CESAR. "California Farm Workers' Struggle." *Black Scholar*, Vol 7 (Jun 1976), 16-19.

4413 CHEVALIER, HAAKON M. *For Us the Living* (a murder mystery). NY: Knopf, 1948.

4414 Clive, Alan. "The Michigan Farmer in World War II." *Michigan History*, Vol 60 (1976), 291-314.

4415 Coalson, George O. *The Development of the Migratory Farm Labor System in Texas, 1900-1954*. San Francisco: R & E Research Associates, 1977.

4416 Coles, Robert. *Uprooted Children: The Early Life of Migrant Farm Workers*. Pittsburgh: U of Pittsburgh Press, 1970.

4417 Conrad, David E. *The Forgotten Farmers: The Story of Sharecroppers in the New Deal*. Urbana: U of Illinois Press, 1965.

4418 Coronado, Richard. *A Conceptual Model of the Harvest Labor Market, the Bracero Program and Factors Involved in Organization among Farm Workers in California, 1946-1970*. Ph D diss, Notre Dame U, 1980.

4419 Corralijo, Jorge. "Report on Proposition 14: Farm Workers vs Big Growers, Big Money and Big Lies." *Radical America*, Vol 11 (Mar-Apr 1977), 74-78.

4420 Cox, LaWanda F. "The American Agricultural Wage Earner, 1865-1900: The Emergence of a Modern Labor Problem." *Agricultural History*, Vol 22 (1948), 95-114.

4421 Daniel, Cletus E. *Bitter Harvest, a History of California Farmworkers, 1870-1941*. Ithaca: Cornell U Press, 1981.

4422 ———. *Labor Radicalism in Pacific Coast Agriculture*. Ph D diss, U of Washington, 1972.

4423 ———. "Radicals on the Farm in California." *Agricultural History*, Vol 49 (1975), 629-46.

4424 Daniel, Franz. "Problems of Union Organization for Migratory Workers." *Labor Law Journal*, Jul 1961, pp 636-43.

4425 Davis, Ronald. *Good and Faithful Labor: a Study in the Origins, Development and Economics of Southern Sharecropping, 1860-1880*. Ph D diss, U of Missouri, 1974.

4426 *A Day Without Sunshine*. 1976. (Documentary film produced for WPBT Public Television in Miami)

4427 *Decision at Delano*. 1967. (Documentary film produced by Jack Copeland)

4428 Dolp, Franz. *Stabilizing Employment of Farm Labor through Cooperative Organization: A Study of Sequoia Farm Labor Association, Tulare County, California*. Ph D diss, U of California, 1964.

4429 Dunbar, Anthony, and Linda Kravity. *Hard Traveling: Migrant Farm Workers in America*. Cambr: Ballinger, 1976.

4430 Dunne, John G. *Delano, the Story of the California Grape Strike*. NY: Farrar, Straus & Giroux, 1967.

4431 Dyson, B. Patricia. "The Farm Workers and the N.L.R.B.: from Wagner to Taft-Hartley." *Federal Bar Journal*, Vol 36 (1977), 121-44.

4432 Dyson, Lowell K. *Red Harvest: the Communist Party and American Farmers*. Lincoln: U of Nebraska Press, 1982.

4433 ———. "The Southern Tenant Farmers Union and Depression Politics." *Political Science Quarterly*, Vol 88 (1973), 230-52.

4434 Elac, John C. *The Employment of Mexican Workers in U.S. Agriculture, 1900-1960: A Biantional Economic Analysis*. San Francisco: R. & E. Research Associates, 1972.

4435 Engler, Robert, and Rosalind Engler. *The Farmers' Union in Washington*. Denver: National Farmers Union, 1948.

4436 Fearis, Donald F. *The California Farm Worker, 1930-1942*. Ph D diss, U of California, 1971.

4437 Folsom, J. C., comp. *Agricultural Labor in the United States, 1943-1952*. Wash.: U.S. Department of Agriculture, Library, 1954.

4438 Friedland, William, and Dorothy Nelkin. *Migrant: Agricultural Workers in America's Northeast*. NY: Holt, Rinehart & Winston, 1972.

4439 ———. "Technological Trends and the Organization of Migrant Farm Workers." *Social Problems*, Vol 19 (1972), 509-12.

4440 FUGITA, STEPHEN, and DAVID O'BRIEN. "Economics, Ideology and Ethnicity: the Struggle between the United Farm Workers Union and the Nisei Farmers League." *Social Problems*, Vol 25 (1977), 146-56.

4441 FULLER, VARDEN, and JOHN W. MAMER. "Constraints on California Farm Worker Unionization." *Industrial Relations*, Vol 17 (1978), 143-55.

4442 GALARZA, ERNESTO. *Farm Workers and Agri-Business in California, 1947-1960.* Notre Dame, IN: Notre Dame Press, 1977.

4443 GLASS, JUDITH C. *Conditions which Facilitate Unionization of Agricultural Workers: A Case Study of the Salinas Valley Lettuce Industry*. Ph D diss, U of California, 1966.

4444 ———. "Organization in Salinas." *Monthly Labor Review*, Vol 51 (Jun 1968), 24-27.

4445 GOLDFARB, RONALD L. *Migrant Farm Workers: A Caste of Despair*. Ames: Iowa State U Press, 1981.

4446 *The Grapes of Wrath*. 1940. (Feature film directed by John Ford)

4447 GRAY, JAMES. *The American Civil Liberties Union of Southern California and Imperial Valley Labor Disturbances, 1930, 1934*. Ph D diss, U of California, 1966.

4448 GREENE, JOSIAH E. *Not in Our Stars* (a novel). NY: Macmillan, 1945.

4449 GREY, ZANE. *Desert of Wheat* (a novel). NY: Grossett & Dunlap, 1918.

4450 GROOM, PHYLLIS. "A Report From the National Farm Labor Conference." *Monthly Labor Review*, Vol 88 (1965), 275-78.

4451 GRUBBS, DONALD H. *Cry from the Cotton: The Southern Tenant Farmers' Union and the New Deal*. Chapel Hill: U of North Cafolina Press, 1971.

4452 ———. "Gardner Jackson, that 'Socialist' Tenant Farmers' Union, and the New Deal." *Agricultural History*, Vol 52 (1968), 125-37.

4453 *Harvest of Shame*. 1960. (Non-fiction film produced by CBS News)

4454 HATHAWAY, DALE E. "The Farm Workers' Transition to Industry." *Monthly Labor Review*, Vol 82 (1966), 34-35.

4455 HAUGHTON, RONALD. "The Influence of Labor-Management Relations on the Settlement of Agricultural Disputes." *Arbitration Journal*, Vol 35 (June 1980), 3-7.

4456 HEAPS, WILLARD A. *Wandering Workers: The Story of American Migrant Farm Workers and Their Problems*. NY: Crown, 1968.

4457 HERBST, JOSEPHINE. *The Rope of Gold* (a novel). NY: Harcourt, Brace, 1939.

4458 HILL, RICHARD B. *California Farm Labor Contractor: A Controversial Occupation in a Rapidly Changing Socio-Economic Environment*. Ph D diss, U of Missouri, 1972.

4459 HOFFMAN, ABRAHAM. "The El Monte Berrypickers' Strike, 1933: International Involvement in a Local Labor Dispute." *Journal of the West*, Vol 12 (1973), 71-84.

4460 HUNTER, ROBERT. "The AAA between Neighbors: Virginia, North Carolina, and the New Deal Farm Program." *Journal of Southern History*, Vol 44 (1978), 537.

4461 HURD, RICHARD W. "Organizing the Working Poor: the California Grape Strike Experience." *Review of Radical Political Economics*, Vol 6 (Spring 1974), 50-75.

4462 ———. "Strategies for Union Growth in Food Manufacturing and Agriculture." *Proceedings of the Twenty-Sixth Annual Winter Meeting of the Industrial Relations Research Association,*, Dec 38-39, 1973, pp 267-74. Madison: IRRA, 1974.

4463 JACKLIN, THOMAS M. "Mission to the Sharecroppers: Neo-Orthodox Radicalism and the Delta Farm Venture, 1936-1940." *South Atlantic Quarterly*, Vol 78 (1979), 302-16.

4464 JAMIESON, STUART M. *Labor Unionism in American Agriculture.*, U.S. Bureau of Labor Statistics Bulletin 836. Wash.: G.P.O., 1945.

4465 JENKINS, J. CRAIG. *Farm Workers and the Powers: Insurgency and Political Conflict (1946-1972)*. Ph D diss, SUNY-Stonybrook, 1976.

4466 ———, and CHARLES PERROW. "Insurgency of the Powerless: Farm Worker Movements (1946-72)." *American Sociological Review*, Vol 42 (1977), 249-67.

4467 JONES, LAMAR B. "Agricultural Labor in the Southwest: the Post Bracero Years." *Social Science Quarterly*, Vol 61 (1980), 85-94.

4468 ———, and LOREN C. SCOTT. "Minimum Wages and Black Employment in the Louisiana Sugarcane Industry." *Proceedings of the Twenty-Fourth Annual Winter Meeting of the Industrial Relations Research Association,*, Dec 27-28, 1971, pp 89-99. Madison: IRRA, 1972.

4469 KESTER, HOWARD. *Revolt Among the Sharecroppers*. NY: Covici-Friede, 1936.

4470 KIRSTEIN, PETER NEIL. "Agribusiness, Labor, and the Wetbacks: Truman's Commission on Migratory Labor." *The Historian*, Vol 40 (1978), 650-67.

4471 KOZIARA, KAREN. "Collective Bargaining in Agriculture: the Policy Alternatives." *Labor Law Journal*, Vol 24 (1973), 424-36.

4472 KUSHNER, SAM. *Long Road to Delano*. NY: International, 1975.

4473 "Labor Department Study Is First of Its Kind: Survey Reports on Earnings of Migrant Farm Workers." *Industrial Bulletin*, (NY State), Vol 40 (1961), 8-11, 18.

4474 LANGE, DOROTHEA, and PAUL S. TAYLOR. *An American Exodus: A Record of Human Erosion in the Thirties*. New Haven: Yale U Press, 1969.

4475 LANHAM, EDWIN M. *The Stricklands* (a novel). Bost.: Little, Brown, 1939.

4476 LEAGUE FOR INDUSTRIAL DEMOCRACY AND NATIONAL SHASRECROPPERS FUND. *Down on the Farm: The Plight of Agricultural Labor*. NY: The League, 1955.

4477 LEVINE, LOUIS. "The Migratory Worker in the Farm Economy." *Labor Law Journal*, July 1961, pp 622-30.

4478 LIEBER, GARY L. "Labor-Management Relations in Agriculture: the Need for Meaningful Collective Bargaining." *Industrial Relations Law Digest*, Vol 17 (Summer 1974), 85-99.

4479 LISS, SAMUEL. "Farm Wage Boards Under the Cooperative Extension Service During World War II." *Agricultural History*, Vol 27 (1953), 103-8.

4480 ———. "Farm Wage Boards Under the Wage Stabilization Program During World War II." *Agricultural History*, Vol 30 (1956), 128-37.

4481 LUMPKIN, GRACE. *A Sign for Cain* (a novel). NY: Lee Furman, 1935.

4482 MCMATH, ROBERT C, JR. "Agrarian Protest at the Forks of the Creek: Three Subordinate Farmers' Alliances in North Carolina." *North Carolina Historical Review*, Vol 51 (1974), 41-63.

4483 MCWILLIAMS, CAREY. *Factories in the Field: The Story of Migratory Farm Labor in California*. Bost.: Little, Brown, 1939.

4484 ———. *Ill Fares the Land: Migrants and Migratory Labor in the United States*. Bost.: Little, Brown, 1942.

4485 MAJKA, LINDA C. *Farm Workers, Labor Unionism and Agrarian Capitalism*. Ph D diss, U of California, 1979.

4486 MAJKA, THEOPHILE J. *Regulating Farm Workers: the Politics of Farm Labor Unionization*. Ph D diss, U of California, 1979.

4487 MARKOFF, DENA S. "The Sugar Industry in the Arkansas River Valley: National Sugar Beet Company." *Colorado Magazine*, Vol 55 (1978), 69-92.

4488 MARSHALL, F. RAY, and LAMAR B. JONES. "Agricultural Unions in Louisiana." *Labor History*, Vol 3 (1962), 287-306.

4489 MARTIN, PHILIP. "Harvest Mechanization and Agricultural Trade Unionism: Obreros Unidos in Wisconsin." *Labor Law Journal*, Vol 28 (1977), 166-73.

4490 MAY, WILLIAM J., JR. "The Colorado Sugar Manufacturing Company: Grand Junction Plant." *Colorado Magazine*, Vol 56 (1978), 328-45.

4491 MEISTER, DICK, and ANNE LOFTIS. *A Long Time Comin': The Struggle to Unionize America's Farm Workers*. NY: Macmillan, 1977.

4492 MEYERS, MIKE. *Farm Labor in the United States: A List of Selected Readings in Labor and Industrial Relations*. Urbana: U of Illinois, Institute of Labor and Industrial Relations, 1971.

4493 MILLS, NICOLAUS. "The Farm Workers Fight It Out." *Dissent*, Vol 20 (1973), 297-98.

4494 ———. "The Ship and the Bee: Diary from the Grape Strike." *Dissent*, Vol 20 (1973), 200-5.

4495 MITCHELL, H. L. "Founding and Early History of the Southern Tenant Farmers Union." *Arkansas Historical Quarterly*, Vol 32 (1973), 340-69.

4496 MITCHELL, ROBERT J. *Peace in the Fields: a Study of the Passage and Subsequent History of the California Agriculture Labor Relations Act of 1975*. Ph D diss, U of California, 1980.

4497 MITCHELL, RUTH C. *Of Human Kindness* (a novel). NY: Appleton-Century, 1940.

4498 MOORE, LINDA LU I. *The Rhetorical Substance and Strategies in the Dispute between California Table Grape Vineyard Owners and the United Farm Workers Organizing Committee: 1965-70*. Ph D diss, Kent State U, 1973.

4499 MORIN, ALEXANDER. *The Organizability of Farm Labor in the United States*. Cambr.: Harvard U Press, 1952.

4500 MULLIGAN, S. "Slave Labor in the Cane Fields." *Progressive*, Vol 45 (May 1981), 36-37.

4501 NASS, DAVID L., ed. "Recollections of Rural Revolt." *Minnesota History*, Vol 44 (1975), 304-8. (Interview with officer of Farmers' Holiday Association during 1930s)

4502 NATIONAL ADVISORY COMMITTEE ON FARM LABOR. *Farm Labor Organizing, 1905-1967: A Brief History*. NY: National Advisory Committee on Farm Labor, 1967.

4503 NATIONAL CHILD LABOR COMMITTEE. *Migrant Farm Labor in Colorado: A Study of Migratory Families*. NY: The Committee, 1951.

4504 NELKIN, DOROTHY. *On the Season: Aspects of the Migrant Labor System*. Ithaca: NY State School of Industrial and Labor Relations, Cornell U, 1970.

4505 NELSON, EUGENE. *Huelga: The First Hundred Days of the Great Delano Grape Strike*. Delano, CA: Farm Worker Press, 1966.

4506 NEWBILL, JAMES G. "Farmers and Wobblies in the Yakima Valley, 1933." *Pacific Northwest Quarterly*, Vol 68 (1977), 80-87.

4507 NEWHOUSE, EDWARD. *This Is Your Day* (a novel). NY: Lee Furman, 1937.

4508 NORQUEST, CARROL. *Rio Grande Wetbacks: Mexican Migrant Workers*. Albuquerque: U of New Mexico Press, 1972.

4509 PETRO, SYLVESTER. "Agriculture and Labor Policy." *Labor Law Journal*, Vol 24 (1973), 24-51.

4510 POWER, JONATHAN. et al. *Migrant Workers in Western Europe and the United States*. NY: Pergamon, 1979.

4511 PRESCOTT, GERALD. "Farm Gentry vs. the Granges: Conflict in Rural America." *California Historical Quarterly*, Vol 56 (Winter 1977), 328-45.

4512 RAPER, ARTHUR M., and IRA DE A. REID. *Sharecroppers All*. Chapel Hill: U of North Carolina, 1940.

4513 RASMUSSEN, WAYNE D. *A History of the Emergency Farm Labor Supply Program, 1943-1947*., U.S. Department of Agriculture Monograph No 13. Wash.: G.P.O., 1951.

4514 RECCOW, LOUIS. *The Orange County Citrus Strikers of 1935-36: The 'Forgotten People' in Revolt*. Ph D diss, U of Southern California, 1971.

4515 REMELE, LARRY. "North Dakota's Forgotten farmers' Union, 1913-1920." *North Dakota History*, Vol 45 (Spring 1978), 4-21.

4516 REUL, MYRTLE R. *Where Hannibal Led Us*. NY: Vantage Press, 1967.

4517 ROBBINS, HAYES. *The Labor Movement and the Farmer*. NY: Harcourt, Brace, 1922.

4518 ROCHIN, REFUGIO. "New Perspectives on Agricultural Labor Relations in California." *Labor Law Journal*, Vol 28 (1977), 395-402.

4519 ROGERS, WILLIAM WARREN. "The Agricultural Wheel in Alabama." *Alabama Review*, Vol 20 (1967), 5-16.

4520 ROSEN, DALE, and THEODORE ROSENGARTEN. "Shoot-out at Reeltown: the Narrative of Jess Hull, Alabama Tenant Farmer." *Radical America*, Vol. ((Nov-Dec 1972), 65-84)

4521 ROWLEY, WILLIAM D. "The Loup City Riot of 1934: Main Street vs. the 'Far-Out' Left." *Nebraska History*, Vol 47 (1966), 295-327.

4522 SABGHIR, IRVING HOWARD. *Mexican Contract Labor in the United States, 1948-1953: A Political and Economic Analysis*. Ph D diss, Harvard U, 1956.

4523 SCARBOROUGH, DOROTHY. *Can't Get a Red Bird* (a novel). NY: Harper, 1929.

4524 SCHWARTZ, HARRY. *Seasonal Farm Labor in the United States*. NY: Columbia U Press, 1945.

4525 SCHWARTZ, MICHAEL. *Radical Protest and Social Structure: The Southen Farmers' Alliance and Cotton Tenancy, 1880-1890*. NY: Academic Press, 1976.

4526 SCRUGGS, OTEY M. "The Bracero Program under the Farm Security Administration, 1942-1943." *Labor History*, Vol 3 (1962), 149-68.

4527 *Seed for Tomorrow*. 1946. ("Dramatized social documentary" film sponsored by the National Farmers Union)

4528 SEGUR, W. H., and VARDEN FULLER. "California's Farm Labor Elections: An Analysis of the Initial Results." *Monthly Labor Review*, Vol 99 (1976), 25-30.

4529 SHLOMOWITZ, R. "Transition from Slave to Freedman Labor Arrangements in Southerm Agriculture, 1865-1870." *Journal of Economic History*, Vol 39 (1979), 333-38.

4530 SHOTWELL, LOUISA R. *The Harvesters: The Story of the Migrant People*. NY: Doubleday, 1961.

4531 SHOVER, JOHN L. *Cornbelt Rebellion: The Farmers' Holiday Association*. Urbana: U of Illinois Press, 1965.

4532 ———. "The Farmers' Holiday Association Strike, August 1932." *Agricultural History*, Vol 39 (1965), 196-203.

4533 ———. "The Penny-Auction Rebellion: Western Farmers Fight against Foreclosure, 1932-1933." *American West*, Vol 2 (Fall, 1965), 64-72.

4534 SIMON, CHARLIE M. *The Share-Cropper* (a novel). NY: Dutton, 1937.

4535 SOUTHERN TENANT FARMERS UNION. *Guide to the Microfilm Edition of the Southern Tenant Farmers Union Papers Located at the Southern Historical Collection, The University of North Carolina Library, Chapel Hill, N.C.* Chapel Hill: U of North Carolina Library, 1972.

4536 STEIN, WALTER J. *California and the Dust Bowl Migration*. Westport, CT: Greenwood Press, 1974.

4537 STEINBECK, JOHN. *The Grapes of Wrath* (a novel). NY: Viking Press, 1939.

4538 ———. *In Dubious Battle* (a novel). NY: Covici-Friede, 1936.

4539 ———. *Of Mice and Men* (a novel). NY: Covici-Friede, 1938.

4540 SYKES, HOPE W. *Second Hoeing* (a novel). NY: Putnam, 1935.

4541 TANGRI, BEVERLY STARIKA. *Federal Legislation as an Expression of United States Public Policy Toward Agricultural Labor, 1914-1954*. Ph D diss, U of California, 1967.

4542 TAYLOR, PAUL S. "California Farm Labor: a Review." *Agricultural History*, Vol 52 (1968), 49-53.

4543 ———. *Mexican Labor in the United States.*, 3 vols. Berkeley: U of California Press, 1928-1934.

4544 TAYLOR, RONALD B. *Sweatshops in the Sun: Child Labor on the Farm*. Bost.: Beacon Press, 1973.

4545 THOMPSON, MARK. *The Agricultural Workers Organizing Committee, 1959-1962*. MS thesis, Cornell U, 1963.

4546 *Tobacco Road*. 1941. (Feature film directed by John Ford)

4547 U.S. CALIFORNIA FARM LABOR PANEL. *Final Report of the California Farm Labor Panel to Secretary of Labor W. Willard Wirtz*. Los Angeles: The Panel, 1965.

4548 U.S. COMMISSION ON INDUSTRIAL RELATIONS (1912). "The Seasonal Labor Problem in Agriculture," Vol 5, pp 4911-5027, *Final Report*, Wash.: G.P.O., 1916.

4549 U.S. CONGRESS. SENATE. Committee on Labor and Public Welfare. Subcommittee on Migratory Labor. *Federal and State Statutes Relating to Farmworkers: A Compilation*. Wash.: G.P.O., 1972.

4550 ———. ———. Committee on Labor and Public Welfare. Subcommittee on Labor and Labor-Management Relations. *Migratory Labor*. Wash.: G.P.O., 1952. (Parts 1 & 2 of Hearings before 82nd Congress, 2nd Session)

4551 U.S. GENERAL ACCOUNTING OFFICE. *Impact of Federal Programs to Improve the Living Conditions of Migrant and Other Seasonal Farmworkers: Report to the Congress [on the] Dept. of Agriculture, Dept. of Health, Education, and Welfare, Dept. of Labor [and] Office of Economic Opportunity, by the Comtroller General of the United States*. Wash.: The Office, 1973.

4552 U.S. PRESIDENT'S COMMISSION ON MIGRATORY LABOR. *Migratory Labor in American Agriculture*. Wash.: G.P.O., 1951.

4553 U.S. WORKS PROJECTS ADMINISTRATION. *Migratory Workers of the Southwest*. Westport, CT: Greenwood, 1978.

4554 VENKATARAMANI, M. S. "Norman Thomas, Arkansas Sharecroppers, and the Roosevelt Agricultural Policies, 1933-1937." *Mississippi Valley Historical Review*, Vol 47 (1960), 225-46.

4555 ———. "Norman Thomas, Arkansas Sharecroppers, and the Roosevelt Agricultural Policies, 1933-1937." *Arkansas Historical Quarterly*, Vol 24 (1965), 3-28. (Reprinted from Mississippi Valley Historical Review, Vol 47(1960), 225-62, but embellished with illustrations not in the original)

4556 WANG, PETER H. "Farmers and the Immigrant Act of 1924." *Agricultural History*, Vol 49 (1975), 647-52.

4557 WARING, P. ALSTON, and CLINTON S. GOLDEN. *Soil and Steel: Exploring the Common Interests of Farmers asnd Wage Earners*. NY: Harper, 1947.

4558 WHITTEN, WOODROW C. "The Wheatland Episode." *Pacific Historical Review*, Vol 17 (1948), 37-42.

4559 WILLIAMS, HARRISON A., JR. "Proposed Legislation for Migratory Workers." *Labor Law Journal*, Jul 1961. pp 630-36.

4560 WOLLENBERG, CHARLES. "*Huelga,* 1928 Style: the Imperial Valley Cantaloupe Workers' Strike." *Pacific Historical Review*, Vol 38 (1969), 45-58.

4561 ———. "Race and Class in Rural California: The El Monte Berry Strike of 1933." *California Historical Quarterly*, Vol 51 (1972), 155-64. (Mexican workers, Japanese Employers)

4562 WRIGHT, DALE. *They Harvest Despair: The Migrant Farm Worker*. Bost.: Beacon Press, 1965.

4563 YOUNG, MARY E., ed. *Migrant Workers: A Bibliography with Abstracts*. Springfield, VA: National Technical Information Service, 1977.

4564 ZERZAN, JOHN. "Cesar Chavez and the Farm Workers." *Politics and Society*, Vol 3 (Fall 1972), 117-23.

Automobile, Aircraft, Agricultural Implements, and Aerospace

4565 AFL-CIO. Executive Council *To Clear the Record: AFL-CIO Executive Council Report on the Disaffiliation of the UAW*. Wash.: The Council, 1969.

4566 ANDERSON, SHERWOOD. *Poor White* (a novel). NY: Huebsch, 1920.

4567 ANDREW, WILLIAM D. "Factionalism and Anti-Communism: Ford Local 600." *Labor History*, Vol 20 (1979), 228-55.

4568 BENNETT, HARRY (AS TOLD TO PAUL MARCUS). *We Never Called Him Henry*. NY: Fawcett, 1951.

4569 BERNSTEIN, BARTON J. "Walter Reuther and the General Motors Strike of 1945-1946." *Michigan History*, Vol 49 (1965), 260-77.

4570 BERNSTEIN, IRVING. *The Automobile Industry: Post War Developments, 1918-1921.*, Historical Studies of Wartime Problems No 52. Wash.: U.S. Bureau of Labor Statistics (Division of Historical Studies of Wartime Problems, 1941-1945), 1942. (Mimeo.)

4571 BLACKWOOD, GEORGE D. *The United Automobile Workers of America, 1935-51*. Ph D diss, U of Chicago, 1952.

4572 BLAUNER, ROBERT. *Alienation and Freedom: The Factory Worker and his Industry*. Chicago: U of Chicago Press, 1964.

4573 BOLES, FRANK. "Walter Reuther and the Kelsey Hays Strike of 1936." *Detroit Perspective*, Vol 4 (Winter 1980), 74-90.

4574 BONOSKY, PHILLIP. *Brother Bill McKie: Building the Union at Ford*. NY: International Publishers, 1953.

4575 BORTZ, NELSON M. "Cost-of-Living Wage Clauses and UAW-GM Pact." *Monthly Labor Review*, Vol 67 (1948), 1-7.

4576 BORYCZKA, RAYMOND. "Militancy and Factionalism in the United Auto Workers Union, 1937-1941." *Maryland Historian*, Vol 8 (1977), 13-25.

4577 ———. "Seasons of Discontent: Auto Union Factionalism and Motor Products Strike of 1935-36." *Michigan History*, Vol 61 (1977), 3-32.

4578 BRODY, CATHERINE. *Nobody Starves* (a novel). NY: Longmans, Green, 1932.

4579 CARLINER, LEWIS. "The Dispute That Never Was." *Labor History*, Vol 12 (1971), 605-13.

4580 CARLTON, FRANCIS. "The G M Strike." *Antioch Review*, Sep 1946, pp 426-41.

4581 CENTER FOR THE STUDY OF DEMOCRATIC INSTITUTIONS. *A Conversation: Labor Looks at Labor. Some Members of the United Auto Workers Undertake a Self-Examination.* Santa Barbara, CA: Center for the Study of Democratic Institutions, 1963.

4582 CHESTER, HARRY. "GM-UAW Wage Settlement." *Labor and Nation*, Jul-Aug 1948, p 12.

4583 CHINOY, ELY. *Automobile Workers and the American Dream*. Garden City: Doubleday, 1955.

4584 COMMUNIST PARTY, U.S. NATIONAL AUTO SECTION. "The '79 Negotiations in Auto." *Political Affairs*, Vol 58 (Jul 1979), 9-16.

4585 CONRAD, LAWRENCE H. *Temper* (a novel). NY: Dodd, Mead, 1924.

4586 CORT, JOHN C. "Fight for the Ford 600." *Commonweal*, Mar 22, 1946, pp 43-45.

4587 CUSHMAN, EDWARD L. "The American Motors—UAW Progress Sharing Agreement." *Proceedings of the Fourteenth Annual Meeting of the Industrial Relations Research Association*, Dec 28-29, 1961, pp 315-24. Madison: IRRA, 1962.

4588 DAHLHEIMER, HARRY. *A History of the Mechanics Educational Society of America in Detroit from Its Inception in 1933 through 1937*. Detroit: Wayne U Press, 1951.

4589 DENNIS, THOMAS. "The Coming Negotiations in Auto." *Political Affairs*, Vol 42 (Jun 1973), 30-40.

4590 "Detroit Auto Worker." *Fortune*, Aug 1946, pp 126-29.

4591 "Due Process vs. Power in Union Trial Procedure." *Union Democracy Review*, Winter 1973, pp 1-3, 6-9, 12.

4592 DUNN, ROBERT W. *Labor and Automobiles*. NY: International Publishers, 1929.

4593 EL-MESSIDI, KATHY G. *The Bargain: The Story Behind the 30-Year Honeymoon of GM and the UAW*. NY: Nollen, 1980.

4594 FABAR, AL. "Auto in the Eighties: Uncar and Unworkers." *Radical America*, Vol 13 (Jan-Feb 1979), 31-37.

4595 FAUNCE, WILLIAM A. "Automation and the Automobile Worker," pp 370-79, *Labor and Trade Unionism: an Interdisciplinary Reader*, Walter Galenson & Seymour Martin Lipset, eds. NY: John Wiley & Sons, 1960.

4596 *Finally Got the News*. 1970. (Non-fiction film by Black Star Productions)

4597 FINE, SIDNEY. *The Automobile Under the Blue Eagle: Labor, Management, and the Automobile Manufacturing Code*. Ann Arbor: U of Michigan Press, 1963.

4598 ———. "The Ford Motor Company and the N.R.A." *Business History Review*, Vol 32 (1958), 353-85.

4599 ———. *Frank Murphy: The Detroit Years*. Ann Arbor: U of Michigan Press, 1975.

4600 ———. *Frank Murphy: The New Deal Years*. Chicago: U of Chicago Press, 1979.

4601 ———. "The General Motors Sit-Down Strike: A Re-examination." *American Historical Review*, Vol 49 (1965), 260-77.

4602 ———. "John L. Lewis Discusses the General Motors Sit-Down Strike: A Document." *Labor History*, Vol 15 (1974), 563-70.

4603 ———. "The Origins of the United Automobile Workers, 1933-1935." *Journal of Economic History*, Vol 18 (1958), 249-82.

4604 ———. "President Roosevelt and the Automobile Code." *Mississippi Valley Historical Review*, Vol 45 (1958), 23-50.

4605 ———. "Proportional Representation of Workers in the Auto Industry, 1934-1935." *Industrial and Labor Relations Review*, Vol 12 (1959), 182-205.

4606 ———. *Sit-Down: The General Motors Strike of 1936-1937*. Ann Arbor: U of Michigan Press, 1969.

4607 ———. "The Toledo Chevrolet Strike of 1935." *Ohio Historical Quarterly*, Vol 67 (1958), 325-56.

4608 ———. "The Tool and Die Makers Strike of 1933." *Michigan History*, Vol 42 (1958), 297-323.

4609 FISHER, THOMAS R. *Industrial Disputes and Federal Legislation, with Special Reference to the Railroad, Coal, Steel, and Automobile Industries in the U.S. Since 1900*. NY: Columbia U Press, 1940.

4610 FOUNTAIN, CLAYTON W. *Union Guy*. NY: Viking Press, 1949.

4611 FRASER, DOUGLAS. "Last Angry Man?— Head of UAW Talks Tough." *Barrons*, June 9, 1980, pp 4-5. (Interview)

4612 FRIEDLANDER, PETER. *The Emergence of a UAW Local*. Pittsburgh: U of Pittsburgh Press, 1975.

4613 ———. *The Emergence of a UAW Local, 1936-1939: a Study in Class and Culture*. Ph D diss, SUNY-Binghamton, 1977.

4614 GABIN, NANCY. "'They Have Placed a Penalty on Womanhood': The Protest Actions of Women Auto Workers in Detroit-Area UAW Locals, 1945-1947." *Feminist Studies*, Vol 8 (1982), 373-98.

4615 ———. "Women Workers and the UAW in the Post-World War II Period: 1945-1954." *Labor History*, Vol 21 (1980), 5-30.

4616 GALENSON, WALTER. "The Automobile Industry," chap. 3, *The CIO Challenge to the AFL*, Cambr.: Harvard U Press, 1960.

4617 GARTMAN, WILLIAM. *Auto Slavery: the Development of the Labor Process in the Auto Industry of the U.S., 1897-1950*. Ph D diss, U of California, 1981.

4618 GEORGAKAS, DAN, and MARVIN SURKIN. "Nigermation in Auto: Company Policy and the Rise of Black Caucuses." *Radical America*, Vol 8 (Jan-Feb 1975), 31-56.

4619 GLABERMAN, MARTIN. "Black Cats, White Cats, Wildcats: Auto Workers in Detroit." *Radical America*, Vol 8 (Jan-Feb 1975), 25-29.

4620 ———. "A Note on Walter Reuther." *Radical America*, Vol 7 (Nov-Dec 1973), 113-17.

4621 ———. *Wartime Strikes: the Struggle against the No-Strike Pledge in the U.A.W. during World War II*. Detroit: Bewick, 1980.

4622 GOODE, BILL. "The Skilled Auto Worker: a Social Portrait." *Dissent*, Vol 23 (1976), 392-97.

4623 *The Great Sitdown.* 1977. (Directed by Stephen Peet for the BBC)

4624 GUEST, ROBERT H. "Quality of Work Life—Learning from Tarrytown." *Harvard Business Review*, Vol 57 (1979), 76-87.

4625 ———. "Work Careers and Aspirations of Automobile Workers," pp 319-28, *Labor and Trade Unionism: an Interdisciplinary Reader*, Walter Galenson & Seymour Martin Lipset, eds. NY: John Wiley & Sons, 1960.

4626 HARBISON, F. H., and ROBERT DUBIN. *Patterns of Union-Management Relations.* Chicago: Science Research Associates, 1947.

4627 HARRINGTON, MICHAEL. "To the Auto Workers Union." *Dissent*, Vol 27 (1980), 371-76.

4628 HAWES, ELIZABETH. *Hurry Up, Please, It's Time.* NY: Reynal and Hitchcock, 1946.

4629 HERO, ALFRED O. *The UAW and World Affairs.* Bost: World Peace Foundation, 1965.

4630 HERRING, NEILL, and SUE THRASHER. "U.A.W. Sit-down Strike: Atlanta, 1936." *Southern Exposure*, Vol 1 (Winter 1973), 64-83.

4631 HIMES, CHESTER B. *Lonely Crusade* (a novel). NY: Knopf, 1947.

4632 HOFFMAN, CLAUDE E. *Sit-Down in Anderson: UAW Local 663, Anderson, Indiana.* Detroit: Wayne State U Press, 1968.

4633 HOWARD, J. WOODFORD, JR. "Frank Murphy and the Sit-Down Strikes of 1937." *Labor History*, Vol 1 (1960), 103-40.

4634 HOWARD, WAYNE E. *The Missile Sites Labor Commission: 1961 Through 1967.* Wash.: G.P.O., 1969.

4635 KEERAN, ROGER R. "Communist Influence in the Automobile Industry, 1920-1933: Paving the Way for an Industrial Union." *Labor History*, Vol 20 (1979), 189-225.

4636 ———. *The Communist Party and the Auto Workers Unions.* Bloomington: Indiana U Press, 1980.

4637 ———. "The Communists and UAW Factionalism, 1937-1939." *Michigan History*, Vol 60 (1976), 115-35.

4638 ———. "'Everything for Victory': Communist Influence in the Auto Industry during World War II." *Science and Society*, Vol 43 (1979), 1-28.

4639 KORNBLUM, WILLIAM. "The UAW: Tooling Up for the '80s." *Dissent*, Vol 26 (1979), 395-405.

4640 KORNHAUSER, ARTHUR W. *Mental Health of the Industrial Worker: A Detroit Study.* NY: Wiley, 1965.

4641 KOVALEFF, THEODORE P. "Divorce American-Style: the Du Pont-General Motors Case." *Delaware History*, Vol 18 (Spring-Summer 1978), 28-42.

4642 KRAUS, HENRY. *The Many and the Few: A Chronicle of the Dynamic Auto Workers.* Los Angeles: Plantin, 1947.

4643 KRUCHKO, JOHN G. *The Birth of a Union Local: The History of UAW Local 647, Norwood, Ohio, 1933 to 1940.* Ithaca: NY State School of Industrial and Labor Relations, Cornell U, 1972.

4644 LEAB, DANIEL J. "Writing History With Film: Two Views of the 1937 Strike Against General Motors by the UAW." *Labor History*, Vol 21 (1980), 102-12.

4645 LEE, HARRY. *Sir and Brother* (a novel). NY: Appleton-Century-Crofts, 1948.

4646 LEIDING, JAMES HERMAN. *Selected Aspects of the Social Action Programs of Muncie's United Automobile Workers' Locals: 1937-1964.* Ph D diss, Ball State U, 1966.

4647 LEVINSON, EDWARD. *Rise of the Auto Workers.* Detroit: UAW, 1946.

4648 LEVINSON, HAROLD M. "Pattern Bargaining by the United Automobile Workers." *Labor Law Journal*, Sep 1958, pp 669-74.

4649 LEWIS, DAVID L. "Ford and Kahn." *Michigan History*, Vol 64 (1980), 17-28.

4650 LICHTENSTEIN, NELSON. "What Happened to the UAW?" *New Politics*, Vol 11 (Fall 1976), 36-45.

4651 LINTON, THOMAS E. *A Historical Examination of the Purposes and Practices of the*

Education Program of the United Automobile Workers of America—1936-1959. Ann Arbor: School of Education, U of Michigan, 1965.

4652 LIPPERT, JOHN. "Fleetwood Wildcat." *Radical America*, Vol 11 (Sep-Oct 1977), 7-37.

4653 ———. "Shopfloor Politics at Fleetwood." *Radical America*, Vol 12 (Jul-Aug 1978), 53-69.

4654 *Loose Bolts.* 1973. (Documentary by Peter Schlaifer)

4655 LOVIN, HUGH T. "The Automobile Workers Unions and the Fight for Labor Parties in the 1930s." *Indiana Magazine of History*, Vol 77 (1981), 128-49.

4656 MCBRIDE, ROBERTA. *Labor Relations in the Automobile Industry.* Detroit: Detroit Public Library, Social Science Department, 1950.

4657 MACDONALD, ROBERT M. *Collective Bargaining in the Automobile Industry: A Study of Wage Structure and Competitive Relations.* New Haven: Yale U Press, 1963.

4658 MCKERSIE, ROBERT B. et al. "Intraorganizational Bargaining in Labor Negotiations." *Journal of Conflict Resolution*, Vol 9 (1969), 463-81.

4659 MCMURRAY, DAVID A. "The Willys-Overland Strike, 1919" *Northwest Ohio Quarterly*, Vol 37 (1965), 33-43, 74-80.

4660 MCPHERSON, WILLIAM H. "Automobiles," chap. 11, *How Collective Bargaining Works*, Harry A Millis, research director. NY: Twentieth Century Fund, 1945.

4661 ———. *Labor Relations in the Automobile Industry.* Wash.: Brookings Institution, 1940.

4662 MALTZ, ALBERT. *The Underground Stream* (a novel). Bost.: Little, Brown, 1940.

4663 MARQUART, FRANK. *The UAW from Crusade to One-Party Union.* University Park, PA: Pennsylvania State U Press, 1976.

4664 MEIER, AUGUST, and ELLIOTT RUDWICK. *Black Detroit and the Rise of the UAW.* NY: Oxford U Press, 1979.

4665 MEYER, STEPHEN. "Adapting the Immigrant to the Line: Americanization in the Ford Factory, 1914-1921." *Journal of Social History*, Vol 14 (1980), 67-82.

4666 ———. *The Five Dollar Day: Labor, Management, and Social Control in the Ford Motor Company, 1908-1921.* Albany: State U of NY Press, 1981.

4667 MEYERS, GEORGE. "Communists in Auto—As It Really Was." *Political Affairs*, Vol 59 (Dec 1980), 33-36. (Review of Keeran's *The C.P. and the Auto Workers Union*)

4668 MILKMAN, RUTH. "Redefining 'Women's Work': The Sexual Division of Labor in the Auto Industry During World War II." *Feminist Studies*, Vol 8 (1982), 336-72.

4669 MOORE, GILBERT. *Poverty, Class Consciousness, and Racial Conflict: the Social Basis of Trade Union Politics in the UAW-CIO, 1937-1955.* Ph D diss,, Princeton U, 1978.

4670 MORRIS, BRUCE R. "Industrial Relations in the Automobile Industry," chap. 17, *Labor in Postwar America*, Colston E. Warne, ed. Brooklyn: Remsen Press, 1949.

4671 MUSTE, ABRAHAM J. *The Automobile Industry and Organized Labor.* Balt.: Christian Social Justice Fund, 1936.

4672 NASH, AL. "The Local Union: Center of Life in the UAW." *Dissent*, Vol 25 (1978), 398-408.

4673 ———. "Quality of Working Life of Auto Assemblers." *Labor Studies Journal*, Vol 2 (Spring 1977), 23-35.

4674 ———. "A Unionist Remembers: Militant Unionism and Political Factions." *Dissent*, Vol 24 (1977), 181-89.

4675 "No-Raid Agreement between UAW and IAM." *Monthly Labor Review*, Vol 70 (1950), 278-79.

4676 NORWOOD, E. P. *Men and Methods.* Garden City: Doubleday, Doran, 1931.

4677 OPINION RESEARCH CORPORATION. *The General Motors Strike.* Princeton: The Corporation, 1945.

4678 OZANNE, ROBERT. *A Century of Labor-Management Relations at McCormick and International Harvester.* Madison: U of Wisconsin Press, 1967.

4679 ———. "Union Wage Impact: A Nineteenth-Century Case." *Industrial and Labor Relations Review*, Vol 15 (1962), 350-75.

4680 ———. "Union-Management Relations: McCormick Harvesting Machine Company, 1862-1886" *Labor History*, Vol 4 (1963), 132-60.

4681 PESOTTA, ROSE. *Bread Upon the Waters* (description of Fisher Body sitdown strike). NY: Dodd, Mead, 1945.

4682 PETERSON, JOYCE S. "Auto Workers and Their Work, 1900-1933." *Labor History*, Vol 22 (1981), 213-36.

4683 ———. "Black Automobile Workers in Detroit, 1910-1930." *Journal of Negro History*, Vol 64 (1979), 177-90.

4684 ———. *A Social History of Automobile Workers before Unionization, 1900-33*. Ph D diss, U of Wisconsin, 1977.

4685 PETRO, SYLVESTER. *The Kohler Strike: Union Violence and Administrative Law*. Chicago: Regnery, 1961.

4686 PIERSON, FRANK C. *Collective Bargaining Systems: A Study of Union-Employer Responsibilities and Problems*. Wash.: American Council on Public Affairs, 1942. (See pp 109-32)

4687 POLLACK, JEROME. "Kaiser-Frazer UAW-CIO Social Security Program." *Industrial and Labor Relations Review*, Vol 6 (1952), 94-109.

4688 POLLARD, SPENCER D. *Some Problems of Democracy in the Government of Labor Unions, with Special Reference to the United Mine Workers of America and the United Automobile Workers of America*. Ph D diss, Harvard U, 1940.

4689 PRICKETT, JAMES R. "Communism and Factionalism in the United Automobile Workers, 1939-1947." *Science & Society*, Vol 32 (1968), 257-77.

4690 ———. "Communists and the Automobile Industry in Detroit before 1935." *Michigan History*, Vol 47 (1973), 185-208.

4691 RAMIREZ, ARMANDO, and THOMAS DENNIS. "The UAW Reaffiliation Move." *Political Affairs*, Vol 57 (Apr 1978), 37-39.

4692 RAUSHENBUSH, CARL. *Fordism: Ford and the Workers, Ford and the Community*. NY: League for Industrial Democracy, 1937.

4693 REUTHER, WALTER P. *Purchasing Power for Prosperity: In the Matter of International Union, UAW, and General Motors Corporation, October 1945—The Case for Maintaining Take-Home Pay without Increasing Prices*. Detroit: The Union, G.M. Department, 1945.

4694 RICE, CHARLES OWEN. "Verdict at Kohler." *The Commonweal*, Nov 11, 1960.

4695 ROSENBERG, BERNARD. "Torn Apart and Driven Apart: A Portrait of a UAW Local in Chicago." *Dissent*, Vol 19 (1972), 61-69.

4696 ROWE, EVAN KEITH. "Health and Welfare Plans in the Automobile Industry." *Monthly Labor Review*, Vol 73 (1951), 277-82.

4697 RUSSELL, JACK. "The Coming of the Line: the Ford Highland Park Plant, 1910-1914." *Radical America*, Vol 12 (May-Jul 1978), 29-45.

4698 SAPERSTEIN, LOU. "Ford is Organized!" *Political Affairs*, Vol 46 (Mar 1977), 29-25; (May 1977), 23-30.

4699 SCHRADE, PAUL. "Growing Bureaucratization of the U.A.W." *New Politics*, Vol 10 (Winter 1973), 13-21.

4700 SCHWARTZ, DONALD A. *The 1941 Strike at Allis-Chalmers*. Madison: U of Wisconsin, 1943. (Mimeo.)

4701 SERRIN, WILLIAM. *The Company and the Union: The "Civilized Relationship" of the General Motors Corporation and the United Automobile Workers*. NY: Knopf, 1973.

4702 *Sitdown*. 1957. (Documentary film produced by the UAW Education Department)

4703 SKEELS, JACK. "The Background of UAW Factionalism." *Labor History*, Vol 2 (1961), 158-81.

4704 SMITTER, WESSEL. *F.O.B., Detroit* (a novel). NY: Harper, 1938.

4705 SRODES, J. "Defending the Motor Workers." *Far Eastern Economic Review*, Vol 107 (1980), 42.

4706 STANLEY, J. PERHAM. "Pension Plans Negotiated by the UAW-CIO." *Monthly Labor Review*, Vol 77 (1954), 13-15.

4707 STANLEY, MARJORIE THINES. "The Amalgamation of Collective Bargaining and Political Activity by the UAW." *Industrial and Labor Relations Review*, Vol 10 (1956), 40-47.

4708 STEELE, JAMES. *Conveyor* (a novel). NY: International Publishers, 1935.

4709 STIEBER, JACK. *Governing the UAW*. NY: John Wiley & Sons, 1962.

4710 SWADOS, HARVEY. *On the Line* (a novel). Bost.: Atlantic, Little, Brown 1957.

4711 ———. *A Radical at Large*. London: Hart-Davis, 1967. (See "The UAW—Over the Top of Over the Hill?," pp 69-92)

4712 SWARD, KEITH. *The Legend of Henry Ford*. NY: Rinehart, 1948.

4713 SWARTHOUT, GLENDON F. *Willow Run* (a novel). NY: Crowell, 1943.

4714 THOMAS, R. J. *Automobile Unionism*., Reports of the President of the U.A.W. Submitted to the 1941 Convention of the U.A.W., Vol 6. Detroit: The Union, 1941.

4715 TICKNOR, THOMAS. *Motor City: the Impact of the Automobile Industry upon Detroit, 1900-1975*. Ph D diss, U of Michigan, 1978.

4716 "UAW: 40 Years of Struggle." *Solidarity*, May 13, 1977, entire issue.

4717 *United Action Means Victory*. 1940. (Non-fiction film produced by the UAW Education Department)

4718 U.S. CONGRESS. Joint Committee on Labor-Management Relations *Labor-Management Relations*. Wash.: G.P.O., 1948. (Senate Report 986, 80th Congress, 2nd Session, pp 115-31, "UAW and the International Harvester Co"; and pp 154-77, "UAW Local 2 and the Murray Corporation of America)

4719 ———. SENATE. Committee on Government Operations. Permanent Subcommittee on Investigations. *Work Stoppage at Missile Bases*., Report No 1312. Wash.: G.P.O., 1962.

4720 U.S. NATIONAL RECOVERY ADMINISTRATION. *Preliminary Report on Study of Regularization of Employment and Improvement of Labor Conditions in the Automobile Industry*. Wash.: G.P.O., 1935.

4721 UPHOFF, WALTER H. *Kohler on Strike: Thirty Years of Conflict*. Bost.: Beacon, 1966.

4722 VAN DE WATER, JOHN R. "Applications of Labor Law to Construction and Equipping of United States Missile Bases." *Labor Law Journal*, Nov 1961, pp 1003-24.

4723 WALKER, CHARLES R., and ROBERT H. GUEST. *The Man on the Assembly Line*. Cambr.: Harvard U Press, 1952.

4724 WEBER, ARNOLD R. "Craft Representation in Industrial Unions." *Proceedings of the Fourteenth Annual Meeting of the Industrial Relations Research Association*, Dec 28-29, 1961, pp 82-92. Madison: IRRA, 1962.

4725 WEINSTONE, WILLIAM. *The Great Sit-Down Strike*. NY: Worker's Library, 1937. (A pamphlet)

4726 WEIR, STAN. "Doug Fraser's Middle Class Coalition." *Radical America*, Vol 13 (Jan-Feb 1979), 19-29.

4727 WIDICK, B. J., ed. *Auto Work and Its Discontents*. Balt.: Johns Hopkins Press, 1976.

4728 ———, and IRVING HOWE. "The UAW and its Leaders." *Virginia Quarterly Review*, Vol 25 (1949), 34-47.

4729 *With Babies and Banners*. 1978. (Non-fiction film directed by Lorraine Gray)

4730 YETT, JANE. *Farm Labor Struggles in California, 1970-1973, in Light of Reinhold Niebuhr's Concepts of Power and Justice*. Ph D diss, Graduate Theological Union, 1980.

Chemical, Atomic Energy, Oil, Utilities

4731 CHASE, STUART. *A Generation of Industrial Peace: 30 Years of Labor Relations at Standard Oil Company (N.J.).* NY: Standard Oil of New Jersey, 1946.

4732 CRAWFORD, ROBERT C. "Government Intervention in Emergency Labor Disputes in Atomic Energy." *Labor Law Journal,* Jun 1959, pp 414-34.

4733 FEIS, HERBERT. *Labor Relations: A Study Made in the Proctor and Gamble Company.* NY: Adelphi, 1928.

4734 GALENSON, WALTER. "The Petroleum Industry," chap. 12, *The CIO Challenge to the AFL,* Cambr.: Harvard U Press, 1960.

4735 GARRETT, ARTHUR MILTON. *The Impact of an Ambiguous Wage Reopener Clause in a Collective Bargaining Contract and an Employee Poll on Labor Relations in a Petrochemical Plant on the Texas Gulf Coast.* Ph D diss, Texas A&M U, 1971.

4736 HICKS, CLARENCE J. *My Life in Industrial Relations: Fifty Years in the Growth of a Profession.* NY: Harper, 1941.

4737 JOHNSON, DAVID B. "Dispute Settlement in Atomic Energy Plants." *Industrial and Labor Relations Review,* Vol 13 (1959), 38-53.

4738 ———. "Labor Relations in the Atomic Program." *Vanderbilt Law Review,* Vol 12 (1958), 161-78.

4739 MCGREGOR, DOUGLAS, and JOSEPH N. SCANLON. *The Dewey and Almy Chemical Company and the International Chemical Workers Union.* Wash.: National Planning Association, Committee on the Causes of Industrial Peace Under Collective Bargaining, Dec 1948.

4740 MARSHALL, F. RAY. "Independent Unions in the Gulf Coast Petroleum Refining Industry—The Esso Experience." *Labor Law Journal,* Sep 1961, pp 823-40.

4741 MILLER, ERNEST, and T. K. STRATTON. "Oildom's Photographic Historian." *Western Pennsylvania Historical Magazine,* Vol 55 (1972), 1-54.

4742 NATIONAL INDUSTRIAL CONFERENCE BOARD. *Labor Relations in the Atomic Energy Field.* NY: The Board, 1957.

4743 O'CONNOR, HARVEY. *History of the Oil Workers International Union-CIO.* Denver: Oil Workers International Union, CIO, 1950.

4744 PARKER, ALBERT R. *Life and Labor in the Mid-Content Oil Fields, 1859-1945.* Ph D diss, U of Oklahoma, 1951.

4745 ROTHBAUM, MELVIN. *The Government of the Oil, Chemical, and Atomic Workers Union.* NY: Wiley, 1962.

4746 SCAMEHORN, H. LEE. "In the Shadow of Cripple Creek: Florence from 1885 to 1910." *Colorado Magazine,* Vol 55 (1978), 205-29.

4747 SMITH, M. MEAD. "Labor and the Savannah River AEC Project: Part II, Unionization and Industrial Relations." *Monthly Labor Review,* Vol 74 (1952), 12-21.

4748 SOMERS, GERALD G. "Small Establishments and Chemicals." *Proceedings of the Ninth Annual Meeting of the Industrial Relations Research Association,* Dec 28-29, 1956, pp 248-54. Madison: IRRA, 1957.

4749 STRAUS, DONALD B. *The Development of a Policy for Industrial Peace in Atomic Energy.* Wash.: National Planning Association, Committee on the Causes of Industrial Peace Under Collective Bargaining, Jul 1950.

4750 U.S. CONGRESS. Joint Committee on Atomic Energy *Labor Policy in Atomic Energy Plants.* Wash.: G.P.O., 1948.

4751 WEBER, ARNOLD R. "Competitive Unionism in the Chemical Industry." *Industrial and Labor Relations Review,* Vol 13 (1959), 16-37.

4752 ———. "Union-Management Power Relations in the Chemical Industry: The Economic Setting." *Labor Law Journal,* Sep 1958, pp 664-68.

Clothing—Men's

4753 ADAMS, SAMUEL HOPKINS. *Sunrise to Sunset* (a novel). NY: Random House, 1950

4754 ALEXANDER, JOSEPH. *Development of Labor Relations in the New York Garment Industry: A Study in Industry-Wide Collective Bargaining in the Local Area Level.* Ph D diss, NY University, 1955.

4755 AMALGAMATED BANK OF NEW YORK. *The Story of a Bank: The Amalgamated Bank of New York, 1923-1963. Published to Mark the 40th Anniversary of a Unique Banking Institution Established by the Amalgamated Clothing Workers of America, in the Interest of Social Progress.* NY: The Bank, 1963.

4756 AMALGAMATED CLOTHING WORKERS OF AMERICA. *Documentary History.*, 6 vols. NY: The Union, 1914-16.

4757 ———. *Ever Forward: Forty Years of Progress.* NY: The Union, 1954.

4758 ———. NY Joint Boards and Local Unions in NY, 1940 *The Book of the Amalgamated in New York 1914-1940* NY: Amalgamated Joint Boards and Local Unions in New York, 1940.

4759 ———. Research Department *The Clothing Workers of Chicago, 1910-1922.* Chicago: Chicago Joint Board, Amalgamated Clothing Workers of America, 1922. (By Leo Wolman, et al)

4760 BAUM, MORTON J. "Maturity in Industrial Relations: A Case Study." *Industrial and Labor Relations Review*, Vol 4 (1951), 257-64.

4761 BENSMAN, DAVID. *Artisan Culture, Business Union: American Hat Finishers in the 19th Century.* Ph D diss, Columbia U, 1977.

4762 BISNO, BEATRICE. *Tomorrow's Bread* (a novel). NY: Liveright, 1938.

4763 BISSELL, RICHARD P. *7½ Cents* (a novel). Bost.: Little, Brown, 1953.

4764 BOOKBINDER, HYMAN H. and Associates. *To Promote the General Welfare: The Story of the Amalgamated.* NY: Amalgamated Clothing Workers of America, 1950.

4765 BRANDES, JOSEPH. "From Sweatshop to Stability: Jewish Labor between Two World Wars." *YIVO Annual of Jewish Social Science*, Vol 16 (1976), 1-149.

4766 BRAUN, KURT. *Union-Management Cooperation: Experience in the Clothing Industry.* Wash.: Brookings Institution, 1947.

4767 BUDISH, J. M., and GEORGE SOULE. *The New Unionism in the Clothing Industry.* NY: Harcourt, Brace, and Howe, 1920.

4768 CARPENTER, JESSE THOMAS. *Competition and Collective Bargaining in the Needle Trades, 1910-1967.* Ithaca: NY State School of Industrial and Labor Relations, Cornell U, 1972.

4769 CHANDLER, MARGARET K. "Case Study 3, Garment Manufacture." *Labor Management Relations in Illini City*, Vol 1. Champaign: U of Illinois, 1953.

4770 CHICAGO TRADE AND LABOR ASSEMBLY. *New Slavery: Investigation into the Sweating System as Applied to the Manufacturing of Wearing Apparel.* Chicago: Rights of Labor Office, 1891.

4771 COLLINS, GEORGE L. *The Amalgamated Clothing Workers.* (Unpublished manuscript, U of Wisconsin)

4772 COOPER, LYLE W. "The Clothing Workers' Factory in Milwaukee." *Harvard Business Review*, Vol 9 (1930), 89-100.

4773 CROWE, ROBERT. *The Reminiscences of Robert Crowe, the Octogenarian Tailor.* Publisher unknown, n.d. (Can be found at Library of Congress)

4774 ELAZAR, DANIEL J, ed. "Working Conditions in Chicago in the Early 20th Century: Testimony before the Illinois Senatorial Vice Committee, 1913." *American Jewish Archives*, Vol 21 (1969), 149-71.

4775 FELDMAN, EGAL. *Fit for Men: A Study of New York's Clothing Trade.* Wash.: Public Affairs Press, 1960.

4776 FRASER, STEVE. "Dress Rehearsal for the New Deal: Shop Floor Insurgents, Political Elites, and Industrial Democracy in the Amalgamated Clothing Workers," pp

212-55, *Working Class America: Essays on Labor, Community, and American Society*, Michael Frisch & Daniel J. Walkowitz, eds. Urbana: U of Illinois Press, 1983.

4777 GALENSON, WALTER. "The Men's Clothing Industry," chap. 7, *The CIO Challenge to the AFL*, Cambr.: Harvard U Press, 1960.

4778 GALTON, FRANK W., ed. *The Tailoring Trade: Select Documents Illustrating the History of Trade Unionism*. NY: Longmans, Green, 1896.

4779 GOUKE, CECIL GRANVILLE. *The Amalgamated Clothing Workers of America, 1940-1960*. Ph D diss, New York U, 1966.

4780 HAAS, FRANCIS J. *Shop Collective Bargaining: A Study of Wage Determination in the Men's Garment Industry*. Wash.: Catholic U of America, 1922.

4781 HARDMAN, J. B. S. "The Needle-Trades Unions: A Labor Movement at Fifty." *Social Research*, Vol 27 (1960), 321-58.

4782 ———. et al. *Fiftieth Anniversary Souvenir History of the New York Joint Board, Amalgamated Clothing Workers of America, AFL-CIO, 1914-1964*. NY: NY Joint Board, Amalgamated Clothing Workers of America, 1964.

4783 HARDMAN, J. B. S., ed. *The Amalgamated—Today and Tomorrow*. NY: Amalgamated Clothing Workers of America, 1939.

4784 HARDY, JACK. *The Clothing Workers*. NY: International Publishers, 1935.

4785 HELFGOTT, ROY B. "Trade Unionism among the Jewish Garment Workers of Britain and the United States." *Labor History*, Vol 2 (1961), 202-14.

4786 ILLINOIS BUREAU OF LABOR STATISTICS. *Seventh Biennial Report*. Springfield, IL: The Bureau, 1893. (See Part II, "The Sweating System in Chicago.")

4787 KIRSHBAUM, LOUIS. *The Sewing Circle*. Los Angeles: De Vorss, 1952.

4788 "Labor Violence and Corruption." *Business Week*, Aug 31, 1957, pp 76-90. (The Amalgamated Clothing Workers and Louis [Buchalter] Lepke)

4789 LAMAR, ELDEN. *The Clothing Workers in Philadelphia: History of Their Struggles for Union and Security*. Phila.: Amalgamated Clothing Workers of America, Philadelphia Joint Board, 1940.

4790 MARCOVITZ, LAZARUS. "Out of Labor's Past—Way Back in Boston." *Labor and Nation,*, Jan-Feb 1948, pp 33-35.

4791 MARIMPIETRI, A. D. *From These Beginnings—The Making of the Amalgamated*. Chicago: Amalgamated Clothing Workers of America, Chicago Joint Board, 1943.

4792 MITCHELL, BROADUS. "Industrial Relations in the Men's and Women's Garment Industry," chap. 23, *Labor in Postwar America*, Colston Warne, ed. Brooklyn: Remsen Press, 1949.

4793 MORGAN, RITA. *Arbitration in the Men's Clothing Industry in New York City: A Case Study of Industrial Arbitration and Conference Method with Particular Reference to Its Educational Implications*. NY: Teachers' College, Columbia U, 1940.

4794 MYERS, ROBERT J., and JOSEPH W. BLOCH. "Men's Clothing," chap. 8, *How Collective Bargaining Works*, Harry A. Millis, research director. NY: Twentieth Century Fund, 1945.

4795 NATIONAL INDUSTRIAL CONFERENCE BOARD. *Experience with Trade Union Agreements—Clothing Industries*. NY: Century, 1921.

4796 NESTEL, LOUIS P. *Labor Relations in the Laundry Industry in Greater New York*. NY: Claridge, 1950.

4797 NEW YORK CLOTHING MANUFACTURERS' EXCHANGE, INC. *The New York Story—A History of the New York Clothing Industry, 1924-1949*. NY: The Exchange, 1949.

4798 "New York State Survey of Industry—Apparel." *Industrial Bulletin*, Vol 26 (1947), 5-9.

4799 PASSERO, ROSARA. *Ethnicity in the Men's Ready Made Clothing Industry, 1880-1950. The Italian Experience in Philadelphia*. Ph D diss, U of Pennsylvania, 1978.

4800 POPE, JESSE E. *The Clothing Industry in New York*. Columbia: U of Missouri, 1905.

4801 RAYACK, ELTON. "The Impact of Unionism on Wages in the Men's Clothing Industry, 1911-1956." *Labor Law Journal*, Sep 1958, 674-88.

4802 ROVERE, RICHARD H. "Sidney Hillman and the Housebroken Workers." *The Reporter*, Feb 17, 1953, pp 36-40.

4803 SAMUEL, HOWARD D., and LYNNE RHODES. *Profile of a Union.* NY: Amalgamated Clothing Workers of America, 1958.

4804 SCHLOSSBERG, JOSEPH. *The Rise of the Clothing Workers.* NY: Amalgamated Clothing Workers of America, 1921.

4805 SEIDMAN, JOEL. *The Needle Trades.* NY: Farrar and Rinehart, 1942.

4806 STEIN, LEON. "Out of the Sweatshop—a Union." *American Federationist*, Vol 84 (Jun 1977), 6-14.

4807 STOWELL, CHARLES J. *The Journeymen Tailors' Union of North America: A Study in Trade Union Policy.* Urbana: U of Illinois, 1918.

4808 ———. *Studies in Trade Unionism in the Custom Tailoring Trade.* Bloomington: Journeymen Tailors' Union of America, 1913.

4809 STRAUS, DONALD B. *Hickey-Freeman Company and the Amalgamated Clothing Workers of America.* Wash.: National Planning Association, 1949.

4810 STRONG, EARL D. *The Amalgamated Clothing Workers of America.* Grinnell, IA: Herald Register, 1940.

4811 U.S. COMMISSION ON INDUSTRIAL RELATIONS (1912). "Men's Garment Trades of New York City," Vol 2, pp 1963-2050, *Final Report*, Wash.: G.P.O., 1916.

4812 U.S. NATIONAL LABOR RELATIONS BOARD. Division of Economic Research "The Clothing Industry," chap. 5, *Written Trade Agreements in Collective Bargaining*, Wash.: G.P.O., 1940.

4813 WEILER, N. SUE. "Walkout: the Chicago Men's Garment Workers Strike, 1910-1911." *Chicago History*, Vol 8 (Winter, 1979), 238-49.

4814 WOMEN'S TRADE UNION LEAGUE OF CHICAGO. *Official Report of the Strike Committee, Chicago Garment Workers' Strike, October 29, 1910-February 18, 1911* Chicago: The League, 1911.

4815 ZARETZ, CHARLES E. *The Amalgamated Clothing Workers of America: A Study in Progressive Trades Unionism.* NY: Ancon, 1934.

Clothing—Women's

4816 ASCH, SHALOM. *East River* (a novel). NY: Putnam, 1946.

4817 BARBASH, JACK. "The I.L.G.W.U. as an Organization in the Age of Dubinsky." *Labor History*, Vol 9 (1968), Special Supplement, 98-115.

4818 BERMAN, HYMAN. *The Era of the Protocol: A Chapter in the History of the International Ladies' Garment Workers' Union, 1910-16.* Ph D diss, Columbia U, 1956.

4819 BISNO, BEATRICE. *Tomorrow's Bread* (a novel). NY: Liveright, 1938.

4820 BRISSENDEN, PAUL F., and JOHN M. KEATING. "Union-Management Cooperation in Millinery Manufacturing in the New York Metropolitan Area." *Industrial and Labor Relations Review*, Vol 2 (1948), 3-32.

4821 BRYNER, EDNA. *The Garment Trades.* Cleveland: Survey Committee of the Cleveland Foundation, 1916.

4822 BUHLE, MARI JO. "Socialist Women and the 'Girl Strikers,' Chicago, 1910." *Signs*, Vol 1 (1976), 1039-51.

4823 BULLARD, ARTHUR (ALBERT EDWARDS, PSEUD.). *Comrade Yetta* (a novel). NY: Macmillan, 1913.

4824 CARPENTER, JESSE THOMAS. *Competition and Collective Bargaining in the Needle Trades, 1910-1967.* Ithaca: NY State School of Industrial and Labor Relations, Cornell U, 1972.

4825 CARSEL, WILFRED. *A History of the Chicago Ladies' Garment Workers' Union.* Chicago: Normandie House, 1940.

4826 CHICAGO TRADE AND LABOR ASSEMBLY. *New Slavery: Investigation into the Sweating System as Applied to the Manufacturing of Wearing Apparel.* Chicago: Rights of Labor Office, 1891.

4827 CLARK, SUE, and EDITH WYATT. *Making Both Ends Meet.* NY: Macmillan, 1911. (See chap. 2, "The Shirtwaist Makers' Strike," & chap. 5, "The Cloak Makers' Strike and the Preferential shop.")

4828 COHEN, HYMAN, and LESTER COHEN. *Aaron Traum* (a novel). NY: Liveright, 1930.

4829 COHEN, JULIUS H. *Law and Order in Industry: Five Years' Experience.* NY: Macmillan, 1916.

4830 ———. *They Builded Better Than They Knew.* NY: Messner, 1946.

4831 CRONE, HARRY. *35 Northeast: A Short Story of the Northeast Department, International Ladies' Garment Workers' Union, AFL-CIO, Based on the Reminiscences and Diaries of David Gingold and Official ILGWU Records.* NY: Northeast Department, ILGWU, 1970.

4832 DANISH, MAX D., and LEON STEIN, eds. *ILGWU News—History, 1900-1950.* NY: International Ladies' Garment Workers' Union, 1950.

4833 DAVIS, PHILIP. *And Crown Thy Good.* NY: Philosophical Library, 1952.

4834 EISNER, J. MICHAEL. "Politics, Legislation and the ILGWU." *American Journal of Economics and Sociology*, Vol 28 (1969), 301-14.

4835 *The Fight's Just Begun: Fifty Years with Local 66, 1913-1963.* NY: ILGWU, 1963.

4836 GALENSON, WALTER. "The Women's Clothing Industry," chap. 8, *The CIO Challenge to the AFL*, Cambr.: Harvard U Press, 1960.

4837 *The Garment Jungle.* 1957. (Feature film directed by Vincent Sherman & an uncredited Robert Aldrich)

4838 "The Garment Workers." *Fortune*, Nov 1946, pp 173-79, 226-29.

4839 GOMBERG, WILLIAM. "Union Policy Experimentation in a Volatile Industry." *Labor History*, Vol 9 (1968), Special Supplement, 69-81.

4840 GUROWSKY, DAVID. *Factional Disputes within the ILGWU, 1919-1928.* Ph D diss, SUNY-Binghamton, 1978.

4841 HALL, BURTON. "I.L.G.W.U.: Its Enemies and its Friends." *New Politics*, Vol 11 (Fall 1976), 46-50.

4842 HERBERT, WILL. "Trade Unions and Minority Problems—The Old-Timers and the Newcomers: Ethnic Group Relations in a Needle Trades Union." *The Journal of Social Issues*, Vol (1953), 12-19.

4843 "I.L.G. Archives: The Past's Role in our Present." *Justice*, Aug 1, 1976, p 9.

4844 INTERNATIONAL LADIES' GARMENT WORKERS' UNION. *The Position of the International Ladies' Garment Workers' Union in Relation to CIO and AFL, 1934-1938.* NY: The Union, 1938.

4845 ———. *Souvenir History of the Strike of the Ladies' Waist Makers' Union.* NY: The Union, 1910.

4846 ———. General Executive Board *The Hourwich Affair.* NY: The Union, 1914.

4847 ———. Welfare and Health Benefits Department *The Thread of Life.* Atlantic City, NJ: The Union, 1956.

4848 KAZIN, ALFRED. "A Brooklyn Childhood—The Kitchen." *The New Yorker*, Sep 15, 1951, pp 53-63.

4849 LANG, HARRY. *"62": Biography of a Union* (Undergarment and Negligee Workers Union). NY: The International Ladies' Garment Workers' Union, Local 62, 1940.

4850 LAZAR, ROBERT E. "The International Ladies Garment Workers' Union Archives." *Labor History*, Vol 22 (1982), 528-33.

4851 LORWIN, LEWIS (LOUIS LEVINE). *The Women's Garment Workers: A History of the International Ladies' Garment Workers' Union.* NY: Huebsch, 1924.

4852 M., D. "Der Onhoib fun der International Ladies' Garment Workers' Union." *Bund Archives. Bulletin*, Nov 1965, pp 1-4.

4853 Magarik, Larry L. "Clothing Workers vs. Farah." *Dissent*, Vol 21 (1974), 14-15.

4854 Malkiel, T. *The Diary of a Shirtwaist Striker*. NY: Co-operative Press, 1910.

4855 Meyersburg, Dorothy. *Seventh Avenue* (a novel). NY: Dutton, 1940.

4856 Mitchell, Broadus. "Industrial Relations in the Men's and Women's Garment Industries," chap. 23, *Labor in Postwar America*, Colston Warne, ed. Brooklyn: Remsen Press, 1949.

4857 *Mother is on Strike*. 1960. (Non-fiction film produced by the ILGWU)

4858 Munts, Raymond, and Mary Louise Munts. "Welfare History of the I.L.G.W.U." *Labor History*, Vol 9 (1968), Special Supplement, 82-97.

4859 Myerson, Michael. "ILGWU: Fighting for Lower Wages." *Ramparts*, Vol 8 (Oct 1969), 50-55.

4860 National Industrial Conference Board. *Experience with Trade Union Agreements—Clothing Industries*. NY: Century, 1921.

4861 New York State. *Report of the Governor's Advisory Commission, Cloak, Suit and Skirt Industry, New York City*. NY: Bureau of Research, Cloak, Suit and Skirt Industry, 1926.

4862 Newman, Pauline. "How Women Forged Early Union." *Allied Industrial Worker*, Vol 19 (Aug 1976), 7.

4863 ———. "We Needed Hope More." *GBBA Horizons*, Vol 24 (Sep 1976), 5. (1909 Triangle Shirt-waist Co strike)

4864 Oko, Dorothy Kuhn. "David Dubinsky and the International Ladies' Garment Workers' Union. A Selected Bibliography." *Labor History*, Vol ((1968), Special Supplement, 116-26.

4865 Oneal, James. *A History of the Amalgamated Ladies' Garment Cutters' Union, Local 10, Affiliated with the International Ladies' Garment Workers' Union*. NY: International Ladies' Garment Workers' Union, Local 10, 1927.

4866 "Panorama of Progress—Eight I.L.G.W.U. Decades." *Justice*, Vol 62 (Jun 1980), 9-16.

4867 Pierson, Frank C. *Collective Bargaining Systems*. Wash.: American Council on Public Affairs, 1942. (See pp 133-69)

4868 Rabinowitz, Dorothy. "Case of the I.L.G.W.U." *Dissent*, Vol 19 (1972), 83-90.

4869 Rich, J. C. "How the Garment Unions Licked the Communists." *Saturday Evening Post*, Aug 9, 1947, pp 3-26, 39.

4870 Rivera A. "The Saga of the 'Shirt Capital' of America and the Role of the Amalgamated." *Advance*, Vol 62 (Jan 1976), 12.

4871 Robinson, Dwight E. *Collective Bargaining and Market Control in the New York Coat and Suit Industry*. NY: Columbia U Press, 1949.

4872 Rosenberg, Abraham. *The Cloakmakers and Their Unions: Memoirs of a Cloakmaker* (in Yiddish). NY: Cloak Operators' Union, Local 1, 1920.

4873 Seaman, Bernard, and Max D. Danish. *The Story of the ILGWU*. NY: International Ladies' Garment Workers' Union, 1947.

4874 Seidman, Joel. "The I.L.G.W.U. in the Dubinsky Period." *Labor History*, Vol 9 (1968), Special Supplement, 55-68.

4875 ———. *The Needle Trades*. NY: Farrar & Rinehart, 1942.

4876 Stein, Leon. *The Triangle Fire*. Phila.: Lippincott, 1962.

4877 Stolberg, Benjamin. *Tailor's Progress: The Story of a Famous Union and the Men Who Made It*. Garden City: Doubleday, 1944.

4878 Tax, Meredith. *Rivington Street* (a novel). NY: Morrow, 1982.

4879 Teper, Lazare. *The Women's Garment Industry*. NY: International Ladies' Garment Workers' Union, 1937.

4880 U.S. Commission on Industrial Relations (1912). "Cloak, Suit, and Waist Industry," Vol 2, pp 1025-161, *Final Report*, Wash.: G.P.O., 1916.

4881 ———. "The Women's Garment Industry of Philadelphia," Vol 4, pp 2091-171, *Final Report*, Wash.: G.P.O., 1916.

4882 U.S. CONGRESS. HOUSE. Committee on Education and Labor. *Investigation of the Garment Industry*. Wash.: G.P.O., 1962.

4883 U.S. NATIONAL LABOR RELATIONS BOARD. Division of Economic Research "The Clothing Industry," chap. 5, *Written Trade Agreements in Collective Bargaining*, Wash.: G.P.O., 1940.

4884 VANDECARR, ANNIE B. *Frances Neureld* (a novel). NY: Warwick, 1950.

4885 WEISS, SAMUEL. "*Die Gleichheit*, sof fun artikl A. T. Die Zeitungen un shurneln fund I.L.G.W.U." *Bund Archives. Bulletin*, Vol 6 (1965), 12-15.

4886 *With These Hands*. 1950. (Non-fiction film produced by the ILGWU)

4887 WOLFSON, THERESA. "Role of the ILGWU in Stabilizing the Women's Garment Industry." *Industrial and Labor Relations Review*, Vol 4 (1950), 33-43.

Coal

4888 *An Account of the Coal Bank Disaster at Blue Rock, Ohio*. Malta, OH: no publisher indicated, 1856.

4889 ACKERMAN, JOHN A. "The Impact of the Coal Strike of 1977-1978." *Industrial and Labor Relations Review*, Vol 32 (1979), 175-88.

4890 AKURAND, HAROLD. "The Anthracite Miner: An Occupational Analysis." *Pennsylvania Magazine of History and Biography*, Vol 104 (1980), 462-73.

4891 AMSDEN, JON, and STEPHEN BRIER. "Coal Miners on Strike: The Transformation of Strike Demands and the Formation of a National Union." *Journal of Interdisciplinary History*, Vol 7 (1977), 583-616.

4892 ANGLE, PAUL M. *Bloody Williamson: A Chapter in American Lawlessness*. NY: Knopf, 1952.

4893 ANSLEY, FRAN, and BRENDA BELL. "Strikes at Davidson and Wilder, 1932." *Southern Exposure*, Vol 1 (Winter 1973), 114-36.

4894 ———, and BRENDA BELL, eds. "Miners Insurrections/Convict Labor." *Southern Exposure*, Vol 1 (Winter 1973), 144-59.

4895 ANTHRACITE BUREAU OF INFORMATION. *The Anthracite Strike of 1922: A Chronological Statement*. Phila.: The Bureau, 1922.

4896 ———. *The Anthracite Strike of 1925-1926: A Chronological Statement*. Phila.: The Bureau, 1926.

4897 "The Anthracite Coal Production Control Plan." *University of Pennsylvania Law Review*, Vol 102 (1954), 368-94.

4898 ARBLE, MEADE. *The Long Tunnel: A Coal Miner's Journal*. NY: Atheneum, 1976.

4899 ARMBRISTER, TREVOR. *Act of Vengeance: the Yablonski Murders and Their Solution*. NY: Saturday Review Press/Dutton, 1975.

4900 ARONOWITZ, STANLEY. "Miners for Democracy." *Liberation*, Vol 17 (1973), 4, 36.

4901 ATHERTON, SARAH H. *Mark's Own* (a novel). Indianapolis: Bobbs-Merril, 1941.

4902 ATKINSON, HENRY. *The Church and Industrial Warfare: A Report on the Labor Troubles in Colorado and Michigan*. NY: Federal Council of the Churches of Christ in America, 1914.

4903 AURAND, HAROLD W. *The Anthracite Mine Workers, 1869-1897: A Functional Approach to Labor History*. Ph D diss, Pennsylvania State U, 1969.

4904 ———. "The Anthracite Strike of 1887-1888." *Pennsylvania History*, Vol 35 (1968), 169-85.

4905 ———. *From the Molly Maguires to the United Mine Workers: the Social Ecology of an Industrial Union, 1869-1897*. Phila: Temple U Press, 1971.

4906 ———. "Social Motivation of the Anthracite Mine Workers: 1901-1920." *Labor History*, Vol 18 (1977), 360-65.

4907 ———. "The Workingmen's Benevolent Association." *Labor History*, Vol 7 (1966), 19-34.

4908 Bailey, Kenneth. "'Grim Visaged Men' and the West Virginia National Guard in the 1912-1913 Paint and Cabin Creek Strike." *West Virginia History*, Vol 41 (1980), 111-25.

4909 Baker, Ralph H. *The National Bituminous Coal Commission: Administration of the Bituminous Coal Act, 1937-1941*. Balt.: Johns Hopkins Press, 1942.

4910 Baratz, Morton S. *The Union and the Coal Industry*. New Haven: Yale U Press, 1955.

4911 Bauman, John F. "Ethnic Adaptation in a Southwestern Pennsylvania Coal Patch, 1910-1940." *Journal of Ethnic Studies*, Vol 7 (Fall 1979), 1-23.

4912 Beame, Edmond M. "The Jacksonville Agreement: Quest for Stability in Coal." *Industrial and Labor Relations Review*, Vol 8 (1955), 195-203.

4913 Beard, Daniel C. *Moonblight and Six Feet of Romance* (a novel). NY: Charles Webster, 1892.

4914 Bensman, David. "Trouble in the Coal Field." *Dissent*, Vol 25 (1978), 253-60.

4915 Benson, H. W. "Four Hundred Miners in Washington Demand Help for Union Democracy." *Union Democracy in Action*, May 1971, pp 1-2.

4916 ———. "Miners for Democracy: A Report From West Virginia." *Dissent*, Vol 19 (1972), 632-38.

4917 Berney, Barbara. "The Rise and Fall of the UMW Fund." *Southern Exposure*, Vol 6 (Summer 1978), 95-102.

4918 Bernstein, Irving, and Hugh G. Lovell. "Are Coal Strikes National Emergencies?" *Industrial and Labor Relations Review*, Vol 6 (1953), 352-67.

4919 Berthoff, Rowland. "The Social Order of the Anthracite Region, 1825-1902." *Pennsylvania Magazine of History and Biography*, Vol 89 (1965), 261-91.

4920 *Black Fury*. 1935. (Warner Brothers feature film)

4921 Blankenhorn, Heber. *The Strike for Union: A Study of the Non-Union Question in Coal and the Problems of a Democratic Movement Based on the Record of the Somerset Strike*. NY: Wilson, 1924.

4922 Bloch, Louis. *The Coal Miners' Insecurity*. NY: Russell Sage Foundation, 1922.

4923 ———. *Labor Agreements in Coal Mines: A Case Study of the Administration of Agreements Between Miners and Operators' Organizations in the Bituminous Coal Mines of Illinois*. NY: Russell Sage Foundation, 1931.

4924 Bowman, John, and Thomas Coode. "'Old Bell': A New Deal Chronicle of Poverty and Isolation in South Western Pennsylvania." *Western Pennsylvania Historical Magazine*, Vol 63 (1980), 215-29.

4925 Branscome, J. "Mine Workers Disunited: Alienation in Appalachia." *Christianity and Crisis*, Vol 38 (1978), 8-10.

4926 Brett, Jeanne, and Stephen Goldberg. "Wildcat Strikes in Bituminous Coal Mining." *Industrial and Labor Relations Review*, Vol 32 (1979), 465-83.

4927 "Brookside Mine 1974." *Southern Exposure*, Vol 2 (Spring-Summer 1974), 52-55.

4928 Brophy, John. "Long Range Plans for the Coal Industry and Union." *Labor and Nation*, Sep-Oct 1947, pp 32-35.

4929 Brown, Rollo W. *Firemakers* (a novel). NY: Coward-McCann, 1931.

4930 Bubka, Tony. "The Harlan County Coal Strike of 1931." *Labor History*, Vol 11 (1970), 41-57.

4931 Carpenter, Thomas. *Labor Conflict in the Mining Industry of Coeur d'Alenes, 1892 and 1899*. Ph D diss, New York U, 1973.

4932 Carter, John F., Jr. *The Destroyers* (a novel). Wash.: Neale, 1907.

4933 Cary, Lorin Lee. "The Reorganized United Mine Workers of America, 1930-1931." *Illinois State Historical Society Journal*, Vol 66 (1973), 245-70.

4934 Chandler, Alfred D. "Anthracite Coal and the Beginnings of the Industrial Revolution in the United States." *Business History Review*, Vol 46 (1972), 141-47.

4935 CHRISTENSON, C. L. "The Theory of the Offset Factor: The Impact of Labor Disputes upon Coal Production." *The American Economic Review*, Vol 43 (1953), 513-47.

4936 CLAP, THOMAS C. *The Bituminous Coal Strike of 1934*. Ph D diss, U of Toledo, 1974.

4937 "Coal I: The Industrial Darkness," *Fortune*, Mar 1947, pp 86-95, 221-32.

4938 "Coal II: The Coal Miner Speaks," *Fortune*, Mar 1947, pp 97-99, 202-6.

4939 "Coal III: The Fuel Revolution," *Fortune*, Apr 1947, 99-105, 238-54.

4940 COLEMAN, MCALISTER. *Men and Coal*. NY: Farrar and Rinehart, 1943.

4941 ———, and H. S. RAUSHENBUSH. *Red Neck* (a novel). NY: Random House, 1936.

4942 CONROY, JACK. *The Disinherited* (a novel). NY: Civici-Friede, 1933.

4943 COOKE, GRACE M. *The Grapple* (a novel). Bost.: Page, 1905.

4944 CORBIN, DAVID. *Life, Work and Rebellion in the Coal Fields: The Southern West Virginia Miners, 1880-1922*. Urbana: U of Illinois Press, 1981.

4945 CORNELL, ROBERT J. *The Anthracite Coal Strike of 1902*. Wash.: Catholic U of America Press, 1957.

4946 CRAFT, JAMES A. "Transition in the Mineworkers Union and the Impact on Labor Relations." *Pittsburgh Business Review*, Vol 45 (Summer 1976), 1-7.

4947 CRAVENS, JOHN N. "Two Miners and Their Families in the Thurber-Strawn Coal Mines, 1905-1918." *Year Book of the West Texas Historical Association*, Vol 48 (1969), 115-26.

4948 CULIN, STEWART. *A Trooper's Narrative of Service in the Anthracite Coal Strike, 1902*. Phila.: Jacobs, 1903.

4949 DARGAN, OLIVE T. (FIELDING BURKE, PSEUD.). *Sons of the Stranger* (a novel). NY: Longmans, Green, 1947.

4950 ———. *Sons of the Stranger* (a novel). NY: Longman's Green, 1947.

4951 DESTLER, CHESTER M. "On the Eve of the Anthracite Coal Strike Arbitration: Henry Demerest Lloyd at United Mine Workers Headquarters." *Labor History*, Vol 13 (1972), 279-95.

4952 DIX, KEITH. *Work Relations in the Coal Industry: The Hand-Loading era, 1880-1930*. Morgantown: West Virginia U, 1977.

4953 EKLUND, MONICA. "Massacre at Ludlow." *Southeast Economy and Society*, Vol 14 (Fall, 1978), 26-31.

4954 ELLIOTT, RUSSELL R. *Radical Labor in the Nevada Mining Booms, 1900-1920*. Carson City, NV: State Printing Office, 1961.

4955 EVANGELA, MARY, SISTER. "Bishop Spalding's Work on the Anthracite Coal Strike Commission." *Catholic Historical Review*, Vol 38 (1942), 184-205.

4956 EVANS, CHRIS. *History of the United Mine Workers of America*. Indianapolis: The United Mine Workers of America, 1918.

4957 EVERLING, ARTHUR C. *Tactics over Strategy in the United Mine Workers of America: Internal Politics and the Question of the Nationalization of the Mines, 1908-1923*. Ph D diss, Pennsylvania State U, 1977.

4958 EWEN, LYNDA ANN. *Which Side Are You On? The Brookside Mine Strike in Harlan County, Kentucky*. Chicago: Vanguard, 1979.

4959 FEDERAL COUNCIL OF THE CHURCHES OF CHRIST IN AMERICA. Commission on the Church and Social Service *The Coal Controversy*. NY: The Council, 1922.

4960 ———. Department of Research and Education *The Coal Strike in Western Pennsylvania*. NY: The Council, 1928.

4961 FILIPPELLI, RONALD L. "Diary of a Strike: George Medrick and the Coal Strike of 1927 in Western Pennsylvania." *Pennsylvania History*, Vol 43 (1976), 253-66.

4962 FINLEY, JOSEPH E. *The Corrupt Kingdom: The Rise and Fall of the United Mine Workers*. NY: Simon & Schuster, 1972.

4963 FISHER, THOMAS R. *Industrial Disputes and Federal Legislation, with Special Reference to the Railroad, Coal, Steel, and Automobile Industries in the United States since 1900*. NY: Columbia U Press, 1940.

4964 FISHER, WALDO E. "Anthracite," chap. 6, *How Collective Bargaining Works*, Harry A. Millis, research director. NY: Twentieth Century Fund, 1945.

4965 ———. "Bituminous Coal," chap. 5, *How Collective Bargaining Works*, Harry A. Millis, research director. NY: Twentieth Century Fund, 1945.

4966 ———. *Collective Bargaining in the Bituminous Coal Industry*. Phila.: U of Pennsylvania Press, 1948.

4967 ———. *Economic Consequences of the Seven-Hour Day and Wage Changes in the Bituminous Coal Industry*. Phila.: U of Pennsylvania Press, 1939.

4968 ———, and A. BEZANSON. *Wage Rates and Working Time in the Bituminous Coal Industry, 1912-1922*. Phila.: U of Pennsylvania Press, 1932.

4969 ———, and CHARLES M. JAMES. *Minimum Price Fixing in the Bituminous Coal Industry*. Princeton: Princeton U Press, 1955.

4970 FOSTER, JACK R. "The Coal Strike of 1943." *Connecticut Review*, Oct 1972, pp 57-69.

4971 ———. *Union on Trial: The United Mine Workers of America, District No 11 of Indiana, 1930-1940*. Ph D diss, Ball State U, 1968.

4972 FOSTER, JAMES C. "The Western Federation Comes to Alaska." *Pacific Northwest Quarterly*, Vol 66 (1975), 161-73.

4973 FOWLER, CHARLES B. *Collective Bargaining in the Bituminous Coal Industry*. NY: Prentice-Hall, 1927.

4974 FOX, DANIEL, and JUDITH STONE. "Black Lung: Miners' Militancy and Medical Uncertainty, 1968-72." *Bulletin of Historical Medicine*, Vol 54 (1980), 43-63.

4975 FRISCH, PAUL. "Labor Conflict at Eureka, 1886-1897." *Utah Historical Quarterly*, Vol 49 (1981), 145-56.

4976 GALENSON, WALTER. "Coal Mining," chap. 4, *The CIO Challenge to the AFL*, Cambr.: Harvard U Press, 1960.

4977 GIBBONS, WILLIAM F. *Those Black Diamond Men* (a novel). NY: Revell, 1902.

4978 GILFILLAN, LAUREN. *I Went to Pit College*. NY: Viking, 1934.

4979 GINGER, RAY. "Company-Sponsored Welfare Plans in the Anthracite Industry before 1900." *Bulletin of the Business Historical Society*, Vol 27 (1953), 112-20.

4980 GLASSER, CARRIE. "Union Wage Policy in Bituminous Coal." *Industrial and Labor Relations Review*, Vol 1 (1948), 609-23.

4981 GOODRICH, CARTER L. *The Miner's Freedom*. Bost.: Marshall Jones, 1925.

4982 GOWASKIE, JOSEPH MICHAEL. "From Conflict to Cooperation: John Mitchell and Bituminous Coal Operators, 1898-1908." *The Historian*, Vol 38 (1976), 669-88.

4983 GRAEBNER, WILLIAM. *Coal Mining Safety in the Progressive Period*. Lexington: U of Kentucky Press, 1976.

4984 ———. "The Coal-Mine Operator and Safety: A Study of Business Reform in the Progressive Period." *Labor History*, Vol 14 (1973), 483-505.

4985 GRAHAM, JOHN. "Upton Sinclair and the Ludlow Massacre." *Colorado Quarterly*, Vol 21 (Summer, 1972), 55-67.

4986 GRAHAM, MARGARET (GRACE LOIS MCDONALD, PSEUD.). *Swing Shift* (a novel). NY: Citadel, 1951.

4987 GREEN, ARCHIE. "The Death of Mother Jones." *Labor History*, Vol 1 (1960), 68-80.

4988 ———. "A Discography of American Coal Miners' Songs." *Labor History*, Vol 2 (1961), 101-15.

4989 ———. *Only a Miner: Studies in Recorded Coalmining Songs*. Urbana: U of Illinois Press, 1972.

4990 GREEN, JAMES R. "Holding the Line: Miners' Militancy and the Strike of 1978." *Radical America*, Vol 12 (May-Jul 1978), 3-27.

4991 GREENE, HOMER. *Coal and the Coal Mines*. Bost.: Houghton Mifflin, 1889.

4992 GREENE, VICTOR R. *The Slavic Community on Strike: Immigrant Labor in Pennsylvania Anthracite*. Notre Dame: Notre Dame U Press, 1968.

4993 GREENSLADE, RUSH V. *The Economic Effects of Collective Bargaining in Bituminous Coal Mining*. Ph D diss, U of Chicago, 1953.

4994 GROGAN, DENNIS S. "Unionization in Boulder and Weld Counties to 1890." *Colorado Magazine*, Vol 44 (1967), 324-41.

4995 GROSSMAN, JONATHAN. "The Great Coal Strike of 1902." *Worklife*, Vol 1 (Jul 1976), 28-32.

4996 GUTMAN, HERBERT G. "The Braidwood Lockout of 1874." *Journal of the Illinois State Historical Society*, Vol 53 (1960), 5-28.

4997 ———. "The Buena Vista Affair, 1874-1875." *The Pennsylvania Magazine of History and Biography*, Vol 88 (1964), 251-93.

4998 ———. "Reconstruction in Ohio: Negroes in the Hocking Valley Coal Mines in 1873 and 1874." *Labor History*, Vol 3 (1962), 243-64.

4999 ———. "Two Lockouts in Pennsylvania 1873-1874." *The Pennsylvania Magazine of History and Biography*, Vol 88 (1959), 307-26.

5000 HADSELL, RICHARD M., and WILLIAM COFFEY. "From Law and Order to Class Warfare: Baldwin-Felts Detectives in the Southern West Virginia Coal Fields." *West Virginia History*, Vol 40 (1979), 268-86.

5001 HAMILTON, WALTON H. *A Way of Order for Bituminous Coal*. NY: Macmillan, 1928.

5002 ———, and HELEN R. WRIGHT. *The Case of Bituminous Coal*. NY: Macmillan, 1925.

5003 *Harlan County, U.S.A.* 1976. (Documentary produced & directed by Barbara Kopple)

5004 HARRIS, SHELDON H. "Letters from West Virginia: Management's Version of the 1902 Coal Strike." *Labor History*, Vol 10 (1969), 229-40.

5005 HARVEY, KATHERINE A. *The Best-Dressed Miners: Life and Labor in the Maryland Coal Region, 1835-1910*. Ithaca: Cornell U Press, 1969.

5006 ———. "The Knights of Labor in the Maryland Coal Fields, 1878-1882." *Labor History*, Vol 10 (1969), 555-83.

5007 HARVEY, KATHERINE A., ed. *The Lonaconing Journals: The Founding of a Coal and Iron Community, 1837-1840*. Phila.: American Philosophical Society, 1977.

5008 HICKEN, VICTOR. "The Virden and Pana Mine Wars of 1898." *Journal of the Illinois State Historical Society*, Vol 52 (1959), 263-78.

5009 HINKLE, STACY C. "The Miners' War." *American Aviation Historical Society Journal*, Vol 20 (1975), 161.

5010 HINRICHS, A. F. *The United Mine Workers of America and the Non-Union Coal Fields*. NY: Columbia U Press, 1923.

5011 HOPKINS, GEORGE W. *The Miners for Democracy: Insurgency in the United Mine Workers of America, 1970-72*. Ph D diss, U of North Carolina, 1977.

5012 HORNBEIN, MARJORIE. "Josephine Roche: Social Worker and Coal Operator." *Colorado Magazine*, Vol 53 (1976), 243-60.

5013 HOWE, FREDERICK. *The Confessions of a Reformer*. NY: Scribner, 1925.

5014 HUDSON, HARRIET D. *The Progressive Mine Workers of America: A Study in Rival Unionism*. Urbana: U of Illinois, 1952.

5015 HUME, BRIT. *Death and the Mines: Rebellion and Murder in the United Mine Workers*. NY: Grossman, 1971.

5016 HUNT, EDWARD E. et al, eds. *What the Coal Commission Found*. Balt.: Williams & Wilkins, 1925.

5017 HUSBAND, JOSEPH. *A Year in a Coal-Mine*. Bost.: Houghton Mifflin, 1911.

5018 IDELL, ALBERT. *Stephen Hayne* (a novel). NY: Sloane, 1951.

5019 IGNATIN, GEORGE. *The Antitrust Laws and Labor: the General Problem and the UMW's Experience*. Ph D diss, U of Texas, 1969.

5020 ITTER, WILLIAM A. "Early Labor Troubles in the Schuylkill Anthracite District." *Pennsylvania History*, Vol 1 (1934), 28-37.

5021 JENSEN, BILLIE BARNES. "Woodrow Wilson's Intervention in the Coal Strike of 1914." *Labor History*, Vol 15 (1974), 63-77.

5022 JOHNSON, JAMES P. "Drafting the NRA Code of Fair Competition for the Bituminous Coal Industry." *Journal of American History*, Vol 53 (1966), 521-41.

5023 KALISCH, PHILIP. "Death Down Below: Coal Mine Disasters in Three Illinois Counties, 1904-1962." *Illinois State Historical Society Journal*, Vol 55 (1972), 5-21.

5024 KANAREK, HAROLD K. "Disaster for Hard Coal: The Anthracite Strike of 1925-1926." *Labor History*, Vol 15 (1974), 44-62.

5025 ———. "The Pennsylvania Anthracite Strike of 1922." *Pennsylvania Magazine of History and Biography*., Vol 99 (1975), 45-71.

5026 ———. *Progressivism in Crisis: the United Mine Workers and the Anthracite Coal Industry during the 1920s*. Ph D diss, U of Virginia, 1972.

5027 KARSH, BERNARD, and JACK LONDON. "The Coal Miners: A Study of Union Control." *Quarterly Journal of Economics*, Vol 55 (1954), 415-86.

5028 KEENAN, CHARLES M. *Historical Documentation of Major Coal-Mine Disasters in the United States Not Classified as Explosions of Gas or Dust: 1846-1962*. Wash.: G.P.O., 1963.

5029 KEISER, JOHN H. "The Union Miners Cemetery at Mt. Olive, Illinois—a Spirit-Thread of Labor History." *Journal of the Illinois State Historical Society*, Vol 52 (1969), 229-66.

5030 KERR, K. AUSTIN. "Labor-Management Cooperation: an 1897 Case." *Pennsylvania Magazine of History and Biography*., Vol 99 (1975), 45-71.

5031 ———. "The Movement for Coal Mine Safety in 19th Century Ohio." *Ohio History*, Vol 86 (1977), 3-18.

5032 KLOCK, JOSEPH J., and DORIS PALYER. "Democracy in the UMW?" *Labor Law Journal*, Vol 25 (1974), 625-31.

5033 KORSON, GEORGE G. *Coal Dust on the Fiddle: Songs and Stories of the Bituminous Industry*. Phila.: U of Pennsylvania Press, 1943.

5034 ———. *Minstrels of the Mine Patch: Songs and Stories of the Anthracite Industry*. Phila.: U of Pennsylvania Press, 1938.

5035 KORSON, GEORGE G., ed. *Songs and Ballads of the Anthracite Miner*. NY: Hitchcock, 1926.

5036 LANE, WINTHROP D. *Civil War in West Virginia: A Story of the Industrial Conflict in Coal Mines*. NY: Huebsch, 1921.

5037 LANGDON, EMMA F. *Labor's Greatest Conflict: The Formation of the Western Workers of America*. Denver: Great Western, 1908.

5038 LEO KRAMER, INC. *The Health-Impaired Miner Under Black Lung Legislation*. NY: Praeger, 1973.

5039 LEVY, ELIZABETH, and TAD RICHARDS. *Struggle and Lose, Struggle and Win: The United Mine Workers*. NY: Four Winds Press, 1977.

5040 LEWIS, ARTHUR H. *Murder by Contract: The People v. "Tough Tony" Boyle*. NY: Macmillan, 1975.

5041 LEWIS, JOHN L. *The Miners' Fight for American Standards*. Indianapolis: Bell, 1925.

5042 LEYENDECKER, LISTON. "The Lebanon Mill and Mine Complex." *Colorado Magazine*, Vol 55 (1978), 161-80.

5043 LLOYD, HENRY D. *A Strike of Millionaires against Miners: Or the Story of Spring Valley*. Chicago: Belford-Clarke, 1890.

5044 LUBIN, ISADORE. *Miners' Wages and the Cost of Coal*. NY: McGraw-Hill, 1924.

5045 MCCLURG, DONALD J. "The Colorado Coal Strike of 1927—Tactical Leadership of the IWW." *Labor History*, Vol 4 (1963), 68-92.

5046 MCDONALD, DAVID, and EDWARD A. LYNCH. *Coal and Unionism: A History of the American Coal Miners' Unions*. Silver Spring, MD: Cornelius Printing Co., 1939.

5047 MCGOVERN, GEORGE S. *The Colorado Coal Strike, 1913-1914*. Ph D diss, Northwestern U, 1953.

5048 ———, and LEONARD F. GUTTRIDGE. *The Great Coalfield War*. Bost.: Houghton Mifflin, 1972.

5049 MCKENNEY, RUTH. *Jake Home* (a novel). NY: Harcourt, Brace, 1943.

5050 MADDALA, G. S. "Productivity and Technological Change in the Bituminous Coal

Industry, 1919-1954." *Journal of Political Economy*, Vol 73 (1965), 352-65.
5051 MALTZ, ALBERT. *The Black Pit* (a drama). NY: Putnam, 1935.
5052 MANFREDINI, DOLORES M. "The Italians Come to Herrin." *Journal of the Illinois State Historical Society*, Vol 37 (1944), 317-28.
5053 MARCUS, IRWIN M. "Labor Discontent in Tioga County, Pennsylvania, 1865-1905." *Labor History*, Vol 14 (1973), 414-22.
5054 MARSCHALL, DANIEL. "The Miners and the UMW: Crisis in the Reform Process." *Socialist Review*, Vol 8 (Jul-Oct 1978), 65-115.
5055 MARTIN, JOHN B. "The Blast in Centralia No. 5: A Mine Disaster No One Stopped." *Harper's*, Mar 1948, pp 193-220.
5056 MASON, DANIEL. "John L. Lewis—Hero or Villain?" *Political Affairs*, Vol 59 (Aug 1980), 28-35.
5057 MERRICK, MARY A., SISTER. *A Case in Practical Democracy: Settlement of the Anthracite Coal Strike of 1902*. Notre Dame, IN: U of Notre Dame Library, 1942.
5058 MEYERHUBER, CARL. "The Alle-Kiski Coal Wars, 1913-1919." *Western Pennsylvania Historical Magazine*, Vol 63 (1980), 197-213.
5059 MILLER, ARNOLD. "UMWA Recommendations for Black Lung Amendments." *Labor Law Journal*, Vol 26 (1975), 199-206.
5060 MILLER, STANLEY. *The United Mine Workers of America: A Study of How Trade Union Policy Relates to Technological Change*. Ph D diss, U of Wisconsin, 1957.
5061 MITCHELL, JOHN. *Organized Labor*. Phila.: American Book and Bible House, 1903.
5062 *The Molly Maguires*. 1969. (Feature film directed by Martin Ritt)
5063 MONROE, DOUGLAS K. *A Decade of Turmoil: John L. Lewis and the Anthracite Miners, 1926-1936*. Ph D diss, Georgetown U, 1977.
5064 MORRIS, HOMER L. *The Plight of the Bituminous Coal Miner*. Phila.: U of Pennsylvania Press, 1934.
5065 MYERS, ROBERT J. "Experience of the UMWA Welfare and Retirement Fund." *Industrial and Labor Relations Review*, Vol 10 (1956), 93-100.
5066 ———. "The Mine Workers' Welfare and Retirement Fund: Fifteen Years' Experience." *Industrial and Labor Relations Review*, Vol 20 (1967), 265-74.
5067 NATHAN, ROBERT L. *Coal Mine No. 7* (a novel). NY: St. Martin's Press, 1981.
5068 NATIONAL COAL ASSOCIATION. *The Herrin Conspiracy*. Wash.: The Association, 1922.
5069 NATIONAL COMMITTEE FOR THE DEFENSE OF POLITICAL PRISONERS. *Harlan Miners Speak: Report on Terrorism in the Kentucky Coal Fields*. NY: Harcourt, Brack, 1932.
5070 NEARING, SCOTT. *Anthracite*. Phila.: John C. Winston, 1915.
5071 NELSON, JAMES. *The Mine Workers' District 50*. NY: Exposition Press, 1955.
5072 NEWELL, ARTHUR. *A Knight of the Toilers* (a novel). Phila.: F. L. Marsh, 1905.
5073 NICHOLS, FRANCES H. "Children of the Coal Shadow." *McClure's Magazine*, Vol 20 (1903), 435-44.
5074 NORRIS, JOHN. "The Vancouver Island Coal Miners, 1912-1914: a Study of Organizational Strike." *BC Studies*, Vol 45 (1980), 56-72.
5075 NOVAK, MICHAEL. *The Guns of Lattimer: The True story of a Massacre and a Trial, August 1897-March 1898*. NY: Basic, 1978.
5076 NYDEN, LINDA. "Black Miners in Western Pennsylvania, 1925-31: the NMW and the United Mine Workers of America." *Science & Society*, Vol 41 (1977), 69-101.
5077 O'BRIEN, LARRY D. "The National Guard in the Coal Strike of 1932." *Ohio History*, Vol 84 (1975), 127-44.
5078 O'MALLEY, MICHAEL. *Miner's Hill* (a novel). NY: Harper, 1962.
5079 PALOMBA, CATHERINE, and RONALD ALTHOUSE. "West Virginia Miners View Mine Safety." *Labor Law Journal*, Vol 26 (1975), 139-45.
5080 PAPANIKOLAS, HELEN ZEESE. "Utah's Coal Lands: a Vital Example of how America Became a Great Nation." *Utah Historical Quarterly*, Vol 43 (1975), 105-24.

5081 PARKER, GLEN L. *The Coal Industry: A Study in Social Control.* Wash.: American Council on Public Affairs, 1940.

5082 PARKINSON, GEORGE. et al. *Guide to Coal Mining Collections in the United States.* Morgantown: West Virginia U Library, 1978.

5083 PERRIGO, H. W. *Factional Strife in District No. 12, United Mine Workers of America, 1919-1933.* Ph D diss, U of Wisconsin, 1933.

5084 POLAKOV, WALTER N. "Sufficient unto Himself Is the Coal Digger." *Labor and Nation*, May-Jun 1947, pp 28-29.

5085 POLLARD, SPENCER D. *Some Problems of Democracy in the Government of Labor Unions, with Special Reference to the United Mine Workers of America and the United Automobile Workers of America.* Ph D diss, Harvard U, 1940.

5086 PONKO, VINCENT W., JR. "The Alaskan Coal Commission, 1920 to 1922." *Alaska Journal*, Vol 8 (1978), 118.

5087 PORTER, EUGENE O. "The Colorado Coal Strike of 1913—An Interpretation." *The Historian*, Vol 12 (1949), 3-27.

5088 POWELL, ALLAN KENT. "The 'Foreign Element' and the 1903-4 Carbon County Coal Miners' Strike." *Utah Historical Quarterly*, Vol 43 (1975), 125-54.

5089 ———. "Utah and the Nationwide Coal Miners' Strike of 1922." *Utah Historical Quarterly*, Vol 45 (1977), 135-57.

5090 POWELL, H. BENJAMIN. "The Pennsylvania Anthracite Industry, 1769-1976." *Pennsylvania History*, Vol 46 (1980), 3-27.

5091 REED, MERL E. "Some Additional Material on the Coal Strike of 1943." *Labor History*, Vol 22 (1982), 90-104.

5092 "Remembering Ludlow: April 20, 1914." *United Mine Workers Journal*, Vol 84 (Apr 15, 1973), 12-13. (Photos of the Ludlow, Colorado, organizing)

5093 ROBERTS, PETER. *Anthracite Coal Communities: A Study of the Demography, the Social, Educational, and Moral Life of the Anthracite Regions.* NY: Macmillan, 1904.

5094 ———. *The Anthracite Coal Industry: A Study of the Economic Conditions and Relations of the Co-operative Forces in the Development of the Anthracite Coal Industry of Pennsylvania.* NY: Macmillan, 1901.

5095 ROCHESTER, ANNA. *Labor and Coal.* NY: International Publishers, 1931.

5096 ROE, MARY A. (C. M. CORNWALL, PSEUD.). *Free, Yet Forgiving Their Own Chains* (a novel). NY: Dodd, Mead, 1876.

5097 ROOD, HENRY E. *The Company Doctor* (a novel). Springfield, MA: Merriam, 1895.

5098 ROOSEVELT, THEODORE. "Social and Industrial Justice," chap. 12, *Autobiography*, NY: Macmillan, 1919. (Anthracite strike, 1902)

5099 ROSEN, GEORGE. *The History of Miners' Diseases, a Medical and Social Interpretation.* NY: Schuman's, 1943.

5100 ROSS, MALCOLM H. *Machine Age in the Hills.* NY: Macmillan, 1933.

5101 ROY, ANDREW. *A History of the Coal Miners of the United States, from the Development of the Mines to the Close of the Anthracite Strike of 1902.* Columbus, OH: J. L. Trauger, 1907.

5102 RUBENSTEIN, HARRY R. "The Great Gallup Coal Strike of 1933." *New Mexico Historical Review*, Vol 52 (1977), 173-92.

5103 RYAN, FREDERICK L. *The Rehabilitation of Oklahoma Coal Mining Communities.* Norman: U of Oklahoma Press, 1935.

5104 SCHLEGEL, MARVIN W. "The Workingmen's Benevolent Association: First Union of Anthracite Miners." *Pennsylvania History*, Vol 10 (1943), 243-67.

5105 SCHNELL, JOHN. "The Impact on Collective Bargaining of Oil Co-Ownership of Bituminous Coal Properties." *Labor Studies Journal*, Vol 3 (1979), 201-27.

5106 SEIDMAN, JOEL. et al. "Coal Miners: Unionism as a Tradition," chap. 2, *The Worker Views His Union*, Chicago: U of Chicago Press, 1958.

5107 SELEKMAN, BEN M., and MARY VAN KLEECK. *Employees' Representation in Coal*

Mines: A Study of the Industrial Representation Plan of the Colorado Fuel and Iron Company. NY: Russell Sage Foundation , 1924.

5108 SELTZER, CURTIS. *The United Mine Workers of America and the Coal Operators: the Political Economy of Coal in Appalachia, 1950-1973* Ph D diss, Columbia U, 1978.

5109 SHEPPARD, MURIEL EARLEY. *Cloud by Day: The Story of Coal and Coke and People*. Chapel Hill: U of North Carolina Press, 1947.

5110 SHIELDS, ART. "The Miners Did It!" *Political Affairs*, Vol 53 (Apr 1974), 3-16.

5111 SIMPSON, ALEXANDER G. *The Life of a Miner in Two Hemispheres*. NY: Abbey Press, 1903.

5112 SINCLAIR, UPTON B. *King Coal* (a novel). NY: Macmillan, 1917.

5113 SIZER, SAMUEL A. "'This is Union Man's Country': Sebastian County, 1914." *Arkansas Historical Quarterly*, Vol 22 (1968), 306-29.

5114 SKAGGS, JIMMY M. "To Build a Barony: Colonel Robert D. Hunter." *Arizona and the West*, Vol 15 (1973), 245-56. (A Robber Baron & a coal miners strike at Strawn, Texas, 1888)

5115 SMITH, BARBARA. *Digging Our Own Graves: Coal Miners and the Struggle Over Black Lung Disease*. Ph D diss, Brandeis U, 1981.

5116 SOMERS, GERALD G. *Experience under National Wage Agreements: Grievance Settlement in Coal Mining*. Morgantown: West Virginia U Press, 1953.

5117 SPEKTOR, CHARLEY. "The 1981 Strike in Coal." *Political Affairs*, Vol 60 (Aug 1981), 27-32.

5118 SPRAGUE, STUART SEELY. "Unionization Struggles on Paint and Cabin Creeks, 1912-13." *West Virginia History*, Vol 38 (1977), 185-213.

5119 STERN, MARK. "Black Strikebreakers in the Coal Fields: King County, Washington, 1891." *Journal of Ethnic Studies*, Vol 5 (Fall 1977), 60-70.

5120 STILLMAN, DON. "Murder and the Mines." *New Politics*, Vol 9 (Winter 1972), 22-29.

5121 ———. "The U.M.W.: Historic Breakthrough for Union Democracy." *New Politics*, Vol 10 (1973), 9-13.

5122 STRAW, RICHARD A. "An Act of Faith: Southeastern Ohio Miners in the Coal Strike of 1927." *Labor History*, Vol 21 (1980), 221-38.

5123 ———. *'This is Not a Strike, It is Simply a Revolution': Birmingham Miners Struggle for Power 1849-1908*. Ph D diss, U of Missouri, 1981.

5124 ———. "The United Mine Workers of America and the 1920 Coal Strike in Alabama." *Alabama Review*, Vol 28 (1975), 104-28.

5125 *The Strike at The Mines*. 1911. (Edison Company film directed by Edwin S. Porter)

5126 SUFFERN, ARTHUR E. *The Coal Miners' Struggle for Industrial Status*. NY: Macmillan, 1926.

5127 ———. *Conciliation and Arbitration in the Coal Industry of America*. Bost.: Houghton Mifflin, 1915.

5128 SUGGS, GEORGE G., JR. "The Colorado Coal Miners' Strike, 1903-1904: A Prelude to Ludlow?" *Journal of the West*, Vol 12 (1973), 36-52.

5129 SUNSERI, ALVIN. "The Ludlow Massacre: A Study in the Mis-Employment of the National Guard." *American Chronicle*, Jan 1972, pp 20-32.

5130 SWADOS, HARVEY. *A Radical at Large*. London: Hart-Davis, 1967. (See "The Miners: Men Without Work," pp 13-30)

5131 TAKAMIZA, MAKOTO. *Union Organization and Militancy: Conclusions from a study of the United Mine Workers of America, 1940-1974*. Meisenheim am Glan: Hain, 1978.

5132 TAYLOR, PAUL F. *Coal and Conflict: the UMWA in Harlan County, 1931-1939*. Ph D diss, U of Kentucky, 1970.

5133 TIPPETT, THOMAS. *Horse Shoe Bottoms* (a novel). NY: Harper, 1935.

5134 TRACHTENBERG, ALEXANDER. *The History of Legislation for the Protection of Coal Miners in Pennsylvania, 1824-1915* NY: International Publishers, 1942.

5135 TRIBE, IVAN MATHEWS. *An Empire in Industry: Hocking Valley Mining Towns in the Gilded Age*. Ph D diss, U of Toledo, 1977.

5136 U.S. ANTHRACITE COAL STRIKE COMMISSION. *Report to the President on the Anthracite Coal Strike of May-October, 1902*. Wash.: G.P.O., 1903.

5137 U.S. BOARD OF INQUIRY ON THE LABOR DISPUTE IN THE BITUMINOUS COAL INDUSTRY. *In Re Coal Operators (and others) and United Mine Workers of America (Ind.), March 31, 1948*. Labor Arbitration Reports, Bureau of National Affairs, Wash., 1948, 9 LA 1016.

5138 ———. *The Labor Dispute in the Bituminous Coal Industry*. Wash.: G.P.O., 1950.

5139 U.S. COAL MINES ADMINISTRATION. *A Medical Survey of the Bituminous Coal Industry*. Wash.: G.P.O., 1947.

5140 U.S. COMMISSION ON INDUSTRIAL RELATIONS (1912). "The Colorado Coal Miners' Strike," Vols 7-8, *Final Report*, Wash.: G.P.O., 1916.

5141 ———. *Further Proceedings Relating to the Colorado Strike, Large Foundations and Industrial Control*. Wash.: G.P.O., 1916.

5142 ———. *Rockefeller Interests in Colorado*. Wash.: G.P.O., 1916.

5143 U.S. CONGRESS. HOUSE. Committee on Education and Labor. *Welfare of Miners*. Wash.: G.P.O., 1947.

5144 ———. ———. Committee on Labor. *Investigation of Wages and Working Conditions in the Coal-Mining Industry*. Wash.: G.P.O., 1922.

5145 ———. ———. Committee on Mines and Mining. *Report on the Colorado Strike Investigations Made under House Revolution 387*., Document 1630. Wash.: G.P.O., 1915.

5146 ———. SENATE. Committee on Labor and Public Welfare. Subcommittee on Labor. *UMW Welfare and Retirement Fund*., Hearings, 91st Congress, 2d Session, 1970. Wash.: G.P.O., 1971.

5147 ———. ———. *United Mine Workers' Election*., Hearings, 91st Congress, 2d Session, 1970. Wash.: G.P.O., 1971.

5148 U.S. NATIONAL LABOR RELATIONS BOARD. Division of Economic Research "The Coal Industry," chap. 7, *Written Trade Agreements in Collective Bargaining*, Wash.: G.P.O., 1940.

5149 ———. *The Effect of Labor Relations in the Bituminous Coal Industry upon Interstate Commerce*. Wash.: G.P.O., 1938.

5150 U.S. PRESIDENT'S COMMISSION ON COAL. *The American Coal Miner: A Report on Community and Living Conditions in the Coalfields*. Wash.: The Commission, 1980.

5151 VAN KLEECK, MARY. *Miners and Management: A Study of the Collective Agreement between the United Mine Workers of America and the Rocky Mountain Fuel Company, and an Analysis of the Problem of Coal in the United States*. NY: Russell Sage Foundation, 1934.

5152 VECSEY, GEORGE. *One Sunset a Week: The Story of a Coal Miner*. NY: Saturday Review Press, 1974.

5153 WALSH, WILLIAM J. *The United Mine Workers of America as an Economic and Social Force in the Anthracite Territory*. Wash.: National Capital Press, 1931.

5154 WARE, NORMAN J. "The Miners," pp 209-21, *The Labor Movement in the United States, 1860-1895*, NY: Appleton, 1929.

5155 WARNE, COLSTON E. "Industrial Relations in Coal," chap. 15, *Labor in Postwar America*, Colston E. Warne, ed. Brooklyn: Remsen Press, 1949.

5156 WARNE, FRANK J. *The Coal-Mine Workers: A Study in Labor Organization*. NY: Longmans, Green, 1905.

5157 ———. *The Slav Invasion and the Mine Workers: A Study in Immigration*. Phila.: Lippincott, 1904.

5158 WATKINS, HAROLD M. *Coal and Men: An Economic and Social Study of the British and American Coal Fields*. London: Allen & Unwin, 1934.

5159 WEINBERG, EDGAR. et al. *Technological Change and Productivity in the Bituminous Coal Industry, 1920-60.* Wash.: G.P.O., 1962.

5160 WHEELER, HOYT N. "Mountaineer Mine Wars: an Analysis of the West Virginia Mine Wars of 1912-1913 and 1920-1921." *Business History Review*, Vol 50 (Spring 1976), 69-71.

5161 WICKERSHAM, EDWARD D. *Opposition to the International Officers of the United Mine Workers of America, 1919-1933.* Ph D diss, Cornell U, 1951.

5162 WIECK, EDWARD A. *The American Miners' Association: A Record of the Origin of Coal Miners' Unions in the United States.* NY: Russell Sage Foundation, 1940.

5163 ———. *The Miners' Case and the Public Interest: A Documented Chronology.* NY: Russell Sage Foundation, 1947.

5164 ———. *Preventing Fatal Explosions in Coal Mines: A Study of Recent Major Disasters in the United States as Accompaniments of Technological Change.* NY: Russell Sage Foundation, 1942.

5165 WILLIAMS, BEN AMES. *Owen Glen* (a novel). Bost.: Houghton Mifflin, 1950.

5166 WITT, MATT. *In Our Blood: Four Coal Mining Families.* Wash.: Highlander Research and Education Center, 1979.

5167 ———. "A Venture into Union Journalism." *Columbia Journalism Review*, Vol 17 (Jul-Aug 1978), 50-52.

5168 WOOL, HAROLD. "Coal Industry Resurgence Attracts Variety of New Yorkers." *Monthly Labor Review*, Vol 104 (Jan 1981), 3-8.

5169 WOOLLEY, BRYAN. *We Be Here When the Morning Comes.* Lexington: U Press of Kentucky, 1976.

5170 WORMSER, RICHARD. *All's Fair* (a novel). NY: Modern Age Books, 1937.

5171 YARNELL, SOPHIA. *The Clark Inheritance* (a novel). NY: Walker, 1981.

5172 YOUNG, DALLAS M. *A History of the Progressive Miners of America, 1932-1940.* Ph D diss, U of Illinois, 1941.

5173 ———. "Origin of the Progressive Mine Workers of America." *Journal of the Illinois State Historical Society*, Vol 40 (1947), 313-30.

5174 ZIEGER, ROBERT H. "Pennsylvnia Coal and Politics: the Anthracite Strike of 1925-1926." *Pennsylvania Magazine of History and Biography*, Vol 92 (1969), 244-62.

5175 ———. "Pinchot and Coolidge: The Politics of the 1923 Anthracite Crisis." *Journal of American History*, Vol 52 (1965), 566-81.

Communications

5176 BARBASH, JACK. *Unions and Telephones.* NY: Harper, 1952.

5177 BROOKS, THOMAS R. *Communications Workers of America: The Story of a Union.* NY: Mason/Charter, 1977.

5178 CHAMBERLAIN, NEIL W. *The Union Challenge to Management Control.* NY: Harper, 1948. (See Appendix D, pp 317-29)

5179 CRAYPO, CHARLES. "The Impact of Changing Corporate Structure and Technology on Telegraph Labor, 1870-1978." *Labor Studies Journal*, Vol 3 (1979), 283-303. (See comments by Kenneth Gagala, pp 305-7)

5180 DAVIS, PEARCE, and HENRY J. MEYER, eds. *Labor Dispute Settlements in the Telephone Industry, 1942-1945.* Wash.: Bureau of National Affairs, 1946.

5181 HOWARD, R. "Strung Out at the Phone Company: How AT&T's Workers Are Drugged, Bugged, and Coming Unplugged." *Mother Jones*, Aug 1981, pp 54-56.

5182 KENNEDY, J. C. "Sidelights on the Telegraphers' Strike." *Journal of Political Economy*, Vol 15 (1907), 438-51.

5183 "Labor Unions in Transportation and Communications Industries." *Monthly Labor Review*, Vol 70 (1950), 275-78.

5184 McIsaac, Archibald M. *The Order of Railroad Telegraphers: A Study in Trade Unionism and Collective Bargaining*. Princeton: Princeton U Press, 1933.

5185 Mayer, Henry. "The National Telephone Strike." *Labor and Nation*, Jul-Aug 1947, pp 13-17.

5186 ———, and Abraham Weiner. "The New Jersey Telephone Company Case." *Industrial and Labor Relations Review*, Vol 1 (1948), 492-99.

5187 Nabach, Joseph. "The Telephone Strike: Frozen Militancy." *New Politics*, Vol 9 (Winter 1972), 40-46. (NY Telephone strike, 1971)

5188 Schacht, John N. *The Rise of the Communications Workers of America: Union Organization and Centralization in the Telephone Industry, 1935-1947* Ph D diss, U of Iowa, 1977.

5189 ———. "Toward Industrial Unionism: Bell Telephone Workers and Company Unions, 1919-1937." *Labor History*, Vol 16 (1975), 5-36.

5190 Segal, Melvin J. "Industrial Relations in Communications," chap. 19, *Labor in Postwar America*, Colston E. Warne, ed. Brooklyn: Remsen Press, 1949.

5191 Seidman, Joel. et al. "Telephone Workers: White-Collar Unionism," chap. 7, *The Worker Views His Union*, Chicago: U of Chicago Press, 1958.

5192 Ulriksson, Vidkunn. *The Telegraphers: Their Craft and Their Unions*. Wash.: Public Affairs Press, 1953.

5193 U.S. Commission on Industrial Relations (1912). "Commercial Telegraph Companies," Vol 10, pp 9291-541, *Final Report*, Wash.: G.P.O., 1916.

5194 U.S. Congress. Senate. Committee on Labor and Public Welfare. Subcommittee on Labor and Labor-Management Relations. *Communist Domination of Certain Unions*. Wash.: G.P.O., 1951. (See pp 43-58)

5195 ———. ———. *Labor-Management Relations in the Bell Telephone System.*, Report No 139. Wash.: G.P.O., 1951.

5196 ———. ———. *Labor-Management Relations in the Bell Telephone System —Hearings*. Wash.: G.P.O., 1951.

Construction

5197 Applebaum, Herbert A. *Royal Blue, The Culture of Construction Workers*. NY: Holt, Rinehart & Winston, 1981.

5198 Bates, Harry. *Bricklayers' Century of Craftsmanship*. Wash.: Bricklayers, Masons and Plasterers International Union, 1955.

5199 Bertram, Gordon, and Sherman J. Maisel. *Industrial Relations in the Construction Industry, The Northern California Experience*. Berkeley: Institute of Industrial Relations, U of California, 1955.

5200 Blum, Solomon. "Trade-Union Rules in the Building Trades," chap. 10, *Studies in American Trade Unionism*, Jacob H. Hollander & George E Barnett, eds. NY: Holt, 1907.

5201 Brooks, Thomas R. "Centennial '81: the Carpenters." *American Federationist*, Vol 88 (May 1981), 11-16.

5202 ———. *The Road to Dignity: A Century of Conflict: A History of the United Brotherhood of Carpenters and Joiners of America, AFL-CIO, 1881-1981*. NY: Atheneum, 1981.

5203 Building Trades Employers' Association of the City of New York. Committee on Welfare Funds *A Review of Welfare Funds in the New York City Building Trades*. NY: The Association, 1951.

5204 "Building-Trades Bargaining Plan in Southern California." *Monthly Labor Review*, Vol 70 (1950), 14-18.

5205 "Carpenters' Labor-Firsts." *Carpenter*, Vol 97 (Aug 1977), 16.

5206 Chepesiuk, Ron. "The Winthrop College Archives and Special Collections: Selected Resources for Study of Women's History." *South Carolina History Magazine*, Vol 82 (1981), 145. (Baker, Mary—trade unionist; description of small collection relating to the Construction and General Laborer's Union-International Hod Carriers Local 58, Augusta, GA)

5207 Christie, Robert A. *Empire in Wood: A History of the United Brotherhood of Carpenters and Joiners of America.*, Cornell Studies in Industrial and Labor Relations, Vol 7. Ithaca: NY State School of Industrial and Labor Relations, Cornell U, 1956.

5208 Clark, Kim C. "The Impact of Unionization on Productivity: a Case Study." *Industrial and Labor Relations Review*, Vol 33 (1980), 451-69.

5209 Coffin, Tom. "Busted by Law: Organizing in the Construction Industry." *Southern Exposure*, Vol 8 (Spring 1980), 26-34.

5210 Covington, J.E. "Union Security Elections in the Building and Construction Industry under the Taft-Hartley Act." *Industrial and Labor Relations Review*, Vol 4 (1951), 543-55.

5211 Deibler, Frederick S. *The Amalgamated Wood Workers' International Union of North America.*, Bulletin 511. Madison: U of Wisconsin, 1912.

5212 Derber, Milton. "Case Study 5, Building Construction," *Labor-Management Relations in Illini City*, Vol 1. Champaign: Institute of Labor and Industrial Relations, U of Illinois, 1953.

5213 DiDonato, Pietro. *Christ in Concrete* (a novel). Indianapolis: Bobbs-Merrill, 1939.

5214 Dubinsky, Irwin. *Reform in Trade Union Discrimination in the Construction Industry: Operation Dig and Its Legacy*. NY: Praeger, 1973.

5215 Dunlop, John T., and Arthur D. Hill. *Wage Adjustment Board: Wartime Stabilization in the Building and Construction Industry*. Cambr.: Harvard U Press, 1950.

5216 Ehrenberg, Ronald, and Stephen Goldberg. "Officer Performance and Compensation in Local Building Trades Unions." *Industrial and Labor Relations Review*, Vol 30 (1977), 188-96.

5217 "Exchange on the Painters Union." *New Politics*, Vol 10 (Spring 1973), 45-65. (Herman Benson, Frank Schoenfeld & Burton Hall)

5218 Fewel, Ben. "Ace Jackson." *Southern Exposure*, Vol 8 (Spring 1980), 11-13. (Interview)

5219 "Fifty Years of Peace." *Fortune*, Feb 1953, pp 84-86. (Building Trades Employers' Association of the City of New York)

5220 Foner, Philip S. "An Early Trades Union and Its Fate." *Labor History*, Vol 14 (1973), 423-24.

5221 Galenson, Walter. "The Building Trades," chap. 16, *The CIO Challenge to the AFL*, Cambr.: Harvard U Press, 1960.

5222 Gilpatrick, Thomas V. *A Case Study of Labor Relations in a Construction Company in a Midwestern Community*. MS thesis, U of Illinois, 1947.

5223 Gould, William B. "The Seattle Building Trades Offer: the First Comprehensive Relief against Employment Discrimination in the Construction Industry." *Industrial Relations Law Digest*, Vol 17 (Fall 1974), 62-79.

5224 Grant, Luke. *National Erectors' Association and International Association of Bridge and Structural Ironworkers*. Wash.: G.P.O., 1915.

5225 Gross, Judith M. *Union-Nonunion Wage Differentials in the Construction Industry*. Ph D diss, Princeton U, 1977.

5226 Gruenberg, Gladys W. "Minority Training and Hiring in the Construction Industry." *Labor Law Journal*, Aug 1971, pp 522-36.

5227 Haber, William. "Building Construction," chap. 4, *How Collective Bargaining Works*, Harry A. Millis, research director. NY: Twentieth Century Fund, 1945.

5228 ———. *Industrial Relations in the Building Industry*. Cambr.: Harvard U Press, 1930.

5229 ———, and HAROLD LEVINSON. *Labor Relations and Productivity in the Building Trades*. Ann Arbor: Bureau of Industrial Relations, U of Michigan, 1956.

5230 HALL, BURTON. "Painter's Union: Troubles of an Ex-Reformer." *New Politics*, Vol 10 (Winter 1973), 22-29.

5231 HARRINGTON, R. E. *Proud Man* (a novel). London: Secker & Wargurg, 1983.

5232 HARTMAN, PAUL, and WALTER FRANKE. "The Changing Bargaining Structure in Construction: Wide-Area and Multicraft Bargaining." *Industrial and Labor Relations Review*, Vol 33 (1980), 170-84.

5233 HOROWITZ, MORRIS A. *The Structure and Government of the Carpenters' Union*. NY: Wiley, 1962.

5234 HOSKING, WILLIAM GEORGE. *A Study of Area Wage Structure and Wage Determination in the Building Construction Industry of Central New York State, 1942-1951*. Ph D diss, Cornell U, 1955.

5235 ILLINOIS GENERAL ASSEMBLY. Joint Building Investigation Commission *Report of Illinois Building Investigation Commission*. Springfield: Illinois State Register, 1923. (Dailey Commission)

5236 INTERNATIONAL UNION OF OPERATING ENGINEERS. *Fifty Years of Progress, 1896-1946*. Wash.: The Union, 1946.

5237 JOFFE, JEROME. *Job Ladders and Job Structures: a Study of Labor Stratification within Maintenance and Repair Occupations in New York City*. Ph D diss, New School for Social Research 1975.

5238 JOHNSON, GERALD W. *Hod-Carrier: Notes of a Laborer on an Unfinished Cathedral*. NY: Morrow, 1964.

5239 JOHNSON, W. C. et al. "An Unusual and Successful Organizing Attempt." *Labor Law Journal*, Vol 28 (1977), 734-40. (Laborers International Union)

5240 LANDON, JOHN, and WILLIAM S. PEIRCE. "Discrimination, Monopsony, and Union Power in the Building Trades: A Cross Sectional Analysis." *Proceedings of the Twenty-Fourth Annual Winter Meeting of the Industrial Relations Research Association*, Dec 27-28, 1971, pp 254-61. Madison: IRRA, 1972.

5241 LIPSKY, DAVID B., and HENRY S. FISHER. "The Composition of Strike Activity in the Construction Industry." *Industrial and Labor Relations Review*, Vol 29 (1976), 388-404.

5242 MCMAHON, EARL J., ed. *The Chicago Building Trades Council, Yesterday and Today*. Chicago: Chicago and Cook County Building and Construction Trades Council, 1945.

5243 MANGAN, JOHN. *History of the Steam Fitters' Protective Association of Chicago*. Chicago: The Association, 1930.

5244 MANGUM, GARTH L. *The Operating Engineers: The Economic History of a Trade Union*. Cambr.: Harvard U Press, 1964.

5245 MARTIN, JOHN. *The Labor Market of the U.S. Shipbuilding Industry: 1960-1970*. Ph D diss, George washington U, 1979.

5246 MERCEY, ARCH. *The Laborer's Story, 1903-1953*. Wash: International Hod Carriers', Building and Common Laborers' Union of America (AFL), 1954.

5247 MEYERS, GLENN D. *The Building Trades: a Case of Monopoly in the Labor Market*. Ph D diss, Columbia U, 1972.

5248 MILLS, D. Q. "Construction Wage Stabilization: A Historic Perspective." *Industrial Relations*, Vol 12 (1972), 350-65.

5249 ———. *Industrial Relations and Manpower in Construction*. Cambr.: MIT Press, 1972.

5250 MONTGOMERY, ROYAL E. *Industrial Relations in the Chicago Building Trades*. Chicago: U of Chicago Press, 1927.

5251 "More Trouble in Paradise." *Fortune*, Nov 1946, pp 154-59, 215-25.

5252 MOSKOW, MICHAEL H. "New Initiatives in Public Policy for the Construction Industry." *Proceedings of the Twenty-Fourth Annual Winter Meeting of the Industrial Relations Research Association*, Dec 27-28, 1971, pp 25-33. Madison: IRRA, 1972.

5253 NATIONAL JOINT BOARD FOR SETTLEMENT OF JURISDICTIONAL DISPUTES. "The Agreement Establishing a National Joint Board for the Settlement of Jurisdictional Disputes in Buillding and Construction Industries." *Industrial and Labor Relations Review*, Vol 2 (1949), 411-15.

5254 NEW YORK STATE. Joint Legislative Committee on Housing (C. C. Lockwood, chairman) *Final Report.*, Legislative Document 48. Albany: State Library, 1923.

5255 "Nineteen Seventy-Eight, The Diamond Anniversary of the Laborers' International Union." *Laborer*, Vol 33 (Jan 1978). (Brief history of Laborers begins in 1903)

5256 O'DONNELL, L. A. "From Limerick to the Golden Gate: Odyssey of an Irish Carpenter." *Studies/ An Irish Quarterly Review*, (Spring-Summer 1979), 76-91. (Patrick Henry McCarthy)

5257 ———. "The Greening of a Limerick Man: Patrick Henry McCarthy." *Eire-Ireland*, Vol 11 (1976), 119-28. (pioneer building trades unionist in San Francisco)

5258 PARTRIDGE, BELLAMY (THOMAS BAILEY, PSEUD.). *Big Freeze* (a novel). NY: Crowell, 1948.

5259 RAMSBOTHAM, ANN, and PAM FARMER. "Women Working: the Building Trades Begin to Open Up." *Southern Exposure*, Vol 8 (Spring 1980), 35-39.

5260 RIEMER, JEFFREY W. *Hard Hats: The Work World of Construction Workers*. Beverly Hills: Sage Publications, 1979.

5261 ROOMKIN, M., and H. A. JURIS. "Changing Character of Unionism in Traditionally Organized Sectors." *Monthly Labor Review*, Vol 102 (Feb 1979), 36-38.

5262 ROSE, ARTHUR. "Wage Differentials in the Building Trades." *Monthly Labor Review*, Vol 92 (Oct 1969), 14-17.

5263 ROSE, WILLIAM T. "Daredevil Tradition Dates Back More Than Three Centuries: Mohawk Indians Are World Famous For Their Skills in 'High Steel'." *Industrial Bulletin*, Vol 40 (1961), 21-24.

5264 RYAN, FREDERICK L. *Industrial Relations in the San Francisco Building Trades*. Norman: U of Oklahoma Press, 1936.

5265 SCHEUCH, RICHARD. "Labor Policies in Residential Construction." *Industrial and Labor Relations Review*, Vol 6 (1953), 378-82.

5266 SCOTT, LEROY. *The Walking Delegate* (a novel). NY: Doubleday, Page, 1905.

5267 SEIDMAN, HAROLD. *Labor Czars*. NY: Liveright, 1938. (See chaps. 2, 5, 6, 7, 10)

5268 SEIDMAN, JOEL. et al. "Plumbers: Craft-conscious Unionism," chap. 3, *The Worker Views His Union*, Chicago: U of Chicago Press, 1958.

5269 SHAW, FRANK L. *The Building Trades*. Cleveland: Survey Committee of the Cleveland Foundation, 1916.

5270 SHELDON, HORACE E. *Union Security and the Taft-Hartley Act in the Buffalo Area.*, Research Bulletin 4. Ithaca: NY State School of Industrial and Labor Relations, Cornell U, 1949.

5271 SILVER, HENRY D. "Making a Living in Rochester: The Diary of Henry D. Silver, 1906-1914." *Rochester History*, Vol 15 (1953), 331-42.

5272 SKIDMORE, HUBERT. *Hawk's Nest* (a novel). NY: Doubleday, Doran, 1941.

5273 SOBOTKA, STEPHEN P. *The Influence of Unions on Wages and Earnings of Labor in the Construction Industry*. Ph D diss, U of Chicago, 1952.

5274 *Steel Against the Sky*. 1941. (Feature film produced by Warner Brothers)

5275 STRAND, KENNETH T. *Jurisdictional Disputes in Construction: The Causes, the Joint Board, and the NLRB*. Pullman: Bureau of Economic and Business Research, School of Economics and Business, Washington State U, 1961.

5276 STRAUB, ADELBERT G., JR. *Whose Welfare? A Report on Union and Employer Welfare PLans in New York*. Albany: State of New York Insurance Department, 1954.

5277 STRAUSS, GEORGE. "Business Agents in the Building Trades: A Case Study in a Community." *Industrial and Labor Relations Review*, Vol 10 (1957), 237-51.

5278 ———. "Control by the Membership in Building Trades Unions." *American Journal of Sociology*, Vol 61 (1956), 527-35.

5279 ———. *Unions in the Building Trades*. Buffalo: U of Buffalo, 1958.

5280 U.S. COMMISSION ON CIVIL RIGHTS. New York Committee *Hometown Plans for the Construction Industry in New York State: A Report to the U. S. Commission on Civil Rights, Prepared by the New York Committee*. NY: The Committee, 1972.

5281 U.S. COMMISSION ON INDUSTRIAL RELATIONS (1912). "Building Trades of New York City," Vol 2, pp 1581-1799, *Final Report*, Wash.: G.P.O., 1916.

5282 ———. "Labor Conditions in Construction Camps," Vol 6, pp 5087-168, *Final Report*, Wash.: G.P.O., 1916.

5283 ———. "The Painters' Strike in San Francisco," Vol 6, pp 5473-84, *Final Report*, Wash.: G.P.O., 1916.

5284 U.S. CONGRESS. HOUSE. Committee on Education and Labor. *Construction Site Picketing*. Wash.: G.P.O., 1960.

5285 ———. ———. *Northern New Jersey Jurisdictional Disputes in the A.F. of L. Building Trades*. Wash.: G.P.O., 1947.

5286 ———. SENATE. Committee on Labor and Public Welfare. Subcommittee on Labor and Labor-Management Relations. *Labor-Management Relations in the Bonneville Power Administration*. Wash.: G.P.O., 1951.

5287 ———. ———. *To Amend the National Labor Relations Act, 1947, with Respect to the Building and Construction Industry*. Wash.: G.P.O., 1951.

5288 U.S. DEPARTMENT OF LABOR. LABOR-MANAGEMENT SERVICES ADMINISTRATION. Office of Labor-Management Policy Development. *Exclusive Union Work Referral Systems in the Building Trades*. Wash.: G.P.O., 1970.

5289 VON RHAU, HENRY. *Fraternally Yours* (a novel). NY: Smith & Haas, 1935.

5290 WARE, NORMAN J. "The Carpenters," pp 231-36, *The Labor Movement in the United States, 1860-1895*, NY: Appleton, 1929.

5291 WHITCOMB, ROBERT. *Talk United States!* (a novel). NY: Smith & Haas, 1935.

5292 WHITE, DONALD J. "The Council on Industrial Relations for the Electrical Contracting Industry." *Proceedings of the Twenty-Fourth Annual Winter Meeting of the Industrial Relations Research Association*, Dec 27-28, 1971, pp 16-24. Madison: IRRA, 1972.

5293 WHITNEY, NATHANIEL R. *Jurisdiction in American Building-Trades Unions*. Balt.: Johns Hopkins Press, 1914.

Education

5294 AMERICAN FEDERATION OF TEACHERS. COMMISSION ON EDUCATIONAL RECONSTRUCTION. *Organizing the Teaching Profession*. Glencoe: Free Press, 1955.

5295 ANGELL, GEORGE W., ed. *Faculty and Teacher Bargaining: The Impact of Unions on Education*. Lexington, MA: Lexington Books, 1981.

5296 AUSSIEKER, BILL. "The Incident and Impact of Faculty Union Strikes." *Labor Law Journal*, Vol 28 (1977), 777-84.

5297 ———, and JOSEPH W. GARBARINO. "Measuring Faculty Unionism: Quantity and Quality." *Industrial Relations*, Vol 12 (1973), 117-24.

5298 BAIN, TREVOR. "Academic Governance and Unions: the Case of CUNY." *Industrial Relations*, Vol 14 (1975), 102-9.

5299 ———. "Collective Bargaining and Wages in Public Higher Education: the Case of CUNY." *Journal of Collective Negotiations in the Public Sector*, Vol 5 (1976), 207-14.

5300 BARTSON, R. J. *The Goals of Union Leaders and Union Members in Michigan Higher Education*. Ph D diss, Wayne State U, 1978.

5301 BATLIN, CARL A. "American Federation of Teachers Endorses Merger Talks." *Monthly Labor Review*, Vol 96 ((ct 1973), 43-44.

5302 BEGIN, JAMES. "Grievance Mechanisms and Faculty Collegiality: the Rutgers Case." *Industrial and Labor Relations Review*, Vol 31 (1978), 295-309.

5303 ———. et al. *Academics on Strike*. New Brunswick, NJ: Institute of Management and Labor Relations, University Extension Division, Rutgers U, [c.1975].

5304 BLUM, ALBERT A., ed. *Teacher Unions and Associations, a Comparative Study*. Urbana: U of Illinois Press, 1969.

5305 BOGNANNO, MARIO. et al. "Union-Management Contracts in Higher Education." *Industrial Relations*, Vol 17 (1978), 189-203.

5306 ———, and EDWARD SUNTRUP. "Graduate Assistants' Response to Unionization: the Minnesota Experience." *Labor Law Journal*, Vol 27 (1976), 32-37.

5307 BRAUN, ROBERT J. *Teachers and Power: The Story of the American Federation of Teachers*. NY: Simon & Schuster, 1972.

5308 BROOKS, GEORGE W. "A Case for Teachers' Unions." *Monthly Labor Review*, Vol 87 (Mar 1964), 292.

5309 BROWN, WILLIAM, and COURTENAY STONE. "Student-Faculty Ratios and Unions." *Educational Record*, Vol 60 (1979), 169-74.

5310 BUCHHEIT, SCOTT EDWARD. *Unionizing Among Graduate Students Employees in American Universities, 1965-1975: Its Causes, Legal Status, and History*. MS thesis, Cornell U, 1977.

5311 CANDELORO, DOMINIC. "The Chicago School Board Crisis of 1907." *Illinois State Historical Society Journal*, Vol 68 (1975), 396-406.

5312 CARR, ROBERT K., and DANIEL K. VANEYCK. *Collective Bargaining Comes to the Campus*. Wash.: American Council on Education, 1973.

5313 CHENG, C. W. "Collective Bargaining in Public Education (Symposium)." *Education and Urban Society*, Vol 11 (1979), 123-269.

5314 CLARKE, JAMES EARL. *The American Federation of Teachers: Origins and History from 1870 to 1952*. Ph D diss, Cornell U, 1966.

5315 COLE, STEPHEN. *The Unionization of Teachers: A Case Study of the UFT*. NY: Praeger, 1969.

5316 "Collective Negotiations in Higher Education: A Symposium." *Wisconsin Law Review*, No 1 of 1971.

5317 COLLINWOOD, DEAN W. *Organizational Origins of the Faculty Unionism Movement in American Higher education*. Ph d diss, U of Chicago, 1980.

5318 COLTON, DAVID L., and EDITH E. GRABER. *Teacher Strikes and the Courts*. Lexington, MA: Lexington Books, 1982.

5319 COOKE, GEORGE E. *The Relationship between Pupil Attitudes and Behavior and the Occurrence of Teacher Strikes*. Ph D diss, Pennsylvania State U, 1979.

5320 DEITCH, JOSEPH. "Man On a Hot Seat." *Saturday Review*, May 19, 1962, p 55. (On the NY City teachers' strike, Apr 11, 1962)

5321 DENKER, JOEL. *Unions and Universities: The Rise of the New Labor Leader*. Montclair, NH: Allanheld, Osmun, 1981.

5322 DEWING, ROLLAND LLOYD. *Teacher Organizations and Desegregation, 1954-1964*. Ph D diss, ball State U, 1967.

5323 DOHERTY, ROBERT E. "Teacher Bargaining, Resource Allocation and Representative Rule." *Proceedings of the Twenty-Second Annual Winter Meeting of the Industrial Relations Research Association*, Dec 29-30, 1969, pp 248-56. Madison: IRRA, 1970.

5324 ———, and WALTER E. OBERER. *Teachers, School Boards, and Collective Bargaining: A Changing of the Guard*. Ithaca: NY State School of Industrial and Labor Relations, Cornell U, 1967.

5325 DORROS, SIDNEY. "The Case for Independent Professional Teachers' Associations." *Monthly Labor Review*, Vol 87 (May 1964), 543.

5326 DURYEA, E. D. et al. *Faculty Unions and Collective Bargaining*. San Francisco: Jossey-Bass, 1973.

5327 EATON, WILLIAM E. *The American Federation of Teachers, 1916-1961: A History of the Movement*. Carbondale: Southern Illinois U Press, 1975.

5328 ———. *The Social and Educational Position of the American Federation of Teachers, 1929-1951*. Ph D diss, Washington U, 1971.

5329 EKLUND, JOHN M. *Collective Negotiations Between Boards of Education and Teachers in the Determination of Personnel Policy in the Public Schools*. Ph D diss, Columbia U, 1954.

5330 ELAM, STANLEY M. et al. *Readings on Collective Negoriations in Public Education*. Chicago: Rand McNally, 1967.

5331 ELLMAN, NEIL C. *The Role of the United Federation of Teachers Chapters in the Union and in their Respective Schools*. Ph D diss, Columbia U, 1973.

5332 ETZIONI, AMITAI, ed. *The Semi-Professions and Their Organization: Teachers, Nurses, Social Workers*. NY: Free Press, 1969.

5333 FAGAN, R. A. *A Social History of Teacher Militancy*. Ph D diss, Marquette U, 1980.

5334 FARLEY, JENNIE. *Academic Women and Employment Discrimination: A Critical Annotated Bibliography*. Ithaca: NY State School of Industrial and Labor Relations, Cornell U, 1982.

5335 FITZGERALD, GERALD. *Factors that Relate to Unionization within an Academic Staff*. Ph D diss, U of Missouri, 1978.

5336 FORDYCE, WELLINGTON G. *The Origin and Development of Teachers Unions in the United States*. Ph D diss, Ohio State U, 1945.

5337 FOX, WILLIAM, and MICHAEL WINCE. "The Structure and Determinants of Occupational Militancy among Public School Teachers." *Industrial and Labor Relations Review*, Vol 30 (1976), 4-58.

5338 GARBARINO, JOSEPH W. "Faculty Unionization: the pre-Yeshiva Years, 1966-1979." *Industrial Relations*, Vol 19 (1980), 221-30.

5339 ———, and JOHN LAWLER. "Faculty Union Activity in Higher Education, 1976." *Industrial Relations*, Vol 16 (1977), 105-6.

5340 GATEWOOD, LUCIAN B. "Factfinding in Teacher Disputes: The Wisconsin Experience." *Monthly Labor Review*, Vol 97 (1974), 45-51.

5341 GERHART, PAUL F., and CHARLES MAXEY. "College Administrators and Collective Bargaining." *Industrial Relations*, Vol 17 (1978), 43-52.

5342 GLASS, RONALD W. "Work Stoppages and Teachers: History and Prospect." *Monthly Labor Review*, Vol 90 (Aug 1967), 43-46.

5343 GRIMSHAW, WILLIAM J. *Union Rule in the Schools: Big-City Politics in Transformation*. Lexington, MA: Lexington Books, 1979.

5344 GROSSE, PAUL ELMER. *Competitive Interest Group Politics: the Philadelphia Federation of Teachers and the Philadelphia Teachers Association*. Ph D diss, Pennsylvania State U, 1968.

5345 HALL, W. CLAYTON, and NORMAN E. CARROLL. "The Effect of Teachers' Organizations on Salaries and Class Size." *Industrial and Labor Relations Review*, Vol 26 (1973), 834-41.

5346 HANLEY, EDWARD F., JR. "National Education Association Again Focuses on Merger Issue." *Monthly Labor Review*, Vol 96 (Sep 1973), 67-68.

5347 HECHINGER, FRED M. "The Story Behind the Strike." *Saturday Review*, May 19, 1962, pp 54, 56, 78. (About the NY City teachers' strike, Apr 11, 1962)

5348 HELFANT, DAVID B. *Ivory Tower Unionism: a Study of Unionist Professionals in the American High Quality University*. Ph D diss, U of Chicago, 1977.

5349 HERMAN, E. EDWARD, and GORDON SKINNER. "Faculty Representation: the Vote at Cincinnati." *Monthly Labor Review*, Vol 99 (Mar 1976), 44-48.

5350 HERRICK, MARY. "Research in the Problems of Organized Teachers." *Proceedings of the Tenth Annual Meeting of the Industrial Relations Research Association*, Sep 5-7, 1957, pp 249-53. Madison: IRRA, 1958.

5351 HOCKNEY, D. W. *The Jennings County Teachers Strike: a Case Study*. Ph D diss, Indiana U, 1977.

5352 HRONICEK, FRANCIS. *The Historical Development of Teachers' Unions in U.S. Public Education*. Ph D diss, St. Louis U, 1981.

5353 HUGHES, CLARENCE R. et al., eds. *Collective Negotiations in Higher Education: a Reader*. Carlinville, IL: Blackburn College Press, 1973.

5354 JOHNSON, SUSAN M. *Teacher Unions and the Schools*. Ph D diss, Harvard U, 1981.

5355 JULIAN, BERNADETTE S. "The AFT in Caucus and Convention: New Style for 1967." *Monthly Labor Review*, Vol 90 (Nov 1967), 19-20.

5356 KAHN, KENNETH. "The NLRB and Higher Education: the Failure of Policy Making through Adjudication." *Industrial Relations Law Digest*, Vol 17 (Fall 1974), 1-27.

5357 KERCHNER, CHARLES T. *An Exploration into the Impacts of Faculty Unions on Community Colleges and their Presidents*. Ph D diss, Northwestern U, 1977.

5358 KLEIN, LAWRENCE R. "The NEA Convention and the Organizing of Teachers." *Monthly Labor Review*, Vol 87 (Aug 1964), 882-85.

5359 KOTOWSKI, CASIMIR. *Urban Community College Unionism: a Descriptive Survey and Case Study of the American Federation of Teachers, Local 1600, City Colleges Division*. Loyola U of Chicago, 1980.

5360 LADD, EVERETT, C., JR., and SEYMOUR MARTIN LIPSET. *Professors, Unions, and American Higher Education*. Wash.: American Enterprise Institute for Public Policy Research, 1973.

5361 LEE, ISABELLA J. *A History of the Labor Union Movement Among New York City Public School Teachers*. Ph D diss, New York U, 1972.

5362 LEWIS, LIONEL, and MICHAEL RYAN. "Professionalization and the Professoriate." *Social Problems*, Vol 24 (1976), 282-97.

5363 LONDON, JACK. "Barriers to the Development of Effective Personnel Practice in Public School Organization." *Educational Administration and Supervision*, Vol 43 (1957), 83-93.

5364 ———. "The Development of a Grievance Procedure in the Public Schools." *Educational Administration and Supervision*, Vol 43 (1957), 1-18.

5365 MCCAMEY, MARION B. *Unionism in Academia*. Ph D diss, U of Massachusetts, 1977.

5366 MAEROFF, GENE I. "Taking Stock after Yeshiva." *Educational Record*, Vol 61 (Summer 1980), 14-18.

5367 MAHONEY, J. J., JR. *A Study of the Teacher Collective: Organizational Behavior of the Teachers' Union and Teachers' Association in the State of New Jersey*. Ph D diss, Rutgers U, 1978.

5368 MARKS, KENNETH E., ed. *Collective Bargaining in U.S. Higher Education: 1960-1971; A Selective Bibliography*. Ames: Iowa State U Library, 1972.

5369 MAYER, MARTIN. *The Teacher Strike, New York, 1968*. NY: Harper & Row, 1969.

5370 MILLER, CHARLES. *Democracy in Education: a Study of How the American Federation of Teachers Met the Threat of Communist Subversion through the Democratic Process*. Ph D diss, Northwestern U, 1967.

5371 MOORE, WILLIAM J. "An Analysis of Teacher Union Growth." *Industrial Relations*, Vol 17 (1978), 204-15.

5372 MORTIMER, KENNETH, and MARK JOHNSON. "Faculty Collective Bargaining in Public Higher Education." *Educational Record*, Vol 57 (1976), 34-44.

5373 MOSKOW, MICHAEL H., and KENNETH MCLENNAN. "The Impact of Decentralization on Collective Bargaining in Urban Education." *Proceedings of the Twenty-Second Annual Winter Meeting of the Industrial Relations Research Association*, Dec 29-30, 1969, pp 236-47. Madison: IRRA, 1970.

5374 MUIR, J. DOUGLAS. "The Strike as a Professional Sanction: The Changing Attitude of the National Education Association." *Labor Law Journal*, Vol 19 (Oct 1968), 615-27.

5375 MURASKIN, L. D. *The Teachers Union of the City of New York from Inception to Schism, 1912-1935.* Ph D diss, U of California, 1980.

5376 MURPHY, EILEEN. *Higher Education and Faculty Unionism: the Impact of Arbitration.* Ph D diss, Harvard U, 1981.

5377 MYERS, DONALD A. *Teacher Power: Professionalization and Collective Bargaining.* Lexington, MA: Lexington Books, 1973.

5378 *The New York City Teachers Strike.* 1962. (Documentary film produced by WCBS-TV in New York)

5379 OAKES, RUSSELL C. *Public and Professional Reactions to Teachers' Strikes, 1918-1954.* Ph D diss, New York U, 1958.

5380 ODEWAHN, CHARLES, and ALLAN SPRITZER. "Administrators' Attitudes towards Faculty Unionism." *Industrial Relations*, Vol 15 (1976), 206-15.

5381 ———. "University Administrators' Attitudes Toward Collective Bargaining: A Comparative Analysis." *Labor Law Journal*, Vol 27 (1976), 763-72.

5382 OSTROFF, BETTY S. *The Metamorphosis of a Professional Association into a Union: a Study of the Pressures, Constraints and Actions as They Worked to Effect Change in the Council of Supervisoty Associations of New York.* Ph D diss, New York U, 1972.

5383 PEARSE, ROBERT F. *Studies in White-Collar Unionism: The Development of a Teachers' Union.* Ph D diss, U of Chicago, 1950.

5384 PENSKI, ROBERT J. "John Dewey and the Nature of Democracy: The Case of Local 5, American Federation of Teachers." *Industrial and Labor Relations Forum*, Vol 5 (1968), 271-306.

5385 PETERSON, RICHARD B. "A Cross-Cultural Study of Teacher Attitudes toward Job Satisfaction, Professionalism, and Collective Negotiations." *Proceedings of the Twenty-Fifth Anniversary Meeting of the Industrial Relations Research Association*, Dec 28-29, 1972, pp 399-407. Madison: IRRA, 1973.

5386 RABINOFF, MARC. *Alternatives to Collective Bargaining: a Study of Private Colleges and Universities Where Unionization Has Been Rejected.* Ph D diss, U of Houston, 1978.

5387 RHODES, A. LEWIS. "Some Characterists of Faculty Union Membership and their Implications." *Social Problems*, Vol 24 (1977), 463-68.

5388 ROBINSON, AILEEN W. *A Critical Evaluation of the American Federation of Teachers.* Chicago: American Federation of Teachers, 1934.

5389 SACKLEY, ARTHUR. "Long-Term Trends in Urban Teachers' Compensation." *Monthly Labor Review*, Vol 89 (1966), 1223-29.

5390 SANZARE, JAMES. *A Study of Teacher Unionism in Philadelphia 1941-73; the Case of Local 3, Philadlephia Federation of Teachers.* Ph D diss, Temple U, 1977.

5391 SCHIFF, ALBERT. *A Study and Evaluation of Teachers' Strikes in the United States.* Ph D diss, Wayne State U, 1953.

5392 SCHIRESON, PETER. *The National Labor Relations Board Faculty Bargaining Unit Decision.* Ph D diss, Harvard U, 1981.

5393 SCHRAMM, CARL J. "Union Organizing at Private Colleges and Universities: a Prognosis Revisited." *Labor Law Journal*, Vol 26 (1975), 724-31.

5394 SCIMECCA, JOSEPH, and ROLAND DAMIANI. *Crisis at St. Johns—Strike and Revolution on the Catholic Campus.* NY: Random House, 1967.

5395 SEYMOUR, HAROLD. "Should College Professors Organize into Unions? Divided, the Profession Weighs the Pros and Cons of Unionism." *Industrial Bulletin*, Vol 41 (1962), 17-20.

5396 SHILS, EDWARD B., and C. TAYLOR WHITTIER. "The Other Employees in the School: Nonteacher Bargaining." *Monthly Labor Review*, Vol 90 (Sep 1967), 42-44.

5397 STINNETT, TIMOTHY M. *Turmoil in Teaching: A History of the Organizational Struggle for America's Teachers*. NY: Macmillan, 1968.

5398 SYFERS, JUDY. "San Francisco School Workers' Union Struggle." *Radical America*, Vol 12 (Mar-Apr 1978), 62-71.

5399 TAFT, PHILIP. *United They Teach: The Story of the United Federation of Teachers*. Los Angeles: Nash, 1974.

5400 THOMAS, C. R. *Faculty Union Presidents in Academe: Leadership Behaviors and Participation Strategies*. Ph D diss, West Virginia U, 1980.

5401 TICE, TERRENCE, and GRACE W. HOLMES. *Faculty Power: Collective Bargaining on Campus*. Ann Arbor, MI: Institute of Continuing Legal Education, 1972.

5402 TOMKIEWICZ, JOSEPH. *Public School Teacher Strikes in Third Class School Districts in Pennsylvania, 1970-1975*. Ph D diss, Temple U, 1978.

5403 URBAN, WAYNE. "Organized Teachers and Educational Reform During the Progressive Era: 1890-1920." *History of Education Quarterly*, Vol 16 (1976), 35-52.

5404 ———. *Why Teachers Organized*. Detroit: Wayne State U Press, 1982.

5405 UROFSKY, MELVIN I., ed. *Why Teachers Strike: Teachers' Rights and Community Control*. Garden City, NY: Doubleday, 1970.

5406 WAYNE STATE UNIVERSITY. Archives of Labor and Urban Affairs *An American Federation of Teachers Bibliography*. Detroit: Wayne State U Press, 1980.

5407 WEBBER, ANNA. "The Diary of Anna Webber: Early Day Teacher of Mitchell County." *Kansas Historical Quarterly*, Vol 38 (1972), 320-37. (Edited by Lila Scrimsher)

5408 WIEDENMAN, CHARLES. *A Study of Issues and Trends in Collective Bargaining in the Public Schools in the United States, as Perceived by School Administrators, Educational Negotiators, and Teacher Union Representatives*. Ph D diss, Ohio U, 1978.

5409 WILSON, BENNIE J. *Faculty and Administrator Attitudes Regarding Unionism Before and After Unionization in Institutions of Higher Education*. Ph D diss, Auburn U, 1979.

5410 WITKIN, IRVING. *Diary of a Teacher: The Crisis at George Washington High School*. NY: United Federation of Teachers, 1970.

5411 YABROFF, BERNARD, and LILY MARY DAVID. "Collective Bargaining and Work Stoppages Involving Teachers." *Monthly Labor Review*, Vol 76 (1953), 475-79.

5412 YATES, MICHAEL. *Public School Teachers' Unions in Pennsylvania*. Ph D diss, U of Pittsburgh, 1976.

5413 ZITRON, CELIA L. *The New York City Teachers Union, 1916-1964: A Story of Educational and Social Commitment*. NY: Humanities Press, 1968.

Electrical and Electronic

5414 ANDERSON, F. J. "The Red Electric Machine: Behind the Matles Mask." *Plain Talk*, Sep 1947.

5415 BELLA, S. J. *Boulwarism and Collective Bargaining at General Electric: A Study in Union-Management Relations*. Ph D diss, U of Michigan, 1962.

5416 BLOCH, ED. "PCB, UE, and GE." *Monthly Review*, Vol 33 (Oct 1981), 17-24.

5417 BOULWARE, LEMUEL R. *The Truth about Boulwarism: Trying to Do Right Voluntarily*. Wash.: Bureau of National Affairs, 1969.

5418 BRIGHT, ARTHUR A., JR. *The Electric-Lamp Industry: Technological Change and Economic Development from 1800 to 1947*. NY: Macmillan, 1949.

5419 BROACH, HOWELL H. *Union Progress in New York: Story of the Modernization of Union Structure and Business Methods in the Electrical Field*. NY: International Brotherhood of Electrical Workers, 1929.

5420 CLELAND, HUGH C. *The Political History of a Local Union: Local 601 of the CIO Electrical Workers Union.* Ph D diss, Western Reserve U, 1957.

5421 COHEN, ABRAHAM. *Coordinated Bargaining at General Electric: An Analysis.* Ph D diss, Cornell U, 1973.

5422 COHEN-ROSENTHAL, E. "Enriching Workers' Lives; Education Programs of the IBEW." *Change*, Vol 11 (Jul 1979), 64-66.

5423 DEAN, LOIS. "Union Activity and Dual Loyalty." *Industrial and Labor Relations Review*, Vol 7 (1954), 526-36.

5424 DERBER, MILTON. "Electrical Products," chap. 14, *How Collective Bargaining Works*, Harry A. Millis, research director. NY: Twentieth Century Fund, 1945.

5425 FENNELL, DODIE. "The Life of a Factory." *Radical America*, Vol 10 (Sep-Oct 1976), 21-41.

5426 FILIPPELLI, RONALD L. "UE: The Formative Years, 1933-1937." *Labor History*, Vol 17 (1976), 351-71.

5427 FORD, MATTHEW. "Commie-Day in Clifton, New Jersey," *Plain Talk*, Sep 1947.

5428 GALENSON, WALTER. "The Electrical and Radio Manufacturing Industries," chap. 5, *The CIO Challenge to the AFL*, Cambr.: Harvard U Press, 1960.

5429 GILDEN, K. B. *Between the Hills and the Sea* (a novel). Garden City, NY: Doubleday, 1971.

5430 GROSSMAN, RACHEL. "Women's Place in the Integrated Circuit." *Radical America*, Vol 14 (Jan-Feb 1980), 29-49.

5431 HARRISON, CHARLES YALE. "Van Arsdale's Tight Little Island." *The Reporter*, Apr 11, 1950, pp 11-14. (Local 3, IBEW)

5432 *History of the Westinghouse Strike, East Pittsburgh, Pennsylvania.* Turtle Creek, PA: Foley & Pierce, 1914.

5433 "How a Business Agent Runs His Local." *Business Week*, Oct 20, 1956, pp 92-98.

5434 HOWARD, ROBERT. "Second Class in Silicon Valley." *Working Papers for a New Society*, Vol 8 (Sep-Oct 1981), 21-31.

5435 JOHNSON, RONALD W. "Organized Labor's Postwar Red Scare: the U.E. in St. Louis." *North Dakota Quarterly*, Vol 48 (1980), 28-39.

5436 JULIANELLE, J. A. "Purge in Bridgeport, Connecticut." *Plain Talk*, Sep 1947.

5437 KASHNER, FRANK. "A Rank and File Strike at General Electric." *Radical America*, Vol 12 (Nov-Dec 1978), 43-60.

5438 "Labor: Father of the Twenty-Five-Hour Week." *Fortune*, Mar 1962, pp 189-94.

5439 "Local With a Heart." *Industrial Bulletin*, Vol 43 (Aug 1964), 20-23. (About Electrical, Radio, and Machine Workers International Union, Local 463)

5440 MACHINE RESEARCH CORPORATION. *Plant City Reactions to Electrical Workers' Strike.* Princeton: The Corporation, 1946.

5441 MCLEAN, ROBERT A. "Coalition Bargaining and Strike Activity in the Electrical Equipment Industry, 1950-74." *Industrial and Labor Relations Review*, Vol 30 (1977), 356-63.

5442 MARSH, CHARLES F. *Trade Unionism in the Electric Light and Power Industry.* Urbana: U of Illinois, 1930.

5443 MULCAIRE, MICHAEL. *The International Brotherhood of Electrical Workers: A Study in Trade Union Structure and Functions.* Wash.: Catholic U of America, 1923.

5444 NEUFELD, MAURICE F. *Day In, Day Out with Local 3, IBEW.*, Bulletin 28. Ithaca: NY State School of Industrial and Labor Relations, Cornell U, 1955.

5445 O'CONNELL, TOM. "The Union That Kept the Faith." *North Country Anvil*, No 9 (Dec-Jan 1973-74), 36-38, 51.

5446 OZANNE, ROBERT. *The Effect of Communist Leadership on American Trade Unions.* Ph D diss, U of Wisconsin, 1954. (See chap. 3)

5447 "The Passing of Marion Hedges." *John Herling's Labor Letter*, Jan 17, 1959, pp 3-4.

5448 PETTINGILL, STUART A., and VINCENT ARKELL. "Electronics Employment and Labor Force." *Monthly Labor Review*, Vol 76 (1953), 1049-54.

5449 RASKIN, A. H. "Labor's Welfare State: The New York Electrical Workers." *Atlantic Monthly,*, Apr 1963, pp 37-44.

5450 REICH, LEONARD. "Industrial Research and the Pursuit of Corporate Security: the Early Years of Bell Labs." *Business History Review*, Vol 54 (1981), 504-29.

5451 SAPOSS, DAVID J. *Communism in American Unions.* NY: McGraw-Hill, 1959. (See Part 4, chap. 22, pp 227-36)

5452 SCHATZ, RONALD. *American Electrical Workers: Work, Struggles, Aspirations, 1930-1950.* Ph D diss, U of Pittsburgh, 1978.

5453 ———. *The Electrical Workers: A History of Labor at General Electric and Westinghouse, 1920-1960.* Urbana, U of Illinois Press, 1983.

5454 ———. "The End of Corporate Liberalism: Class Struggle in the Electrical Manufacturing Industry, 1933-1950." *Radical America*, Vol 9 (Jul-Aug 1975), 187-205.

5455 ———. "Union Pioneers: The Founders of Local Unions at General Electric and Westinghouse, 1933-1937." *Journal of American History*, Vol 66 (1979), 586-602.

5456 SEIDMAN, HAROLD. "Electrical Workers Local 3," chap. 9, *Labor Czars*, NY: Liveright, 1938.

5457 SELIGMAN, DANIEL. "UE: The Biggest Communist Union." *American Mercury*, Jul 1949, pp 35-45.

5458 "The Short Work Week: A One-Year Report." *Industrial Bulletin*, Vol 42 (Aug 1963), 8-11.

5459 "Union Receiver." *Business Week*, Jan 31, 1948, pp 74-76.

5460 U.S. CONGRESS. HOUSE. Committee on Education and Labor. *Investigation of Communist Infiltration into Labor Unions which Serve the Industries of the United States: The United Electrical, Radio and Machine Workers of America, CIO.* Wash.: G.P.O., 1948.

5461 VELIE, LESTER. "The Union That Gives More to the Boss." *Reader's Digest*, Jan 1956, pp 126-30.

5462 WEBER, ARNOLD R. "Craft Representation in Industrial Unions." *Proceedings of the Fourteenth Winter Meeting of the Industrial Relations Research Association*, Dec 28-29, 1961, pp 82-92. Madison: IRRA, 1962.

5463 "Westinghouse—The First 'Automation' Strike." *Fortune*, Dec 1955, pp 57-62.

5464 WHITE, DONALD J. "Dispute Settlement in the Electrical Contracting Industry." *Monthly Labor Review*, Vol 95 (Apr 1972), 21-23.

Entertainment

GENERAL

5465 DEMBO, JONATHAN. "John Danz and the Seattle Amusement Trades Strike, 1921-1935." *Pacific Northwest Quarterly*, Vol 71 (1980), 172-82.

5466 FAINE, HYMAN R. "Unions and the Arts." *American Economic Review*, Vol 52 (1972), 70-77.

5467 MOSKOW, MICHAEL H. "Trade Unions in the Performing Arts." *Monthly Labor Review*, Vol 93 (Mar 1970), 16-20.

5468 U.S. CONGRESS. HOUSE. Committee on Education and Labor. *Economic Conditions in the Performing Arts.* Wash.:G.P.O., 1962.

5469 ———. ———. Committee on Un-American Activities. *Communist Methods of Infiltration (Entertainment).* Wash.: G.P.O., 1954.

DANCE

5470 CHASEN, J. S. "Dancer's Business: Unions and the Dancer." *Dance Magazine*, Vol 54 (1980), 46-47.

MOTION PICTURES

5471 CEPLAIR, L., and S. ENGLUND. *The Inquisition in Hollywood: Politics in the Film Community*. Garden City, NY: Doubleday, 1980.

5472 CHRISTENSON, C. LAWRENCE. "Chicago Service Trades" chap. 15, *How Collective Bargaining Works*, Harry A. Millis, research director. NY: Twentieth Century Fund, 1945. (Motion Picture Machine Operators of Chicago; Musicians of Chicago)

5473 MENDE, ROBERT. *Spit and the Stars*. NY: Rinehart, 1949.

5474 ROSS, MURRAY. *Stars and Strikes: Unionization of Hollywood*. NY: Columbia U Press, 1941.

5475 SCHWARTZ, NANCY LYNN, and SHEILA SCHWARTZ. *The Hollywood Writers' Wars*. NY: Knopf, 1982.

5476 SEIDMAN, HAROLD. "The Motion Picture Operators," chap. 11, *Labor Czars*, NY: Liveright, 1938.

5477 *Strike the Set*. 1974. (Documentary film produced by Dave Davis)

5478 SUBER, HOWARD. *The Anti-Communist Blacklist in the Hollywood Motion Picture Industry*. Ph D diss, UCLA, 1968.

5479 ———. "Politics and Popular Culture: Hollywood at Bay, 1933-1953." *American Jewish History*, Vol 68 (1979), 517-33.

5480 U.S. CONGRESS. HOUSE. Committee on Education and Labor. *Jurisdictional Disputes in the Motion Picture Industry*. Wash.: G.P.O., 1948.

5481 ———. ———. Committee on Un-American Activities. *Hearings Regarding the Communist Infiltration of the Motion Picture Industry*. Wash.: G.P.O., 1947.

MUSIC

5482 ARIAN, ED. "Some Problems of Collective Bargaining in Symphony Orchestras." *Labor Law Journal*, Vol 25 (1974), 666-72.

5483 COMMONS, JOHN R. "The Musicians of St. Louis and New York," *Labor and Administration*, NY: Macmillan, 1913.

5484 COUNTRY, VERN. "The Organized Musicians." *University of Chicago Law Review*, Vol 16 (1949), 56-85, 239-97.

5485 LEONARD, ARTHUR S. "Collective Bargaining in Major Orchestras." *Industrial and Labor Relations Forum*, Vol 10 (1975), 386-417.

5486 LOFT, ABRAM. *Musicians Guild and Union: A Consideration of the Evolution of Protective Organization among Musicians*. Ph d diss, Columbia U, 1950.

5487 LUNDE, ANDERS S. "The American Federation of Musicians and the Recording Ban." *Public Opinion Quarterly*, Vol 12 (1948), 45-56.

5488 LUNDEN, LEON E. "The Musicians' Experience: Unions, Legislation, and the Courts." *Monthly Labor Review*, Vol 88 (1965), 1177-81.

5489 SMITH, P. J. "Chorus Singers on Strike: Professionalizing Choruses." *Hi Fi*, Aug 1978, p 28.

5490 U.S. CONGRESS. HOUSE. Committee on Education and Labor. *Investigation of James C. Petrillo, The American Federation of Musicians, et al.* Wash.: G.P.O., 1947.

5491 ———. ———. *Restrictive Union Practices of the American Federation of Musicians*. Wash.: G.P.O., 1948.

SPORTS

5492 CROAK, THOMAS M. "The Professionalization of Prizefighting: Pittsburgh at the Turn of the Century." *Western Pennsylvania History Magazine*, Vol 62 (1979), 333-43.

5493 DWORKIN, JAMES B. *Owners versus Players: Baseball and Collective Bargaining*. Bost.: Auburn House, 1981.

5494 GILROY, THOMAS, and PATRICK MADDEN. "Labor Relations in Professional Sports." *Labor Law Journal*, Vol 28 (1977), 768-76.

5495 JABLE, J. THOMAS. "The Birth of Professional Football: Pittsburgh Athletic Clubs Ring in Professionals in 1892." *Western Pennsylvania History Magazine*, Vol 62 (1979), 131-47.

5496 KAPLAN, H. ROY. "The Convergence of Work, Sport and Gambling in America." *Annals of the American Academy of Political and Social Sciences*, Vol 445 (Sep 1979), 24-38.

5497 RASKIN, A. H. "Garvey and Petrillo." *The New York Times*, Oct 23, 1982, p 27.

5498 SLOANE, ARTHUR. "Collective Bargaining in Major League Baseball: a New Ball Game and its Genesis." *Labor Law Journal*, Vol 28 (1977), 200-210.

TELEVISION AND RADIO

5499 BARKER, A. F. *Attitudes of Metropolitan New York Newscasters Toward a Craft Union.* MA thesis, Brooklyn College, 1969.

5500 BENDER, M. R. *Introduction to Organized Labor in Television.* MA thesis, Michigan State U, 1969.

5501 KOENIG, A. E. "Labor Relations in the Broadcasting Industry: Periodical Literature, 1937-1964." *Journal of Broadcasting*, Vol 9 (1965), 339-56.

5502 KOENIG, ALLEN E., ed. *Broadcasting and Bargaining: Labor Relations in Radio and Television.* Madison: U of Wisconsin Press, 1970.

5503 MAHER, JEWEL G. *Analysis of Organization and Collective Bargaining by Radio Artists (AFRA).* Ph D diss, U of Chicago, 1951.

5504 MARGOLIES, MARJORIE. *The "Girls" in the Newsroom* (a novel). NY: Charter, 1983.

5505 MILLER, MERLE. *The Judges and the Judged.* Garden City: Doubleday, 1952. (Report for the American Civil Liberties Union)

5506 WILHOIT, G. C., JR. *Labor Union Organization in Radio Broadcasting: The Wagner Act to the Taft-Hartley Law.* MA thesis, U of North Carolina, 1963.

THEATER

5507 BAKER, ROBERT O. *The International Alliance of Theatrical Stage Employes and Moving Picture Machine Operators of the United States and Canada.* Lawrence, KS: The Author, 1933.

5508 FAULKENDER, ROBERT EDGASR. *Historical Development and Basic Policies of the Actors Equity.* PhD diss, U of Pittsburgh, 1954.

5509 HARDING, ALFRED. *The Revolt of the Actors.* NY: William Morrow, 1929.

5510 MARONEK, J. "Ins and Outs of a Labor Union: USA Local 350 Chicago." *Theatre Crafts.*, Vol 13 (Oct 1979), 6.

5511 O'CONNOR, JOHN, and LORRAINE BROWN, eds.. *Free, Adult, Uncensored: The Living History of the Federal Theater Project.* Wash.: New Republic, 1978.

5512 PEARLIN, LEONARD I., and HENRY E. RICHARDS. "Equity: A Study of Union Democracy," pp 265-81, *Labor and Trade Unionism: An Interdisciplinary Reader,*, Walter Galenson & Seymour Martin Lipset, eds. NY: Wiley, 1960.

5513 RITTERBUSH, ALICE MCCRACKEN. *Variety's Involvement in Broadway Labor-Management Disputes, 1905-1931.* Ph D diss, Tulane U, 1968.

5514 ROCKWOOD, JEROME. *The Cultural Activities of the Actors' Equity Association: The First Fifty Years, 1913-1963.* Ph D diss, New York U, 1966.

5515 SAPOSS, DAVID J. *Communism in American Unions.* NY: McGraw-Hill, 1959. (See chaps. 4-9, pp 19-81)

5516 U.S. CONGRESS. HOUSE. Committee on Education and Labor. *Investigation of Associated Actors and Artistes of American and Affiliated Unions.* Wash.: G.P.O., 1948.

5517 ———. SENATE. Committee on Government Operations. Permanent Subcommittee on Investigations. *American Guild of Variety Artists.* Wash.: G.P.O., 1962.

Food and Allied Products

5518 ADADEJI, MOSES. *Crossing the Color Line: Three Decades of the United Packinghouse Workers of America Crusade AGainst Racism in the Trans-Mississippi West, 1936-1968.* Ph D diss, North Texas State U, 1979.

5519 ARMOUR AND COMPANY; UNITED PACKINGHOUSE FOOD AND ALLIED WORKERS, AFL-CIO; AND AMALGAMATED MEAT CUTTERS AND BUTCHER WORKMEN OF NORTH AMERICA, AFL-CIO. Automation Committee *Progress Report: Automation Committee.* Chicago: The Committee, June 19, 1961.

5520 BELSKY, JOSEPH. *I, the Union: Being the Personalized Trade Union Story of the Hebrew Butcher Workers of America.* Yonkers: Raddock, 1953.

5521 BLUM, FRED H. *Toward a Democratic Work Process: The Hormel-Packinghouse Workers' Experiment.* NY: Harper, 1954.

5522 BONGARTZ, ROY. "The Chocolate Camelot." *American Heritage*, Vol 24 (Jun 1973), 5-11, 91-99. (Labor troubles at Hershey factory)

5523 BRODY, DAVID. *The Butcher Workmen.* Cambr.: Harvard U Press, 1964.

5524 BYRNES, JOSEPH FRANCIS. *Union Development in the Chicago Area Food Distribution Industry, 1900-1972.* Ph D diss, Northwestern U, 1974.

5525 CARVER, ARTHUR H. *Personnel and Labor Problems in the Packing Industry.* Chicago: U of Chicago Press, 1928.

5526 CONANT, EATON H. "Report and Appraisal: The Armour Fund's Sioux City Project." *Monthly Labor Review*, Vol 88 (1965), 1297-1301.

5527 COREY, LEWIS. *Meat and Man: A Study of Monopoly, Unionism, and Food Policy.* NY: Viking, 1950.

5528 DERBER, MILTON. "Case Study 1—Grain Processing." *Labor-Management Relations in Illini City*, Vol 1. Champaign: Institute of Labor and Industrial Relations, U of Illinois, 1953.

5529 EDDY, ARTHUR J. *Ganton and Company* (a novel). Chicago: McClurg, 1908.

5530 ELDREDGE, DAVID S. "The Gloucester Fishing Industry in World War II." *American Neptune*, Vol 27 (1967), 202-10.

5531 ENGELMANN, LARRY D. "'We Were the Poor People.' The Hormel Strike of 1933." *Labor History*, Vol 15 (1974), 483-510.

5532 FOGEL, WALTER. "Union Impact on Retail Food Wages in California." *Industrial Relations*, Vol 6 (1966), 79-94.

5533 GALENSON, WALTER. "The Meat Industry," chap. 10, *The CIO Challenge to the AFL*, Cambr.: Harvard U Press, 1960.

5534 GARSIDE, EDWARD B. *Cranberry Red* (a novel). NY: Little, Brown, 1938.

5535 GREENBERG, JACLYN. "Organizing the Great Cannery Strike of 1917." *Harvest Quarterly*, No 3/4 (1976), 5-11.

5536 GREENE, JOSIAH E. *Not in Our Stars* (a novel). NY: Macmillan, 1945.

5537 HURD, RICHARD W. "Strategies for Union Growth in Food Manufacturing and Agriculture." *Proceedings of the Twenty-Sixth Annual Winter Meeting of the Industrial Relations Research Association*, Dec 28-29, 1973, pp 267-74. Madison: IRRA, 1974.

5538 KROOTH, ANN BAXANDALL, and JACLYN GREENBERG. "Elizabeth Nicholas: Working in the California Canneries." *Harvest Quarterly*, No 3/4 (1976), 12-25. (Interview)

5539 LEGRANDE, L. "Merger of Retail Clerks, Meat Cutters Creates Union Exceeding 1.2 Million." *Monthly Labor Review*, Vol 102 (Sep 1979), 56-57.

5540 McDONALD, GRACE L (MARGARET GRAHAM, PSEUD). *Swing Shift* (a novel). NY: Citadel, 1951.

5541 MAURER, FLEISHER & ASSOCIATES, INC., WASHINGTON, D.C. *Union with a Heart: International Union of United Brewery, Flour, Cereal, Soft Drink and Distillery Workers of America, 75 Years of a Great Union, 1886-1961.* Cincinnati: The Union, 1961.

5542 MONTGOMERY, LOUISE. *The American Girl in the Stockyards District.* Chicago: U of Chicago Press, 1913.

5543 O'BRIEN, HOWARD V. *New Men for Old* (a novel). NY: Kennerley, 1914.

5544 OREAR, LESLIE F., and STEPHEN H. DIAMOND. *Out of the Jungle: The Packinghouse Workers Fight for Justice and Equality.* [N.p.]: Hyde Park Press, 1968.

5545 PURCELL, THEODORE V. *Blue Collar Man: Patterns of Dual Allegiance in Industry.* Cambr.: Harvard U Press, 1960.

5546 ———. *The Worker Speaks His Mind on Company and Union.* Cambr.: Harvard U Press, 1953.

5547 RANDALL, ROGER L. "Labor Agreements in the West Coast Fishing Industry: Restraint of Trade or Basis of Industrial Stability?" *Industrial and Labor Relations Review,* Vol 3 (1950), 514-41.

5548 SCARPACI, JEAN ANN. *Italian Immigrants in Louisiana's Sugar Parishes: Recruitment, Labor Conditions, and Community Relations, 1880-1910.* Ph D diss, Rutgers U, 1973.

5549 SEIDMAN, HAROLD. "The Markets," chap. 12, *Labor Czars,* NY: Liveright, 1938.

5550 SEIDMAN, JOEL. "Unity in Meat Packing: Problems and Prospects," chap. 2, *New Dimensions in Coillective Bargaining,* H. W. Davey, et al., eds. NY: Harper, 1959.

5551 SHELTON, BRENDA K. "The Grain Shovellers' Strike of 1899." *Labor History,* Vol 9 (1968), 210-38.

5552 SHULTZ, GEORGE P., and ARNOLD R. WEBER. "The Fort Worth Project of the the Armour Automation Committee." *Monthly Labor Review,* Vol 87 (1964), 53-57.

5553 SINCLAIR, UPTON B. *The Jungle* (a novel). NY: Doubleday, Doran, 1906.

5554 THOMPSON, CARL W. "Labor in the Packing Industry." *Journal of Political Economy,* Vol 15 (1907), 88-107.

5555 TUTTLE, WILLIAM M., JR. "Some Strikebreakers' Observations of Industrial Warfare." *Labor History,* Vol 7 (1966), 193-96. (Chicago packinghouse strike, 1904)

5556 *Union With a Heart.* 1974. (Documentary film produced by the Brewery Workers Union)

5557 UNITED PACKINGHOUSE WORKERS OF AMERICA. *20 Years with UPWA.* Chicago: The Union, Oct 1957.

5558 U.S. COMMISSION ON INDUSTRIAL RELATIONS (1912). "Life and Labor Conditions of Chicago Stockyards Employees," Vol 4, pp 3459-531, *Final Report,* Wash.: G.P.O., 1916.

5559 U.S. CONGRESS. HOUSE. Committee on Education and Labor. *Communist Infiltration of Maritime and Fisheries Unions.* Wash.: G.P.O., 1948.

5560 ———. ———. *Labor Practices in the Food Industry.* Wash.: G.P.O., 1948.

5561 WALKER, KENNETH P. "The Pecan Shellers of San Antonio and Mechanization." *Southwestern Historical Quarterly,* Vol 69 (1965), 44-58.

5562 WITTE, EDWIN E. "Industrial Relations in Meat Packing," chap. 22, *Labor in Postwar America,* Colston E Warne, ed. Brooklyn: Remsen Press, 1949.

Furniture

5563 ARROYO, L. L. *Industrial Unionism and the Los Angeles Furniture Industry, 1918-1954.* Ph D diss, U of California, 1980.

Glass, Stone, Pottery

5564 ALDRICH, THOMAS B. *The Stillwater Tragedy* (a novel). Bost.: Houghton Mifflin, 1880.

5565 BAIN, TREVOR. "Flat Glass: 'Industrial Peace' Revisited." *Industrial Relations*, Vol 8 (1969), 259-68.

5566 ———. *The Impact of Technological Change on the Flat Glass Industry and the Union's Reactions to Change: Colonial Period to the Present*. Ph D diss, U of California, 1964.

5567 ———. "Internal Union Conflict: the Flat Glass Workers, 1936-1937." *Labor History*, Vol 9 (1968), 106-109.

5568 BERCOWITZ, ANNA. "Labor-Management Relations in the Cement Industry." *Monthly Labor Review*, Vol 72 (1951), 17-21.

5569 BLOCH, HOWARD RUBEN. *An Analysis of an Attempt to Cut Labor Costs Despite Strong Union Opposition*. Ph D diss, Princeton U, 1964.

5570 GLASS BOTTLE BLOWERS ASSOCIATION. *Our Home: Back Through the Years*. Phila.: The Association, 1951.

5571 HARBISON, FREDERICK H., and KING CARR. *Libbey-Owens-Ford Glass Company and the Federation of Glass, Ceramic and Silica Sand Workers of America*. Wash.: National Planning Association Committee on the Causes of Industrial Peace Under Collective Bargaining, 1948.

5572 HOFFMAN, MILES E. *A Contemporary Analysis of a Labor Union: Development - Structure - Functions (Glass Bottle Blowers Association of the U.S. and Canada, AFL-CIO)*. Phila.: Department of Economics and Management, Temple U, 1959.

5573 LARNER, JOHN WILLIAMS, JR. "The Glass House Boys: Child Labor Conditions in Pittsburgh's Glass Factories, 1890-1917." *Western Pennsylvania Historical Magazine*, Vol 48 (1965), 353-64.

5574 MCCABE, DAVID A. *National Collective Bargaining in the Pottery Industry*. Balt.: Johns Hopkins U Press, 1932.

5575 MEASELL, JAMES. "The Indiana Tumbler and Goblet Company, 1894-1903." *Indiana Magazine of History*, Vol 76 (1980), 319-333.

5576 ROWE, THOMAS W., and HARRY H. COOK. *History, 1878-1957* (of American Flint Glass Workers' Union of North America). Toledo, OH: The Union, 1958.

5577 SHOTLIFF, DON A. "The 1894 Tariff and the Pottery Strike: the Rebirth of the National Brotherhood of Operative Potters." *Western Pennsylvania History Magazine*, Vol 58 (1975), 307-25.

5578 STEELE, H. ELLSWORTH. "The Consolidation Issue in the American Glass Worker Unions." *Industrial and Labor Relations Review*, Vol 3 (1950), 561-66.

5579 ———. "An Evaluation of the American Flint Glass Workers' Apprenticeship Program." *Industrial and Labor Relations Review*, Vol 5 (1951), 50-61.

5580 ———. *The Flint Glass Workers' Union*. Ph D diss, Ohio State U, 1947.

5581 ———. "The Flint Glass Workers Union in the Indiana Gas Belt and the Ohio Valley in the 1890's." *Indiana Magazine of History*, Vol 50 (1954), 229-50.

5582 U.S. NATIONAL LABOR RELATIONS BOARD. Division of Economic Research "The Pottery and Glass Industries," pp 80-92, *Written Trade Agreements in Collective Bargaining*., Wash.: G.P.O., 1939.

5583 UPHOFF, WALTER H. *Kohler on Strike: Thirty Years of Conflict*. Bost.: Beacon, 1966.

Government

5584 AFL-CIO. GOVERNMENT EMPLOYEES COUNCIL. *Report of the American Bar Association Committee on Labor Relations of Governmental Employees*. Wash.: The Council, 1955.

5585 Alexander, L. B. "Professionalization and Unionization: Compatible After All?" *Social Work*, Vol 25 (1980), 476-82.

5586 American Civil Liberties Union. *Policy Statement on Civil Rights in Government Employment*. NY: ACLU, Apr 13, 1959.

5587 Anderson, Arvid. "Labor Relations in the Public Service." *Labor Law Journal*, Nov 1961, pp 1069-94.

5588 Ashenfelter, Orley. "The Effect of Unionization on Wages in the Public Sector: The Case of Fire Fighters." *Industrial and Labor Relations Review*, Vol 24 (1971), 191-202.

5589 "At the Bargaining Table." *Public Management*, Vol 62 (1980), 1-16. (Symposium)

5590 Baarslag, Karl. *History of the National Federation of Post Office Clerks*. Wash.: The Union, 1945.

5591 Baim, Julian. *Work Alienation and its Impact on Political Life: Case Study of District Council 37 Workers*. Ph D diss, City U of NY, 1981.

5592 Bakke, E. Wight. "Reflections on the Future of Bargaining in the Public Sector." *Monthly Labor Review*, Vol 93 (July 1970), 21-25.

5593 Balkin, David B. *The Effect of Unionization, Strike Experience, and Arbitration Experience on Relative Wages in the Minnestoa Public Sector*. Ph D diss, U of Minnesota, 1981.

5594 Barrett, Jerome, and Ira B. Lobel. "Public Sector Strikes—Legislative and Court Treatment." *Monthly Labor Review*, Vol 97 (Sep 1974), 19-22.

5595 Belasco, James A. "Resolving Dispute over Contract Terms in the State Public Service: An Analysis." *Labor Law Journal*, Sep 1965, pp 533-44.

5596 Berger, Harriet. *Exclusive Recognition of Employee Organizations in the Public Service: Federal Agencies in Philadelphia and the City of Philadelphia*. Ph D diss, U of Pennsylvania, 1967.

5597 ———. "The Grievance Process in the Philadelphia Public Service." *Industrial and Labor Relations Review*, Vol 13 (1960), 568-80.

5598 ———, and Edward Blomstedt. "Clerk versus Mail Handler: Jurisdictional Disputes in the Postal Service." *Labor Law Journal*, Vol 27 (1976), 641-47.

5599 Bers, Melvin K. "The Right to Strike in the Public Sector—A Comment." *Labor Law Journal*, Aug 1970, pp 482-84.

5600 Beyer, Janice M. et al. "The Impact of Federal Sector Unions on Supervisor's Use of Personnel Policies." *Industrial and Labor Relations Review*, Vol 33 (1980), 212-31.

5601 *Blue-Collar Soldiers?: Unionization and the U.S. Military*. Phila.: Foreign Policy Research Institute, 1977.

5602 Bowen, Don L., ed. *Public Service Professional Associations and the Public Interest*. Phila.: American Academy of Political and Social Science, 1973.

5603 Brickner, Dale G. "The Status of Public Employee Bargaining." *Labor Law Journal*, Aug 1971, pp 492-98.

5604 Brooks, Thomas R. "Public Unions: Parallels to the 1930s." *American Federationist*, Vol 83 (Dec 1976), 107-22.

5605 Brooks, William W. et al. "A Current Perspective on Military Unionization: Can It Happen Here?" *Journal Collective Negotiations Public Sector*, Vol 8 (1979), 97-104.

5606 Brookshire, Michael L., and Fred Holly. "Resolving Bargaining Impasses Through Gradual Pressure Strikes." *Labor Law Journal*, Vol 24 (1973), 662-70.

5607 ———, and Michael D. Rogers. *Collective Bargaining in Public Employment: The TVA Experience*. Lexington, MA: Lexington Books, 1977.

5608 Bunker, Charles S. *Collective Bargaining: Non-Profit Sector*. Columbus, OH: Grid, 1973.

5609 Burpo, John H. *The Police Labor Movement: Problems and Perspectives*. Springfield, IL: Thomas, 1971.

5610 Burton, John F., Jr. "Can Public Employees Be Given the Right to Strike?" *Labor Law Journal*, Vol 21 (Aug 1970), 472-78.

5611 ———. "Local Government Bargaining and Management Structure." *Industrial Relations*, Vol 11 (1972), 123-40.

5612 Bussey, Ellen M. "Labor Relations in the Public Sector." *Labor Law Journal*, Aug 1973, pp 512-14.

5613 Caddell, Harold. *Attitudes of Air Force Officers Towards Professional Unionism.* Ph D diss, U.S. International U, 1981.

5614 California, U of. Bureau of Governmental Research *Organized Public Employee Relations: An Annotated Bibliogoraphy of Periodical Literature.* Los Angeles: The Bureau, 1961.

5615 Calister, Richard W. "Policemen View Collective Bargaining." *Industrial and Labor Relations Forum*, Vol 6 (1969), 319-36.

5616 Capozzola, Jolen M. "Public Employees Strikes: Myth and Realities." *National Civic Review*, Vol 68 (Apr 1979), 178-88.

5617 Case, Harry L. *Personnel Policy in a Public Agency: The TVA Experience.* NY: Harper, 1955.

5618 Chickering, A. Lawrence, ed. *Public Employee Unions: A Study of the Crisis in Public Sector Labor Relations.* San Francisco: Institute for Contemporary Studies, 1976.

5619 Cipollina, Natale. *No Past, and No Future: the Politics of Reform, Budgets, Unions, and Crises.* Ph D diss, Brandeis, 1981.

5620 Clark, R. Theodore, Jr. *Compulsory Arbitration in Public Employment.* Chicago: Public Personnel Association, 1972.

5621 Cling, Edwin Layne. *Industrial Labor Relations Policies and Practices in Municipal Government—Milwaukee, Wisconsin.* PhD diss, Northwestern U, 1957.

5622 Cohany, Harry P., and Lucretia M. Dewey. "Union Membership Among Government Employees." *Monthly Labor Review*, Vol 93 (Jul 1970), 15-20.

5623 Cohen, David M. "Grievance Arbitration in the United States Postal Service." *Arbitration Journal*, Vol 28 (1973), 258-67.

5624 Cohen, Sanford. "Does Public Employee Unionism Diminish Democracy?" *Industrial and Labor Relations Review*, Vol 32 (1979), 189-95.

5625 Cole, David L. "Devising Alternatives to the Right to Strike." *Monthly Labor Review*, Vol 92 (Jul 1969), 60-62.

5626 Compton, Luvenia. *Municipal Workers and the Labor Movement: a Bibliography.* Monticello, IL: Council of Planning Librarians, 1977.

5627 Connery, Robert H., and William V. Farr, eds.. "Unionization of Municipal Employees." *Proceedings of the Academy of Political Science*, Vol 30 (Dec 1970), entire issue.

5628 Cook, Alice H. "Public Employee Bargaining in New York City." *Industrial Relations*, Vol 9 (1970), 249-67.

5629 Cortright, David, and Strom Thurmond. *Unions in the Military?* Wash.: American Enterprise Institute, 1977.

5630 Davey, Harold W. "The Structural Dilemma in Public Sector Bargaining at State and Local Levels: A Preliminary Analysis." *Proceedings of the Twenty-Sixth Annual Winter Meeting of the Industrial Relations Research Association*, Dec 28-29, 1973, pp 67-73. Madison: IRRA, 1974.

5631 Derber, Milton. "Collective Bargaining in the Quasi-Public Sector: A Survey of Policies and Practices in the United States." *Canadian CIRIEC Review*, Vol 2 (Jun-Dec 1970), 1-20.

5632 ———. "Labor-Management Policy for Public Employees in Illinois: The Experience of the Governor's Commission, 1966-1967." *Industrial and Labor Relations Review*, Vol 21 (1968), 541-58.

5633 DOHERTY, ROBERT E. "Public Employee Bargaining and the Conferral of Public Benefits." *Labor Law Journal*, Aug 1971, pp 485-92.

5634 DOHERTY, WILLIAM C. *Mailman, U.S.A.* (history of the National Association of Letter Carriers). NY: David McKay, 1960.

5635 DOUGLAS, J. M. "Labor Injunction: Enjoining Public Sector Strikes in New Jersey." *Labor Law Journal*, Vol 31 (1980), 34-52.

5636 DUDRA, MICHAEL, ed. *Experiences Under the Pennsylvania Public Employee Relations Act: A Symposium, September 29, 1972*. Loretto, PA: Graduate Program in Industrial Relations, Saint Francis College, 1972.

5637 EDWARDS, HARRY T. "The Impact of Private Sector Principles in the Public Sector: Bargaining Rights for Supervisors and the Duty to Bargain," chap. 3, *Union Power and Public Policy*, David B. Lipsky, ed. Ithaca: NY State School of Industrial and Labor Relations, Cornell U, 1975.

5638 EHRENBERG, RONALD. "Municipal Government Structure, Unionization, and the Wages of Fire Fighters." *Industrial and Labor Relations Review*, Vol 27 (1973), 36-48.

5639 ENSIGN, TOD, and MICHAEL UHL. "Why a GI Union?" *Win*, Vol 14 (Aug 1977), 13-28.

5640 ERICKSON, HERMAN. "WPA Strike and Trials of 1939." *Minnesota History*, Summer 1971, pp 203-14.

5641 ERRANT, JAMES W. *Trade Unionism in the Civil Service of Chicago, 1895-1930*. PhD diss, U of Chicago, 1939.

5642 "Executive Order Governing Procedures of Departments Agencies of New York State for Resolution of Employee Complaints." *Industrial and Labor Relations Review*, Vol 4 (1950), 102-9.

5643 FEUILLE, PETER. "Police Labor Relations and Multilateralism." *Proceedings of the Twenty-Sixth Annual Winter Meeting of the Industrial Relations Research Association*, Dec 28-29, 1973, pp 170-77. Madison: IRRA, 1974.

5644 FEUILLE, PETER, ed. "Public Sector Impasses: a Symposium." *Industrial Relations*, Vol 16 (1977), 264-314.

5645 GAMMAGE, ALLEN Z., and STANLEY L. SACHS. *Police Unions*. Springfield, IL: Thomas, 1972.

5646 GENTEL, WILLIAM D. *Police Strikes: Causes and Prevention*. Gaithersburg, MD: International Association of Chiefs of Police, 1979.

5647 GERHART, PAUL F. "The Scope of Bargaining in Local Government Labor Negotiations." *Labor Law Journal*, Aug 1969, pp 545-52.

5648 GIBBONS, JAMES J. *The International Association of Fire Fighters*. Wash.: The Association, 1944.

5649 GODINE, MORTON R. *The Labor Problem in the Public Service: A Study of Political Pluralism*. Cambr.: Harvard U Press, 1951.

5650 GOLDBERG, JOSEPH P. "Changing Policies in Public Employee Labor Relations." *Monthly Labor Review*, Vol 93 (Jul 1970), 5-14.

5651 ———. "The Government's Industrial Employees: I—Extent of Employment, Status, Organization." *Monthly Labor Review*, Vol 77 (1954), 1-6.

5652 ———. "The Government's Industrial Employees: II—Consultation, Bargaining, and Wage Determination." *Monthly Labor Review*, Vol 77 (1954), 249-56.

5653 GOTBAUM, V. "Training for Transition: Union View; AFSCME, with Discussion." *Change*, Vol 11 (Jul 1979), 44-49.

5654 GRODIN, JOSEPH R., and MARK A. HARDIN. *Public Employee Bargaining in Oregon*. Wash.: Labor Management Services Administration, 1972.

5655 HANSLOWE, KURT L. *The Emerging Law of Labor Relations in Public Employment*. Ithaca: NY State School of Industrial and Labor Relations, Cornell U, 1967.

5656 HARPER, DEAN. "Labor Relations in the Postal Service." *Industrial and Labor Relations Review*, Vol 17 (1964), 443-53.

5657 Harring, Sydney. *The Buffalo Police: 1872-1915: Industrialization, Social Unrest, and the Development of the Police Institution.* Ph D diss, U of Wisconsin, 1976.

5658 Hart, Wilson R. *Collective Bargaining in the Federal Civil Service: A Study of Labor-Management Relations in United States Government Employment.* NY: Harper, 1961.

5659 ———. "The U.S. Civil Service Learns to Live with Executive Order 10,988: An Interim Appraisal." *Industrial and Labor Relations Review*, Vol 17 (1964), 203-20.

5660 Harvey; O. L. "The 10-Hour Day in the Philadelphia Navy Yard, 1835-36." *Monthly Labor Review*, Vol 85 (1962), 258-60.

5661 Hasson, David. *The Historical Development of Public Employee Unionism: the Performance and Effectiveness of the American Postal Union.* Ph D diss, U of California, 1977.

5662 Hayes, Robert E. *The Structure of Collective Bargaining in the Internal Revenue Service.* MS thesis, Cornell U, 1973.

5663 Hedburn, I. B. "Public Employee Labor Relations in Texas: the Widening Gap." *Labor Law Journal*, Vol 27 (1976), 107-22.

5664 Helsby, Robert D. "A Political System for a Political World—In Public Sector Labor Relations." *Labor Law Journal*, Aug 1973, pp 504-11.

5665 Herman, E. Edward. "Policy Concerns in Public Employee Bargaining: Introduction." *Labor Law Journal*, Aug 1971, pp 484-85.

5666 Herron, Robert. "The Police Strike of 1918." *Bulletin of the Historical and Philosophical Society of Ohio*, Vol 17 (1959), 181-94.

5667 Hilligan, Thomas J. "Police Employee Organizations: Past Developments and Present Problems" *Labor Law Journal*, Vol 24 (1973), 288-305.

5668 Hopkins, Anne. et al. "Public Employee Unionization in the States; a Comparative Analysis." *Administration and Society*, Vol 8 (1976), 319-41.

5669 Ichniowski, Casey. "Economic Effects of the Firefighters' Union." *Industrial and Labor Relations Review*, Vol 33 (1980), 198-211.

5670 Imundo, Louis Victor. *Why Government Employees Join Unions: A Study of AFGE Local 916.* Ph D diss, U of Oklahoma, 1971.

5671 Inter-University Seminar on the Armed Forces and Society. *Special Symposium on Trade Unionism in the Military.* Chicago: The Seminar, 1976.

5672 Jedel, Michael Jay, and William T. Rutherford. "Public Labor Relations in the Southeast: Review, Synthesis and Prognosis." *Labor Law Journal*, Aug 1974, pp 483-95.

5673 Jennings, Kenneth. et al. *Labor Relations in a Public Service Industry: Unions, Management, and the Public Interest in Mass Transit.* NY: Praeger, 1978.

5674 Juris, H. A., and Peter Feuille. *Police Unionism: Power and Impact in Public-Sector Bargaining.* Lexington: Lexington Books, 1973.

5675 Kampelman, Max M. "TVA Labor Relations: A Laboratory in Democratic Human Relations." *Minnesota Law Review*, Vol 30 (1946), 332-71.

5676 Kaplan, H. Eliot. "Concepts of Public Employee Relations." *Industrial and Labor Relations Review*, Vol 1 (1948), 206-30.

5677 Kienast, Philip K. *Policemen and Fire Fighters Employee Organizations: A Comparative Study of Historical and Sociological Factors Affecting Employee Organization Structure.* Ph D diss, Michigan State U, 1972.

5678 Killingsworth, Charles C. "Grievance Adjudication in Public Employment." *The American Arbitration Journal*, Vol 13 (1958), 3-15.

5679 Klaus, Ida. "Collective Bargaining by Government Employees," pp 21-38, *Proceedings, Conference on Labor, New York University*, NY: M. Bender, 1959.

5680 Koss, Frederick Manuel. *The Boston Police Strike of 1919.* Ph D diss, Boston U, 1966.

5681 Kovach, K. A. "Federal Employee Unions." *Business and Society Review*, Vol 29 (Spring 1979), 69-70.

5682 ———. et al. "Unions and the Military Services in the United States." *Labor Law Journal*, Vol 29 (Feb 1978), 87-94.

5683 KRAMER, LEO. *Labor's Paradox—The American Federation of State, County, and Municipal Employees AFL-CIO*. NY: Wiley, 1962.

5684 KRENDEL, EZRA S., and BERNARD L. SAMOFF, eds. *Unionizing the Armed Forces*. Phila.: U of Pennsylvania Press, 1977.

5685 KRINSKY, EDWARD B. "Avoiding Public Employee Strikes—Lessons from Recent Strike Activity." *Labor Law Journal*, Vol 21 (Aug 1970), 464-72.

5686 KRISLOV, JOSEPH. "The Independent Public Employee Association: Characteristics and Functions." *Industrial and Labor Relations Review*, Vol 15 (1962), 510-20.

5687 ———. "The Union Quest for Recognition in Government Service." *Labor Law Journal*, Jun 1958, pp 421-24, 461.

5688 ———. "The Union Shop, Employment Security, and Municipal Workers." *Industrial and Labor Relations Review*, Vol 12 (1959), 256-58.

5689 KRUGER, DANIEL H. "Trends in Public Employment." *Proceedings of the Fourteenth Annual Meeting of the Industrial Relations Research Association*, Dec 28-29, 1961, pp 354-66. Madison: IRRA, 1962.

5690 KUPFERBERG, SETH. "AFSCME: Profile of a Union." *Working Papers for a New Society*, Vol 6 (Mar-Apr 1979), 44-54.

5691 "Labor Relations Program for Employees of the City of New York." *Industrial and Labor Relations Review*, Vol 12 (1959), 618-25.

5692 LAWRENCE, LARRY J. *Attitudes of Air Force Junior Enlisted Personnel Toward Professional Unionism*. Ph D diss, U.S. International U, 1981.

5693 LEE, JOHN, and JEAN DIEMUNSCH. *Bibliography of Public Labor Relations*. Tempe: Center for Public Affairs, Arizona State U, 1979.

5694 LEE, R. ALTON. "The Army 'Mutiny' of 1946." *Journal of American History*, Vol 53 (1966), 555-71.

5695 LEKACHMAN, ROBERT. "Public Jobs: The Need for National Policy." *Proceedings of the Twenty-Fourth Annual Winter Meeting of the Industrial Relations Research Association*, Dec 27-28, 1971, pp 296-304. Madison: IRRA, 1972.

5696 LELCHOOK, JERRY, and HERBERT J. LAHNE, comps.. *Collective Bargaining in Public Employment and the Merit System*. Wash.: U.S. Office of Labor-Management Policy Development, 1972.

5697 LEVI, MARGARET. "The Political Economy of Public-Employee Unionism." *Monthly Review*, Vol 32 (Sep 1980), 46-54.

5698 LEWIN, DAVID. "Collective Bargaining Impacts on Personnel Administration in the American Public Sector." *Labor Law Journal*, Vol 27 (1976), 426-36.

5699 ———. "Public Sector Labor Relations." *Labor History*, Vol 18 (1977), 133-44.

5700 ———. et al. *Public Sector Labor Relations: Analysis and Readings*. Sun Lakes, AZ: T Horton, 1981.

5701 ———, and M. MCCORMICK. "Coalition Bargaining in Municipal Government: the New York City Experience." *Industrial and Labor Relations Review*, Vol 34 (1981), 175-90.

5702 LOEWENBERG, J. JOSEPH. *Compulsory Arbitration for Police and Fire Fighters in Pennsylvania in 1968*. Industrial and Labor Relations Review., Vol 23 (1970), 367-79.

5703 LOMBARDO, NANCY. *The Political Behavior of Boston Municipal Employee Unions in the early 1970s*. Ph D diss, Yale U, 1980.

5704 LOVE, THOMAS M., and GEORGE T. SULZNER. "Political Implications of Public Employee Bargaining." *Industrial Relations*, Vol 11 (1972), 18-33.

5705 MCANDREW, IAN C. *The Politics of the Public Workers Unions: a Case Study of AFSCME in Illinois*. Ph D diss, U of Illinois, 1976.

5706 McCollum, James K. *Status and Function of Northern Virginia Public Sector Local Unions after Commonwealth v. Arlington County Board.* Ph D diss, Virginia Polytechnic Institute, 1980.

5707 McFadden, Richard Charles. *Labor-Management Relations in the Illinois State Service, 1952.* Urbana: Institute of Labor and Industrial Relations, Cooperating with Institute of Government and Public Affairs, U of Illinois, 1954.

5708 McKelvey, Jean T. "The Role of State Agencies in Public Employee Labor Relations." *Industrial and Labor Relations Review,* Vol 20 (1967), 179-97.

5709 McLennan, Kenneth, and Michael H. Moskow. "Proceedings of the Twenty-First Annual Winter Meeting of the Industrial Relations Research Association" *Dec 29-30, 1968, pp 31-40, 59-69. Madison: IRRA, 1969*

5710 Maier, Mark H. *The City and the Unions: Collective Bargaining in New York City, 1954-1973.* Ph D diss, New School for Social Research, 1980.

5711 Martin, James F. "Union-Management Consultation in the Federal Government: Problems and Promise." *Labor Law Journal,* Vol 27 (1976), 11-17.

5712 Millett, John H. *Public Employee Unionism in Downstate Illinois Municipalities.* Ph D diss, U of Illinois, 1951.

5713 Mire, Joseph. "Unions in the Public Services." *Labor and Nation,* Sep-Oct 1947, pp 41-42.

5714 Miserendino, C. Richard. "Arbitration in the Federal Service." *Arbitration Journal,* Vol 30 (1975), 129-45.

5715 Montilla, M. Robert. *Prison Employee Unionism: Management Guide for Correctional Administrators.* Wash.: G.P.O., 1978.

5716 Morse, John R. *Strategies for Job Mobility of Minority Workers: A Study of Mobility among Unionized Civil Service Municipal Employees in New York City.* Ph D diss, New York U, 1974.

5717 Murphy, Richard J., and Morris Sackman, eds. *The Crisis in Public Employee Relations in the Decade of the Seventies: Proceedings of a Seminar Conducted by the Public Employee Relations Center, Harbridge House, Inc., February 1970.* Wash.: Bureau of National Affairs, 1970.

5718 Nelson, Nels E. "Union Security in the Public Sector." *Labor Law Journal,* Vol 27 (1976), 334-42.

5719 Nevin, Jack, and Lorna Nevin. *AFGE-Federal Union: The Story of the American Federation of Government Employees.* Wash.: The Federation, 1976.

5720 New York City Department of Labor. *Experience of New York City Municipal Agencies in the Operation of Their Grievance Procedures and Joint Labor Relations Committees.* NY: The Department, 1955.

5721 ———. *Studies on the Organizing of Public Employees.* NY: The Department, 1955. (9 numbers in 1 volume)

5722 Nigro, Felix A., ed. "Collective Bargaining in the Public Service: A Reappraisal." *Public Administration Review,* Vol 32 (Mar-Apr 1972), entire issue.

5723 Nolan, Loretto R., and James T. Hall, Jr. "Strikes of Government Employees, 1942-61." *Monthly Labor Review,* Vol 86 (1963), 52-54.

5724 Ocheltree, Keith, ed. *Government Labor Relations in Transition.* Chicago: Public Personnel Association, 1966.

5725 Olson, Craig A. "The Impact of Arbitration on the Wages of Firefighters." *Industrial Relations,* Vol 19 (1980), 325-39.

5726 Paulson, Darryl, and Janet Stiff. "An Empty Victory: the St. Petersburg Sanitation Strike, 1968." *Florida Historical Quarterly,* Vol 57 (1979), 421-33.

5727 Pendleton, Edwin C., and Paul D. Staudohar. "Arbitration and Strikes in Hawaii Public Employment." *Industrial Relations,* Vol 13 (1974), 299-307.

5728 Pezdek, Robert V. *Public Employment: Bibliography.* Ithaca: NY State School of Industrial and Labor Relations, Cornell U, 1973.

5729 PRASOW, PAUL. et al. *Scope of Bargaining in the Public Sector: Concepts and Problems.* Wash.: U.S. Department of Labor, 1972.

5730 QUESTER, GEORGE H. *The Politics of Public-Sector Labor Relations: Some Predictions.* Ithaca: NY State School of Industrial and Labor Relations, Cornell U, 1973.

5731 REHMUS, CHARLES M. "Labor Relations in the Public Sector." *Labor Law Journal,* Aug 1973, pp 514-16.

5732 ———. "Legislated Interest Arbitration." *Proceedings of the Twenty-Seventh Annual Winter Meeting of the Industrial Relations Research Association,* Dec 28-29, 1974, pp 307-14. Madison: IRRA, 1975.

5733 REINER, ROBERT. *The Blue-Coated Worker: A Sociological Study of Police Unions.* NY: Cambridge U Press, 1978.

5734 REPAS, ROBERT. *Collective Bargaining in Federal Employment.* Honolulu: Industrial Relations Center, U of Hawaii, 1970.

5735 RHYNE, CHARLES S. *Labor Unions and Municipal Employee Law.* Wash.: National Institute of Municipal Law Officers, 1946. *A Supplementary Report,* Aug 1949.

5736 ROBERTS, HAROLD S., comp. *Labor-Management Relations in the Public Service.* Honolulu: U of Hawaii Press, 1970.

5737 ROCK, ELI. "Unions and Local Government: A Review Essay." *Monthly Labor Review,* Vol 95 (Apr 1972), 33-36.

5738 ROSS, JEFFREY K. "Collective Bargaining in the Prison Sector." *Industrial and Labor Relations Forum.,* Vol 8 (1972), 1-30.

5739 SALERNO, CHARLES A. *Police at the Bargaining Table.* Springfield, IL: Thomas, 1981.

5740 SASO, CARMEN, D. *Coping with Public Employee Strikes.* Chicago: Public Personnel Association, 1970.

5741 SCHNEIDER, B. V. H. "Collective Bargaining and the Federal Civil Service." *Industrial Relations,* Vol 3 (May 1964), 97-120.

5742 SCHWEPPE, EMMA. *The Firemen's and Patrolmen's Unions in the City of New York.* NY: King's Crown Press, 1948.

5743 SEGAL, DAVID R. et al. "The Changing American Soldier: Work-Related Attitudes of U.S. Army Personnel in World War II and the 1970s." *American Journal of Sociology,* Vol 85 (1979), 95-108.

5744 SEIDMAN, JOEL. "Collective Bargaining in the Postal Service." *Industrial Relations,* Vol 9 (1969), 11-26.

5745 ———. "Discipline of Union Officers by Public Management." *Arbitration Journal,* Vol 32 (1977), 256-69.

5746 ———, and PAUL D. STAUDOHAR. "The Hawaii Public Employment Relations Act: A Critical Analysis..." *Industrial and Labor Relations Review,* Vol 26 (1973), 919-37.

5747 SIME, COLBEN K. *The Issue of Military Unionism: Genesis, Current Status and Resolution.* Wash.: National Defense University, 1977.

5748 SIMPSON, DOROTHY. *Selected References on Collective Bargaining in the Public Service.* Berkeley: Bureau of Public Administration Library, U of California, 1960.

5749 SMITH, R. L., and W. LYONS. "Impact of Fire Fighter Unionization on Wages and Working Hours in American Cities." *Public Administration Review,* Vol 40 (1980), 568-74.

5750 SMITH, RUSSELL A., and ANNE HOPKINS. "Public Employee Attitudes toward Unions." *Industrial and Labor Relations Review,* Vol 32 (1979), 484-95.

5751 ———, and DORIS B. MCLAUGHLIN. "Public Employment: A Neglected Area of Research and Training in Labor Relations." *Industrial and Labor Relations Review,* Vol 1. ((1962), 30-44)

5752 SMITH, SHARON P. "Are Postal Workers Over- or Underpaid?" *Industrial Relations,* Vol 15 (1976), 168-76.

5753 SPERO, STERLING D. *Government as Employer.* NY: Remsen Press, 1948.

5754 ———. *The Labor Movement in a Government Industry: A Study of Employee Organization in the Postal Service.* NY: Doran, 1924.

5755 ———, and JOHN M. CAPOZZOLA. *The Urban Community and its Unionized Bureaucracies: Pressure Politics in Local Government Labor Relations.* NY: Dunellen, 1973.

5756 STANLEY, DAVID T. *Managing Local Government under Union Pressure.* Wash.: Brookings Institution, 1972.

5757 STATE OF NEW YORK. GOVERNOR'S COMMITTEE ON PUBLIC EMPLOYEE RELATIONS. *Final Report, March 31, 1966.* Albany: The Committee, 1966. (Committee was: George W. Taylor, chairman, E. Wight Bakke, David L. Cole, John T. Dunlop & Frederick H. Harbison)

5758 STAUDOHAR, PAUL D. "Prison Guard Labor Relations in Ohio." *Industrial Relations,* Vol 15 (1976), 177-90.

5759 STERN, JAMES. "The Kennedy Policy: A Favorable View." *Industrial Relations,* Vol 3 (1964), 21-32.

5760 STIEBER, JACK. "The Future of Public Employee Unionism in the U.S." *Relations Industrielles-Industrial Relations,* Vol 29 (1974), 825-37.

5761 ———. *Public Employee Unionism: Structure, Growth, Policy.* Wash.: Brookings Institution, 1973.

5762 STUTZ, ROBERT L. *Collective Dealing by Units of Local Government in Connecticut.* Storrs: Labor-Management Institute, Connecticut U, 1960.

5763 "Symposium: Public Sector Labor Relations; a Canadian-United States Comparison." *Industrial Relations,* Vol 19 (1980), 239-324.

5764 TAYLOR, GEORGE W. "Public Employment: Strikes or Procedures?" *Industrial and Labor Relations Review,* Vol 20 (1967), 617-36.

5765 THE AMERICAN ASSEMBLY. *The Federal Government Service: Its Character, Prestige, and Problems.* NY: Graduate School of Business, Columbia U, 1954. (See chap. 4, pp 139-45)

5766 TOMPKINS, DOROTHY, comp. *Strikes by Public Employees, Professional Personnel and Social Workers: A Bibliography.* Berkeley: Institute of Governmental Studies, U of California, 1966.

5767 TRECKEL, KARL F. "Collective Bargaining and the Federal Reserve System." *Labor Law Journal,* Vol 24 (1973), 724-32.

5768 "Trends in Labor Legislation for Public Employees." *Monthly Labor Review,* Vol 83 (1960), 1293-96.

5769 UNIFORMED SANITATIONMEN'S ASSOCIATION. *Nine Days That Shook New York City.* NY: The Association, 1968.

5770 U.S. CIVIL SERVICE COMMISSION. Library *Labor Management Relations in the Public Service.* Wash.: The Library, 1972.

5771 U.S. CONGRESS. Joint Committee on Atomic Energy *Labor Policy in Atomic Energy Plants.* Wash.: G.P.O., 1948.

5772 ———. Joint Committee on Labor-Management Relations *Labor-Management Relations in TVA.* Wash.: G.P.O., 1949.

5773 ———. HOUSE. Committee on Education and Labor. *Investigation of GSI Strike.* Wash.: G.P.O., 1948. (Strike of workers in DC government cafeterias against General Services, Inc., the contractor)

5774 ———. SENATE. Committee on Labor and Public Welfare. Subcommittee on Labor and Labor-Management Relations. *Communist Domination of Certain Unions.* Wash.: G.P.O., 1951. (See pp 111-33 on United Public Workers of America)

5775 ———. ———. *Labor-Management Relations in the Bonneville Power Administration.* Wash.: G.P.O., 1951.

5776 ———. ———. Committee on Post Office and Civil Service. *Labor-Management Relations in the Federal Service. Hearing, 93rd Congress, 1st Session, on S. 351 to Provide for Improved Labor-Management Relations in the Federal Service...Hearing Held May 31, 1973.* Wash.: G.P.O., 1973.

5777 U.S. Department of Labor. Labor-Management Services Administration *Collective Bargaining in Public Employment and the Merit System*. Wash.: G.P.O., 1972.

5778 ———. Office of the Secretary *Draft Report of the President's Review Committee on Employee-Management Relations in the Federal Service*. Wash.: The Office, Apr 1968.

5779 U.S. General Accounting Office. *Information on Military Unionization and Organization: Report to the Congress by the Comptroller General of the United States*. Wash.: The Office, 1977.

5780 U.S. President's Task Force on Employee-Management Relations in the Federal Service. *A Policy for Employee-Management Cooperation in the Federal Service: Report, November 30, 1961*. Wash.: U.S. President's Task Force, 1961.

5781 Wagner, Aubrey J. "TVA Looks at Three Decades of Collective Bargaining." *Industrial and Labor Relations Review*, Vol 22 (1968), 20-30.

5782 Walsh, Justin E. *The Fraternal Order of Police, 1915-1976: A History*. Indianapolis: J. Munson, 1977.

5783 Weitzman, Joan. *City Workers and Fiscal Crisis: Cutbacks, Givebacks, and Survival: A Study of the New York City Experience*. New Brunswick, NJ: Rutgers U, 1979.

5784 Wellington, Harry, and Ralph K. Winter, Jr.. *The Unions and the Cities*. Wash.: Brookings Institution, 1971.

5785 Wheeler, Hoyt N. "An Analysis of the Fire Fighter Strikes." *Labor Law Journal*, Vol 26 (1975), 17-20.

5786 White, Donald J. "The Right to Strike in the Public Sector—a Discussion." *Labor Law Journal*, Vol 21 (Aug 1970), 479-82.

5787 White, Leonard D. "Strikes in the Public Service." *Public Personnel Review*, Vol 10 (1949), 3-10.

5788 White, Sheila C. "Work Stoppages of Government Employees." *Monthly Labor Review*, Vol 92 (Dec 1969), 29-34.

5789 ———. "Work Stoppages of Government Employees." *Monthly Labor Review*, Vol 92 (1969), 29-34.

5790 Woolf, Donald A. "Labor Problems in the Post Office." *Industrial Relations*, Vol 9 (1969), 27-35.

5791 Wynne, John M., Jr. "Unions and Bargaining among Employees of State Prisons." *Monthly Labor Review*, Vol 101 (Mar 1978), 10-16.

5792 Yager, Paul. "The Federal Experience." *Proceedings of the Twenty-Sixth Annual Winter Meeting of the Industrial Relations Research Association*, Dec 28-29, 1973, pp 93-97. Madison, IRRA, 1974.

5793 Yancy, Dorothy C. *The Spectre of Public Unionism from 1966 to 1976: a Critical Analysis of the Labor Polities of the City of Atlanta*. Ph D diss, Atlanta U, 1979.

5794 Zagoria, Sam, ed. *Public Workers and Public Unions*. Englewood Cliffs: Prentice-Hall, 1972.

5795 Ziskind, David. *One Thousand Strikes of Government Employees*. NY: Columbia U Press, 1940.

Health Services

5796 Alexander, L. B. *Organizing the Professional Social Worker: Union Development in Voluntary Social Work, 1930-1950*. Ph D diss, Bryn Mawr College, 1978.

5797 Alper, Philip R., ed. *Doctors' Unions and Collective Bargaining*. Berkeley: Center for Labor Research and Education, U of California, 1974.

5798 *I Am Somebody*. 1970. (Non-fiction film produced by Local 1199 of the National Union of Hospital and Health Care Employees)

5799 American Federation of Physicians and Dentists. *Doctors' Unions and Collective Bargaining*. Berkeley: Institute of Industrial Relations, U of California, 1975.

5800 "'As We See It'—the NLRB and the Courts Accomodate Union Solicitation Rights and Hospital Patient-Care Responsibilities." *William and Mary Law Review*, Vol 20 (Summer 1979), 741-67.

5801 BARRIS, BERLEAN. *Nurses' Attitudes Toward Collective Bargaining in the State of Illinois.* Ph D diss, Northwestern U, 1980.

5802 BECKER, BRIAN E. *The Impact of Unions on Labor Costs in Hospitals: a Three State Study.* Ph D diss, U of Wisconsin, 1977.

5803 ———. "Union Impact on Wages and Fringe Benefits of Hospital Nonprofessionals." *Quarterly Review of Economics and Business*, Vol 19 (Winter 1979), 27-44.

5804 BOHLANDER, GEORGE, and KEVIN O'NEIL. "Health Care Bargaining Unit Determination: Congressional Intent and the N.L.R.B. Decisions." *Labor Studies Journal*, Vol 5 (1980), 25-41.

5805 BUNKER, CHARLES S. *A Study to Determine the Impact of Unionization and the Threat Thereof on New York City's Voluntary, Nonprofit Hospitals: 1959-1966.* Ph D diss, George Washington U, 1968.

5806 BURROW, JAMES G. *AMA: Voice of American Medicine.* Balt.: Johns Hopkins Press, 1963.

5807 DELANEY, JOHN. "Union Success in Hospital Representation Elections." *Industrial Relations*, Vol 20 (1981), 149-61.

5808 DENTON, DAVID. *The Union Movement in American Hospitals, 1847-1976.* Ph D diss, Boston U, 1976.

5809 EHRENREICH, JOHN, and BARBARA EHRENREICH. "Hospital Workers: a Case Study in the 'New Working Class'." *Monthly Review*, Vol 24 (1973), 288-305.

5810 ETZIONI, AMITAI, ed. *The Semi-Professions and Their Organization: Teachers, Nurses, Social Workers.* NY: Free Press, 1969.

5811 GAMM, SARA. *Toward Collective Bargaining in Non-Profit Hospitals: Impact of New York Law.* Ithaca: NY State School of Industrial and Labor Relations, Cornell U, 1968.

5812 HEPNER, JAMES O. et al. *Personnel Administration and Labor Relations in Health Care Facilities.* St. Louis: Mosby, 1969.

5813 HEPTON, ESTELLE. *Battle for the Hospitals: A Study of Unionization in Non-profit Hospitals.* Ithaca: NY State School of Industrial and Labor Relations, Cornell U, 1963.

5814 HERSHEY, NATHAN. "Labor Relations in Hospitals in the Private Sector." *Proceedings of the Twenty-Second Annual Winter Meeting of the Industrial Relations Research Association*, Dec 29-30, 1969, pp 217-25. Madison: IRRA, 1970.

5815 HOTTLER, MYRON D. "The Union Impact on Hospital Wages." *Industrial and Labor Relations Review*, Vol 30 (1977), 342-55.

5816 JURIS, H. A. "Collective Bargaining in Hospitals." *Labor Law Journal*, Vol 28 (1977), 504-11.

5817 KHEEL, THEODORE W., and LEWIS B. KADEN. "Collective Bargaining in Hospitals: A Plan to Resolve Impasses." *Proceedings of the Twenty-Second Annual Winter Meeting of the Industrial Relations Research Association*, Dec 29-30, 1969, pp 210-16. Madison: IRRA, 1970.

5818 KOCHERY, DAVIS R., and GEORGE STRAUSS. "The Nonprofit Hospital and the Union." *Buffalo Law Review*, Vol 9 (1960), 255-82.

5819 KORN, R. "Nurses United! One Staff's Decision to Strike." *American Journal of Nursing*, Vol 80 (1980), 2218-2221.

5820 KOSSORIS, MAX D. "The San Francisco Bay Area 1966 Nurses' Negotiations." *Monthly Labor Review*, Vol 90 (Jun 1967), 8-12.

5821 LAGEMANN, ELLEN CONDLIFFE, ed. *Nursing History: New Perspectives, New Possibilities.* NY: Teachers College Press, 1983. (See especially Mary Ann Dzuback's "Nursing Historiography, 1960-1980: An Annotated Bibliography," pp 181-210)

5822 *Like a Beautiful Child.* 1967. (Documentary sponsored by Local 1199 of the National Union of Hospital and Health Care Employees)

5823 McLaughan, Catherine. *The Impact of Unions on Hospital Wages.* Ph D diss, U of Wisconsin, 1981.

5824 McMenemy, Agnes C. *The History of Collective Bargaining in Professional Nursing in Michigan.* Ph D diss, Wayne State U, 1979.

5825 Melosh, Barbara. *"The Physician's Hand": Work Culture and Conflict in American Nursing.* Phila.: Temple U Press, 1982.

5826 Metzger, Norman, and Dennis D. Pointer. *Labor-Management Relations in the Health Services Industry: Theory & Practice.* Wash.: Science & Health Publication, 1972.

5827 O'Rourke, Karen A., and Salley R. Barton. *Nurse Power: Unions and the Law.* Bowie, MD: R. J. Brady Co, 1981.

5828 Osterhaus, Leo Benedict. *Labor Unions in the Hospital and Their Effect on Management.* Ph D diss, U of Texas, 1966.

5829 Peterson, Devereaux. *The Rationale and Development of House Staff Unionization.* Ph D diss, U of Pittsburgh, 1980.

5830 Pointer, Dennis D., and Harry Graham. "Recognition, Negotiation, and Work Stoppages in Hospitals." *Monthly Labor Review,* Vol 94 (May 1971), 54-58.

5831 Ponak, Allen. *Registered Nurses and Collective Bargaining: an Analysis of Job Related Goals.* Ph D diss, U of Wisconsin, 1978.

5832 ———. "Unionized Professionals and the Scope of Bargaining: a Study of Nurses." *Industrial and Labor Relations Review,* Vol 34 (1981), 396-412.

5833 Reverby, Susan. "Hospital Organizing the the 1950s: an Interview with Lilian Roberts." *Signs,* Vol I (1976), 1053-63.

5834 Rothman, William A. *A Bibliography of Collective Bargaining in Hospitals and Related Facilities, 1959-1968.* Ann Arbor: Institute of Labor and Industrial Relations, U of Michigan—Wayne State U, 1970.

5835 ———. *A Bibliography of Collective Bargaining in Hospitals and Related Facilities, 1969-1971.* Ann Arbor: Institute of Labor and Industrial Relations, U of Michigan—Wayne State U, 1972.

5836 Sakmyster, Mary Ann. *Professionals and Social Reform: a Case Study of Unionized Physicians.* Ph D diss, 1981.

5837 Schorr, T. M. "Good News on the Speak-Up Front." *American Journal of Nursing,* Vol 79 (1979), 1387.

5838 Schutt, R. K. *The Politics of Work: Union Involvement by Social Service Employees.* Ph D diss, U of Illinois, 1978.

5839 Spano, Richard. *The Rank and File Movement in Social Work.* Ph D diss, U of Minnesota, 1979.

5840 U.S. Congress. House. Committee on Education and Labor. *Extension of NLRA to Nonprofit Hospital Employees. Hearings, 93rd Congress, 1st Session on H.R. 1236. Hearings Held April 12 and 19, 1973, in Washington, D.C.* Wash.: G.P.O., 1973.

Independent Organizations

5841 Bow, Frank T. *Independent Labor Organizations and the National Labor Relations Act.* NY: Prentice-Hall, 1940.

5842 "The Case for the Local Independent Union." *Personnel,* Nov 1955, pp 226-33.

5843 Cook, D. D. "Did Union's Success Dethrone Akron's King?" *Industry Week,* Vol 195 (Nov 1977), 70-71.

5844 Foulkes, Fred K. *Personnel Policies in Large Non-Union Companies.* Englewood Cliffs, NJ: Prentice-Hall, 1980.

5845 GILLETT, ALEXANDER. "Independent Unionism in the Midwest: The Case of the Associated Employees Organization." *Industrial and Labor Relations Forum*, Vol 5 (1969), 357-93.

5846 MARSHALL, F. RAY. "Independent Unions in the Gulf Coast Petroleum Refining Industry—The Esso Experience." *Labor Law Journal*, Sep 1961, pp 823-40.

5847 NORTHRUP, HERBERT R., and RICHARD L. ROWAN. "Multinational Union Activity in the 1976 U.S. Rubber Tire Strike." *Sloan Management Review*, Vol 18 (Spring 1977), 17-28.

5848 REPAS, ROBERT. "History of the Christian Labor Association." *Labor History*, Vol 5 (1964), 168-82.

5849 REZLER, JULIUS. "Labor Organization at Du Pont: A Study in Independent Local Unionism." *Labor History*, Vol 4 (1963), 178-95.

5850 ROTHSTEIN, WILLIAM G. "The American Association of Engineers." *Industrial and Labor Relations Review*, Vol 22 (1968), 48-72.

5851 SHOSTAK, ARTHUR B. *America's Forgotten Labor Organization: A Survey of the Role of the Single-Firm Independent Union in American Industry*. Princeton: Industrial Relations Section, Department of Economics, Princeton U, 1962.

5852 TILLERY, WINSTON L. "Local and Single-Employer Unions." *Monthly Labor Review*, Vol 92 (Sep 1969), 46-47.

5853 TROY, LEO. "Local Independent and National Unions: Competitive Labor Organizations." *The Journal of Political Economy*, Oct 1960, pp 4817-506.

5854 ———. *Local Independent Unionism: Two Case Studies*. New Brunswick, NJ: Institute of Management and Labor Relations, Rutgers State U, 1961.

5855 ———. "Local Independent Unions and the American Labor Movement." *Industrial and Labor Relations Review*, Vol 14 (1961), 331-49. (See also "Communication" by Philip Taft, pp 102-6; "Reply" by Leo Troy, pp 106-10, Vol 15, Oct 1961)

5856 U.S. BUREAU OF LABOR STATISTICS. *Characteristics of Company Unions, 1935*. Wash.: G.P.O., 1937.

5857 ———. *Unaffiliated Local and Single-Employer Unions in the United States, 1961*. Wash.: G.P.O., 1962.

5858 U.S. CONGRESS. HOUSE. Committee on Education and Labor. *Labor-Management Reform Legislation,*, Part 3. Wash.: G.P.O., 1959. (See "Statement of J. W. Dunnebeck, President, International Society of Skilled Trades, Linden, Michigan," pp 1157-81; "Statement of Joseph Gritter, Secretary, Christian Labor Association of the United Stastes of America," pp 1198-1212)

Iron, Steel, and Metal

5859 ADAMS, LARRY T. "Abel-Dominated Convention Endorses No-Strike Policy, Seeks Job Guarantee." *Monthly Labor Review*, Vol 99 (1976), 44-46.

5860 ALBERY, FAXON F.D. *Michael Ryan, Capitalist* (a novel). Columbus, OH: Rowfant, 1913.

5861 AMERICAN MANAGEMENT ASSOCIATION. *Labor Relations in United States Steel,*, Personnel Series No 164. NY: The Association, 1955.

5862 *An American Romance*. 1944. (Feature film directed by King Vidor)

5863 ASHER, ROBERT. "Painful Memories: the Historical Consciousness of Steelworkers and the Steel Strike of 1919." *Pennsylvania History*, Vol 45 (1978), 61-86.

5864 ATTAWAY, WILLIAM. *Blood on the Forge* (a novel). NY: Doubleday, Doran, 1941.

5865 BART, PHIL. "Observations on the McNamara Case." *Political Affairs*, Vol 59 (Nov 1980), 31-33.

5866 BATLIN, CARL A. "United Steelworkers of America Convention." *Monthly Labor Review*, Vol 95 (Nov 1972), 53-54.

5867 Bauder, Russell. *Industrial Relations in the Machinery and Jobbing Branch of the Foundry Industry*. (Unpublished manuscript, U of Wisconsin Library)

5868 Baughman, James L. *The 1937 Little Steel Strike in Three Ohio Communities*. MA thesis, Columbia U, 1975.

5869 ———. "Classes and Company Towns: Legends of the 1937 Little Steel Strike." *Ohio History*, Vol 87 (1978), 175-84.

5870 Bell, Thomas. *Out of This Furnace* (a novel). Bost.: Little, Brown, 1941.

5871 Belman, Albert A. "Wage Chronology No 11: Aluminum Company of America, 1939-1950." *Monthly Labor Review*, Vol 71 (1950), 688-92.

5872 Bennett, John. *Iron Workers in Woods Run and Johnstown: the Union Era, 1865-1895*. Ph D diss, U of Pittsburgh, 1978.

5873 Bernstein, Meyer. *The Steelworkers Election 1965*. Wash.: United Steelworkers of America, 1966.

5874 Betheil, Richard. "The ENA in Perspective: the Transformation of Collective Bargaining in the Basic Steel Industry." *Review of Radical Political Economics*, Vol 10 (Summer 1978), 1-24.

5875 Brody, David. *Labor in Crisis: The Steel Strike of 1919*. Phila.: Lippincott, 1965.

5876 ———. *Steelworkers in America: The Nonunion Era*. Cambr.: Harvard U Press, 1960.

5877 Bromfield, Louis. *The Green Bay Tree* (a novel). NY: Grosset & Dunlap, 1927.

5878 Brooks, Robert R. R. *As Steel Goes,...Unionism in a Basic Industry*. New Haven: Yale U Press, 1940.

5879 Brooks, Thomas R. "A Steelworker's Local in New England." *Dissent*, Vol 19 (1972), 47-52.

5880 Byington, M. F. *Homestead: The Households of a Mill Town*. NY: Charities Publication Committee, 1910.

5881 Caldwell, Janet Taylor. *Strong City* (a novel). NY: Scribner's, 1942.

5882 Close, K. "Steel Makers: 1937-1947." *Survey Graphic*, Mar, 1947.

5883 Cohen, Steven R. "Steelworkers Rethink the Homestead Strike of 1892." *Pennsylvania History*, Vol 48 (1981), 155-77.

5884 Coleman, Glen M. *The Growth of Management-Labor Understanding in the Steel Industry of Western Pennsylvania, with Special Emphasis on Job Security and Seniority*. Ph D diss, U of Pittsburgh, 1953.

5885 Cook, Philip L. "Tom Girdler and the Labor Policies of the Republic Steel Corporation." *Social Science History*, Vol 42 (1967), 21-30.

5886 Cortner, Richard C. *The Jones and Laughlin Case*. NY: Knopf, 1970.

5887 Craft, James A. "The ENA, Consent Decrees, and Cooperative in Steel Labor Relations: a Critical Appraisal." *Labor Law Journal*, Vol 27 (1976), 633-40.

5888 Craypo, Charles. "Collective Bargaining in the Conglomerate, Multinational Firm: Litton's Shutdown of Royal Typewriter." *Industrial and Labor Relations Review*, Vol 29 (1975), 3-25.

5889 Crowell, F. Elisabeth. "Painter's Row and the Commons." *Charities and the Commons*, Vol 21 (1909), 899-910. (Periodical later known as *Survey Graphic*)

5890 D'Agostino, Therese. "Women as Steelworkers." *Political Affairs*, Vol 55 (May 1976), 11-19.

5891 Daugherty, Carroll R. et al. *The Economics of the Iron and Steel Industry*. NY: McGraw-Hill, 1937.

5892 Davenport, Susan. *A Job in the Mills: Women Workers in Steel Production in the Chicago Area During World War II*. MA thesis, U of Illinois, 1981.

5893 David, Henry. "Upheaval at Homestead" chap. 7, *America in Crisis*, Daniel Aaron, ed. NY: Knopf, 1952.

5894 Davis, Horace B. *Labor and Steel*. NY: International Publishers, 1933.

5895 De Vyver, Frank T. "Collective Bargaining in Steel," chap. 16, *Labor in Postwar America*, Colston E. Warn, ed. Brooklyn: Remsen Press, 1949.

5896 DERBER, MILTON. "Labor Participation in Management: Some Impressions of Experience in the Metal Working Industries of Britain, Israel and the United States." *Proceedings of the Seventeenth Annual Meeting of the Industrial Relations Research Association*, Dec 28-29, 1964, pp 261-69. Madison: IRRA, 1965.

5897 DIX, KEITH. *A Study of Collective Bargaining in the Non-ferrous Metals Industry*. Ph D diss, U of Maryland, 1967.

5898 DOERINGER, PETER B. "Piece Rate Wage Structures in the Pittsburgh Iron and Steel Industry—1880-1900." *Labor History*, Vol 9 (1968), 262-74.

5899 EGGERT, GERALD G. *Steelmasters and Labor Reform, 1886-1923*. Pittsburgh: U of Pittsburgh Press, 1981.

5900 EMSPAK, FRANK. "Labor Process and Capitalism Corporate Planning." *Science & Society*, Vol 44 (1980), 224-28.

5901 FACT FINDING BOARD. *Steel Producing Subsidiaries of U.S. Steel Corp. and United Steelworkers of America (CIO),*, Feb 25, 1946. Labor Arbitration Reports, Bureau of National Affairs. Wash.:, 1946. 1 LA 630.

5902 *Factory*. 1969. (Non-fiction film by Arthur Barron)

5903 FEDERAL COUNCIL OF THE CHURCHES OF CHRIST IN AMERICA. Commission on the Church and Social Service *Report of Special Committee...Concerning the Industrial Situation in South Bethlehem, Pennsylvania*. NY: The Council, 1912.

5904 ———. Research Department *The Twelve Hour Day in the Steel Industry*. NY: The Council, 1923.

5905 *The Fight Against Black Monday*. 1977. (Non-fiction film by ABC-News)

5906 FISCHER, BEN. "Arbitration: The Steel Industry Experiment." *Monthly Labor Review*, Vol 95 (1972), 7-10.

5907 FISHER, THOMAS R. *Industrial Disputes and Federal Legislation, with Special Reference to the Railroad, Coal, Steel and Automobile Industries in the U.S. since 1900*. NY: Columbia U Press, 1940.

5908 FITCH, JOHN. *The Steel Workers*. NY: Charities Publications, 1911.

5909 FOSTER, WILLIAM Z. *The Steel Workers and the Fight for Labor's Rights*. NY: New Century, 1952.

5910 ———. *Unionizing Steel*. NY: Workers Library, 1936.

5911 GALENSON, WALTER. "The Organization of Steel," chap. 2, *The CIO Challenge to the AFL*, Cambr.: Harvard U Press, 1960.

5912 GALLAGHER, DANIEL J. *MIRA and the Molders' Union: the Conference Committee as an Alternative Form of Grievance Settlement*. Ph D diss, U of Cincinnati, 1980.

5913 GARRATY, JOHN A. "The United States Steel Corporation Versus Labor: The Early Years." *Labor History*, Vol 1 (1960), 3-38.

5914 GORDON, MAX. "The Communists and the Drive to Organize Steel, 1936." *Labor History*, Vol 22 (1982), 254-65.

5915 GOTTLIEB, PETER. "Migration and Jobs: the New Black Workers in Pittsburgh, 1916-1930." *Western Pennsylvania Historical Magazine*, Vol 61 (1978), 1-15.

5916 GOULD, E. R. L. *The Social Condition of Labor*. Balt.: Johns Hopkins Press, 1893.

5917 GOULD, HELEN M. "Aliquippa." *Labor and Nation,*, Apr-May 1946, pp 27-30. (Steel strike, 1946)

5918 GRAUBMAN, MELODY W. "Kennecott: Alaskan Origins of a Copper Empire, 1900-1938." *Western Historical Quarterly*, Vol 9 (1978), 197-211.

5919 GREENE, JOSIAH E. *The Man with One Talent* (a novel). NY: McGraw-Hill, 1951.

5920 GREER, EDWARD. "Monopoly and Competitive Capital in the Making of Gary, Indiana." *Science & Society*, Vol 40 (1976), 465-78.

5921 GROSSMAN, JONATHAN. "Co-Operative Foundries." *New York History*, Vol 24 (1943), 196-210.

5922 ———. "The Molders' Struggle Against Contract Prison Labor." *New York History*, Vol 23 (1942), 449-57.

5923 GULICK, CHARLES A. *Labor Policy of the United States Steel Corporation.* NY: Columbia U Press, 1924.

5924 GURNEY, JOHN L. "Union Conventions: United Steelworkers of America." *Monthly Labor Review*, Vol 93 (Dec 1970), 33-34.

5925 GUTMAN, HERBERT G. "An Iron Workers' Strike in the Ohio Valley, 1873-1874." *The Ohio Historical Quarterly*, Vol 68 (1959), 353-70.

5926 ———. "Two Lockouts in Pennsylvania 1873-1874." *The Pennsylvania Magazine of History and Biography*, Vol 83 (1959), 307-26.

5927 HALL, GUS. "Thirty Years of Struggle for a Steelworkers' Union and Working Class Ideology." *Political Affairs*, Vol 53 (Sep 1974), 20-36.

5928 HALPER, ALBERT. *The Foundry* (a novel). NY: Viking, 1934.

5929 HARBISON, FREDERICK H. "Steel," chap. 10, *How Collective Bargaining Works*, Harry A. Millis, research director. NY:L Twentieth Century Fund, 1945.

5930 ———, and ROBERT C. SPENCER. "The Politics of Collective Bargaining: The Postwar Record in Steel." *American Political Science Review*, Vol 48 (1954), 705-20.

5931 HARRIS, CYRIL. *The Trouble at Hungersford* (a novel). Bost: Little, Brown, 1952.

5932 HARVEY, G. B. M. *Henry Clay Frick.* NY: Scribner's, 1928.

5933 HENLE, PETER. "Reverse Collective Bargaining? A Look at Some Union Concession Situations." *Industrial and Labor Relations Review*, Vol 26 (1973), 956-68.

5934 HERLING, JOHN. *Right to Challenge: People and Power in the Steelworkers Union.* NY: Harper & Row, 1972.

5935 HESSEN, ROBERT. "The Bethlehem Steel Strike of 1910." *Labor History*, Vol 15 (1974), 3-18.

5936 ———. "The Transformation of Bethlehem Steel, 1904-09." *Business History Review*, Vol 46 (1972), 339-60.

5937 HILL, CHARLES. "Fighting the Twelve-Hour Day in the American Steel Industry." *Labor History*, Vol 15 (1974), 19-35.

5938 HILL, JOSEPH. "Steel: Changing Workplace, How It Looks in Allegheny County." *Dissent*, Vol 19 (1972), 37-47.

5939 HOLT, JAMES. "Trade Unionism in the British and U.S. Steel Industries, 1888-1912: A Comparative Study." *Labor History*, Vol 18 (1977), 5-35.

5940 HOOPES, ROY. *The Steel Crisis.* NY: John Day, 1963.

5941 "How Truth Was almost Lost: Strikers Got Blame until Film Discovered." *Allied Industrial Worker*, Vol 17 (Aug 1974). (Memorial Day Massacre)

5942 INGHAM, JOHN NORMAN. *Elite and Upper Class in the Iron and Steel Industry, 1874 to 1965.* Ph D diss, U of Pittsburgh, 1973.

5943 "It Happened in Steel: Story of the M. C. Taylor Labor Formula." *Fortune*, May 1937, pp 91-94.

5944 JENSEN, VERNON H. *Heritage of Conflict: Labor Relations in the Nonferrous Metals Industry up to 1930.* Ithaca: Cornell U Press, 1950.

5945 ———. *Nonferrous Metals Industry Unionism, 1932-1954.* Ithaca: NY State School of Industrial and Labor Relations, Cornell U, 1954.

5946 JONES, IDWAL. *Steel Chips* (a novel). NY: Knopf, 1919.

5947 KEITEL, ROBERT S. "The Merger of the International Union of Mine, Mill and Smelter workers into the United Steel Workers of America." *Labor History*, Vol 15 (1974), 36-43.

5948 KORNBLUM, WILLIAM. "A Crisis in Basic Steel." *Dissent*, Vol 25 (1978), 146-49.

5949 ———. "Insurgency in the Steel Union." *Dissent*, Vol 22 (1975), 220-22.

5950 KREMEN, BENNETT. "No Pride in This Dust: Young Workers in the Steel Mills." *Dissent*, Vol 19 (1972), 21-28.

5951 LAGES, JOHN D. *The SWOC-CIO Attempt to Organize the Steel Industry, 1936-1942: A Restatement and Economic Analysis.* Ph D diss, Iowa State U, 1967.

5952 LAHNE, HERBERT J. "The Welder's Search for Craft Recognition." *Industrial and Labor Relations Review*, Vol 11 (1958), 591-607.

5953 LAUDERBAUGH, RICHARD A. *American Steel Makers and the Coming of the Second World War*. Ph D diss, Washington U, 1979.

5954 LAVELLE, MICHAEL. *Red, White and Blue-Collar Views: A Steelworker Speaks his Mind about America*. NY: Saturday Review Press/Dutton, 1975.

5955 LEAB, DANIEL J. "The Memorial Day Massacre." *Midcontinent American Studies Journal*, Vol 8 (Fall 1967), 3-17.

5956 LEE, HARRY. *Sir and Brother* (a novel). NY: Viking, 1940.

5957 LEOTTA, LOUIS, JR. *Republic Steel Corporation in the Steel Strike of 1937*. MA thesis, Columbia U, 1960.

5958 LEVIN, MEYER. *Citizens* (a novel). NY: Viking, 1940.

5959 LEVINSON, HAROLD M. *Collective Bargaining in the Steel Industry: Pattern Setter or Pattern Follower?* Ann Arbor: Institute of Labor and Industrial Relations, U of Michigan—Wayne State U, 1962.

5960 LIBERTELLA, ANTHONY F. *The Steel Strike of 1959: Labor, Management and Government Relations*. Ph D diss, Ohio State U, 1972.

5961 LIVERNASH, EDWARD R. *Collective Bargaining in the Basic Steel Industry: A Study of the Public Interest and the Role of Government*. Westport, CT: Greenwood, 1976.

5962 LOVEDAY, AMOS. *The Cut Nail Industry, 1776-1890: Technology, Cost Accounting and the Upper Ohio Valley*. Ph D diss, Ohio State U, 1980.

5963 LYND, STAUGHTON. "What Happened in Youngstown; an Outline." *Radical America*, Vol 15 (Jul-Aug 1981), 37-48.

5964 MCCAFFREE, KENNETH M. *Bargaining in the Metal Trades in the Northwest*. Wash.: U.S. Bureau of Labor Statistics, 1957.

5965 MCCLYMER, JOHN F. "The Pittsburgh Survey, 1907-1914: Forging an Ideology in the Steel District." *Pennsylvania History*, Vol 41 (1974), 169-86.

5966 MCCONNELL, GRANT. *Steel and the Presidency, 1962*. NY: Norton, 1963.

5967 MACDONALD, JEFF. "New Directions: the Allied Industrial Workers Locus on Bargaining Committees and Contract Negotiation." *Labor Studies Journal*, Vol 6 (1981), 95-103.

5968 MCGIBENY, DONALD. *Slag: a Story of Steel and Stocks* (a novel). Indianapolis: Bobbs-Merrill, 1922.

5969 MACILVAINE, C. A. "Appraisal of Kaiser's Sharing Plan." *Monthly Labor Review*, Vol 87 (Apr 1964), 401-4.

5970 MCPHERSON, DONALD S. "The 'Little Steel' Strike of 1937 in Johnstown, Pennsylvania." *Pennsylvania History*, Vol 39 (Apr 1972), 45-56.

5971 MCSORLEY, EDWARD. *Our Own Kind*. NY: Harper, 1946.

5972 MAIRS, E. D. "Extended Vacations at Alcoa." *Monthly Labor Review*, Vol 87 (1964), 404-6.

5973 MANN, HENRY. *Adam Clarke* (a novel). NY: Popular Book Co., 1904.

5974 MANZARDO, M. "Death on a Prairie." *Steel Labor*, Vol 37 (May 1972), 5. (Participants report of the Republic Steel Southside Chicago plant strike on Memorial Day 1937)

5975 MARCUS, MAEVA. *The Steel Seizure Case of 1952*. Ph D diss, Columbia U, 1978.

5976 MARSH, JOHN L. "Captain Fred, Col. I, and the Workers of Homestead." *Pennsylvania History*, Vol 46 (1979), 291-311.

5977 MARTIN, JAMES M. *Which Way, Sirs, the Better?* (a novel). Bost.: Arena, 1895.

5978 MATERA, VINCENT L. "Steel Industry Equal Employment Consent Decrees." *Proceedings of the Twenty-Seventh Annual Winter Meeting of the Industrial Relations Research Association*, Dec 28-29, 1974, pp 217-24. Madison: IRRA, 1975.

5979 *Memorial Day Massacre of 1937*. 1977. (Documentary film produced by the Illinois Labor History Society)

5980 *Men and Dust*. 1940. (Documentary film produced by Lee & Sheldon Dick)
5981 MERGEN, BERNARD. "Blacksmiths and Welders: Identity and Phenomenal Change." *Industrial and Labor Relations Review*, Vol 25 (1972), 354-62. (See also Vol 26(1973), pp 860-64 for comment & reply)
5982 METZGAR, JACK. "Plant Shutdowns and Worker Response: the Case of Johnstown, Pennsylvania." *Socialist Review*, Vol 10 (Sep-Oct 1980), 9-49.
5983 MEYERHUBER, CARL. "Organizing Alcoa: the Aluminum Workers Union in Pennsylvania's Allegheny Valley, 1900-1971." *Pennsylvania History*, Vol 48 (1981), 195-219.
5984 ———. "Black Valley: Pennsylvania's Allekiski and the Great Strike of 1919." *Western Pennsylvania History Magazine*, Vol 69 (1979), 251-65.
5985 MILLER, J. WADE. *Sharon Steel Corporation and United Steelworkers of America*. Wash.: National Planning Association, 1949.
5986 MOBERG, DAVID. "Socialism and the Steelworkers." *Socialist Revolution*, Vol 6 (Oct-Dec 1976), 57-76.
5987 MOHL, RAYMOND A. "The Great Steel Strike of 1919 in Gary, Indiana: Working Class Radicalism or Trade Union Militancy." *Mid-America*, Vol 63 (1981), 36-49.
5988 NAGLE, RICHARD. *Collective Bargaining in Basic Steel and the Federal Government, 1945-1960*. Ph D diss, Pennsylvania State U, 1978.
5989 NELSON, DANIEL. "Taylorism and the Workers at Bethlehem Steel, 1898-1901." *Pennsylvania Magazine of History and Biography*, Vol 101 (1977), 487-505.
5990 NOBLE, BOB. *Steel Bibliography*. 1981. (40-page mimeo., copy in Tamiment Library)
5991 NYDEN, PHILIP. *Rank-and-File Insurgency in a Large Industrial Union: A Case Study of the United Steelworkers of America*. Ph D diss, U of Pennsylvania, 1979.
5992 O'CONNOR, HARVEY. *Steel-Dictator*. NY: John Day, 1935.
5993 O'MALLEY, MICHAEL. *Miners Mill* (a novel). NY: Harper, 1962.
5994 ORR, JOHN A. *The Impact of the Product Market upon Labor Relations in the American Basic Steel Industry*. Ph D diss, U of Wisconsin, 1968.
5995 ———. "The Rise and Fall of Steel's Human Relations Committee." *Labor History*, Vol 14 (1973), 69-82.
5996 PACKARD, STEVE. "Steelmill Blues." *Liberation*, Vol 19 (May 1975), 7-15.
5997 PALMER, FRANK L. *Spies in Steel: An Expose of Industrial War*. Denver: Labor Press, 1928.
5998 PITCAITHLEY, DWIGHT. "Zinc and Lead Mining Along the Buffalo River." *Arkansas Historical Quarterly*, Vol 37 (1978), 293-305.
5999 RAIMON, ROBERT L. "Affluence, Collective Bargaining and Steel." *Labor Law Journal*, Nov 1960, pp 979-86.
6000 RAYL, DALLAS G. "Extended Vacations at Timken." *Monthly Labor Review*, Vol 87 (Apr 1964), 406.
6001 ROBERTS, DICK. "The World Crisis in Steel." *International Socialist Review*, Vol 30 (Jan 1972), 18-21.
6002 ROBINSON, JESSE S. *The Amalgamated Association of Iron Steel, and Tin Workers*. Balt.: Johns Hopkins Press, 1920.
6003 ROOT, LAWRENCE S. *Fringe Benefits: Social Insurance in the Steel Industry*. Beverly Hills, CA: Sage, 1982.
6004 ROSS, CLINTON. *The Silent Workman* (a novel). NY: Putnam, 1886.
6005 SAKOLSKI, A. M. "The Finances of the Iron Molders' Union." *Studies in American Trade Unionism*, Jacob H. Hollander & George E. Barnett, eds. NY: Holt, 1906.
6006 SAPOSS, DAVID J. *Organization of Steel Workers*. NY: Bureau of Industrial Research, 1921.
6007 SCHAFFER, BEVERLY. "Experience with Supplementary Unemployment Benefits: A Case Study of the Atlantic Steel Company." *Industrial and Labor Relations Review*, Vol 22 (1968), 85-94.

6008 SCHEUERMAN, WILLIAM. "Economic Power in the United States: the Case of Steel." *Politics and Society*, Vol 5 (1975), 337-66.
6009 SCHULTZ, GEORGE P., and ROBERT P. CRISARA. *The LaPoint Machine Tool Company and United Steelworkers of America.* Wash.: National Planning Association, 1952.
6010 SCOTT, LEROY. *The Walking Delegate* (a novel). NY: Doubleday, Page, 1905.
6011 SEIDMAN, JOEL. et al. "Metal Workers: Factionalism and Conflict," chap. 5, *The Worker Views His Union*, Chicago: U of Chicago Press, 1958.
6012 ———. "Steel Workers: Militant Unionism," chap. 4, *The Worker Views His Union*, Chicago: U of Chicago Press, 1958.
6013 SELEKMAN, BEN M. *Employees' Representation in Steel Works: A Study of the Industrial Representation Plan of the Minnequa Steel Works of the Colorado Fuel and Iron Company*. NY: Russell Sage Foundation, 1924.
6014 SELTZER, GEORGE. "The United Steelworkers and Unionwide Bargaining." *Monthly Labor Review*, Vol 84 (1961), 129-36.
6015 SERENE, FRANK H. *Immigrant Steelworkers in the Monongahela Valley: Their Communities and the Development of a Labor Class Consciousness*. Ph D diss, U of Pittsburgh, 1979.
6016 SHIELDS, ART. "The Class Struggle in Steel." *Political Affairs*, Vol 55 (Jan 1976), 14-28.
6017 SHINER, JOHN F. "The 1937 Steel Labor Dispute and the Ohio National Guard." *Ohio History*, Vol 84 (1975), 182-95.
6018 SINCLAIR, UPTON B. *Little Steel* (a novel). NY: Farrar and Rinehart, 1938.
6019 SKAGGS, J. C., and RICHARD L. EHRLICH. "Profits, Paternalism, and Rebellion: a Case Study in Industrial Strife." *Business History Review*, Vol 54 (1980), 155-74.
6020 SMITH, WILLIAM DALE. *A Multitude of Men* (a novel). NY: Simon and Schuster, 1959.
6021 SOFCHALK, DONALD G. "The Chicago Memorial Day Incident: An Episode of Mass Action." *Labor History*, Vol 6 (1965), 3-43.
6022 ———. *The Little Steel Strike of 1937.* Ph D diss, Ohio State U, 1961.
6023 SPEER, MICHAEL. "The 'Little Steel' Strike: Conflict for Control." *Ohio History*, Vol 78 (1969), 273-87.
6024 SPIER, WILLIAM. "A Social History of Manganese Mining in the Batesville District of Independence County." *Arkansas Historical Quarterly*, Vol 36 (1977), 130-57.
6025 "Steel Negotiation Documents." *Monthly Labor Review*, Vol 82 (1959), 1330-47. (George W. Taylor, "Remarks upon Conclusion of Steel Board Testimony," pp 1330-32; "The Steel Board's Report to the President," pp 1333-41; "The Supreme Court's Ruling in the Injunction Appeal," pp 1342-44; "The Kaiser-Steelworkers Agreement," pp 1345-46; and "A Long-Range Plan for Preventing Bargaining Crises," p 1347)
6026 *Steeltown*. 1943. (Documentary film by Willard Van Dyke, for OWI)
6027 "Steelworker Roots." *Steel Labor*, Vol 42 (Sep 1977), 8-9. (Steelworkers archives)
6028 "Steelworkers Are Tough and Their Union Is the Best Organized in the C.I.O." *Life*, Feb 4, 1946.
6029 "Steelworkers Want Wartime Justice." *Fortune*, Feb 1944, pp 164-66.
6030 STEFFEN, CHARLES. "The Pre-Industrial Iron Worker: Northampton Iron Works, 1780-1820." *Labor History*, Vol 20 (1979), 89-110.
6031 STIEBER, JACK. "Occupational Wage Differentials in the Basic Steel Industry." *Industrial and Labor Relations Review*, Vol 12 (1959), 167-81.
6032 ———. *The Steel Industry Wage Structure: A Study of the Joint Union-Management Job Evaluation Program in the Basic Steel Industry*. Cambr.: Harvard U Press, 1959.
6033 STOCKTON, FRANK T. *The International Molders' Union of North America.* Balt.: Johns Hopkins Press, 1921.
6034 STONE, KATHERINE. "The Origin of Job Structure in the Steel Industry." *Radical America*, Vol 7 (Nov-Dec 1973), 19-64.

6035 STRAUS, DONALD B. "Laws Won't Stop Strikes." *Harper's*, Jul 1, 1952, pp 21-27.

6036 SWETNAM, G. "Labor-Management Relations in Pennsylvania's Steel Industry, 1800-1959." *Western Pennsylvania History Magazine*, Vol 62 (1979), 321-32.

6037 TILLETT, DOROTHY S. (JOHN STEPHEN STRANGE, PSEUD.). *Angry Dust* (a novel). NY: Doubleday, 1946.

6038 TILOVE, ROBERT. *Collective Bargaining in the Steel Industry*. Phila.: U of Pennsylvania Press, 1948.

6039 TROUTMANN, WILLIAM E., and PETER HAGBOLDT. *Hammers of Hell* (a novel). Chicago: New World Press, 1921.

6040 ULMAN, LLOYD. *The Government of the Steel Workers' Union*. NY: Wiley, 1962.

6041 U.S. BOARD OF INQUIRY ON THE 1959 LABOR DISPUTE IN THE STEEL INDUSTRY. *Final Report*. Wash.: The Board, Jan 6, 1960.

6042 ———. *Report to the President Submitted by the Board of Inquiry under Executive Orders 10843 and 10848 Pursuant to the "National Emergencies" Sections of the Labor Management Relations Act, 1947*. Wash.: The Board, Oct 19, 1959.

6043 U.S. BUREAU OF LABOR. *Report on Conditions of Employment in the Iron and Steel Industry in the United States*. Wash.: G.P.O., 1911-13. (Senate Document No 110)

6044 U.S. BUREAU OF LABOR STATISTICS. *Work Stoppages: Basic Steel Industry, 1901-1958*. Wash.: G.P.O., 1959.

6045 U.S. COMMISSION ON INDUSTRIAL RELATIONS (1912). "The Metal Trades of Philadelphia," Vol 3, pp 2817-927, *Final Report*, Wash.: G.P.O., 1916.

6046 U.S. CONGRESS. HOUSE. Committee on Education and Labor. *Investigation of Riot at Shakespeare Company, Kalamazoo, Michigan*. Wash.: G.P.O., 1948.

6047 ———. ———. *Investigation of the Wage Stabilization Board*. Wash.: G.P.O., 1952.

6048 ———. ———. Committee on the Judiciary. *Investigation of the Employment of Pinkerton Detectives in Connection with the Labor Troubles at Homestead, Pennsylvania*. Wash.: G.P.O., 1892.

6049 ———. SENATE. Committee on Labor and Public Welfare. Subcommittee on Labor and Labor-Management Relations. *Disputes Functions of the Wage Stabilization Board*. Wash.: G.P.O., 1952.

6050 ———. ———. *National Emergency Labor Disputes*. Wash.: G.P.O., 1952.

6051 ———. ———. Committee on the Judiciary. *Relationship Between Teamsters Union and Mine, Mill & Smelter Workers*. Wash.: G.P.O., 1962.

6052 U.S. DEPARTMENT OF LABOR. *Collective Bargaining in the Basic Steel Industry: A Study of the Public Interest and the Role of Government*. Wash.: G.P.O., 1961.

6053 U.S. NATIONAL LABOR RELATIONS BOARD. Division of Economic Research "The Steel Industry," chap. 12, *Written Trade Agreements in Collective Bargaining*, Wash.: G.P.O., 1940.

6054 UNITED STATES OF AMERICA. defendant *The Steel Seizure Case*. Wash.: G.P.O., 1952. (House Document No 534, Parts 1 & 2. Youngstown Sheet and Tube Co., et al. vs. Charles Sawyer)

6055 "United Steelworkers of America." *Fortune*, Nov 1946, pp 142-44, 252-64.

6056 *Valley Town*. 1940. (Documentary film by Willard Van Dyke)

6057 VORSE, MARY H. *Men and Steel*. NY: Boni and Liveright, 1920.

6058 WALKER, CHARLES R. *Bread and Fire* (a novel). Bost.: Houghton Mifflin, 1927.

6059 ———. *Steel, the Diary of a Furnace Worker*. Bost.: Atlantic Monthly Press, 1922.

6060 ———. *Steeltown: An Industrial Case History of the Conflict between Progress and Security*. NY: Harper, 1950.

6061 WARE, NORMAN J. "The Iron and Steel Workers," pp 228-31, *The Labor Movement in the United States, 1860-1895*, NY: Appleton, 1929.

6062 WEBER, ARNOLD R. "Craft Representation in Industrial Unions." *Proceedings of the Fourteenth Annual Meeting of the Industrial Relations Research Association*, Dec 28-29, 1961, pp 82-92. Madison: IRRA, 1962.

6063 WESTIN, ALAN F. *The Anatomy of a Constitutional Law Case: Youngstown Sheet and Tube Co. v. Sawyer; the Steel Seizure Decision.* NY: Macmillan, 1958.

6064 WHITE, VICTOR. *Peter Domanig in America: Steel* (a novel). Indianapolis: Bobbs-Merrill, 1954.

6065 WILSON, JOSEPH F. *Cold Steel: the Political Economy of Black Labor and Reform in the United Steelworkers of America.* Ph D diss, Columbia U, 1980.

6066 WOLFF, LEON. *Lockout: The Story of the Homestead Strike of 1892.* NY: Harper & Row, 1965.

6067 YATES, W. ROSS. "Discovery of the Process for Making Anthracite Iron." *Pennsylvania Magazine of History and Biography*, Vol 98 (1974), 206-23.

6068 ———. "Samuel Wetherill, Joseph Wharton, and the Founding of the American Zinc Industry." *Pennsylvania Magazine of History and Biography*, Vol 98 (1974), 469-514.

6069 YOUNG, ERNEST W. *Comments on the Interchurch Report on the Steel Strike of 1919.* Bost.: R. G. Badger, 1921.

6070 ZINKE, GEORGE W. *Minneque Plant of Colorado Fuel and Iron Corporation and Two Locals of United Steelworkers of America.* Wash.: National Planning Association, 1951.

6071 ZIPSER, ARTHUR. "The Life of William Z. Foster—the Steel Strike Chapter." *Political Affairs*, Vol 60 (Feb 1981), 13-20.

Leather and Fur

6072 BROWN, LEO C, S. J. *Union Policies in the Leather Industry*. Cambr.: Harvard U Press, 1947.

6073 FONER, PHILIP S. *The Fur and Leather Workers Union.* Newark, NJ: Nordan Press, 1950.

6074 LEITER, ROBERT D. "The Fur Workers Union." *Industrial and Labor Relations Review*, Vol 3 (1950), 163-86.

6075 MORGAN, J. W. "The History of Labor Relations in the Leather Industry"; "Labor Union Development in the Tanning Industry"; "The Leather Union Now a Potent Industry Force"; "Communism in the Leather Labor Unions"; "Communist Tactics in the Leather Unions"; "Combatting Communism in Leather Unions"; "The T-H Act and the Leather Industry"; "The Unions are Held Responsible"; "Recent Effects of the T-H Act in the Leather Industry." *Leather and Shoes*, Jun 1, Jul 10, Jul 24, Aug 14, Aug 28, Sep 11, Sep 25, Oct 9, Oct 23, 1948.

6076 NESTOR, AGNES. *Brief History of the International Glove Workers Union of America.* Chicago: The Union, 1942.

6077 ROWLAND, ANDREW. "Tanning Leather Tanning Hides: Health and Safety Struggles in a Leather Factory." *Radical America*, Vol 14 (Nov-Dec 1980, 23-27.

6078 WALINSKY, OSSIP, ed. *Industrial Peace in Action: Thirty Years of Collective Bargaining in the Pocketbook Industry of New York.* NY: Pocketbook Workers Union, 1948.

Lumber, Woodworking, Paper, Pulp

6079 ALLEN, RUTH A. *East Texas Lumber Workers: An Economic and Social Picture.* Austin: U of Texas Press, 1961.

6080 ALTON, LEO R. "The Eradication of Phossy Jaw: a Unique Development of Federal Police Power." *The Historian*, Vol 29 (1966), 1-21. (Match industry, 1909-12)

6081 BAXANDALL, LEE. "The Great Oshkosh Woodworker Strike." *Green Mountain Quarterly*, No 3 (May 1976), 15-34.

6082 BELLAS, CARL J. *Industrial Democracy and the Worker-Owned Firm: A Study of Twenty-one Plywood Companies in the Pacific Northwest.* NY: Praeger, 1972.

6083 BENSON, BARBARA. *Logs and Lumber: the Development of the Lumber Industry in Michigan's Lower Peninsula, 1837-1870.* Ph D diss, Indiana U, 1977.

6084 BURNS, MATTHEW J. *History of the Papermakers.* Albany, 1922. (Microfilm in Library of NY State School of Industrial and Labor Relations made from typewritten copy)

6085 CANTWELL, ROBERT. *Land of Plenty* (a novel). NY: Farrar and Rinehart, 1934.

6086 COLMAN, LOUIS. *Lumber* (a novel). Bost.: Little, Brown, 1931.

6087 COX, THOMAS R. "Transition in the Woods: Log Drivers, Raftsmen, and the Emergence of Modern Lumbering in Pennsylvania." *Pennsylvania Magazine of History and Biography*, Vol 104 (1980), 345-64.

6088 DANA, JOHN L. "Bargaining in the Western Lumber Industry." *Monthly Labor Review*, Vol 88 (1965), 925-31.

6089 DEIBLER, FREDERICK S. *The Amalgamated Wood Workers' International Union of America: A Historical Study of Trade Unionism in Its Relation to the Development of an Industry.* Madison: U of Wisconsin, 1912.

6090 DOERFLINGER, WILLIAM M. *Shantymen and Shantyboys: Songs of Sailor and Lumberman.* NY: Macmillan, 1951.

6091 EISTERHOLD, JOHN A. "Lumber and Trade in the Lower Mississippi Valley and New Orleans, 1800-1860." *Louisiana History*, Vol 13 (1972), 71-91.

6092 ———. "Savannah: Lumber Center of the South Atlantic." *Georgia History Quarterly*, Vol 47 (1973), 526-43.

6093 ELIEL, PAUL. "Industrial Peace and Conflict: A Study of Two Pacific Coast Industries." *Industrial and Labor Relations Review*, Vol 2 (1949), 477-501.

6094 ENGBERG, GEORGE B. "Collective Bargaining in the Lumber Industry of the Upper Great Lakes States." *Agricultural History*, Vol 24 (1950), 205-11.

6095 ———. "Lumber and Labor in the Lake States." *Minnesota History*, Vol 36 (1959), 153-66.

6096 FICKEL, JAMES F. "Management Looks at the 'Labor Problem': The Southern Pine Industry during World War I and the Postwar Era." *Journal of Southern History*, Vol 40 (1974), 61-78.

6097 FICKEN, ROBERT E. *Lumber and Politics: The Career of Mark E. Reed.* Seattle: U of Washington Press, 1979.

6098 FLEMING, R. W., and EDWIN E. WITTE. *Marathon Corporation and Seven Labor Unions.* Wash.: National Planning Association, 1950.

6099 FONES-WOLF, ELIZABETH, and KENNETH FONES-WOLF. "Knights versus the Trade Unionists: The Case of the Washington, D.C. Carpenters, 1881-1896." *Labor History*, Vol 22 (1981), 192-212.

6100 GALENSON, WALTER. "The Lumber Industry," chap. 11, *The CIO Challenge to the AFL*, Cambr.: Harvard U Press, 1960.

6101 GLOCK, MARGARET S. *Collective Bargaining in the Pacific Northwest Lumber Industry.* Berkeley: Institute of Industrial Relations, U of California, 1955.

6102 GOODSTEIN, ANITA SHAFER. "Labor Relations in the Saginaw Valley Lumber Industry, 1865-1885." *Bulletin of the Business Historical Society*, Vol 27 (1953), 193-221.

6103 GRAHAM, HARRY. *History of the Formation of Western Pulp and Paper Workers.* Ph D diss, U of Wisconsin, 1967.

6104 ———. *The Paper Rebellion: Development and Upheaval in Pulp and Paper Unionism.* Iowa City: U of Iowa Press, 1970.

6105 GREEN, JAMES R. "The Brotherhood of Timber Workers, 1910-1913: A Radical Response to Industrial Capitalism in the Southern U.S.A." *Past and Present*, Aug 1973, pp 161-200.

6106 HAPGOOD, HUTCHINS. *The Spirit of Labor* (a novel). NY: Duffield, 1907.

6107 HARRIS, CYRIL. *The Trouble at Hungersford* (a novel). Bost.: Little, Brown, 1952.

6108 HART, ALAN. *In the Lives of Men* (a novel). NY: Norton, 1937.

6109 HYMAN, HAROLD. *Soldiers and Spruce: Origins of the Loyal Legion of Loggers and Lumbermen.* Los Angeles: Institute of Industrial Relations, U of California, 1963.

6110 INDUSTRIAL WORKERS OF THE WORLD. *The Lumber Industry and Its Workers.* Chicago: The Union, 1921.

6111 JENSEN, VERNON H. "Industrial Relations in the Lumber Industry," chap. 24, *Labor in Postwar America,* Colston E. Warne, ed. Brooklyn: Remsen Press, 1949.

6112 ———. *Lumber and Labor.* NY: Farrar and Rinehart, 1945.

6113 KERR, CLARK, and ROGER L. RANDALL. *Crown Zellerbach and the Pacific Coast Pulp and Paper Industry and International Brotherhood of Pulp, Sulphite and Paper Mill Workers and International Brotherhood of Paper Makers.* Wash.: National Planning Association, 1948.

6114 KLEINSORGE, PAUL L., and WILLIAM C. KERBY. "The Pulp and Paper Rebellion: A New Pacific Coast Union." *Industrial Relations,* Vol 6 (1966), 1-20.

6115 KUSNERZ, PEG. "Winter Camp: Lumbering in Michigan, 1860-1900." *Chronicle,* Vol 8 (3rd quarter 1972), 10-19. (Photo essay)

6116 LEMBECKE, J. L. "Capital and Labor in the Pacific Northwest Products Industry." *Humboldt Journal of Social Relations,* Vol 3 (Spring-Summer 1976), 8-15.

6117 ———. *The International Woodworkers of America: an Internal Comparative Study of Two Regions.* Ph D diss, U of Oregon, 1979.

6118 LUNDBERG, WILLIAM T. "Black and White Woodsmen Form New Union in the South." *The New Leader,* Mar 6, 1972, pp 10-12.

6119 MACDONALD, ROBERT M. "Unionism and the Wage Structure in the United States Pulp and Paper Industry" pp 99-166, *The Evolution of Wage Structure,* Lloyd G. Reynolds & Cynthia H. Taft, eds. New Haven: Yale U Press, 1956.

6120 MCKELVEY, BLAKE. "Lumber and Wood Processing in Rochester's History." *Rochester History,* Vol 40 (Jan 1978), 1-24.

6121 MAHER, RICHARD A. *Gold Must Be Tried by Fire* (a novel). NY: Macmillan, 1917.

6122 MORGAN, GEORGE T., JR. "No Compromise—No Recognition: John Henry Kirby, the Southern Lumber Operators' Association, and Unionism in the Piney Woods, 1906-1916." *Labor History,* Vol 10 (1969), 193-204.

6123 MORGAN, MURRAY C (CROMWELL MURRAY, PSEUD.). *The Viewless Winds* (a novel). NY: Dutton, 1949.

6124 MYERS, CHARLES A., and GEORGE P. SCHULTZ. *Nashua Gummed and Coated Paper Company and Seven AFL Unions.* Wash.: National Planning Association 1950.

6125 NICHOLS, CLAUDE W. *Brotherhood in the Woods: The Loyal Legion of Loggers and Lumbermen, a Twenty Year Attempt at "Industrial Cooperation."* Ph D diss, U of Oregon, 1959.

6126 NORTHRUP, HERBERT R., and RICHARD ROWKEN. "Multinational Union Activity in the Paper Industry." *Relations Industrielles-Industrial Relations,* Vol 34 (1979), 722-31.

6127 OLIVER, EGBERT S. "Sawmilling on Grays Harbor in the Twenties." *Pacific Northwest Quarterly,* Vol 69 (1978), 1-18.

6128 RADER, BENJAMIN G. "The Montana Lumber Strike of 1917." *Pacific Historical Review,* Vol 36 (1967), 189-207.

6129 RANDALL, ROGER L. *Labor Relations in the Pulp and Paper Industry of the Pacific Northwest.* Portland, OR: Northwest Regional Council, 1942.

6130 ROSE, GERALD A. "The Westwood Lumber Strike." *Labor History,* Vol 13 (1972), 171-99.

6131 SHERRARD, WILLIAM R. "Labor Productivity for the Firm: A Case Study." *Quarterly Review of Economics and Business,* Vol 7 (1967), 49-61.

6132 ———. *Measuring Labor Productivity for the Firm: A Case Study.* Ph D diss, U of Washington, 1964. (St. Paul & Tacoma Lumber Co,, 1903-38)

6133 SHIELDS, JAMES M. "The Amazing Timberworkers." *North Country Anvil,* Dec-Jan 1973-74, pp 21-24.

6134 SHOFNER, JERRELL. "Forced Labor in the Florida Forests, 1880-1950." *Journal of Forest History*, Vol 23 (Jan 1981), 14-30.

6135 ———. "Mary Grace Quackenbos, a Visitor Florida Did Not Want." *Florida Historical Quarterly*, Vol 58 (1980), 273-90.

6136 ———. "Postscript to the Martin Tabert Case: Peonage as Usual in the Florida Turpentine Camps." *Florida Historical Quarterly*, Vol 59 (1981), 161-73.

6137 SMITH, JAMES ALLAN. *The Structure of Wages in the Pacific Northwest Lumber Industry, 1939-1964*. Ph D diss, Washington State U, 1967.

6138 STRITE, DONALD D. "Up the Kilchis." *Oregon Historical Quarterly*, Vol 73 (1972), 5-30, 171-92, 212-27.

6139 TELLER, CHARLOTTE. *The Cage* (a novel). NY: Appleton, 1907.

6140 TODES, CHARLOTTE. *Labor and Lumber*. NY: International Publishers, 1931.

6141 TYGIEL, JULES. "Tramping Artisans: The Case of the Carpenters in Industrial America." *Labor History*, Vol 22 (1981), 325-76.

6142 TYLER, ROBERT L. "The United States Government as Union Organizer: The Loyal Legion of Loggers and Lumbermen." *Mississippi Valley Historical Review*, Vol 47 (1960), 434-51.

6143 VAN TINE, WARREN R. et al, eds. *A Centennial History of the United Brotherhood of Carpenters and Joiners of America in Ohio*. Columbus: Labor Education and Research Service, 1982.

6144 WEATHERWAX, CLARA. *Marching! Marching!* (a novel about lumber workers in the Northwest during the 1930s). NY: John Day, 1935.

6145 WEBER, ARNOLD R. "Craft Representation in Industrial Unions." *Proceedings of the Fourteenth Annual Meeting of hte Industrial Relations Research Association*, Dec 28-29, 1961, pp 82-92. Madison: IRRA, 1962.

6146 ZIEGER, ROBERT H. "The Limits of Militancy: Organizing Paper Workers, 1933-1935." *Journal of American History*, Vol 53 (1976), 638-57.

Machinery

6147 BLACK-LISTED MACHINIST. *Capital and Labor* Chicago: Publisher not indicated, 1902.

6148 CUOMO, GEORGE. *Family Man: An American Life* (a novel). Garden Ctiy: Doubleday, 1983.

6149 DAHLHEIMER, HARRY. *A History of the Mechanics Educational Society of America in Detroit from Its Inception in 1933 through 1937*. Detroit: Mechanics Educational Society of America, 1951.

6150 GALENSON, WALTER. "The Machinists," chap. 15, *The CIO Challenge to the AFL*, Cambr.: Harvard U Press, 1960.

6151 GROVES, HAROLD M. *The Machinist in Industry*. Ph D diss, U of Wisconsin, 1928.

6152 HEDGES, MARION HAWTHORNE. *The Iron City* (a novel). NY: Boni and Liveright, 1919.

6153 "IAM History Preserved in Southern Labor Archives." *Machinist*, Vol 29 (May 2, 1974), 3.

6154 INGHAM, JOHN N. "A Strike in the Progressive Era: McKees Rocks, 1909." *Pennsylvania Magazine of History and Biography*, Vol 90 (1966), 353-77.

6155 INTERNATIONAL ASSOCIATION OF MACHINISTS. *Half a Century with the International Association of Machinists*. Wash.: The Union, 1938.

6156 ———. *Machinists on the March, 1888-1950*. Wash.: The Union, May, 1950.

6157 JACOBS, PAUL. "Mr. Hayes Settles a Local Disturbance." *The Reporter*, Apr 2, 1959, pp 18-21.

6158 KERR, CLARK, and GEORGE HALVERSON. *Lockheed Aircraft Corporation and the International Association of Machinists*. Wash.: National Planning Association, 1949.

6159 LICHLITER, MARCELLUS D. *History of hte Junior Order United American Mechanics of the United States of North America*. Phila.: Lippincott, 1908.

6160 MCCULLOUGH, FRANK. *Strike! A Confidential Reort on Labor-Management Conflict by an Undercover Agent*. NY: American Press, 1954.

6161 "No-Raid Agreement between UAW and IAM." *Monthly Labor Review*, Vol 70 (1950), 1962.

6162 PERLMAN, MARK. *Democracy in the International Association of Machinists*. NY: Wiley, 1962.

6163 ———. *The Machinists: A New Study in American Trade Unionism*. Cambr.: Harvard U Press, 1961.

6164 U.S. NATIONAL LABOR RELATIONS BOARD. Division of Economic Research "The Machinists," chap. 10, *Written Trade Agreements in Collective Bargaining*, Wash.: G.P.O., 1940.

6165 WARD, ESTOLV. *The Piecard* (a novel). NY: Associated Authors, 1954.

6166 WEBSTER, HENRY K. *An American Family: A Novel of Today*. Indianapolis: Bobbs-Merrill, 1918.

6167 WHARTON, A. O. "Fifty Years of the Machinists Union." *Labor Information Bulletin*, Vol 5 (1938), 1-4.

Manufacturing

6168 "Centennial 1981: the Boilermakers." *American Federationist*, Vol 88 (May 1981), 17-20.

6169 HESHIZER, BRIAN P. *Employee Benefits, Trade Unions and the Union Impact on Employee Benefits in Manufacturing*. Ph D diss, U of Wisconsin, 1979.

6170 MEDOFF, JAMES. "Layoffs and Alternatives under Trade Unions in U.S. Manufacturing." *American Economic Review*, Vol 69 (1979), 380-95.

6171 MOLL, TIMOTHY. "The Deshler Broom Factory." *Nebraska History*, Vol 62 (1981), 73-79.

6172 SCHLESINGER, TOM. "Trailers the Factory." *Southern Exposure*, Vol 8 (Spring 1980), 14-25.

Metal Mining

6173 ANDREWS, CLARENCE A. "Big Anne and the 1913 Michigan Copper Strike." *Michigan History*, Vol 48 (1973), 53-68.

6174 BETTEN, NEIL. "Strike on the Mesabi-1907." *Minnesota History*, Vol 40 (1967), 340-47.

6175 BIBERMAN, HERBERT. *Salt of the Earth*. Bost.: Beacon Press, 1965. (Includes screenplay)

6176 BRINGHURST, NEWELL. "The 'New' Labor History and Hard Rock Miners in Nevada and the West." *Nevada Historical Society Quarterly*, Vol 24 (1981), 170-75.

6177 BRINKS, HERBERT J. "Marquette Iron Range Strike, 1895." *Michigan History*, Vol 50 (1966), 293-305.

6178 BRINLEY, JOHN E. *The Western Federation of Miners*. Ph D diss, U of Utah, 1972.

6179 BROOKS, THOMAS R. *Toil and Trouble: A History of American Labor*. NY: Delacorte Press, 1971.

6180 BROWN, RONALD C. *Hard-Rock Miners: The Intermountain West, 1860-1920*. College Station: Texas A & M U Press, 1979.

6181 Byrkit, James W. *Forging the Copper Collar: Arizona's Labor-Management War, 1901-1921.* Tucson: U of Arizona Press, 1982.

6182 Cash, Joseph Harper. *Labor in the West: The Homestake Mining Company and Its Workers, 1877-1942.* Ph D diss, U of Iowa, 1966.

6183 Davidson, Lallah S. *South of Joplin* (a novel). NY: Norton, 1939.

6184 Delli Quadri, Carmen Leonard. *Labor Relations on the Mesabi Range.* MA thesis, U of Colorado, 1944.

6185 Dersch, Virginia Jonas. "Copper Mining in Northern Michigan: a Social History" *Michigan History*, Vol 61 (1977), 291-321.

6186 Dubofsky, Melvyn. "The Leadville Strike of 1896-1897: an Appraisal." *Mid-America*, Vol 48 (1966), 99-118.

6187 Elliott, Russell R. "Labor Troubles in the Mining Camp at Goldfield, Nevada, 1906-1908." *Pacific Historical Review*, Vol 19 (1950), 369-84.

6188 ———. *Radical Labor in the Nevada Mining Booms, 1900-1920.* Carson City, NV: State Printing Office, 1961.

6189 Foote, Mary H. *Coeur d'Alene* (a novel). Bost.: Houghton Mifflin, 1894.

6190 Garland, Hamlin. *Hesper* (a novel). NY: Harper, 1903.

6191 Gazzam, Joseph P. "The Leadville Strike of 1896." *Bulletin of the Missouri Historical Society*, Vol 7 (1950), 89-94.

6192 Gedicks, Al. "Ethnicity, Class Solidarity, and Labor Radicalism among Finnish Immigrants in Michigan Copper County." *Politics and Society*, Vol 7 (1977), 127-56.

6193 Gutfeld, Arnon. "The Speculator Disaster in 1917: Labor Resurgence at Butte, Montana." *Arizona and the West*, Vol 11 (1969), 27-38.

6194 Hough, Merrill. "Leadville and the Western Federation of Miners." *Colorado Magazine*, Vol 49 (1972), 19-34.

6195 Hurt, Walter. *The Scarlet Shadow* (a novel). Girard, KS: Appeal to Reason, 1907.

6196 Jensen, Vernon H. *Heritage of Conflict: Labor Relations in the Nonferrous Metals Industry Up to 1930.* Ithaca: Cornell U Press, 1950.

6197 ———. *Nonferrous Metals Industry Unionism, 1932-1954.* Ithaca: NY State School of Industrial and Labor Relations, Cornell U, 1954.

6198 Kluger, James R. *The Clifton-Morenci Strike: Labor Difficulty in Arizona, 1915-1916.* Tucson: U of Arizona Press, 1970.

6199 Langdon, Emma F. *The Cripple Creek Strike: A History of Industrial Wars in Colorado, 1903-4-5.* Denver: Great Western, 1904-5.

6200 ———. *Labor's Greatest Conflict: The Formation of the Western Federation of Miners, a Brief Account of the Rise of the United Mine Workers of America.* Denver: Great Western, 1908.

6201 Levinne, Marvin J. "The Homestakes Mining Company: the Strategy and Semantics of Organizational Conflict—1877-1963." *Report and Historical Collections*, South Dakota, Department of History, Vol 32 (1966), 512-41.

6202 Lingenfelter, Richard E. *The Hardrock Miners: A History of the Mining Labor Movement in the American West, 1863-1893.* Berkeley: U of California Press, 1974.

6203 Mellinger, P. J. *The Beginnings of Modern Industrial Unionism in the Southwest: Labor Trouble Among Unskilled Copper Workers, 1903-1917.* Ph D diss, U of Chicago, 1979.

6204 Miller, Darlis A. "Carleton's California Column: a Chapter in New Mexico's Mining History." *New Mexico Historical Review*, Vol 53 (1978), 5-38.

6205 Murray, Robert A. "Miner's Delight, Investor's Despair: the Ups and Downs of a Sub-Marginal Mining Camp in Wyoming." *Annals of Wyoming*, Vol 44 (1972), 25-56.

6206 Ozanne, Robert. "Mine, Mill and Smelter Workers Union" chap. 3, *The Effect of Communist Leadership on American Trade Unions*, Ph D diss, U of Wisconsin, 1954.

6207 PETERSEN, WILLIAM J. "Regulating the Lead Miners." *Palimpsest*, Vol 17 (1936), 185-200.

6208 PETERSON, RICHARD H. "Conflict and Consensus: Labor Relations in Western Mining." *Journal of the West.*, Vol 12 (1973), 1-17.

6209 RASTALL, BENJAMIN M. *The Labor History of the Cripple Creek District*. Madison: U of Wisconsin, 1908.

6210 ROOSEVELT, THEODORE. "Social and Industrial Justice," chap. 13, *Autobiography*, NY: Macmillan, 1919. (Western Federation of Miners)

6211 *Salt of the Earth*. 1953. (Feature film produced in cooperation with the International Union of Mine, Mill and Smelter Workers)

6212 SCHWARTZ, JEROME L. "Prepayment Medical Clinics of the Mesabi Iron Range: 1904-19643" *Journal of the History of Medicine and Allied Sciences*, Vol 22 (1967), 139-51.

6213 SHELDON, CHARLES M. *His Brother's Keeper* (a novel about Western iron miners based on events in an actual strike during the 1890s). Bost.: Congregationsl Sunday-School and Publishing Society, 1896.

6214 SMITH, ROBERT W. *The Coeur d'Alene Mining War of 1892: A Case Study of an Industrial Dispute*. Gloucester, MA: Smith, 1968.

6215 STAVIS, BARRIE. *The Man Who Never Died: A Play About Joe Hill*. NY: Haven Press, 1954.

6216 STEGNER, S. PAGE. "Protest Songs from the Butte Mines." *Western Folklore*, Vol 26 (1967), 157-67.

6217 STITZEL, JAMES A. "Inflammatory Speaking in the Victor, Colo., Mass Meeting —June 6, 1904." *Western Speech*, Vol 32 (1968), 11-18.

6218 "'Strike for Liberty.' Songs, Poetry, and Comments by Workers of the Western Federation of Miners: 1900-1907." *Southwest Economy and Society*, Vol 51 (1979-80), 1-139.

6219 SUGGS, GEORGE G., JR. "Catalyst for Industrial Change: The WFM, 1893-1903." *Colorado Magazine*, Vol 45 (1968), 322-39.

6220 ———. "Prelude to Industrial Warfare: the Colorado City Strike." *Colorado Magazine*, Vol 44 (1967), 241-62.

6221 ———. "Strike-Breaking in Colorado: Governor James H. Peabody and the Telluride Strike, 1903-1904." *Journal of the West*, Vol 5 (1966), 454-76.

6222 SULLIVAN, WILLIAM A. "The 1913 Revolt of the Michigan Copper Miners." *Michigan History*, Vol 43 (1959), 3-23.

6223 THOMASON, FRANK. "The Bellevue Stranglers." *Idaho Yesterdays*, Vol 13 (1969), 26-32. (Galena ore miners strike, 1885)

6224 U.S. COMMISSION ON INDUSTRIAL RELATIONS (1912). "Western Federation of Miners," Vol 9, pp 10569-72, *Final Report*, Wash.: G.P.O., 1916.

6225 U.S. CONGRESS. SENATE. Committee on Labor and Public Welfare. Subcommittee on Labor and Labor-Management Relations. *Communist Domination of Certain Unions*. Wash.: G.P.O., 1951. (See pp 97-100)

6226 ———. ———. Committee on the Judiciary. *Relationship Between Teamsters Union and Mine, Mill & Smelter Workers*. Wash.: G.P.O., 1962.

6227 WELLS, MERLE W. "The Western Federation of Miners." *Journal of the West*, Vol 12 (1973), 18-35.

6228 WHITE, EARL BRUCE. "A Note on the Archives of the Western Federation of Miners and the International Union of Mine, Mill and Smelter Workers." *Labor History*, Vol 17 (1976), 613-17.

6229 WOOD, FREMONT. *The Introductory Chapter to the History of the Trials of Moyer, Haywood, and Pettibone*. Caldwell, ID: Caxton, 1931.

6230 WYMAN, MARK. *Hard-Rock Epic: Western Miners and the Industrial Revolution, 1860-1910*. Berkeley: U of California Press, 1979.

6231 ———. "Industrial Revolution in the West: Hard Rock Miners and the New Technology." *Western Historical Quarterly*, Vol 5 (1974), 39-57.

6232 WYMAN, WALKER DEMARQUIS. *The Underground Miner, 1860-1910: Labor and Industrial Change in the Northern Rockies.* Ph D diss, U of Washington, 1971.

Newspapers

6233 ALLEN, WALTER M. "A Survey of the Extent of Unionization of Daily Newspaper Pressrooms by the I.P.P. & A.U. of N.A." *Proceedings of the Tenth Annual Meeting of the Industrial Relations Research Association*, Sep 5-7, 1957, pp 254-59. Madison: IRRA, 1958.

6234 BENDINER, ROBERT. "One for All—and All for Nothing." *The Reporter*, Apr 2, 1959, pp 13-17.

6235 BROWN, BERNARD D. "Labor's Shotgun Wedding." *New Leader,*, Apr 15, 1963, pp 16-17.

6236 BURNS, ROBERT K. "Daily Newspapers," chap. 2, *How Collective Bargaining Works*, Harry A Millis, research director. NY: Twentieth Century Fund, 1945.

6237 ———. *Collective Bargaining and Arbitration: The Case of the Newspaper Industry.* Ph D diss, U of Chicago, 1943.

6238 CARLISLE, RODNEY. "William Randolph Hearst's Reaction to the American Newspaper Guild: A Challenge to New Deal Labor Legislation." *Labor History*, Vol 10 (1969), 74-99.

6239 ELDER, S. "Journalist versus the Unions at the *Washington Post*." *Columbia Journalism Review*, Vol 15 (May 1976), 42-45.

6240 FEDLER, F., and P. TAYLOR. "Reporters and Newspaper Guild: Membership, Attitudes, and Salaries." *Journalism Quarterly*, Vol 58 (1981), 83-88.

6241 FEDLER, FRED, and PHILIP TAYLOR. "Reporters and the Newspaper Guild: Membership Attitudes and Salaries." *Journalism Quarterly*, Vol 58 (Jan 1981), 83-88.

6242 *Five Star Final.* 1931. (Feature film produced by Warner Brothers)

6243 *The Front Page.* 1931. (Feature film produced by Howard Hughes)

6244 GRENIER, JUDSON. "Upton Sinclair and the Press: *The Brass Check* Reconsidered." *Journalism Quarterly*, Vol 49 (19972), 427-36.

6245 GUIMARY, DONALD L. "Strike-Born Newspapers." *Journalism Quarterly*, Vol 46 (1969), 594-97.

6246 HARRIS, HERBERT. *American Labor.* NY: Yale U Press, 1938. (See pp 173-92 on American Newspaper Guild)

6247 HENTOFF, NAT. "Labor Odyssey: the Unionization of the *Village Voice*." *Social Policy*, Vol 8 (Mar 1978), 47-49.

6248 HERSHFIELD, DAVID C. "The Choice Between Obstruction and Control in the New York City Newspaper Industry." *Proceedings of the Twenty-Fourth Annual Winter Meeting of the Industrial Relations Research Association*, Dec 27-28, 1971, pp 246-53. Madison: IRRA, 1972.

6249 HOLDEN, W. SPRAGUE. "The Anatomy of Two Newspaper Industrial Disputes, U.S. and Australian." *Journal of Industrial Relations*, Vol 9 (1967), 1-12.

6250 HUENERGARD C. "I.T.U., Guild, Mailers Make Merger Progress." *Editor and Publisher*, Sep 3, 1977, p 15.

6251 KRITZBERG, BARRY. "An Unfinished Chapter in White-Collar Unionism: The Formative Years of the Chicago Newspaper Guild." *Labor History*, Vol 14 (1973), 397-413.

6252 KUCZUN, SAM. *History of the American Newspaper Guild.* Ph D diss, U of Minnesota, 1970.

6253 ———. "International Affairs and the American Newspaper Guild." *Journalism Quarterly*, Vol 43 (1966), 655-64.
6254 LEAB, DANIEL J. "Strike with Ukuleles." *Columbia Journalism Review*, Vol 2 (Fall 1963), 36-37.
6255 ———. "Towards Unionization: The *Newark Star Ledger* Strike of 1934-1935." *Labor History*, Vol 11 (1970), 3-22.
6256 ———. *A Union of Individuals; the Formation of the American Newspasper Guild, 1933-1936*. Ph D diss, Columbia U, 1969.
6257 ———. *A Union of Individuals; the Formation of the American Newspasper Guild, 1933-1936*. NY: Columbia U Press, 1970.
6258 LENS, SIDNEY. "Reunion: Celebrating Fortieth Anniversary of Chicago's Hearst Papers Strike." *Progressive*, Vol 43 (Feb 1979), 66.
6259 MURASKEN, ESTELLE. *Newswriters' Unions in English-Speaking Countries*. NY: U.S. Works Progress Administration, 1937. (Mimeo.)
6260 "The Nation: Labor." *Time*, Mar 1, 1963, pp 13-176New York City Newspaper Strike, Dec 1962-Mar 1963.
6261 PALOMBO, RAYMOND N. *Collective Bargaining and the Merit System in the City of New York*. Ph D diss, New York U, 1970.
6262 RASKIN, A. H. "Reporter at Large; New York City." *New Yorker*, Jan 29, 1979, 56-63.
6263 SERRIN, WILLIAM. "The Ultimate Shutdown: the Detroit Strike of 1967-1968." *Columbia Journalism Review*, Vol 8 (Summer 1969), 36-44.
6264 SHAPIRO, FRED C. "The Negotiations." *The New Yorker*, Apr 10, 1965, pp 161-92.
6265 TAFT, PHILIP. "The Limits of Labor Unity: The Chicago Newspaper Strike of 1912." *Labor History*, Vol 19 (1978), 100-29.
6266 U.S. NATIONAL LABOR RELATIONS BOARD. Division of Economic Research *Collective Bargaining in the Newspaper Industry*. Wash.: G.P.O., 1939.
6267 WAGNER, DAVE, and PAUL BUHLE. "Worker's Control and the News: the Madison, Wisconsin *Press Connection*." *Radical America*, Vol 14 (Jul-Aug 1980), 7-20.
6268 WATKINS, THOMAS L. *The Relation of Certain Environmental Factors to the Difficulty with White Labor Agreements are Negotiated in Public Employment*. Ph D diss, U of Cincinnati, 1971.

Printing and Publishing

6269 BAKER, ELIZABETH F. "The Development of the International Printing Pressmen and Assistants' Union." *Proceedings of the Tenth Annual Meeting of the Industrial Relations Research Association*, Sep 5-7, 1957, pp 156-62. Madison: IRRA, 1958.
6270 ———. *Displacement of Men by Machines: Effects of Technological Change in Commercial Printing*. NY: Columbia U Press, 1933.
6271 ———. *Printers and Technology: A History of the International Printing Pressmen and Assistants' Union*. NY: Columbia U Press, 1957.
6272 ———. "The Printing Foreman—Union Man: A Historical Sketch." *Industrial and Labor Relations Review*, Vol 4 (1951), 223-35.
6273 ———. "The Printing Pressroom Foreman—Union Man: A Case Study." *Industrial and Labor Relations Review*, Vol 4 (1951), 367-85.
6274 BALUNER, ROBERT. *Alienation and Freedom: The Factory Worker and his Industry*. Chicago: U of Chicago Press, 1964.
6275 BARNETT, GEORGE. *The Printers: A Study in American Trade Unionism*. Cambr.: American Economic Association, 1909.
6276 BEVIS, A. S. "ITU's Two-Party System Unique." *Typographical Journal*, 172 (Apr 1978), 41. (President reviews 65-year history of union's two-party system)

6277 BIGGS, M. "Neither Printer's Wife nor Widow: American Women in Typesetting, 1830-1950." *Library Quarterly*, Vol 50 (1980), 431-52.

6278 BIGGS, MARY. "Neither Printer's Wife nor Widow: American Women in Typesetting, 1830-1950." *Library Quarterly*, Vol 50 (1980), 431-52.

6279 BLAINE, HARRY. "Discipline and Discharge in the United States Postal Service: Adverse Action and Appeal." *Industrial and Labor Relations Review*, Vol 19 (1965), 92-98.

6280 BROWN, EMILY C. "Book and Job Printing," chap. 3, *How Collective Bargaining Works*, Harry A. Millis, research director. NY: Twentieth Century Fund, 1945.

6281 BURNS, ROBERT K. "Industrial Relations in Printing," chap. 18, *Labor in Postwar America*, Colston E. Warne, ed. (Brooklyn: Remsen Press, 1949)

6282 CLARK, FLORENCE ELIZABETH. *The Printing Trades and Their Workers*. Scranton: International Text Books, 1932.

6283 CORKERY, JAMES P. "Wage Chronology No. 16: Chicago Printing, 1939-50." *Monthly Labor Review*, Vol 73 (1951), 49-56.

6284 DENKER, DAVID. "The Printers: Craft Unionism." *Current History*, Jul 1954, pp 26-30.

6285 DERTOUZOS, JAMES. *Union Objectives, Wage Determination, and the International Typographical Union*. Ph D diss, Stanford U, 1980.

6286 FEIN, MARVIN. *The International Typographical Union 1910-29* (Unpublished manuscript, U of Wisconsin)

6287 GALENSON, WALTER. "Printing and Publishing," chap. 17, *The CIO Challenge to the AFL*, Cambr.: Harvard U Press, 1960.

6288 GIEBEL, GREGORY. "Corporate Structure, Technology, and the Printing Industry." *Labor Studies Journal*, Vol 3 (1979), 228-51. (See comments by Carl Torgoff, pp 251-56)

6289 HARD, WILLIAM. "The Typographical Union—Model for All." *Reader's Digest*, Jun 1943, pp 1-5.

6290 HIGGINS, JOE. "Struggle of the New York Printers." *Political Affairs*, Vol 53 (Aug 1974) 13-27.

6291 HOAGLAND, HENRY E. *Collective Bargaining in the Lithographic Industry*. NY: Columbia U Press, 1917.

6292 INTERNATIONAL PRINTING PRESSMEN AND ASSISTANTS' UNION OF NORTH AMERICA. *History of the Suit of the Chicago Printing Pressmen's Union against the Officers of the International Printing Pressmen and Assistants' Union of North America* (pamphlet). Chicago: The Union, 1919.

6293 INTERNATIONAL TYPOGRAPHICAL UNION OF NORTH AMERICA. *A Study of the History of the International Typographical Union, 1852-1963*. Colorado Springs: The Union, 1964.

6294 KELBER, HARRY. *The Response of New York Typographical Union No. 6 to Technological Changes in the Printing Industry since 1947*. Ph D diss, New York U, 1966.

6295 ———, and CARL SCHLESINGER. *Union Printers and Controlled Automation*. NY: Free Press, 1967.

6296 KOVNER, JOSEPH. "Basic Issue Between ITU and the T-H Law." *Labor and Nation*, Jan-Feb 1948, pp 13-14.

6297 LAMPMAN, BEN HUR. *Tramp Printer*. Portland, OR: Metropolitan, 1934.

6298 LEESE, CHARLES. *Collective Bargaining among Photo-Engravers in Philadelphia*. Phila.: U of Pennsylvania Press, 1929.

6299 LIPSET, SEYMOUR MARTIN. et al. *Union Democracy: The Internal Politics of the International Typographical Union*. Glencoe, IL: Free Press, 1956.

6300 LOFT, JACOB. "Backgrounds and Perspectives in the Printers-Publishers Fight." *Labor and Nation,*, Mar-Apr 1948, pp 19-20, 48.

6301 ———. *The Printing Trades*. NY: Farrar and Rinehart, 1944.

6302 LYNCH, JAMES M. *Epochal History of the International Typographical Union.* Indianapolis: The Union, 1925.

6303 MCCOWAN, ARCHIBALD (LUKE A. HEDD, PSEUD.). *Philip Meyer's Scheme: A Story of Trades Unionism* (a novel). NY: J. S. Ogilvie, 1892.

6304 MUNSON, FRED C. *Labor Relations in the Lithographic Industry.* Cambr.: Harvard U Press, 1963.

6305 PASCHELL, WILLIAM. "The International Typographical Union." *Monthly Labor Review,* Vol 74 (1952), 493-98.

6306 PERLMAN, SELIG, and PHILIP TAFT. *History of Labor in the United States, 1896-1932.* NY: Macmillan, 1935. (See pp 51-60, 456-60, 497-99)

6307 PETRO, SYLVESTER. *The Kingsport Strike.* New Rochelle, NY: Arlington House, 1967.

6308 PORTER, ARTHUR R., JR. *Job Property Rights: A Study of the Job Controls of the International Typographical Union.* NY: King's Crown Press, 1954.

6309 POWELL, LEONA M. *The History of the United Typothetae of America.* Chicago: U of Chicago Press, 1926.

6310 RAYMOND, MARGARET T. *Bend in the Road* (a novel). NY: Longmans, Green, 1934.

6311 ROSE, WILLIAM T. "New York Union Advertises to Tell Its Story: Lithographers Condemn Featherbedding, Welcome Automation as Tool for Progress." *Industrial Bulletin,* Vol 41 (1962), 3-7.

6312 ROSEMONT, HENRY P. "Benjamin Franklin and the Philadelphia Typographical Strikers of 1786." *Labor History,* Vol 22 (1981), 398-429.

6313 SACKLEY, ARTHUR. "Trends in Salaries of Firemen and Policemen." *Monthly Labor Review,* Vol 88 (1965), 159-63.

6314 SEYBOLD, JOHN W. *The Philadelphia Printing Industry: A Case Study.* Phila.: U of Pennsylvania Press, 1949.

6315 SOFFER, BENSON. "The Role of Union Foremen in the Evolution of the International Typographical Union." *Labor History,* Vol 2 (1961), 62-81.

6316 STEVENS, GEORGE A. *New York Typographical Union No 6: A Study of a Modern Trade Union and Its Predecessors.* Albany: NY State Department of Labor, 1913.

6317 STEWART, ETHELBERT. "A Documentary History of the Early Organizations of Printers." *Bulletin of the Bureau of Labor,* Wash.: G.P.O., 1905. (Document 61, pp 857-1033)

6318 TRACY, GEORGE A. *History of the Typographical Unions: Its Beginnings, Progress and Development, Its Beneficial and Educational Features together with a Chapter on the Early Organization of Printers.* Indianapolis: The Union, 1913.

6319 U.S. CONGRESS. HOUSE. Committee on Education and Labor. *Chicago ITU-Publishers Dispute.* Wash.: G.P.O., 1948.

6320 ———. ———. *The Philadelphia Record Case.* Wash.: G.P.O., 1947.

6321 U.S. NATIONAL LABOR RELATIONS BOARD. Division of Economic Research "The Printing Industry," chap. 4, *Written Trade Agreements in Collective Bargaining,* Wash.: G.P.O., 1940.

6322 WALLIHAN, JAMES P. *Workplace Politics and Leadership in a Chicago Printing Trades Union.* Ph D diss, Indiana U, 1974.

6323 WARE, NORMAN J. "The Printers," pp 236-42, *The Labor Movement in the United States, 1860-1895,* NY: Appleton, 1929.

6324 WILKINS, JOHN. "The New Assembly Line." *Working Papers for a New Society.,* Vol 7 (May-Jun 1980), 24-32.

Prisons

6325 CHRISTIANSON, SCOTT. "How Unions Affect Prison Administration." *Criminal Law Bulletin,* Vol 15 (May/Jun 1979), 238-47.

6326 CONLEY, JOHN. "Prisons, Production and Profit: Reconsidering the Importance of Prison Industries." *Journal of Social History*, Vol 14 (1980), 257-75.

6327 "Future of Prisoners' Unions." *Harvard Civil Rights Law Review*, Vol 13 (Summer 1978), 799-826.

6328 HUFF, CLARENCE R. *Unionization behing the Walls: an Analytic Study of the Ohio Prisoners' Labor Union Movement*. Ph D diss, Ohio State U, 1974.

6329 "Inmate Unions: an Appraisal of Prisoner Rights and Labor Implications." *University of Miami Law Review*, Vol 32 (Jun 1978), 613-35.

6330 KUHL, CHARLES. *Collective Bargaining in Correctional Institutions: Guidelines and Preparation Activities*. Ph D diss, Brigham Young U, 1978.

6331 PETERSON, ANDREW A. "Deterring Strikes by Public Employees: New York's Two-for-One Salary Penalty and the '79 Prison Guard Strike." *Industrial and Labor Relations Review*, Vol 34 (1981), 545-62.

6332 WOOLPERT, S. "Prisoners' Unions, Inmate Militancy, and Correctional Policy-Making." *Federal Probation*, Vol 42 (Jun 1978), 40-45.

6333 ZIMMER, L., and J. B. JACOBS. "Challenging the Taylor Law: Prison Guards on Strike." *Industrial and Labor Relations Review*, Vol 34 (1981), 531-44.

Rubber

6334 ANTHONY, DONALD. "Rubber Products," chap. 12, *How Collective Bargaining Works*, Harry A. Millis, research director. NY: Twentieth Century Fund, 1945.

6335 GALENSON, WALTER. "The Rubber Industry," chap. 6, *The CIO Challenge to the AFL*, Cambr.: Harvard U Press, 1960.

6336 GEORGE, ED, and JEFF PAUL. "Work in America: The Rubber Factory." *Radical America*, Vol 6 (Mar-Apr 1972), 108-20.

6337 JONES, ALFRED W. *Life, Liberty, and Property: A Story of Conflict and a Measurement of Conflicting Rights*. Phila.: Lippincott, 1941.

6338 LUDOLF, GORDON WILLIAMS. *Pattern Bargaining in the Rubber Industry*. Ph D diss, Ohio State U, 1964.

6339 MCKENNEY, RUTH. *Industrial Valley* (a novel). NY: Harcourt, Brace, 1939.

6340 NELSON, DANIEL. "Origins of the Sit-Down Era: Worker Militancy and Innovation in the Rubber Industry, 1934-38." *Labor History*, Vol 22 (1982), 198-225.

6341 PARSONS, EDGAR A. *Some Economic Aspects of Collective Bargaining in the Rubber Industry*. Ph D diss, Cornell U, 1950.

6342 ROBERTS, HAROLD S. *The Rubber Workers*. NY: Harper, 1944.

6343 SOBEL, IRVIN. *Economic Impact of Collective Bargaining upon the Rubber Tire Industry*. Ph D diss, U of Chicago, 1951.

6344 THURBER, JOHN NEWTON. *Rubber Workers' History (1935-1955)*. Akron: United Rubber, Cork, Linoleum and Plastic Workers of America, 1955.

6345 UNITED RUBBER WORKERS OF AMERICA. *Five Years: The Story of the United Rubber Workers of America*. Akron: The Union, [c.1940].

6346 "United Rubber Workers of America, 1935-1945." *Monthly Labor Review*, Vol 62 (1946), 601-6.

6347 U.S. NATIONAL LABOR RELATIONS BOARD. Division of Economic Research "The Rubber Industry," chap. 11, *Written Trade Agreements in Collective Bargaining*, Wash.: G.P.O., 1940.

Shoes

6348 BLATT, MARTY. et al. "A Reunion of Shoeworkers: the First Massachusetts History Workshop." *Radical America*, vol 14 (Jan-Feb 1980), 67-77.

6349 Blewett, Mary H. "I Am Doomed to Disappointment: the Diaries of a Beverly, Mass., Shoebinder, Sarah E. Trask, 1849-1851." *Essex Institute Historical Collections*, Vol 117 (1981), 192-212.

6350 Burt, Edward W. *The Shoe-Craft: Its Organization*. Bost.: The Everett Press, 1917.

6351 Commons, John R. "American Shoemakers, 1648-1895," chap. 14, *Labor and Administration*, NY: Macmillan, 1913.

6352 Condon, Richard. "Bayonets at the North Bridge: the Lewiston-Auburn Shoe Strike, 1937." *Maine Historical Society Quarterly*, Vol 21 (1981), 75-98.

6353 Davis, Horace B. *Shoes: The Workers and the Industry*. NY: International Publishers, 1940.

6354 Dodd, Martin H. "Marlboro, Massachusetts and the Shoeworkers' Strike of 1898-1899." *Labor History*, Vol 20 (1979), 376-97.

6355 Faler, Paul. "Cultural Aspects of the Industrial Revolution: Lynn, Massachusetts Shoemakers and Industrial Morality, 1826-1860." *Labor History*, Vol 15 (1974), 367-94.

6356 Galster, Augusta E. *The Labor Movement in the Shoe Industry, Especially in Philadelphia*. NY: Ronald, 1924.

6357 Hall, John P. *The Gentle Craft: A Narrative of Yankee Shoemakers*. Ph D diss, Columbia U, 1953.

6358 ———. "The Knights of St. Crispin in Massachusetts, 1869-1878." *Journal of Economic History*, Vol 18 (1958), 161-75.

6359 Jeter, Goetze. *The Strikers* (a novel about a shoe factory in New England during the 1930s). Phila.: Stokes, 1937.

6360 Lescohier, Don D. *The Knights of St. Crispin, 1867-1874: A Study in the Industrial Causes of Trade Unionism*. Madison: U of Wisconsin, 1910.

6361 McNeill, George E., ed. *The Labor Movement: The Problem of Today*. NY: M. W. Hazen, 1892. (See pp 209-13. An account of the Brockton strike of 1885 and the settlement reached based upon the "Philadelphia Rules," so-called from their previous adoption and use by the Philadelphia Shoe manufacturers and operatives)

6362 Mayer, Stephen. "*People v. Fisher*: The Shoemakers' Strike of 1833." *New-York Historical Society Quarterly*, Vol 42 (1978), 7-21.

6363 Morris, James M. "The Cincinnati Shoemakers' Lockout of 1888." *Labor History*, Vol 13 (1972), 505-19.

6364 Mulligan, William. "Mechanization and Work in the American Shoe Industry: Lynn, Mass., 1852-1883." *Journal of Economic History*, Vol 41 (1981), 59-63.

6365 Norton, Thomas L. *Trade Union Policies in the Massachusetts Shoe Industry, 1919-1929*. NY: Columbia U Press, 1932.

6366 Nunn, Henry L. *Partners in Production: A New Role for Management and Labor*. Englewood Cliffs, NJ: Prentice-Hall, 1961. (Nunn-Bush Shoe Co.)

6367 Schultz, George P. *Pressures on Wage Decisions: A Case Study in the Shoe Industry*. NY: Wiley & Technology Press, Massachusetts Institute of Technology, 1951. (The Brotherhood of Shoe and Allied Craftsmen, an independent union)

6368 Trefry, Clarence, and N. Chamberlain. "The Shoemaking Industry in Marblehead: a Reminiscence." *Essex Institute Historical Collections*, Vol 117 (1981), 213-22.

6369 Twentieth Century Association, Boston. *The Strike of the Shoe Workers in Marlboro, Mass, November 14, 1898-May 5, 1899*. Bost.: Boston Co-operative Press, 1900.

6370 Ware, Norman J. "The Shoemakers," pp 200-9, *The Labor Movement in the United States, 1860-1895*, NY: Appleton, 1929.

6371 Yellowitz, Irwin. "Skilled Workers and Mechanization: The Lasters in the 1890's." *Labor History*, Vol 18 (1977), 197-212.

Supervision

6372 BAKER, ELIZABETH F. "The Printing Foreman—Union Man: A Historical Sketch." *Industrial and Labor Relations Review*, Vol 4 (1951), 223-35.

6373 ———. "The Printing Pressroom Foreman—Union Man: A Case Study." *Industrial and Labor Relations Review*, Vol 4 (1951), 367-85.

6374 CABE, J. CARL. *Collective Bargaining by Foremen*. Urbana: U of Illinois, Institute of Labor and Industrial Relations, Sep 1947.

6375 ———. *Foremen's Unions: a New Development in Industrial Relations*. Urbana: U of Illinois, Bureau of Economic and Business Research, 1947.

6376 "Collective Bargaining by Supervisory Employees under the Wagner Act." *Univeristy of Chicago Law Review*, Vol 13 (1946), 332-46.

6377 COOPER, HERMAN E. "The Status of Foremen as 'Employees' under the National Labor Relations Act." *Fordham Law Review*, Vol 15 (Nov 1946), 191-221.

6378 LARROWE, CHARLES P. "A Meteor on the Industrial Relations Horizon: The Foreman's Association of America." *Labor History*, Vol 2 (1961), 259-94.

6379 LEITER, ROBERT D. *The Foreman in Industrial Relations*. NY: Columbia U Press, 1948.

6380 MANN, FLOYD C., and JAMES K. DENT. "The Supervisory: Member of two Organizational Families." *Harvard Business Review*, Vol 32 (1954), 103-12.

6381 NORTHRUP, HERBERT R. "The Foreman's Association of America." *Harvard Business Review*, Vol 23 (1945), 187-202.

6382 ROSENTHAL, ROBERT J. "Exclusions of Employees under the Taft-Hartley Act." *Industrial and Labor Relations Review*, Vol 4 (1951), 556-70.

6383 SLICHTER, SUMNER H. et al. "The Changing Position of Foremen in American Industry." *Advanced Management*, Vol 10 (1945), 155-61.

6384 SUFRIN, SIDNEY C. "Foremen and Their Social Adjustment." *Industrial and Labor Relations Review*, Vol 4 (1951), 386-92.

Textiles

6385 ANDERSON, SHERWOOD. *Beyond Desire* (a novel). NY: Liveright, 1932.

6386 BARKIN, SOLOMON. "Labor Relations in the United States Textile Industry." *International Labor Review*, Vol 75 (1957), 391-411.

6387 BASSO, HAMILTON. *In Their Own Image* (a novel). NY: Scribner, 1935.

6388 BEAL, FRED E. *Proletarian Journay*. NY: Hillman-Curl, 1937.

6389 BELLAMY, CHARLES J. *The Breton Mills* (a novel). NY: Putnam, 1879.

6390 BENJAMIN, CHARLES A. (PUBLISHED ANONYMOUSLY). *The Strike in the B—Mill* (a novel). Bost.: Ticknor, 1887.

6391 BERNSTEIN, IRVING. *The Lean Years: A History of the American Worker 1920-1933*. Bost.: Houghton Mifflin 1960. (See "Prologue: Revolt in the Piedmont," pp 1-43)

6392 BLAUNER, ROBERT. *Alienation and Freedom: The Factory Worker and his Industry*. Chicago: U of Chicago Press, 1964.

6393 BOYTE, HARRY. "The Textile Industry: Keel of Southern Industrialization." *Radical America*, Vol 6 (Mar-Apr 1972), 4-49.

6394 BROCK, E. J. *Background and Recent Status of Collective Bargaining in the Cotton Industry of Rhode Island*. Wash.: Catholic U of America Press, 1942.

6395 BROOKS, ROBERT R. R. *The United Textile Workers of America*. New Haven: Yale U Microfilms, 1935.

6396 ———. *The United Textile Workers of America*. Ph D diss, Yale U, 1935.

6397 CAHN, BILL. *Mill Town*. NY: Cameron and Kahn, 1954.

6398 CARLSON, LEONARD. "Labor Supply, the Acquisition of Skills, and the Location of Southern Textile Mills, 1880-1900." *Journal of Economic History*, Vol 41 (1981), 65-73.

6399 CARLTON, DAVID. *Mill and Town: the Cotton Mill Workers and the Middle Class in South Carolina, 1880-1920.* Ph D diss, Yale U, 1977.

6400 CHURCHILL, WINSTON. *The Dwelling Place of Light* (a novel). NY: Macmillan, 1917.

6401 COLE, DONALD B. "Lawrence, Massachusetts: Model Town to Immigrant City, 1845-1912." *Historical Collections of the Essex Institute*, Vol 92 (1956), 349-75.

6402 CONWAY, MIMI. *Rise Gonna Rise: A Portrait of Southern Textile Workers.* Garden City, NY: Anchor, 1979.

6403 COSTELLO, ANTHONY. *Jericho* (a novel). NY: Bantam Books, 1982.

6404 CUTHBERT, CLIFTON. *Another Such Victory* (a novel). NY: Hillman-Curl, 1937.

6405 DALLAS, SHERMAN, and BEVERLY SCHAFFER. "Whatever Happened to the Darlington Case?" *Labor Law Journal*, Vol 24 (1973), 3-11.

6406 DARGAN, OLIVE T (FIELDING BURKE, PSEUD.). *Call Home the Heart* (a novel). NY: Longmans, Green, 1932.

6407 ———. *A Stone Came Rolling* (a novel). NY: Longmans, Green, 1935.

6408 DAVIDSON, ELIZABETH H. *Child Labor Legislation in Relation to the Textile Industry in the South.* Ph D diss, Duke U, 1932.

6409 DAVIS, REBECCA HARDING. *Margaret Howth* (a novel). Bost.: Ticknor & Fields, 1862.

6410 DE VYVER, FRANK T. "Union Fratricide: The Textile Workers Split." *South Atlantic Quarterly*, Vol 63 (1964), 363-84.

6411 DELL, FLOYD. *Diana Stair* (a novel). NY: Farrar and Rinehart, 1932.

6412 DOUGLAS, AMANDA M. *Hope Mills* (a novel). Bost.: Lee & Shepard, 1880.

6413 DUBLIN, THOMAS. "Women, Work and Protest in the Early Lowell Mills: 'The Oppressing Hand of Avarice Would Enslave Us.'" *Labor History*, Vol 16 (1975), 99-116.

6414 DUNN, ROBERT W., and HARDY J.. *Labor and Textiles.* NY: International Publishers, 1931.

6415 DUNNE, WILLIAM F. *Gastonia, Citadel of the Class Struggle in the South.* NY: Workers Library, 1929.

6416 EARLE, JOHN R. et al. *Spindles and Spires: A Restudy of Religion and Social Change in Gastonia.* Atlanta: John Knox Press, 1976.

6417 EBERT, JUSTUS. *The Trial of a New Society.* Cleveland: I.W.W. Publishing Bureau, 1913.

6418 EBNER, MICHAEL H. "Strikes and Society: Civil Behavior in Passaic, 1875-1926." *New Jersey History*, Vol 97 (1979), 7-24.

6419 EDMUNDS, MURRELL. *Between the Devil* (a novel). NY: Dutton, 1939.

6420 FAST, HOWARD. *Clarkton* (a novel). NY: Duell, Sloan & Pearce, 1947.

6421 FOGELSON, NANCY. "They Paved the Streets with Silk: Paterson, New Jersey Silk Workers, 1913-1924." *New Jersey History*, Vol 97 (1979), 133-48.

6422 FRANKLIN, J. R., and JORMAN SOMPLATSKY. "Which Way Does the Boycott Cut at J. P. Stevens." *Business and Society Review*, Vol 24 (Winter 1977), 47-54.

6423 FRY, JOSEPH A. "Rayon, Riot and Repression: Covington Sit Down Strike of 1937." *Virginia Magazine of History and Biography*, Vol 84 (1976), 3-18.

6424 GALENSON, WALTER. "The Renascence of Textile Unionism," chap. 9, *The CIO Challenge to the AFL*, Cambr.: Harvard U Press, 1960.

6425 GAMBINO, RICHARD. *Bread and Roses* (a novel). NY: Seaview Books, 1981.

6426 GERSUNY, CARL. "New England Mill Casualties, 1890-1910." *New England Quarterly*, Vol 52 (1979), 467-82.

6427 ———. "Work Injuries and Adversary Processes in Two New England Textile Mills." *Business History Review*, Vol 51 (1977), 326-40.

6428 GINGER, RAY. "Labor in a Massachusetts Cotton Mill, 1853-60." *Business History Review*, Vol 28 (1954), 67-91.

6429 GITELMAN, HOWARD M. "The Waltham System and the Coming of the Irish." *Labor History*, Vol 8 (1967), 227-53.

6430 GLASER, MARTHA. "Paterson, 1924: the ACLU and Labor." *New Jersey History*, Vol 94 (1976), 155-72.

6431 GRIFFIN, RICHARD W. "Poor White Laborers in Southern Cotton Factories, 1789-1865." *South Carolina Historical Magazine*, Vol 61 (1960), 26-40.

6432 HADCOCK, EDITHA. "Labor Problems in the Rhode Island Cotton Mills—1790-1940." *Rhode Island History*, Vol 14 (1955), 82-85, 88-93, 110-19.

6433 HALE, EDWARD E. *How They Lived at Hampton* (a novel). Bost.: J. S. Smith, 1888.

6434 HAMMOND, PATRICIA A. *The Failure of Unionization in the Southern Textile Industry: A Case Study*. MS thesis, Cornell U, 1964.

6435 HAREVEN, TAMARA K. "The Laborers of Manchester, New Hampshire, 1912-1922: the Role of Family and Ethnicity in Adjustment to Industrial Life." *Labor History*, Vol 16 (1975), 249-65.

6436 ———, and RANDOLPH LANGENBACH. *Amoskeag: Life and Work in an American Factory-City*. NY: Pantheon, 1978.

6437 HAVIRA, BARBARA. "At Work in Belding: Michigan's Silk Mill City." *Michigan History*, Vol 65 (May-Jun 1981), 33-41.

6438 HODGES, JAMES A. *The New Deal Labor Policy and the Southern Cotton Textile Industry, 1933-1941*. Ph D diss, Vanderbilt U, 1964.

6439 HUTCHINS, GRACE. *Labor and Silk*. NY: International Publishers, 1929.

6440 JOSEPHSON, HANNAH. *The Golden Threads: New England's Mill Girls and Magnates*. NY: Duell, Sloan & Pearce, 1949.

6441 KENNEDY, DONALD. "Corporate Structure, Technology, and Unionism in the Full-Fashioned Hosiery Industry: the Berkshire Knitting Mills Strike of 1936-37." *Labor Studies Journal*, Vol 3 (1979), 257-80. (See comment by Mark Brown, pp 280-82)

6442 KENNEDY, JOHN W. *The General Strike of the Textile Industry, September 1934*. MA thesis, Duke U, 1947.

6443 KENNEDY, THOMAS. *Effective Labor Arbitration: The Impartial Chairmanship of the Full-Fashioned Hosiery Industry*. Phila.: U of Pennsylvania Press, 1948.

6444 KIDDER, ALICE. "Federal Compliance Efforts in the Carolina Textile Industry: A Summary Report." *Proceedings of the Twenty-Fifth Anniversary Meeting of the Industrial Relations Research Association*, Dec 28-29, 1972, pp 353-61. Madison: IRRA, 1973.

6445 LAHNE, HERBERT J. *Cotton Mill Worker*. NY: Farrar and Rinehart, 1944.

6446 LARCOM, LUCY. *An Idyl of Work* (narrative poem based on her experiences in the Lowell Mills). Bost.: James R. Osgood, 1875.

6447 ———. *A New England Girlhood*. Bost.: Houghton Mifflin, 1889.

6448 LEA, ARDEN J. "Cotton Textiles and the Federal Child Labor Act of 1916." *Labor History*, Vol 16 (1975), 485-94.

6449 LEFTWICH, RICHARD. *Some Effects of Collective Bargaining on Resource Allocation: the Fullfashioned Hosiery Industry*. Ph D diss, U of Chicago, 1950.

6450 LEVINE, SUSAN. "Honor Each Noble Maid: Women Workers and the Yonkers Carpet Weavers' Strike of 1833." *New York History*, Vol 62 (1981), 153-76.

6451 LUMPKIN, GRACE. *To Make My Bread* (a novel). NY: Macaulay, 1932.

6452 LUMPKIN, KATHERINE D. *Shutdowns in the Connecticut Valley*. Northampton, MA: Department of History, Smith College, 1934.

6453 MCCURRY, DAN, and CAROLYN ASHBAUGH, eds. "Gastonia, 1919: Strike at the Loray Mill." *Southern Exposure*, Vol 1 (Winter 1973), 185-203.

6454 MACDONALD, LOIS. *Southern Mill Hills*. NY: Alex Hillman,, 1928.

6455 McHugh, Cathy L. "Child Labor in the Postbellum Southern Cotton Textile Industry." *Business and Economic History*, 2nd Series, Vol 11 (1982), 136-46.
6456 McLaurin, Melton A. *Paternalism and Protest: Southern Cotton Mill Workers and Organized Labor, 1875-1905.* Westport, CT: Greenwood, 1971.
6457 ———. *The Southern Cotton Textile Operative and Organized Labor, 1880-1905.* Ph D diss, U of South Carolina, 1967.
6458 McMahon, Thomas F. *United Textile Workers of America.* NY: Workers Education Bureau Press, 1926.
6459 Mims, Henry N., and Guy B. Arthur, Jr. *Analysis of 31 Southern Textile Labor Contracts.* Toccoa, CA: Management Evaluation Services, 1949.
6460 Mitchell, George S. *Textile Unionism and the South.* Chapel Hill: U of North Carolina Press, 1931.
6461 Moore, John T. *The Bishop of Cottontown* (a novel). Phila.: Winston, 1906.
6462 Muste, Abraham J. "Not So Long Ago: Autobiography." *Liberation*, 1958. (Part 7: "The Lawrence Strike of 1919," Feb 1958, pp 15-29; Part 8: "They Can't Weave Wool with Machine Guns," Mar 1958, pp 16-19; Part 9: "Nonviolence and the Lawrence Strike," Apr 1958, pp 16-19; Part 10: "The Attempt to Build a Union," May 1958, pp 16-18)
6463 Neill, Charles P. *Report on the Strike of Textile Workers in Lawrence, Massachusetts in 1912.* Wash.: G.P.O., 1912. (Senate Document No 870. U.S. Bureau of Labor Study)
6464 Nisonoff, Laurie. "Bread and Roses: the Proletarianization of Women Workers in New England Textile Mills, 1827-1848." *Historical Journal of Massachusetts*, Vol 9 (Jan 1981), 3-14.
6465 *Norma Rae.* 1979. (Feature film directed by Martin Ritt)
6466 Norton, Nancy P. "Labor in the Early New England Carpet Industry." *Bulletin of the Business Historical Society*, Vol 26 (1952), 19-26.
6467 Nyman, Richmond C., and Elliott D. Smith. *Union-Management Cooperation on the "Stretch-Out": Labor Extension at the Pequot Mills.* New Haven: Yale U Press, 1935.
6468 O'Connell, Lucille. "The Lawrence Textile Strike of 1912: Testimony of Two Polish Women." *Polish American STudies*, Vol 36 (Autumn 1979) 44-62.
6469 Page, Dorothy Myra. *Gathering Storm* (a novel). NY: International Publishers, 1932.
6470 ———. *Southern Cotton Mills and Labor.* NY: Workers Library, 1929.
6471 *The Pajama Game.* 1957. (Feature film produced by Warner Brothers)
6472 Palmer, Gladys. *Union Tactics and Economic Change.* Phila.: U of Pennsylvania Press, 1932.
6473 *The Passaic Textile Strike.* 1926. (Non-fiction film distributed by International Workers Aid.)
6474 Paul, George S. *American Velvet Company and Textile Workers Union of America.* Wash.: National Planning Association, 1953.
6475 Phillips, Edward L. *Collective Bargaining and Craft Unions: An Historical and Analytical Study of a Strike...in the Textile Industry of Fall River, Massachusetts.* Fall River: Loomfixers' Union, 1950.
6476 Poirier, Clarisse. *Pemberton Mills, 1852-1938: a Case Study of the Industrial Labor History of Lawrence, Massachusetts.* Ph D diss, Boston U, 1978.
6477 Pope, Liston. *Millhands and Preachers: A Study of Gastonia, North Carolina.* New Haven: Yale U Press, 1942.
6478 Potwin, Marjorie A. *Cotton Mill People of the Piedmont.* NY: Columbia U Press, 1927.
6479 Rankin, Carl E. *The University of North Carolina and the Problems of the Cotton Mill Employee.* Ph D diss, Columbia U, 1938.

6480 REED, MERL E. "The Augusta Textile Mills and the Strike of 1886." *Labor History*, Vol 14 (1973), 228-46.

6481 RHYNE, JENNINGS J. *Some Southern Cotton Mill Workers and Their Villages.* Chapel Hill: U of North Carolina Press, 1930.

6482 RICHARDS, PAUL D. *The History of the Textile Workers Union of America, CIO, in the South, 1937-1945.* Ph D diss, U of Wisconsin, 1978.

6483 RIEVE, EMIL. "TWUA-CIO." *Labor and Nation,*, Sep-Oct 1947, p 30.

6484 ROBINSON, HARRIET H. *Loom and Spindle: Or, Life Among the Early Mill Girls.* NY: Crowell, 1898.

6485 ROGIN, LAWRENCE. *Making History in Hosiery: The Story of the American Federation of Hosiery Workers.* Phila.: The Federation, 1938.

6486 ROLLINS, WILLIAM. *The Shadow Before* (a novel). NY: McBride, 1934.

6487 SAVAGE, SARAH (WRITING ANONYMOUSLY AS "A LADY"). *The Factory Girl* (a novel). Bost.: Munroe, Francis & Parker, 1814.

6488 SEIDMAN, JOEL. et al. "Knitting Mill Workers: The Impact of an Organizing Strike," chap. 6, *The Worker Views His Union,* Chicago: U of Chicago Press, 1958.

6489 SELEKMAN, BEN M. et al. *The Clothing and Textile Industries in New York and Its Environs.* NY: Regional Plan of New York and Its Environs, 1925.

6490 SHANKER, A. "The J. P. Stevens Struggle." *Free Trade Union News*, Vol 32 (Mar 1977), 13.

6491 SHELDON, CHARLES M. *The Crucifixion of Philip Strong* (a novel). Chicago: McClurg, 1894.

6492 SHERRY, P. H., and R. STROMMEN. "Boycott in Behalf of Workers' Rights: the Textile Workers vs J. P. Stevens." *Christianity and Crisis*, Vol 37 (Apr 1977), 59-63.

6493 SIEGEL, MORTON. *The Passaic Textile Strike of 1926.* Ph D diss, Columbia U, 1952.

6494 SILVIA, PHILIP T. "The Position of Workers in a Textile Community: Fall River in the Early 1880's." *Labor History*, Vol 16 (1975), 230-48.

6495 SIMON, JEAN-CLAUDE. *Textile Workers, Trade Unions, and Politics: Comparative Case Studies, France and the United States, 1885-1914.* Ph D diss, Tufts U, 1981.

6496 SMITH, THOMAS R. *The Cotton Textile Industry of Fall River, Massachusetts.* NY: King's Crown Press, 1944.

6497 SNYDER, ROBERT E. "Women, Wobblies and Workers' Rights: the 1912 Textile Strike in Little Falls, New York." *New York History*, Vol 60 (1979), 29-57.

6498 SPARKS, PHILIP. "The Darlington Case: Justice Delayed is Justice Denied." *Labor Law Journal*, Vol 26 (1975), 759-66.

6499 STOKES, ALLEN. *Black and White Labor and the Development of the Southern Textile Industry, 1800-1920.* Ph D diss, U of South Carolina, 1978.

6500 STORROW, CHARLES S. *Report of the Treasurer of the Committee of Relief for the Sufferers by the Fall of the Pemberton Mill in Lawrence, Massachusetts.* NY: no publisher indicated, 1860.

6501 "Struggles of Textile Workers Depicted by Labor Cartoonists." *Textile Labor*, Vol 34 (Feb 1973), 5.

6502 SYLVESTER, DAVID. "Lowell's Labors Lost." *Progressive*, Vol 45 (Jul 1981), 34-35.

6503 TABER, GLADYS B. *A Star to Steer By* (a novel). Phila.: Macrae Smith, 1938.

6504 TAYLOR, GEORGE W. *The Full-Fashioned Hosiery Worker: His Changing Economic Status.* Phila.: U of Pennsylvania Press, 1931.

6505 ———. "Hosiery," chap. 9, *How Collective Bargaining Works*, Harry A. Millis, research director. NY: Twentieth Century Fund, 1945.

6506 *Testimony: Justice vs. J. P. Stevens.* 1976. (Non-fiction film produced by Harold Mayer & Lynne Rhodes Mayer)

6507 TEXTILE WORKERS UNION OF AMERICA. *Almost Unbelieveable: The Story of an Industry, a Union and a Law.* NY: The Union, [1961].

6508 ———. *Building a Textile Union.* NY: The Union, 1948.

6509 ———. *Half a Million Forgotten People: The Story of the Cotton Textile Workers.* NY: The Union, 1944.

6510 ———. *Taft-Hartleyism in Textiles with Special Reference to Conditions in the Southern Branch of the Industry*. NY: The Union, 1953.

6511 TIPPETT, THOMAS. *Mill Shadows: A Drama of Social Forces in Four Acts.* Katonah, NY: Brookwood Labor College, 1932.

6512 ———. *When Southern Labor Stirs.* NY: Cape & Smith, 1931.

6513 TUCKER, GEORGE. "The Struggle to Organize J. P. Stevens." *Political Affairs*, Vol 57 (May 1978), 2-9.

6514 TURNER, GEORGE K. *The Taskmasters* (a novel). NY: McClure, Phillips, 1902.

6515 U.S. COMMISSION ON INDUSTRIAL RELATIONS (1912). "The Textile Industry in Philadelphia," Vol 4, pp 3033-90, *Final Report*, Wash.: G.P.O., 1916.

6516 U.S. CONGRESS. HOUSE. Committee on Rules. *The Strike at Lawrence, Massachusetts.* Wash.: G.P.O., 1912. (House Document No 671)

6517 ———. SENATE. Committee on Labor and Public Welfare. Subcommittee on Labor and Labor-Management Relations. *Labor-Management Relations in the Southern Textile Industry*. Wash.: G.P.O., 1952.

6518 ———. ———. *Labor-Management Relations in the Southern Textile Manufacturing Industry,,* Parts 1 & 2. Wash.: G.P.O., 1950-51.

6519 U.S. DEPARTMENT OF LABOR. Bureau of Labor Statistics *Union Agreements in the Cotton-Textile Industry.*, Bulletin 885. Wash.: G.P.O., 1947.

6520 UNITED TEXTILE WORKERS OF AMERICA. *The AFL Textile Workers.* Wash.: The Union, 1950.

6521 VAN OSDELL, JOHN GARRETT, JR. *Cotton Mills, Labor and the Southern Mind: 1880-1930.* Ph D diss, Tulane U, 1966.

6522 VAN VORST, MARIE. *Amanda of the Mill* (a novel). NY: Dodd-Mead, 1905.

6523 VORSE, MARY H. *The Passaic Textile Strike, 1926-1927.* Passaic, NJ: General Relief Committee of Textile Strikers, 1927.

6524 ———. *Strike!* (a novel). NY: Liveright, 1930.

6525 WALTON, PERRY. *The Story of Textiles.* Bost.: Walton Printing Co., 1912.

6526 WARD, ELIZABETH S. PHELPS. *The Silent Partner* (a novel). Bost.: Osgood, 1871.

6527 WEISBORD, ALBERT. *Passaic: The Story of a Struggle against Starvation Wages and for the Right to Organize.* Chicago: Daily Worker, 1926.

6528 WORTZEL, HEIDI. *Lowell: the Corporations and the City, 1859-1869.* Ph D diss, Brown U, 1980.

6529 WRIGHT, GAVIN. "Cheap Labor and Southern Textiles Before 1880." *Journal of Economic History*, Vol 29 (1979), 655-80.

6530 YABROFF, BERNARD, and ANN J. HERLIHY. "History of Work Stoppages in Textile Industries." *Monthly Lasbor Review*, Vol 76 (1953), 367-71.

6531 YELLEN, SAMUEL. "The Great Lawrence Strike!," *American Labor Struggles*, NY: Harcourt, Brace, 1936.

6532 ZEISEL, ROSE N. "Technology and Labor in the Textile Industry." *Monthly Labor Review*, Vol 91 (Feb 1968), 49-55.

Tobacco

6533 APPEL, JOHN C. "The Unionization of Florida Cigarmakers and the Coming of the War with Spain." *Hispanic American Historical Review*, Vol 36 (1956), 38-49.

6534 BANKS, ANN. "Tobacco Talk." *Southern Exposure*, Vol 8 (Winter 1980), 35-45.

6535 LONG, DURWARD. "The Open-Closed Shop Battle in Tampa's Cigar Industry, 1919-1921." *Florida Historical Quarterly*, Vol 42 (1968), 121.

6536 PEREZ, LOUIS A., JR. "Cubans in Tampa: from Exiles to Immigrants, 1892-1901." *Florida Historical Quarterly*, Vol 62 (1978), 129-40.

6537 ———. "Reminiscences of a *lector*: Cuban Cigar Workers in Tampa." *Florida Historical Quarterly*, Vol 53 (1975), 443-49.

6538 WARE, NORMAN J. "The Cigar Makers," pp 258-79, *The Labor Movement in the United States, 1860-1895*, NY: Appleton, 1929.

Transportation—Air

6539 BLUM, ALBERT A. "Fourth Man Out: The Background of the Flight Engineer —Airline Pilot Conflict." *Labor Law Journal*, Aug 1962, pp 649-57.

6540 BRIGGS, VERNON M., JR. "The Mutual Aid Pact of the Airline Industry." *Industrial and Labor Relations Review*, Vol 19 (1965), 3-20.

6541 CIMINI, MICHAEL H. "Emergency Boards in the Airline Industry, 1936-69." *Monthly Labor Review*, Vol 93 (Jul 1970), 57-65.

6542 DALE, ERNEST, and ROBERT L. RAIMON. "Management Unionism and Public Policy on the Railroads and the Airliness." *Industrial and Labor Relations Review*, Vol 11 (1958), 551-71.

6543 HOLLOWAY, H. A. *A Dramatic Examination of Changing Image: the Airline Pilots Association, 1931-1938.* Ph D diss, Wayne State U, 1979.

6544 HOPKINS, GEORGE E. *The Airline Pilots: A Study in Elete Unionization.* Cambr.: Harvard U Press, 1971.

6545 ———. "ALPA Wins its Legislative Wings." *Air Line Pilot*, Vol 45 (Sep 1976), 18-20.

6546 ———. "Howard Hughes (1905-1976): ALPA Member." *Air Line Pilot*, Vol 45 (Oct 1976), 14, 47.

6547 ———. "Pilot Strike: 1919." *Airline Pilot*, Vol 43 (Jul 1974), 12-15.

6548 KAHN, MARK L. "Airline Flight Crews: Adjustment to Technological Change in a Regulated Growth Industry." *Proceedings of the Eighteenth Annual Winter Meeting of the Industrial Relations Research Association*, Dec 28-29, 1965, pp 124-38. Madison: IRRA, 1966.

6549 ———. "Mutual Strike Aid in the Airlines." *Labor Law Journal*, Vol 11 (Jul 1960), 595-606.

6550 ———. "Wage Determination for Airlines Pilots." *Industrial and Labor Relations Review*, Vol 6 (1953), 317-36.

6551 KRISLOV, JOSEPH. "Representation Disputes in the Railroad and Airline Industries." *Labor Law Journal,*, Feb 1956, pp 98-103.

6552 KROLICK, REUBEN HARRISON. *A Study of the Changing Economic Status of Skilled Occupations: Railroad Engineers and Airline Pilots.* Ph D diss, Stanford U, 1966.

6553 LEIDING, OSCAR. *A Story of the Origin and Progression of the Air Line Pilots Association and of Its Key Figure and Organizer, 1930-1944.* Chicago (?): The Association, 1945.

6554 LEYERZAPF, JAMES W. "Aviation Promotion in Kansas City: 1925-1931." *Missouri Historical Review*, Vol 46 (1972), 246-67.

6555 MARQUARDT, MARTIN WILLIAM. *The Scope of Bargaining at U.S. Air Force Installations Within the Forty-Eight Coterminous States Under Executive Order 11491: An Analysis and Projection.* Ph D diss, U of Alabama, 1972.

6556 MATER, DAN H., and GARTH L. MANGUM. "The Integration of Seniority Lists in Transportation Mergers." *Industrial and Labor Relations Review*, Vol 16 (1963), 343-65.

6557 MODES, ED, ed. *The ALPA Story* (a history and Study of the background, functions, and organization of the Air Line Pilots Association). Chicago (?): Air Line Pilots Association, 1954.

6558 NIELSEN, GEORGIA PAINTER. *From Sky Girl to Flight Attendant: Women and the Making of a Union.* Ithaca: ILR Press, NY State School of Industrial and Labor Relations, Cornell U, 1982.

6559 NORTHRUP, HERBERT R. "Airline Strike Insurance: a Study in Escalation." *Industrial and Labor Relations Review*, Vol 30 (1977), 364-72.

6560 OLIVER, ELI L. "Labor Problems of the Transportation Industry." *Law and Contemporary Problems*, Vol 25 (1960), 3-21.

6561 PRICE, WESLEY. "Labor's Biggest Wind." *Saturday Evening Post*, Aug 2, 1947, pp 25, 117-18.

6562 "Recommendations on the Airlines-Flight Engineers Dispute." *Monthly Labor Review*, Vol 84 (1961), 750-53.

6563 REDENIUS, CHARLES MELVIN. *The Railway Act and the Airline Industry*. Ph D diss, U of Michigan, 1968.

6564 RUPPENTHAL, KARL M. "Compulsory Retirement of Air Line Pilots." *Industrial and Labor Relations Review*, Vol 14 (1961), 528-47.

6565 TULLY, PAUL. *Attitudes of Air Force Personnel Toward Unionization*. Ph D diss, U of Houston, 1980.

6566 U.S. CONGRESS. HOUSE. Committee on Post Office and Civil Service. *Oversight on Grievances of Air Traffic Control Specialists*. Wash.: G.P.O., 1981.

6567 UNTERBERGER, S. HERBERT, and EDWARD C. KOZIARA. "Airline Strike Insurance: A Study in Escalation." *Industrial and Labor Relations Review*, Vol 29 (1975), 26-45.

6568 ———. "Reply." *Industrial and Labor Relations Review*, Vol 30 (1977), 373-79.

Transportation—Railroads

GENERAL

6569 ADLER, PHILIP, JR. *A Historical Study of Management-Labor Relations Pertaining to the Dieselization of Railroads in the United States*. Ph D diss, Ohio State U, 1966.

6570 AFROS, JOHN L. "Guaranteed Employment Plan of Seaboard Railroad." *Monthly Labor Review*, Vol 65 (1947), 167-71.

6571 AGNEW, ROBERT J. *The Diesel-electric Locomotive and Railway Employees*. PhD diss, Massachusetts Institute of Technology, 1953.

6572 ALLEN, RUTH A. *The Great Southwest Strike*. Austin: U of Texas Press, 1942.

6573 ARNOW, PHILIP. "Findings of the Presidential Railroad Commission." *Labor Law Journal*, Aug 1963, pp 677-85.

6574 ASHLEY, WILLIAM J. *The Railroad Strike of 1894*. Cambr.: The Church Social Union, 1895.

6575 BACKMAN, JULES. *Economics of New York State Fullcrew Laws*. NY: NY State Association of Railroads, 1964.

6576 BARNARD, HARRY. *Eagle Forgotten: The Life of John Peter Altgeld*. Indianapolis: Bobbs-Merrill, 1938.

6577 BERNHARDT, JOSHUA. *The Railroad Labor Board: Its History, Activities and Organization*. Balt.: Johns Hopkins Press, 1923.

6578 BEYER, OTTO. "Union-Management Cooperation in the Railway Industry." *Bulletin of the Taylor Society*, Feb 1926.

6579 BLACK, PAUL V. "Experiment in Bureaucratic Centralization; Employee Blacklisting on the Burlington Railroad, 1877-1892." *Business History Review*, Vol 51 (1977), 444-59.

6580 BLANK, IRA L., ed. *Railroad Labor and Government Transportation Policy, 1962-1972: A Selected Bibliography*. Ithaca: Labor Management Documentation Center, NY State School of Industrial and Labor Relations, Cornell U, 1972.

6581 "BLE Played a Major Role in Organizing Railway Labor Executives' Association." *Locomotive Engineer*, Vol 108 (Aug 30, 1974), 4-5.

6582 BOYLE, OHIO D. *History of Railroad Strikes: A History of the Railroad Revolt of 1887....* Wash.: Brotherhood Publishing Co., 1935.

6583 BRADLEY, WALTER, comp. *An Industrial War: History of the Missouri and North Arkansas Railroad Strike.* Harrison, AR: Bradley and Russell, 1923.

6584 BRIGGS, VERNON M., JR. "The Strike Insurance Plan of the Railroad Industry." *Industrial Relations*, Vol 6 (1967), 205-12.

6585 BRUCE, ROBERT V. *1877: Year of Violence.* NY: Bobbs-Merrill, 1959.

6586 BUREAU OF INFORMATION OF THE EASTERN RAILWAYS. *Wages and Labor Relations in the Railroad Industry, 1900-1941.* NY: The Bureau, 1942.

6587 BURNS, WILLIAM F. *The Pullman Boycott.* St. Paul: McGill, 1894.

6588 CHRISTIE, HUGH K., and JAMES MCKINNEY. *The Railway Foreman and His Job.* Chicago: American Technical Society, 1947.

6589 CIMINI, MICHAEL H. "Government Intervention in Railroad Disputes." *Monthly Labor Review*, Vol 94 (1971), 27-34.

6590 CLARK, CHARLES HUGH. *The Railroad Safety Movement in the United States: Origins and Development, 1869-1893.* Ph D diss, U of Illinois, 1966.

6591 CLEVELAND, GROVER. *The Government in the Chicago Strike of 1894.* Princeton: Princeton U Press, 1913.

6592 COTTRELL, FRED. *Technological Change and Labor in the Railroad Industry: A Comparative Study.* Lexington, MA: Heath, 1970.

6593 COTTRELL, WILLIAM F. *The Railroader.* Stanford: CA: Stanford U Press, 1940.

6594 DENISON, THOMAS S. *An Iron Crown: A Tale of the Great Republic* (a novel). Chicago: T. S. Denison, 1885.

6595 DEWSNUP, ERNEST R. *Railway Organization and Working.* Chicago: U of Chicago Press, 1906.

6596 DOWLING, GEORGE T. *The Wreckers* (a novel). Phila.: Lippincott, 1886.

6597 DUCKER, JAMES. *Men of the Steel Rails: Workers on the Atchison, Topeka and Santa Fe Railroad, 1869-1900.* Ph D diss, U of Illinois, 1980.

6598 EGGERT, GERALD G. "A Missed Alternative: Federal Court Arbitration of Railway Labor Disputes, 1877-1895." *Labor History*, Vol 7 (1966), 287-306.

6599 ———. *Railroad Labor Disputes: The Beginnings of Federal Strike Policy.* Ann Arbor: U of Michigan Press, 1967.

6600 FAGAN, J. O. *Labor and the Railroads.* Bost.: Houghton Mifflin, 1909.

6601 FISHER, THOMAS R. *Industrial Disputes and Federal Legislation, with Special Reference to the Railroad, Coal, Steel, and Automobile Industries in the U.S. since 1900.* NY: Columbia U Press, 1940.

6602 FORAN, MARTIN A. *The Other Side* (a novel). Cleveland: Ingham, Clark & Wash.: Gray & Clarkson, 1886.

6603 FORD, PAUL LEICESTER. *The Honorable Peter Stirling and What People Thought of Him* (a novel). NY: Holt, 1894.

6604 GALENSON, WALTER. "Railroad Unionism," chap. 18, *The CIO Challenge to the AFL*, Cambr.: Harvard U Press, 1960.

6605 GINGER, RAY. *Altgeld's America.* NY: Funk & Wagnalls, 1958.

6606 GUTMAN, HERBERT G. "Trouble on the Railroads in 1873-1874: Prelude to the 1877 Crisis?" *Labor History*, Vol 2 (1961), 215-35.

6607 HALL, JOHN A. *The Great Strike on the "Q," with a History of the Organization and Growth of the Brotherhood of Locomotive Firemen, and Switchmen's Mutual Air Association of North America.* Chicago: Elliott and Beezley, 1889.

6608 HAMBLEN, HERBERT ELLIOTT. *The General Manager's Story: Old Time Reminiscences of Railroading in the United States* (a novel). NY: Macmillan, 1898.

6609 HARRIS, HERBERT. *American Labor.* New Haven: Yale U Press, 1938. (See pp 225-66)

6610 HARRIS, LEE O. *The Man Who Tramps* (a novel). Indianapolis: Douglass & Carlon, 1878.

6611 HAY, JOHN (PUBLISHED ANONYMOUSLY). *The Bread-Winners* (a novel). NY: Harper, 1884.

6612 HEADLEY, JOEL T. *Pen and Pencil Sketches of the Great Riots: An Illustrated History of the Railroad and Other Great American Riots.* NY: E. B. Treat, 1877.

6613 HENDERSON, A. B. "F.E.P.C. and the Southern Railway Case: an Investigation into the Discriminatory Practices of Railroads during World War II." *Journal of Negro History*, Vol 61 (1976), 173-87.

6614 HENDERSON, JAMES A. "The Railroad Riots in Pittsburgh, Saturday and Sunday, April 21st and 22nd, 1877." *Western Pennsylvania Historical Magazine*, Vol 11 (1928), 194-97.

6615 HERRICK, ROBERT. *The Web of Life* (a novel). NY: Macmillan, 1900.

6616 HOROWITZ, MORRIS A. *Manpower Utilization in the Railroad Industry: An Analysis of Working Rules and Practices.* Bost.: Bureau of Business and Economic Research, Northeastern U, 1960.

6617 ———. "The Railroads' Dual System of Payment: A Make-Work Rule?" *Industrial and Labor Relations Review*, Vol 8 (1955), 177-94.

6618 HORTON, GEORGE R., and H. ELLSWORTH STEELE. "The Unity Issue among Railroad Engineers and Firemen." *Industrial and Labor Relations Review*, Vol 10 (1956), 48-69.

6619 JAKUBAUSKAS, EDWARD B. "Technological Change and Recent Trends in the Composition of Railroad Employment." *Quarterly Review of Economics & Business*, Vol 2 (1962), 81-90.

6620 JEBSEN, HARRY, JR. "The Role of Blue Island in the Pullman Strike of 1894." *Illinois State Historical Society Journal*, Vol 57 (1974), 275-93.

6621 JONES, HARRY E. *Inquiry of the Attorney General's Committee on Administrative Procedure Relating to the National Railroad Adjustment Board—Historical Background and Growth of Machinery Set Up for the Handling of Railroad Labor Disputes, 1888-1940* Wash.: U.S. Department of Justice, 1941.

6622 ———. *Railroad Wages and Labor Relations, 1900-1952: An Historical Survey and Summary of Results.* NY: Bureau of Information of the Eastern Railways, 1953.

6623 KAUFMAN, JACOB JOSEPH. *Collective Bargaining in the Railroad Industry.* NY: King's Crown Press, 1954.

6624 ———. "Emergency Boards Under the Railway Labor Act." *Labor Law Journal,*, Dec 1958, pp 910-20, 949.

6625 ———. "Government Intervention in Railroad Labor Disputes." *Current Economic Comment*, Vol 20 (Aug 1958), 9-16.

6626 ———. "Grievance Arbitration in the Railroad Industry." *Labor Law Journal,*, Mar 1958, pp 244-47.

6627 ———. "Grievance Procedure under the Railway Labor Act." *Southern Economic Journal*, Vol 14 (1952), 66-78.

6628 ———. "Logic and Meaning of Work Rules on the Railroads." *Proceedings of the Fourteenth Annual Meeting of the Industrial Relations Research Association*, Dec 28-29, 1961, pp 378-88/ Madison: IRRA, 1962.

6629 ———. "The Railroad Labor Dispute: A Marathon of Maneuver and Improvisation." *Industrial and Labor Relations Review*, Vol 18 (1965), 196-212.

6630 ———. "Representation in the Railroad Industry." *Labor Law Journal*, Jul 1955, pp 437-512.

6631 ———. "Wage Criteria in the Railroad Industry." *Industrial and Labor Relations Review*, Vol 6 (1952), 119-26.

6632 KEENAN, HENRY F. *The Money-Makers* (a novel). NY: Appleton, 1885.

6633 KERLEY, JAMES W. *The Failure of Railway Labor Leadership: A Chapter in Railroad Labor Relations.* Ph D diss, Columbia U, 1959.

6634 KILGOUR, JOHN G. "Alternatives to the Railway Labor Act: An Appraisal." *Industrial and Labor Relations Review*, Vol 25 (1971), 72-84.

6635 KRISLOV, JOSEPH. "Mediation under the Railway Labor Act: a Process in Search of a Name." *Labor Law Journal*, Vol 27 (1976), 310-15.

6636 ———. "Representation Disputes in the Railroad and Airline Industries." *Labor Law Journal*, Feb 1956, pp 98-103.

6637 KROLICK, REUBEN HARRISON. *A Study of the Changing Economic Status of Skilled Occupations: Railroad Engineers and Airline Pilots*. Ph D diss, Stanford U, 1966.

6638 "Labor Unions in Transportation and Communications Industries." *Monthly Labor Review*, Vol 70 (1950), 275-78.

6639 "Labor-Management Relations Under the Railway Labor Act, 1934-57." *Monthly Labor Review*, Vol 81 (1958), 879-81.

6640 LAZAR, JOSEPH. *Due Process on the Railroads*. Los Angeles: U of California Press, 1953.

6641 ———. *Due Process on the Railroads: Disciplinary Grievance Procedures before the National Railroad Adjustment Board*. Los Angeles: Institute of Industrial Relations, U of California, 1958.

6642 LECHT, LEONARD. *Experience under Railway Labor Legislation*. NY: Columbia U Press, 1955.

6643 LICHT, WALTER. *Nineteenth Century American Railway Men: a Study in the Nature and Organization of Work*. Ph D diss, Princeton U, 1978.

6644 LIGHTNER, DAVID. "Construction Labor on the Illinois Central Railroad." *Illinois State Historical Society Journal*, Vol 46 (1973), 285-301.

6645 LINDSEY, ALMONT. "Paternalism and the Pullman Strike." *American Historical Review*, Vol 44 (1939), 272-89.

6646 ———. *The Pullman Strike*. Chicago: U of Chicago Press, 1942.

6647 LOGAN, SAMUEL C. *A City's Danger and Defense: Or, Issues and Results of the Strikes of 1877, Containing the Origin and History of the Scranton City Guard*. Phila.: J. B. Rodgers Printing Co., 1887.

6648 MCCABE, DOUGLAS M. *The Crew Size Dispute in the Railroad Industry*. Wash.: U.S. Department of Transportation, Federal Railroad Administration, 1977.

6649 MCCABE, JAMES D. (EDWARD W. MARTIN, PSEUD.). *The History of the Great Riots*. Phila.: National Publishing Co., 1877.

6650 MCDONALD, GRACE L. (MARGARET GRAHAM, PSEUD.). *Swing Shift* (a novel). NY: Citadel Press, 1951.

6651 MACKEY, PHILIP ENGLISH. "Law and Order, 1877: Philadelphia's Response to the Railroad Riots." *Pennsylvania Magazine of History and Biography*, Vol 96 (1973), 183-202.

6652 MCMURRY, DONALD L. "Federation of the Railroad Brotherhoods, 1889-1894." *Industrial and Labor Relations Review*, Vol 7 (1953), 73-92.

6653 ———. *The Great Burlington Railroad Strike of 1888*. Cambr.: Harvard U Press, 1956.

6654 ———. "Labor Policies of the General Managers' Association of Chicago, 1886-1894." *Journal of Economic History*, Vol 13 (1953), 160-78.

6655 ———. "The Legal Ancestry of the Pullman Strike Injunctions." *Industrial and Labor Relations Review*, Vol 14 (1961), 235-56.

6656 MANDEL, BERNARD. "The Great Uprising of 1877." *Cigar Makers Official Journal*, Dec 1953.

6657 ———. "Notes on the Pullman Boycott." *Explorations in Entrepreneurial History*, Vol 6 (1954), 184-89.

6658 MANGUM, GARTH L. "Grievance Procedures for Railroad Operating Employees." *Industrial and Labor Relations Review*, Vol 15 (1962), 474-99.

6659 MANNING, THOMAS G. *The Chicago Strike of 1894: Industrial Labor in the Late Nineteenth Century*. NY: Holt, 1960.

6660 MATER, DAN H. *The Railroad Seniority System: History, Description and Evaluation*. Ph D diss, U of Chicago, 1942.

6661 ———, and GARTH L. MANGUM. "The Integration of Seniority Lists in Transportation Mergers." *Industrial and Labor Relations Review*, Vol 16 (1963), 343-65.

6662 MATTHEWS, JOHN MICHAEL. "The Georgia 'Race Strike' of 1909." *Journal of Southern History*, Vol 40 (1974), 613-30.

6663 MEYERS, FREDERIC. "Criteria in the Making of Wage Decisions by 'Neutrals': The Railroads as a Case Study." *Industrial and Labor Relations Review*, Vol 4 (1951), 343-55.

6664 MIDDLETON, P. H. *Railways and Organized Labor*. Chicago: Railway Business Association, 1941.

6665 MILLER, J. F. *Report to Joseph Wood, General Manager, Pennsylvania Lines West of Pittsburgh, on the 1894 Strike of the American Railroad Union*. (Carbon typescript at the Labor-Management Documentation Center, NY State School of Industrial and Labor Relations, Cornell U)

6666 MISSOURI. Bureau of Labor Statistics and Inspection *The Official History of the Great Strike of 1886 on the Southwestern Railway System*. (Jefferson City: The Bureau, 1887)

6667 MORRIS, JAMES O. *Bibliography of Industrial Relations in the Railroad Industry*. Ithaca: NY State School of Industrial and Labor Relations, Cornell U, 1975.

6668 MURPHY, FRANK J., S. J. "Agreement on the Railroads—The Joint Railway Conference of 1926." *Labor Law Journal*, Sep 1960, pp 823-36.

6669 NEWBORN, NORTON. "Restrictions on the Right to Strike on the Railroads: A History and Analysis." *Labor Law Journal*, Vol 24 (1973), 142-63, 234-50.

6670 NORRIS, FRANK. *The Octopus* (a novel). Long Island, NY: Garden City Publishing Co., 1901.

6671 NORTHRUP, HERBERT R. "Industrial Relations on the Railroads," chap. 20, *Labor in Postwar America*, Colston Warne, ed. Brooklyn: Remsen Press, 1949.

6672 ———. "The Railway Labor Act: A Critical Reappraisal." *Industrial and Labor Relations Review*, Vol 25 (1971), 3-31.

6673 ———. "The Railway Labor Act and Railway Labor Disputes in Wartime." *American Economic Review*, Jun 1946.

6674 ———. "Unfair Labor Practice Prevention under the Railway Labor Act." *Industrial and Labor Relations Review*, Vol 3 (1950), pp 323-40.

6675 ———, and MARK L. KAHN. "Railroad Grievance Machinery: A Critical Analysis." *Industrial and Labor Relations Review*, Vol 5 (1952), 365-82, 540-59.

6676 OLIVER, ELI. "Job and Income Security in Railway Mergers and Abandonments." *Automation and Major Technological Change: Collective Bargaining Problems*, papers presented at a conference held under the auspices of the Industrial Union Department, AFL-CIO, Apr 22, 1958, pp 21-27.

6677 ———. "Labor Problems of the Transportation Industry." *Law and Contemporary Problems*, Vol 25 (1960), 3-21.

6678 PERSON, CARL E. *The Lizard's Trail: A Story from the Illinois Central and Harrison Lines Strike of 1911 to 1915 Inclusive*. Chicago: Lake Publishing Co., 1918.

6679 POLLACK, JEROME. "Workmen's Compensation for Railroad Work Injuries and Diseases." *Cornell Law Quarterly*, Vol 36 (1951).

6680 PRESIDENTIAL RAILROAD COMMISSION. *Report of the Presidential Railroad Commission*. Wash.: The Commission, Feb 1962.

6681 PULLMAN, GEORGE M. *The Strike at Pullman*. Cambr.: Church Social Union, 1895.

6682 RAILROAD BROTHERHOOD UNITY MOVEMENT. *Revolt in the Railroad Unions*. Chicago: no publisher indicated, 1935.

6683 "Railroads," chap. 7, *How Collective Bargaining Works*, Harry A. Millis, research director. NY: Twentieth Century Fund, 1945.

6684 RAILWAY LABOR EXECUTIVES' ASSOCIATION. *Labor and Transportation—Program and Objectives of Transporation Labor in the Post-War Period*. Wash.: The Association, 1946.

6685 REHMUS, CHARLES M. "Railway Labor Act Modifications: Helpful or Harmful?" *Industrial and Labor Relations Review*, Vol 25 (1971), 85-94.

6686 Reinhardt, Richard, comp. *Working on the Railroad: Reminiscences from the Age of Steam*. Palo Alto, CA: American West Publishing Co., 1970.

6687 Richberg, Donald R. "Legal Battles for Labor," chap. 9, *My Hero: The Indiscreet Memoirs of an Eventful but Unheroic Life*, NY: Putnam, 1954. (On the Railway Labor Act of 1926)

6688 Salmons, Charles H., comp. *The Burlington Strike*. Aurora, IL: Bunnell & Ward, 1889.

6689 Saxton, Alexander. *Great Midland* (a novel). NY: Appleton-Century-Crofts, 1948.

6690 Schlager, W. L., Jr. "Expedited Arbitration on the Long Island Railroad." *Arbitration Journal*, Vol 30 (1975), 273-82.

6691 Schubert, Richard, and Jean S. Cooper. "The Florida East Coast Railway Case: A Study of Governmental Decision Making." *Labor Law Journal*, Vol 25 (1974), 131-49.

6692 Sigmund, Elwin W. *Federal Laws Concerning Railroad Labor Disputes: A Legislative and Legal History, 1877-1934*. Ph D diss, U of Illinois, 1961.

6693 Smith, D. J. "The American Railroad Novel." *Markham Review*, Vol 3 (1972), 61-71.

6694 Speirs, Rosemary E. *Technological Change and the Railway Unions, 1945-72*. Ph D diss, U of Toronto, 1977.

6695 Spencer, William H. *The National Railroad Adjustment Board*. Chicago: U of Chicago Press, 1938.

6696 St. Louis Project Team. Task Force on Rail Transportation of the Labor/Management Committee *A Cooperative Program of Experiments Involving Changes in Railroad Operations: St. Louis Project: 1975 Progress Report*. Wash.: The Task Force, 1976.

6697 Stockett, Joseph Noble. *The Arbitral Determination of Railway Wages*. Bost.: Houghton Mifflin, 1918.

6698 Stoesen, Alexander. "Road from Receivership: Claude Pepper, the Dupont Trust and the Florida East Railroad." *Florida History Quarterly*, Vol 42 (1973), 132-56.

6699 Stromquist, Howard S. *A Generation of Boomers: Work, Community Structure, and the Pattern of Industrial Conflict on Late 19th Century American Railroads*. Ph D diss, U of Pittsburgh, 1981.

6700 Troy, Leo. "Labor Representation on American Railways." *Labor History*, Vol 2 (1961), 295-322.

6701 Turner, Ralph V., and William Warren Rogers. "Arkansas Labor in Revolt: Little Rock and the Great Southwestern Strike." *Arkansas Historical QWuarterly*, Vol 24 (1965), 29-46.

6702 "Twenty Years of Benefit Programs for Railroad Workers." *Monthly Labor Review*, Vol 79 (1956), 815-17.

6703 Uhl, Alexander. *Trains and the Men Who Run Them*. Wash.: Public Affairs Institute, 1954.

6704 U.S. Attorney General's Committee on Administrative Procedure. *Railroad Retirement Board*. Wash.: The Committee, 1939.

6705 ———. *Railway Labor: The National Railroad Adjustment Board and the National Mediation Board*. Wash.: The Committee, 1940.

6706 U.S. Commission on Industrial Relations (1912). "Conditions of Labor on the Pennsylvania Railroad," Vol 11, pp 10067-449, *Final Report*, Wash.: G.P.O., 1916.

6707 ———. "Harriman Railroad System Strike," Vol 10, pp 9697-10066, *Final Report*, Wash.: G.P.O., 1916.

6708 ———. "Pullman Employees," Vol 10, pp 9543-695, *Final Report*, Wash.: G.P.O., 1916.

6709 U.S. Congress. House. Committee on Education and Labor. *Investigation of Communist Influence in the Bucyrus-Erie Strike*. Wash.: G.P.O., 1948.

6710 ———. Senate. Committee on Interstate Commerce. *Government Investigation of Railway Disputes*. Wash.: G.P.O., 1917.

6711 ———. ———. Committee on Labor and Public Welfare. Subcommittee on Labor and Labor-Management Relations. *Labor Dispute between the Railroad Carriers and Four Operating Railroad Brotherhoods.* Wash.: G.P.O., 1951.

6712 U.S. Department of Labor. Bureau of Labor Statistics *Employment Outlook in Railroad Occupations.*, Bulletin 961. Wash.: G.P.O., 1949.

6713 ———. *Use of Federal Power in Settlement of Railway Labor Disputes.*, Bulletin 303. Wash.: G.P.O., 1922.

6714 U.S. Eight-Hour Commission. *Report of the Eight-Hour Commission.* Wash.: G.P.O., 1918. (See especially Appendix VI, "Railway Wage Schedules and Agreements," by William Z. Ripley, and Appendix VII, "Employment Conditions in Road and Yard Service," by Victor S. Clark)

6715 U.S. Emergency Board, 1943. Carriers and Employees, Diesel-Electric Operators *Transcript of Proceedings of the National Railway Labor Panel Emergency Board. So-Called "Diesel Case."* NY: Eastern Printing Corp., 1943.

6716 ———. Carriers and Employees, Non-Operating *Transcript of Proceedings of the National Railway Labor Panel Emergency Board. Union Shop Wage Increase Case.* NY: Eastern Printing Corp., 1943.

6717 ———. Carriers and Employees, Operating *Transcript of Proceedings of the National Railway Labor Panel Emergency Board. Wage Increase Case.* NY: Eastern Printing Corp., 1943.

6718 U.S. National Labor Relations Board. Division of Economic Research "The Railway Industry," chap. 8, *Written Trade Agreements in Collective Bargaining*, Wash.: G.P.O., 1940.

6719 U.S. National Mediation Board. *Administration of the Railway Labor Act by the National Mediation Board, 1934-1957.* Wash.: G.P.O., 1958.

6720 ———. *Fifteen Years under the Railway Labor Act, Amended, and the National Mediation Board, 1934-1949.* Wash.: G.P.O., 1950.

6721 ———. *Labor Relations in the Railroad Industry.* Wash.: G.P.O., 1940.

6722 U.S. Strike Commission. *Report on the Chicago Strike of June-July, 1894.* Wash.: G.P.O., 1895. (Senate Executive Document No 7)

6723 Varg, Paul A. "The Political Ideas of the American Railway Union." *The Historian*, Vol 10 (1948), 85-100.

6724 Ward, Frank B. *The United States Railroad Labor Board and Railway Labor Disputes.* Phila.: U of Pennsylvania Press, 1929.

6725 Warman, Cy. *Snow on the Headlight* (a novel). NY: Appleton, 1899.

6726 Weltz, G. "Railroads and the UTU: What Does History Teach." *Railway Age*, Oct 31, 1977, pp 35-42.

6727 Wetzel, Kurt. "Railroad Management's Response to Operating Employees Accidents, 1890-1913." *Labor History*, Vol 21 (1980), 351-68.

6728 White, William T. *A History of Railroad Workers in the Pacific Northwest, 1883-1934.* Ph D diss, U of Washington, 1981.

6729 Whittaker, Frederick. *Nemo, King of the Tramps; or, The Romany Girl's Vengeance. A Story of the Great Railroad Riots* (a novel). NY: M. J. Ivers, 1881.

6730 Wish, Harvey. "The Pullman Strike: A Study in Industrial Warfare." *Journal of the Illinois State Historical Society*, Vol 32 (1939), 288-312.

6731 Wolf, Harry D. *The Railroad Labor Board.* Chicago: U of Chicago Press, 1927.

6732 Wollenberg, Charles. "Working on the El Traque: the Pacific Electric Strike of 1903." *Pacific Historical Review*, Vol 42 (1973), 358-69.

6733 Wood, Louis A. *Union-Management Cooperation on the Railroads.* New Haven: Yale U Press, 1931.

6734 Yearley, Clifton K., Jr. "The Baltimore and Ohio Railroad Strike of 1877." *Maryland Historical Magazine*, Vol 51 (1956), 188-211.

6735 Yen, Tzu-Kuei. *Chinese Workers and the First Transcontinental Railroad of the USA.* Ph D diss, St. John's U, 1977.

6736 ZIEGER, ROBERT H. "From Hostility to Moderation: Railroad Labor Policy in the 1920s." *Labor History*, Vol ((1968), 23-38.

CARMEN

6737 CHRISTIE, HUGH K. *The Carman's Helper*. Chicago: Trade Educational Bureau of the Brotherhood of Railway Carmen of America, 1920.

6738 HOGAN, EDMOND K. *The Work of the Railway Carman*. Kansas City, MO: Brotherhood of Railway Carmen of America, 1921.

6739 PAINTER, LEONARD. *Through 50 Years with the Brotherhood of Railway Carmen of America*. Kansas City, MO: Brotherhood of Railway Carmen of America, 1941.

CLERKS

6740 HENIG, HARRY. *The Brotherhood of Railway Clerks*. NY: Columbia U Press, 1927.

CONDUCTORS

6741 ROBBINS, EDWIN C. *Railway Conductors: A Study in Organized Labor*. NY: Columbia U Press, 1914.

LOCOMOTIVE ENGINEERS

6742 BROOKS, HAROLD C. "Story of the Founding of the Brotherhood of Locomotive Engineers." *Michigan History*, Vol 27 (1943), 611-19.

6743 BROTHERHOOD OF LOCOMOTIVE ENGINEERS. *A Century of Service*. Phila.: National Publishing Co., 1963.

6744 FULTON, JUSTIN D. *Sam Hobart*. NY: Funk & Wagnalls, 1883. (See especially chap 8: "The Brotherhood of Locomotive Engineers," pp 83-109)

6745 RICHARDSON, REED C. *The Locomotive Engineer: 1863-1963, A Century of Railway Labor Relations and Work Rules*. Ann Arbor: Bureau of Industrial Relations, U of Michigan, 1963.

6746 STEVENSON, GEORGE JAMES. *The Brotherhood of Locomotive Engineers and Its Leaders, 1863-1920*. Ph D diss, Vanderbilt U, 1954.

LOCOMOTIVE FIREMEN AND ENGINEMEN

6747 BROTHERHOOD OF LOCOMOTIVE FIREMEN AND ENGINEMEN. *Fiftieth Anniversary, Brotherhood of Locomotive Firemen and Enginemen, December 1, 1873-December 1, 1923*. Kansas City, MO: The Brotherhood, 1923.

6748 ———. "Historical Sketch, 1873-1947." *Brotherhood of Locomotive Firemen and Enginemen's Magazine*, Vol 123 (1947), 17-49.

6749 ———. *An Historical Sketch of the Brotherhood*. Cleveland: The Brotherhood, 1937.

6750 FEDERAL COUNCIL OF THE CHURCHES OF CHRIST IN AMERICA. Department of Research and Education *The Enginemen's Strike on the Western Maryland Railroad*. NY: Davis Press, 1927.

6751 HOROWITZ, MORRIS A. "The Diesel Firemen Issue on the Railroads." *Industrial and Labor Relations Review*, Vol 13 (1960), 550-58.

6752 ———. "The Diesel-Firemen Issue—A Comparison of Treatment—A Discussion." *Labor Law Journal*, Aug 1963, pp 694-99.

6753 LOOMIS, WILLIAM. "Union Policies of Reaction to Technological Change—An Examination of the Brotherhood of Locomotive Firemen and Enginemen." *Industrial and Labor Relations Forum*, Vol 2 (1966), 225-50.

6754 THOMAS, WILLIAM E. "The Vanishing Fireman: A Case Study in Compulsory Arbitration." *Loyola Law Review*, Vol 14 (1967-68), 125-64.

MAINTENANCE OF WAY

6755 Brotherhood of Maintenance of Way Employees. *Pictorial History, 1877-1951.* Detroit: The Brotherhood, 1952.

6756 Hertel, Denver Willard. *History of the Brotherhood of Maintenance of Way Employees: Its Birth and Growth, 1877-1955.* Wash.: Ransdell, 1955.

6757 "History Recalled: a Great Union is No Longer." *Brotherhood of Maintenance of Way Employees Journal*, Vol 82 (Jul 1974), 7.

6758 Thompson, Mark. "Rival Unionism as it Faced the Brotherhood of Maintenance of Way Employees." *Industrial and Labor Relations Forum*, Vol 1 (1964), 5-40.

SHOPMEN

6759 American Federation of Labor. Railway Employees' Department *The Case of the Railway Shopmen: A Brief Statement of Facts Concerning the Controversies Which Precipitated the Strike.* Wash.: The Department, 1922.

SIGNALMEN

6760 Brotherhood of Railroad Signalmen of America. *50 Years of Railroad Signaling: A History of the Brotherhood of Railroad Signalmen of America.* Chicago: The Brotherhood, [n.d.].

6761 Fagan, J. O. *Confessions of a Railroad Signalman.* Bost.: Houghton Mifflin, 1908.

6762 Lyon, Arlon E. *The First 75: History of the Brotherhood of Railroad Signalmen, 1901-1976.* Mount Prospect, IL: The Brotherhood, 1976.

SLEEPING CAR PORTERS

6763 Brazeal, Brailsford. *The Brotherhood of Sleeping Car Porters: Its Origin and Development.* NY: Harper, 1946.

6764 Harris, William H. *Keeping the Faith: A. Philip Randolph, Milton P. Webster, and the Brotherhood of Sleeping Car Porters, 1925-37.* Urbana: U of Illinois Press, 1977.

6765 Mergen, Bernard. "The Pullman Porter: from 'George' to Brotherhood." *South Atlantic Quarterly*, Vol 73 (1974), 224-35.

6766 Pfeffer, Paula. *A. Philip Randolph: a Case Study in Black Leadership.* Ph D diss, Northwestern U, 1980.

6767 Posadas, Barbara M. "The Hierarchy of Color and Psychological Adjustment in an Industrial Environment: Filipinos, The Pullman Company and the Brotherhood of Sleeping Car Porters." *Labor History*, Vol 22 (1982), 349-73.

TELEGRAPHERS

6768 McIsaac, Archibald M. *The Order of Railroad Telegraphers: A Study in Trade Unionism and Collective Bargaining.* Princeton: Princeton U Press, 1933.

TRAINMEN

6769 McCaleb, Walter F. *Brotherhood of Railroad Trainmen: With Special Reference to the Life of Alexander F. Whitney.* NY: Boni and Liveright, 1936.

6770 Seidman, Joel. *The Brotherhood of Railroad Trainmen: The Internal Political Life of a National Union.* NY: Wiley, 1962.

6771 "Trainmen: When They Fight, the U.S. Is Involved." *Business Week*, Oct 10, 1953, pp 170-73.

6772 U.S. Congress. House. Committee on Labor. *Investigation of the Causes of Labor Disputes,*, Part II, "General Labor Conditions" (Testimony of A. F. Whitney). Wash.: G.P.O., 1946.

6773 WHITNEY, ALEXANDER F. *Report of A. F. Whitney, President, Brotherhood of Railroad Trainmen, on Railroad Rules-Wage Movement, U.S., 1944-45-446*. Cleveland: The Brotherhood, 1946.

6774 ZIEGER, ROBERT H. "From Hostility to Moderation: Railroad Labor Policy in the 1920's." *Labor History*, Vol 9 (1968), 23-28.

Transportation—Trucking

6775 ANNABLE, JAMES E, JR. "The I.C.C., the I.B.T., and the Cartelization of the American Trucking Industry." *Quarterly Review of Economics and Business*, Vol 13 (Summer 1973), 33-42.

6776 BARRY, DESMOND A., and JOHN E. RASCO. *Too Hot to Handle*. Garden City: Doubleday, 1962.

6777 "Beck and Reuther." *The Reporter*, Jul 5, 1949, pp 4-7.

6778 BELL, JOHN F. "The Teamsters: Big Unionism." *Current History*, Vol 27 (1954), 36-41.

6779 BENSON, H. W. "Growth of Reform Group Among Teamsters." *Dissent*, Vol 26 (1979), 153-57.

6780 BERNSTEIN, IRVING. "The Politics of the West Coast Teamsters and Truckers." *Proceedings of the Tenth Annual Meeting of the Industrial Relations Research Association*, Sep 5-7, 1957, 12-34. Madison: IRRA, 1958.

6781 BLAKE, JOSEPH A. "Occupational Thrill, Mystique and the Truck Driver." *Urban Life and Culture*, Vol 3 (1974), 205-20.

6782 BOFFO, LOUIS S. "Study 4, Trucking." *Labor-Management Relations in Illini City*, Vol 1. Champaign: U of Illinois Press, 1953.

6783 BOWERS, ROBERT S. *The International Brotherhood of Teamsters and a Theory of Jurisdiction*. Ph D diss, U of Wisconsin, 1951.

6784 BRILL, STEVEN. *The Teamsters*. NY: Simon & Schuster, 1978.

6785 BRINKER, PAUL A., and BENJAMIN TAYLOR. "Secondary Boycott Analysis by Industry." *Labor Law Journal*, Vol 24 (1973), 671-83.

6786 DEARMOND, FREDERICK F. *Managers vs. Teamsters: The New Tactics in Labor Bargaining*. Springfield, MO: Mycroft Press, 1959.

6787 DOBBS, FARRELL. *Teamster Politics*. NY: Monad Press, 1975.

6788 ———. *Teamster Power*. NY: Monad, 1973.

6789 EDDY, ARTHUR J. *Ganton and Company* (a novel). Chicago: McClurg, 1908.

6790 FEINSINGER, NATHAN P. *Collective Bargaining in the Trucking Industry*. Phila.: U of Pennsylvania Press, 1949.

6791 *F.I.S.T.* 1978. (Feature film directed by Norman Jewison)

6792 GALENSON, WALTER. "The Teamsters," chap. 14, *The CIO CHallenge to the AFL*, Cambr.: Harvard U Press, 1960.

6793 GARNEL, DONALD. *The Rise of Teamster Power in the West*. Berkeley: U of California Press, 1972.

6794 ———. *Teamsters and Highway Truckers in the West: the Evolution of Multi-Employer Bargaining in the Western Highway Trucking Industry*. Ph D diss, U of California, 1966.

6795 GILLINGHAM, J. B. *The Teamsters Union on the West Coast*. Berkeley: Institute of Industrial Relations, U of California, 1956.

6796 HEFFERMAN, NATHAN (WRITTEN IN COLLABORATION WITH DALE KRAMER). *The Man in the Middle*. Garden City: Doubleday, 1961.

6797 HILL, SAMUEL. *Teamsters and Transportation: Employee-Employer Relationships in New England*. Wash.: American Council on Public Affairs, 1942.

6798 HOSTETTER, GORDON L., and THOMAS Q. BEESLEY. *It's a Racket!* Chicago: Les Quin, 1929.

6799 Industrial Relations Counselors. *A Profile of the Teamsters Union.* NY: Industrial Relations Counselors, 1961.

6800 International Brotherhood of Teamsters, Chauffeurs, Warehousemen and Helpers of America. "Papers, 1904-1952." *Collection* (At State Historical Society of Wisconsin. 234 boxes)

6801 ———. *Teamsters All: Pictorial Highlights in Our History.* Wash.: Merule Press, 1976.

6802 James, Ralph C., and Estelle James. "Hoffa's Manipulation of Pension Benefits." *Industrial Relations,* Vol 4 (1965), 46-60.

6803 ———. "The Purge of the Trotskyites from the Teamsters." *Western Political Quarterly,* Vol 19 (1966), 5-15.

6804 Kay, Ira. *Inter-industry Wage Differentials Among Unionized Truck Drivers in a Local Labor Market: a Case Study.* Ph D diss, Wayne State U, 1976.

6805 Leiter, Robert D. "The Relationship Between Structure and Policy in the Teamsters Union." *Proceedings of the Tenth Annual Meeting of the Industrial Relations Research Association,* Sep 5-7, 1957, pp 148-55. Madison: IRRA, 1958.

6806 Lens, Sidney. "Dave Beck's Teamsters: Sour Note in Labor Harmony." *Harper's,* Feb 1956, pp 74-82.

6807 Lipsitz, George. "Beyond the Fringe Benefits: Rank and File Teamsters in St. Louis." *Liberation,* Vol 18 (Jul-Aug 1973), 31-45, 53.

6808 Lynd, Staughton. "Where is the Teamster Rebellion Going?" *Radical America,* Vol 13 (Mar-Apr 1979), 67-74.

6809 McLellan, John L. (as told to Beverly Smith, Jr.). "What We Learned about Labor Gangsters." *Saturday Evening Post,* May 3, 1958, pp 23-24; May 10, 1958, p 35.

6810 Milk Drivers and Dairy Employees Union, Local 471. *Status of Free Man.* Minneapolis: The Union, 1947.

6811 Moldea, Dan E. *The Hoffa Wars: Teamsters, Rebels, Politicians and the Mob.* NY: Padington, 1978.

6812 Neuberger, Richard. *Our Promised Land.* Minneapolis: The Union, 1947.

6813 PROD (Professional Over-the-Road Drivers, Teamster's Union). *Teamster Democracy and Financial Responsibility: A Factual and Structural Analysis.* Wash.: PROD, 1976.

6814 Raskin, A. H. "What the 'Little Fellow' Says to the Teamsters Is What Counts." *New York Times Magazine,* May 30, 1971, pp 12-13, 35, 40-43.

6815 Rinaldi, Matthew. "Dissent in the Brotherhood: Organizing in the Teamsters Union." *Radical America,* Vol 11 (Jul-Aug 1977, pp 43-55.

6816 Robinson, Robert M. "San Francisco Teamsters at the Turn of the Century." *California Historical Society Quarterly,* Vol 35 (1956), 59-69, 145-53.

6817 Romer, Sam. *The International Brotherhood of Teamsters: Its Government and Structure.* NY: Wiley, 1962.

6818 ———. "The Teamster Monitors and the Administration of the International Union." *Labor Law Journal,* Jul 1961, pp 604-13.

6819 Rose, Arnold. "The Influence of a Border City Union on the Race Attitudes of Its Members." *The Journal of Social Issues,* Vol 9 (1953).

6820 ———. *Union Solidarity: The Internal Cohesion of a Labor Union* (Local 688, St. Louis, IBT). Minneapolis: U of Minnesota Press, 1952.

6821 Schnepp, Gerald J., and Isabelle Morello. "Approaches to the Industry Council Idea in the U.S." *Industrial Relations,* (Quebec, Canada), Vol 9 (1954), 381-94.

6822 Seidman, Harold. "The Markets" chap. 11, *Labor Czars,* NY: Liveright, 1938.

6823 Sikorski, John. "Fitzsimmons and Beyond." *New Politics,* Vol 12 (Winter 1978), 53-58.

6824 Sloane, Arthur. "Collective Bargaining in Trucking: Prelude to a National Contract." *Industrial and Labor Relations Review,* Vol 19 (1965), 21-40.

6825 *The St. Louis Kid.* 1934. (Feature film produced by Warner Brothers)
6826 STRAUB, ADELBERT G., JR. *Whose Welfare? A Report on Union and Employer Welfare Plans in New York.* Albany: State of NY Insurance Department, 1954. (See sections on Locals 804 & 805, IBT)
6827 "Teamster Union Welfare, Pension Plans." *Industrial Bulletin*, Jun 1954, pp 19-20.
6828 "Teamsters Drive Tests the Hard-Boiled Approach." *Business Week*, Sep 8, 1956, pp 60-70.
6829 "Teamsters Face Their Judges." *Business Week*, Sep 7, 1957, pp 171-72.
6830 "Teamsters Strengthen Davd Beck's Hand." *Business Week*, Mar 31, 1956, pp 156-58.
6831 *They Drive by Night.* 1940. (Feature film produced by Warner Brothers)
6832 TOBIN, DAN. "As to Being One's Brothers' Keeper." *Teamster*, Jun 1948.
6833 U.S. CONGRESS. SENATE. Committee on Government Operations. *James R. Hoffa and Continued Underworld Control of New York Teamster Local 239.* Wash.: G.P.O., 1962.
6834 ———. ———. Committee on Governmental Affairs. Permanent Subcommittee on Investigations. *Oversight Inquiry of the Department of Labor's Investigation of the Teamsters Central States Pension Fund: Report.* Wash.: G.P.O., 1981.
6835 ———. ———. Committee on the Judiciary. *Relationship Between Teamsters Union and Mine, Mill & Smelter Workers.* Wash.: G.P.O., 1962.
6836 VOTAW, ALBERT N. "The Teamsters and the Hoods." *The New Leader*, May 14, 1951, pp 6-7.
6837 WALKER, CHARLES R. *American City: A Rank and File History* (Minneapolis truck drivers strike of 1934). NY: Farrar and Rinehart, 1937.
6838 WALSH, ED, and CHARLES CRAYPO. "Union Oligarchy and the Grass Roots: the Case of the Teamsters' Defeat in Farmwork Organizing." *Sociology and Social Research*, Vol 63 (1979), 269-93.

Transportation—Urban

6839 AMALGAMATED ASSOCIATION OF STREET, ELECTRIC RAILWAY AND MOTOR COACH EMPLOYEES OF AMERICA. "Golden Jubilee." *Motorman, Conductor and Motor Coach Operator*, Vol 50 (1942), entire Sep issue.
6840 BARNUM DAROLD T. "From Private to Public: Labor Relations in Urban Transit." *Industrial and Labor Relations Review*, Vol 25 (1971), 95-115.
6841 ———. "National Public Labor Relations Legislation: the Case of Urban Mass Transit." *Labor Law Journal*, Vol 27 (1976), 168-76.
6842 BURRAN, JAMES A. "Labor Conflict in Urban Appalachia: the Knoxville Streetcar Strike of 1919." *Tennessee History Quarterly*, Vol 38 (1979), 62-78.
6843 CRAYPO, CHARLES. "Bargaining Units and Corporate Merger: NLRB Policy in the Inter-City Bus Industry." *Industrial Relations Law Journal*, Vol 1 (Summer 1976), 285-322.
6844 DUNCAN, DAVID. *Serpent's Egg* (a novel). NY: Macmillan, 1949.
6845 FABER, GUSTAV. *And Then Came T.W.U.: The Brooklyn Trolley Strike.* NY: Transport Workers Union of America, CIO, 1950.
6846 FLEMING, RALPH D. *Labor Conditions and Wages in Street Railway, Motor and Wagon Transporation Services in Cleveland.* Menasha, WI: Banta, 1916.
6847 FREEMAN, JOSHUA B. "Catholics, Communists, and Republicans: Irish Workers and the Organization of the Transport Workers Union," pp 256-83, *Working Class America: Essays on Labor, Community, and American Society*, Michael Frisch & Daniel J. Walkowitz, eds. Urbana: U of Illinois Press, 1983.
6848 HUBERMAN, LEO. *The Great Bus Strike.* NY: Modern Age, 1941.

6849 Hunt, Carder. et al. *Labor-Management Relations in Urban Mass Transit: An Annotated Bibliography*. Irvine: U of California, 1976.

6850 Jennings, Kenneth. et al. *Study of Unions, Management Rights, and the Public Interest in Mass Transit: Final Report*. Wash.: U.S. Department of Transportation, 1977.

6851 Kheel, Theodore W., and J. K. Turcott. *Transit and Arbitration: A Decade of Decisions and The Path to Transit Peace*. Englewood Cliffs: Prentice-Hall, 1960.

6852 Lawrence, James S. "T.W.U.-Transit Authority Compromise on Issue: Agreement Between Labor, Management Smooths Shuttle Train Differences." *Industrial Bulletin*, Vol 41 (1962), 8-11, 15.

6853 MacDonald, Lois. et al. *The Grievance Process in New York City Transit*. NY: Graduate School of Public Administration and Social Service, New York U, 1956.

6854 McGinley, James J. *Labor Relations in the New York Rapid Transit Systems, 1904-1944*. NY: King's Crown Press, 1949.

6855 Nash, Abraham. *The Making of the New York City Taxi Drivers' Union*. MA thesis, Columbia U, 1967.

6856 New York (State) Board of Inquiry on Rochester Transit Work Stoppage. *Final Report to the Industrial Commissioner from a Board of Inquiry on Rochester Transit Work Stoppage, May 1-May 23, 1952*. Rochester (?): no publisher indicated, 1952.

6857 ———. *Proceedings in the Matter of the Arbitration between the Rochester Transit Corporation and Local 282 of Amalgamated Association of Street, Electric Railway and Motor Coach Employees of America*. Rochester (?): no publisher indicated, 1952.

6858 Odets, Clifford. *Waiting for Lefty....* NY: Covici-Friede, 1935.

6859 Oliphant, Herman. *Interborough Rapid Transit Company against William Green, et al., Brief for Defendants*. NY: Workers Education Bureau Press, 1928.

6860 Saposs, David J. *Communism in American Unions*. NY: McGraw-Hill, 1959. (See pp 119-270 *passim* on Transport Workers Union of America)

6861 Schmidt, Emerson P. *Industrial Relations in Urban Transportation*. Minneapolis: U of Minnesota Press, 1937.

6862 Sussna, Edward. "Collective Bargaining on the New York City Transit System, 1940-1957." *Industrial and Labor Relations Review*, Vol 11 (1958), 518-33.

6863 *Taxi*. 1932. (Feature film produced by Warner Brothers)

6864 Tourgee, Albion W. *Murvale Eastman, Christian Socialist* (a novel). NY: Fords, Howard, and Hulbert, 1890.

6865 U.S. Commission on Industrial Relations (1912). "The Cooperative Plan of the Philadelphia Rapid Transit Co.," Vol 3, pp 2731-816, *Final Report*, Wash.: G.P.O., 1916.

6866 Weinberg, J. "Priests, Workers and Communists: What Happened in a New York Transit Workers Union." *Harpers*, Nov 1948, pp 49-56.

6867 Winkler, Allan M. "The Philadelphia Transit Strike of 1944." *Journal of American History*, Vol 59 (1972), 73-89.

6868 Young, Dallas M. "Fifty Years of Labor Arbitration in Cleveland Transit." *Monthly Labor Review*, Vol 83 (1960), 464-71.

Transportation—Water and Longshoring

6869 Albion, Robert G. *Maritime and Naval History: An Annotated Bibliography*. Mystic, CT: Marine Historical Association, 1955.

6870 Albrecht, Arthur E. *The International Seamen's Union of America,*, Bulletin 342, Bureau of Labor Statistics. Wash.: G.P.O., 1923.

6871 Alcorn, Rowena L., and Gordon D. Alcorn. "Tacoma Seamen's Rest: Waterfront Mission, 1897-1903." *Oregon Historical Quarterly*, Vol 66 (1965), 101-13.

6872 Anderson, Thomas. *Here Comes Pete Now* (a novel). NY: Random House, 1961.

6873 Auerbach, Jerold S. "Progressives at Sea: The LaFollette Act of 1915." *Labor History*, Vol 2 (1961), 344-60.

6874 Ball, Joseph H. *The Government-Subsidized Union Monopoly: A Study of Labor Practices in the Shipping Industry*. Wash.: Labor Policy Association, 1966.

6875 Barnes, Charles B. *The Longshoremen*. NY: Russell Sage Foundation, 1915.

6876 Bell, Daniel. "Last of the Business Rackets." *Fortune*, Jun 1951, pp 89-91, 193-203.

6877 ———. "The Racket-Ridden Longshoremen: The Web of Economics and Politics," chap. 9, *The End of Ideology: On the Exhaustion of Political Ideas in the Fifties,* NY: Collier, 1961.

6878 Benson, H. W. "Democracy and Union Conglomerates: a Report on Recent Trends in the N.M.U." *Dissent*, Vol 20 (1973), 392-97.

6879 Bissell, Richard. *A Stretch on the River* (a novel). Bost.: Little, Brown, 1950.

6880 "'Bloody Thursday' Gets Varied Observance." *Dispatcher*, Jul 19, 1974, p 4.

6881 Boyden, Richard. "Why the I.L.W.U. Strike Failed." *New Politics*, Vol 10 (Fall 1972), 61-69.

6882 Boyer, Richard O. *The Dark Ship* (a novel). Bost.: Little, Brown, 1947.

6883 Brissenden, Paul F. *Employment System of the Lake Carriers' Association,*, Bulletin 235, Bureau of Labor Statistics. Wash.: G.P.O., 1918.

6884 Brown, Giles T. "The West Coast Phase of the Maritime Strike of 1921." *Pacific Historical Review*, Vol 19 (1950), 385-96.

6885 Catherwood, Martin P. et al. *Final Report to the Industrial Commissioner, State of New York, from Board of Inquiry on Longshore Industry Work Stoppage, October-November 1951, Port of New York*. Albany: State of New York, 1952.

6886 Chevalier, Haakon M. *For Us the Living* (a novel). NY: Knopf, 1948.

6887 "CIO to Sea." *Time*, July 19, 1937, pp 12-14.

6888 Clark, William H. *Ships and Sailors: The Story of Our Merchant Marine*. Bost.: Page, 1938.

6889 Collins, John J. *Bargaining at the Local Level*. NY: Fordham U Press, 1974.

6890 ———. *The Mobil Story, 1907-1978: A Saga of Labor Progress and Peace*. NY: Mobil Tanker Officers Association, 1978.

6891 ———. *Never Off Pay: The Story of the Independent Tanker Union, 1937-1962*. NY: Fordham U Press, 1964.

6892 Daitsman, George. "Labor and the Welfare State in Early New York." *Labor History*, Vol 4 (1963), 248-56.

6893 Doerflinger, William M. *Shantymen and Shantyboys: Songs of Sailor and Lumberman*. NY: Macmillan, 1951.

6894 Eliel, Paul. "Industrial Peace and Conflict: A Study of Two Pacific Coast Industries." *Industrial and Labor Relations Review*, Vol 2 (1949), 477-501.

6895 ———. *The Waterfront and General Strikes*. San Francisco: Hooper Printing Co., 1934.

6896 "Employment Conditions in the Longshore Industry." *Industrial Bulletin*, Vol 31 (1952), 7-14.

6897 Fact-Finding Board. *In re Waterfront Employers Association of the Pacific Coast...and International Longshoremen's and Warehousemen's Union (CIO), May 13, 1946.*, Labor Arbitration Reports, Vol 3, pp 165-81. Wash.: Bureau of National Affairs, 1946.

6898 Fairley, Lincoln. *Facing Mechanization: the West Coast Longshore Plan*. Los Angeles; Institute of Industrial Relations, U of California, 1979.

6899 ———. "The ILWU-PMA Mechanization and Modernization Agreement." *Labor Law Journal*, Jul 1961, pp 664-80.

6900 ———. "The ILWU-PMA Mechanization and Modernization Agreement: An Evaluation of the Experience under the Agreement: The Union's Viewpoint." *Proceedings of the Sixteenth Annual Meeting of the Industrial Relations Research Association*, Dec 27-28, 1963, pp 34-47. Madison: IRRA, 1964.

6901 FALL, JAMES. *British Merchant Seamen in San Francisco, 1892-1898.* London: publisher not indicated, 1899.

6902 FARNAM, H. W. "The Seamen's Act of 1915." *American Labor Legislation Review*, Vol 6 (1916), 41-60.

6903 FRANCIS, ROBERT E. *A History of Labor on the San Francisco Waterfront*. Ph D diss, U of California, 1934.

6904 FURUSETH, ANDREW. "The Seamen's Act and Its Critics." *American Labor Legislation Review*, Vol 6 (1916), 61-68.

6905 GALENSON, WALTER. "The Maritime Industry," chap. 13, *The CIO Challenge to the AFL*, Cambr.: Harvard U Press, 1960.

6906 GODDARD, DONALD. *All Fall Down: ONe Man Against the Waterfront Mob*. NY: Times Books, 1980.

6907 GOLDBERG, JOSEPH P. "Collective Bargaining in Maritime Shipping Industry." *Monthly Labor Review*, Vol 71 (1950), 332-37.

6908 ———. "Containerization as a Force for Change on the Waterfront." *Monthly Labor Review*, Vol 91 (Jan 1968), 8-13.

6909 ———. "Longshoremen and the Modernization of Cargo Handling in the United States." *International Labor Review*, Vol 107 (1973), 253-79.

6910 ———. *The Maritime Story: A Study in Labor-Management Relations*. Cambr.: Harvard U Press, 1958.

6911 ———. "Seamen and the International Labor Organization." *Monthly Labor Review*, Vol 81 (1958), 974-81.

6912 GORTER, WYTZE, and GEORGE H. HILDEBRAND. *The Pacific Coast Maritime Shipping Industry, 1930-1948.*, 2 vols. Berkeley: U of California Press, 1954.

6913 GOULD, JOHN P. et al. *Impact of Longshore Strikes on the National Economy*. Wash.: U.S. Department of Labor, 1970.

6914 GROAT, GEORGE G. *An Introduction to the Study of Organized Labor in America*. NY: Macmillan, 1926.

6915 GROOM, PHYLLIS. "Hiring Practices for Longshoremen: The Diversity of Arrangements Shown by a Labor Department Study of 10 East and Gulf Coast Ports." *Monthly Labor Review*, Vol 88 (1965), 1289-96.

6916 HARRIS, ED. "The Trouble with Harry Bridges." *International Socialist Review*, Vol 34 (Sep 1973), 6-11, 39.

6917 HARRISON, CHARLES YALE. "Stalin's American Merchant Marine." *American Mercury*, Oct 1940, pp 135-44.

6918 HARTMAN, PAUL. *Collective Bargaining and Productivity: The Longshore Mechanization Agreement*. Berkeley: U of California Press, 1969.

6919 ———. *Work Rules and Productivity in the Pacific Coast Longshore Industry*. Ph D diss, U of California, 1966.

6920 HAVIGHURST, WALTER. *Pier 17* (a novel). NY: Macmillan, 1935.

6921 HEALEY, JAMES C. *Foc's'le and Glory-Hole, a Study of the Merchant Seaman and his Occupation*. NY: Merchant Marine Publishing Association, 1936.

6922 HEALY, JAMES J. et al. "Maritime Policy and Program of the United States: Recommendation for Maritime Labor Relations Policies." *Monthly Labor Review*, Vol 89 (Jan 1966), 19-21.

6923 HERZOG, DONALD ROSWELL. *A Study of Labor Relations Relating to American Seamen in the Maritime Industry*. Ph D diss, U of Iowa, 1955.

6924 HIELD, WAYNE. "What Keeps Harry Bridges Going?" *Labor and Nation*, Jan-Mar 1952, pp 38-40.

6925 Hoagland, Henry E. *Wage Bargaining on the Vessels of the Great Lakes*. Urbana: U of Illinois Press, 1917.

6926 Hohman, Elmo P. *The American Whaleman: A Study of Life and Labor in the Whaling Industry*. NY: Longmans, Green, 1928.

6927 ———. *History of American Merchant Seamen*. Hamden, CT: The Shoe String Press, 1956.

6928 ———. "Labor Problems in the Merchant Marine." *Proceedings of the Fourteenth Annual Meeting of the Industrial Relations Research Association*, Dec 28-29, 1961, pp 346-53. Madison: IRRA, 1962.

6929 ———. "Maritime Labor Economics as a Determinant of the Structure and Policy of Seamen's Unions." *Proceedings of the Tenth Annual Meeting of the Industrial Relations Research Association*, Sep 5-7, 1957, pp 163-70. Madison: IRRA, 1958.

6930 ———. "Maritime Labor in the U.S." *International Labour Review*, Vol 38 (1938).

6931 ———. "Work and Wages of American Merchant Seamen." *Industrial and Labor Relations Review*, Vol 15 (1962), 221-29.

6932 Holmes, Thomas. *The Specter of Communism in Hawaii, 1947-1953*. Ph D diss, U of Hawaii, 1976.

6933 Horvitz, Wayne L. "The ILWU-PMA Mechanization and Modernization Agreement: An Experiment in Industrial Relations." *Proceedings of the Sixteenth Annual Meeting of the Industrial Relations Research Association*, Dec 27-28, 1963, pp 22-33. Madison: IRRA, 1964.

6934 Huberman, Leo. *The National Maritime Union—What It Is, What It Does*. NY: National Maritime Union, 1943.

6935 Hughes, I. B. *Port Workers in Britain and the United States, 1870-1914*. Ph D diss, Edinburgh U, 1972.

6936 "I.L.W.U. Wins Grant to study its Past." *Dispatcher*, Jul 10, 1981, p 4.

6937 "Impact of Longshore Strikes on the Economy." *Monthly Labor Review*, Vol 93 (Mar 1970), 51-53.

6938 International Juridical Association. *Report on the Status and Working Conditions of Seamen in the American Merchant Marine*. NY: publisher not indicated, 1936.

6939 International Longshoremen's and Warehousemen's Union. *The ILWU Story: Three Decades of Militant Unionism*. San Francisco: The Union, 1963.

6940 ———. *Union Busting: New Model: The Case Against the Coast Guard Screening Program*. San Francisco: The Union, 1951.

6941 International Longshoremen's Association, AFL. *Answer of the International Longshoremen's Association, AFL, to the Report of the New York State Crime Commission Dealing with the Waterfront of the Port of New York Submitted to the Governor and the Members of the Legislature of the State of New York*. NY: The Association, 1953.

6942 ———. *The ILA Program to Improve and Further Stabilize Labor and Industrial Conditions in the Port of New York* (submitted to Board of Inquiry, Dec 1951). NY: Waldman and Waldman, Attorneys, 1951. (Mimeo.)

6943 Jensen, Vernon H. "Computer Hiring of Dock Workers in the Port of New York." *Industrial and Labor Relations Review*, Vol 20 (1967), 414-32.

6944 ———. "Decasualization of Employment on the New York Waterfront." *Industrial and Labor Relations Review*, Vol 11 (1958), 534-50.

6945 ———. "Dispute Settlement in the New York Longshore Industry." *Industrial and Labor Relations Review*, Vol 10 (1957), 588-608.

6946 ———. *Hiring of Dock Workers: And Employment Practices in the Ports of New York, Liverpool, London, Rotterdam, and Marseilles*. Cambr.: Harvard U Press, 1964.

6947 ———. "Hiring Practices and Employment Experience of Longshoremen in the Port of New York." *International Labour Review*, Vol 77 (1958), 1-28.

6948 ———. *Strife on the Waterfront: The Port of New York Since 1945.* Ithaca: Cornell U Press, 1974.

6949 JOHNSON, MALCOLM. *Crime on the Labor Front.* NY: McGraw-Hill, 1950.

6950 KAHN, LAWRENCE M. "Union and Internal Labor Markets: The Case of the San Francisco Longshoremen." *Labor History*, Vol 21 (1980), 369-91.

6951 KELLER, KENNETH W. "The Philadelphia Pilots' Strike of 1792." *Labor History*, Vol 18 (1977), 36-48.

6952 KELLER, MARVEL. *Decasualization of Longshore Work in San Francisco.* Phila.: Works Project Administration, National Research Project, 1939.

6953 KELLEY, FLORENCE. "The LaFollette Law from the Consumers League Point of View." *Proceedings of the Academy of Political Science*, Vol 6 (1915), 90-96.

6954 KENNEDY, P. B. "The Seamen's Act." *Annals of the American Academy of Political and Social Science*, Vol 63 (1916), 232-43.

6955 KERR, CLARK. "Collective Bargaining on the Pacific Coast." *Monthly Labor Review*, Vol 64 (1947), 650-74. (Seafaring)

6956 KILLINGSWORTH, CHARLES C. "The Modernization of West Coast Longshore Work Rules." *Industrial and Labor Relations Review*, Vol 15 (1962), 295-306. (Note also: Fairly, Lincoln, "West Coast Longshore Work Rules," in Vol 16 (1962), 134-35; and Killingsworth, Charles C., "Reply," same issue, 135-36)

6957 KOSSORIS, MAX D. "Working Rules in West Coast Longshoring." *Monthly Labor Review*, Vol 84 (1961), 1-10.

6958 KUECHLE, DAVID. *The Story of the Savannah: An Episode in Maritime Labor-Management Relations.* Cambr.: Harvard U Press, 1971.

6959 LAFOLLETTE, ROBERT. "The American Sailor, a Free Man." *The Survey*, May 1, 1915.

6960 LANG, F. J. *Maritime: An Historical Sketch—A Worker's Program.* NY: Pioneer, 1945.

6961 LARROWE, CHARLES P. *Maritime Labor Relations on the Great Lakes.* East Lansing: Labor and Industrial Relations Center, 1959.

6962 ———. *Shape-Up and Hiring Hall: A Comparison of Hiring Methods and Labor Relations on the New York and Seattle Waterfronts.* (Berkeley: U of California Press, 1955)

6963 "Legislative Recommendations of the New York Waterfront Commission" *Monthly Labor Review*, Vol 84 (1961), 510-12.

6964 LEMISCH, JESSE. "Jack Tar in the Streets: Merchant Seamen in the Politics of Revolutionary America." *William and Mary Quarterly*, 3rd Series, Vol 25 (1968), 371-407.

6965 LIEBES, RICHARD A. *Longshore Labor Relations on the Pacific Coast, 1934-1942.* Ph D diss, U of California, 1943.

6966 "The Longshoremen of the Great Lakes," chap 15, *Labor and Administration*, NY: Macmillan, 1951.

6967 LUCY, GEORGE E. *Group Employer-Employee Industrial Relations in the san Francisco Maritime Industry, 1888-1947.* Ph D diss, St. Louis U, 1948.

6968 MCFEE, W. "Seagoing Soviets: Will Communist Waterfronters Take Over Our Merchant Marine?" *Saturday Evening Post*, Sep 21, 1940, p 27ff.

6969 MCLAUGHLIN, FRANCIS M. "The Development of Labor Peace in the Port of Boston." *Industrial and Labor Relations Review*, Vol 20 (1967), 221-33.

6970 MALM, F. THEODORE. "Wage Differentials in Pacific Coast Longshoring." *Industrial and Labor Relations Review*, Vol 5 (1951), pp 33-49.

6971 MARITIME LABOR BOARD. *Report to the President and to the Congress. March 1, 1940.* Wash.: G.P.O., 1940.

6972 "The Maritime Unions." *Fortune*, Sep 1937, pp 123-28, 132-37.

6973 "Maritime's Highest Award Honors the late Paul Hall." *Seafarers Log*, Vol 43 (Oct 1981), 8.

6974 Martin, Harry. *Merchant Marine Machinations*. NY: Merchant Manuals Distributing Co., 1949.

6975 Mears, Eliot Grinnell. *Maritime Trade of Western United States*. Stanford, CA: Stanford U Press, 1935.

6976 National Maritime Union of America. *On a True Course: The Story of the National Maritime Union of America, AFL-CIO*. Wash.: The Union, 1967.

6977 ———. *This Is the NMU: A Picture History of the National Maritime Union of America, CIO*. NY: Publishers Printing Co., 1953.

6978 New York State Crime Commission. *Record of the Public Hearing Held by Governor Thomas E. Dewey on the Recommendations of the New York State Crime Commission for Remedying Conditions on the Waterfront of the Port of New York* (June 8 & 9, 1953). NY: Publishers Printing Co., 1953.

6979 New York State School of Industrial and Labor Relations, Cornell University. *Longshore Industry with Emphasis on the Situation in New York City*. Urbana: Institute of Labor and Industrial Relations, U of Illinois, Apr 30, 1953. (Industrial Relations Libraries Exchange Bibliographies No 810 & Cornell List, NYSSILR, No 87. Mimeo.)

6980 "New York's Waterfront." *Fortune*, Dec 1949, pp 210-213.

6981 "NMU—40 Years on a True Course." *NMU Pilot*, Vol 42 (May 1977), 12-13.

6982 Norris, Charles G. *Flint* (a novel). NY: Doubleday, Doran, 1944.

6983 Norris, Martin J. *The Law of Seamen* NY: Baker, Voorhis, 1951.

6984 Ogg, Elizabeth. *Longshoremen and Their Homes*. NY: Greenwich House, 1939.

6985 *On the Waterfront*. 1954. (Feature film directed by Elia Kazan)

6986 Ozanne, Robert. "Marine Cooks and Stewards," chap. 3, *The Effect of Communist Leadership on American Trade Unions*, Ph D diss, U of Wisconsin, 1954.

6987 Pacific Maritime Association. *Analysis of Strikes and Work Stoppages in the West Coast Maritime Industry*. San Francisco: The Association, 1952.

6988 "Pages from the History of the American Seamen's Labor Movement." *Seafarers Log*, Vol 39 (Mar 1977), 27.

6989 Palmer, Dwight L. *Pacific Coast Maritime Labor*. Ph D diss, Stanford U, 1936.

6990 Pawa, Jay M. "The *Jefferson Borden* Pirates and Samuel Gompers: Aftermath of a Mutiny." *American Neptune*, Vol 27 (1967), 46-60.

6991 Phelps, E. A. M., ed. *The Open Shop, a Debate* (between Andrew Furuseth and W. G. Merritt). NY: Wilson, 1920.

6992 Phleger, Herman. *Pacific Coast Longshoremen's Strike of 1934*. San Francisco (?): publisher not indicated, 1934.

6993 Pilcher, William W. *The Portland Longshoremen: A Dispersed Urban Community*. NY: Holt, Rinehart & Winston, 1972.

6994 "Polluted Port." *Fortune*, Dec 1953, pp 64-68.

6995 Poole, Ernest. *The Harbor* (a novel). NY: Macmillan, 1915.

6996 Purrington, Philip F. "Anatomy of a Mutiny." *American Neptune*, Vol 27 (1967), 98-110.

6997 Rapping, Leonard A. "The Impact of Atlantic-Gulf Unionism on the Relative Earnings of Unlicensed Merchant Seamen." *Industrial and Labor Relations Review*, Vol 17 (1963), 75-95.

6998 Record, Jane Cassels. "The Rise and Fall of a Maritime Union." *Industrial and Labor Relations Review*, Vol 10 (1956), 81-92.

6999 *Riffraff*. 1935. (Feature film produced by MGM)

7000 Robinson, Donald. "How Our Seamen Bounced the Commies." *Saturday Evening Post*, Dec 25, 1948.

7001 Ross, Philip. "Distribution of Power Within the ILWU and the ILA." *Monthly Labor Review*, Vol 91 (Jan 1968), 1-7.

7002 Ruchlin, Hirsch S. "Industrial Relations in the U.S. Maritime Industry and its Impact on Maritime Manpower." *Proceedings of the Twenty-Second Annual Winter Meeting of the Industrial Relations Research Association*, Dec 29-30, 1969, pp 330-38. Madison: IRRA, 1970.

7003 Ryan, Paul W (Mike Quin, pseud.). *The Big Strike*. Olema, CA: Olema Publishing Co., 1949. (Pacific Coast Longshoremen's strike, 1934)

7004 ———. *On the Drumhead: A Selection from the Writings of Mike Quin*. San Francisco: Pacific Publishing Foundation, 1948.

7005 Sanderson and Porter, Engineers and Constructors. *Study of the Port of New York*. NY: NY Crime Commission, 1953.

7006 Sarbaugh, Timothy. "Father Yorke and the San Francisco Waterfront, 1901-1916." *Pacific Historian*, Vol 25 (1981), 29-35.

7007 Schenker, Eric. et al. *Maritime Labor Organizations on the Great Lakes—St. Lawrence Seaway System*. Madison: U of Wisconsin Sea Grant College Program, 1978.

7008 Schneider, Betty V., and Abraham Siegel. *Industrial Relations in the Pacific Coast Longshore Industry*. Berkeley: Institute of Industrial Relations, U of California, 1956.

7009 Schulberg, Budd. "How One Pier Got Rid of the Mob." *New York Times Magazine*, Sep 27, 1953, pp 17, 58-60.

7010 ———. "Joe Docks, Forgotten Man of the Waterfront." *New York Times Magazine*, Dec 28, 1952, pp 3, 28-30.

7011 ———. *On The Waterfront: A Screenplay*. Carbondale: Southern Illinois U Press, 1980.

7012 ———. *Waterfront* (a novel). NY: Random House, 1955.

7013 Schwartz, Harvey. "A Union Combats Racism: the I.L.W.U.'s Japanese-American 'Stockton Incident' of 1945." *Southern California Quarterly*, Vol 62 (1980), 161-75.

7014 Seafarers Historical Research Department. "Pages from the History of the American Seamen's Labor Movement." *Seafarers Log*, Vol 38 (Jun 1976), 18; (Nov 1976), 24-25.

7015 Seafarers International Union of North America. *The Seafarers in World War II*. San Francisco: The Union, 1951.

7016 "Settlement of Hawaiian Longshoremen's Strike." *Monthly Labor Review*, Vol 69 (1949), 653-56.

7017 "Seven Seamen." *Fortune*, Sep 1937, pp 121-22, 130-32.

7018 Sherman, L. "How I.T.W.U. Local 26 Got Started." *Dispatcher*, Vol 31 (Feb 1973), 8.

7019 Shils, Edward B., and Sidney L. Miller, Jr.. "Foreign Flags on U.S. Ships: Convenience or Necessity?" *Industrial Relations*, Vol 2 (1963), 131-52.

7020 Sklar, George, and Paul Peters. *Stevedore* (a play). NY: Covici-Friede, 1934.

7021 Smith, Francis H. *Tom Grogan* (a novel). Bost.: Houghton Mifflin, 1896.

7022 Spritzer, Allan. *Trade Union Sponsored Occupational Training in the U.S. Maritime Industry: The Upgrading and Retraining Program of the National Maritime Union*. Ph D diss, Cornell U, 1971.

7023 Standard, William L. *Merchant Seamen: A Short History of Their Struggles*. NY: International Publishers, 1947.

7024 Stocahj, John Michael. *The Development of the Atlantic and Gulf Coast District of the Seafarers International Union of North America*. Ph D diss, New York U, 1963.

7025 Sturm, Herman M. "Postwar Labor Relations in the Maritime Industry" chap. 21, *Labor in Postwar America*, Colston Warne, ed. Brooklyn: Remsen Press, 1949.

7026 Swanstrom, Edward E. *The Waterfront Labor Problem: A Study in Decasualization and Unemployment Insurance*. NY: Fordham University Press, 1938.

7027 TAFT, PHILIP. "Problems of Labor Relations in the Maritime Industry." *American Seamen*, Winter, 1941.

7028 ———. "Strife in the Maritime Industry." *Political Science Quarterly*, Vol 54 (1939), 216-36.

7029 ———. "The Unlicensed Seafaring Unions." *Industrial and Labor Relations Review*, Vol 3 (1950), 187-212.

7030 TAFT-HARTLEY BOARD OF INQUIRY. *In re Maritime Industry (Atlantic Coast Employers) and International Longshoremen's Assn. (AFL). Final Report of Board of Inquiry, October 21, 1948.*, Labor Arbitration Reports, Vol 11, pp 388-93. Wash.: Bureau of National Affairs, 1949.

7031 TANK, HERB. *Communists on the Water Front*. NY: New Century, 1946.

7032 TAYLOR, PAUL S. *The Sailor's Union of the Pacific*. NY: Ronald Press, 1923.

7033 ———, and NORMAN GOLD. "San Francisco and the General Strike." *Survey Graphic*, Sep 1934.

7034 TOY, ECKARD V., JR. "The Oxford Group and the Strike of the Seattle Longshoremen in 1934." *Pacific Northwest Quarterly*, Vol 69 (1978), 174-84.

7035 TRAVERS, ROBERT. *A Funeral for Sabella* (a novel). NY: Harcourt, Brace, 1952.

7036 TURNBULL, JOHN G. *Labor-Management Relations on the Mississippi Waterway System*. Minneapolis: U of Minnesota Press, 1951.

7037 UHLINGER, CHARLES W. *Bibliography on History of Labor in the American Merchant Marine, 1850-1915*. (Manuscript, NY State Maritime College)

7038 ———. *Collective Bargaining on Government Operated Vessels in World War II*. (Mimeo. manuscript. NY State Maritime College)

7039 U.S. BOARD OF INQUIRY ON THE LABOR DISPUTE INVOLVING LONGSHOREMEN AND ASSOCIATED OCCUPATIONS IN THE MARITIME INDUSTRY ON THE ATLANTIC AND GULF COAST. *Report to the President by the Board of Inquiry Appointed October 6, 1959*. Wash.: The Board, 1959.

7040 U.S. COMMISSION ON INDUSTRIAL RELATIONS (1912). "The Dock Workers of New York City," Vol 3, pp 2051-212, *Final Report*, Wash.: G.P.O., 1916.

7041 U.S. CONGRESS. HOUSE. Committee on Education and Labor. *Communist Infiltration of Maritime Fisheries Unions*. Wash.: G.P.O., 1948.

7042 ———. ———. *Emergency Legislation to Settle the West Coast Dock Dispute*. Wash.: G.P.O., 1972.

7043 ———. ———. *Hiring Practices, Maritime Industry*. Wash.: G.P.O., 1949.

7044 ———. ———. *Hiring Seamen*. Wash.: G.P.O., 1949.

7045 ———. ———. *Investigation of Communist Infiltration into Labor Unions Which Serve the Industries of the United States, the International Fishermen and Allied Workers of America, CIO*. Wash.: G.P.O., 1948.

7046 ———. ———. *Investigation of Steamship Unions*. Wash.: G.P.O., 1948.

7047 ———. ———. Committee on Merchant Marine and Fisheries. *Labor-Management Problems of the American Merchant Marine*. Wash.: G.P.O., 1955.

7048 ———. ———. Committee on Un-American Activities. *Communist Activities among Seamen and on Waterfront Facilities.*, Hearings, Part 1. Wash.: G.P.O., 1960. (See pp 1747-1854)

7049 ———. SENATE. Committee on Commerce. Subcommittee on Merchant Marine and Fisheries. *Hawaii Public Interest Protection Act of 1971*. Wash.: G.P.O., 1972.

7050 ———. ———. *Settlement of Maritime Interunion Disputes*. Wash.: G.P.O., 1965.

7051 ———. ———. Committee on Interstate and Foreign Commerce. *Waterfront Investigation.*, Hearings, 2 parts. Wash.: G.P.O., 1953.

7052 ———. ———. Committee on Labor and Public Welfare. Subcommittee on Labor and Labor-Management Relations. *Communist Domination of Certain Unions*. Wash.: G.P.O., 1951.

7053 ———. ———. *Labor-Management Relations in the East Coast Oil Tanker Industry*. Wash.: G.P.O., 1950 & 1951.

7054 ———. ———. *The Marine Cooks and Stewards Union.* Wash.: G.P.O., 1953.
7055 ———. ———. *Maritime Hiring Halls.* Wash.: G.P.O., 1950, 1951 & 1952.
7056 ———. ———. *West Coast Dock Dispute, January-February 1972.* Wash.: G.P.O., 1972.
7057 ———. ———. *West Coast Maritime Industry.* Wash.: G.P.O., 1948.
7058 ———. ———. Committee on the Judiciary. *Scope of Soviet Activity in the United States, Commission on the Waterfront.*, Hearings. Wash.: G.P.O., 1956.
7059 U.S. MARITIME ADMINISTRATION. *Guide to Seafaring Collective Bargaining.* Wash.: G.P.O., 1959.
7060 ———. *Review of Labor-Management Relations in the Maritime Industry and the Subsidization of Seamen Wages.* Wash.: The Administration, 1955.
7061 U.S. NATIONAL ARCHIVES. *Preliminary Inventory of the Records of the Maritime Labor Board.* Wash.: National Archives, 1949.
7062 U.S. NATIONAL LABOR RELATIONS BOARD. Division of Economic Research "The Maritime Industry," chap. 9, *Written Trade Agreements in Collective Bargaining*, Wash.: G.P.O., 1940.
7063 VARNEY, H. L. "Sovietizing Our Merchant Marine." *American Mercury*, May 1938, pp 31-43.
7064 WALDMAN, LOUIS, and SEYMOUR WALDMAN. *Final Report on Survey of ILA Locals.* NY: ILA, 1952.
7065 WARNER, AARON. "Technology and the Labor Force in the Offshore Maritime Industry." *Proceedings of the Eighteenth Annual Winter Meeting of the Industrial Relations Research Association*, Dec 28-29, 1965, pp 139-50. Madison: IRRA, 1966.
7066 WATERFRONT COMMISSION OF NEW YORK HARBOR. *Waterfront Commission Act.* NY: The Commission, 1953. (Mimeo.)
7067 "Waterfront Mess." *Fortune*, Apr 1953, pp 94-98.
7068 WELLS, DAVEE, and JIM STODDER. "A Short History of New Orleans Dockworkers." *Radical America*, Vol 10 (Jan-Feb 1976), 43-69.
7069 WHALEN, ROBERT G. "Two Generals Patrol the Docks." *New York Times Magazine*, Nov 29, 1953, p 20.
7070 WOLLETT, DONALD H., and ROBERT J. LAMPMAN. "The Law of Union Factionalism —The Case of the Sailors." *Stanford Law Review*, Vol 4 (1952).
7071 YELLEN, SAMUEL. *American Labor Struggles.* NY: Harcourt, Brace, 1936. (Longshoremen, San Francisco)

White Collar and Service

GENERAL

7072 "Aiming at White-Collar Target." *Business Week*, May 12, 1956, pp 169-71.
7073 BAMBRICK, JAMES J., and HAROLD STIEGLITZ. *White Collar Unionization: Union Strategy and Tactics, Analysis of Contracts, Problems after Unionization.* NY: National Industrial Conference Board, 1949.
7074 BLUM, ALBERT A. *Management and the White-Collar Union.* NY: American Management Association, 1964.
7075 ———. *White-Collar Workers.* NY: Random House, 1971.
7076 BOLLENS, LEO F. *White Collar or Noose? The Occupation of Millions.* NY: North River Press, 1947.
7077 BRUNER, DICK. "Why White Collar Workers Can't Be Organized." *Harper's*, Aug 1957, pp 44-50.
7078 BURNS, ROBERT K. *Unionization of the White Collar Worker.* NY: American Management Association, 1947.

7079 Chicago, University of, Industrial Relations Center. *Studies in White Collar Unionism*. Chicago: The Center, 1954.

7080 Croner, Fritz. "Salaried Employees in Modern Society." *International Labour Review*, Vol 69 (1954), 97-110.

7081 Curtin, Edward R. *White-Collar Unionization*. NY: National Industrial Conference Board, 1970.

7082 *Developments in White Collar Unionism: A Panel Discussion by Harold J. Gibbons, Everett M. Kassalow, and Joel Seidman*. Chicago: A. G. Bush Library, Industrial Relations Center, U of Chicago, 1962.

7083 Doolan, Robert J. *Attitudes of White-Collar Workers Toward Unionization*. Ann Arbor: U of Michigan, Bureau of Industrial Relations, 1959.

7084 Dowd, Douglas F. "The White Collar Worker." *Monthly Review*, Jul-Aug 1958, pp 127-33.

7085 Finley, Joseph E. *White Collar Union: The Story of the OPEIU and Its People*. NY: Octagon, 1977.

7086 Forsyth, George. *Private Sector White Collar Workers: Examining their Propensity for Unionism*. Ph D diss, U of Western Ontario, 1977.

7087 Greenbaum, J. *In the Name of Efficiency: Management Theory and Shopfloor Practice in Data Processing Work*. Phila.: Temple U Press, 1979.

7088 *In White Collar America*. 1974. (Produced by NBC-TV)

7089 Kassalow, Everett M. *Automation and Technological Change: A Challenge to the American Labor Movement*. Bost, June 27, 1958. (Mimeo.)

7090 ———. "The Prospects for White-Collar Union Growth." *Industrial Relations*, Vol 5 (Oct 1965), 37-47.

7091 Kocka, Juergen. *Angestellte zwischen Faschismus und Demokratie: Zur politischen Sozialgeschichte der Angestellten, USA 1890-1940 im internationalen Vergleich*. Goettingen: Vandenhoeck & Ruprecht, 1977.

7092 ———. *White Collar Workers in America, 1890-1940: A Social-Political History in International Perspective*. Beverly Hills, CA: Sage Publication, 1980.

7093 "Labor's Centennial—a Celebration Shared by all Workers." *International Presidents Bulletin*, Vol 45 (1981), 48-55.

7094 Levison, Andrew. *The Working-Class Majority*. NY: Coward, McCann & Geoghegan, 1974.

7095 Lombardi, Vincent, and Andrew J. Grimes. "A Primer for a Theory of White-Collar Unionization." *Monthly Labor Review*, Vol 90 (May 1967), 46-49.

7096 Lynch, R. "Women in the Workforce: Clerical Workers Unrest." *Progressive*, Vol 43 (Oct 1979), 28-31.

7097 McColloch, Mark David. *White Collar Electrical Machinery, Banking and Public Welfare Workers, 1940-1970*. Ph D diss, U of Pittsburgh, 1976.

7098 Mills, C. Wright. *White Collar: The American Middle Classes*. NY: Oxford U Press, 1951.

7099 *Nine to Five*. 1980. (Feature film produced by Twentieth Century-Fox)

7100 Nurnberger, T. S. *Experiences with White-Collar Unions*. Ann Arbor: U of Michigan, Bureau of Industrial Relations, 1959.

7101 Robinson, R. "Politics Always Play a Part in Fixing Broad Boundaries." *Insurance Worker*, Vol 21 (Feb 1979), 4.

7102 ———. "Routing Convention Rebels was UPOWA's Last Victory." *Insurance Worker*, Vol 21 (Mar 1979), 4.

7103 ———. "Secession Turmoil Rocked Union as Pro Talks Neared." *Insurance Worker*, Vol 21 (Apr 1979), 4.

7104 Snyder, Carl D. *White-Collar Workers and the UAW*. Urbana: U of Illinois Press, 1973.

7105 ———. *White-Collar Workers and the UAW*. Urbana: U of Illinois Press, 1973.

7106 SOLOMON, BENJAMIN. "The Problems and Areas of Union Expansion in the White-Collar Sector." *Proceedings of the Ninth Annual Meeting of the Industrial Relations Research Association*, Dec 28-29, 1956, pp 238-43. Madison: IRRA, 1957.

7107 STRAUSS, GEORGE. "White Collar Unions Are Different." *Harvard Business Review*, Sep-Oct 1954, pp 73-82.

7108 STURMTHAL, ADOLF, ed. *White-Collar Trade Unions: Contemporary Developments in Industrialized Societies*. Urbana: U of Illinois Press, 1966.

7109 "A Union Target: The White-Collar Worker." *Business Week*, Feb 7, 1948, pp 88-94.

FINANCE

7110 BAKER, HELEN. *Current Policies in Personnel Relations in Banks*. Princeton: Industrial Relations Section, Princeton U, 1940.

7111 BELL, THOMAS. *There Comes a Time* (a novel). Bost.: Little, Brown, 1946.

7112 CLERMONT, HARVEY J. *Organizing the Insurance Worker: A History of Labor Unions of Insurance Employees*. Wash.: Catholic U of America Press, 1966.

7113 COLEMAN, CHARLES J., and JANE A. ROSE. "Bank Unionization: Status and Prospects." *Monthly Labor Review*, Vol 98 (Oct 1975), 38-41.

7114 GROAT, MARGARET SCHAER. *Collective Bargaining in Wall Street*. MS thesis, Cornell U, 1948.

7115 MASSE, BENJAMIN L. "The Strike on Wall Street." *America*, Apr 24, 1948.

OFFICE

7116 AHERN, EILEEN. *Survey of Personnel Practices in Unionized Offices*. NY: American Management Association, 1948.

7117 AMATO, J. et al "Year on the Line: Women's Strike Against the Citizen's National Bank of Willmar, Minnesota." *Progressive*, Vol 43 (Feb 1979), 41.

7118 AMERICAN MANAGEMENT ASSOCIATION. *Collective Bargaining in the Office*. NY: The Association, 1948.

7119 ARON, CINDY S. "'To Barter their Souls for Gold': Female Clerks in Federal Government Offices, 1862-1890." *Journal of American History*, Vol 67 (1981), 835-53.

7120 BECKER, ESTHER R., and EUGENE F. MURPHY. *The Office in Transition: Meeting the Problems of Automation*. NY: Harper, 1957. (See especially chap. 13: "The Future of White Collar Unionization")

7121 BLUM, ALBERT A. "The Prospects for Office Employee Unionism." *Proceedings of the Sixteenth Annual Meeting of the Industrial Relations Research Association*, Dec 27-28, 1963, pp 182-93. Madison: IRRA, 1964.

7122 *The Crowd*. 1928. (Feature film directed by King Vidor)

7123 FELDBERG, ROSLYN. "'Union Fever': Organizing Among Clerical Workers, 1900-1930." *Radical America*, Vol 14 (May-Jun 1980), 53-67.

7124 FREEDMAN, AUDREY. "Office Automation in the Insurance Industry." *Monthly Labor Review*, Vol 88 (Nov 1965), 1313-19.

7125 HELFGOTT, ROY B. "EDP and the Office Work Force." *Industrial and Labor Relations Review*, Vol 19 (1966), 503-16.

7126 LAWRENCE, JOSEPHINE. *Sound of Running Feet* (a novel). Phila.: Stokes, 1937.

7127 LUBIN, JOHN F. *Clerical and Office Unionism in the United States: The Unit for Collective Bargaining*. Ph D diss, U of Pennsylvania, 1956.

7128 NUSSBAUM, KAREN. "Women Clerical Workers and Trade Unionism." *Socialist Review*, Vol 10 (Jan-Feb 1980), 151-59.

7129 PELL, ORLIE. *The Office Worker—Labor's Side of the Ledger*. NY: League for Industrial Democracy, Oct 1938.

7130 PROSSER, WILLIAM H. *Nine to Five* (a novel). Bost.: Little, Brown, 1953.

7131 RICE, ELMER. *The Adding Machine: A Play in Seven Scenes.* NY: Samuel French, 1929.

7132 ROBINSON, R. "Big UOPWA Breakthroughs Featured the Middle 1940s." *Insurance Worker*, Vol 20 (Apr 1978), 4.

7133 ———. "Early Struggles in Chicago." *Insurance Worker*, Vol 18 (Aug 1976). (Profile of Local 20817, Insurance Debit Employees Union)

7134 SANSBURG, GAIL G. "'Now What's the Matter with You Girls?' Clerical Women Organize." *Radical America*, Vol 14 (Nov-Dec 1890), 67-75.

7135 SULLIVAN, DANIEL. "Labor Looks to Enlisting White Collar Workers: Office Employees International Union has 15,000 Members in New York State." *Industrial Bulletin*, Vol 39 (1960), 15-19.

7136 TEPPERMAN, JEAN. *Not Servants, Not Machines: Office Workers Speak Out!* Bost.: Beacon, 1976.

7137 ———. "Organizing Office Workers." *Radical America*, Vol 10 (Jan-Feb 1976), 3-20.

7138 U.S. CONGRESS. SENATE. Committee on Labor and Public Welfare. Subcommittee on Labor and Labor-Management Relations. *Communist Domination of Certain Unions.* Wash.: G.P.O., 1951. (See pp 3-18 for United Office and Professional Workers of America)

7139 WAHN, E. V. "Collective Bargaining Rights of Managerial Employees in the United States and Canada." *Labor Law Journal*, Vol 27 (1976), 343-60.

PROFESSIONAL

7140 AFL-CIO. INDUSTRIAL UNION DEPARTMENT. *Summary Report and Conclusion of IUD Seminar; Collective Bargaining Problems of Professional and Technical Workers in Industry, Harvard University, January 14-17, 1960.* Wash.: The Department, Jan 1960. (Mimeo.)

7141 ALEXANDER, KENNETH O. "Scientists, Engineers and the Organization of Work." *American Journal of Economics and Sociology*, Vol 40 (1981), 51-66.

7142 BAILEY, PERCIVAL, R. *Progressive Lawyers: a History of the National Lawyers Guild, 1936-1958.* Ph D diss, Rutgers U, 1979.

7143 BAIRSTOW, FRANCES, and LEONARD SAYLES. "Bargaining Over Work Standards by Professional Unions," chap. 6, *Collective Bargaining and Productivity*, Gerald Somers et al., eds. Madison: IRRA, 1975.

7144 BAMBRICK, JAMES J., JR. et al. *Unionization among American Engineers.* NY: National Industrial Conference Board, 1956.

7145 BARRETT, JEROME. "The Reaction to Technological Change by a Local Union of Engineers." *Labor Studies Journal*, Vol 5 (1980), 134-45.

7146 BOGNANNO, MARIO. et al. "Physicians' and Dentists' Bargaining Organizations: A Preliminary Look." *Monthly Labor Review*, Vol 98 (Jun 1975), 33-35.

7147 BOUGHTON, V. T. "Engineering Societies and Unions." *Civil Engineering*, Oct 1939, pp 418-19.

7148 BUREAU OF NATIONAL AFFAIRS. *Unionization in the Legal Profession.* Wash.: The Bureau, 1981.

7149 BUTTERWORTH, CHARLES E. "When Diplomats Engage in Collective Bargaining." *Proceedings of the Twenty-Fifth Anniversary Meeting of the Industrial Relations Research Association*, Dec 28-29, 1972, pp 408-15. Madison: IRRA, 1973.

7150 CHAPLAN, MARGARET, and CHARLES MAXEY. "The Scope of Faculty Bargaining: Implications for Academic Librarians." *Library Quarterly*, Vol 46 (1976), 231-47.

7151 CHAPLAN, MARGARET, ed. "Employee Organizations and Collective Bargaining in Libraries." *Library Trends*, Vol 25 (1976), 419-557.

7152 CULLEY, JACK F. *A Primer on Engineering Unionism.* Iowa City: Bureau of Labor and Management, Iowa U, 1959.

7153 DVORAK, ELDON J. "Will Engineers Unionize?" *Industrial Relations*, Vol 2 (1963), 45-65.

7154 Engineering Societies Library. *Bibliography on Unionization of Professional Engineers.* NY: The Library, 1954.

7155 Finer, Herman. *Administration and the Nursing Services.* NY: Macmillan, 1952.

7156 Fisher, Waldo E. "Collective Bargaining for Engineers." *Engineering and Science Monthly*, Jun 1946, pp 24-25.

7157 Goldstein, Bernard. "The Perspective of Unionized Professionals." *Social Forces*, May 1959, pp 323-27.

7158 ———. "Some Aspects of the Nature of Unonism Among Salaried Professionals in Industry," pp 329-36, *Labor and Trade Unionism: An Interdisciplinary Reader*, Walter Galenson & Seymour Martin Lipset, ets. NY: Wiley, 1960.

7159 ———, and Bernard P. Indik. "Unionism as a Social Choice: The Engineers' Case." *Monthly Labor Review*, Vol 86 (1963), 365-69.

7160 Greenwood, David C. *The Engineering Profession and Unionization.* Wash.: Public Affairs Press, 1960.

7161 Guyton, Theodora L. *Unionization: the Viewpoint of Librarians.* Chicago: American Library Association, 1975.

7162 Hansen, W. Lee. "Professional Engineers: Salary Structure Problems." *Industrial Relations*, Vol 2 (1963), 33-44.

7163 Indik, Bernard P., and Bernard Goldstein. "Professional Engineers Look at Unions." *Proceedings of the Sixteenth Annual Meeting of the Industrial Relations Research Association*, Dec 27-28, 1963, pp 209-18. Madison: IRRA, 1964.

7164 Kaufman, Harold G. *Professionals in Search of Work: Coping with the Stress of Job Loss and Underemployment.* NY: Wiley, 1982.

7165 Kleingartner, Archie. "Professional and Engineering Unionism." *Industrial Relations*, Vol 8 (1969), 224-35.

7166 ———. *Professional and Quasi-Union Organization and Bargaining Behavior: A Bibliography.* Los Angeles: Institute of Industrial Relations, U of California, 1972.

7167 ———. "Unionization of Engineers and Technicians." *Monthly Labor Review*, Vol 90 (Oct 1967), 29-35.

7168 Kornhauser, William. *Scientists in Industry, Conflict and Accomodation.* Berkeley: U of California Press, 1962.

7169 Kotaschnig, Walter W. *Unemployment in the Learned Professions: An International Study of Occupational and Educational Planning.* London: Oxford U Press, 1937.

7170 Kruger, Daniel H. "Bargaining and the Nursing Profession." *Monthly Labor Review*, Vol 84 (1961), 699-705.

7171 Kuhn, James W. "Success and Failure in Organizing Professional Engineers." *Proceedings of the Sixteenth Annual Meeting of the Industrial Relations Research Association*, Dec 27-28, 1963, pp 194-208. Madison: IRRA, 1964.

7172 Latta, Geoffrey. "Union Organization among Engineers: a Current Assessment." *Industrial and Labor RElations Review*, Vol 35 (1981), 29-42.

7173 McKenzie, Richard D. *A New Deal for Artists.* Princeton: Princeton U Press, 1973.

7174 Mangione, Jerre. *The Dream and the Deal: The Federal Writers' Project 1935-1943.* Bost.: Little, Brown, 1972.

7175 Manley, T. Roger, and Charles W. McNichols. "Attitudes of Federal Scientists and Engineers Toward Unions." *Monthly Labor Review*, Vol 98 (Apr 1975), 57-60.

7176 Mendes, Richard Henry P. *The Professional Union: a Study of the Social Service Employees Union of the New York City Department of Social Services.* Ph D diss, Columbia U 1974.

7177 Michener, Roger. "Library Unions: a Review Article." *Library Quarterly*, Vol 46 (1976), 171-75.

7178 Michigan State University, Labor and Industrial Relations Center. *Effective Utilization of Engineering Personnel.* East Lansing: The Center, 1957.

7179 Miller, Richard Lurie. "Collective Bargaining in Banking." *Bankers Magazine*, Vol 163 (May-Jun 1980), 67-74.

7180 Myers, Hugh L. "The Engineer and Organized Labor." *Cornell Engineer*, Vol 11 (1946), 13-14, 32-36.

7181 National Society of Professional Engineers. *Tabulation of Unions Representing Engineering and Technical Employees*. Wash.: The Society, 1959.

7182 Northrup, Herbert R. "Collective Bargaining by Professional Societies," chap. 6, *Insights into Labor Issues*, Richard A. Lester & Joseph Shister, eds. NY: Macmillan, 1948.

7183 Orrell, Herbert M. "Engineers Turn to Unionism." *The Nation*, Jun 21, 1952, p 605.

7184 Peckworth, H. F. *The Engineer and Collective Bargaining*. NY: American Society of Civil Engineers, July 1943.

7185 Penkower, Monty. *The Federal Writers' Project: A Study in Government Patronage of the Arts*. Urbana: U of Illinois Press, 1977.

7186 Princeton University, Industrial Relations Section. *Personnel Management and the Professional Employee*. Princeton: The Section, 1957.

7187 Riegel, John W. *Collective Bargaining as Viewed by Unorganized Engineers and Scientists*. Ann Arbor: Bureau of Industrial Relations, U of Michigan, 1959.

7188 Robinson, R. "PRU Agents Stirred Up Fuss in Unchartered A.F.L. Council." *Insurance Worker*, Vol 22 (Mar 1980), 4.

7189 ———. "Rocky Road for George Russ." *Insurance Worker*, Vol 22 (Feb 1980), 4.

7190 Rothstein, William G. "The American Association of Engineers." *Industrial and Labor Relations Review*, Vol 22 (1968), 48-72.

7191 Shea, T. E. "The Implications of Engineering Unionism—Western Electric Experience." *Research Management*, Autumn 1959, pp 149-57.

7192 Somers, Gerald G. "Small Establishments and Chemicals." *Proceedings of the Ninth Annual Meeting of the Industrial Relations Research Association*, Dec 28-29, 1956, pp 248-55. Madison: IRRA, 1957.

7193 Strauss, George. "Professional or Employee-Oriented: Dilemma for Engineering Unions." *Industrial and Labor Relations Review*, Vol 17 (1964), 519-33.

7194 ———. "Professionalism and Occupational Associations." *Industrial Relations*, Vol 2 (1963), 7-31.

7195 Taft, Everett. "Unions among Engineers." *Proceedings of the Ninth Annual Meeting of the Industrial Relations Research Association*, Dec 28-29, 1956, pp 244-47. Madison: IRRA, 1957.

7196 "Unionization of Law Firms." *Fordham Law Review*, Vol 46 (1978), 1008-36.

7197 U.S. Congress. House. Special Committee on Un-American Activities. *Investigation of Un-American Propaganda Activities in the United States*. Wash.: G.P.O., 1944. (See pp 703-18 for Federation of Architects, Engineers, Chemists and Technicians)

7198 Wallach, Anne Tolstoi. *Women's Work* (a novel). NY: New American Library, 1981.

7199 Walton, Richard E. *The Impact of the Professional Engineering Union: A Study of Collective Bargaining among Engineers and Scientists and Its Significance for Management*. Bost.: Graduate School of Business Administration, Harvard U, 1961.

7200 Weber, Arnold R. "Paradise Lost; or Whatever Happened to the Chicago Social Workers?" *Industrial and Labor Relations Review*, Vol 22 (1969), 323-38.

7201 Wex, J. H., and W. S. McGee. "Unionization of Court Employees Has Raised Legal Practical Questions." *Monthly Labor Review*, Vol 102 (Aug 1979), 20-24.

7202 Wirfs, R. M. "Surviving the 70s—I.U.O.E. Local 3." *Job Safety and Health*, Vol 5 (Sep 1977), 8-16.

RETAIL, WHOLESALE, DEPARTMENT STORES

7203 Allaway, Richard. *Four Analytical Approaches Toward an Understanding of the Decision-Making Process in Three Retail Unions*. Ph D diss, Cornell U, 1950.

7204 Baker, Helen, and Robert R. France. *Personnel Administration and Labor Relations in Department Stores: An Analysis of Developments and Practices.* Princeton: Industrial Relations Section, Princeton U, Aug 1950.

7205 Bedolis, Robert A. "Miracle on Astor Place: The District 65 Story." *The Nation,* Sep 25, 1954, pp 255-57.

7206 Benson, Susan P. "The Cinderella of Occupations: Managing the Work of Department Store Sales Women, 1900-1940." *Business History Review,* Vol 55 (Spring 1981), 1-25.

7207 ———. "'The Customer Ain't God': The Work Culture of Department Store Saleswomen, 1890-1940," pp 185-211, *Working Class America: Essays on Labor, Community, and American Society,* Michael Frisch & Daniel J. Walkowitz, eds. Urbana: U of Illinois Press, 1983.

7208 *The Devil and Miss Jones.* 1940. (Feature film directed by Sam Wood)

7209 Estey, Marten S. "The Grocery Clerks: Center of Retail Unionism." *Industrial Relations,* Vol 7 (1968), 249-61.

7210 ———. "Patterns of Union Membership in Retail Trades." *Industrial and Labor Relations Review,* Vol 8 (1955), 557-64.

7211 ———. *Some Factors Influencing Labor Organizations in the Retail Trades.* Princeton: Princeton U, 1952.

7212 Fogel, Walter. "Union Impact on Retail Food Wages in California." *Industrial Relations,* Vol 6 (1966), 79-94.

7213 Greenberg, Max. "The Retail, Wholesale and Department Store Union." *AFL-CIO American Federationist,* Vol 66 (1959), 23-25.

7214 Halper, Albert. *The Chute* (a novel). NY: Viking, 1937.

7215 ———. *The Little People* (a novel). NY: Harper, 1942.

7216 Harrington, Michael. *The Retail Clerks.* NY: Wiley, 1962.

7217 Healy, Paul F. "He Runs a White-Collar Union." *Saturday Evening Post,* Mar 16, 1957, pp 49, 125-26.

7218 Hill, Anne. "District 925: a New Union for Office Workers." *Socialist Revolution,* No 59 (Sep-Oct 1981), 142-46.

7219 Howard, George (Jason Striker, pseud.). *Haste to Succeed* (a novel). NY: Appleton-Century-Crofts, 1961.

7220 Hughes, Rupert. *Miss 318 and Mr. 37* (a novel). NY: REvell, 1912.

7221 Job, Barbara C. "Employment and Pay Trends in the Retail Trade Industry." *Monthly Labor Review,* Vol 103 (Mar 1980), 40-43.

7222 Kirstein, George G. *Stores and Unions: A Study of the Growth of Unionism in Dry Goods and Department Stores.* NY: Fairchild, 1950.

7223 La Dame, Mary. *The Filene Store: A Study of Employees' Relation to Management in a Retail Store.* NY: Russell Sage Foundation, 1930.

7224 "Looking Backward—1933-1937." *Distributive Worker,* Vol 9 (Oct 1977), 9.

7225 Michman, Ronald D. *Unionization of Salespeople in Department Stores in the United States, 1888-1964.* Ph D diss, New York U, 1966.

7226 Rogow, Robert. "Membership Participation and Centralized Control." *Industrial Relations,* Vol 7 (1968), 132-45.

7227 Seidman, Harold. *Labor Czars.* NY: Liveright, 1938. (See chap. 12, pp 185-98 & chap. 13, pp 199-213)

7228 U.S. Commission on Industrial Relations (1912). "The Department Stores of New York City," Vol 3, pp 2213-410, *Final Report,* Wash.: G.P.O., 1916.

7229 Wilson, Andrew Austin. *Wage Determination in the Los Angeles Retail Food Industry.* Ph D diss, Claremont Graduate School, 1966.

7230 Zugsmith, Leane. *A Time to Remember* (a novel). NY: Random House, 1936.

SERVICES

7231 Building Service Employees International Union, AFL, Local 32B. *Going Up!: The Story of 32B*. NY: The Union, 1955.

7232 Christenson, C. Lawrence. "Chicago Service Trades," chap. 15, *How Collective Bargaining Works*, Harry A. Millis, research director. NY: Twentieth Century Fund, 1945.

7233 DeArmond, Frederick F. *The Laundry Industry*. NY: Harper, 1950.

7234 Dubofsky, Melvyn. "Neither Upstairs nor Downstairs: Domestic Service in Middle-Class Homes" *Reviews in American History*, Vol 8 (1980), 86-91.

7235 "Employment in Social Welfare and Related Organizations." *Monthly Labor Review*, Vol 77 (1954), 1126-29.

7236 Fisher, William. *The Waiters* (a novel). Cleveland: World, 1953.

7237 "Foot-note to Labor History: After 30 Years, the Automats Are Organized." *Industrial Bulletin*, Vol 45 (May 1966), 10-11.

7238 Hall, William S. *Journeymen Barbers' International Union of America*. Balt.: Johns Hopkins Press, 1936.

7239 Henderson, John P. *Labor Market Institutions and Wages in the Lodging Industry*. East Lansing: Graduate School of Business Administration, Michigan State U, 1966.

7240 Hobby, Daniel T. "'We Have Got Results': A Document on the Organization of Domestics in the Progressive Era." *Labor History*, Vol 17 (1976), 103-8.

7241 Horowitz, Morris A. *The New York Hotel Industry: A Labor Relations Study*. Cambr.: Harvard U Press, 1960.

7242 Josephson, Matthew. *Union House, Union Bar: The History of the Hotel and Restaurant Employees and Bartenders' International Union (AFL-CIO)*. NY: Random House, 1956.

7243 Katzman, David M. *Seven Days a Week: Women and Domestic Service in Industrializing America*. NY: Oxford U Press, 1978.

7244 Kennedy, Van Dusen. *Arbitration in the San Francisco Hotel and Restaurant Industries*. Phila.: U of Pennsylvania, 1952.

7245 "Local 144: 'A Miniature U.N.'" *Industrial Bulletin*, Vol 42 (1963), 16-18. (health and welfare)

7246 Moore, Mack A. "The Temporary Help Service Industry: Historical Development, Operation, and Scope." *Industrial and Labor Relations Review*, Vol 18 (1965), 554-69.

7247 Nestel, Louis P. *Labor Relations in the Laundry Industry in Greater New York*. NY: Claridge, 1950.

7248 Richmond, Al. "The San Francisco Hotel Strike." *Socialist Revolution*, No 56 (May-Jun 1981), 87-113.

7249 Russ, George L. "The Insurance Agents Are Sold on Unionism." *American Federationist*, Vol 16 (1954), 22-23.

7250 Saposs, David J. *Communism in American Unions*. NY: McGraw-Hill, 1959. (See Part 2, chaps. 10, 12, pp 82-115 for hotel, restaurant, bar)

7251 Scherer, Joseph. *Collective Bargaining in the Service Industries: A Study of the Year-Round Hotels*. Ph D diss, U of Chicago, 1951.

7252 ———. "The Union Impact on Wages: The Case of the Year-Round Hotel Industry." *Industrial and Labor Relations Review*, Vol 9 (1956), 213-24.

7253 Seidman, Harold. *Labor Czars*. NY: Liveright, 1938. (See chap. 13, pp 199-213 for hotel, restaurant, bar)

7254 Skinner, Wickham, and Kishore Chakraborty. *The Impact of New Technology: People and Organizations in Service Industries*. NY: Pergamon, 1982.

7255 Slocum, John Howard. *A Study of the Labor Relations of Selected Colleges and Universities and Their Maintenance Employees*. Ph D diss, Cornell U, 1950.

7256 Stigler, George J. *Domestic Servants in the United States, 1900-1940.* NY: National Bureau of Economic Research, 1946.

7257 Sutherland, Daniel E. *Americans and Their Servants: Domestic Service in the United States from 1800 to 1920.* Baton Rouge: Louisiana State U Press, 1981.

7258 U.S. Commission on Industrial Relations (1912). "Conditions of Employment of Waiters and Cooks," Vol 14, pp 3533-36, *Final Report*, Wash.: G.P.O., 1916.

7259 U.S. Industrial Commission (1898). *Report.* Wash.: G.P.O., 1901. (Vol 14 includes a special report on domestic service)

7260 "We Celebrate our 90th Year." *Journeyman Barber*, Vol 73 (Sep 1977), 8. (first in a series of 12)

7261 Whyte, William F. *Human Relations in the Restaurant Industry.* NY: McGraw-Hill, 1948.

Appendix

The following is a list of possible resources for the rental or purchase of films cited in the text. While not comprehensive, it should prove of assistance. Remember that many of these films are also available on videotape from the following sources.

AFL-CIO Dept. of Education, Film Division
815 16 St. N.W.
Washington, DC 20006
(202) 637-5000

California Newsreel
630 Natoma St.
San Francisco, CA 94103
(415) 621-6196

Films Incorporated
1144 Wilmette Ave.
Wilmette, IL 60091
(312) 256-4730

First Run Features
144 Bleecker St.
New York, NY 10012
(212) 673-6881

Illinois Labor History Society
20 E. Jackson Ave.
Chicago, IL 60604
(312) 663-4107

Kit Parker Films
1245 Tenth St.
Monterey, CA 93940
(408) 649-5573

Museum of Modern Art
Film Circulation
11 W. 53 St.
New York, NY 10019
(212) 956-4204

National AudioVisual Center
National Archives and Record Service
General Services Administration
Washington, DC 20409
(301) 763-1896

New Day Films
Box 315
Franklin Lakes, NJ 07417
(201) 891-8240

New Yorker Films
16 W. 61 St.
New York, NY 10023
(212) 247-6110

Unifilm, Inc.
419 Park Ave. South
New York, NY 10016
(212) 686-9890

United Auto Workers
Education Dept., Film Library
8000 E. Jefferson Ave.
Detroit, MI 48214
(313) 926-5474

Index